The Bloomsbury Group:
A Collection of Memoirs and Commenta

D0380562

Revised Edition

Also by S.P. Rosenbaum

Edwardian Bloomsbury:
The Early Literary History of the Bloomsbury Group, volume 2

Victorian Bloomsbury:
The Early Literary History of the Bloomsbury Group, volume 1

Edited Works

A Bloomsbury Group Reader

Virginia Woolf's Women & Fiction:
The Manuscript Versions of *A Room of One's Own*

English Literature and British Fiction:
A Collection of Critical Essays

Henry James's *The Ambassadors*: A Norton Critical Edition

A Concordance to the Poems of Emily Dickinson

The Bloomsbury Group

A Collection of Memoirs and Commentary

REVISED EDITION

Edited by S.P. Rosenbaum

UNIVERSITY OF TORONTO PRESS

Toronto Buffalo London

Rancho Santiago College
Orange Campus Library

© University of Toronto Press Incorporated 1995
Toronto Buffalo London
Printed in Canada

ISBN 0-8020-0690-6 (cloth)
ISBN 0-8020-7640-8 (paper)

Printed on acid-free paper

Canadian Cataloguing in Publication Data

Main entry under title:
The Bloomsbury group : a collection of memoirs
and commentary

Rev. ed.
Includes bibliographical references and index.
ISBN 0-8020-0690-6 (bound) ISBN 0-8020-7640-8 (pbk.)

1. Bloomsbury group.   2. London (England) –
Intellectual life.   3. London (England) – Biography.
I. Rosenbaum, S. P. (Stanford Patrick), 1929–   .

PR478.B46B65 1995   700'.92'242   C95-931667-1

Cover illustration: *The Memoir Club* (Vanessa
Bell 1943). Courtesy of Bryan Ferry.
Seated from left to right are Duncan Grant,
Leonard Woolf, Vanessa Bell, Clive Bell, David
Garnett, J.M. Keynes, Lydia Keynes, Desmond
MacCarthy, Molly MacCarthy, Quentin Bell, and
E.M. Forster. On the walls are Bloomsbury
portraits of the three deceased members, Virginia
Woolf, Lytton Strachey, and Roger Fry.

University of Toronto Press acknowledges the
financial assistance to its publishing program
of the Canada Council and the Ontario Arts
Council.

PR 478
B46 B65
1995

Contents

Contents

Foreword

In the twenty years since this collection of memoirs and commentary by and about the members of the Bloomsbury Group was first published, knowledge about the Group has increased considerably. The publication of biographies, bibliographies, autobiographies, letters, and diaries, as well as studies in Bloomsbury art and literary history, have all supported the original assumptions of the collection that there was such a thing as the Bloomsbury Group and that it was worth studying seriously.

The difference in the understanding of Bloomsbury can be illustrated by two definitions of the Group. The 1972 supplement to the most authoritative dictionary of the language, *The Oxford English Dictionary*, defined Bloomsbury as 'a school of writers and aesthetes living in or associated with Bloomsbury, that flourished in the early twentieth century; a member of this school.' In the 1989 second edition of *The Oxford English Dictionary*, Bloomsbury was now defined as 'a set of writers, artists, and intellectuals living in or associated with Bloomsbury in the early 20th century; a member of this set.' 'Set' is certainly a better term than 'school,' for Bloomsbury had no body of doctrine, code of conduct, or masters. And certainly 'artists and intellectuals' is a more adequate description than 'aesthetes,' though it really does not encompass the achievements of a great art critic or a world-changing economist. Nor is 'set,' with its emphasis on social relations, a very exact designation of the values and beliefs that connected Bloomsbury together as much as friendship did.

In the course of its history Bloomsbury has been called a clique, coterie, cénacle, clan, commune, gang, and mafia; it has been described as Gloomsbury or Boomsbury, and its members have been named Bloomsberries (a term one of them invented), Bloomburyites, even Bloomsbuggers. Of the more neutral terms such as 'circle' or 'group,' the latter, vaguer term seems the more precise because, as Quentin Bell has observed, Bloomsbury cannot really be called a circle,

if by a circle we mean something that has a regular circumference all the
parts of which would be equi-distant from the centre. Bloomsbury had
no centre or any regular or indeed any definable shape. Rather we should
say that it was a continually changing agglomeration of individuals united
by friendship and by a similarity of opinions. (*Who's Who,* 19)

Because Bloomsbury was a collectivity of friends and relations who
knew and loved one another for over two generations, it is not a
simple matter to enumerate the individuals of the Group or identify
principles they held in common. The ideas, beliefs, and tastes of the
original members of Bloomsbury display that overlapping and criss-
crossing similarity that Ludwig Wittgenstein (who knew some of
them) has called a family resemblance. In art and literature, love and
friendship, in celebration and defamations, the Bloomsbury Group
displays a unique, intricate resemblance that cannot be reduced to
a creed or argued away because of its complexity. The importance
of G.E. Moore's philosophy for Bloomsbury, for instance, was not
merely a question of ideals of love and beauty; at least as significant
was his fundamental distinction between intrinsic and instrumental
value - between things valuable as ends in themselves and actions
valued as means to those ends. Again, Bloomsbury's formative beliefs
are not to be simplistically equated with those enumerated by John
Maynard Keynes in the famous memoir of his early beliefs. What
Bloomsbury stood for is what they were and what they did. That
is why a collection of descriptions of Bloomsbury's lives and works
may be the only wholly satisfactory way of defining the Bloomsbury
Group.
    Essentialist definitions of Bloomsbury's beliefs and polemical mis-
representations of the Group's membership led some of the members themselves to deny Bloomsbury's existence or confine it to
their relationships before the First World War. But the continuing
reality of Bloomsbury is corroborated midway through their history
in the formation of the Memoir Club in 1920. Members of Bloomsbury formed many clubs from their undergraduate days at Cambridge
onward, but the significance of the Memoir Club can be seen not
only in its longevity - its last meeting was 1956 - but also in its
purpose, which appears to confirm the shared experience of a group
of old friends that was the original and enduring basis of Bloomsbury. The least that can be said of the thirteen members of the Memoir
Club in 1920 is that no roster of Bloomsbury ought to leave them

out. According to Leonard Woolf they were the same thirteen members of what came to be called Old Bloomsbury. Their names were Leonard and Virginia Woolf, Vanessa and Clive Bell, Lytton Strachey, Roger Fry, Duncan Grant, J.M. Keynes, Molly and Desmond MacCarthy, E.M. Forster, Saxon Sydney-Turner, and Adrian Stephen. In all Bloomsbury lists there seem to be room for disagreement and need for qualification, however. Adrian Stephen did not in fact belong to the Memoir Club, while Sydney Waterlow did, though he was not part of Old Bloomsbury. Yet Leonard Woolf's list is as reasonable a one as has been made by anyone in Bloomsbury of the Group's core. With one addition I have accepted it for the purposes of this collection, the addition being David Garnett, who became permanently involved with Bloomsbury during the First World War.

It should be emphasized that this is a minimum list of a changing group, and that there are many other names that could be plausibly added to it. Edwardian Bloomsbury included, in addition to the original thirteen, Waterlow, H.T.J. Norton, Gerald Shove, and various Stracheys, especially James, Marjorie, and Oliver. Wartime Bloomsbury saw the advent of a second generation, which included, in addition to Garnett, Francis Birrell, Mary Hutchinson, Karin Costelloe, Barbara Hiles Bagenal, Arthur Waley, Alix Sargant-Florence Strachey, Dora Carrington. Ralph Partridge, Raymond Mortimer, George Rylands, Angus Davidson, Stephen Tomlin, Frances Marshall Partridge, Roger Senhouse, and Lydia Lopokova Keynes were all involved, in one way or another, with Bloomsbury during the twenties. By the thirties the Bell children Julian, Quentin, and Angelica were active in the Group along with friends such as John Lehmann and Jane Bussy. But Bloomsbury cannot be stretched to include all the well-known contemporaries of Bloomsbury. Despite the attention recently given to the friendship of Virginia Woolf with Vita Sackville-West, for example, Vita and her husband Harold Nicolson were never considered members of Bloomsbury by the Group or themselves.

Death changed Bloomsbury as much as new friends. Thoby Stephen, whose introduction of his Cambridge friends to his sisters was the starting point for Bloomsbury, died tragically young in 1906. Lytton Strachey died in 1932, Roger Fry in 1934, Virginia Woolf in 1941. Late in 1917 Roger Fry wrote to Vanessa Bell that Clive had proposed 'a great historical group portrait of Bloomsbury.' Fry thought he would like to attempt the picture, but it was left to Vanessa to paint Bloomsbury's portrait in the form of an oil sketch of the Memoir

Club as it existed around 1943. The painting is reproduced on the
cover of this collection. Seated together from left to right are Duncan
Grant, Leonard Woolf, Vanessa Bell, Clive Bell, David Garnett, J.M.
Keynes, Lydia Keynes, Desmond MacCarthy, Molly MacCarthy,
Quentin Bell, and E.M. Forster. Desmond MacCarthy is reading a
paper while the others listen. On the walls are Bloomsbury portraits
of the three deceased members, Virginia Woolf, Lytton Strachey, and
Roger Fry. (In a preliminary version Angelica Garnett is shown entering the room.) Vanessa Bell's sketch illustrates the changing nature
of Bloomsbury and also serves to remind readers that in Bloomsbury
the art of painting was a highly regarded as the art of writing.

The pieces in this collection have been arranged under three head-
ings. These divisions are not absolute, and several pieces collected
under one heading could have been placed under another. For the
revision of the second edition of this collection, several of the texts
have been rearranged. The first section, *Bloomsbury on Bloomsbury*,
contains the basic memoirs and discussions of the Group itself by
twelve of the original members of Bloomsbury plus David Garnett.
These recollections range from sometimes unpublished private correspondence and diaries to formal autobiographies, and they were
written over a period of sixty years. There is a certain amount of
repetition, but sometimes what may seem to be repetitious actually
reveals an interesting difference in points of view. In the revised and
expanded edition Virginia Woolf's complete Memoir Club paper on
Old Bloomsbury and excerpts on Bloomsbury from her letters and
diaries have replaced parts of her recollections of Bloomsbury and
of Julian Bell. Also added are letters about Bloomsbury by Lytton
Strachey, Roger Fry, E.M. Forster, and Vanessa Bell, together with
the remainder of Desmond MacCarthy's unpublished memoir on the
Group.

The second section, entitled *Bloomsberries*, contains observations
on individual Bloomsberries by other members of the Group and their
children. Descriptions by people outside the Group have been omitted
from the second edition and replaced by additional pieces by Leonard
Woolf, Quentin Bell, David Garnett, Angelica Garnett, Henrietta Garnett, and Virginia Woolf, whose unpublished biographical fantasy
of J.M. Keynes is collected here for the first time. Accounts of Molly
MacCarthy, Carrington, Lydia Lopokova, and David Garnett have
also now been included among the Bloomsberries.

Bloomsbury Observed, the last section, consists of reminiscences
of the Group mainly by their contemporaries. Additions to the revised

edition include an early anonymous newspaper account of Bloomsbury, and other observations by Quentin Bell, Beatrice Webb, Gerald
Brenan, Ann Synge, Christopher Isherwood, Frances Partridge, Richard Morphet, Julian Bell, and Charles Mauron. (Several of the original pieces have been slightly reduced for the second edition.) To
make more room for the additions in this new edition, a fourth section
of the first edition has been omitted, and the title of the book shortened to *The Bloomsbury Group: A Collection of Memoirs and Commentaries.* The fourth section consisted of Bloomsbury criticisms by
Wyndham Lewis, D.H. Lawrence, George Bernard Shaw, Dimitri
Mirsky, F.R. Leavis, and Bertrand Russell. These now somewhat dated
controversies and the renewed criticisms of Bloomsbury that have followed during the past twenty years contribute less to the understanding of Bloomsbury than the letters, memoirs, and descriptions that
have been added to this collection. (See for example Roger Fry's unpublished letter on the criticism of Bloomsbury by J.M. Murry and
Wyndham Lewis, p. 37.) More than a third of the revised edition
consists of new material. About a quarter of the original edition has
been removed, along with the black and white portraits of the Group's
members, which are now available in books of colour reproductions
devoted to Bloomsbury's art.

The three sections of this revised collection are preceded by an
updated chronology recording the principal events in the careers of
Bloomsbury's members. Individual sections and selections are introduced by headnotes that give the setting of the texts and clarify their
allusions. The headnotes have been revised throughout for the second
edition; quotations in them are keyed to references at the end of the
volume, following identifications of various people and works mentioned in the text. (All footnotes in the text are those of the original
authors.) After the headnote references come the sources for the selections. Selected bibliographies and an index of names and works
in the selections conclude the volume.

*The Bloomsbury Group: A Collection of Memoirs and Commen-
taries* was originally begun as a preparation for writing a literary
history of the Bloomsbury Group. The first volume of that history,
Victorian Bloomsbury, was published in 1987, and the second,
Edwardian Bloomsbury, in 1994. *Georgian Bloomsbury* is now in
preparation.

S.P.R.   Toronto, 1 January 1995

Acknowledgments

The editor and publishers wish to thank The Hogarth Press for excerpts from Adrian Stephen, *The Dreadnought Hoax*, © 1936; Quentin Bell, excerpt from *Virginia Woolf: A Biography*, Hogarth Press, © 1972; Virginia Woolf, 'Old Bloomsbury,' *Moments of Being*, ed. Jeanne Schulkind, © 1985; excerpts from *The Diaries of Virginia Woolf*, ed. Anne Olivier Bell and Andrew McNeillie, © 1977–84; excerpts from *The Letters of Virginia Woolf*, ed. Nigel Nicolson and Joanne Trautmann, © 1975–80; Angelica Garnett, from *Deceived with Kindness*, © 1984; Leonard Woolf, from *Sowing: An Autobiography of the Years 1880–1904*, © 1960, *Beginning Again: An Autobiography of the Years 1911–1918*, © 1964; *Downhill All the Way: An Autobiography of the Years 1919–1939*, © 1967. Harcourt Brace & Co. and the Estate of Leonard Woolf from *Sowing: An Autobiography of the Years 1880–1904*, © 1960; *Beginning Again: An Autobiography of the Years 1911–1918*, © 1964; *Downhill All the Way: An Autobiography of the Years 1919–1939*, © 1967. C.A. Cole for an extract from an unpublished letter of Roger Fry, © 1995. Chatto & Windus for excerpts from Roger Fry, *Letters of Roger Fry*, ed. Denys Sutton, © 1972; Clive Bell, 'Bloomsbury,' 'Roger Fry,' 'Maynard Keynes,' *Old Friends: Personal Recollections*, © 1956; David Garnett, from *The Familiar Faces*, vol. 3 of *The Golden Echo*, © 1962; from *The Flowers of the Forest*, vol. 2 of *The Golden Echo*, © 1955; 'Preface,' *Carrington: Letters and Extracts from her Diaries*, © 1970. A.P. Watt, Ltd. on behalf of the Estate of David Garnett for 'Preface,' *Carrington: Letters and Extracts from her Diaries*, © 1970. The Society of Authors as agents of the Strachey Trust for 'Monday June 26th 1916'; *Lytton Strachey by Himself: A Self-Portrait*, ed. Michael Holroyd, © 1971; extract from unpublished letter, © 1995; as agents of the Estate of Virginia Woolf for the unpublished 'JMK,' © 1995. Henry W. and Albert A. Berg Collection, The New York Public Library (Astor, Lenox and Tilden Foundations) for Virginia Woolf, for permission to reproduce 'JMK.' Quentin Bell and the Estate of Virginia Woolf, extract from 'Some

New Woolf Letters,' ed. Joanne Trautmann Banks, *Modern Fiction Studies*, © 1984. King's College Cambridge and The Society of Authors as literary representatives of the E.M. Forster Estate for 'Tributes to Desmond MacCarthy,' *The Listener*, © 1952; 'Bloomsbury, An Early Note,' *Commmonplace Book*, ed. Philip Gardner, © 1985; from 'Bloomsbury, An Interview,' *Forster in Egypt: A Graeco-Alexandrian Encounter*, ed. Hilda D. Spear and Abdel Moneim Aly, © 1987; excerpts from *Selected Letters of E.M. Forster*, ed. Mary Lago and P.N. Furbank, © 1985; 'Virginia Woolf,' *Two Cheers for Democracy*, ed. Oliver Stallybrass, © 1951, 1972. Hugh Cecil and the Estate of Desmond MacCarthy for 'Bloomsbury, An Unfinished Memoir'; unpublished typescript with holograph revisions, MacCarthy Papers, Lilly Library, Indiana University, © 1995; excerpt from 'Roger Fry and the Post-Impressionist Exhibition of 1910,' *Memories*, © 1953. Royal Economic Society, Macmillan Press and Cambridge University Press, New York, for 'My Early Beliefs,' *The Collected Writings of John Maynard Keynes*, ed. D.E. Moggridge, © 1972. Henrietta Garnett and the Duncan Grant Estate for 'Virginia Woolf,' *Horizon*, © 1978. Henrietta Garnett for 'Aspects of My Father,' *Telegraph Weekend Magazine*, © 1989. Angelica Garnett and the Estate of Vanessa Bell for 'Notes on Bloomsbury,' © 1975; unpublished letter to Molly MacCarthy, Lilly Library, Indiana University, © 1995. Quentin Bell for 'Ludendorff Bell,' *Selected Letters of Vanessa Bell*, ed. Regina Marler, © 1993; 'Introduction,' Leonard Woolf, *An Autobiography, 1: 1880–1911*, © 1980; 'Bloomsbury and Lydia,' *Lydia Lopokova*, ed. Milo Keynes, Weidenfeld and Nicolson, © 1983; 'Foreward,' Judith Collins, *The Omega Workshops*, vi–x, © 1983. Weidenfeld and Nicolson for Quentin Bell, 'The Character of Bloomsbury,' *Bloomsbury*, © 1968. Trekkie Parsons and the Leonard Woolf Estate for 'Virginia Woolf; Writer and Personality,' *The Listener*, © 1965; 'Lytton Strachey,' *The New Statesman and Nation*, © 1932. Murray Pollinger, agent for the Ottoline Morrell Estate, from *The Early Memoirs of Lady Ottoline Morrell*, ed. Robert Gathorne-Hardy, © 1963. Constable Publishers for Peter Stansky and William Abrahams, from *Journey to the Frontier: Julian Bell and John Cornford: Their Lives in the 1930s*, © 1966; Arthur Waley from 'Introduction,' *One Hundred and Seventy Chinese Poems*, © 1962. Stanford University Press for Peter Stansky and William Abrahams, from *Journey to the Frontier: Julian Bell and John Cornford: Their Lives in the 1930s*, © 1966. Harper-Collins for *The Harold Nicolson Diaries and Letters*, ed. Nigel Nicolson, © 1966. Nigel Nicolson for 'Vita and Virginia and Vanessa,' *A Cézanne in the Hedge and Other Memories of Charleston,* ed.

Hugh Lee, © 1992. David Higham Associates for Edith Sitwell from *Taken Care Of: The Autobiography of Edith Sitwell,* © 1965; Osbert Sitwell, *Laughter in the Next Room,* © 1949; John Lehmann, from *The Whispering Gallery,* © 1955; *I Am My Brother,* © 1960. Virago Press for extracts from *The Diary of Beatrice Webb,* vol. 4, 1924–1943, ed. Norman and Jean MacKenzie, © 1985; Penguin Books for Gerald Brenan, from *South from Granada,* © 1957. Ann Synge for 'Childhood on the Edge of Bloomsbury,' *Charleston Newsletter,* 10 March 1985, 14–15, © 1985. Rupert Hart-Davis for William Plomer, extract from *At Home,* © 1958. Donadio & Ashworth Inc. for Christopher Isherwood, from *Exhumations: Stories, Articles, Verses,* © 1966. Farrar, Straus & Giroux for extracts from Christopher Isherwood, *Christopher and His Kind: 1929–1939,* © 1976. Curtis Brown Ltd. on behalf of the Estate of Christopher Isherwood for *Christopher and His Kind: 1929–1939,* © 1976; *Exhumations: Stories, Articles, Verses,* © 1966. Mrs. T.S. Eliot and the Estate of T.S. Eliot for T.S. Eliot, 'Virginia Woolf,' *Horizon,* © 1941. Faber and Faber for Stephen Spender, from *World Within World,* © 1951. St. Martin's Press for Stephen Spender, *World Within World,* © 1951, 1994. Frances Partridge and Rogers, Coleridge & White Ltd. for Frances Partridge, from *Memories,* Victor Gollancz, © 1981; 'Bloomsbury Houses,' *Charleston Newsletter,* © 1985. Richard Morphet for 'The Significance of Charleston,' *Apollo,* © 1967. Julian Bell for 'Monk's House and the Woolfs,' *Virginia Woolf's Rodmell: An Illustrated Guide to a Sussex Village,* ed. Marie McQueeney, Rodmell, East Sussex: Rodmell Village Press, © 1991. Alice Mauron for Charles Mauron, unpublished remarks on Bloomsbury, © 1995. Bryan Ferry for permission to reproduce Vanessa Bell's painting of the Memoir Club.

The editor and publishers apologize for any errors or omissions in the above list and would be grateful for information and corrections that can be incorporated in the next edition.

In addition to those thanked in the first edition and those mentioned above, I would also like to thank again Quentin Bell, whom I have continued to bother in innumerable ways, and Naomi Black, who has continued to provide aid and comfort. For the revised edition I am also indebted to Judith Williams for her scrupulous editing.

A Bloomsbury Chronology

1866
Roger Fry born

1877
Desmond MacCarthy born

1879
E.M. Forster born
Vanessa Stephen born

1880
Lytton Strachey born
Thoby Stephen born
Saxon Sydney-Turner born
Leonard Woolf born

1881
Clive Bell born

1882
Virginia Stephen born
Mary Warre-Cornish born

1883
J.M. Keynes born
Adrian Stephen born

1885
Duncan Grant born
Roger Fry enters King's College, Cambridge

1888
Roger Fry obtains a First Class honours in natural sciences and decides to
  study painting

1892
Roger Fry studies painting in Paris
David Garnett born

1893
Dora Carrington born

1894
Roger Fry gives university extension lectures at Cambridge mainly on Italian
    art
Desmond MacCarthy enters Trinity College, Cambridge

1895
Death of Mrs Leslie Stephen
Virginia Stephen's first breakdown

1896
Roger Fry and Helen Coombe married

1897
E.M. Forster enters King's College, Cambridge
Desmond MacCarthy leaves Trinity College
Virginia Stephen attends Greek and history classes at King's College, London

1899
Roger Fry: *Giovanni Bellini*
Clive Bell, Thoby Stephen, Lytton Strachey, Saxon Sydney-Turner, Leonard
    Woolf all enter Trinity College, Cambridge
The Midnight Society – a 'reading society' – founded at Trinity by Bell,
    Sydney-Turner, Stephen, and Woolf

1900
Roger Fry gives university extension lectures on art at Cambridge

1901
Roger Fry becomes art critic for the *Athenaeum*
Vanessa Stephen enters the Royal Academy Schools
E.M. Forster leaves Cambridge, travels in Italy and Greece, begins *A Room
    with a View*

1902
Duncan Grant attends the Westminster Art School
Leonard Woolf, Saxon Sydney-Turner, and Lytton Strachey elected to 'The

Apostles' (older members include Roger Fry, Desmond MacCarthy, E.M. Forster)

Clive Bell does historical research in London after leaving Cambridge

Adrian Stephen enters Trinity College, Cambridge

J.M. Keynes enters King's College, Cambridge

Virginia Stephen starts private Greek lessons

1903

G.E. Moore: *Principia Ethica*

Roger Fry's first exhibition of paintings and drawings

Desmond MacCarthy writes criticism for the *Speaker*

J.M. Keynes elected to 'The Apostles'

E.M. Forster's first short story published

1904

Virginia Stephen publishes her first review

Leslie Stephen dies, and the Stephen children move to 46 Gordon Square, Bloomsbury

E.M. Forster acts as tutor to Countess von Arnim's children in Germany

Clive Bell lives in Paris and does historical research

Leonard Woolf leaves Cambridge, takes the Civil Service examination and sails for Ceylon as a cadet in the Ceylon Civil Service

Saxon Sydney-Turner leaves Cambridge and becomes a clerk in the Estate Duty Office

Lytton Strachey works on a fellowship dissertation

Virginia Stephen's second breakdown

1905

Euphrosyne: A Collection of Verse, with anonymous contributions by Clive Bell, Saxon Sydney-Turner, Leonard Woolf, and Lytton Strachey

Roger Fry edits *The Discourses of Sir Joshua Reynolds*

E.M. Forster: *Where Angels Fear to Tread*

Adrian Stephen leaves Trinity College

Virginia Stephen teaching at Morley College, London

Thoby Stephen begins the Thursday evenings at Gordon Square for his friends

Vanessa Stephen organizes the Friday Club, which is concerned with the arts

Lytton Strachey leaves Cambridge

J.M. Keynes bracketed Twelfth Wrangler

1906

Clive Bell reads for the Bar

Desmond MacCarthy and Mary Warre-Cornish married
Roger Fry accepts curatorship of the Department of Painting, Metropolitan
    Museum of New York
Duncan Grant studies art in Paris
J.M. Keynes joins the India Office
Thoby Stephen dies of typhoid fever

1907
E.M. Forster: *The Longest Journey*
Desmond MacCarthy: *The Court Theatre: A Commentary and Criticism*
Vanessa Stephen and Clive Bell married
Duncan Grant lives in Paris after studying a term at the Slade School
Virginia and Adrian Stephen move to 29 Fitzroy Square; Thursday evenings
    begin again
Virginia Stephen begins work on her first novel
Roger Fry resigns curatorship and becomes European advisor to the
    Metropolitan Museum
Desmond MacCarthy edits the *New Quarterly* (until 1910)
Lytton Strachey begins weekly reviews for the *Spectator* (until 1909)
Play-reading Society begun at 46 Gordon Square with the Bells, Adrian and
    Virginia Stephen, Strachey, and Sydney-Turner; meets intermittently until
    1914

1908
E.M. Forster: *A Room with a View*
Julian Bell born
Leonard Woolf becomes Assistant Government Agent, Hambantota, Ceylon
J.M. Keynes leaves the Civil Service

1909
Roger Fry: 'An Essay in Aesthetics'
Lytton Strachey proposes to Virginia Stephen
Duncan Grant moves to 21 Fitzroy Square
Roger Fry becomes editor of the *Burlington Magazine*
Lady Ottoline Morrell comes to Thursday evenings in Fitzroy Square
J.M. Keynes elected to a fellowship at King's

1910
E.M. Forster: *Howards End*
The *Dreadnought* hoax takes place in February; Virginia Stephen, Adrian
    Stephen, Duncan Grant participate.
Roger Fry meets Duncan Grant, the Bells; talks to the Friday Club; is
    dismissed from the Metropolitan Museum by J.P. Morgan
Helen Fry confined to a mental institution as incurably insane (dies in 1937)

Virginia Stephen doing volunteer work for women's suffrage
Lytton Strachey and Lady Ottoline Morrell meet
Quentin Bell born
First Post-Impressionist Exhibition at the Grafton Galleries organized by
     Roger Fry, with Desmond MacCarthy as secretary (from November to
     January 1911)

1911
E.M. Forster: *The Celestial Omnibus and Other Stories*
Virginia Stephen leases a house at Firle, Sussex
Roger Fry declines the directorship of the Tate Gallery; starts lecturing at the
     Slade School
Leonard Woolf returns from Ceylon
J.M. Keynes becomes a lecturer in economics at Cambridge
Virginia and Adrian Stephen move to 38 Brunswick Square where they share
     a house with Woolf, Keynes, and Grant
Vanessa Bell, Roger Fry affair

1912
Lytton Strachey: *Landmarks in French Literature*
E.M. Forster travels in India
J.M. Keynes becomes editor of the *Economic Journal* (until 1945)
Leonard Woolf resigns from the Colonial Service
Virginia Stephen and Leonard Woolf married; they live in Clifford's Inn,
     London, and at Asham House, Sussex, after travelling in France, Spain,
     and Italy
Second Post-Impressionist Exhibition organized by Roger Fry with Leonard
     Woolf as secretary (from November to February 1913)

1913
Virginia Woolf finishes *The Voyage Out*
Leonard Woolf: *The Village and the Jungle*
J.M. Keynes: *Indian Currency and Finance*
E.M. Forster returns from India, begins *A Passage to India* and writes
     Maurice
Saxon Sydney-Turner joins the Treasury
Leonard Woolf begins reviewing for the *New Statesman* and studying the
     Co-operative Movement
Vanessa Bell falls in love with Duncan Grant
Desmond MacCarthy becomes drama critic for the *New Statesman*
Omega Workshops founded by Roger Fry with Duncan Grant as co-director;
     quarrel with Wyndham Lewis
Virginia Woolf suffers another breakdown and attempts suicide

Novel Club exists for about a year

1914
Clive Bell: *Art*
Leonard Woolf: *The Wise Virgins*
Adrian Stephen and Karin Costelloe married
Desmond MacCarthy joins the Red Cross and serves in France (until 1915)
J.M. Keynes joins the Treasury
The Woolfs move to Richmond, Surrey, from Clifford's Inn
Clive Bell, Mary Hutchinson relationship begins (until 1927)

1915
Clive Bell: *Peace at Once* (ordered destroyed by the Lord Mayor of London)
Virginia Woolf: *The Voyage Out*
E.M. Forster in Alexandria with the Red Cross (until 1918)
The Woolfs move to Hogarth House, Richmond
Carrington meets Lytton Strachey and Bloomsbury

1916
Leonard Woolf: *International Government: Two Reports*
Lytton Strachey's claim of conscientious objection to conscription is denied,
    but he is granted exemption for medical reasons
Leonard Woolf is exempted from conscription for medical reasons
Clive Bell does alternative service on the Morrells' farm at Garsington
Vanessa Bell, her children, Duncan Grant, and David Garnett move to
    Wissett in Suffolk so that Garnett and Grant can do alternative service on a
    farm; later in the year they move to Charleston, Firle, Sussex, where the
    Bells and Duncan Grant live permanently
J.M. Keynes and friends take over 46 Gordon Square, which remains
    Keynes's London home

1917
Leonard Woolf: *The Future of Constantinople*
Clive Bell: *Ad Familiares*
The Woolfs buy a printing press: *Two Stories Written and Printed by
    Virginia Woolf and L.S. Woolf* is publication #1 of the Hogarth Press
Leonard Woolf edits *The Framework for a Lasting Peace*; founds the 1917
    Club; and becomes secretary to the Labour party advisory committee on
    imperial and international questions for more than twenty years
Virginia Woolf begins keeping a regular diary
Lytton Strachey and Carrington set up house at the Mill House, Tidmarsh,
    Berkshire

1918
Lytton Strachey: *Eminent Victorians*
Clive Bell: *Pot-Boilers*
Mary MacCarthy: *A Pier and a Band*
Desmond MacCarthy: *Remnants*
Leonard Woolf: *Co-operation and the Future of Industry*
Leonard Woolf becomes editor of the *International Review*
Katherine Mansfield's *Prelude* published by the Hogarth Press
At the suggestion of Roger Fry and Duncan Grant, J.M. Keynes persuades
    the Treasury to purchase works of art from the Degas sale in Paris
Angelica Bell, daughter of Vanessa Bell and Duncan Grant, born

1919
Virginia Woolf: *Night and Day*
The Hogarth Press publishes Virginia Woolf's *Kew Gardens* and T.S. Eliot's
    Poems, but is unable to publish James Joyce's *Ulysses* offered to it the year
    before
J.M. Keynes in Paris as the principal respresentative of the Treasury at the
    Peace Conference; he resigns in June and writes *The Economic
    Consequences of the Peace* at Charleston, which is published at the end of
    the year
The Bells, Woolfs, Keynes, Fry, and Grant meet Diaghileff's troupe in
    London, including Picasso, Derain, Stravinsky, Massine, Ansermet,
    Nijinsky, and Lydia Lopokova
Woolfs move from Asham to Monk's House, Rodmell, Sussex
Clive Bell in Paris; friendship with Derain, Braque, Dunoyer de Segonzac,
    Picasso, Cocteau, and others
Lady Strachey and daughters move to 51 Gordon Square
Francis Birrell and David Garnett open a bookstore

1920
Roger Fry: *Vision and Design*
Leonard Woolf: *Economic Imperialism* and *Empire and Commerce in Africa*
The Hogarth Press publishes Maxim Gorky's *Reminiscences of Tolstoy*,
    translated by S.S. Koteliansky and Leonard Woolf, and E.M. Forster's *The
    Story of the Siren*
Leonard Woolf writes leaders on foreign affairs for the *Nation* for three
    months
Omega Workshops close
First meeting of the Memoir Club
Duncan Grant has his first one-man show in London

Desmond MacCarthy becomes literary editor of the *New Statesman* (until
    1927), reviews under the pen name 'Affable Hawk'
E.M. Forster becomes literary editor of the London *Daily Herald* for a year

1921
Clive Bell: *Poems*
Virginia Woolf: *Monday or Tuesday*
Lytton Strachey: *Queen Victoria*
Roger Fry: *Twelve Original Woodcuts*
Leonard Woolf: *Stories from the East* and *Socialism and Co-operation*
J.M. Keynes: *A Treatise on Probability*
E.M. Forster in India as temporary secretary to the Maharajah of Dewas
    State Senior
Virginia Woolf is ill and inactive for four months
Carrington and Ralph Partridge married

1922
Clive Bell: *Since Cézanne*
Lytton Strachey: *Books and Characters: French and English*
E.M. Forster: *Alexandria: A History and a Guide*
Virginia Woolf: *Jacob's Room*
J.M. Keynes: *A Revision of the Treaty*
Vanessa Bell and Duncan Grant decorate Keynes's rooms at King's College
Leonard Woolf defeated as the Labour candidate for the Combined
    University constituency

1923
Clive Bell: *On British Freedom*; also writes *The Legend of Monte della Sibilla*
    or *Le Paradis de la Reine Sibille,* with illustrations by Vanessa Bell and
    Duncan Grant published by the Hogarth Press
Roger Fry: *Duncan Grant* and *A Sampler of Castile*
E.M. Forster: *Pharos and Pharillon*
J.M. Keynes: *A Tract on Monetary Reform*
The Hogarth Press publishes T.S. Eliot's *The Waste Land*
Virginia Woolf: *Freshwater: A Comedy,* a play about Julia Margaret
    Cameron, performed; revised 1935 for another performance
Leonard Woolf edits *Fabian Essays on Co-operation*
J.M. Keynes becomes chairman of the board of the *Nation and Athenaeum*;
    Leonard Woolf becomes the literary editor (until 1930)
David Garnett: *Lady into Fox*

1924
E.M. Forster: *A Passage to India*

Mary MacCarthy: *A Nineteenth-Century Childhood*
Virginia Woolf: *Mr Bennett and Mrs Brown*
Roger Fry: *The Artist and Psycho-analysis*
The Hogarth Press publishes Freud's *Collected Papers* and begins the
  Psycho-Analytic Library; 'The Hogarth Essays' also begun
Lytton Strachey, Carrington, and Ralph Partridge move to Ham Spray
  House, Berkshire
The Woolfs (and the Hogarth Press) move to 52 Tavistock Square in Blooms-
  bury
David Garnett: *The Man in the Zoo*

1925
Virginia Woolf: *The Common Reader* and *Mrs Dalloway*
Leonard Woolf: *Fear and Politics: A Debate at the Zoo*
J.M. Keynes: *The Economic Consequences of Mr Churchill* and *A Short View
  of Russia*
E.M. Forster: *Anonymity*
Lytton Strachey's play *The Son of Heaven* (written in 1912) performed;
  Strachey lectures on Pope at Cambridge
J.M. Keynes and Lydia Lopokova married; Keynes visits Russia; then takes a
  lease on Tilton, near Charleston, which remains his country home
Virginia Woolf ill for three months
Virginia Woolf becomes friends with Vita Sackville-West

1926
Roger Fry: *Transformations* and *Art and Commerce*
*Julia Margaret Cameron, Victorian Photographs of Famous Men and Fair
  Women*, with introductions by Roger Fry and Virginia Woolf, published
  by the Hogarth Press
Adrian and Karin Stephen obtain bachelor of medicine degrees to become
  psycho-analysts
David Garnett: *The Sailor's Return*

1927
Virginia Woolf: *To the Lighthouse*
Clive Bell: *Landmarks in Nineteenth-Century Painting*
Leonard Woolf: *Essays on Literature, History, Politics, etc.* and *Hunting the
  Highbrow*
E.M. Forster gives the Clark lectures at Cambridge, which are published as
  Aspects of the Novel; becomes a Fellow of King's College
Roger Fry: *Flemish Art* and *Cézanne*; translates Charles Mauron's *The
  Nature of Beauty in Art and Literature*; lectures on Flemish Art at the
  Queen's Hall, becomes an honorary fellow at King's

The 'Hogarth Lectures on Literature' started
Julian Bell enters King's College, Cambridge
David Garnett: *Go She Must!*

1928
Clive Bell: *Civilization* and *Proust*
Leonard Woolf: *Imperialism and Civilization*
E.M. Forster: *The Eternal Moment and Other Stories*
Virginia Woolf: *Orlando: A Biography*
Lytton Strachey: *Elizabeth and Essex: A Tragic History*
Desmond MacCarthy succeeds Edmund Gosse as senior literary critic for the
    Sunday Times; also edits *Life and Letters* (until 1933)
The Bells, Duncan Grant, occasionally the Woolfs and Roger Fry, stay at 'La
    Bergère,' Cassis, near Marseille, regularly until 1938
Lady Strachey dies

1929
Virginia Woolf: *A Room of One's Own*
Duncan Grant: a retrospective exhibition (1910-29)
Desmond MacCarthy delivers the Clark Lectures at Cambridge on Byron

1930
Mary MacCarthy: *Fighting Fitzgerald and Other Papers*
Roger Fry: *Henri Matisse*
J.M. Keynes: *A Treatise on Money*, 2 vols
Vanessa Bell: exhibition of her paintings in London
Leonard Woolf helps to found the *Political Quarterly* and becomes an editor
    next year (until 1959)
The 'Hogarth Day to Day Pamphlets' started

1931
Virginia Woolf: *The Waves*
Clive Bell: *An Account of French Painting*
Desmond MacCarthy: *Portraits*
Leonard Woolf: *After the Deluge*, vol. 1
Lytton Strachey: *Portraits in Miniature*
J.M. Keynes: *Essays in Persuasion*
E.M. Forster: *A Letter to Madan Blanchard* (first of the Hogarth Letters)
Roger Fry: retrospective exhibition of paintings
John Lehmann joins the Hogarth Press (leaves in 1932)

1932
Virginia Woolf: *The Common Reader* Second Series and *A Letter to a Young
    Poet*

Desmond MacCarthy: *Criticism*
Roger Fry: *Characteristics of French Art* and *The Arts of Painting and
  Sculpture*
Lytton Strachey dies; Carrington commits suicide
Roger Fry lectures at the Queen's Hall
Exhibition of recent paintings by Vanessa Bell and Duncan Grant in
  London
New Signatures begun by the Hogarth Press

1933
Roger Fry: *Art-History as an Academic Study*
J.M. Keynes: *Essays in Biography*
Leonard Woolf edits *The Intelligent Man's Way to Prevent War*
Virginia Woolf: *Flush: A Biography*
Lytton Strachey: *Characters and Commentaries*
Roger Fry appointed Slade Professor at Cambridge
Clive Bell becomes art critic of the *New Statesman and Nation* (until 1943)

1934
Clive Bell: *Enjoying Pictures: Meditations in the National Gallery and
  Elsewhere*
E.M. Forster: *Goldsworthy Lowes Dickinson*
Roger Fry: *Reflections on British Painting*
Virginia Woolf: *Walter Sickert: A Conversation*
Roger Fry dies
Exhibition of Vanessa Bell's paintings

1935
Desmond MacCarthy: *Experience*
Leonard Woolf: *Quack, Quack!*
Vanessa Bell and Duncan Grant execute decorations for the *Queen Mary*
  which are then rejected
J.M. Keynes helps to build the Arts Theatre in Cambridge

1936
J.M. Keynes: *The General Theory of Employment, Interest and Money*
E.M. Forster: *Abinger Harvest*
Mary MacCarthy: *Handicaps: Six Studies*
Leonard Woolf: *The League and Abyssinia*
Adrian Stephen: *The 'Dreadnought' Hoax*
Stephane Mallarmé's *Poems*, translated by Roger Fry with commentaries by
  Charles Mauron
Virginia Woolf ill for two months

1937
Virginia Woolf: *The Years*
Mary MacCarthy: *The Festival, Etc.*
Desmond MacCarthy gives the Leslie Stephen Lecture on Leslie Stephen at
  Cambridge
Vanessa Bell: exhibition of paintings
Duncan Grant: exhibition of paintings
Julian Bell killed in Spain
J.M. Keynes seriously ill

1938
Virginia Woolf: *Three Guineas*
Clive Bell: *Warmongers*
E.M. Forster: *England's Pleasant Land: A Pageant Play* produced
Julian Bell: *Essays, Poems and Letters*, ed. Quentin Bell
The Greville Memoirs, ed. Lytton Strachey and Roger Fulford, 8 vols
John Lehmann rejoins the Hogarth Press as general manager and partner,
  buying Virginia Woolf's interest in the Press
Leonard Woolf appointed a member of the Civil Service Arbitration
  Tribunal (for seventeen years)
J.M. Keynes reads 'My Early Beliefs' to the Memoir Club

1939
Leonard Woolf: *After the Deluge*, vol. 2, *The Barbarians at the Gate*, and
  The Hotel
E.M. Forster: *What I Believe*
Roger Fry: *Last Lectures*
Woolfs and the Hogarth Press move to 37 Mecklenburgh Square
Angelica Bell's twenty-first birthday: 'the last Bloomsbury party'

1940
Virginia Woolf: *Roger Fry: A Biography*
Desmond MacCarthy: *Drama*
Leonard Woolf: *The War for Peace*
Hogarth Press bombed in Mecklenburgh Square; moved to Hertfordshire
E.M. Forster broadcasts regularly throughout the war to India

1941
Virginia Woolf: *Between the Acts*
Virginia Woolf commits suicide
Vanessa Bell: exhibition of paintings

1942
E.M. Forster: *Virginia Woolf*

Virginia Woolf: *The Death of the Moth and Other Essays*
Angelica Bell and David Garnett married
J.M. Keynes becomes chairman of the Committee for the Encouragement of
　　Music and the Arts (which becomes the Arts Council in 1945); awarded a
　　peerage

1943
Virginia Woolf: *A Haunted House and Other Short Stories*
Vanessa Bell, Duncan Grant, and Quentin Bell complete paintings for the
　　parish church at Berwick near Firle, Sussex

1944
J.M. Keynes at the Bretton Woods international conference

1945
E.M. Forster elected honorary fellow of King's College and takes up
　　residence there after his mother's death
J.M. Keynes: 'The Arts Council: Its Policy and Hopes,' BBC broadcast
Duncan Grant: one-man exhibition
J.M. Keynes goes to America to negotiate a loan for Britain

1946
J.M. Keynes awarded the Order of Merit but dies before it is conferred
John Lehmann offers to buy the Hogarth Press, but Leonard Woolf sells out
　　to Chatto & Windus instead

1947
E.M. Forster: *Collected Tales*
Virginia Woolf: *The Moment and Other Essays*

1948
Adrian Stephen dies

1949
J.M. Keynes: *Two Memoirs*

1950
Virginia Woolf: *The Captain's Death Bed and Other Essays*

1951
Desmond MacCarthy: *Shaw*
E.M. Forster: *Two Cheers for Democracy*; writes the libretto for Benjamin
　　Britten's opera *Billy Budd*
Desmond MacCarthy knighted

1952
Desmond MacCarthy dies

1953
Desmond MacCarthy: *Humanities* and *Memories*
Leonard Woolf: *Principle Politica* (vol. 3 of *After the Deluge*)
Virginia Woolf: *A Writer's Diary*, ed. Leonard Woolf
E.M. Forster: *The Hill of Devi*
Mary MacCarthy dies
David Garnett: *The Golden Echo*

1954
Desmond MacCarthy: *Theatre*

1955
David Garnett: *Aspects of Love* and *The Flowers of the Forest*

1956
Clive Bell: *Old Friends: Personal Recollections*
E.M. Forster: *Marianne Thornton: A Domestic Biography*
Virginia Woolf and Lytton Strachey: *Letters*
Vanessa Bell: exhibition of paintings
Last meeting of the Memoir Club

1957
Duncan Grant: exhibition of paintings

1958
Virginia Woolf: *Granite and Rainbow: Essays*
Duncan Grant decorates Russell Chantry, Lincoln Cathedral

1959
Duncan Grant: retrospective exhibition at the Tate Gallery

1960
Leonard Woolf: *Sowing: An Autobiography of the Years 1880-1904*; revisits
    Ceylon

1961
Leonard Woolf: *Growing: An Autobiography of The Years 1904-1911*
Vanessa Bell dies; memorial exhibition of her paintings

1962
Leonard Woolf: *Diaries in Ceylon: 1908-1911*
Saxon Sydney-Turner dies
David Garnett: *The Familiar Faces*

1964
Leonard Woolf: *Beginning Again: An Autobiography of the Years 1911-1918*

Lytton Strachey: *Spectatorial Essays*
Duncan Grant and His World: An Exhibition
Vanessa Bell: A Memorial Exhibition of her Paintings by the Arts Council
Clive Bell dies

1965
Virginia Woolf: *Contemporary Writers*

1967
Leonard Woolf: *Downhill All the Way: 1919–1939*

1969
Leonard Woolf: *The Journey Not the Arrival Matters: An Autobiography of
    the Years 1939–1969*
Portraits by Duncan Grant: an Arts Council exhibition
E.M. Forster awarded the Order of Merit
Leonard Woolf dies

1970
E.M. Forster dies
Carrington: *Letters and Extracts from Her Diaries*, ed. David Garnett

1971
E.M. Forster: *Maurice* and *Albergo Empedocle and Other Writings*
Lytton Strachey by Himself: A Self-Portrait

1972
Roger Fry: *Letters*, 2 vols
E.M. Forster: *The Life to Come and Other Stories*
Lytton Strachey: *The Really Interesting Question and Other Papers*
Duncan Grant: exhibition of watercolours and drawings

1973
Virginia Woolf: *Mrs Dalloway's Party: A Short Short Sequence*

1975
The Letters of Virginia Woolf (6 vols to 1980)

1976
Virginia Woolf: *Moments of Being* (expanded edition, 1985)

1977
The Diary of Virginia Woolf (5 vols to 1984)
Virginia Woolf: *Books and Portraits*

1978
Duncan Grant dies

E.M. Forster: *Commonplace Book* facsimile published; transcribed 1985

1979
David Garnett: *Great Friends*

1980
E.M. Forster: *Arctic Summer and Other Fiction*

1981
David Garnett, Lydia Keynes die

1983
Selected Letters of E.M. Forster (2 vols to 1985)

1985
Virginia Woolf, *The Complete Shorter Fiction* (expanded edition, 1989)

1986
Essays of Virginia Woolf (6 vols to -)

1989
Letters of Leonard Woolf

1990
The Early Journals of Virginia Woolf

1993
Selected Letters of Vanessa Bell

PART ONE

Bloomsbury on Bloomsbury

Introduction

The Memoir Club first met on 4 March 1920, but long before then Bloomsbury had been discussing themselves in letters, in diaries, and in essays written for friends. The portrait, in words or paint, was a preferred mode of expression for members of the Group. Biography was their favourite form of history; along with fiction it was the genre in which their most important literary writing was done. The philosophical justification for Bloomsbury's high valuation of personal relations came from the book Bloomsbury liked to refer to as their Bible, G.E. Moore's *Principia Ethica*. In his chapter on The Ideal, Moore concluded 'that personal affections and aesthetic enjoyments include *all* the greatest, and *by far* the greatest, goods we can imagine' (238). In Bloomsbury's aesthetic treatment of personal affections these ideals were combined.

The texts in *Bloomsbury on Bloomsbury* range from private correspondence and diaries to public memoirs. All are accounts of Bloomsbury's various relationships and activities by those individuals who made up the immediate family of Bloomsbury. Some are contemporary descriptions, and others rather distant recollections. The selections have been arranged in two different ways: they have been placed for the most part in chronological order of their writing and also grouped together under their authors. Readers who wish to begin with general views of Bloomsbury can start with the excerpts from Leonard Woolf's autobiographies and then read the memoirs of Virginia Woolf, Desmond MacCarthy, J.M. Keynes, and the Bells.

Adrian Stephen: A Bloomsbury Evening in 1909

After the death of their father Leslie Stephen in 1904, Vanessa, Thoby, Virginia, and Adrian moved from Hyde Park Gate near Kensington Gardens to 46 Gordon Square in Bloomsbury. In 1905 Thoby began to hold his Thursday evenings at which his sisters met his Cambridge friends. 'It was there,' wrote Duncan Grant, 'that what has since been called "Bloomsbury" for good or ill came into being' (see p. 99). Accounts of these gatherings are to be found in the memoirs of Virginia Woolf and Vanessa Bell. After Thoby's death in 1906 and Vanessa's marriage to Clive Bell in 1907, the two remaining Stephens moved to Fitzroy Square near Bloomsbury, where they lived on not wholly amicable terms and continued in a somewhat less serious vein the Thursday evenings that Thoby had begun. (For a later account of Adrian Stephen's connections with Bloomsbury, see the account by his daughter on pp. 380-2.)

A contemporary account of what one of those Thursday evenings in Fitzroy Square was like is given in a diary that Adrian Stephen kept in June and July, 1909. 'The Goat' was a pet family name for Virginia. Miss Cole was the sister of Horace, the instigator of the Dreadnought hoax described in the next selection.

Thursday July 1st

On my way home I went to Gordon Square where I found the Goat and walked home with her. We dined alone together and after dinner waited a long time before anybody appeared. Saxon as usual came in first but was quickly followed by Norton and he by James and Lytton Strachey. We were very silent at first, Virginia and Lytton and I doing all the talking, Saxon being in his usual state of torpor and Norton and James occasionally exchanging a whisper. Later on Vanessa and Clive came in bringing with them Duncan Grant. After this the conversation became more lively. Vanessa sat with Lytton on the sofa and from half heard snatches I gathered they were talking about his and James's obscene loves. Whatever it was they were discussing they were brought to an abrupt stop by a sudden silence, this pleased them very much, especially Vanessa, and I kindly added to their joy by asking why they stopped. Soon afterwards Henry Lamb came in having returned from doing some portraits at Oxford. The conversation kept up a good flow, though it was not very interesting, until at about half past eleven Miss Cole arrived.

She went and sat in the long wicker chair with Virginia and Clive on the floor beside her. Virginia began in her usual tone of frank admiration to compliment her on her appearance. 'Of course, you Miss Cole are always dressed so exquisitely. You look so original, so like a sea shell. There is something so refined about you coming in among our muddy boots and pipe smoke, dressed in your exquisite creations.' Clive chimed in with more heavy compliments and then began asking her why she disliked him so much, saying how any other young lady would have been much pleased with all the nice things he had been saying but that she treated him so sharply. At this Virginia interrupted with 'I think Miss Cole has a very strong character' and so on and so on. Altogether Miss Cole was as unhappy and uncomfortable as she could be; it was impossible not to help laughing at the extravagance of Virginia and Clive and all conversation was stopped by their noisy choruses, so the poor woman was the centre of all our gaze, and did not know what to do with herself. At last, a merciful diversion was made and Virginia took my seat and I hers and with, I may say, some skill I managed to keep Clive under control.

James and Lytton Strachey left and we played an absurd game which Vanessa and Clive had learnt at the Freshfields. The principle of the game was as follows: that person won who in half a minute could say the most words beginning with any given letter. Clive held the watch and gave us each a turn. Norton being given G started off with Jerusalem and Jesus, which I am afraid must have added another pain to poor Miss Cole's already lengthy list. We all had our turns, Vanessa trying to sail as near to the wind as she could, she is always trying to bring out some bawdy remark and is as pleased when she has done it as a spoilt child. Miss Cole went at one and Duncan Grant at about the same time, when a great discussion was started, I know not by whom, about vice. Very soon Virginia with exquisite art made herself the centre of the argument making the vaguest statements with the intensest feeling and ready to snap up anybody who laughed. Her method is ingenious and at first is rather disconcerting for when someone has carefully examined her argument and certainly refuted it she at once agrees with him enthusiastically saying that he has put her point exactly.

The argument such as it was degenerated into mere phrase-making and so regarded was quite amusing; this gave way in its turn to the game of bantering Saxon. He was chaffed and laughed at for all his little peculiarities and all the time he kept his silence, only giving an occasional smile. He could not be provoked into saying anything even by Virginia's most daring sallies which never fail of their guffaw when Clive is present. At last everybody went except Saxon. Saxon went on to discuss different ways to Germany having obtained further information from Cooks. Virginia and I were however so sleepy that we managed by sheer indifference to oust him. We got to bed as the dawn was coming up about 3.

Adrian Stephen: The *Dreadnought* Hoax

*Two famous events in the early history of Bloomsbury occurred in
1910. How Roger Fry's first post-impressionist exhibition, which
opened in November, stunned the English art establishment is described later in this section by Desmond MacCarthy. The previous
January Adrian Stephen, his sister Virginia, and Duncan Grant joined
three of Adrian's friends to hoax the Royal Navy so successfully that
it made newspaper headlines and caused questions in Parliament. The
celebrated* Dreadnought *hoax was organized by Horace Cole, a wealthy
practical joker and college friend of Adrian's, and participated in by
two other friends of theirs, Anthony Buxton and Guy Ridley.*

*Adrian Stephen became a psychiatrist and wrote his account of the
hoax a quarter of a century after the event. It begins with the story
of how Cole and his friends had hoaxed the mayor of Cambridge
several years before by disguising themselves as the sultan of Zanzibar
and his suite. For Stephen these hoaxes had a purpose beyond that
of simply having fun at other people's expense: 'It had seemed to
me ever since I was very young, just as I imagine it had seemed to
Cole, that anyone who took up an attitude of authority over anyone
else was necessarily also someone who offered a leg for everyone to
pull' (10). The* Dreadnought *was the largest and most powerful bat-
tleship of the time. The coming world war is implicit in Stephen's
retelling of the hoax, but it is the class, race, and gender setting of
the story that is most noticeable now.*

*Virginia Woolf retold the story of the ceremonial beatings in her
feminist story of 1920, 'A Society,' and also left a later fragmentary
account of the hoax mentioning that one of its results was the tight-
ening up of naval regulations concerning official visitors. 'I am glad
to think that I too have been of help to my country,' she observed.
And when Admiral Sir William Fisher, the Stephens' first cousin who
had been chief of the Admiral's staff on the* Dreadnought, *died the
year after Adrian Stephen's account was published, she remarked in
a letter, 'Yes I'm sorry about William – our last meeting was on the
deck of the Dreadnought in 1910 I think; but I wore a beard. And
I'm afraid he took it to heart a good deal. . . .' (quoted in Quentin
Bell,* Virginia Woolf, *1:215–16).*

The *Dreadnought* Hoax . . . took place a few years later. The 'Channel Fleet' (I believe it was called this) was then lying at Weymouth
under the command of Admiral X, whose flagship was the *Dread-*

nought, and, in short, we proposed to visit it in the characters of the Emperor of Abyssinia and his suite. The idea was suggested to Cole by a naval officer as a matter of fact, and those who made a to-do about the honour of the Navy would have been interested to hear this. I am afraid I may be letting something out of the bag, too, if I say that one of his first aims was to pull the leg of another naval officer, a cousin of my own. My cousin was chief of the Admiral's staff at that time and so might be considered to be involved.

Cole asked me to meet his friend at luncheon, and he and I took to the plan at once, and the next thing was to collect our troupe of hoaxers. Cole got hold of two friends, Mr Anthony Buxton and Mr Guy Ridley, and I got hold of my sister Virginia, now Mrs Woolf, and Mr Duncan Grant.

The plan which had worked so well at Cambridge was to be repeated as nearly as possible, but this time Cole was to be a young gentleman from the Foreign Office, Buxton was to be the Emperor of Abyssinia, Virginia, Guy Ridley and Duncan Grant were to form the suite, and I was to be the interpreter.

Virginia and I lived in Fitzroy Square in those days, and it was arranged that the whole troupe should meet in our house early one morning to be made up for their parts. Clarksons undertook to dress us up, and I believe the great Mr Willy Clarkson himself came to superintend, though, of course, we let no one into our plot. Horace Cole just had to wear a top-hat and tail coat, but the Emperor and his suite, including Virginia, had to have their faces blackened, to wear false beards and moustaches and elaborate Eastern robes. I was merely disguised with a false beard, a moustache and a little sunburn powder. I wore a bowler hat and a great coat and looked, I am afraid, like a seedy commercial traveller.

When all was ready we took taxis to Paddington Station and got into a train with a luncheon car bound for Weymouth. The telegram, warning the Admiral to expect us, was to be sent off after we started, and it was to be signed 'Hardinge', though the friend who sent it was named in sober fact Tudor Castle. Hardinge, however, was the name of the permanent head of the Foreign Office.

There is little to tell of the journey down. Cole and I insisted that the others should not go with us into the luncheon car, as we were afraid of accidents to their make-up. He and I went and lunched together, however, and spent our time largely in the attempt to teach me the Swahili language. Swahili is, I believe, spoken in some parts of East Africa. Whether it is spoken in Abyssinia or not I don't know, but we thought it might be as well for me to know a few phrases, and to that end we had bought a grammar from the Society for the Propagation of the Gospel. Of course, when the time came, I could hardly remember two words, though some newspapers later described us as having talked 'fluent Abyssinian'. However, if it did nothing else, the study of Swahili helped Cole and me, at any rate, to pass the time, for to tell the truth we were feeling rather nervous. Something might so easily go wrong. It might be that the telegram ought to have been written in some special code, or it might be that the Admiral would send a message by wireless to get it confirmed, or perhaps my cousin might recognize me (he would hardly recognize Virginia) and then we should get into trouble.

I think that perhaps the most exciting moment for me that day was first the arrival at Weymouth – that was the plunge into the cold bath. As the train slowed down for the station we were all agog. I think I half expected that no notice would be taken of us at all, and we should just have to slink back to London but no, there on the platform stood a naval officer in full uniform, and the hoax had begun.

As we got out of the train the officer stepped smartly up and saluted the Emperor formally, and Cole and I made whatever introductions seemed necessary.

In spite of the short notice we had given, everything was ready for our reception. Inside the station a red carpet was laid down for us to walk on, and there was a barrier in position to keep sightseers at a proper distance. Outside we were conducted to cabs which took us down to the harbour and there, again, was the smart little steam launch which was to take us out to the Fleet.

By the time we reached the *Dreadnought* the expedition had become for me at any rate almost an affair of every day. It was hardly a question any longer of a hoax. We were almost acting the truth. Everyone was expecting us to act as the Emperor and his suite, and it would have been extremely difficult not to.

It may have seemed to some an odd introduction to the story of a hoax in which I took part to say that I am incapable of deception. Of course, I did not mean the words to be taken too pedantically. Suppose someone sent word to an unwelcome visitor that he was not at home you could hardly on that grounds describe him as a liar without being so misleading as to be guilty of falsehood yourself. Pedantically speaking, he would, of course, be a liar, and, pedantically speaking, I must admit myself capable of deception when I took part in the hoax. But once the telegram had been sent off, and we had arrived and been received, it would not have been an easy matter to tell the truth, and we almost, I think, believed in the hoax ourselves.

We steamed out then in our little brass-funnelled launch into the bay where we saw the *Dreadnought* lying among the Fleet, with lines of marines drawn up on her deck and flags flying from her mast. Then, as we came alongside and approached the ship's gangway, the band struck up its music.

As a matter of fact, the ship was smaller than I expected, I remember, and uglier, with its funnels and its great tripod mast and its gun turrets and what not, stuck all about. However, I had not much time for criticism. When we arrived the Admiral and his staff and the captain of the ship, all in their gold-laced uniforms, were ready to receive us.

Cole went on board first, I think, and then the Emperor and his suite, and I was last. I had one or two surprises at this point. Cole was performing the introductions, and I was a little taken aback to hear myself introduced as Kauffmann. We had all chosen our own names coming down in the train and Cole, who was rather deaf, had misheard me. I had chosen an English name that sounded a little like Kauffmann and Kauffmann with a German name I was to be. I was a little alarmed at this, because German spy scares were for ever being started in those days, and I was afraid of an extra close scrutiny. At the same time I was conscious of looking the most awful 'outsider' and of not knowing in what form to return the Admiral's welcome, whether to take my hat off or shake hands or what. On the top of this I saw my cousin standing staring at me from a few yards off, and since I stood 6 ft 5 in. in my socks I was afraid he might observe me. Then I became aware of another source of danger, too, that was quite unexpected, for the captain of the ship also turned out to be a man with whom I was personally acquainted. I belonged at that time to a small club which took long country walks on Sundays, and the captain had several times joined in and spent whole days in our company. I knew, of course, that he was a Captain in the Navy, but did not know his ship.

The situation, then, was becoming very embarrassing, but I was saved by the naval officers' proverbial tact. Their cordiality was such that it put me at my ease at once and the inspection of the ship began.

I am afraid that my memory of the visit must necessarily refer mainly to my own experience, and it is rather scrappy, but a few moments seem to stand out specially. The first thing to do was to inspect the Guard of Honour, and this put the first strain on my powers of interpretation. There were two kinds of marines in the guard, and some of them had blue uniforms and some red, some were, I think, artillery and some infantry. The Admiral explained this to me and told me to pass it on to the Emperor. For a moment I boggled at this, I could not think what to say. 'I am afraid it will be rather hard to put that into Abyssinian, sir,' I said. 'However, I'll try.' 'Entaqui, mahai, kustufani,' I started, addressing Anthony Buxton, and whether those were real Swahili words learnt from the grammar, or whether they were invented on the spur of the moment, I don't remember, but they have stuck in my memory ever since. If they were real Swahili they were the only native African words that any of us used, and I could get no further. I don't find it easy to speak fluent gibberish impromptu, and I was again in something of a difficulty. I must somehow produce something that would not be too jerky, and too unplausible. After a pause I began again as follows: 'Tahli bussor ahbat tahl aesque miss. Erraema, fleet use . . .' and so on. My language may have sounded a bit odd, but at any rate I could be fluent enough. When I was a boy I had spent years on what is called a classical education, and now I found a use for it. It was the habit in the middle forms of my school to learn by heart the fourth book of Virgil's *Aeneid* as 'repetition'. I was able, therefore, to repeat whole stretches of it, and I knew a good deal of Homer in the same way. I was provided by my education, then, with a fine repertory of nonsense and did not have to fall back entirely on my own invention. I had to take care that neither the Latin nor the Greek should be recognized, of course, but I felt that probably few naval officers had suffered an education like mine and, in any case, I so broke up the words and so mispronounced them that probably they would have escaped; notice even of the best scholar. The quotation that I started with by the way is from the *Aeneid* Book IV, line 437.

I found that my plan worked excellently, and even began to improve on it as in some emergencies that occurred more than once such as telling the Emperor to mind his head in a doorway, I would remember what I had said last time and use the same phrase again. This may have given us a little plausibility, especially as Anthony Buxton was very quick in picking up some of my words, and using them in his replies. I remember, though, hearing two officers who were eavesdropping behind some corner remark on the oddness of our lingo.

There was only one further precaution that I had to take about our speech. Since there were two men on board, with one of whom, indeed, I had to converse a great deal, who might be expected to know my voice, some disguise was clearly necessary. Instead of my usual rather high register and Cambridge accent, therefore, I used a most unnatural deep bass, and an accent that was meant to be German. With that our disguise was as good as I could make it, but there was one other moment of suspense in connection with our speech, though I don't remember exactly when it occurred. Someone told me that there was one man in the Fleet who could speak to the Abyssinians in their own tongue, but mercifully added that he was away on leave.

The Admiral received us then and inspected the Guard of Honour with us, and then handed us over to Captain Y (my acquaintance) to be taken over the ship. I cannot remember now all that we saw, but I remember going down long corridors, looking at the wireless room, the sick bay if that is what it is called, and the Mess, having the big guns turned and aimed in different directions and so forth and so on. All these things I duly described in a mixture of Homer and Virgil.

As one might have expected the officers were almost too hospitable, and pressed us hard to eat and drink, but I was too afraid of the effect on our make-up. I excused us on the grounds that the religious beliefs of Abyssinia made it impossible for the Royal family to touch food unless it was prepared in quite special ways. The feeding problem was easily dealt with, but a worse moment was when I saw the Duncan's moustache was beginning to peel off. A slight breeze had got up, and a little rain began to fall, so that I was terrified what might happen next. I did what I could with an umbrella, but there were five people to cover, and then I saw the obvious solution. I spoke to the captain of the heat of the Abyssinian climate and the chill of England, and he saw my point at once and took us below. For a moment or two I had to separate Duncan from the rest and dab hastily at his upper lip, but I was able to be quick enough to escape notice.

Another problem arose about a salute. The Emperor of Abyssinia might expect to be saluted by the firing of guns, and I was consulted as to whether this should be done. I took the course which I think at any rate most of us approved of and said that it was not necessary at all. The French Fleet had not saluted us at Toulon, why should the English? The real fact was that I understood that firing salutes meant cleaning guns afterwards, and it seemed too much of a shame to cause such unnecessary trouble – besides, it was almost as grand to refuse a salute as to accept one.

After going all over the ship, there was nothing left but to return home. Cole who had been enjoying himself in the ward room rejoined the party, and we embarked again on our little steam launch.

We were accompanied again by a young officer, and I remember his pleasure at the astonishment of the simple natives when he switched on the electric light. I think it was this young man, too, who spoke to me about the tune with which the band had welcomed us. The band-master had been unable to get a copy of the Abyssinian National Anthem, but had played, as the next best thing, the Anthem of Zanzibar. I said I thought it did excellently, and considering Cole's and my history, I thought it did.

Another incident happened, I believe, during this short passage to the shore, but I did not notice it – another vessel crossed our bows. But our launch contained Royalty and it is, apparently, a great breach of etiquette to cross the bows of Royalty, so the young officer who was responsible was had up by his Captain and reprimanded. Now the officer who was reprimanded was the young Prince of A. I had this story from another naval officer, and whether it is true or not I feel it ought to be.

When we reached the shore Cole tipped the sailors who came with us royally, and tried to pin a fancy-dress order on the breast of our young officer. He refused it rather shyly, saying he could not accept it without permission from his superiors. He was a nice young man, I thought, and I was really saddened a few years later when I saw what I believed to be his name in the list of those killed in some battle.

We drove to the station, then, and I think when we got into the train we were all except, perhaps, Cole, thoroughly exhausted. The only thing we could think of was our dinner, and luckily we were able to have it in our own compartment, so we ate it in comfort. We only kept up the hoax so far as to insist on the waiters wearing white gloves to serve us. I believe they had to dash out and buy them.

I suppose that most of us imagined that with our arrival home the whole incident was finished. We had decided not to tell the newspapers and, though something was bound to leak out, we did not expect what happened. We had had a photograph taken of ourselves in our fancy dress as a memento, and one day walking in the street I saw this reproduced on the poster of (I think) the *Mirror*. I believe that was how I first realized that someone had given the story away, and I have never felt the slightest doubt that it was Cole who did it, and he would certainly never contradict it.

After this we heard nothing more for some time, till one day walking with Cole near the top of Sloane Street, I saw Captain Y and his wife. He saw us, too, and recognized us and pretended at first to be horrified and then to call a policeman. After a second or two, though, he began to laugh and, in fact, took the whole affair in the best of good humours. There were certain other officers, however, who took it in a different spirit.

It was several weeks after the hoax was over when I was called down early one Sunday morning to see my cousin Z and found him waiting for me in the hall with an expression that I felt to be grim. He told me that he had come to find out just who had taken part in the hoax and that he wanted us all to apologize. He said that he already knew Cole's name, and that Virginia was involved, but he did not know who the others were. For my own part, I said, I did not mind apologizing in the least if it would make things easier for the Admiral. There had been questions asked in Parliament, and we had never meant to cause serious trouble, so if trouble could be avoided by an apology I should be quite ready to make one; though, of course, the others would have to be asked what they felt. My cousin asked me who the others were and, innocent as a lamb, I gave him their names. I, of course, had been hoaxed in my own turn, for the names were needed for another purpose.

My cousin almost snorted with contempt when I suggested that an apology might make things easier for the Admiral – as though such miserable creatures as the hoaxers could possibly make things easier or harder for such an exalted being as an Admiral. I gathered, though, what he minded even more than the questions of the gentlemen in Parliament was the behaviour of the little boys in the streets of Weymouth. When the hoax became so widely known as it did through the *Daily Mirror*, one of the newspapers published an interview. I think it was supposed to be with one of the assistants at Clarksons, who professed to know a great deal more than he did, and in particular stated that we had used the expression 'Bunga-Bunga'. Anyhow, the words 'Bunga-Bunga' became public catchwords for a time, and were introduced as tags into music-hall songs and so forth. Apparently the Admiral was unable to go on shore without having them shouted after him in the streets, and I suppose that other officers suffered in the same way. Naturally, I was very sorry about this – we had no wish to make anyone really uncomfortable – and I expressed my sympathy to my cousin. He left me, then, but as he went he asked me whether I know what the officers were saying about Virginia in the Mess. 'They are saying that she is a common woman of the town – and *I* have to sit and hear this in silence.' With this, holding his right hand in a marked way aloof from mine, he closed the door.

Of course, I got into touch at once with Cole, and then I heard his story. Things had gone very differently with him. The evening before my cousin and another naval officer had arrived at his house and asked to see him. Cole received them in his sitting-room, and they announced that they had come to avenge the honour of the Navy. They proposed to achieve this by beating him with a cane. In ordinary circumstances there would probably have been a free fight, and as Cole was pretty formidable, and as his manservant had scented trouble and was waiting outside the door in case he was needed, there is no telling who would have won. There was one thing which complicated matters, though. Cole was only just recovering from an illness which would have made violent exercise rather a serious danger. This was pointed out to the officers, and it put them in a dilemma. This was the third week-end, they said, that they had journeyed up to London to avenge the Navy, and they could not be foiled again. Eventually Cole made a proposal: he would agree to be beaten if he was allowed to reply in kind. This was agreed to, and the whole party adjourned to a quiet back street. Here they were safe from interruption, either from Cole's manservant or from the public, and here six ceremonial taps were administered to Cole's hindquarters, and six ceremonial taps were administered by him in return.

After this the Navy's honour was at least partly cleared, and the two sides shook hands and parted.

The only other adventure of this kind that I heard of was Duncan's. Whether Buxton or Ridley received visits from the Navy I never heard, and I have scarcely seen either of them since, but Duncan certainly did. He was sitting at breakfast with his father and mother one Sunday morning when a maid announced that some gentlemen had called to see him. It must have been the same morning that my cousin called on me, because Duncan had no warning, and went to see his friends who were waiting outside. Looking out of the window, Mrs Grant saw her son tripped up and pushed into a taxi, the door slammed and the taxi driven off. She was naturally alarmed, and appealed to her husband to know what they should do. 'I expect it's his friends from the *Dreadnought*,' said Major Grant, with his usual beaming smile, and so, of course, it was. When he looked about him in the taxi Duncan found himself seated on the floor at the feet of three large men who were carrying a bundle of canes. They drove on for a bit in silence and Duncan asked where they were going. 'You'll see plenty of *Dreadnoughts* where you are going,' answered my cousin in an ominous voice. Then they asked Duncan whether he was ill, fearing, I suppose, a repetition of the night before.

At last they arrived somewhere in the region of Hendon, and here they stopped, and Duncan was told to get out and go into a field. There was no use in fighting against overwhelming odds, as Duncan said, and out he got and did as he was told.

'I can't make this chap out,' said one of the officers, 'he does not put up any fight. You can't cane a chap like that.' In the end it proved that they could cane a chap like that, but only with some difficulty. My cousin was unable to do it himself, but he could order his inferior officer to do so and the inferior officer could carry out his orders. Duncan, then, received two ceremonial taps, also, and the little party broke up. It so happened, though, that Duncan had only his bedroom slippers on, and no hat, and this so distressed the officers that they pressed him to accept a lift home. 'You can't go home like that,' they said, but Duncan felt it less embarrassing to travel home by tube.

And now I come to what was, so far as I know, the last episode. A great many people – even those who had been thoroughly amused at the Cambridge joke – were profoundly shocked at the idea of hoaxing the Navy. I had an elderly relation, for instance, who had been delighted with the first hoax, and who kindly wrote offering his help in case there were legal proceedings in connection with the second. In his letter, however, he implored me 'for God's sake' to 'keep Virginia's name out of it,' and felt bound to state his opinion that 'His Majesty's ships are not suitable objects for practical jokes'. Other people, and especially a certain military gentleman, began to ask questions in Parliament, and word came round to me that some form of reprimand was going to be administered to the Admiral. Whether the rumour was true I don't know, but it reached me apparently very directly from Mrs McKenna, who was the wife of the First Lord of the Admiralty. It was suggested again that an apology might make things easier. If the hoaxers were to apologize that might appease

those who wanted the Admiral punished. When I heard this, there
was no time to waste. Cole was either ill or away, and I could not
get hold of either Ridley or Buxton, but I did get hold of Duncan,
and together we went down to Whitehall. The door-keeper at the
Admiralty seemed a little surprised to see us, but when we told him
that we wished to see the First Lord about the *Dreadnought* hoax
he gave us an interested look and went to make inquiries. We did
not have to wait long, but were taken upstairs to what I suppose
was Mr McKenna's private room. Mr McKenna took it for granted
at once that we had come to beg for mercy. He told us that at least
one of us had committed a forgery under the Post Office Acts, and
was liable to go to gaol and he at any rate had better lie low, while
the position of the rest of us was doubtful. We tried to get him to
see that we were not in the least concerned with what the Government
proposed to do to us and were, indeed, extremely sceptical as to
whether they could do anything at all. We were only offering, if he
wanted it, an easy way of smoothing things over, but he would have
none of it, and bundled us out. I think I really felt quite ill-used
about this. We had come absolutely gratuitously to make what seemed
a generous offer, and I did not see why this politician should treat
us *de haut en bas*, not even if he had rowed in the Cambridge boat
before he was First Lord of the Admiralty. Perhaps, really, we had
put him in an awkward position, and he did not know quite what
to say; perhaps, indeed, he was laughing up his sleeve.

This was the end of the whole affair. I waited expecting to receive
some sort of visitation from the Navy, but none came. Just why they
beat Cole and Duncan, and not me, I have never understood. Anyone
who does not know me may possible think that it was because I was
6 ft 5 in. high, and might have been a formidable customer. That
is not so, however; if matters had come to a trial of strength I should
have fallen a much easier victim than Cole. In any case, had I been
a Goliath I am sure the Navy's gallantry would have risen to the
occasion. I should be sorry, indeed, if anything I wrote were taken
as intended to cast doubts on the bravery of naval officers. These
men have very particular feelings on this point. Bravery is as much
a matter of professional pride to them as is the quality of his potatoes
to a greengrocer. I should be sorry without the strongest reasons to
cast doubts on either.

Personally, I have always felt, as I expect most of those concerned
did, that the officers' wisest course would have been that which the
Vice-Chancellor recommended to the Mayor of Cambridge – to take

no notice of us. As for 'revenge', if they wanted any they had already had plenty before the hoax was over. They treated us so delightfully while we were on board that I, for one, felt very uncomfortable at mocking, even in the friendliest spirit, such charming people.

Lytton Strachey: Monday June 26th 1916

Lytton Strachey never wrote an account of Bloomsbury as such, though his letters, diaries, and Memoir Club papers reflect Bloomsbury life. It was also in 1910, for example, that Lytton Strachey kept a brief diary, in which he wrote on 8 March that he found 'no Bloomby' at a gathering at Lady Ottoline Morrell's in Bedford Square. This is, I believe, the first recorded use of 'Bloomsbury' to stand for the Bloomsbury Group. Two days later Strachey dined with the Bells at Gordon Square and noted in his diary 'complaints of Clive as to collective affectation and dullness of set. "Everyone tries to make his individuality tell." I couldn't believe it' (120). The internal criticism of Bloomsbury, of which there was to be a great deal through its history, thus accompanied the first use of the word that came to identify the Group.

Lytton Strachey's most important description of life in Bloomsbury was written during the First World War and read later to the Memoir Club. The idea occurred to him, he says, towards the end of the essay, of writing a 'microscopic description of a day.' The aim of such a description is given in the opening words of the memoir and bears a striking family resemblance to Virginia Woolf's famous manifesto in her essay 'Modern Fiction' where she urged writers to give 'the life of Monday or Tuesday' by recording 'the atoms as they fall upon the mind in the order in which they fall . . . however disconnected and incoherent in appearance. . . .' She had in fact written such a description in the sketch 'Monday or Tuesday.' The 'luminous halo' she evokes there shows how different were the atoms that fell on her consciousness from those that fell on Lytton Strachey's (Woolf, Essays, 4:160–1).

The life of Monday or Tuesday that Strachey chose to describe took place at Wissett Lodge, a farmhouse in Suffolk that had belonged to an aunt of Duncan Grant's named Florence Ewbank. Grant and David 'Bunny' Garnett moved in to do fruit farming and thus avoid conscription. Wissett was presided over by Vanessa Bell and her young children Julian and Quentin. For Strachey it was one of the places,

like Lady Ottoline's at Garsington, where he could stay with friends.
On this particular visit he was accompanied by Harry Norton, a Cam-
bridge friend and mathematician, who helped Strachey out financially;
Eminent Victorians, which Strachey was in the midst of writing, is
dedicated to him. Norton had been in love with Vanessa, who was
in love with Duncan, who had been in love with Lytton and was
now in love with 'Bunny.' These relationships lie mostly under the
surface in Strachey's narrative. ('L' in the memoir probably refers to
Strachey's friend the painter Henry Lamb.)

To understand the particular tone of Strachey's memoir, it is im-
portant to remember, first, that it was read to and perhaps even written
for close friends who could be expected to respond to the ironic nu-
ances of Strachey's self-portrait, and secondly, that its setting is war-
time. 'It is horrid to sit helpless while those poor creatures are going
through such things,' Strachey had recently written to Keynes. 'But
really one would have to be God Almighty to be of any effective use'
(138). (All ellipses in the memoir are Strachey's.)

To come close to life! To look at it, not through the eyes of Poets
and Novelists, with their beautifying arrangements or their selected
realisms, but simply as one actually *does* look at it, when it happens,
with its minuteness and its multiplicity and its intensity, vivid and
complete! To do that! To do that even with a bit of it – with no
more than a single day – to realize absolutely the events of a single
and not extraordinary day – surely that might be no less marvellous
than a novel or even a poem, and still more illuminating, perhaps!
If one *could* do it! But one can't, of course. One has neither the power
nor the mere physical possibility for enchaining that almost infinite
succession; one's memory is baffled; and then – the things one remembers most one cannot, one dares not – no! one can only come
close to *them* in a very peculiar secrecy; and yet . . . there remains
a good deal that one can and may even perhaps positively *ought*
to give a fixity to, after all!

I had already had some vague, half-dreaming thoughts about the
Piero della Francesca portrait downstairs, and whether what Duncan
had said about the goodness of the composition was really true, and
whether Norton's exclamation about both his and Nessa's self-
delusion . . . when I was woken up properly by Blanche putting my
breakfast-tray down on the table beside me, and pulling the curtains.
It was eight o'clock. I was happy – as usual – to find food before
me, all ready to be eaten; I certainly wanted nothing else in the world

just then; but, having put on my eye-glasses, I saw two letters crouching under a plate, and realized that I was very glad to have letters too. One was some damned bill, and the other was a huge affair from Ottoline; I opened it, and saw that it covered sheets and that it had enclosures, so I thought that before reading it I'll have my breakfast. And then, as I ate my boiled egg and drank my rather thick tea – but the toast was on its accustomed royal scale – I suddenly remembered the dubiousness of my position, and all that I had decided the night before. Nessa's – yes, one could only call it sulkiness – that oppressed silence all the evening after our late return – how could I doubt its meaning? – 'For heaven's sake – *can't* you leave me with Duncan for a moment? Is it *never* to be?' How her dumb animality – like some creature *aux abois*, as I've often thought – came out more unmistakably than I'd even known! And yet, perhaps it was a mistake! How can one tell, I reflected, what that woman's thinking, with her extraordinary simplicities? But I was as certain as ever that I must do something to settle it one way or the other, that I should have to suggest my going, which meant of course Norton's too, I'd no doubt, and then – I could judge from how she took it what I was to do next. I did not like the thought of going away, though why I didn't I could not be sure. Certainly it might have been a much happier visit; somehow, I had been lonely – and why? There was Norton to talk to about the war and mathematics – wasn't that enough to satisfy me? – And they were all very kind; but had they been kind enough? Was it their married state that oppressed me? But then – were *they* married? – Perhaps it was their *un*married state. Perhaps if I could have lain with Bunny – and then I smiled to think of my romantic visions before coming – of a recrudescence of that affair, under Duncan's nose – and of his dimness on my arrival, and of how very very little I wanted to lie with him now! – Only, all the same, the thought of going away depressed me. Perhaps it was simply because of the easy-goingness of the place and the quantities of food, or was it because . . . and then the vision of that young postman with the fair hair and lovely country complexion who had smiled at me and said 'Good evening, sir', as he passed on his bicycle, flashed upon me, and that other unexpected meeting – but I felt that *that* train of thought was too exciting to be hurried over, and decided, as I'd finished my breakfast, to get through Ott's letter before anything else.

I enjoyed reading it; for it was one of her tremendously expansive and affectionate letters, which invariably carry me off my feet. And it showed me (*apparently*) that she was not annoyed with me (though why one should care whether she was annoyed or not . . .) and that she was ready to have me back again at Garsington, which was a relief, because, if I *had* to go away, it was as well to have somewhere to go to. As for the enclosure, it was an appalling coloured photograph of a young man by Titian, all vague and turd-tinted, and incredibly sentimental, which I was to give to Duncan with her love.

It took a long time getting all the writing clear, but I did it at last; and then, feeling considerably more cheerful, I fished my manuscripts out of the big envelope which I'd put the night before on the lower shelf of the table and began brooding over my poem on Kisses, but I added nothing, and my digestion beginning to work, I fell back drowsily on the pillow, and for a moment there was L. before my eyes. But only for a moment; it was the post-youth who fascinated me now. My scheme of meeting him in the long lane past the village recurred to me, and then I began embroidering romantic and only *just* possible adventures which might follow – the bedroom in the inn at Norwich, and all the rest; but there was the necessity of talking to him first; and I went once more through the calculations of time and place, and saw that my plan really might, if I had the nerve, come off. The down on his cheek, the delicious down on his cheek! It was true that his nose had looked stupid, but perhaps not *too* stupid. Oh! there was no doubt that he was nice. Why, why, had Norton been with me at that second meeting? And he had not even looked in his direction! He had not even been aware that a bicycle had passed!

It was about eleven by the time I was dressed, and when I came down I found Norton and Duncan in the drawing-room. I had hardly finished reading them Ott's letter when Vanessa came in. I gave it to her to read to herself, and of course she could hardly spell out a word of it, and thought a good deal of it dull. I was slightly annoyed, and went off to the dreadful E.C., where I could only just scrape together enough earth out of the tin coalscuttle to cover my addition to the mountain, which, even before my addition, had been far too high.

The sun was shining, and there was my chair in the little arbour at the corner of the lawn. And Blanche came with my midday cocoa, and after that I studied the Bishop of Oxford's book on the Sermon on the Mount. It was a foolish book, but I found in it a charming little poem by an old lady in Torquay to Florrie Ewbank about the coal-strike and the neighbours and 'Sweep' who turned out to be a

new dog – 'such a companion'. It was as good any anything in Samuel
Butler. Then I saw that the time had come to face Vanessa. I went
upstairs, and knocked at the door of her studioroom, which I'd never
been in before, and went in, and there she was in front of me in
the white room, on a dilapidated basket chair, and in one of her
most collapsed and dreamy attitudes.

Was she plain or beautiful? I could not decide. I talked vaguely
– about the room, about Ottoline – and she was very nice. I suddenly
wondered why I had knocked at the door; was it idiotic? How well
I know her! – And how little – how very little! Even her face, which
seemed now almost chocolate-coloured, was strangely unfamiliar. If
I could only have flung myself into her arms! – But I knew so well
what would happen – her smile – her half-bewilderment, half infinitely sensible acceptance – and her odd relapse. As it was, I walked
about uncomfortably, looking at moments vaguely out of the window;
and I was decidedly uneasy when I said at last 'I think I shall have
to drift off'. Of course she simply answered 'Shall you really?' I said,
'Yes – I think so – I think tomorrow.' She said 'Will you go to Garsington?' And I saw then, in the same moment, both that I couldn't
bear the thought of going, and that I should have to go. I thought
that perhaps she would have liked me to stay if that hadn't involved
Norton's also staying; but I felt unable to disentangle that – and I
got no atom of encouragement. When I had got out of the room,
I entirely failed to shut the door, after repeated efforts; there was
something wrong with the lock. She called out, still in her chair,
that she would shut it. Before going, I had wildly glanced at a picture
half-painted on an easel, representing a group of people, with what
was apparently a saint in a halo in mid-air. It looked very niggly,
and the colours were extremely garish – altogether it alarmed me.
In the drawing-room I found the Daily News and the Daily Mirror,
and went out with them into the garden again.

Norton had vanished; his chair in the sun was empty. There were
only the children playing by the pond. I was terrified of their coming
and pulling me to pieces, but for some reason or other they didn't,
and I could read my newspaper in peace. I read the Daily News,
but there was nothing to interest me. As for the Daily Mirror, what
could there be to interest me in that? A face perhaps . . . but for weeks
past I had never found a single one that wasn't disgusting; and I
thought of that time at the Lacket, when every day I had found some
living creature in it – usually killed. And then I *did* come on a face
– a charming one – of a young boxer – 'Jimmy Wilde, the famous fly-

weight', whom I'd never heard of before. I longed to go and see him
boxing: I have never seen a boxing-match. What would happen? I
wondered. Would the blood pour down over his eyes? But the match
he was to box was to be that very night, so that was impossible –
though for a second I actually envisaged going up to London on
some excuse that afternoon. But then – the post-boy? No! It was all
ridiculous: the boxing match would come and go without me; and
after that what chance would I have of ever seeing Jimmy Wilde
again? At that moment I looked up, and saw, slowly pounding along
the farm-road on the other side of the house, a waggon and horses,
driven by a youth. It was too far off to be sure, but he seemed hand-
some, I was feeling *désoeuvré* and distracted, and so I thought I'll
go and see what he was like. But then I thought after all I wouldn't,
and remained sitting there – undecided, vague and miserable. I was
in my slippers, I reflected: and how could I go through the dirt?
The cart and horses and young man had vanished; but they might
still be in the farm-yard: should I go after all? I still waited. I begun
to think that I should have to tell Norton that I was going next day,
and that he would certainly then say that he was going too, so that
we should have to travel together to London; oh! was there no way
out of that? Or should I rather like it, really? He was so amusing,
and so agreeable, and I liked talking to him; but how could one
have adventures when he was there? Suddenly, for no apparent reason,
I got up, went in, went up to my room, put on my boots, and came
down again, and walked by the back way into the farm-yard.

There was no sign of a waggon; but I noticed, what I'd never noticed before, that the farm-road did not end in the farm-yard, but
continued past some indefinite pig-styes, through a field, and then
turned round a corner out of sight. So after all the waggon – and
the waggoner – might be further on – not very far away – engaged
in some promiscuous occupation. I began to walk through the farm-
yard, when Bunny appeared, at the door of a barn.

He was in his shirt, with the sleeves rolled us, engaged also, apparently, in some extremely promiscuous occupation. What *was* he
always doing in those odd purlieus? Something with the rabbits I
suppose.

I talked with him – vaguely; and felt once more the pleasure of
being able to do that. And the happier I felt, the more my heart
sank at the thought of going away. It sank down and down, and
I kept chattering with him about the hens, and wanted to take hold
of his large brown bare arm. *That* I knew was beautiful; and then

my heart sank so very low that I conceived the possibility of *his* asking me to stay on, if I could suggest adroitly enough that I should like to. But who can be adroit with his heart in his boots? My attempt was really feeble; and when I blurted out, apropos of nothing, that I was going tomorrow, he said, in his charming way 'Oh, I *am* sorry', and I saw that I was dished again.

Then, after a little more talking - about the new Dostoievsky - I went on along the path, and he disappeared into the recesses of the barn. I passed the indeterminate pig-styes, went through a gate, turned the corner, and found myself in a field. No waggon was anywhere in view, but, as I crossed the field, I forgot all about it - I could think of nothing but the mere pleasure and beauty of the summer day. I came into a second field, and then, to one side of me, the country dipped down at a little distance, rising again in a lovely little landscape - lovely and yet perfectly ordinary - of fields and trees and hedges and blue sky. And the field I was in was full of splendid grasses, and there were wild flowers scattered all about, and wild roses in the hedge at my left hand. I walked entranced; that feeling of a sudden explanation came upon me - a sudden easy mysterious explanation of all the long difficult mysterious embroilments of the world. 'Est-ce que j'ai trouvé le grand Peut-être?' I thought. 'Am I luckier even than Rabelais? - How miraculously lucky I am!' And I sat down, absolutely comfortable, with a little bank of earth under the hedge for my back to lean against, and the charming English prospect before my eyes. I thought of my friends, and my extraordinary happiness. I thought of Death, of Keats and the Ode to the Nightingale, of 'easeful Death' - 'half in love with easeful Death' - and I was convinced, as I'd been convinced in the train coming down from London that if Death would only come to one in a mood of serene happiness, he would be very welcome. I thought of suddenly dying, painlessly, where I lay. I wondered whether that was morbid; and then I imagined them finding my dead body - so singularly thin - and what their thoughts would be. All the time the sun warmed me deliciously, and the landscape beamed in front of me, and visions of Jimmy Wilde, half naked, with bruised ears, floated in my imagination - or dressed, in a fascinating tweed suit, rather too big for him, staying with me for a week-end at my cottage at Garsington, coming out through the door onto the lawn . . . And L? . . . The dazzling happiness, coming, in flood after flood, over my soul, was so intense that it was like a religious conversion. And through it all there was an odd waft of melancholy - a kind of vi-

bration of regret. A strange importance seemed to invest and involve
into a unity of scene, the moment, and my state of feeling. But at
last I knew it was time to go back to the house. As I walked back,
I felt as if I had made an advance – as if I had got somewhere new.
But it seemed far shorter going back than going, and very soon I
was through the back premises, and, coming onto the lawn through
the gap in the bushes, found them all quite close to me sitting in
the verandah, having lunch. I was late – they had almost finished
their meat – and it occurred to me that all the time I had been there
I had never been late for lunch before. Nessa seemed slightly surprised,
and asked me whether I'd been for a long walk. My plate was filled
with food, and as I ate I began to ask Duncan about the National
Sporting Club – whether he had ever been there, and what boxing
was like. The wretch saw at once what I was up to and said 'You've
been looking at the Daily Mirror'; I didn't attempt to deny it, and
went on with my questions; but his answers were unsatisfactory. He
said that I would certainly enjoy the National Sporting Club very
much, because one had to go there in evening dress, and that I might
get Lord Henry Bentinck to take me; but he admitted that he'd never
been there himself; and Nessa said that he didn't understand me at
all. Bunny advised me to go to some boxing haunt in the East End
that he knew of, where he said the blood flowed by the bucket-full.
Norton pursed himself up, and said that all this was very disgusting,
and said that I was like Nero at a gladiatorial show. I rather testily
replied that he was an 'anachoret', and Nessa again took my side.
Then the conversation somehow got on to George, and my relations
with him, and Duncan's relations with him; and Duncan was very
amusing, confessing that he still sometimes thought of him senti-
mentally, and that at one time he would have been willing to give
him a hundred a year, to have him as his mistress. We asked him
where he would have got a hundred a year from, to give to George.
He said he would have borrowed it. We asked 'Who from?' And Norton and I at once saw that of course it would have been from Maynard,
and everybody laughed. After that Ottoline loomed up in her accustomed style, and there was a long and rather fierce argument as
to whether she had any artistic capacity, and whether she was 'creative'; I said that she was, and that Garsington proved it; but all
the others were against me. Norton declared that Garsington was
the work of a bower-bird, and that to talk of its showing 'creativeness'
was absurd. I answered in a voice more contemptuous than my feeling
but gradually I felt my feeling growing as contemptuous as my voice.

Then Nessa began on the 'artistic' tack, and for a moment I almost became better; all that violent discussion of my second evening shimmered in the background, and I got as far as saying that I didn't think I agreed with her notion of art. But it passed off, and the children appeared, and we all got up from the table. I found myself standing next to Duncan on the lawn, and he was holding the Daily Mirror open at the picture of Jimmy Wilde. I said 'Don't you think he's beautiful?' And he said 'Yes'; but added almost immediately, 'I expect it's only because he hasn't got a collar on. If his neck was covered he'd probably look like anyone else.' I didn't believe it, and I was slightly annoyed.

Then I went upstairs, heavy with all that eating, and lay down on my bed, where I began again thinking out my plan of campaign with the postboy, until I fell asleep; and I slept solidly for over an hour. I was woken up by the piercing screams of the children, as they played on the little piece of grass outside my window. The noise gradually penetrated my sleep, and reached a climax with Quentin bursting into sobs. I heard Julian's cockney voice, full of guilt and self-justification, calling out to Flossie ('Flossay') that Quentin was very naughty and would *not* play with him. After a confused interval, Nessa's voice emerged – low and plaintive – 'I've *told* you, Julian, that you must *not* . . . You're much stronger than Quentin, and he can't defend himself . . . I've *told* you . . .' And then utter silence on the part of Julian. Irritation came upon me at the woman's weakness. – Or *was* it weakness? Wasn't it perhaps simply common sense? Did she see that no amount of punishment would ever prevent Julian from being cruel? That it would only make him dislike her to no purpose? Perhaps; but still I was angry with her for her lack of indignation; and my hatred of Julian was intense.

However, silence was re-established, and I picked up the copy of Temple Bar on the bed-table, to see if there was anything in it that I hadn't already read. I struck at once upon an article by some woman or other on political parties in Bohemia. It was all entirely new to me, and most interesting; I had never before seen the names of Rieger or Gregr; I knew nothing whatever of the history of those movements. The article was not very profound, but it was not badly done either. I was amazed and appalled by my ignorance – that at the age of 36 it should only be by a chance article in a back number of a second-rate magazine, written by an unknown woman, that I should have become acquainted with facts of that magnitude, with names as important in Austrian history as those of O'Connell and Parnell in ours. And I, and my likes, are supposed to be well educated persons! I then skimmed an article on Thurlow, which was slightly interesting too; by that time it was four o'clock, and I got up and went downstairs for my afternoon stroll.

On the lawn I saw Norton reading mathematics so I took the opportunity of telling him that I had decided to go away next day; and he immediately announced that he would go with me. I assented, and drifted off, leaving him with his mathematics.

I drifted down the dreary road that goes in the opposite direction to the village. My mind, which (with exception of the interval of sleep) had been in a state of constant activity since 8 o'clock in the morning, now relapsed into dreaminess. The expectation of tea was one of the few things definitely present to it, as I walked along between the hedges on the empty road. - That, and the feeling that it was only *after* tea that anything exciting could happen - that *then* something exciting would happen - that *then* there would be the crisis of the meeting with the bicycle, and the conversation, and all the possibilities involved - so that *until* then I had nothing to do but to meander about and fill up the interval as best I could. I fancy I thought a little about Sarah Bernhardt, and, after I'd turned back, the puzzle of my relations with women flickered before me. Carrington occurred to me, and then, for some odd reason, Maria. Why on earth had I been so chaste during those Latin lessons? I saw how easily I could have been otherwise - how I might have put my hand on her bare neck, and even up her legs, with considerable enjoyment; and probably she would have been on the whole rather pleased. I became certain that the solution was that I was restrained by my knowledge that she would certainly inform 'Auntie' of every detail of what had happened, at the earliest possible opportunity. It would be practically copulating with Ott looking through the keyhole - which I was by no means prepared to do. There are limits in these matters, I reflected; strange that it should be so, but there are. I turned in at the gate, passed the angle of the house, and saw to my delight that tea was ready and Vanessa actually pouring it out.

Norton appeared immediately, and Duncan and Bunny a little later. There was not very much conversation; what there was chiefly circled round the question of the train that Norton and I should go by. He wanted to go after lunch, and I wanted to go after tea. As he had no motive to produce and I had - viz that dinner in a train was so amusing - it was eventually settled that I should have my way. I ate my frugal sponge fingers contentedly, listening to their gibes.

Duncan at last got up and went into the drawing-room, where he began to play his Bach composition. I followed him, with what I hoped was an air of detachment, pretended to look for a book, went out through the drawing-room door into the passage, and so through the front door out of the house.

My fear had been that Norton would want to walk out with me, but I seemed to have escaped him successfully. He would hardly follow me now. The time, too, was exactly right, so far as I could judge. I had nothing to do now but to walk forward, and I was bound to meet . . . the bicycle, either before I got to the pillar-box at the cross-roads, or, if necessary, *at* it. I walked down the road towards the village, wondering how it would turn out. I felt to see that I had my letter to Ottoline in my pocket, and rehearsed the meeting – my stopping him, my asking him if he would mind taking the letter, and then, somehow, my offering him a cigarette. It was fairly clear, although I foresaw that the actual stopping of the bicycle might be difficult – especially if he was coming down hill – so far it was fairly clear; but after the opening – *after* the preliminary conversation and the cigarette – then everything was a blank, to be filled in at the moment according to his amiability, and as my presence of mind would suggest. But both his amiability and my presence of mind were highly dubious entities. I had the wildest, and the bleakest, visions – of amusement and charm and successes culminating in Norwich, and of crushing failure – sheer stupidity, or undisguised annoyance – or perhaps of missing him altogether by some unforeseen mischance. It was a preposterous errand! I laughed, and imagined myself reading about myself in a novel by Tolstoy – reading quickly, and turning over the pages as fast as I could, in my excitement to know what would happen in the end. What *would* happen? I took the short-cut by the field with the poppies, emerged onto the high road, turned to the left, away from the village, and then off to the right, up the long narrow lane, at the end of which was the pillar-box. It was half-past five; the collection at the pillar-box was due at five minutes to six; the lane was probably about two miles long; therefore, if he was punctual, it seemed certain that I should meet him in it, as there was no other way from the pillar-box to the village, and he had to be in the village at half-past six. I had remembered the lane as being fairly level, but now it seemed to go up and down in the most alarming manner. If I were to come upon him as he was on a downward dip – should I have the nerve – or even the strength of voice – to stop him? And wouldn't he be furious if I did? Perhaps he would be mol-

lified if he saw that my letter was to a Ladyship. Or perhaps . . .
my mind lost itself in speculations. I imagined his nose, his cheek,
and his complexion with a tantalizing mixture of indistinctness and
intensity. His cap, too, and his yellow hair, lighter than his skin
– and that odd armlet . . . and why, to be sure, *wasn't* he in the army?
Surely he wasn't under age? . . . A woman in a drab mackintosh appeared on the road in front of me, going in the same direction. I
passed her easily, and sped on. It seemed almost probable that I should
reach the pillar-box before he did, in which case I should have to
linger about; and then – if there were other people there? – old gaffers
posting letters to their sons at the front? I might be done for in that
case. I had passed the turning down which Norton and I had gone
after meeting him the time before, so that, supposing the time to
have been the same on that occasion, he might appear at any moment
now. But he didn't appear: the lane went on and on indefinitely,
its only merit being that it kept more or less straight, so that one
could see people approaching from a good distance, and prepare accordingly. But no one did approach. Meanwhile the sky had been
growing darker and darker, and I expected it to rain at any moment;
that would be an additional complication. Then I saw that the pillar-
box could not be far off; it was almost in sight, in a group of trees
in front of me, I had no doubt; I recognized the place from some
cottages on the right hand, so I *should* have to wait there, after all.
Suddenly I heard a whistle – and an immediate reminiscence flashed
upon me: it was of 'Signor Grasso', the postman on the Loch-an-
Eilan road, when he came on his bicycle with the letters in the morning. My mind shot back for an instant to Milton Cottage – how many
years ago? – with Pippa and Pernel in the garden, and Sharp Cottage,
too, and its dreariness, and James of course – it all came and went
in a moment; was it possible that *he* too – ? That he was whistling
to warn those cottages that he was coming? Oh no! Such things were-
n't done out of the Highlands . . . and then his bicycle appeared,
slowly advancing: it *was* he, there could be no doubt. But he did
not stop at the cottage. He came on, and we should meet almost
at once. He looked rather bigger than I had remembered him, and
he had something in his mouth – a cigarette? Then *that* plan was
shattered. But I saw at once that it was the whistle, and as I took
the letter out of my pocket he actually began slowing down, almost
as if he was expecting me to give it him. 'This is a very favourable
beginning', I thought. And on the very heels of that, came the perception that something was all wrong, hopelessly wrong, that he

wasn't - that he couldn't be - that it was somebody else. Yes, it was
another postman, with black hair, and a red Presbyterian face, and
a most unattractive briskness about him altogether, stopping with
an *écoeurant* politeness to take my letter, as I handed it to him, saying
'Would you mind taking this?' with the most natural air in the world.
'So *that's* all over,' I said to myself, as he vanished, and I turned
automatically on my tracks, for obviously there was now nothing
to be done but to trudge back home. I nearly burst out laughing
aloud at the farcicality of my proceedings, but was restrained by the
re-appearance of the woman in the mackintosh, who I now saw, as
I passed her, looked like a lower-class Vernon Lee. I began to wonder
what had happened - why he had failed me - whether it was only
a temporary change, or whether . . . Perhaps he'd joined the army,
perhaps that armlet meant that he was going to be called up, and
very likely, as today was Monday . . . anyhow it was just like my
luck. There was a servant-maid waiting at the corner of the branch
road - waiting rather mysteriously; she was pretty, and sad. Could
she have been waiting for . . . ? I passed on, and by this time the
clouds had disappeared from the sky and the sun was out again. I
thought of the youth at Lockeridge who had been obliterated in the
same silent way: but, after all, I considered, some remain. There are
so many possibilities in this world, and I shouldn't have been much
surprised if something extraordinary had happened almost at once.
But nothing happened, except that, quite suddenly and apparently
irrelevantly, a phrase from Handel sounded in my mind - a phrase
that I don't believe I'd thought of for years. - 'Rejoice! Rejoice! Rejoi-
oi-oi-oi-oice greatly!' And then the thought occurred to me of writing
this microscopic description of a day. I was delighted with the idea
and went on elaborating it for a long time, until at last I drifted
into the plan of a satirical poem on Winston in the style of the cho-
russes in Samson Agonistes, which should begin

   Strange are the ways of men;
   And the ways of God are still more curious;

and I was still murmuring these lines when I reached the house;
and as I went upstairs to my room I saw that they would have to
end the poem too.
   In my room, I fell with extraordinary energy on my Arabian story,
which I had a wild notion that I might finish before dinner. It was
obvious, really, that I couldn't, yet I wrote on at top speed for more

than an hour, covering the pages in a most unusual manner. I heard them calling to me to come to dinner, but still wrote. They called again, and then I realized that it was useless going on - the wretched thing wasn't nearly finished; so I went down into the kitchen and had dinner with them - rather silent, while they discussed the superfetation of rabbits, and whether wildflowers might be legitimately classified as yellow, blue and red.

I went out of the room before anyone else, and walked through the drawing-room out onto the lawn. It was still quite light, though it must have been past nine o'clock. I paced once or twice up and down the lawn, when Bunny appeared and immediately joined me. I had a sharp and most queer feeling that it was somehow done by arrangement - though of course we had arranged nothing of the sort. We went at once through the pergola into the strip of kitchen garden, and began walking up and down the path. I felt nervous, almost neurasthenic - what used to be called 'unstrung'. He was so calm and gentle, and his body was so large, with his shirt (with nothing under it) open all the way down - that I longed to throw myself onto him as if he were a feather-bed, to tell him everything - everything, and to sob myself asleep. And yet, at the same time, the more I longed to expand, the more I hated the thought of it. It would be disgusting and ridiculous - it was out of the question. And I became astringent, and would talk of nothing but the vegetables as we walked up and down. The vegetables and still the vegetables - it almost seemed at last that there was nothing else that one could possibly talk about; and, as the subject was not very interesting, why not give it up and go in? I was in terror that this would happen, and yet my congealment was such that when, at the end of one of our turns, we got to the pergola, I made as if to go through it, back on to the lawn. At that, he came out in that lovely firm way that he sometimes so unexpectedly has, and turned right off through an asparagus bed into that other more remote part of the garden, where the grass is so thick and lush, and everything is tangled and overgrown with weeds and roses - a place that trembles on the edge of sentimentality, but is saved by being so small and unkempt and tumbledown. We went and sat on a dirty wooden seat at the farthest end of it, and I thought that if it had been a clean stone seat, and if he had been dressed in white knee-breeches and a blue coat with brass buttons, and if I had been a young lady in a high waist - or should it have been the other way round? - the scene would have done very well for an Academy picture by Marcus Stone.

And so we did talk at last – about other things than vegetables – about Barbara, and that fandango of the letter; and he made me realize what a charming creature she was. And he chaffed me about my 'affair with Carrington'; and I explained in great detail that it couldn't be called that; and as we talked I grew comfortable, and in fact happy; and then, when the conversation touched upon the changeability of moods, I said that I had been in a wretched mood all day, that I had felt everything with an unnatural acuteness, as if I had had no skin. It wasn't at all an accurate statement, and his sympathy – 'Oh Lytton, how dreadful!' – made me feel myself a silly beast, and I quickly covered my tracks by bringing up the subject of his life at Wissett, and his prospects, and his general state. He talked for a long time about these things – about his settled happiness and the problems of his future – and I felt very sympathetic, and wished I had several thousand a year. He was amusing, too, very amusing, and I saw how shy and distrustful of himself he was in company. It grew darker and colder, but we stayed on. At last it seemed quite natural to ask him whether he thought they really liked me. 'Who, Lytton?' – 'Duncan and Vanessa – no, not really; but sometimes they seem very severe. Perhaps I'm too uppish.' 'Oh Lytton, how absurd you are. They call you "the old gentleman". I heard them saying that they hoped the old gentleman was happy.' – The darling! How beautifully he had smoothed me down! So that everything was now calm and good – so that that was the ordinary state of the world – and all those doubts and itches – how futile and preposterous! I laughed, and said 'Do *you* call me "the old gentleman?"' He answered, flirting, 'The Prince of Darkness is a gentleman.' Without any difficulty I stretched out my hand and put it into his breast, which was glowing a warm pink in the twilight. I said 'An *old* gentleman?' and he answered 'No; that's just the difference.' 'Have I more experience than the Devil?' I murmured as we laughed. We came nearer to one another, and, with a divine vigour, embraced. I was amused to notice, just before it happened, that he looked very nervously in the direction of the house. We kissed a great deal, and I was happy. Physically, as well as mentally, he had assuaged me. That was what was so wonderful about him – he gave neither too little nor too much. I felt neither the disillusionment of having gone too far, nor any of the impatience of desire. I knew that we loved each other, and I was unaware that my cock had moved.

It was too cold to stay out any longer, and we came in to find the room in almost pitch darkness, with three figures over the fire.

He went out with Duncan; left alone with Norton and Nessa, I instantly realized that we must have been out rather a long time. Norton
said something which I took for an indecent joke, and I answered
with unnecessary self-consciousness; then, of course, he said that he
had meant nothing at all. There was a long pause, during which
I imagined Duncan furious in the kitchen, and Bunny pacifying him.
But when they appeared at last with the lamp, Duncan seemed perfectly cheerful, and the evening at once became very gay. We ranged
over Ka and her complicated history, we discussed our private weaknesses, and ended in a fantastic [blank in MS] of idiotic rhymes.

Ka is my Ma,
But who is my Pa?

was Norton's first inspiration, which set us all off in a string. How
adorable was Nessa, as she sat, rocking with laughter at the bawdiness
of the jokes! We got up from our chairs somehow, at about one
o'clock. Duncan and Bunny disappeared as usual, to lock up. Nessa
went off, and Norton briskly mounted his attic-ladder. I tore off my
clothes in my bedroom, with only one desire – to sleep. In bed, I
thought of Bunny, and then, as I was dozing off, something strange
happened. I suddenly found myself with Duncan under the bushes
in the drizzle on that first afternoon on Hampstead Heath. The vividness of it was so great that I woke up with a start. Then that too
melted in oblivion; and it was L. who was with me when I finally
fell asleep.

Lytton Strachey: Letters

*Going through Lytton Strachey's letters after his death, Carrington
wrote of their Bloomsbury significance,*

> *I am not surprised, reading Lytton's old Cambridge letters, that their friend-
> ship for each other survived all 'frenzies', even removes to other countries
> and old age. . . . After reading a great many letters I suddenly felt the quin-
> tessence of what had so often puzzled me. It was a marvellous combination
> of the higher intelligence and appreciation of literature with a lean humour
> and tremendous affection. They gave it backwards and forwards to each
> other like shuttlecocks, only the shuttlecocks multiplied as they flew in
> the air. (Noel Carrington, 32)*

Unfortunately Strachey's letters – unlike those of Virginia and Leonard Woolf, E.M. Forster, Roger Fry, Vanessa Bell, and even Carrington herself – have yet to be collected and published. The following two brief excerpts suggest something of what Carrington found in them. The first was written to J.M. Keynes shortly after Strachey came down from Cambridge, and refers to their mutual Oxford friend Bernard Swithinbank, who soon left for the Indian Civil Service. The second excerpt is from a letter to James Strachey during a visit to Charleston and Rodmell fifteen years later.

From a letter to John Maynard Keynes, 1905 Oh dear me, when will my Heaven be realized? – My Castle in Spain? Rooms, you know, for you, Duncan and Swithin, as fixtures – Woolf of course, too, if we could lure him from Ceylon; and several suites for guests. Can you conceive anything more supreme! I should write tragedies; you would revolutionize political economy, Swithin would compose French poetry, Duncan would paint our portraits in every conceivable combination and permutation, and Woolf would criticize us and our works without remorse.

From a letter to James Strachey, 19 September 1920 The company in this house is its sempiternal self. Duncan and Vanessa painting all day in each other's arms. Pozzo writing on Probability, on the History of Currency, controlling the business of King's, and editing the Economic Journal. Clive pretending to read Stendhal, Mary writing letters on blue note-paper, the children screaming and falling into the pond. I went over for a day to Leonard and Virginia in their new Rodmell establishment, which is a most peculiar structure – small, higgledy-piggledy with rooms like cupboards and cupboards like lavatories, gardens projecting among various walls, a plaster bust of Juno on a cistern, an orchard with hens and onions, but altogether quite attractive, and I fancied even comfortable – but I shall discover this more fully tomorrow. They strike one as being absolutely happy; he looks more gaunt and eminent than ever, and she a school girl, almost, in cheap red beads.

Saxon Sydney-Turner: A Description of Bloomsbury

The most obscure member of the Bloomsbury Group was Saxon Sydney-Turner. A close friend of Leonard Woolf's at Cambridge, an

*Apostle and also a friend of Thoby Stephen and Lytton Strachey, he
spent his life in the Treasury. 'He was an eccentric in the best English
tradition,' Woolf wrote of him in* The Times *after his death; he possessed 'an extraordinarily supple, subtle, and enigmatic mind,' and
'wrote elegant verse and music, but published nothing' (see also
Woolf's description on pp. 123–6).*

*The following extract is from a letter written to Virginia Woolf
in 1919 while Sydney-Turner was staying with Lytton Strachey. It was
found among her papers and labelled as a description of Bloomsbury by Leonard Woolf. The pages of Virginia Woolf's that Sydney-
Turner refers to are now unknown, though she has written him three
years before that she wanted 'somehow to give you back what you
lost in Thoby. For I've often thought that you were the one person
who understood about him – I mean his death meant almost more
to you and me than anyone, and I think we shared together some
of the worst things' (Letters, 2:126). The interest of Sydney-Turner's
letter lies in the attempt to suggest how Bloomsbury came about. The
influence of G.E. Moore and his 'black box' analytic method receives
an early emphasis here, and just who the members of Bloomsbury
were – in this instance whether Oliver Strachey and Barbara Bagenal
should be included – appears to have been a question as early as 1919.*

. . . I must try – to show myself not ungrateful for your three large
pages to induce you to send some more.

So far you certainly avoid the dangers you foresaw: I should like
that chapter (? with illustrations) on the difficulty of getting into
touch. But I don't really remember in my own case any acute discomfort in the process of getting intimate. Perhaps this is entirely
due to chance. Partly the fact that some of them started at Cambridge
accounts for the ease of the early stages of the intimacies. One was
the right age and the conditions were right. Looking back it seems
as if there were no early stages in some cases, as if one just fell in.
Then if you take Clive and Adrian there was the fairly long period
there of, at any rate, getting accustomed, which laid a foundation
against the time when we came together again in London. Perhaps
also it's easier between man and man. I remember that at one time
I thought you rather difficult, which was at least as reasonable as
you thinking me shocked [?]. One may have been the result of the
other.

I agree though – and I think that if I were a quite dispassionate
outsider I should still agree – that our friends do come out of it rather

well. Whether this is because of Gordon Square and Fitzroy Square
I don't know: I'm not clear whether you think so. But I fancy there
was something there first that made those aggregations natural, and
this suggests that our distinctive characteristic isn't simply middle
age. Is there really any except that we are all rather nice and that
about certain things we have much the same point of view derived
by some of us from Moore's black box? And won't a descriptive definition like this include, say, Oliver and Barbara? Of course the black
box influenced Oliver too. . . . [*sic*]

But perhaps this is all beside the real point, and that is what has
come of it not how it came. And this is very complicated. I see in
the collection each of us connected up with each of the others by
particular peculiar links: some are more and some less important
but they all have some meaning. . . .

Roger Fry: Two Letters on Bloomsbury

*Roger Fry was the oldest member of Bloomsbury and yet the last to
join the core of what became known as Old Bloomsbury. Fry's ad-
vocacy of post-impressionism through his two celebrated exhibitions
of 1910 and 1912 and then his founding of the Omega Workshops
in 1913 brought him into sharp conflict not only with the art establishment of the time but also with some radical younger painters,
the most articulate of whom was Wyndham Lewis. Lewis was originally a member of the Omega but quit in a highly publicized attack
on Fry, accusing him of dishonesty in running the workshops. The
only basis of the charge appears to be some confusion over a commission, yet Fry and his Bloomsbury friends would not respond to
Lewis's charges. (See Q. Bell and Stephen Chaplin's 'The Ideal Home
Rumpus.') As 'The Enemy' – a persona he developed in one of his
magazines – Lewis attacked Bloomsbury's painting, criticism, and fiction in a variety of works written over three decades.*

*Fry left no memoirs of Bloomsbury and rarely mentions the Group
in his correspondence. Parts of two letters show, however, his awareness of the Group's existence and his attitude towards those who attacked him and Bloomsbury. In the first letter, to Vanessa Bell, Fry
enumerates a list of Bloomsbury that leaves out some central members,
such as Forster and Leonard Woolf, and includes others, such as Mary
Hutchinson, who according to Quentin Bell was 'the most important
woman in Clive's life . . . and this of course meant that she became,*

*if not a "member", at least a very frequent visitor in Bloomsbury'
(Bell, Virginia Woolf, 2:59). The painting Fry calls for was finally
done by Vanessa Bell some twenty-five years later and is reproduced
on the cover of this volume (see the Foreword, pp. xi–xii).*

*Fry's second, hitherto unpublished, letter to Virginia Woolf was writ-
ten on a train, partly in response to a review of Fry's 1921 pamphlet
'Architectural Heresies of a Painter' by John Middleton Murry. In the
pamphlet Fry dismisses English architecture as concerned only with
the snobbery of dressing up buildings in fashionable historical costumes instead of trying to develop 'plastic' forms suitable to the times.
Murry's review begins by praising Wyndham Lewis as an earlier and
more effective polemicist against British architecture, and goes on to
deny that plastic form was of any use because the only vital idea in
architecture now is the commercial one of getting the most for one's
money. Murry and his wife, Katherine Mansfield, were not enemies
of Bloomsbury in the way Lewis was (the Woolfs had published works
by both a few years before when starting their Hogarth Press), yet
Fry's letter makes an interesting connection between two different
sources of criticism directed at Bloomsbury early in its history. Fry
also reveals in his letter the refusal of himself and many of his Bloomsbury friends to be drawn into the politics of art as well as the contempt
they felt for the values and the cultures of critics like Murry and Lewis.
Such attitudes were not intended, of course, to decrease the enmity
towards Bloomsbury.*

From a letter to Vanessa Bell, 12 December 1917   Clive and Mary
came for Sunday and as it was wet and cold we never stirred from
the fire all day long, and talked incessantly. Clive was in great form;
Mary sympathetic and discreet. I enjoyed it very much. Clive is amazing in the quantity and flow of his mind, and the quality gets better,
I think. I expect it's good for him being a good deal alone in the
country and doing a lot of reading.

He suggested a great historical portrait group of Bloomsbury. I
think I shall have a shot at it - it would be rather fun. Lytton, Maynard, Clive, Duncan, me, you, Virginia, Mary, Molly, Desmond. Is
there anyone else that ought to be in? P'raps Walter Sickert coming
in at the door and looking at us all with a kind of benevolent
cynicism.

But p'raps it's too hideously difficult and p'raps you ought to do
it, as being so brilliant at likeness, though I seem to be getting rather
better.

From a letter to Virginia Woolf, 4–5 September 1921   Now I rush by the help of a tunnel to get back to England and its J.M.M's.

I confess I was very much pleased and consoled that you and Leonard resented his article on my architecture tract, for it had really irritated and annoyed me – what annoys me most is that he can produce any effect on me for goodness knows there was no criticism in it. It was pure partizanship – and then this abject prostration before a vulgar charlatan like Wyndham Lewis. I can't make out exactly why he shows such bitterness against me – he always proposes something like affection – I think he really detests any sort of detached thought. He's by nature an arrivist politician and he resents anyone who won't take a hand in the party politics of literature and art. One thing interested me very much in his article the evidence in it of an alliance which I've long suspected – an alliance between the old cultured and the cubist-vorticist-Murryist group who are joining hands to crush what both hate most, our group. If one comes to think of it it's very natural – we shocked the old cultured because we had their culture but were not bound by their shibboleths and we enraged the under-world that Murry and K.M. come from and really belong to because however much they read they never could get the cultured attitude.

Since they both hate us they're making this unholy alliance the common ground being envy and a hatred of intellectual freedom. I think it's a most interesting development. They've got as a battle cry art for life – art and morals and it's a clever demagogic move which moreover comes to them naturally because they hate pure and disinterested thought and feeling. As for exposing J.M.M. I should love to see it done because his pretentious self-sufficiency and vanity irritate me – but it's against my principles. I'd let him be and take as little notice of him as possible. He'll probably have a huge success and become a kind of prophet for the public but we shall just go on in our insignificant way and do what we want to do or as much as we can. I'm sure one must not meddle with politics.

David Garnett: Bloomsbury Parties

Though too young to belong to Old Bloomsbury, David Garnett became closely identified with the Group during the First World War, as Lytton Strachey's Memoir Club paper indicates. Garnett's own discussions of Clive Bell, Grant, Keynes, and Carrington collected here demonstrate how useful a source for the study of Bloomsbury his writ-

ings are, especially his three-volume autobiography The Golden Echo. *The two parties he describes below took place in 1923 and 1926. The play of Virginia Woolf's referred to is* Freshwater, *which she wrote in 1923 and then revised for another performance in 1935. 'Tommy' is the sculptor Stephen Tomlin; the famous author of sentimental fiction was Berta Ruck.*

Bloomsbury parties were of all sorts except the formal. Those which took place in Duncan's studio were really the best of them. These often included Clive and Vanessa Bell's children and were to celebrate one of their birthdays. If the Bells were still at Charleston, their house in Sussex, as they often were for Quentin's birthday in September, there was a traditional feast with grouse and fireworks sent up on the further side of the pond. But when they were in London, birthday parties would be in Duncan's studio, and on these occasions a dramatic performance was usually presented. One such was written by Virginia Woolf on the subject of the marriage of Ellen Terry as a young girl to the famous painter Watts. Angelica Bell took the part of Ellen Terry and Duncan was Watts. Angelica's school-friend Eve Younger was Queen Victoria and Julian Bell was Tennyson. Another year the play was Julian's work and was largely aimed at making fun of Virginia.

There were many much grander parties than those given in Duncan's studio – the grandest I suppose being given by Maynard and Lydia Keynes at 46 Gordon Square. At several of these parties Lydia sang, usually Victorian drawing-room ballads chosen for her by Duncan whose father Major Bartle Grant had written the music for a number of them. Putting her hands together and her exquisite little head on one side she would invite our compassion with such lines as:

My earrings! Oh my earrings!
I have dropped them in the well.
And how to tell my Mirza,
I cannot cannot tell.

These grand parties were by no means limited to the inhabitants of Bloomsbury. Anyone might be there, and the worlds of Society, Art, Politics and Finance mingled with those of Old Bloomsbury and Young Cambridge. At one such party, given I think by Clive and

Vanessa, I remember seeing Picasso talking to Douglas Fairbanks senior. At another, given by Maynard and Lydia, the most striking figure was a famous writer of sentimental novelettes.

The servants had learned that the authoress of their favourite works of fiction was in the house and they stole upstairs on to the landing in order to peep through the half-opened door at the woman whom they worshipped. Unfortunately Walter Richard Sickert, who had been paying court to her, had discovered that she could sing and had an extensive repertoire of the old risqué music-hall songs which he adored. She was delighting us with:

Never trust a sailor an inch above your knee.

At its conclusion I noticed that the housemaid supported by the cook, was being led downstairs sobbing. Both were bitterly disillusioned by the lack of refinement of their idol.

Sometimes Lydia danced, being partnered by Duncan, who acquitted himself with character and originality. But at one party Maynard danced a delightful *pas-de-deux* with Lydia in which she showed an exquisitely graceful solicitude in supporting him and making his part easier for him. By a lucky chance the programme of this ambitious entertainment has survived and I reproduce it here. The topical references which need explanation are that Mr Hayley Morris, a wealthy gentleman who had retired from the trade with China, and lived at Pippingford Park near Uckfield, had received unwelcome notoriety in the gutter press while being convicted for an offence against *les moeurs* involving a young woman under the age of consent. He also kept a number of large dogs which featured in the case. 'Georgeston' is of course Charleston; Clarissa, Vanessa Bell who was impersonated by Molly MacCarthy who could not have looked less like, a fact which added to the audience's amusement. Before the performance Molly wrote to Vanessa asking whether she minded her playing the part. Vanessa grimly replied: 'How can I possibly tell until I have seen it?'

Tommy, who wrote most of the songs, played the part of Hayley Morris. Molly turned a deaf ear to his overtures until he offered her a Cézanne and a Giotto when she accepted and went off with him. I should add perhaps that the parts of Messrs Sickert, Grant and Fry were performed by these distinguished painters. In Act I the Beauty Chorus consisted of three ladies, each of them over six foot, whose parts were taken by Angus and Douglas Davidson and Dadie Rylands.

They were partnered by three gentlemen, Barbara Bagenal, Frances Marshall and Bea Howe.

DON'T BE FRIGHTENED or PIPPINGTON PARK

Act I   The Front at Brighton
         1. Beauty (Welcome to Brighton)
         2. Art (Abide with me)
         3. Truth (I simply should like to remark)
         4. Ensemble (Come, come, come to the Metropole)

Act II   The Drawing-Room at Georgeston
         1. The abduction
         2. The rescue party sets out (Is Clarissa still alive?)
         Ballet The London Group – Messrs Sickert, Fry and Grant
             disguised as dogs.

Act III The Park at Pippington
         1. Clarissa settles down (Bloomsbury never gave me a bow-
             wow)
         2. The dogs arrive (Take her back to dear old Bloomsbury)

Interval

Act IV   Garden Square rejoices. Clarissa's friends arrive to a select
             entertainment 'A little bit of sea-weed'.
         Pas-de-deux   The Keynes-Keynes.
         A Veteran does her best (Taraboumtia)

Virginia Woolf: Old Bloomsbury

Virginia Woolf's memoir of Old Bloomsbury was written around 1922 at the instigation of Molly MacCarthy, the secretary of the Memoir Club. It continues, less hyperbolically, the last scene from a preceding memoir for the Club in which Woolf described George Duckworth as the lover of his half-sisters Vanessa and herself. Members of three families at the Stephens' family home in Hyde Park Gate are referred to at the beginning of the memoir: Leslie Stephen's daughter by his first marriage to Thackeray's daughter, the three children George, Stella, and Gerald Duckworth of Julia Stephen's first marriage to Herbert Duckworth; and the four Stephen children. Woolf's memoir swarms with names from the past, including Stephen family friends and relations such as Jack Hills, who was Stella's young widower. (Some of the people mentioned are included in the identifications at the end of this volume.)

The memoir describes two of what Woolf calls the three chapters of Old Bloomsbury's history. After Leslie Stephen's death and Virginia's breakdown in 1904, the Stephen children moved to Bloomsbury where chapter one of Old Bloomsbury began when Thoby's Cambridge friends (who had just published their poetry anonymously in a collection called Euphrosyne) *met his sisters and discussed Moore's philosophy with them. The chapter ended with Thoby Stephen's death in 1906 and Vanessa's marriage to Clive Bell early the next year. During chapter two, which culminated in Fry's first post-impressionist exhibition of 1910, Virginia became aware of homosexuality in Bloomsbury, and Lytton Strachey liberated the Group's conversation. Early in chapter three, which was ended by the First World War, Virginia was sharing a house in Brunswick Square with Adrian, Keynes, Grant, and Leonard Woolf, who had just returned from Ceylon.*

Though 'Old Bloomsbury' was posthumously published, it appears to have been heard or read by a number of the following memoirists, who pick up some of its tone and repeat some of its questions. (The original editing of the memoir has been modified in some places.)

At Molly's command I have had to write a memoir of Old Bloomsbury – of Bloomsbury from 1904 to 1914. Naturally I see Bloomsbury only from my own angle – not from yours. For this I must ask you to make allowances. From my angle then, one approaches Bloomsbury through Hyde Park Gate – that little irregular cul-de-sac which lies next to Queen's Gate and opposite to Kensington Gardens. And we must look for a moment at that very tall house on the left hand side near the bottom which begins by being stucco and ends by being red brick; which is so high and yet – as I can say now that we have sold it – so rickety that it seems as if a very high wind would topple it over.

I was undressing at the top of that house when my last memoir ended, in my bedroom at the back. My white satin dress was on the floor. The faint smell of kid gloves was in the air. My necklace of seed-pearls was tangled with hairpins on the dressing table. I had just come back from a party – from a series of parties indeed, for it was a memorable night in the height of the season of 1903. I had dined with Lady Carnarvon in Bruton Street; I had seen George undoubtedly kiss her among the pillars in the hall; I had talked much

too much – about my emotions on hearing music – at dinner; Lady
Carnarvon, Mrs Popham, George and myself had then gone to the
most indecent French play I have ever seen. We had risen like a flock
of partridges at the end of the first act. Mrs Popham's withered cheeks
had burnt crimson. Elsie's grey locks had streamed in the wind. We
had parted, with great embarrassment on their side, on the pavement,
and Elsie had said she did hope I wasn't tired – which meant, I felt,
she hoped I wouldn't lose my virginity or something like that. And
then we had gone on – George and I in a hansom together to another
party, for George said, to my intense shame, I had talked much too
much and I must really learn how to behave – we had gone on to
the Holman Hunts, where 'The Light of the World' had just come
back from its mission to the chief cities of the British Empire, and
Mr Edward Clifford, Mrs Russell Barrington, Mrs Freshfield and I
know not what distinguished old gentlemen with black ribbons attached to their eyeglasses and elderly ladies with curious vertebrae
showing through their real but rather ragged old lace had talked
in hushed voices of the master's art while the master himself sat in
a skull cap drinking, in spite of the June night, hot cocoa from a
mug.

It was long past midnight that I got into bed and sat reading a
page or two of *Marius the Epicurean* for which I had then a passion.
There would be a tap at the door; the light would be turned out
and George would fling himself on my bed, cuddling and kissing
and otherwise embracing me in order, as he told Dr Savage later,
to comfort me for the fatal illness of my father – who was dying
three or four storeys lower down of cancer.

But it is the house that I would ask you to imagine for a moment
for, though Hyde Park Gate seems now so distant from Bloomsbury,
its shadow falls across it. 46 Gordon Square could never have meant
what it did had not 22 Hyde Park Gate preceded it. It was a house
of innumerable small oddly shaped rooms built to accommodate not
one family but three. For besides the three Duckworths and the four
Stephens there was also Thackeray's grand-daughter, a vacant-eyed
girl whose idiocy was becoming daily more obvious, who could hardly
read, who would throw the scissors into the fire, who was tongue-
tied and stammered and yet had to appear at table with the rest of
us. To house the lot of us, now a storey would be thrown out on
top, now a dining room flung out at bottom. My mother, I believe,
sketched what she wanted on a sheet of notepaper to save the ar-
chitect's fees. These three families had poured all their possessions

into this one house. One never knew when one rummaged in the many dark cupboards and wardrobes whether one would disinter Herbert Duckworth's barrister's wig, my father's clergyman's collar, or a sheet scribbled over with drawings by Thackeray which we afterwards sold to Pierpont Morgan for a considerable sum. Old letters filled dozens of black tin boxes. One opened them and got a terrific whiff of the past. There were chests of heavy family plate. There were hoards of china and glass. Eleven people aged between eight and sixty lived there, and were waited upon by seven servants, while various old women and lame men did odd jobs with rakes and pails by day.

The house was dark because the street was so narrow that one could see Mrs Redgrave washing her neck in her bedroom across the way; also because my mother who had been brought up in the Watts-Venetian-Little Holland House tradition had covered the furniture in red velvet and painted the woodwork black with thin gold lines upon it. The house was also completely quiet. Save for an occasional hansom or butcher's cart nothing ever passed the door. One heard footsteps tapping down the street before we saw a top hat or a bonnet; one almost always knew who it was that passed; it might be Sir Arthur Clay; the Muir-MacKenzies or the white-nosed Miss or the red-nosed Mrs Redgrave. Here then seventeen or eighteen people lived in small bedrooms with one bathroom and three water-closets between them. Here the four of us were born; here my grandmother died; here my mother died; here my father died; here Stella became engaged to Jack Hills and two doors further down the street after three months of marriage she died too. When I look back upon that house it seems to me so crowded with scenes of family life, grotesque, comic and tragic; with the violent emotions of youth, revolt, despair, intoxicating happiness, immense boredom, with parties of the famous and the dull; with rages again, George and Gerald; with love scenes with Jack Hills; with passionate affection for my father alternating with passionate hatred of him, all tingling and vibrating in an atmosphere of youthful bewilderment and curiosity – that I feel suffocated by the recollection. The place seemed tangled and matted with emotion. I could write the history of every mark and scratch in my room, I wrote later. The walls and the rooms had in sober truth been built to our shape. We had permeated the whole vast fabric – it has since been made into an hotel – with our family history. It seemed as if the house and the family which had lived in it, thrown together as they were by so many deaths, so many emotions, so many traditions, must endure for ever. And then suddenly in one night both vanished.

When I recovered from the illness which was not unnaturally the result of all these emotions and complications, 22 Hyde Park Gate no longer existed. While I had lain in bed at the Dickinsons' house at Welwyn thinking that the birds were singing Greek choruses and that King Edward was using the foulest possible language among Ozzie Dickinson's azaleas, Vanessa had wound up Hyde Park Gate once and for all. She had sold; she had burnt; she had sorted; she had torn up. Sometimes I believe she had actually to get men with hammers to batter down – so wedged into each other had the walls and the cabinets become. But now all the rooms stood empty. Furniture vans had carted off all the different belongings. For not only had the furniture been dispersed. The family which had seemed equally wedged together had broken apart too. George had married Lady Margaret. Gerald had taken a bachelor flat in Berkeley Street. Laura had been finally incarcerated with a doctor in an asylum; Jack Hills had entered on a political career. The four of us were therefore left alone. And Vanessa – looking at a map of London and seeing how far apart they were – had decided that we should leave Kensington and start life afresh in Bloomsbury.

It was thus that 46 Gordon Square came into existence. When one sees it today, Gordon Square is not one of the most romantic of the Bloomsbury squares. It has neither the distinction of Fitzroy Square nor the majesty of Mecklenburgh Square. It is prosperous middle class and thoroughly mid-Victorian. But I can assure you that in October 1904 it was the most beautiful, the most exciting, the most romantic place in the world. To begin with it was astonishing to stand at the drawing room window and look into all those trees; the tree which shoots its branches up into the air and lets them fall in a shower; the tree which glistens after rain like the body of a seal – instead of looking at old Mrs Redgrave washing her neck across the way. The light and the air after the rich red gloom of Hyde Park Gate were a revelation. Things one had never seen in the darkness there – Watts pictures, Dutch cabinets, blue china – shone out for the first time in the drawing room at Gordon Square. After the muffled silence of Hyde Park Gate the roar of traffic was positively alarming. Odd characters, sinister, strange, prowled and slunk past our windows. But what was even more exhilarating was the extraordinary increase of space. At Hyde Park Gate one had only a bedroom in which to read or see one's friends. Here Vanessa and I each had a sitting room; there was the large double drawing room; and a study on the ground floor. To make it all newer and fresher, the house had been completely done up. Needless to say the Watts-Venetian tradition of red plush and black paint had been reversed; we had entered the Sargent-Furse era; white and green chintzes were everywhere; and instead of Morris wall-papers with their intricate patterns we decorated our walls with washes of plain distemper. We were full of experiments and reforms. We were going to do without table napkins, we were to have Bromo instead; we were going to paint; to write; to have coffee after dinner instead of tea at nine o'clock. Everything was going to be new; everything was going to be different. Everything was on trial.

We were, it appears, extremely social. For some months in the winter of 1904-5 I kept a diary from which I find that we were for ever lunching and dining out and loitering about the book shops – 'Bloomsbury is ever so much more interesting than Kensington,' I wrote – or going to a concert or visiting a picture gallery and coming home to find the drawing room full of the oddest collections of people. 'Cousin Henry Prinsep, Miss Millais, Ozzie Dickinson and Victor Marshall all came this afternoon and stayed late, so that we had only just time to rush off to a Mr Rutter's lecture on Impressionism at the Grafton Gallery . . . Lady Hylton, V. Dickinson and E. Coltman came to tea. We lunched with the Shaw Stewarts and met an art critic called Nicholls. Sir Hugh seemed nice but there isn't much in him . . . I lunched with the Protheroes and met the Bertrand Russells. It was very amusing. Thoby and I dined with the Cecils and went on to the St Loe Stracheys where we knew a great many people . . . I called for Nessa and Thoby at Mrs Flower's and we went on to a dance at the Hobhouses'. Nessa was in a state of great misery today waiting for Mr Tonks who came at one to criticise her pictures. He is a man with a cold bony face, prominent eyes and a look of serenity and boredom. Meg Booth and Sir Fred Pollock came to tea . . .' So it goes on; but among all these short records of parties, of how the chintzes came home and how we went to the Zoo and how we went to *Peter Pan*, there are a few entries which bear on Bloomsbury. On Thursday March 2nd 1905 Violet Dickinson brought a clergyman's wife to tea and Sydney-Turner and Strachey came after dinner and we talked till twelve. On Wednesday the 8th of March: 'Margaret [Duckworth] sent round her new motor car this afternoon and we took Violet to pay a series of calls, but we, of course, forgot our cards. Then I went on to the Waterloo Road and lectured (a class

of working men and women) on the Greek Myths. Home and found
Bell, and we talked about the nature of good till almost one!'

On the 16th March Miss Power and Miss Malone dined with us.
Sydney-Turner and Gerald came in after dinner – the first of our
Thursday evenings. On the 23rd March nine people came to our eve-
ning and stayed till one.

A few days later I went to Spain, and the duty which I laid on
myself of recording every sight and sound, every wave and hill, sick-
ened me with diary writing so that I stopped – with this last entry:
May the 11th – 'Our evening: Gaye, Bell, D. MacCarthy and Gerald
– who shocked the cultured.'

So my diary ends just as it might have become interesting. Yet I
think it is clear even in this brief record in which every sort of doing
is piled up higgledy-piggledy that these few meetings of Bloomsbury
in its infancy differed from the rest. These are the only occasions
when I do not merely say I had met so and so and thought him
long-faced like Reginald Smith or pompous like Moorsom, or quite
easy to get on with, but nothing much in him, like Sir Hugh Shaw
Stewart. I say we talked to Strachey and Sydney-Turner. I add with
a note of exclamation that we talked with Bell about the nature of
good till one! And I did not use notes of exclamation often – and
once more indeed – when I say that I smoked a cigarette with Beatrice
Thynne!

These Thursday evening parties were, as far as I am concerned,
the germ from which sprang all that has since come to be called
– in newspapers, in novels, in Germany, in France – even, I daresay,
in Turkey and Timbuktu – by the name of Bloomsbury. They deserve
to be recorded and described. Yet how difficult – how impossible.
Talk – even the talk which had such tremendous results upon the
lives and characters of the two Miss Stephens – even talk of this interest and importance is as elusive as smoke. It flies up the chimney
and is gone.

In the first place it is not true to say that when the door opened
and with a curious hesitation and self-effacement Turner or Strachey
glided in – that they were complete strangers to us. We had met them
– and Bell, Woolf, Hilton Young and others – in Cambridge at May
Week before my father died. But what was of much greater importance, we had heard of them from Thoby. Thoby possessed a great
power of romanticizing his friends. Even when he was a little boy
at a private school there was always some astonishing fellow, whose
amazing character and exploits he would describe hour after hour

when he came home for the holidays. These stories had the greatest fascination for me. I thought about Pilkington or Sidney Irwin or the Woolly Bear whom I never saw in the flesh as if they were characters in Shakespeare. I made up stories about them myself. It was a kind of saga that went on year after year. And now just as I had heard of Radcliffe, Stuart, or whoever it might be, I began to hear of Bell, Strachey, Turner, Woolf. We talked of them by the hour, rambling about the country or sitting over the fire in my bedroom.

'There's an astonishing fellow called Bell,' Thoby would begin directly he came back. 'He's a sort of mixture between Shelley and a sporting country squire.'

At this of course I pricked up my ears and began to ask endless questions. We were walking over a moor somewhere, I remember. I got a fantastic impression that this man Bell was a kind of Sun God – with straw in his hair. He was an [illegible] of innocence and enthusiasm. Bell had never opened a book till he came to Cambridge, Thoby said. Then he suddenly discovered Shelley and Keats and went nearly mad with excitement. He did nothing but spout poetry and write poetry. Yet he was a perfect horseman – a gift which Thoby enormously admired – and kept two or three hunters up at Cambridge.

'And is Bell a great poet?' I asked.

No, Thoby wouldn't go so far as to say that; but it was quite on the cards that Strachey was. And so we discussed Strachey – or 'the Strache', as Thoby called him. Strachey at once became as singular, as fascinating as Bell. But it was in quite a different way. 'The Strache' was the essence of culture. In fact I think his culture a little alarmed Thoby. He had French pictures in his rooms. He had a passion for Pope. He was exotic, extreme in every way – Thoby describe him – so long, so thin that his thigh was no thicker than Thoby's arm. Once he burst into Thoby's rooms, cried out, 'Do you hear the music of the spheres?' and fell in a faint. Once in the midst of a dead silence, he piped up – and Thoby could imitate his voice perfectly – 'Let's all write Sonnets to Robertson.' He was a prodigy of wit. Even the tutors and the dons would come and listen to him. 'Whatever they give you, Strachey,' Dr Jackson had said when Strachey was in for some examination, 'it won't be good enough.' And then Thoby, leaving me enormously impressed and rather dazed, would switch off to tell me about another astonishing fellow – a man who trembled perpetually all over. He was as eccentric, as remarkable in his way as Bell and Strachey in theirs. He was a Jew. When I asked why he trembled, Thoby somehow made me feel that it was part of his nature – he was so violent, so savage; he so despised the whole human race. 'And after all,' Thoby said, 'it is a pretty feeble affair, isn't it?' Nobody was much good after twenty-five, he said. But most people, I gathered, rather rubbed along, and came to terms with things. Woolf did not and Thoby thought it sublime. One night he dreamt he was throttling a man and he dreamt with such violence that when he woke up he had pulled his own thumb out of joint. I was of course inspired with the deepest interest in that violent trembling misan-thropic Jew who had already shaken his fist at civilization and was about to disappear into the tropics so that we should none of us ever see him again. And then perhaps the talk got upon Sydney-Turner. According to Thoby, Sydney-Turner was an absolute prodigy of learning. He had the whole of Greek literature by heart. There was practically nothing in any language that was any good that he had not read. He was very silent and thin and odd. He never came out by day. But late at night if he saw one's lamp burning he would come and tap at the window like a moth. At about three in the morn-ing he would begin to talk. His talk was then of astonishing bril-liance. When later I complained to Thoby that I had met Turner and had not found him brilliant Thoby severely supposed that by brilliance I meant wit; he on the contrary meant truth. Sydney-Turner was the most brilliant talker he knew because he always spoke the truth.

Naturally then, when the bell rang and these astonishing fellows came in, Vanessa and I were in a twitter of excitement. It was late at night; the room was full of smoke; buns, coffee and whisky were strewn about; we were not wearing white satin or seed-pearls; we were not dressed at all. Thoby went to open the door; in came Sydney-Turner; in came Bell; in came Strachey.

They came in hesitatingly, self-effacingly, and folded themselves up quietly [in] the corners of sofas. For a long time they said nothing. None of our old conversational openings seemed to do. Vanessa and Thoby and Clive, if Clive were there – for Clive differed in many ways from the others [and] was always ready to sacrifice himself in the cause of talk – would start different subjects. But they were almost always answered in the negative. 'No,' was the most frequent reply. 'No, I haven't seen it'; 'No, I haven't been there.' Or simply, 'I don't know.' The conversation languished in a way that would have been impossible in the drawing room at Hyde Park Gate. Yet the silence was difficult, not dull. It seemed as if the standard of what was worth saying had risen so high that it was better not to break it unworthily. We sat and looked at the ground. Then at last Vanessa, having said perhaps that she had been to some picture show, incautiously used the word 'beauty'. At that, one of the young men would lift his head slowly and say, 'It depends what you mean by beauty.' At once all our ears were pricked. It was as if the bull had at last been turned into the ring.

The bull might be 'beauty', might be 'good', might be 'reality'. Whatever it was, it was some abstract question that now drew out all our forces. Never have I listened so intently to each step and half-step in an argument. Never have I been at such pains to sharpen and launch my own little dart. And then what joy it was when one's contribution was accepted. No praise has pleased me more than Saxon's saying – and was not Saxon infallible after all? – that he thought I had argued my case very cleverly. And what strange cases those were! I remember trying to persuade Hawtrey that there is such a thing as atmosphere in literature. Hawtrey challenged me to prove it by pointing out in any book any one word which had this quality apart from its meaning. I went and fetched *Diana of the Crossways*. The argument, whether it was about atmosphere or the nature of truth, was always tossed into the middle of the party. Now Hawtrey would say something; now Vanessa; now Saxon; now Clive; now Thoby. It filled me with wonder to watch those who were finally left in the argument piling stone upon stone, cautiously, accurately, long after it had completely soared above my sight. But if one could not say anything, one could listen. One had glimpses of something miraculous happening high up in the air. Often we would still be sitting in a circle at two or three in the morning. Still Saxon would be taking his pipe from his mouth as if to speak, and putting it back again without having spoken. At last, rumpling his hair back, he would pronounce very shortly some absolutely final summing up. The marvellous edifice was complete, one could stumble off to bed feeling that something very important had happened. It had been proved that beauty was – or beauty was not – for I have never been quite sure which – part of a picture.

From such discussions Vanessa and I got probably much the same pleasure that undergraduates get when they meet friends of their own for the first time. In the world of the Booths and the Maxses we were not asked to use our brains much. Here we used nothing else. And part of the charm of those Thursday evenings was that they were astonishingly abstract. It was not only that Moore's book had

set us all discussing philosophy, art, religion; it was that the atmosphere – if in spite of Hawtrey I may use that word – was abstract
in the extreme. The young men I have named had no 'manners' in
the Hyde Park Gate sense. They criticized our arguments as severely
as their own. They never seemed to notice how we were dressed or
if we were nice looking or not. All that tremendous encumbrance
of appearance and behaviour which George had piled upon our first
years vanished completely. One had no longer to endure that terrible
inquisition after a party – and be told, 'You looked lovely.' Or, 'You
did look plain.' Or, 'You must really learn to do your hair.' Or, 'Do
try not to look so bored when you dance.' Or, 'You did make a con-
quest,' or, 'You *were* a failure.' All this seemed to have no meaning
or existence in the world of Bell, Strachey, Hawtrey and Sydney-
Turner. In that world the only comment as we stretched ourselves
after our guests had gone, was, 'I must say you made your point
rather well'; 'I think you were talking rather through your hat.' It
was an immense simplification. And for my part it went deeper than
this. The atmosphere of Hyde Park Gate had been full of love and
marriage. George's engagement to Flora Russell, Stella's to Jack Hills,
Gerald's innumerable flirtations were all discussed either in private
or openly with the greatest interest. Vanessa was already supposed
to have attracted Austen Chamberlain. My Aunt Mary Fisher, poking
about as usual in nooks and corners, had discovered that there were
six drawings of him in Vanessa's sketchbook and [had] come to her
own conclusions. George rather suspected that Charles Trevelyan was
in love with her. But at Gordon Square love was never mentioned.
Love had no existence. So lightly was it treated that for years I believed
that Desmond had married an old Miss Cornish, aged about sixty,
with snow-white hair. One never took the trouble to find out. It
seemed incredible that any of these young men should want to marry
us or that we should want to marry them. Secretly I felt that marriage
was a very low-down affair, but that if one practised it, one practised
it – it is a serious confession I know – with young men who had
been in the Eton Eleven and dressed for dinner. When I looked round
the room at 46 I thought – if you will excuse me for saying so –
that I had never seen young men so dingy, so lacking in physical
splendour as Thoby's friends. Kitty Maxse who came in once or twice
sighed afterwards, 'I've no doubt they're very nice but, oh darling,
how awful they do look!' Henry James, on seeing Lytton and Saxon
at Rye, exclaimed to Mrs Prothero, 'Deplorable! Deplorable! How
could Vanessa and Virginia have picked up such friends? How could

Leslie's daughters have taken up with young men like that?' But it was precisely this lack of physical splendour, this shabbiness! that was in my eyes a proof of their superiority. More than that, it was, in some obscure way, reassuring; for it meant that things could go on like this, in abstract argument, without dressing for dinner, and never revert to the ways, which I had come to think so distasteful, at Hyde Park Gate.

I was wrong. One afternoon that first summer Vanessa said to Adrian and me and I watched her, stretching her arms above her head with a gesture that was at once reluctant and yielding, in the great looking-glass as she said it – 'Of course, I can see that we shall all marry. It's bound to happen' – and as she said it I could feel a horrible necessity impending over us; a fate would descend and snatch us apart just as we had achieved freedom and happiness. She, I felt, was already aware of some claim, some need which I resented and tried to ignore. A few weeks later indeed Clive proposed to her. 'Yes,' said Thoby grimly when I murmured something to him very shyly about Clive's proposal, 'That's the worst of Thursday evenings!' And her marriage in the beginning of 1907 was in fact the end of them. With that, the first chapter of Old Bloomsbury came to an end. It had been very austere, very exciting, of immense importance. A small concentrated world dwelling inside the much larger and looser world of dances and dinners had come into existence. It had already begun to colour that world and still I think colours the much more gregarious Bloomsbury which succeeded it.

But it could not have gone on. Even if Vanessa had not married, even if Thoby had lived, change was inevitable. We could not have gone on discussing the nature of beauty in the abstract for ever. The young men, as we used to call them, were changing from the general to the particular. They had ceased to be Mr Turner, Mr Strachey, Mr Bell. They had become Saxon, Lytton, Clive. Then too one was beginning to criticize, to distinguish, to compare. Those old flamboyant portraits were being revised. One could see that Walter Lamb whom Thoby had compared to a Greek boy playing a flute in a vineyard was in fact rather bald, and rather dull; one could wish that Saxon could be induced either to go or to say something perhaps that was not strictly true; one could even doubt, when *Euphrosyne* was published, whether as many of the poems in that famous book were sure of immortality as Thoby made out. But there was something else that made for a change though I at least did not know what it was. Perhaps if I read you a passage from another diary which

I kept intermittently for a month or two in the year 1909 you will guess what it was. I am describing a tea-party in James Strachey's rooms at Cambridge.

'His rooms,' I wrote, 'though they are lodgings, are discreet and dim. French pastels hang upon the walls and there are cases of old books. The three young men – Norton, Brooke and James Strachey – sat in deep chairs; and gazed with soft intent eyes into the fire. Mr Norton knew that he must talk; he and I talked laboriously. The others were silent. I should like to account for this silence, but time presses and I am puzzled. For the truth is that these young men are evidently respectable; they are not only able but their views seem to me honest and simple. They lack all padding; so that one has convictions to disagree with if one disagrees. Yet we had nothing to say to each other and I was conscious that not only my remarks by my presence was criticized. They wished for the truth and doubted if I could speak it or be it. I thought this courageous of them but unsympathetic. I admired the atmosphere – was it more? – and felt in some respects at ease in it. Yet why should intellect and character be so barren? It seems as if the highest efforts of the most intelligent people produce a negative result; one cannot honestly be anything.'

There is a great change there from what I should have written two or three years earlier. In part, of course, the change was due to circumstances; I lived alone with Adrian now in Fitzroy Square; and we were the most incompatible of people. We drove each other perpetually into frenzies of irritation or into the depths of gloom. We still went to a great many parties: but the combination of the two worlds which I think was so [illegible] was far more difficult. I could not reconcile the two. True, we still had Thursday evenings as before. But they were always strained and often ended in dismal failure. Adrian stalked off to his room, I to mine, in complete silence. But there was more in it than that. What it was I was not altogether certain. I knew theoretically, from books, much more than I knew practically from life. I knew that there were buggers in Plato's Greece; I suspected – it was not a question one could just ask Thoby – that there were buggers in Dr Butler's Trinity [College], Cambridge; but it never occurred to me that there were buggers even now in the Stephens' sitting room at Gordon Square. It never struck me that the abstractness, the simplicity which had been so great a relief after Hyde Park Gate were largely due to the fact that the majority of the young men who came there were not attracted by young women. I did not realize that love, far from being a thing they never mentioned, was in fact a thing which they seldom ceased to discuss. Now I had begun to be puzzled. Those long sittings, those long silences, those long arguments – they still went on in Fitzroy Square as they had done in Gordon Square. But now I found them of the most perplexing nature. They still excited me much more than any men I met with in the outer world of dinners and dances – and yet I was, dared I say it or think it even? – intolerably bored. Why, I asked, had we nothing to say to each other? Why were the most gifted of people also the most barren? Why were the most stimulating of friendships also the most deadening? Why was it all so negative? Why did these young men make one feel that one could not honestly be anything? The answer to all my questions was, obviously – as you will have guessed – that there was no physical attraction between us.

The society of buggers has many advantages – if you are a woman. It is simple, it is honest, it makes one feel, as I noted, in some respects at one's ease. But it has this drawback – with buggers one cannot, as nurses say, show off. Something is always suppressed, held down. Yet this showing off, which is not copulating, necessarily, nor altogether being in love, is one of the great delights, one of the chief necessities of life. Only then does all effort cease; one ceases to be honest, one ceases to be clever. One fizzes up into some absurd delightful effervescence of soda water or champagne through which one sees the world tinged with all the colours of the rainbow. It is significant of what I had come to desire that I went straight – on almost the next page of my diary indeed – from the dim and discreet rooms of James Strachey at Cambridge to dine with Lady Ottoline Morrell at Bedford Square. Her rooms, I noted without drawing any inferences, seemed to me instantly full of 'lustre and illusion'.

So one changed. But these changes of mine were part of a much bigger change. The headquarters of Bloomsbury have always been in Gordon Square. Now that Vanessa and Clive were married, now that Clive had shocked the Maxses, the Booths, the Cecils, the Protheroes, irretrievably, now that the house was done up once more, now that they were giving little parties with their beautiful brown table linen and their lovely eighteenth-century silver, Bloomsbury rapidly lost the monastic character it had had in Chapter One; the character of Chapter Two was superficially at least to be very different.

Another scene has always lived in my memory – I do not know if I invented it or not – as the best illustration of Bloomsbury Chapter Two. It was a spring evening. Vanessa and I were sitting in the drawing room. The drawing room had greatly changed its character since

1904. The Sargent-Furse age was over. The age of August John was
dawning. His *Pyramus* filled one entire wall. The Watts' portraits
of my father and my mother were hung downstairs if they were hung
at all. Clive had hidden all the match boxes because their blue and
yellow swore with the prevailing colour scheme. At any moment Clive
might come in and he and I should begin to argue – amicably, im-
personally at first; soon we should be hurling abuse at each other
and pacing up and down the room. Vanessa sat silent and did something mysterious with her needle or her scissors. I talked, egotistically,
excitedly, about my own affairs no doubt. Suddenly the door opened
and the long and sinister figure of Mr Lytton Strachey stood on the
threshold. He pointed his finger at a stain on Vanessa's white dress.
   'Semen?' he said.
   Can one really say it? I thought and we burst out laughing. With
that one word all barriers of reticence and reserve went down. A flood
of the sacred fluid seemed to overwhelm us. Sex permeated our conversation. The word bugger was never far from our lips. We discussed
copulation with the same excitement and openness that we had discussed the nature of good. It is strange to think how reticent, how
reserved we had been and for how long. It seems a marvel now that
so late as the year 1908 or 9 Clive had blushed and I had blushed
too when I asked him to let me pass to go to the lavatory on the
French Express. I never dreamt of asking Vanessa to tell me what
happened on her wedding night. Thoby and Adrian would have died
rather than discuss the love affairs of undergraduates. When all intellectual questions had been debated so freely, sex was ignored. Now
a flood of light poured in upon that department too. We had known
everything but we had never talked. Now we talked of nothing else.
We listened with rapt interest to the love affairs of the buggers. We
followed the ups and downs of their chequered histories; Vanessa sympathetically; I – had I not written in 1905, women are so much more
amusing than men – frivolously, laughingly. 'Norton tells me', Vanessa would say, 'that James is in utter despair. Rupert has been twice
to bed with Hobhouse' and I would cap her stories with some equally
thrilling piece of gossip; about a divine undergraduate with a head
like a Greek God – but alas his teeth were bad – called George Mallory.
   All this had been the result that the old sentimental views of marriage in which we were brought up were revolutionized. I should
be sorry to tell you how old I was before I saw that there is nothing
shocking in a man's having a mistress, or in a woman's being one.
Perhaps the fidelity of our parents was not the only or inevitably

the highest form of married life. Perhaps indeed that fidelity was not so strict as one had supposed. 'Of course Kitty Maxse has two or three lovers,' said Clive – Kitty Maxse, the chaste, the exquisite, the devoted! Again, the whole aspect of life was changed.

So there was now nothing that one could not say, nothing that one could not do, at 46 Gordon Square. It was, I think, a great advance in civilization. It may be true that the loves of buggers are not – at least if one is of the other persuasion – of enthralling interest or paramount importance. But the fact that they can be mentioned openly leads to the fact that no one minds if they are practised privately. Thus many customs and beliefs were revised. Indeed the future of Bloomsbury was to prove that many variations can be played on the theme of sex, and with such happy results that my father might have hesitated before he thundered out the one work which he thought fit to apply to a bugger or an adulterer; which was Blackguard!

Here I come to a question which I must leave to some other memoir writer to discuss – that is to say, if we take it for granted that Bloomsbury exists, what are the qualities that admit one to it, what are the qualities that expel one from it? Now at any rate between 1910 and 1914 many new members were admitted. It must have been in 1910 I suppose that Clive one evening rushed upstairs in a state of the highest excitement. He had just had one of the most interesting conversations of his life. It was with Roger Fry. They had been discussing the theory of art for hours. He thought Roger Fry the most interesting person he had met since Cambridge days. So Roger appeared. He appeared, I seem to think, in a large ulster coat, every pocket of which was stuffed with a book, a paint box or something intriguing; special tips which he had bought from a little man in a back street; he had canvases under his arms; his hair flew; his eyes glowed. He had more knowledge and experience than the rest of us put together. His mind seemed hooked on to life by an extraordinary number of attachments. We started talking about [Marguerite Audoux's] *Marie-Claire*. And at once we were all launched into a terrific argument about literature; adjectives? associations? overtones? We had down Milton; we re-read Wordsworth. We had to think the whole thing over again. The old skeleton arguments of primitive Bloomsbury about art and beauty put on flesh and blood. There was always some new idea afoot; always some new picture standing on a chair to be looked at, some new poet fished out from obscurity and stood in the light of day. Odd people wandered through 46; Rothenstein, Sickert, Yeats, Tonks – Tonks who could, I suppose, make Vanessa miserable no more. And

sometimes one began to meet a queer faun-like figure, hitching his
clothes up, blinking his eyes, stumbling oddly over the long words
in his sentences. A year or two before, Adrian and I had been standing
in front of a certain gold and black picture in the Louvre when a
voice said: 'Are you Adrian Stephen? I'm Duncan Grant.' Duncan
now began to haunt the purlieus of Bloomsbury. How he lived I
do not know. He was penniless. Uncle Trevor indeed said he was
mad. He lived in a studio in Fitzroy Square with an old drunken
charwoman called Filmer and a clergyman who frightened girls in
the street by making faces at them. Duncan was on the best of terms
with both. He was rigged out by his friends in clothes which seemed
always to be falling to the floor. He borrowed old china from us
to paint; and my father's old trousers to go to parties in. He broke
the china and he ruined the trousers by jumping into the Cam to
rescue a child who was swept into the river by the rope of Walter
Lamb's barge, the 'Aholibah'. Our cook Sophie called him 'that Mr
Grant' and complained that he had been taking things again as if
he were a rat in her larder. But she succumbed to his charm. He
seemed to be vaguely tossing about in the breeze; but he always
alighted exactly where he meant to.

And once at least Morgan flitted through Bloomsbury lodging for
a moment in Fitzroy Square on his way even then to catch a train.
He carried, I think, the same black bag with the same brass label
on it that is now in the hall outside at this moment. I felt as if a
butterfly – by preference a pale blue butterfly – had settled on the
sofa; if one raised a finger or made a movement the butterfly would
be off. He talked of Italy and the Working Men's College. And I
listened – with the deepest curiosity, for he was the only novelist
I knew – except Henry James and George Meredith; the only one
anyhow who wrote about people like ourselves. But I was too much
afraid of raising my hand and making the butterfly fly away to say
much. I used to watch him from behind a hedge as he flitted through
Gordon Square, erratic, irregular, with his bag, on his way to catch
a train.

These, with Maynard – very truculent, I felt, very formidable, like
a portrait of Tolstoy as a young man to look at, able to rend any
argument that came his way with a blow of his paw, yet concealing,
as the novelists say, a kind and even simple heart under that immensely impressive armour of intellect – and Norton; Norton who
was the essence of all I meant by Cambridge; so able; so honest; so
ugly; so dry; Norton with whom I spent a whole night once talking

and with whom I went at dawn to Covent Garden, whom I still see in memory scowling in his pince-nez – yellow and severe against a bank of roses and carnations – these I think were the chief figures in Bloomsbury before the war.

But here again it becomes necessary to ask – where does Bloomsbury end? What is Bloomsbury? Does it for instance include Bedford Square? Before the war, I think we should most of us have said 'Yes'. When the history of Bloomsbury is written – and what better subject could there be for Lytton's next book? – there will have to be a chapter, even if it is only in the appendix, devoted to Ottoline. Her first appearance among us was, I think, in 1908 or 9. I find from my diary that I dined with her on March the 30th 1909 – I think for the first time. But a few weeks before this, she had swooped down upon one of my own Thursday evenings with Philip, Augustus John and Dorelia in tow: she had written the next morning to ask me to give her the names and addresses of all 'my wonderful friends'. This was followed by an invitation to come to Bedford Square any Thursday about ten o'clock and bring anyone I liked. I took Rupert Brooke. Soon we were all swept into the extraordinary whirlpool where such odd sticks and straws were brought momentarily together. There was Augustus John, very sinister in a black stock and a velvet coat; Winston Churchill, very rubicund, all gold lace and medals, on his way to Buckingham Palace; Raymond Asquith crackling with epigrams; Francis Dodd telling me most graphically how he and Aunt Susie had killed bugs: she held the lamp; he a basin of paraffin; bugs crossed the ceiling in an incessant stream. There was Lord Henry Bentinck at one end of the sofa and perhaps Nina Lamb at the other. There was Philip fresh from the House of Commons humming and hawing on the hearth-rug. There was Gilbert Cannan who was said to be in love with Ottoline. There was Bertie Russell, whom she was said to be in love with. Above all, there was Ottoline herself.

'Lady Ottoline', I wrote in my diary, 'is a great lady who has become discontented with her own class and is trying to find what she wants among artists and writers. For this reason, as if they were inspired with something divine, she approaches them in a deferential way and they see her as a disembodied spirit escaping from her world into one where she can never take root. She is remarkable to look at if not beautiful. Like most passive people she is very careful and elaborate in her surroundings. She takes the utmost pains to set off her beauty as though it were some rare object picked up in a dusky Florentine back street. It always seems possible that the rich American

women who finger her Persian cloak and call it "very good" may
go on to finger her face and call it a fine work in the late renaissance
style; the brow and eyes magnificent, the chin perhaps restored. The
pallor of her cheeks, the way she has of drawing back her head and
looking at you blankly gives her the appearance of a marble Medusa.
She is curiously passive.' And then I go on to exclaim rather rhap-
sodically that the whole place was full of 'lustre and illusion'.

When indeed one remembers that drawing room full of people,
the pale yellows and pinks of the brocades, the Italian chairs, the
Persian rugs, the embroideries, the tassels, the scent, the pomegran-
ates, the pugs, the pot-pourri and Ottoline bearing down upon one
from afar in her white shawl with the great scarlet flowers on it and
sweeping one away out of the large room and the crowd into a little
room with her alone, where she plied one with questions that were
so intimate and so intense, about life and one's friends, and made
one sign one's name in a little scented book - it was only last week
that I signed my name in another little scented book in Gower Street
- I think my excitement may be excused.

Indeed lustre and illusion tinged Bloomsbury during those last
years before the war. We were not so austere; we were not so exalted.
There were quarrels and intrigues. Ottoline may have been a Medusa;
but she was not a passive Medusa. She had a great gift for drawing
people under. Even Middleton Murry, it is said, was pulled down
by her among the vegetables at Garsington. And by this time we were
far from drab. Thursday evenings with their silences and their arguments were a thing of the past. Their place was taken by parties
of a very different sort. The Post-Impressionist movement had cast
- not its shadow - but its bunch of variegated lights upon us. We
bought poinsettias made of scarlet plush; we made dresses of the
printed cotton that is specially loved by negroes; we dressed ourselves
up as Gauguin pictures and careered round Crosby Hall. Mrs Whitehead was scandalized. She said that Vanessa and I were practically
naked. My mother's ghost was invoked once more - by Violet Dickinson - to deplore the fact that I had taken a house in Brunswick
Square and had asked young men to share it. George Duckworth
came all the way from Charles Street to beg Vanessa to make me
give up the idea and was not comforted perhaps when she replied
that after all the Foundling Hospital was handy. Stories began to
circulate about parties at which we all undressed in public. Logan
Pearsall Smith told Ethel Sands that he knew for a fact that Maynard
had copulated with Vanessa on a sofa in the middle of the drawing

room. It was a heartless, immoral, cynical society it was said; we were abandoned women and our friends were the most worthless of young men.

Yet in spite of Logan, in spite of Mrs Whitehead, in spite of Vanessa and Maynard and what they did on the sofa at Brunswick Square, Old Bloomsbury still survives. If you seek a proof – look around.

Virginia Woolf: Diaries

The diaries that Virginia Woolf kept for a quarter of a century supplement her picture of Old Bloomsbury. In them she reflects its development as well as contrasting Bloomsbury to other places and styles of life she knew in London. (See also her diary descriptions of E.M. Forster in the second section, pp. 193–6.)

Monday 14 January 1918 On Sunday Clive came to tea. . . . We talked chiefly about the hypnotism exerted by Bloomsbury over the younger generation. . . . The dominion that 'Bloomsbury' exercises over the sane & the insane alike seems to be sufficient to turn the brains of the most robust. Happily I'm 'Bloomsbury' myself, & thus immune; but I'm not altogether ignorant of what they mean. & its a hypnotism very difficult to shake off, because there's some foundation for it. Oddly, though, Maynard seems to be the chief fount of the magic spirit.

Wednesday 23 October 1918 Edith Sichel, whose entire soul is now open to me through her letters, makes me determine to write descriptions neither of pictures nor of music. She makes me consider that the gulf which we crossed between Kensington & Bloomsbury was the gulf between respectable mummified humbug & life crude & impertinent perhaps, but living. The breath of South Kensington lives in her pages – almost entirely, I believe, because they would not mention either copulation or w.c.'s. However this bring me to our dinner with the MacCarthy's, when I borrowed this book. The book [*New and Old*] has a sort of fascination for me. I see the outside of that world so clearly, & take a kind of ribald pleasure in putting those figures into action – sending them slumming, to Pops [concerts], to the National Gallery, always full of high thoughts, morality, kindliness, & never seeing beyond High St. Kensington. Molly, thanks to Bloomsbury, has escaped the Ritchie touch.

Friday 27 November 1925 People die; Madge dies, & one cannot beat up a solitary tear. But then, if 6 people died, it is true that my life would cease: by wh. I mean, it would run so thin that though it might go on, would it have any relish? Imagine Leonard, Nessa, Duncan, Lytton, Clive, Morgan all dead.

Tuesday 2 September 1930 I seldom see Lytton; that is true. The reason is that we dont fit in, I imagine, to his parties nor he to ours; but that if we can meet in solitude, all goes as usual. Yet what do one's friends mean to one, if one only sees them 8 times a year? Morgan I keep up with in our chronically spasmodic way. We are all very much aware of life, & seldom do anything we do not want to. My Bell family relations are young, fertile & intimate. Julian & Quentin change so much. This year Q. is shabby easy natural & gifted; last year he was foppish, finicky & affected. Julian is publishing with Chatto & Windus. As for Nessa & Duncan I am persuaded that nothing can be now destructive of that easy relationship, because it is based on Bohemianism. My bent that way increases – in spite of the prodigious fame (it has faded out since July 15th: I am going through a phase of obscurity; I am not a writer: I am nothing: but I am quite content) I am more & more attracted by looseness, freedom, & eating one's dinner off a table anywhere, having cooked it previously. This rhythm (I say I am writing The Waves to a rhythm not to a plot) is in harmony with the painters'. Ease & shabbiness & content therefore are all ensured. Adrian I never see. I keep constant with Maynard. I never see Saxon. I am slightly repelled by his lack of generosity; yet would like to write to him. Perhaps I will. George Duckworth, feeling the grave gape, wishes to lunch with Nessa; wishes to feel again the old sentimental emotions. After all, Nessa & I are his only women relations. A queer cawing of homing rooks this is. I daresay the delights of snobbishness somewhat fail in later life – & we have done – 'made good' – that is his expression.

Thursday 27 June 1935 A good thing for old Bloomsbury to be shaken up no doubt: a good thing to dine with R[ebecca]. West & Mr Andrews last night in their flat in P[ortman]. Sqre. with the view, with the £750 book case, & the fish carved out of a yew branch, & the modern pictures, period furniture, letter box in the wall & which dont work (nor did Arnold Bennett's – you have to poke with a stick). But the electric light in the coat cupboard does work. And what's wrong? The plumbers nose – the miner's canary, again. I mean scent-

ing out differences, & let us hope inferiorities. Of course its admirable
in its way – impersonal, breezy, yes, go ahead, facing life, eating
dinner at Savoy, meeting millionaires, woman & man of the worldly;
but – no, I must add the kindness intelligence & erudition of the
admirable effete spectacled swollen eyed Andrews – the cultivated don
turned banker, with his devotion to R. – Cecily he calls her, for whom
he buys these fish & bookcases. Whats wrong then? Where does the
gas escape? I think its the emptiness, the formality, the social strata
they live on – appearances, as the Apostles would say: the sense of
Now we're having a dinner party & must talk till 11: tomorrow another. Hospitality to American publisher & the Woolves. Nothing
said of any naturalness or spontaneity. Yet thats not quite so; that
one cd. go on having dinner every night & never know each other
better. No intimacy at the end of that Oxford Street. And I was a
little diminished in my own esteem – why? Because. . [*sic*] did they
differentiate me from other people? No. Or Leonard? But then isnt
this Bloomsbury conceit – our d—d refinement? . . .

Thursday 29 April 1937 Many things have happened – a crowd of
little engagements – the pleasantest, indeed a happy one, was the
Memoir Club meeting. We dined in a kind of sitting room behind
the Etoile [restaurant] – & soon kindled, though it was a wet night:
D[uncan]. had a cold; Bunny the whooping cough; & Morgan dined
with Forrest Reid. But Desmond was babbling as a nightingale – never
have I known him in such a jubilant good temper as this year. As
if he worked only to enjoy to radiate. And my thimble of vanity was
filled instantly because Maynard said my Gibbon [article] was 20 times
better than anyone elses; & praised The Years – a lovely book: &
D[esmond]. said he is going to write a long essay on me altogether.
(but he wont) And then Molly & I kissed; & Maynard suggested that
D[esmond]. should give the L[eslie]. S[tephen]. lecture [at Cambridge]
on L.S.: & we had a nice slice of savoury meat; & so round to the
Studio. D[uncan]. read a good account of his adventure at Florence,
when he misrepresented Maynard. And then old Desmond 'obliged'.
That is he had a few notes in his hand, took a comfortable chair,
& gave us with perfect ease & fluency & form a character of Wilfred
Blunt. . . . Oh but it was beautifully done – & stopped when it might
have gone on without boring us. Then Morgan read his condemned
introduction to the [T.E.] Lawrence letters, which Bunny is now to
do. And then we went off in the rain. Desmond said We're not a
day older, & we enjoy our society as much as we ever did. And Morgan

said I felt so fond of everyone, I almost wept – I think he said that. Anyway, it was a great success; & no nonsense about it.

Sunday 20 October 1940 . . . So to Tavistock Sq. With a sigh of relief saw a heap of ruins. Three houses, I sh. say gone. Basement all rubble. Only relics an old basket chair (bought in Fitzroy Sqre days) & Penmans board To Let. Otherwise bricks & wood splinters. One glass door in the next door house hanging. I cd just see a piece of my studio wall standing: otherwise rubble where I wrote so many books. Open air where we sat so many nights, gave so many parties. . . .

Virginia Woolf: Letters

In Virginia Woolf's letters on Bloomsbury she is often concerned to defend the Group against the misapprehensions of outsiders. This is particularly evident in the excerpts from letters to her old Neo-Pagan friend Gwen Raverat in 1925, to a student planning a book about her in 1932, to her older friend and fierce admirer Ethel Smyth (who lived in Woking, Surrey) in 1936, and finally during the war to Vita Sackville-West's son Ben Nicolson, who had criticized Woolf's biography of Roger Fry. Nicolson's view of Bloomsbury later changed, thanks perhaps to Virginia Woolf's letters (see p. 115).

From a letter to Barbara Bagenal, 23 December 1920 Carrington has been in London; Gordon Square is like nothing so much as the lions house at the Zoo. One goes from cage to cage. All the animals are dangerous, rather suspicious of each other, and full of fascination and mystery. I'm sometimes too timid to go in, and trail along the pavement, looking in at the windows.

From a letter to Gwen Raverat, 1 May 1925 Now I want to discuss your view, or Rupert [Brooke]'s view of Bloomsbury but have no time. After all, I always wind up, if six people, with no special start except what their wits give them, can so dominate, there must be some reason in it. And what Rupert never allowed for was that half of them were every bit as lacerated and sceptical and unhappy as he was. Where they seem to me to triumph is in having worked out a view of life which was not by any means corrupt or sinister or merely intellectual; rather ascetic and austere indeed; which still

holds, and keeps them dining together, and staying together after
20 years; and no amount of quarrelling or success or failure has altered this. Now I do think this rather creditable. But tell me who
is Bloomsbury in your mind?

From a letter to Vita Sackville-West, 28 February 1927 Oh and does
it strike you that one's friendships are long conversations, perpetually
broken off, but always about the same thing with the same person?
With Lytton I talk about reading; with Clive about love; with Nessa
about people; with Roger about art; with Morgan about writing; with
Vita – well, what do I talk about with Vita? Sometimes we snore. . . .

From a letter to Vanessa Bell, 27 December 1928 Roger is the only
civilised man I have ever met, and I continue to think him the plume
in our cap; the vindication, asseveration – and all the rest of it –
If Bloomsbury had produced only Roger, it would be on a par with
Athens at its prime (little though this will convey to you) We dined
with him, and came away – fed to the lips, but impressed almost
to tears with his charm.

From a letter to Harmon H. Goldstone, 16 August 1932   *The Bloomsbury Period.* I do not want to impose my views, but I feel that Bloomsbury is a word that stands for very little. The Bloomsbury group
is largely a creation of the journalists. To dwell upon Bloomsbury
as an influence is liable to lead to judgments that, as far as I know
have no basis in fact.

From a letter to Julian Bell, 21 May 1936 I wish I had spent three
years in China at your age – the difference was, though, that at your
age, what with all the family deaths and extreme intensities – father,
mother, Stella, Thoby, George, Jack – I felt I had lived through all
emotions and only wanted peace and loneliness. All the horrors of
life had been pressed in to our eyes so very crude and raw. And then
came the burst of splendour, those two years at Gordon Square before
Thoby died, a kind of Elizabethan renaissance, much though I disliked the airs that young Cambridge gave itself. I found an old diary
which was one violent shriek of rage at Saxon and Lytton sitting
there saying nothing, and with no emotional experience, I said. But
I musn't begin writing my autobiography. How I wish I had known
you in those days. Only I should have fallen in love with you, after

my fashion, and you would have loved Nessa, because I always thought her so very much more lovable than I was. More autobiography!

To Ethel Smyth, 13 August 1936 I send back the [Maurice] Baring article; but I am not going to say what I think of it, for two reasons. First, I should have to write some serious criticism, for which my brain is at the moment unfit (I'm such a prig, I cant bear to write frivolously about books) Second: you'll be amused to hear, you made the blood come to my head the other day by some remarks of yours in a letter on 'Bloomsbury' Now here on the very second page I think you say 'important – to use the great Bloomsbury word' and again the blood rushes. To explain would take too long. But I daresay you'll twig from the following quotation. A young man the other day sent me a book in which he perpetually used 'Bloomsbury' as a convenient hold all for everything silly, cheap, indecent, conceited and so on. Upon which I wrote to him: All the people I most respect and admire have been what you call 'Bloomsbury'. Thus, though you have every right to despise and dislike them, you cant expect me to agree. More-over, to use a general term like this, without giving instances and names, so that people you sneer at can defend themselves, seems to me a cowardly subterfuge, of which you ought to be ashamed. Any-how, never come and see me, who live in Bloomsbury, again. (Maurice I see talks of Bloomsbury too)

And as you have once more trodden on that toe – I admit all the cheap journalists, ever since Roger and Lytton died, have been jump-ing on it, – I see red: which colour is not favourable to criticism: an art that should be impersonal; and so I wont tell you what I think of your article, for this second reason too. The first however, is the more important (to use a Bloomsbury word) I've read almost all Bar-ing; and to sum up our differences would, as I say, use more time and brain power than are mine.

Lord! How I loathe Wokingism.

From a draft of a letter to Benedict Nicolson, 24 August 1940 'My quarrel' you say 'is not with art but with Bloomsbury.' What do you mean by Bloomsbury? It is rather as if I should say, My quarrel is not with art but with Mayfair, meaning by Mayfair Ben Nicolson, Vita, Eddie Sackville, the Sitwells, Stephen Tennant and David Cecil. You would feel I meant something vaguely abusive, but you would find it very difficult to say what. Apparently you mean by 'Blooms-

bury' a set of people who sat on the floor at Bernard Street saying
'More and more I understand nothing of humanity in the mass' and
were content with that, instead of trying to make humanity in the
mass understand and appreciate what you know and say. It was Roger
Fry who said 'I understand nothing of humanity in the mass.' I did
not say that: if you impute that to me, then you must also impute
to me his saying 'More and more I dread the imprisonment of egotism.' You must make me responsible for teaching elementary school
children in the black country how to dress, for setting up the Omega,
for decorating the walls of the Boro Polytechnic.

But in fact I am not responsible for anything Roger did or said.
My own education and my own point of view were entirely different
from his. I never went to school or college. My father spent perhaps
£100 on my education. When I was a young woman I tried to share
the fruits of that very imperfect education with the working classes
by teaching literature at Morley College; by holding a Womens Co-
operative Guild meeting weekly; and, politically, by working for the
vote. It is true I wrote books and some of those books, like the Common Reader, A Room of One's Own and Three Guineas (in which
I did my best to destroy Sackvilles and Dufferins) have sold many
thousand copies. That is, I did my best to make them reach a far
wider circle than a little private circle of exquisite and cultivated
people. And to some extent I succeeded. Leonard too is Bloomsbury.
He has spent half his life in writing books like International Government, like the Barbarians at the gates, like Empire and Commerce,
to prevent the growth of Nazism; and to create a League of Nations.
Maynard Keynes is Bloomsbury. He wrote the Consequences of the
Peace. Lytton Strachey was Bloomsbury. His books had a very large
circulation and certainly influenced a wider circle than any small
group. Duncan has made a living ever since he was a boy by painting.
These are facts about Bloomsbury and they do seem to me to prove
that they have done their very best to make humanity in the mass
appreciate what they knew and saw. . . .

Desmond MacCarthy: Bloomsbury, An Unfinished Memoir

*Desmond MacCarthy appears to have been the most genial member
of Bloomsbury. He was a little older than most of the others, and
although his career was a disappointment to himself and his friends,
he did become the most influential English newspaper critic of his*

time and gave wide currency to certain Bloomsbury values. An auto-
biographical digression in an essay on Henry James in 1931 sum-
marized those values as derived from G.E. Moore, whose best friend
was MacCarthy. (They can be compared with Keynes's later description
on pp. 85-6.)

> *Our generation, at least that part of it with which I was best acquainted*
> *and most at home, was interested in those parts of experience which could*
> *be regarded as ends in themselves. Morality was either a means to attaining*
> *those goods of the soul, or it was nothing. . . . Those ends naturally fined*
> *themselves down to personal relations, aesthetic emotions and the pursuit*
> *of truth. We were perpetually in search of distinctions; our most ardent*
> *discussions were attempts to fix some sort of scale of values for experience.*
> *The tendency was for the stress to fall on feeling rightly rather than upon*
> *action. It would be an exaggeration to say we cared not a sprat either for*
> *causes or for our own careers (appetite in both directions comes with eating,*
> *and we had barely begun to nibble); but those interests were subordi-*
> *nate. (Portraits, 164-5)*

MacCarthy's Bloomsbury memoir was included in his Memories *in*
1953, and it is completely characteristic of him that it should be un-
finished. One reason for this, however, is that the published memoir
was part of a longer, more personal unpublished reminiscence that
he wrote for the Memoir Club after hearing Virginia Woolf's memoir.
An edited version of the unpublished part has been added to the pub-
lished memoir here (minus a digression on MacCarthy's eccentric
friend Reymond Abbott). MacCarthy's attitude towards his own as-
sociation with Bloomsbury is rather paradoxical, but his identification
of Bloomsbury with Old or Early Bloomsbury recurs in a number
of other Bloomsbury memoirs, such as Vanessa Bell's. More revealing
is his emphasis on the importance of Clive Bell to the Group. Mac-
Carthy's reflections on Lytton Strachey's influence are continued in
his portrait of Strachey in the Bloomsberries *part of this collec-*
tion.

'Bloomsbury' is a regional adjective which has been used as a label
for a few writers and painters who dwell, or have some time or other
dwelt, in that part of London; and who used to, or do, see a good
deal of each other. It is chiefly used as a term of abuse in reviews.
In the shorthand of colloquial criticism and gossip it connotes,
vaguely, a certain arrogant exclusiveness, anti-herd intellectualism,

and a superior moral frivolity. 'Bloomsbury', as a word, has also found its way into the jargon of French and German criticism of contemporary English literature, where it takes on the significance of a literary movement. But in England, where spectators see, at any rate, that there is little in common between the work of Lytton Strachey, Virginia Woolf, Clive Bell, David Garnett, Roger Fry, Maynard Keynes, Leonard Woolf, Vanessa Bell, Duncan Grant, E.M. Forster, it does not suggest so much a movement as a 'push'; a mutual-admiration society, to which some, suffering from suspicion-mania, have attributed a sinister power over the Press. Writers and painters who are indignant, sometimes rightly, sometimes wrongly, at their works not meeting with universal praise, and looking about for an explanation of the inexplicable, have been known to mutter darkly 'Bloomsbury' and find relief.

> Of all the clever people round me here
> > I most delight in Me –
> Mine is the only voice I hear,
> > And mine the only face I see.

Roy Campbell's epigram, which he calls *Home Thoughts in Bloomsbury*, expresses a conception of it which is only an exaggeration of one that is fairly common. But, in fact, 'Bloomsbury' is neither a movement, nor a push, but only a group of old friends; whose affection and respect for each other has stood the test of nearly thirty years and whose intellectual candour makes their company agreeable to each other. It never was a movement. In taste and judgment 'Bloomsbury' from the start has been at variance with itself. Indeed, here lay its charm as a social circle. There was enough mutual respect and affection, well tested by time, to supply cement; enough difference of temperament and opinion to stimulate talk; enough intellectual honesty to enable them to learn from each other. Their association began when they were far too young (with the exception of Roger Fry) to have achieved anything; and by the time the world heard of 'Bloomsbury', 'Bloomsbury' as a group had ceased to exist. Though old ties remained, friends were scattered; and most of them were seeing much more of new friends than of each other: 'Marriage and death and division make barren our lives.'

And so far from being a mutual admiration society, 'Bloomsbury' is the last place where a Bloomsburian, who has just written a book, would look for that enthusiastic amazement at his achievement which

authors enjoy most. A considerate silence, a carefully measured com-
mendation veering at once into a discussion of generalities, is the
most he, or she, ever hopes to get *there*. In early days, before they
had done anything, they did believe in one another – perhaps more
than each believed in himself or herself.

'Bloomsbury' has never been a spiritual home to me; but let me
add that I have not got one, although at Cambridge for a few years
I fancied that I had. 'Bloomsbury' had been to me, rather, what those
who cater for sailors (like theirs, my home is a floating one) call
'a home from home'. Looking back I see that I converged upon
'Bloomsbury' by three ways: through making friends with Clive Bell,
through getting to know some Cambridge 'Apostles' junior to me,
and through my introduction into the home-life of Miss Vanessa and
Miss Virginia Stephen. Although the second of these approaches was
prior in time I will begin with my first encounter (it was strikingly
accidental) with Clive Bell.

My undergraduate days were over, and I was going down to Cambridge one November afternoon in 1901 to visit George Moore, the
philosopher, who still had rooms in Neville's Court. It must have
been that train which gets us up to Cambridge in time for dinner.
My mood was one of dejection; and when such moods come upon
me I take any modest steps handy to relieve them. If I happen, for
instance, to be travelling, and to have money in my pocket, I will
travel first-class. It does me hardly any perceptible good, but still
perhaps – a little. There was on this occasion one other occupant
of the carriage that I entered that afternoon. He was a youth with
a noticeable head of wavy auburn hair, and that mild-white skin
which often goes with it. I cannot visualize him completely, but I
think I am safe in saying that he was dressed with careless opulence,
and that he wore, flung open, a dark fur coat with a deep astrakhan
collar. I thought his appearance distinctly enviable, and I was prepared by my melancholy to take a pathetically unselfish interest in
the good fortune of others. It was not his aspect which struck me
as proclaiming him to be one of the fortunate; not even his youth,
a quality, which, at the age of twenty-four, I thought even more enviable than I think it now, but his eager and enjoying temperament,
with which in the first ten minutes of conversation I came in contact.
I forgot in talk with him the weight of troubles, cosmic and private,
which were oppressing me; and I fancied myself to be enjoying, vi-
cariously at any rate, through him, the prospect of helping myself

in a generous manner to the pleasures of life. My attitude towards
this young man (it was inevitable in one so rent and bruised by experience as myself) was distinctly avuncular. Happily either he did
not perceive this or he did not resent it. I delighted in him because
I could see in imagination the enormous rich hunk he was about
to cut from the cake of life. What we talked about I cannot remember,
but that was the residual impression. I must, of course, have asked
him if he did not know 'So-and-So, and So-and-So', mentioning those
younger Cambridge 'Apostles' who, as I said, also proved to be roads
leading to 'Bloomsbury' – Lytton Strachey certainly was one of them.
Anyhow we got on so well together that he asked me to lunch with
him the next day. One other thing interested me in him, the ori-
entation of his life at the moment seemed to resemble what my own
had been when I first went up to Cambridge.

He appeared to have a foot in two communities which, in the University, and indeed in the world itself, are separated from each other
by as deep a trench as divides, say, Roman Catholics from the rest
of mankind. He seemed to live, half with the rich sporting-set, and
half with the intellectuals; and sure enough the next day I found
my host in a white hunting-stock and a dressing gown. His aspect
was reminiscent of a sporting young man in a Leech picture at that
delicious moment when he has pulled off his top-boots and is about
to take his hot shower-bath. That it was a Sunday and he could not
have thrown a leg over a horse that morning, added to his character
a touch of fantasy, which was in harmony with my first impression
of him.

[*The unpublished part of MacCarthy's memoir continues*] When I describe him [Clive Bell] as an intellectual I must distinguish by saying
that he clearly did not belong to the hard-boiled type, towards which
I had gravitated on disentangling myself from the bloods who had
called upon me when I arrived at Trinity and had sat smoking cigars
and drinking port on my packing cases, and with whom, during my
first term, I did occasionally 'beat the floor and crash the glass'. He
seemed to have artistic rather than philosophical leanings, and not
those of the safe kind in the direction, say, of Michael Angelo or
Bellini. No reproductions of these undoubted masterpieces hung
upon the walls of his manly and comfortable rooms. On the contrary
there was a whiff of Aubrey Beardsley and Wilde about his preferences. . . . He had prepared me to believe that it was possible to enjoy

aspects of things which were not noble, and this no doubt helped me on the way to subsequent intimacy with this pleasure-loving youth, in whom I was afterwards to discover other qualities.

I was to discover in him first and foremost a capacity for warm and generous, even extravagant, admiration for others, a capacity which years and increasing self-confidence has no doubt since dimmed. He rayed forth a warmth upon his friends which was almost more than a mere premonition of fame. It was fame itself. It was an utterly and even extravagantly generous appreciation – and I am speaking now of early years – the disseminator of this glow was himself apparently utterly content with the merely refracted glory of his own shedding. To be one (he did not seem to stop to determine his own contribution to it) of such a very remarkable group of people as his particular friends was enough. It was enough, it was enough. In retrospect it seems to me impossible to over-estimate the part played by him in the creation of Bloomsbury. For in so far as that entity has ever existed, it was due to him that Bloomsbury, composed as it was of most varying and highly individualized personalities – endowed in very different directions – and all highly critical – learnt to think of themselves as a 'we', and found a kind of attitude towards the rest of the world thrust upon them. Some resented this. They sometimes thought it blatant, but I seem to remember that even those who did so, took full advantage of the recuperating properties of a frequent bath in this extemporised sea of glory. As each in turn made his or her mark on the world, the comforting and hygienic properties of private fame became of course less important to them. While the self-confidence of the dispenser of it also waxed in proportion, the issuing rays became mixed with criticism and patronage. It is only in youth that the 'We-band-of-brothers', 'we-salt-of-the-earth' feeling is salutary or indeed even possible. By the time that the big common world had begun to hear of Bloomsbury, Bloomsbury had ceased as a coherent entity to exist. Clive's work in that direction was over. Every tub was sitting on its own bottom, every herring hanging by its own head, every cheese, whether soft or hard, depending from its own hook. We, who are in this room now, are in a sense Bloomsbury, but the whole is no longer greater than the sum of its parts. Bloomsbury had ceased to exist.

I was very much interested in the distinction which Virginia in the delightful paper she read us last time made between the early and the later Bloomsbury. The early Bloomsbury from her account and from my own recollections of very occasional dips into it, was an attempt to colonise the Spirit of the Apostles in London. But the emigrants from Cambridge were not remarkable for that strength and clearness of intellect which made such gatherings supportable. Discussion guttered down too readily in Bloomsbury into the darkness of sincere but inconclusive silence. Saxon might breathe forth the true apostolic spirit, Clive might trot out his recollections of *Principia Ethica*, but the dialectical energy and intellectual force of Cambridge was absent, and I do not wonder that the Misses Stephen, though at first impressed, soon grew slightly bored.

Virginia has described the releasing effect of the appearance of Lytton upon the scene, bringing with him freedom of speech. What is of some interest to the social historian – the historian of influences – is that he had already exerted a similar change at Cambridge. Cambridge had long been ruled by metaphysicians. My sojourn there coincided with the deposition of idealist philosophy in the person of McTaggart by the realistic common-sense school embodied in Moore. In all departments of thought Moore was concerned to prove that, say, the views of his old nurse were the last word. He succeeded in showing that certainly the views of the Idealists were less well-founded. He was succeeded by Lytton. That generation were quite incapable of arguing such matters closely. They were not convinced and yet they were not unconvinced. They turned their attention to the discussion of what they understood better than abstract ideas, personal emotions and personal relations: to literature, art and themselves. This implied the discovery that they were far from being 'good' in Moore's sense of the word – except in regard to fundamental intellectual sincerity, the while the extirpation of the word shyness was essential to the nature of their discussions and interests, and Lytton's own proclivities abolished the last of the taboos. Thus, as I see it, the free-speech movement which was the mark of Bloomsbury had its origin elsewhere, and the only difference between Bloomsbury and contemporary Cambridge was that when the latter was transplanted it flourished in a company in which women were not excluded – from the point of view of the social historian, a most important change.

But I am wandering from my true aim, that of reminiscence – not analysis. Let me return to the subject of my own approach to Bloomsbury. But before I do so, let me put before you the notion that there were not two Bloomsburys, but three. Not merely the Early and the Late, which Virginia described, but an Early, a Late and a Decadent.

By the Decadent period I mean that in which there was a con-

siderable infiltration of inferior persons. Now the influence of Lytton
though beneficent and inspiring was, wherever he went, subject to
one great draw-back. His estimate of people was apt to depend to
a large extent upon the way their hair grew on their foreheads or
the brightness of their eyes and teeth. I do not say that he failed to
arrive soon himself at a truer estimate of their total value, but this
was only liable to happen *after* he had thrust them on his friends
as most remarkable human beings. Of course with age he grew wiser,
and allowed for the effect of the juice which had been squeezed into
his own eyes. I am not prepared to say that he was responsible for
the Decadent Period of Bloomsbury, but the same kind of thing struck
me as happening in Gordon Square. I remember a Bloomsbury period
which I called to myself the Dicky-bird period, when a flock of those
otherwise harmless creatures descended upon Bloomsbury and pecked
conversation to death. For those on whose knees they perched there
was doubtless some compensation, but not for others. But I am forgetting again my own second avenue of approach – the Misses Stephen. We have listened to a fascinating account of their early attempts
to become normal young ladies. I never met Virginia in society, but
I have a vivid recollection of Vanessa at parties. She had the aspect
of a beautiful captive; her large grey eyes appeared to be homes of
silent prayer; one could almost see the chains upon her wrists. Any
young man introduced to her would presently appear to be in difficulties. You might have supposed, indeed, that he was shyly en-
deavouring to communicate something of an intimate nature, which
she was receiving with the painful reserve necessitated by a drawing-
room full of people. Appearances were deceptive, he was only trying
to follow up say the question of whether she had heard Joachim
play at St. James Hall last week. At the Freshfields I was myself introduced to her. I got on perhaps a little better, having hit upon
the topics of dogs and boxing, but I dare say I, too, looked as though
I were asking her why she had been so unkind to me. From the background of people 'that angel' George Duckworth, for so all the dow-
agers spoke of him, would throw her a bright smile of encouragement.
'He's a mother you know to those girls – he really is.'

One memorable afternoon 'Aunt Anny' took me to tea at Hyde
Park Gate. I had (and still have) a great admiration for Leslie Stephen.
I had heard him grumble gently but despairingly in Mrs Freshfield's
boudoir about Sainte-Beuve, but it was his work of course that had
created in me that deep respect. He belonged to the type of mind
and character which my Cambridge education had led me to admire.

What happened was a thrilling play to me. L.S. though polite was sunk in a most respectworthy gloom. And I enjoyed the comedy of its gradual thawing. I was hardly conscious of his daughters so absorbed was I in admiration of Aunt Anny's reckless intrepidity. She seized the speaking end of the serpent which he held to his ear and proceeded to shout down it a series of remarks of a most trivial nature which for a short time only elicited groans. 'Leslie, Desmond and I saw a little dog – such an odd little dog – run outside your gate.' 'Oh, Anny, Anny.' 'King Edward motored all the way to Windsor with this terrier.' 'Oh Anny, Anny.' 'Herbert Paul fell downstairs yesterday on his head.' 'Oh, Anny, Anny.' 'I do hope it has knocked those dreadful headaches out of him.' – 'Oh, Anny, Anny' – but at last this time the groan ended in half-a-laugh. The Misses Stephen also smiled.

I called again several times and had a try myself at performing on the serpent. Leslie Stephen was very indulgent. This gave me also an opportunity of talking a little with Vanessa, who, I think always presided over tea. Once I called with Theodore Davies, and on our walk back we spoke of those frail ethereal creatures the Misses Stephen. They had impressed us. Theodore quoted Meredith: 'The breast of them a sounding shell; the blood of them a lighted dew.' I remember, and I still think it does credit to my perspicacity, that I replied, 'yes, but you know I believe that the Misses Stephen would rather enjoy a sponge-fight.' An extravagant suggestion so it seemed at the time, but implying a certain insight which subsequent experience confirmed. They were not so frail and ethereal as they appeared.

The glamour of Leslie Stephen invested and increased my admiration for Virginia, in whom I thought I saw a resemblance to him. It hurt me a little that the family referred to her casually as 'goat'. But there was an intensity in her father's eye which vaguely reminded me of that animal – and had I not seen a resemblance between them? Allowing for family brutality I could, while deprecating the nickname, account for it.

Once after L.S.'s death I saw her looking very pale and young floating vaguely about Hatchards shop in a long black dress. I preferred to watch her rather than to speak to her and when she left the shop after turning over a few books I followed her. She went across into the then existing St. James's Hall. In those happy unhappy days I had no occupation – time was no object. I followed and took a ticket for the concert and the music mixed with my contemplation of her.

I did not get to know her at all till she was living with Adrian

in Fitzroy Square, and then not very well – for it appeared to me
an ideal menage. I have gathered since it was not quite that.

Desmond MacCarthy: The Post-Impressionist Exhibition of 1910

*Post-impressionist painting was in certain respects the justification
for the aesthetics of Bloomsbury's two art critics, Roger Fry and Clive
Bell. But the violent public reaction to the exhibition that Fry organized in 1910 was almost as interesting to Bloomsbury as the paintings themselves. Desmond MacCarthy was the secretary for the first
exhibition, and Leonard Woolf the secretary for the second (see his
account, pp. 146–8). In 1945 MacCarthy recalled his experience as
secretary.*

When Roger Fry proposed that I should go abroad and help assemble
a representative exhibition of pictures by Cézanne, Matisse, Van Gogh,
Gauguin, Seurat, Picasso and other now familiar French painters (incidentally he promised me a few days' bicycling in France) I don't
think he chose me because he had special trust in my judgment. Of
course he knew I was fond of pictures and that if confronted with
one I could look at it with interest for more than two minutes –
a faculty not so common as you might suppose. (Next time you are
in a gallery you can verify this by timing people as they go round.)
And then, though I could not generalize about artists, I did occasionally say something about a picture which would interest him,
though it might be only 'I'm almost sure that cow is too near the
tree' or 'that crimson blob next her nose – of course, I see something
of the kind is necessary and I didn't notice it at all at first, but now
I have – it bothers me'. But what really influenced him in choosing
me was that we were happy together. My failings were not the sort
which annoyed him, nor (equally important) were my virtues. Masterful men often prefer a rather incompetent colleague to an over-
confident one. Fry was capable of making muddles himself; he would
not have been quite comfortable with anyone implacably efficient.
And here I must mention that he was also a most persuasive man.

   Hearing that the Grafton Galleries had no show for the months
between their usual London Season exhibition and the new year's,
he proceeded to convince them that they might do worse than hold
a stop-gap exhibition of modern foreign artists – also that Desmond
MacCarthy was an excellent man of business which indeed, in my

opinion (but of this you must judge for yourselves) he did turn out to be. It was all settled in a tremendous hurry. I had just time to interview the director of the Galleries. He apologized for the smallness of my fee (a hundred pounds). But if – he added, with a pitying smile – if there were profits, I might have half of them. Neither the committee of the Grafton Galleries nor Roger Fry thought for one moment that the show could be a financial success.

Then I was stricken down with an influenza. However, Roger wasn't a man to be put out by a little thing like that. He made me rise from bed, drink a bottle of champagne and catch the boat for Calais with him. I arrived in Paris feeling as though my head were about the size and weight of an apple.

Of course, the first people we went to see in Paris were dealers who had modern pictures. If they could be persuaded to lend, then the London show would be representative. We spent day after day looking at the pictures, and nearly all those which Roger preferred were at our disposal. I remember his raptures. He would sit in front of them with his hands on his knees groaning repeatedly 'Wonderful! wonderful!' I don't think at that date anybody in England possessed any specimens of these artists' works, except Sutro, the playwright, who had a small Van Gogh. At these interviews with dealers I used to pose as M. le Publique, and on one point my verdict was final: Was there, or was there not, anything in some nude which might create an outcry in London?

Then off we went for our little tour, after which Roger returned to London and I was sent on to Munich and Holland to get other pictures. In Amsterdam Van Gogh's sister, Madame Gosschalk Bonger, had, of course, many of her late brother's, and they were still admirably cheap. When we came to price them she was asking a hundred and twenty pounds or less for some admirable examples of his art. Then I returned to Paris to settle the business side.

Now, though I was supposed to be a man of affairs, when the biggest dealer asked me what percentage the Galleries wanted on sales, I confess I was floored. It was a point on which I had neglected to inform myself before starting. At a venture I murmured, 'twenty per cent', and he replied, *'Parfaitement, Monsieur.'* Then he went on, 'If you get an offer for a picture, do not communicate at once with the artist, but with me first. He may accept less and then we can share the difference.' Now the success of the exhibition largely depended on keeping on good terms with him. How would you have behaved? Well, I summoned up all the tact for which an aunt of mine had been famous, and replied: 'I don't think I can agree to anything not down in black and white, but if you write to me. . . .' He looked a little hard at me and then repeated, *'Parfaitement, Monsieur.'* Of course, I never received that letter. We remained on excellent terms, and all was well.

On my return to London I reported that several hundred interesting pictures were available (transit insurance probably £150). I was told that expenses had to be kept down as the venture was a certain loss; still, one hundred pounds might be spent on advertising; *that* was satisfactory. I was about to leave when the director casually remarked: 'I suppose you secured our usual percentage on sales?' Feebly, I murmured: 'You never told me what it was.' There was an oppressive pause. 'Do you mean to say you didn't ask if you didn't know? What *did* you get?' 'Twenty per cent.' 'Twenty? Why, we've *never* got more than eleven!' For several days after that I was convinced that I was cut out for a business career.

What was the exhibition to be called? That was the next question. Roger and I and a young journalist who was to help us with publicity, met to consider this; and it was at that meeting that a word which is now safely embedded in the English language – 'post-impressionism' – was invented. Roger first suggested various terms like 'expressionism', which aimed at distinguishing these artists from the impressionists; but the journalist wouldn't have that or any other of his alternatives. At last Roger, losing patience, said: 'Oh, let's just call them post-impressionists; at any rate, they came after the impressionists.' Later he handed over to me, with a few notes, the ticklish job of writing the preface to the catalogue – the unsigned preface. This work of mine was far more widely quoted than anything I was ever destined to write, and phrases from it like 'A good rocking-horse is more like a horse than the snapshot of a Derby winner' were quoted and re-quoted with laughter.

The hurried agonies of that picture-hanging are still vivid to me. Roger was entirely absorbed in deciding which picture would look best next another, while it lay with me to number them. As he was continually shifting them about when I was elsewhere, I was terrified that the numbers and titles wouldn't always correspond, with the effect of increasing the mockery, which I now felt certain the exhibition would excite. It was four AM. before I got to bed the night before Press day, and then I couldn't sleep for worrying. When the newspaper was brought to me with coffee in bed, although it happened to contain a long and laudatory review of a book I had just published, I couldn't even read that. The prospect of public ridicule owing to having, say, catalogued a nude girl as "Station-master at Arles', made my walk to the gallery more like a walk to the gallows. Soon after ten, the Press began to arrive. Now anything new in art is apt to provoke the same kind of indignation as immoral conduct, and vice is detected in perfectly innocent pictures. Perhaps any mental shock is apt to remind people of moral shocks they have received, and the sensations being similar, they attribute this to the same cause. Anyhow, as I walked about among the tittering newspaper critics busily taking notes (they saw at once that the whole thing was splendid copy) I kept overhearing such remarks as 'Pure pornography', 'Admirably indecent'. Not a word of truth, of course, in this. As M. le Publique I had been careful to exclude too frankly physiological nudes and, indeed, at the last moment, instead of hanging two of the pictures, I told Roger they had better be kept, for a time, in my sanctum downstairs.

The Press notices were certainly calculated to rouse curiosity. And from the opening day the public flocked, and the big rooms echoed with explosions of laughter and indignation. Sometimes I hovered about trying to explain what I thought was the point of a picture, drawing attention to colour or arrangement, and here and there, now and then, I did find a receptive listener. One young lady seemed to come nearly every day for a lecture and presently proposed to me, which was almost a fault in the opposite direction. I hit on a device for calming those of the furious who stormed down in a rage to my sanctum beneath the galleries. To these I would first explain that I was, after all, only the secretary, so I could not very well close the exhibition on my own initiative that very evening. But I would add, 'Your point of view is most interesting, and if you will write it down and sign it, I shall be most happy to pin it up in the entrance for all to read.' This suggestion acted as a sedative. The indignant one would reply, 'Oh, I don't know that I want to put anything on paper; only I did feel that what I have said ought to be said.' Occasionally I did get a document to pin up. I wish I had kept them.

The people who annoyed me most were, I think, cultivated women who went deliberately into trills of silvery laughter in front of pic- tures. With those who were genuinely amused I had some sympathy. I remember, for instance, a stout, elderly man of a good appearance, led in by a young woman, who went into such convulsions of laughter on catching sight of Cézanne's portrait of his wife in the first little room that his companion had to take him out and walk him up and down in the fresh air. When they re-entered, I watched him going round the other rooms, where there really were some startling pictures. He did so without a smile. Now when one has laughed oneself weak, one can't laugh again even at something far funnier. This man's amusement had been genuine, not wilful, or superior, or offensive, and I forgave it.

Presently we actually began to sell pictures. The Art Gallery at Helsinki bought a very fine Cézanne for £800, I remember; and when we closed, my share of the profits amounted to – what do you think? – over £460 – such a lump sum as I had never earned before, and would never earn again! Not only had the exhibition been the theme of non-stop correspondence in the papers and of pamphlet wars – all the best known painters were, alas, against us – but it also provoked lectures from mental specialists. Fry himself did not make one penny out of the exhibition, nor did he out of the Omega workshops, which he started seven years later. Indeed, by introducing the works of Cézanne, Matisse, Seurat, Van Gogh, Gauguin and Picasso to the British public, he smashed for a long time his reputation as an art critic. Kind people called him mad, and reminded others that his wife was in an asylum. The majority declared him to be a subverter of morals and art, and a blatant self-advertiser. . . .

E.M. Forster: Bloomsbury, An Early Note

E.M. Forster was a Cambridge Apostle at the turn of the century, an early member of the Memoir Club, a close friend for many years of Leonard and Virginia Woolf as well as a good friend of Lytton Strachey, Desmond MacCarthy, and Roger Fry. Yet he felt, as he says in his early note on Bloomsbury, that he did not belong automatically to the Group, especially after 1916 when he went to Alexandria to work for the Red Cross and fell in love with an Egyptian. If further evidence of Forster's involvement with Bloomsbury were needed, it could be found in an unpublished and undated draft of a paper for the Memoir Club on his early approaches to Bloomsbury. They began with Roger Fry's lectures at Cambridge, which Forster attended at the end of the last century – lectures in which Forster first detected the essential Bloomsbury undertone that maintained it was not the subject but the treatment that mattered in art. Encounters with Lytton Strachey and Duncan Grant followed at Cambridge, and later in London he met Clive Bell (they quarrelled over Bell's praise of the France's Second Empire), Grant again, and finally Virginia and Adrian Stephen in Fitzroy Square. Forster's tone in his fragmentary memoir is more affectionate than in the note included here, and it suggests why the Woolfs tried to get him to write a comic guide to Bloomsbury in the 1930s; he was tempted but never finally wrote it (see p. 193).

Forster's early note on Bloomsbury was written in his Commonplace Book, *then published in a cut form under the title 'Bloomsbury, An Early Note (February 1929)' in* Pawn, a King's College magazine, *in 1956. It alludes not only to Virginia Woolf's* Orlando, *which was published in 1928, but also to the death that year of Lytton Strachey's mother, whose obituary Virginia wrote for* The Times. *Gerald Heard's book* The Ascent of Humanity *(published in 1929 and dedicated to 'E.M.F. and K.W.') is subtitled* The Evolution of Civilization from Group Consciousness through Individuality to Super-Consciousness. *In the fifth chapter Heard explains how the divergence of thought and feeling in 'upper individuals' needs to be reconciled through a new super-individuality.*

Bloomsbury, hopes W.J. Turner, will not enjoy Schnabel, a pianist whom he enjoys himself. Why drag the place in, I wonder? I suppose because it is the only genuine *movement* in English civilisation, though that civilisation contains far better and more genuine individuals. The other movements are anti-Bloomsbury and self-conscious/ cheap, envious – wh. Bl. as a movement is not, being composed of people who hold similar opinions and dont quarrel violently with one another – But unkind, despite irritable protests to the contrary; Orlando regards the centuries of flesh and spirit as fresh fuel for her bonfire, and death can only be laughed at (I remember their laughter at Massingham's) or adorned with a tasteful garland like Lady Strachey's. – Its contempt of the outsider plays a very small part of its activity, and rests on inattention rather than arrogance. Once convinced that he is not a figure of fun, it welcomes and studies him, but the rest of humanity remains in a background of screaming farce as before. Meanwhile the intellect – thinking and talking things out – goes steadily ahead, 'things' looking rather like small Xmas trees when they come into the room, and trees minus their leaves and decorations when they are carried out. The final bareness isn't tragic, the horrors of the universe being surveyed in physical comfort, and suffering apprehended only intellectually.

Essentially *gentlefolks*. Would open other people's letters, but wouldn't steal, bully, slander, or blackmail like many of their critics, and have acquired a culture in harmony with their social position.

Hence their stability. Contrast them with (a) gamindom – Joyce, D.H. Lawrence, Wyndham Lewes (b) aristocracy who regard culture as an adventure and may at any moment burn their tapering fingers and drop it. Academic background, independent income. Continental enthusiasms sex-talk, and all, they are in the English tradition.

I dont belong automatically – from 1916 the gulf was bound to widen. And I couldn't go there for any sort of comfort or sympathy.

G. Heard, the Ascent of Society, Ch. V, tho dealing with the wider subject of intellectualism explains *Bloomsbury* without denouncing it – never done before, I think. Why are intellectuals so irritated at emotionalism? because they are not wholly intellectual.

> Their intelligence permits them to see the future as the emotionalists cannot but their own emotions will not let them give the true reason of their fear at what they see. They will not face or at least give expression to the fact that what lies before us is a revolution and that the only choice before us is a metamorphosis so drastic as to the individualist to be scarcely distinguishable from death.

The irritation is 'a by-product, a strain-symptom'.

cf. also in this connection a letter from Frances Marshall, a Bloomsbury hanger on in which she complains of Miss MacMunn as having a strong streak of the octopus in her, and making a bee line for one's soul at the first opportunity. Fear of being interfered with emotionally soon turns to hysteria.

G.H. argues that the intellectual always ascribes intellectual motives to his opponents and argues that even if the emotionalist rank and file don't know what they are up to, their leaders do.   26-2-29.

E.M. Forster: Interview on Bloomsbury

Later in 1929 Forster returned briefly to Alexandria, where he was interviewed by a Greek newspaper. His public attitude towards Bloomsbury complements his private one. The inclusion of Arthur Waley in Bloomsbury is a little surprising, though he did live there and was friends with various members of the Group (see pp. 319–21).

In our conversation with Mr Forster, literary societies were another subject of discussion.

'In England,' he told us, 'there are very few literary and artistic societies and this distinguishes England, for better or worse, from other countries. Writers tend to work in isolation and they do not make a group effort except when their literary freedom is threatened, as was recently the case involving ridiculous police intervention. The only society which comes to my mind is the "Bloomsbury Group" which is composed of people of high intelligence, who have spiritual integrity, great critical ability, economic independence and liberal opinions. Their enemies sarcastically call them "highbrow" and impute sterility to them. This society, however, has already produced Lytton Strachey, J.M. Keynes, Virginia Woolf (the poetic novelist with great talent), Roger Fry (our principal art critic), Arthur Waley (the great Japanese scholar and translator), not to mention other writers of the younger generation like David Garnett.

'Of course, the Bloomsbury Group is not wholly representative of English literature. It is sophisticated, has a sense of its own importance and is often lacking in spontaneity and warmth. However, it is certainly a creative force and the literary historian of the future will probably hold it in high esteem. . . .'

E.M. Forster: Letters

To his friend W.J.H. Sprott, who had complained about that quintessential Bloomsbury book Virginia Woolf's The Waves *and also grumbled about various members of the Group, Forster replied expressing his qualified exasperation with Bloomsbury in 1931. Sprott, an Apostle, psychologist, and close friend of Forster and Keynes, was a younger associate of the Group. All members of Bloomsbury expressed their irritation with the Group at one time or another, of course. To another Bloomsbury associate, William Plomer, Forster showed a different attitude towards Bloomsbury in 1946. The 'rumps' referred to were presumably Memoir Club memoirs by three of the deceased members.*

From a letter to W.J.H. Sprott, 16 July 1931 Oh the Bells, the Woolves – or rather Virginia, for I do like Leonard! Oh how I do agree, and if to become anti-Bloomsbury were not to become Bloomsbury, how I would become it! But to turn one's backside to them is the only course – they will never have the grace to penetrate it, their inquisitiveness never had any spunk, that is why one loathes it so. Turned well away from them, let one read their books, which are *very* good, and look at their mural designs, which may be good too, and that is the end. I am sorry what you say about Lytton, and surprised – I thought his curiosity was of the pardonable type, and that he was getting both solid and charming. . . .

From a letter to William Plomer, April 1943 We had a very good meeting of the Memoir Club last week. Virginia's, Lytton's, and Roger's rumps were brilliant, . . . and made me realise how much is past and passing and how, for understandable reasons, no civilisation or attempt at civilisation has succeeded Bloomsbury, and how much of my own time I waste with second rate people to whom I haven't even any obligation to be kind.

John Maynard Keynes: My Early Beliefs

Of all the memoirs of Bloomsbury, J.M. Keynes's 'My Early Beliefs' is the most widely known and the most influential. Since its 1949 posthumous publication in Two Memoirs, *Keynes's brilliant description of how Moore converted him and his friends to a limited yet pure religion of love, beauty, and truth has been taken by Bloomsbury friends and foes alike as the definitive account of the Group's intellectual background at Cambridge. It was only later that authorities such as Leonard Woolf showed the confusion in Keynes's chronology and his misinterpretation of G.E. Moore's influence on the Bloomsbury Apostles (see pp. 133–41).*

Keynes's memoir was originally published with an introduction by David Garnett, who explained that it was written for the Memoir Club following a paper of his own recollecting D.H. Lawrence. Lawrence was fond of Garnett and his parents but disliked his friends such as Duncan Grant, Francis Birrell, and the Stracheys, as well as Keynes. Garnett's introduction quotes a letter from Lawrence saying Garnett's friends made him dream of beetles and that his meeting with Keynes in Cambridge in 1915 'sent me mad with misery and hostility and rage . . .' (Keynes, 10:431). Garnett did not reveal in his own memoir or his introduction, however, what Lawrence had said, in parts of the letter not quoted – that it was 'men loving men' among Garnett's friends that had brought on one of the crises in his life. (Garnett gave the full text of the letter only in his 1979 memoirs, Great Friends, *88–9.) Homosexuality is also a missing belief in 'My Early Beliefs.'*

*At the end of his memoir Keynes says that the ignoring by himself
and his friends of 'both the reality and the value of the vulgar passions'
helped to arouse Lawrence's passionate distaste for Cambridge (see
p. 97). But Keynes himself continues in his memoir to ignore one
particular kind of 'vulgar passion' whose reality and value so repelled
Lawrence.*

*The occasion on which Keynes read 'My Early Beliefs' was also
recalled by one of the younger members of the Memoir Club. Quentin
Bell's recollection completes the setting for this famous essay and suggests further qualifications of its interpretation of Bloomsbury. 'It was
in the summer of 1938, the summer before Munich; the audience consisted of the Memoir Club, that is to say a more or less Bloomsbury
audience, and two persons who were not in any real sense Bloomsbury, Jane Bussy, a niece of Lytton Strachey, and myself. A certain
part of the paper was addressed to, or at, us – the younger generation.
Maynard knew that we, and indeed some of his contemporaries, considered that he had become very reactionary. His plea for the traditional values, his attacks on Marxism, his sympathy for Lawrence's
attitude towards intuition as opposed to reason was meant to shock
and irritate us; it succeeded in doing so' (Bloomsbury, 74).*

*Garnett's introduction identifies a number of the names mentioned
in the memoir; these have been included, instead, in the identifications
at the end of this volume.*

I can visualize very clearly the scene of my meeting with D.H. Lawrence in 1914 (Bunny seems to suggest 1915, but my memory suggests
that it may have been earlier than that) of which he speaks in the
letter from which Bunny quoted at the last meeting of the Club. But
unfortunately I cannot remember any fragment of what was said,
though I retain some faint remains of what was felt.

It was at a breakfast party given by Bertie Russell in his rooms
in Neville's Court. There were only the three of us there. I fancy
that Lawrence had been staying with Bertie and that there had been
some meeting or party the night before, at which Lawrence had been
facing Cambridge. Probably he had not enjoyed it. My memory is
that he was morose from the outset and said very little, apart from
indefinite expressions of irritable dissent, all the morning. Most of
the talk was between Bertie and me, and I haven't the faintest recollection of what it was about. But it was not the sort of conversation
we should have had if we had been alone. It was *at* Lawrence and
with the intention, largely unsuccessful, of getting him to participate.
We sat round the fireplace with the sofa drawn across. Lawrence

sat on the right-hand side in rather a crouching position with his
head down. Bertie stood up by the fireplace, as I think I did, too,
from time to time. I came away feeling that the party had been a
failure and that we had failed to establish contact, but with no other
particular impression. You know the sort of situation when two familiar friends talk *at* a visitor. I had never seen him before, and I
never saw him again. Many years later he recorded in a letter, which
is printed in his published correspondence, that I was the only
member of Bloomsbury who had supported him by subscribing for
Lady Chatterley.

That is all I *remember*. But Bunny's story suggests some inferences
to me. In the passage of his life which Bunny had described I think
that Lawrence was influenced by two causes of emotional disturbance.
One of them centred around Ottoline. As always, Ottoline was keeping more than one world. Except for Bertie, the Cambridge and
Bloomsbury world was only just beginning to hold her. Lawrence,
Gertler, Carrington were a different strand in her furbelows. Lawrence was jealous of the other lot; and Cambridge rationalism and
cynicism, then at their height, were, of course, repulsive to him. Bertie
gave him what must have been, I think, his first glimpse of Cambridge. It overwhelmed, attracted and repulsed him – which was the
other emotional disturbance. It was obviously a civilisation, and not
less obviously uncomfortable and unattainable for him – very repulsive and very attractive. Now Bunny had come into his life quite
independently, neither through Ottoline nor from Cambridge and
Bloomsbury; he was evidently very fond of Bunny; and when he saw
him being seduced by Cambridge, he was yet more jealous, just as
he was jealous of Ottoline's new leanings that way. And jealousy
apart, it is impossible to imagine moods more antagonistic than those
of Lawrence and of pre-war Cambridge.

But when all that has been said, was there something true and
right in what Lawrence felt? There generally was. His reactions were
incomplete and unfair, but they were not usually baseless. I have said
that I have forgotten what the conversation was about. But I expect
it was pretty brittle stuff – not so brittle as Frankie Birrell's – but
pretty brittle all the same. And although it was silly to take it, or
to estimate it, at its face value, did the way of responding to life
which lay behind it lack something important? Lawrence was oblivious of anything valuable it may have offered – it was a *lack* that
he was violently apprehending. So Bunny's memoir has thrown my
mind back to reflections about our mental history in the dozen years
before the war; and if it will not shock the club too much, I should

like in this contribution to its proceedings to introduce for once, mental or spiritual, instead of sexual, adventures, to try and recall the principal impacts on one's virgin mind and to wonder how it has all turned out, and whether one still holds by that youthful religion.

I went up to Cambridge at Michaelmas 1902, and Moore's *Principia Ethica* came out at the end of my first year. I have never heard of the present generation having read it. But, of course, its effect on *us*, and the talk which preceded and followed it, dominated, and perhaps still dominate, everything else. We were at an age when our beliefs influenced our behaviour, a characteristic of the young which it is easy for the middle-aged to forget, and the habits of feeling formed then still persist in a recognisable degree. It is those habits of feeling, influencing the majority of us, which make this Club a collectivity and separate us from the rest. They overlaid, somehow, our otherwise extremely different characters – Moore himself was a puritan and precisian, Strachey (for that was his name at that time) a Voltairean, Woolf a rabbi, myself a nonconformist, Sheppard a conformist and (as it now turns out) an ecclesiastic, Clive a gay and amiable dog, Sydney-Turner a quietist, Hawtrey a dogmatist and so on. Of those who had come just before, only MacCarthy and Ainsworth, who were much influenced by their personal feelings for Moore, came under his full influence. We did not see much of Forster at that time; who was already the elusive colt of a dark horse. It was only for us, those who were active in 1903, that Moore completely ousted McTaggart, Dickinson, Russell. The influence was not only overwhelming; but it was the extreme opposite of what Strachey used to call *funeste*; it was exciting, exhilarating, the beginning of a renaissance, the opening of a new heaven on a new earth, we were the forerunners of a new dispensation, we were not afraid of anything. Perhaps it was because we were so brought up that even at our gloomiest and worst we have never lost a certain resilience which the younger generation seem never to have had. They have enjoyed, at most, only a pale reflection of something, not altogether superseded, but faded and without illusions.

Now what we got from Moore was by no means entirely what he offered us. He had one foot on the threshold of the new heaven, but the other foot in Sidgwick and the Benthamite calculus and the general rules of correct behaviour. There was one chapter in the *Principia* of which we took not the slightest notice. We accepted Moore's religion, so to speak, and discarded his morals. Indeed, in our opinion, one of the greatest advantages of his religion, was that it made morals unnecessary – meaning by 'religion' one's attitude towards oneself and the ultimate and by 'morals' one's attitude towards the outside world and the intermediate. To the consequences of having a religion and no morals I return later.

Even if the new members of the Club know what the religion was (do they?), it will not do any of us any harm to try and recall the crude outlines. Nothing mattered except states of mind, our own and other people's of course, but chiefly our own. These states of mind were not associated with action or achievement or with consequences. They consisted in timeless, passionate states of contemplation and communion, largely unattached to 'before' and 'after'. Their value depended, in accordance with the principle of organic unity, on the state of affairs as a whole which could not be usefully analysed into parts. For example, the value of the state of mind of being in love did not depend merely on the nature of one's own emotions, but also on the worth of their object and on the reciprocity and nature of the object's motions; but it did not depend, if I remember rightly, or did not depend much, on what happened, or how one felt about it, a year later, though I myself was always an advocate of a principle of organic unity through time, which still seems to me only sensible. The appropriate subjects of passionate contemplation and communion were a beloved person, beauty and truth, and one's prime objects in life were love, the creation and enjoyment of aesthetic experience and the pursuit of knowledge. Of these love came a long way first. But in the early days under Moore's influence the public treatment of this and its associated acts was, on the whole, austere and platonic. Some of us might argue that physical enjoyment could spoil and detract from the state of mind as a whole. I do not remember at what date Strachey issued his edict that certain Latin technical terms of sex were the correct words to use, that to avoid them was a grave error, and, even in mixed company, a weakness, and the use of other synonyms a vulgarity. But I should certainly say that this was later. In 1903 those words were not even esoteric terms of common discourse.

Our religion closely followed the English puritan tradition of being chiefly concerned with the salvation of our own souls. The divine resided within a closed circle. There was not a very intimate connection between 'being good' and 'doing good'; and we had a feeling that there was some risk that in practice the latter might interfere with the former. But religions proper, as distinct from modern 'social service' pseudo-religions, have always been of that character; and perhaps it was a sufficient offset that our religion was altogether unworldly – with wealth, power, popularity or success it had no concern whatever, they were thoroughly despised.

How did we know what states of mind were good? This was a matter of direct inspection, of direct unanalysable intuition about which it was useless and impossible to argue. In that case who was right when there was a difference of opinion? There were two possible explanations. It might be that the two parties were not really talking about the same thing, that they were not bringing their intuitions to bear on precisely the same object, and, by virtue of the principle of organic unity, a very small difference in the object might make a very big difference in the result. Or it might be that some people had an acuter sense of judgment, just as some people can judge a vintage port and others cannot. On the whole, so far as I remember, this explanation prevailed. In practice, victory was with those who could speak with the greatest appearance of clear, undoubting conviction and could best use the accents of infallibility. Moore at this time was a master of this method – greeting one's remarks with a gasp of incredulity – *Do* you *really* think *that,* an expression of face as if to hear such a thing said reduced him to a state of wonder verging on imbecility, with his mouth wide open and wagging his head in the negative so violently that his hair shook. *Oh!* He would say, goggling at you as if either you or he must be mad; and no reply was possible. Strachey's methods were different; grim silence as if such a dreadful observation was beyond comment and the less said about it the better, but almost as effective for disposing of what he called death-packets. Woolf was fairly good at indicating a negative, but he was better at producing the effect that it was useless to argue with *him* than at crushing *you.* Dickinson knew how to shrug his shoulders and retreat unconvinced, but it was a retreat all the same. As for Sheppard and me we could only turn like worms, but worms who could be eventually goaded into voluble claims that worms have at least the *right* to turn. Yet after all the differences were about details. Broadly speaking we all knew for certain what were good states of mind and that they consisted in communion with objects of love, beauty, and truth.

I have called this faith a religion, and some sort of relation of neo-platonism it surely was. But we should have been very angry at the time with such a suggestion. We regarded all this as entirely rational and scientific in character. Like any other branch of science, it was nothing more than the application of logic and rational analysis to the material presented as sense-data. Our apprehension of good was exactly the same as our apprehension of green, and we purported to handle it with the same logical and analytical technique which was appropriate to the latter. Indeed we combined a dogmatic treatment as to the nature of experience with a method of handling it which was extravagantly scholastic. Russell's *Principles of Mathematics* came out in the same year as *Principia Ethica*; and the former, in spirit, furnished a method for handling the material provided by the latter. Let me give you a few examples of the sort of things we used to discuss.

If A was in love with B and believed that B reciprocated his feelings, whereas in fact B did not, but was in love with C, the state of affairs was certainly not so good as it would have been if A had been right, but was it worse or better than it would become if A discovered his mistake? If A was in love with B under a misapprehension as to B's qualities, was this better or worse than A's not being in love at all? If A was in love with B because A's spectacles were not strong enough to see B's complexion, did this altogether, or partly, destroy the value of A's state of mind? Suppose we were to live our lives backwards, having our experiences in the reverse order, would this affect the value of our successive states of mind? If the states of mind enjoyed by each of us were pooled and then redistributed, would this affect their value? How did one compare the value of a good state of mind which had bad consequences with a bad state of mind which had good consequences? In valuing the consequences did one assess them at their actual value as it turned out eventually to be, or their probable value at the time? If at their probable value, how much evidence as to possible consequences was it one's duty to collect before applying the calculus? Was there a separate objective standard of beauty? Was a beautiful thing, that is to say, by definition that which it was good to contemplate? Or was there an actual objective quality to 'beauty', just like 'green' and 'good'? And knowledge, too, presented a problem. Were all truths equally good to pursue and contemplate? – as for example the number of grains in a given tract of sea-sand. We were disposed to repudiate very strongly the idea that useful knowledge could be preferable to useless knowledge. But we flirted with the idea that there might be some intrinsic quality – though not, perhaps, quite on a par with 'green' and 'good' and 'beautiful' – which one could call 'interesting', and we were prepared to think it just possible that ' interesting' knowledge might be better to pursue than 'uninteresting' knowledge. Another competing adjective was 'important', provided it was quite clear that 'important' did not mean 'useful'. Or to return again to our favourite subject, was a violent love affair which lasted a short time better than a more tepid one which endured longer? We were inclined to think it was. But I have said enough by now to make it clear that the problems of mensuration, in which we had involved ourselves, were somewhat formidable.

It was all under the influence of Moore's method, according to which you could hope to make essentially vague notions clear by using precise language about them and asking exact questions. It was a method of discovery by the instrument of impeccable grammar and an unambiguous dictionary. 'What *exactly* do you mean?' was the phrase most frequently on our lips. If it appeared under cross-examination that you did not mean *exactly* anything, you lay under a strong suspicion of meaning nothing whatever. It was a stringent education in dialectic; but in practice it was a kind of combat in which strength of character was really much more valuable than subtlety of mind. In the preface to his great work, bespattered with the numerous italics through which the reader who knew him could actually hear, as with Queen Victoria, the vehemence of his utterance, Moore begins by saying that error is chiefly 'the attempt to answer questions, without first discovering precisely *what* question it is which you desire to answer. . . . Once we recognize the exact meaning of the two questions, I think it also becomes plain exactly what kind of reasons are relevant as arguments for or against any particular answer to them'. So we spent our time trying to discover *precisely* *what* questions we were asking, confident in the faith that, if only we could ask precise questions, everyone would know the answer. Indeed Moore expressly claimed as much. In his famous chapter on 'The Ideal' he wrote:

> Indeed, once the meaning of the question is clearly understood, the answer to it, in its main outlines, appears to be so obvious, that it runs the risk of seeming to be a platitude. By far the most valuable things, which we know or can imagine, are certain states of consciousness, which may be roughly described as the pleasures of human intercourse and the enjoyment of beautiful objects. No one, probably, who has asked himself the question, has ever doubted that personal affection and the appreciation of what is beautiful in Art or Nature, are good in themselves; nor if we consider strictly what things are worth having *purely for their own sakes*, does it appear probable that any one will think that anything else has *nearly* so great a value as the things which are included under these two heads.

And then there was the question of pleasure. As time wore on towards the nineteen-tens, I fancy we weakened a bit about pleasure. But, in our prime, pleasure was nowhere. I would faintly urge that if two states of mind were similar in all other respects except that one was pleasurable and the other was painful there *might* be a little

to be said for the former, but the principle of organic unities was
against me. It was the general view (though not quite borne out by
the *Principia*) that pleasure had nothing to do with the case and,
on the whole, a pleasant state of mind lay under grave suspicion
of lacking intensity and passion.

In those days X. had not taken up women, nor Woolf monkeys,
and they were not their present blithe selves. The two of them, sunk
deep in silence and in basket chairs on opposite sides of the fireplace
in a room which was at all times pitch dark, would stop sucking
their pipes only to murmur that all good states of mind were extremely painful and to imply that all painful states of mind were
extremely good. Strachey seconded them – it was only in his second
childhood that Lytton took up pleasure – though his sorrow was
more fitful than their settled gloom. But with Sheppard and myself
cheerfulness could not but break through, and we were in great dis-
grace about it. There was a terrible scene one evening when we turned
insubordinate and reckless and maintained that there was nothing
wrong in itself in being cheerful. It was decided that such low habits
were particularly characteristic of King's as opposed to the austerity
of Trinity.

Socrates had persuaded Protarchus that pure hedonism was absurd.
Moore himself was only prepared to accept pleasure as an enhance-
ment of a state of affairs otherwise good. But Moore hated evil and
he found a place in his religion for vindictive punishment.

> Not only is the pleasantness of a state *not* in proportion to its intrinsic
> worth; it may even add positively to its vileness. . . . The infliction of pain
> on a person whose state of mind is bad may, if the pain be not too intense,
> create a state of things that is better *on the whole* than if the evil state
> of mind had existed unpunished. Whether such a state of affairs can ever
> constitute a *positive* good is another question.

I call attention to the qualification 'if the pain be not too intense'.
Our Ideal was a merciful God.

Thus we were brought up – with Plato's absorption in the good
in itself, with a scholasticism which outdid St Thomas, in calvinistic
withdrawal from the pleasures and successes of Vanity Fair, and oppressed with all the sorrows of Werther. It did not prevent us from
laughing most of the time and we enjoyed supreme self-confidence,
superiority and contempt towards all the rest of the unconverted
world. But it was hardly a state of mind which a grown-up person

in his senses could sustain literally. When MacCarthy came down for a week-end, he would smile affectionately, persuade Moore to sing his German Lieder at the piano, to hear which we all agreed was a very good state of mind indeed, or incite Bob Trevy to deliver a broken oration which was a frantic travesty of the whole method, the charm of it lying in the impossibility of deciding whether Bob himself meant it, half at least, seriously or not.

It seems to me looking back, that this religion of ours was a very good one to grow up under. It remains nearer the truth than any other that I know, with less irrelevant extraneous matter and nothing to be ashamed of; though it is a comfort to-day to be able to discard with a good conscience the calculus and the mensuration and the duty to know *exactly* what one means and feels. It was a purer, sweeter air by far than Freud cum Marx. It is still my religion under the surface. I read again last week Moore's famous chapter on 'The Ideal'. It is remarkable how wholly oblivious he managed to be of the qualities of the life of action and also of the pattern of life as a whole. He was existing in a timeless ecstasy. His way of translating his own particular emotions of the moment into the language of generalised abstraction is a charming and beautiful comedy. Do you remember the passage in which he discusses whether, granting that it is mental qualities which one should chiefly love, it is important that the beloved person should also be good-looking? In the upshot good looks win a modest victory over 'mental qualities'. I cannot forbear to quote this sweet and lovely passage, so sincere and passionate and careful:

> I think it may be admitted that wherever the affection is most valuable, the appreciation of mental qualities must form a large part of it, and that the presence of this part makes the whole far more valuable than it could have been without it. But it seems very doubtful whether this appreciation, by itself, can possess as much value as the whole in which it is combined with an appreciation of the appropriate *corporeal* expression of the mental qualities in question. It is certain that in all actual cases of valuable affection, the bodily expressions of character, whether by looks, by words, or by actions, do form a part of the object towards which the affection is felt, and that the fact of their inclusion appears to heighten the value of the whole state. It is, indeed, very difficult to image what the cognition of mental qualities *alone*, unaccompanied by *any* corporeal expression, would be like; and, in so far as we succeed in making this abstraction, the whole considered certainly appears to have less value. I therefore conclude that the importance of an admiration of admirable men-

tal qualities lies chiefly in the immense superiority of a whole, in which
it forms a part, to one in which it is absent, and not in any high degree
of intrinsic value which it possesses by itself. It even appears to be doubtful,
whether, in itself, it possesses so much value as the appreciation of mere
corporeal beauty undoubtedly does possess; that is to say, whether the appreciation of what has great intrinsic value is so valuable as the appreciation of what is merely beautiful.

But further if we consider the nature of admirable mental qualities, by
themselves, it appears that a proper appreciation of them involves a reference to purely material beauty in yet another way. Admirable mental
qualities do, if our previous conclusions are correct, consist very largely
in an emotional contemplation of beautiful objects; and hence the appreciation of them will consist essentially in the contemplation of such
contemplation. It is true that the most valuable appreciation of persons
appears to be that which consists in the appreciation of their appreciation
of other persons: but even here a reference to material beauty appears
to be involved, *both* in respect of the fact that what is appreciated in the
last instance may be the contemplation of what is merely beautiful, *and*
in respect of the fact that the most valuable appreciation of a person appears to *include* an appreciation of his corporeal expression. Though,
therefore, we may admit that the appreciation of a person's attitude towards
other persons, or, to take one instance, the love of love, is far the most
valuable good we know, and far more valuable than the mere love of
beauty, yet we can only admit this if the first be understood to *include*
the latter, in various degrees of directness.

The New Testament is a handbook for politicians compared with
the unworldliness of Moore's chapter on 'The Ideal'. I know no equal
to it in literature since Plato. And it is better than Plato because
it is quite free from *fancy*. It conveys the beauty of the literalness
of Moore's mind, the pure and passionate intensity of his vision,
*un*fanciful and *un*dressed-up. Moore had a nightmare once in which
he could not distinguish propositions from tables. But even when
he was awake, he could not distinguish love and beauty and truth
from the furniture. They took on the same definition of outline, the
same stable, solid, objective qualities and common-sense reality.

I see no reason to shift from the fundamental intuitions of *Principia
Ethica*; though they are much too few and too narrow to fit actual
experience which provides a richer and more various content. That
they furnish a justification of experience wholly independent of outside events has become an added comfort, even though one cannot

live to-day secure in the undisturbed individualism which was the extraordinary achievement of the early Edwardian days, not for our little lot only, but for everyone else, too.

I am still a long way off from D.H. Lawrence and what he might have been justified in meaning when he said that we were 'done for'. And even now I am not quite ready to approach that theme. First of all I must explain the other facet of our faith. So far it has been a question of our attitude to ourselves and one another. What was our understanding of the outside world and our relation to it?

It was an important object of Moore's book to distinguish between goodness as an attribute of states of mind and rightness as an attribute of actions. He also has a section on the justification of general rules of conduct. The large part played by considerations of probability in his theory of right conduct was, indeed, an important contributory cause to my spending all the leisure of many years on the study of that subject: I was writing under the joint influence of Moore's *Principia Ethica* and Russell's *Principia Mathematica*. But for the most part, as I have said, we did not pay attention to this aspect of the book or bother much about it. We were living in the specious present, nor had begun to play the game of consequences. We existed in the world of Plato's *Dialogues*; we had not reached the *Republic*, let alone the *Laws*.

This brought us one big advantage. As we had thrown hedonism out of the window and, discarding Moore's so highly problematical calculus, lived entirely in present experience, since social action as an end in itself and not merely as a lugubrious duty had dropped out of our Ideal, and, not only social action, but life of action generally, power, politics, success, wealth, ambition, with the economic motive and the economic criterion less prominent in our philosophy than with St Francis of Assisi, who at least made collections for the birds, it follows that we were amongst the first of our generation, perhaps alone amongst our generation, to escape from the Benthamite tradition. In practice, of course, at least so far as I was concerned, the outside world was not forgotten or forsworn. But I am recalling what our Ideal was in those early days when the life of passionate contemplation and communion was supposed to oust all other purposes whatever. It can be no part of this memoir for me to try to explain why it was such a big advantage for us to have escaped from the Benthamite tradition. But I do now regard that as the worm which has been gnawing at the insides of modern civilisation and is responsible for its present moral decay. We used to regard the Christians

as the enemy, because they appeared as the representatives of tradition, convention and hocus-pocus. In truth it was the Benthamite
calculus, based on an over-valuation of the economic criterion, which
was destroying the quality of the popular Ideal.

Moreover, it was this escape from Bentham, joined with the un-
surpassable individualism of our philosophy, which has served to
protect the whole lot of us from the final *reductio ad absurdum* of
Benthanism known as Marxism. We have completely failed, indeed,
to provide a substitute for these economic bogus-faiths capable of
protecting or satisfying our successors. But we ourselves have remained – am I not right in saying *all* of us? – altogether immune
from the virus, as safe in the citadel of our ultimate faith as the Pope
of Rome in his.

This is what we gained. But we set on one side, not only that part
of Moore's fifth chapter on 'Ethics in Relation to Conduct' which
dealt with the obligation so to act as to produce by causal connection
the most probable maximum of eventual good through the whole
procession of future ages (a discussion which was indeed riddled with
fallacies), but also the part which discussed the duty of the individual
to obey general rules. We entirely repudiated a personal liability on
us to obey general rules. We claimed the right to judge every individual case on its merits, and the wisdom, experience and self-control
to do so successfully. This was a very important part of our faith,
violently and aggressively held, and for the outer world it was our
most obvious and dangerous characteristic. We repudiated entirely
customary morals, conventions and traditional wisdom. We were, that
is to say, in the strict sense of the term, immoralists. The consequences
of being found out had, of course, to be considered for what they
were worth. But we recognised no moral obligation on us, no inner
sanction, to conform or to obey. Before heaven we claimed to be our
own judge in our own case. I have come to think that this is, perhaps,
rather a Russian characteristic. It is certainly not an English one.
It resulted in a general, widespread, though partly covert, suspicion
affecting ourselves, our motives and our behaviour. This suspicion
still persists to a certain extent, and it always will. It has deeply coloured the course of our lives in relation to the outside world. It is,
I now think, a justifiable suspicion. Yet so far as I am concerned,
it is too late to change. I remain, and always will remain, an
immoralist.

I am not now concerned, however, with the fact that this aspect
of our code was shocking. It would have been not less so, even if

we had been perfectly right. What matters a great deal more is the fact that it was flimsily based, as I now think, on an *a priori* view of what human nature is like, both other people's and our own, which was disastrously mistaken.

I have said that we were amongst the first to escape from Benthanism. But of another eighteenth-century heresy we were the unrepentant heirs and last upholders. We were among the last of the Utopians, or meliorists as they are sometimes called, who believe in a continuing moral progress by virtue of which the human race already consists of reliable, rational, decent people, influenced by truth and objective standards, who can be safely released from the outward restraints of convention and traditional standards and inflexible rules of conduct, and left, from now onwards, to their own sensible devices, pure motives and reliable intuitions of the good. The view that human nature is reasonable had in 1903 quite a long history behind it. It underlay the ethics of self-interest – rational self-interest as it was called – just as much as the universal ethics of Kant or Bentham which aimed at the general good; and it was because self-interest was *rational* that the egoistic and altruistic systems were supposed to work out in practice to the same conclusions.

In short, we repudiated all versions of the doctrine of original sin, of there being insane and irrational springs of wickedness in most men. We were not aware that civilisation was a thin and precarious crust erected by the personality and the will of a very few, and only maintained by rules and conventions skilfully put across and guilefully preserved. We had no respect for traditional wisdom or the restraints of custom. We lacked reverence, as Lawrence observed and as Ludwig with justice also used to say – for everything and everyone. It did not occur to us to respect the extraordinary accomplishment of our predecessors in the ordering of life (as it now seems to me to have been) or the elaborate framework which they had devised to protect this order. Plato said in his *Laws* that one of the best of a set of good laws would be a law forbidding any young man to enquire which of them are right or wrong, though an old man remarking any defect in the laws might communicate this observation to a ruler or to an equal in years when no young man was present. That was a *dictum* in which we should have been unable to discover any point or significance whatever. As cause and consequence of our general state of mind we completely misunderstood human nature, including our own. The rationality which we attributed to it led to a superficiality, not only of judgment, but also of feeling. It was not

only that intellectually we were pre-Freudian, but we had lost something which our predecessors had without replacing it. I still suffer
incurably from attributing an unreal rationality to other people's feelings and behaviour (and doubtless to my own, too). There is one
small but extraordinarily silly manifestation of this absurd idea of
what is 'normal', namely the impulse to *protest* – to write a letter
to *The Times*, call a meeting in the Guildhall, subscribe to some
fund when my presuppositions as to what is 'normal' are not fulfilled.
I behave as if there really existed some authority or standard to which
I can successfully appeal if I shout loud enough – perhaps it is some
hereditary vestige of a belief in the efficacy of prayer.

I have said that this pseudo-rational view of human nature led to
a thinness, a superficiality, not only of judgment, but also of feeling.
It seems to me that Moore's chapter on 'The Ideal' left out altogether
some whole categories of valuable emotion. The attribution of rationality to human nature, instead of enriching it, now seems to me
to have impoverished it. It ignored certain powerful and valuable
springs of feeling. Some of the spontaneous, irrational outbursts of
human nature can have a sort of value from which our schematism
was cut off. Even some of the feelings associated with wickedness
can have value. And in addition to the values arising out of spontaneous, volcanic and even wicked impulses, there are many objects
of valuable contemplation and communion beyond those we know
of – those concerned with the order and pattern of life amongst communities and the emotions which they can inspire. Though one must
ever remember Paley's *dictum* that 'although we speak of communities
as of sentient beings and ascribe to them happiness and misery, desires,
interests and passions, nothing really exists or feels but *individuals*',
yet we carried the individualism of our individuals too far.

And as the years wore on towards 1914, the thinness and superficiality, as well as the falsity, of our view of man's heart became,
as it now seems to me, more obvious; and there was, too, some falling
away from the purity of the original doctrine. Concentration on moments of communion between a pair of lovers got thoroughly mixed
up with the, once rejected, pleasure. The pattern of life would sometimes become no better than a succession of permutations of short
sharp superficial 'intrigues', as we called them. Our comments on
life and affairs were bright and amusing, but brittle – as I said of
the conversation of Russell and myself with Lawrence – because there
was no solid diagnosis of human nature underlying them. Bertie in
particular sustained simultaneously a pair of opinions ludicrously

incompatible. He held that in fact human affairs were carried on after a most irrational fashion, but that the remedy was quite simple and easy, since all we had to do was to carry them on rationally. A discussion of practical affairs on these lines was really very boring. And a discussion of the human heart which ignored so many of its deeper and blinder passions, both good and bad, was scarcely more interesting. Indeed it is only states of mind that matter, provided we agree to take account of the pattern of life through time and give up regarding it as a series of independent, instantaneous flashes, but the ways in which states of mind can be valuable, and the objects of them, are more various, and also much richer, than we allowed for. I fancy we used in old days to get round the rich variety of experience by expanding illegitimately the field of aesthetic appreciation (we would deal, for example, with all branches of the tragic emotion under this head), classifying as aesthetic experience what is really human experience and somehow sterilizing it by this misclassification.

If, therefore, I altogether ignore our merits – our charm, our intelligence, our unworldliness, our affection – I can see us as waterspiders, gracefully skimming, as light and reasonable as air, the surface of the stream without any contact at all with the eddies and currents underneath. And if I imagine us as coming under the observation of Lawrence's ignorant, jealous, irritable, hostile eyes, what a combination of qualities we offered to arouse his passionate distaste; this thin rationalism skipping on the crust of the lava, ignoring both the reality and the value of the vulgar passions, joined to libertinism and comprehensive irreverence, too clever by half for such an earthy character as Bunny, seducing with its intellectual *chic* such a portent as Ottoline, a regular skin-poison. All this was very unfair to poor, silly, well-meaning us. But that is why I say that there may have been just a grain of truth when Lawrence said in 1914 that we were 'done for'.

9th September 1938

Duncan Grant: Virginia Woolf and the Beginnings of Bloomsbury

In trying to convey the effect of Virginia Woolf on her closest friends, Clive Bell wrote,

*I remember spending some dark, uneasy winter days during the first war
in the depth of the country with Lytton Strachey. After lunch, as we watched
the rain pour down and premature darkness roll up, he said in his search-
ing, personal way, 'Loves apart, whom would you most like to see coming
up the drive?' I hesitated a moment, and he supplied the answer: 'Virginia
of course.' (118)*

*Duncan Grant's memoir of Virginia Woolf, written after her death
in 1941, shows Woolf's attractiveness to her Bloomsbury friends in
the making. Grant wrote very little, but his brief recollections of the
Thursday evenings in Fitzroy Square are among the most interesting
of Bloomsbury memoirs by one of the Group's original members.
Grant's friendship with Virginia developed with his love for her
brother Adrian, which followed his affairs with Strachey, then Keynes,
and preceded his long life with Vanessa Bell. Indeed, one waggish
definition of Bloomsbury is that of a group of men and women all
of whom were in love with Duncan Grant. Grant's memoir was originally entitled simply 'Virginia Woolf.' (Cézanne's* grappin dessus *refers to his fear that anyone might get control of him.)*

I first knew Virginia Stephen when she and her brother Adrian took
No 29 Fitzroy Square, soon after her sister Vanessa married Clive
Bell. It was a house on the south-west corner of the square with a
view of the two fine Adams' façades. It was a derelict square. The
houses of the great had gradually decayed and were taken as offices,
lodgings, nursing homes and small artisans' workshops.

I had taken for a studio two rooms on the second floor of a house
on the same side of the square. There was certainly not much gentility
left in the district; the only relic of grandeur was a beadle to march
round the square and keep order among the children, in a top-hat
and a tail-coat piped with red and brass buttons. The Stephens were
the only people I remember who had a complete house there; complete
with their cook Sophie Farrell, their maid Maud, a front-door bell
and a dog, Hans. A close friendship sprang up between Adrian Stephen and myself, and I had only to tap at the window of the ground-
floor room to be let in. 'That Mr Grant gets in everywhere,' Maud
once remarked to Virginia. But irregular as my visits were, in a sense
they soon became frequent enough to escape notice.

The house was conveniently divided to suit the inhabitants. On
the ground floor was Adrian's study lined with books. Behind was
the dining room. The first floor was entirely a drawing room – the
room least used in the house. It was a pleasantly proportioned room,

with long windows overlooking the square. It had a green carpet, red brocade curtains; a Dutch Portrait of a Lady and Watts' portrait of Sir Leslie Stephen were the only pictures on the walls. In the back part of the room there was an instrument called a Pianola, into which one put rolls of paper punctured by small holes. You bellowed with your feet and Beethoven or Wagner would appear.

Anyone coming into the room might have thought that Adrian was a Paderewski – the effort on the bellows gave him a swaying movement very like that of a great performer, and his hands were hidden.

I do not remember that Virginia ever performed on this instrument, but it must have played a part in her life, for Adrian on coming home from work would play in the empty room by the hour. Entirely empty it nearly always was and kept spotlessly clean.

It was here that Virginia sometimes saw her less intimate friends and it was here that the dog Hans made a mess on the hearthrug when Lady Strachey was paying her first visit, and no mention was made of the fact by either lady.

The more lively rooms were Virginia's own workroom above this, and Adrian's downstairs. Her room was full of books untidily arranged and a high table at which she would write standing. The windows on this floor were double. She was very sensitive to sound, and the noise from the mews and street was severe. The time she gave to her writing was two and a half hours in the morning. She never, I believe, wrote for more than this time, but very regularly.

The study on the ground floor had the air of being much lived in. It was to this room that their friends came on Thursday evenings – a continuation of those evenings which began in Gordon Square before Thoby Stephen died and before Vanessa married. It was there that what has since been called 'Bloomsbury' for good or ill came into being.

About ten o'clock in the evening people used to appear and continue to come at intervals till twelve o'clock at night, and it was seldom that the last guest left before two or three in the morning. Whisky, buns and cocoa were the diet, and people talked to each other. If someone had lit a pipe he would sometimes hold out the lighted match to Hans the dog, who would snap at it and put it out. Conversation; that was all. Yet many people made a habit of coming, and few who did so will forget those evenings.

Among those who constantly came in early days were Charles Sanger, Theodore Llewelyn Davies, Desmond MacCarthy, Charles Tennyson, Hilton Young (now Lord Kennet), Lytton Strachey.

It was certainly not a 'salon'. Virginia Stephen in those days was
not at all the sort of hostess required for such a thing. She appeared
very shy and probably was so, and never addressed the company. She
would listen to general arguments and occasionally speak, but her
conversation was mainly directed to someone next to her. Her brother's Cambridge friends she knew well by this time, but I think there
was always something a little aloof and even a little fierce in her
manner to most men at the time I am speaking of. To her women
friends, especially older women like Miss Pater and Miss Janet Case,
who had taught her Greek, she was more open and less reserved.
They were alive to her, by remembrance as well as presence, and had
already their place in her imagination as belonging to the world she
knew and had left – that life with her parents and her half-brothers
at Hyde Park Gate. Henceforward she and her brother and sister had
tacitly agreed to face life on their own terms.

I do not think that her new existence had 'become alive' to Virginia's
imagination in those first years. She gave the impression of being
so intensely receptive to any experience new to her, and so intensely
interested in facts that she had not come across before, that time was
necessary to give it a meaning as a whole. It took the years to complete
her vision of it.

It is very difficult for one who is no writer to attempt to describe
so subtle a thing as the 'feeling' of long ago. But I must make the
attempt to explain why it was that the effect of these young people
on a contemporary was so remarkable. To begin with they were not
Bohemians. The people I had come across before who had cut themselves off from respectable existence had been mainly painters and
Bohemians. If the Stephens defied the conventions of their particular
class, it was from being intellectually honest.

They had suffered much, had struggled and finally arrived at an
attitude of mind which I think had a great influence on their friends.

If it was an influence Virginia Stephen and her sister were unconscious of the fact.

The impression generally given must have been that these two
young women were absorbing the ideas of their new Cambridge
friends. And of course this was true up to a point. Saxon Sydney-
Turner, Clive Bell, Lytton Strachey, Maynard Keynes, were willing
to discuss anything and everything with them or before them. It was
a gain all round. What the Cambridge of that time needed was a
little feminine society. It was a little arid, and if it took almost everything seriously it had mostly left the Arts out of account. It took
some things religiously. 'This is my Bible' was said by one, pointing

to the *Principia Ethica*, by G. Moore. This eminent philosopher was
certainly the overwhelming influence on these young men. Conversations on the 'Good' and the value of certain states of mind were
a frequent subject of discussion; and these Apostolic young men found
to their amazement that they could be shocked by the boldness and
scepticism of two young women.

To be intimate with Virginia Stephen in those days was not to
be on easy terms. Indeed the greater the intimacy the greater the
danger – the danger of sudden outbursts of scathing criticism. I have
the impression that no one had much encouragement for anything
they produced. Nor was it looked for. Nothing was expected save
complete frankness (of criticism) and a mutual respect for the point
of view of each. To work for immediate success never entered anyone's
head, perhaps partly because it seemed out of the question. Virginia
Stephen was working on her first novel, *The Voyage Out*. It took
seven years to finish. But I do not remember that this was thought
to be an out of the way length of time in which to produce a novel.

The inner fierceness of her attitude to which I have already alluded
is worth remembering, and will possibly surprise those who only
knew her in later life when it seemed to have entirely disappeared
or to have found expression in quite other ways.

It then expressed itself sometimes, as I have said, by an appearance
of acute shyness. Upon an unforeseen introduction, for instance, there
was an expression of blazing defiance, a few carefully chosen banal-
ities, and a feeling of awkwardness. It came from a sort of variant
of Cézanne's *grappin dessus*, which made her literally turn tail from
misadventure. As when she saw Mrs Humphry Ward advancing along
a narrow passage in the Louvre and hid herself behind a totally inadequate post.

No one so beautiful and so fierce could give offence except to the
very stupid. But she was capable of inspiring feelings of respect in
the most philistine.

This shyness or fierceness was a necessary self-defence in her war
with the world. The world must, she surmised, accept her on her
own terms or not at all.

If these notes have any interest it is because they may to some revive
the memory, to others suggest the existence, of that seemingly very
different Virginia Woolf known to a variety of people in later years.

Marriage and possibly a growing appreciation of her work had
the effect of seeming to make her very much more at ease in the
world.

Vanessa Bell: Notes on Bloomsbury

Bloomsbury has occasionally been described as a matriarchy, the ma-
triarch being Vanessa Bell. As the eldest child of Leslie and Julia Ste-
phen and as the first to have children, she was certainly the most
maternal figure at the centre of Bloomsbury. The fact that she painted
rather than wrote may have added to the slightly mysterious aura
that apparently surrounded her. Vanessa did write several papers on
Bloomsbury for the Memoir Club; she published none of them but
they are among the most delightful and revealing accounts of the Group.

Vanessa Bell's most extended recollection of Bloomsbury, which she
entitled 'Notes on Bloomsbury', shows that though a painter, she could
still write like a Stephen. In addition to detailing the London be-
ginnings of Bloomsbury, her memoir argues, as Desmond MacCarthy's
does, for an interpretation of the Group that would equate it with
what she calls Old Bloomsbury. According to this view, Bloomsbury
ceased to exist with the First World War – before the major works
of Virginia Woolf, Lytton Strachey, and Maynard Keynes had been
written. The continuity of Bloomsbury as manifested in the Memoir
Club itself is denied by this conception of the Group, yet such was
the reaction of Vanessa Bell and others in the Group to the loose
and pejorative way that the term 'Bloomsbury' had come to be used
by the time she wrote her memoir in 1951. In 1919, however, she
wondered in a letter to Lytton Strachey if Old Bloomsbury was going
to be revived after the war, and in another to Leonard Woolf in 1928
she alluded to the continuing charm of Old Bloomsbury.

In editing the memoir I have spelled out abbreviations and ignored
some cancellations. Several alternative sheets to the memoir have also
been omitted, as they develop slightly different topics already treated
in the main part of the memoir.

It is lucky perhaps that Bloomsbury has a pleasant reverberating
sound, suggesting old fashioned gardens and out of the way walks,
and squares; otherwise how could one bear it? If every review, every
talk on the radio, every biography, every memoir of the last fifty years,
were to talk instead incessantly of Hoxton or Brixton, surely one's
nerves would be unbearably frayed. Perhaps they are even as it is,
yet here am I proposing to add to the chaos. What excuse have I?
Simply that of having been one of the original members of Old
Bloomsbury, and so thinking that I may possibly know more of the
relevant facts than do later-comers.

Yet I know very well, having always lived among them, that I am no writer and that all I can hope to do is to jot down notes for others to use. They will be as true as I can make them and at least I shall not claim distinguished writers like T.S. Eliot or W.B. Yeats as members of Bloomsbury. Perhaps some other original member (for not all of us are dead yet) will be induced to write his or her account, and though no doubt we should see the whole from different angles yet possibly with luck each might paint one true facet of the whole. I may be told that just as Mrs Thrale considered Boswell to be a most inaccurate biographer of her friend Dr Johnson so would any two members of Bloomsbury disagree violently about the character of a third – yet each view may throw light and make the subject alive. The two portraits of Chocquet by Cézanne and Renoir give very different views of the same man. That only adds to one's knowledge of the original, but what should we learn from one of those posthumous portraits done from a photograph and advertised as the work of 'an exhibitor at the R.A.'? It would have much the same effect on me as do those brightly written descriptions of a dead society which the author never knew, but to which I happened to belong.

What is to be done then? Perhaps historians should wait till the last survivors have gone and no one lives to say 'Oh no: it wasn't like that.'

If this is too much to ask, at least let us try for accuracy of dates, places and persons. I look in the first account I come across and learn that my sister, Virginia Woolf, was born in Cornwall, instead of being a pure-bred Cockney as I had always believed: that all members of Bloomsbury were rich and independent – unfortunately far from being true; in another I learn that a house on the north side of Gordon Square was one of the homes of Bloomsbury. Do these things matter? Perhaps not very much, but why get them all wrong? And when it comes to painting a picture with many of the figures in it such as never could have been there then I think it does matter. A quite false atmosphere results and it might as well be called by any name other than Bloomsbury.

To begin with then. This is how it all arose.

My father was Leslie Stephen. Anyone who wishes to can find out all they need about the Stephen family from the DNB and I shall leave it at that. He lived with his four children and two stepsons at 22 Hyde Park Gate a pleasant quiet cul-de-sac, then as now, with Kensington Gardens just across the main road at the top. No. 22 was near the bottom of the sac and hardly any traffic came past it.

It was a tall house, having been added on to at the top by my parents
and was very spacious in its own way, with a large double room
on the ground floor a dining room built out in the back garden and
a large light study for my father at the very top. Yet many of the
rooms were pitch dark, Virginian Creeper hung down in a thick curtain over the back drawing room window, the kitchen and other basement rooms could only be seen by candle or lamp light and most
of the paint was black. Not until quite a short time before my father's
death did we have electric light and even then not everywhere.

The atmosphere of the house was melancholy in every way during
those last years. There had been tragedy following on tragedy and
now my father was old and dying. The two stepsons, George and
Gerald Duckworth (the publisher) and we four younger ones made
up the household. When my father died in the spring of 1904 and
the house was evidently too large for us we had to decide where to
live. It was then that Bloomsbury came into our lives and that after
various inspections of other districts we finally took 46 Gordon
Square. When I say 'we' I mean the Stephen members of the household
only, consisting of myself, my brother Julian Thoby, my sister Virginia and my brother Adrian Leslie. We were very near each other
in age. I the eldest 25 and Adrian 21. George Duckworth married
at about that time and Gerald was glad to live a bachelor life in
rooms.

We knew no one living in Bloomsbury then and that I think was
one of its attractions. True, people did live there whom we might
easily have known, but they were of the older generation, such as
the George Protheros in Bedford Square with whom I had actually
once dined. Then there was the Slade in Gower Street to which I
went as an art student for a short time; but to me Professor Tonks,
then in control, was a most depressing master, I made no friends
there and soon left. It seemed as if in every way we were making
a new beginning in the tall clean rather frigid rooms, heated only
by coal fires in the old fashioned open fireplaces. It *was* a bit cold
perhaps, but it was exhilarating to have left the house in which had
been so much gloom and depression, to have come to these white
walls, large windows opening on to trees and lawns, to have one's
own rooms, be master of one's own time, have all the things in fact
which come as a matter of course to many of the young today but
so seldom then to young women at least. The only thing really lacking
to make all easy was money. As my father, like most Victorians, was
mad on the subject, never happy unless he had an enormous balance
at the Bank and constantly telling us we were rapidly heading for

'The Workhouse' we had learnt not to take the subject very seriously. I don't think we ever knew how much we had nor at what rate we were living but just went on gaily as long as we could. No doubt the Workhouse *would* have been our fate if other things had not intervened. For the time being it did not seem important.

Soon after this beginning in Gordon Square, I think in the summer of 1905, Thoby, not long down from Cambridge and now reading for the Bar, began to gather round him such of his Cambridge friends as were also starting life in London. It seemed to him a good plan to be at home one evening a week and though I do not think it had at first occurred to him to include his sisters in the arrangement, still there they were. So it happened that one or two of his Cambridge friends began to drift in on Thursday evenings after dinner. The entertainment was frugal. I believe there was generally some whisky to be had but most of us were content with cocoa and biscuits. In fact as everyone had had something to eat and perhaps even to drink at about 8 o'clock it didn't seem to occur to them to want more at 9 or at any time between then and midnight. Then, perhaps, exhausted by conversation, serious or frivolous, they welcomed some nourishment. It was one of the things which made entertaining cheap in those days.

Among those who first came fairly often were Saxon Sydney-Turner, then living in rooms in Great Ormond Street, Lytton Strachey living when in London with his family in Hampstead, Clive Bell from his lovely rooms in the Temple, Charles Tennyson, Hilton Young, Desmond MacCarthy, Theodore Llewelyn Davies, Robin Mayor. Plenty of odd creatures came too who would I suppose hardly be called 'Bloomsbury' who would in fact have been horrified by the idea of such a thing. A few old family friends or the younger ones of our generation sometimes looked in, even our half-brothers the Duckworths occasionally honoured us. But they did not altogether approve of our way of life and I remember Gerald Duckworth's disdain when Thoby tried to persuade him that it might be profitable to publish the works of Lytton Strachey, Clive Bell and others. (For all Thoby's friends were geniuses in his view.) It was not only the Duckworths who disapproved. It seems as if, as soon as our very innocent society got under way and began to have some life in it, hostility was aroused. Perhaps this always happens. Any kind of clique is sneered at by those outside it as a matter of course and no doubt our ways of behaviour in our own surroundings were sufficiently odd, according to the customs of the day, to stir criticism. Certainly I remember being questioned curiously by a group of young and older people at an ordinary conventional party as to whether we really sat up talking to young men till all hours of the night? What did we talk about? – Who were these young men?, etc. They laughed, even then there was a tone of disapproval.

What *did* we talk about? The only true answer can be anything that came into our heads. Of course the young men from Cambridge were full of the 'meaning of good'. I had never read their prophet G.E. Moore, nor I think had Virginia, but that didn't prevent one from trying to find out what one thought about good or anything else. The young men were perhaps not clear enough in their own heads to mind trying to get clearer by discussion with young women who might possibly see things from a different angle. At any rate talk we all did, it's true, till all hours of the night. Not always, of course about the meaning of good – sometimes about books or painting or anything that occurred to one – or told the company of one's daily doings and adventures. There was nothing at all unusual about it perhaps, except that for some reason we seemed to be a company of the young, all free, all beginning life in new surroundings, without elders to whom we had to account in any way for our doings or behaviour, and this was not then common in a mixed company of our class: for classes still existed. Naturally it made a difference that the company included people like Lytton Strachey and Virginia, but I think we were hardly aware of this. Virginia in fact in those days was apt to be very silent nor could Lytton be relied on to take any trouble in the way of conversation. He might suddenly place some remark in his high voice which was incredibly amusing or shattering – but then again he might not. It all depended upon how he was feeling and too often he was not feeling well. But somehow Thoby's beauty and geniality, Clive Bell's power of starting good subjects and encouraging everyone to pursue them and the feeling that acute intelligence was present even if unexpressed, made a curious atmosphere. That this was real and meant some unusual bond between us is proved I think by the fact that all those who were then young together and are still alive have in spite of violent quarrels and differences of opinions of all kinds, yet kept a certain feeling about members of Bloomsbury.*

Not that Bloomsbury was called so by anyone then, not even I

* *Note.* This does not mean that one did not later come to have most intimate friends who were definitely not of Bloomsbury. Even at the time some, for one reason or another, were quite outside it and later, of course, people who probably would have belonged to it could not be members of a circle which no longer existed.

think by its enemies. I believe it was first called Bloomsbury by Mrs Desmond MacCarthy, to distinguish it from Chelsea – where at least as many of the 'high-brows' lived and always have lived. The Mac-Carthys in spite of living in Chelsea themselves were and are a most important ingredient of Bloomsbury. Her slightly mocking attitude had great uses and he naturally knew all the Cambridge people and had also known and admired my father, so he was perhaps the one link with the past. Not that one could or can ever think of him as a 'link' – or is that one of his great gifts? Certainly he seems to be always in touch with more people of more different kinds than anyone else in the world and so he can choose, when it suits him, whether or not to be a 'link'.

Besides these there were other members of the Strachey family, James, Lytton's brother and Marjorie, his sister, whose astonishing gifts as a music-hall artiste were perhaps appreciated only in Blooms-bury. Visitors from other districts were apt to be shocked by her ren-derings of innocent nursery rhymes. Another elusive visitor was E.M. Forster, completely at home when with us but vanishing as completely to a world of his own.

Holidays in the country interrupted Thursday evenings and made a change from Bloomsbury. Its earliest chapter was very short – from the summer of 1905 to the autumn of 1906. Then after a holiday in Greece social evenings and our small circle generally seemed crushed by the tragedy of Thoby's death of typhoid fever at the age of twenty-six. He had seemed essential to the life and structure of our circle, but in youth, I suppose, no one is essential. The young mercifully recover from any blow and though it was true that life was changed for us yet something began to revive.

Then Clive Bell and I were married in the spring of 1907; that and the fact that in those terrible weeks such friends as Lytton and Saxon had become closer and more intimate helped a new life to begin. So when Virginia and Adrian moved from Gordon Square to Fitzroy Square in the spring of 1907 leaving us, a newly married couple, in Gordon Square they began fairly soon to have Thursday evenings again. They were different from the old ones of course. Vir-ginia was now hostess and this made her, I think, much less silent. She also asked what seemed to the rest of us some peculiar guests. I wonder what those who imagine a rarefied atmosphere of wit, in-telligence, criticism, self-conscious brilliance and never any tolerance of ordinary dullness, would have thought of the rather stiff young ladies to whom it never occurred not to talk about the weather, or of Adrian's dog Hans who insisted on entertaining the company by blowing out matches, of a great many rather childish doings and discussions. When it is said that we did not hesitate to talk of anything, it must be understood that this was literally true. If you could say what you liked about art, sex, or religion you could also talk freely and very likely dully about the ordinary doings of daily life. There was very little self-consciousness I think in those early gatherings; but life was exciting, terrible and amusing and we had to explore it, thankful that one could do so freely.

Perhaps it made a difference that no one (at least if you discount the young ladies and a few other curious relics from the past such as Clara Pater, Walter Pater's sister, and Janet Case, both of whom had taught Virginia Greek in Kensington days) had any feelings to be considered. None of us had the slightest respect, for instance, for religion or religious emotions. If we wanted to mock some doctrine which seemed to us laughable we could do so as freely as if we were mocking some ludicrous happening in daily life. I suppose my experience of religion, or something like it had happened to many of us. Having been brought up to believe nothing in particular I was converted to Christianity (of a rather vague kind I admit) when I was about twelve by some well brought up children of the same age. It lasted two or three years, then one day walking through Kensington Gardens and enjoying the sight of the trees, suddenly I knew quite certainly that religion meant nothing to me and that never again need I bother about it. It was a great relief. Possibly others of us had had some experience of the kind, or perhaps had had even less 'bother' than I had had. Anyhow it was a help to ease and intimacy not to have to consider in conversation such 'feelings' as might have existed either about religion or anything else.

This freedom was I believe largely owing to Lytton Strachey. Every one knows his qualities as a writer, his wit and brilliance. But only those just getting to know him well in the days when complete freedom of mind and expression were almost unknown, at least among men and women together, can understand what an exciting world of explorations of thought and feeling he seemed to reveal. His great honesty of mind and remorseless poking fun at any sham forced others to be honest too and showed a world in which one need no longer be afraid of saying what one thought, surely the first step to anything that could be of interest or value.

Some of those who were to become most intimate members of Bloomsbury were still hardly known to the others. When I talk of members I do not mean that there was any sort of club or society. Yet people were definitely 'Bloomsbury' or not and this is a convenient way of classifying them. One of these was Duncan Grant, who was of course already intimate with his Strachey cousins. When after a year as an art student in Paris he settled down in London, I think in 1908 (?) he very soon knew us all. He was living with his family in Hampstead but he also shared rooms in Fitzroy Square with Maynard Keynes and through him and Lytton and James Strachey had known all the Cambridge friends or nearly all. He was penniless but seemed unaware of the fact. If he wanted to go from one place to another he would borrow the exact sum 2½d perhaps, which any of us could afford. If he wanted a meal he appeared, an contributions from each plate were willingly made. So he solved the problem of living on air with satisfaction to everyone, and soon of course selling his pictures solved it even further. As he had a studio of kinds in Fitzroy Square it was easy for him to see a lot of Adrian and Virginia of whom he has published his own account. It was natural too that Maynard Keynes should become one of the circle and I think he very quickly felt at home in it.

Yet one more was to come, perhaps the most important of all – Roger Fry. Older than any of us, though that never seemed of the least importance, he had the advantage of greater experience of life and of art. But how one laughed at him and how ready he was to see the joke, how ready to discuss anything with the most ignorant of us. It is impossible and unnecessary for me to describe him for this has been done by Virginia in her Life. She knew him of course very intimately and he was one of her warmest and greatest admirers. Even now seventeen years after his death one is constantly surprised by the way in which those who knew him speak of him. English and French, both writers and painters, even those who were hardly grown up when he died, all seem to have been stirred by a deep affection and admiration and tell one how they still miss him. 'How honest he was – He never minded admitting that he had been quite wrong and changing his mind if only he could come a little nearer the truth.' So someone who knew him well but who had never been a member of Bloomsbury said to me the other day. Not only did he bring himself to our circle, he knew many people both French and English who were strangers to us and he seemed to draw them to Bloomsbury, not as members necessarily but as delightful and sympathetic visitors. Such were Jacques Copeau, Charles Vildrac, a tiny and charming painter called Doucet (later killed in the War) Auguste

Bréal and others. When we went for jaunts to Paris with him to took
us to see various painters, among them Picasso then quite young
and little known, Matisse, and even to rather stiff and alarming luncheon parties with a dealer like Vollard, made worth while by the
Cézannes and Renoirs mysteriously produced from cellars. When
Roger Fry had been buyer for the Metropolitan Museum of New York
of course every dealer had besieged him and was only too ready to
grant him (and his friends) the great favour of the most private of
views, hoping even then that something to their advantage might
result. They were right, as they always are in matters of business,
for no doubt the great boon in modern French art to follow a little
later was largely owing to Roger Fry's interest and enthusiasm.

During the years 1908 or 09 to 1911, two more, Leonard Woolf
who had been one of Thoby's greatest friends at Cambridge and Oliver
Strachey, Lytton's brother, returned from Ceylon and from India. It
was inevitable that they should be as they have been ever since
members of the innermost circle.

In 1911 Virginia and Adrian decided to give up the house in Fitzroy
Square and move to a large house in Brunswick Square which they
proposed to share with friends of whom Leonard Woolf was one.
Each member of the household was to have their own room, carrying
up their own meals to it and so living completely separate existences,
with the advantages of shared expenses. The other inhabitants, besides
Leonard Woolf, were Maynard Keynes, Duncan Grant and Gerald
Shove. This meant that Thursday evenings were given up, but
members of Bloomsbury met as often or oftener than that before.
Brunswick Square was a little nearer Gordon Square than was Fitzroy
Square and all sorts of parties at all hours of the day or night happened constantly. Rooms were decorated, people made to sit for their
portraits, champagne was produced (rashly left unlocked up by Maynard Keynes who was half the time in Cambridge), to while away
the morning sittings – all seemed a sizzle of excitement. Brunswick
would come round to Gordon when tired of the tray system of meals
and in those easy days the larder always held enough for two or three
unexpected guests, and servants seemed to welcome them with delight.
So it was natural to say 'stay to dinner' and to sit and talk as of
old till all hours, either in the familiar room at No 46 or in the
Square garden. Then (in 1912?) Leonard Woolf and Virginia were
married and presently moved to another part of London and later
to Richmond.

It was in these years, from 1909 or 10 to 1914 that there came the great expansion and development of Bloomsbury, that life seemed fullest of interest and promise and expansion of all kinds. Most of the members were writers or civil servants, only two in the earlier part of this time, Duncan Grant and myself, were painters. But when Roger Fry came bringing in his train painters both English and French the general attention was more directed to painting and less perhaps to the meaning of good. Other painters such as Sickert, Spencer Gore, F. Etchells, Henry Lamb and Francis Dodd, who were often in our company and on the friendliest terms with everyone, without belonging to Bloomsbury, helped to encourage talk about the visual arts. And then came the great excitement of the Post-Impressionist exhibition in 1910–11 which caused even more dismay and disapproval than Bloomsbury itself. How full of life those days seemed. Everything was brim full of interest and ideas and it certainly was for many of us 'very heaven' to be alive.

It must now be almost incredible how unaware we were of the disaster so soon to come. I do not know how much the politicians then foresaw, but I think that we in Bloomsbury had only the haziest ideas as to what was going on in the rest of Europe. How could we be interested in such matters when first getting to know well the great artists of the immediate past and those following them, when beauty was springing up under one's feet so vividly that violent abuse was hurled at it and genius generally considered to be insanity, when the writers were pricking up their ears and raising their voices lest too much attention should be given to painting: when music joined in the general chorus with sounds which excited ecstasy rage and derision: a great new freedom seemed about to come and perhaps would have come, if it had not been for motives and ambitions of which we knew nothing. But surely such unawareness can never come again and it is difficult to explain it to those who cannot hope to feel it.

In 1913 the Omega Workshops were started by Roger Fry at the wrong time for success. It was a difficult venture, with not enough money or experience behind it and temperamental artists to be driven the way they should go by Roger. All the same his pottery, lovely and perfect in its own way, would not have existed without it and many of the textiles, rugs, screens and painted furniture had character and beauty, too soon to be imitated and vulgarized by other shops. Then when it seemed as if in spite of all difficulties the Omega might survive and succeed, came the War. It could struggle on only for another year or so. The difficulties were too great.

Bloomsbury was not destroyed as probably many other circles were destroyed by the departure of all its young men to the wars. Perhaps one reason for much of the later abuse was that many were Conscientious Objectors. For some time therefore they were let alone and quietly pursued their usual professions. Women of course were not conscripted during the war and could do as they liked. So for a time Bloomsbury still existed even if crushed and bored by the outer world. The excitement and joy had gone. The hostility of the general public was real now, no longer a ridiculous and even stimulating joke, and the dreariness of the universal Khaki seemed only too appropriate. There was not even fear to create sympathy in unlikely quarters as in the last war. All the world was hostile close round one and Bloomsbury had no changing atmosphere in which to move and expand and grow. So when the young men were finally forced to take some share in what was going on for the most part they chose to work on farms, and this meant a dispersal and general scattering.

Most went to the country: but some like Maynard Keynes and others from Cambridge came to London to do war work. He took our house, 46 Gordon Square, and lived there with three or four others during the War, eventually continuing to live there for the rest of his life. I was among those who left London in 1916 and when I came back three years later I realized very clearly how all had changed. Nothing happens twice and Bloomsbury had had its day. It dissolved in the newer world and the younger generation, now known as the Twenties. This contained of course many brilliant, possibly more brilliant, writers, than Bloomsbury had known, such as the Sitwells, Raymond Mortimer, Aldous Huxley, Francis Birrell, L.H. Myers, T.S. Eliot and many others. There was I think one figure, David Garnett, who was completely of Bloomsbury in its latest moments of disintegration and yet also outside it, for he had grown up in an entirely different circle.

When therefore the critics of today abuse Bloomsbury let them in the interests of accuracy distinguish it from all that came after the 1914-18 War. Abuse or criticism has never done it much harm that I know of, but why should Bloomsbury be singled out from all other districts? Why not Hampstead or Chelsea? Chelsea had always been the home of painters and writers and highbrows generally. There were George Moore and his circle, universally admired and respected, with Logan Pearsall Smith round the corner and painters of course by the hundred. Augustus John, Tonks, Steer, McEvoy and many others formed a bigger circle than Bloomsbury can even have done. In Hampstead too there must have been a group of the same kind, with

Sir William Rothenstein, D.S. MacColl and Sir Charles Aitken to make a beginning. Yet one never heard a word against them and who now would be understood if he talked sneeringly of Chelsea or Hampstead?

No: say what you like, but while there are still those who remember take the trouble to get your facts right.

V.B. 1951

Vanessa Bell: Letters

Two letters of Vanessa Bell, written more than thirty years apart, illuminate views of Bloomsbury that were shared by others in the Group. The first unpublished one suggests how self-critical Old Bloomsbury could be (the identity of Moor is uncertain, but he seems not to have been the philosopher). The other letter indicates why those in Bloomsbury, such as Clive Bell in the next memoir, came to deny the existence of Bloomsbury. Vanessa Bell founded the Friday Club in 1905 for the discussion of art and related matters; it held exhibitions up through the First World War, though neither Vanessa nor Duncan Grant was involved with it much after 1913.

Letter to Molly MacCarthy, 4 July [1913?]
My Dearest Molly

I don't know your Irish address but hope this will be forwarded. Do sent it to me – I wonder if you're going through that awful journey with the children today – and how you'll survive it.

You would be touched if you knew the consternation you caused in Bloomsbury the other night. They have all been to me since, Duncan, Shove, etc. to know whether it means that you're going to desert Bloomsbury for if so they say it will be too terrible! They want to know what's at the back of it all and whether you *really* find Bloomsbury such an unsympathetic clique. It's very serious for us if that is our reputation for we should then find ourselves more of a clique than ever, all outsiders thinking that we didn't want to know them. As a matter of fact 'Bloomsbury' is a mixed collection of varieties who are really all pining to get away from each other and let in a little new blood. Do help them and don't think they're satisfied with themselves. I don't believe they're so horribly inhuman. Some day I shall give you a true history of my early years and troubles to convince you that I'm not this gigantic arctic character that I know you think me – and probably all the others are really very human too. Anyhow you *mustn't* desert them. You will have time to reflect over all the muddle of London life in Ireland. I hope without the help of Moor, etc. for they *are* inhuman if you like. Will you tell me when you think you could come to Asheham – what part of September would suit you best?

    Yours

      Vanessa

From a letter to Leonard Woolf, 20 July [c. 1950]   I have had a letter sent on to me here [in France] from a Miss Bensen who says you had a talk with her two years ago, and therefore she now writes to me wanting me to tell her about the Friday Club and the 'Bloomsbury Group.' She wants to come and see me at Charleston and also says Morgan told her to come to me.

So this is to warn you in case she approaches you again that I am wandering indefinitely in France and don't know when I shall be back. I have also told her that the Friday Club was a small society which didn't last very long, and implied that it was quite unimportant and that there never was such a thing as the 'Bloomsbury Group.'

I don't want to be brutal to the woman, but I simply cannot go on telling people about such things. They always and inevitably get it hopelessly wrong. It seems to me that if Bloomsbury is to be written about it must be by its own members (most of whom have done so). One can't tell the truth about living people and the world must wait till we're all dead. Don't you agree? I don't mind telling what I can about the past generation, but not about my own – except to my own family and friends.

Clive Bell: Bloomsbury

Clive Bell's essay was originally published under the title 'What Was Bloomsbury?' in 1954 before being collected under the title 'Bloomsbury' in Old Friends: Personal Recollections. *It is based on an unpublished memoir devoted to the Cambridge origins of Bloomsbury. Clive's published essay displays an annoyance similar to that of Vanessa's memoir at the irresponsible way in which the label Bloomsbury was being used by journalists and other critics. The emphasis on the distinctions to be made inside Bloomsbury is valuable, though Clive's insistence that a definition of Bloomsbury identify its common*

*and peculiar characteristics is questionable. Clive Bell's own enthu-
siasm for his friends made him a key figure in the development of
Bloomsbury as a Group, as Desmond MacCarthy's memoir indicates
(see pp. 69-70). An illustration of this is to be found in a letter Clive
wrote to Molly MacCarthy in 1913: 'It seems very absurd that people
who are fond of each other shouldn't all live together always. What's
this modern notion of pairing off instead of living in rookeries? Vanessa and I are happy enough alone, painting and writing and reading
and mooning and pottering about, but we should be happier in the
thick of our friends.'*

*Raymond Mortimer, who is mentioned as at least an associate of
Bloomsbury in Clive Bell's essay (see also pp. 309-12), wrote to him
when the essay was first published that it was 'inevitable and indeed
proper that Bloomsbury should engage public interest, because the
English are habitually less clannishly intellectual than the French . . .'
and he offered two characteristics that united Bloomsbury: 'their rationalism and open-mindedness about patriotism and sex' and 'a preoccupation with quality and a contempt for the third-rate. . . . In any
case your diverting suggestion that there was no such thing as Bloomsbury must be fruitless: the influence has been evident, however indefinite the grouping.'*

The reading society that Bell mentions in another chapter of Old
Friends *was the Midnight Society, 'which met at midnight because
another – the X – of which some of us were members, met earlier
on Saturday evenings . . . and, having strengthened itself with whisky
or punch and one of those gloomy beef-steak pies which it was the
fashion to order for Sunday lunch, proceeded to read aloud some such
trifle as* Prometheus Unbound, The Cenci, The Return of the Druses,
Bartholomew Fair *or* Comus.' *It was in this society that Bell believed
the foundations of Bloomsbury were laid (* Old Friends, *26).*

'Bloomsbury' was illustrated in Old Friends *with a photograph of
Mrs St John Hutchinson, E.M. Forster, Duncan Grant, and Bell him-
self in the garden at Charleston. The* TLS *anonymous review 'The
Air of Bloomsbury' referred to in Bell's first note was a review by
Benedict Nicolson of J.K. Johnstone's* The Bloomsbury Group.

There is mystery in the word, and money too perhaps. Or is it merely
for fun that grave historians and pompous leader-writers no less than
the riff-raff of Fleet Street and Portland Place chatter about the thing?
'The thing', I say, because that is the least committal substantive I
can think of, and it is not always clear whether what the chatterers

are chattering about is a point of view, a period, a gang of con-
spirators or an infectious disease. Beyond meaning something nasty,
what do they mean by 'Bloomsbury'? Assuming, as seems reasonable,
that they all have in mind, amongst other things, a gang or group
or clique (for without human beings you cannot well have a point
of view or a doctrine, and even an epidemic needs 'carriers'), I invite
them to name the men and women of whom this gang or group
or clique was composed. Who were the members of Bloomsbury? Let
them give the names: then they may be able to tell us what were
the tastes and opinions held in common by and peculiar to the people
to whom these names belong, what, in fact, is or was the 'Bloomsbury doctrine'.[1]

But we must not ask too much – and it is much to think clearly
and state one's thought perspicuously – of columnists and broadcasters, so to *The Time's Literary Supplement* and a Fellow of All
Souls I turn. The *Supplement* has before now castigated Bloomsbury in reviews and even in a leading article; while only the other
day I caught one of the most prominent fellows of the glorious foundation writing in *The Times* of 'Bloomsbury historians'. From such
high courts we may expect clear judgments. I implore the
Supplement, I implore Mr Rowse, to give categorical answers to a
couple of straight questions: (*a*) Who are or were the members of
Bloomsbury? (*b*) For what do they, or did they, stand?

I have been stigmatized as 'Bloomsbury' myself, and the epithet
has been applied freely to most of those who are, or were – for many
are dead – my intimate friends, so, if it be true that something that
can fairly be called 'the Bloomsbury group' did exist, presumably
I am entitled to an opinion as to who were the members and what
were their thoughts and feelings. Of course I am aware that people
born in recent years and distant lands hold opinions clean contrary
to mine. By all means let them enjoy a Bloomsbury of their own
invention; only, should they chance to write on the subject, let them

---

1 *The Times Literary Supplement* (20th August 1954) published a long review of a
book the name of which escapes me. This review, or essay rather, was entitled 'The
Air of Bloomsbury'; and is by far the most intelligent and penetrating piece that has
been written on the subject. There were errors of fact to be sure, errors there must be
in an appreciation by someone who is not himself a part of the society described, by
someone who was neither an eye nor an ear witness. But the essay, admirably written, reveals a remarkable power of understanding complex characters and peculiar
points of view. It has value much beyond that of most ephemeral, or rather hebdom-
adal, criticism. And it is to be hoped that it will soon be published in easily accessible and durable form.

state clearly whom and what they are writing about. Otherwise historians unborn will flounder in a sea of doubt. Knowing that 'Bloomsbury' was the curse of a decade or two in the twentieth century, but unable to infer from a mass of woolly evidence who precisely were the malefactors and what precisely was the thing, some will be sure that it was a religious heresy, a political deviation or a conspiracy, while others, less confident, may suspect it was no more than a peculiar vice.

So, having appealed to the highest authorities for simple answers to simple questions, I now repeat my request to the smaller fry. Let everyone have his or her notion of 'Bloomsbury'; but let everyone who uses the name in public speech or writing do his or her best to say exactly what he or she intends by it. Thus, even should it turn out that in fact there never was such a thing, the word might come to have significance independent of the facts and acquire value as a label. I dare say Plato would have been at a loss to discover the connection between his philosophy and the epithet 'platonic' as used by lady-novelists and reviewers in the nineteenth and twentieth centuries; nevertheless in refined conversation the word now has a recognised meaning. 'Bloomsbury' may yet come to signify something definite, though as yet few people, so far as I can make out, understand by it anything more precise than 'the sort of thing we all dislike'. Wherefore I repeat, let publicists and broadcasters be explicit. That is my modest request: which made, I will give what help I can by telling all I know.

The name was first applied to a set of friends by Lady MacCarthy – Mrs Desmond MacCarthy as she then was – in a letter: she calls them 'the Bloomsberries'. The term, as she uses it, had a purely topographical import; and the letter, which doubtless could be found at the bottom of one of five or six tin boxes, must have been written in 1910 or 1911. But the story begins earlier. It begins, as I have recorded in an earlier chapter, in October 1899 when five freshmen went up to Trinity – Cambridge, of course – and suddenly becoming intimate, as freshmen will, founded a society as freshmen almost invariably do. It was a 'reading society' which met in my rooms in the New Court on Saturdays at midnight, and here are the names of the five original members: Lytton Strachey, Sydney-Turner, Leonard Woolf, Thoby Stephen, Clive Bell.[2] After he had gone down,

2 I maintain that A.J. Robertson was also an original member, but he disclaims the honour – or dishonour.

and after the death of his father, Thoby Stephen lived at 46 Gordon Square, Bloomsbury, with his brother Adrian and his two sisters Vanessa (later Vanessa Bell) and Virginia (later Virginia Woolf). These two beautiful, gifted and completely independent young women, with a house of their own, became the centre of a circle of which Thoby's Cambridge friends were what perhaps I may call the spokes. And when, in 1907, the elder married, the circle was not broken but enlarged; for Virginia, with her surviving brother Adrian, took a house in nearby Fitzroy Square: thus, instead of one *salon* – if that be the word – there were two *salons*. If ever such an entity as 'Bloomsbury' existed, these sisters, with their houses in Gordon and Fitzroy Squares, were at the heart of it. But did such an entity exist?

All one can say truthfully is this. A dozen friends – I will try to name them presently – between 1904 and 1914 saw a great deal of each other. They differed widely, as I shall tell, in opinions, tastes and preoccupations. But they liked, though they sharply criticized, each other, and they liked being together. I suppose one might say they were 'in sympathy'. Can a dozen individuals so loosely connected be called a group? It is not for me to decide. Anyhow the first World War disintegrated this group, if group it were, and when the friends came together again inevitably things had changed. Old friends brought with them new and younger acquaintances. Differences of opinion and taste, always wide, became wider. Close relationships with people quite outside the old circle sprang up. Sympathy remained. But whatever cohesion there may have been among those who saw so much of each other in Gordon Square and Fitzroy Square, among Lady MacCarthy's 'Bloomsberries' that is, by 1918 had been lost. That was the end of 'old Bloomsbury'.

Now I will try to name these friends. There were the surviving members of the Midnight Society. Thoby Stephen had died in the late autumn of 1906: Leonard Woolf was in Ceylon between 1904 and 1911: remained in Bloomsbury, Lytton Strachey (who, in fact, lived in Hampstead), Saxon Sydney-Turner, Clive Bell. There were the two ladies. Add to these Duncan Grant, Roger Fry, Maynard Keynes, H.T.J. Norton and perhaps Gerald Shove, and I believe you will have completed the list of those of the elder generation who have been called 'Bloomsbury'. Certainly Desmond and Molly Mac-Carthy and Morgan Forster were close and affectionate friends, but I doubt whether any one of them has yet been branded with the fatal name. So much for the old gang.

As I have said, after the war a few men of a younger generation became intimate with most of us. I will do my best to name these, too; but as the new association was even looser than the old, the classification will be even less precise. First and foremost come David Garnett and Francis Birrell, both of whom we – by 'we' I mean the old Bloomsberries – had known and like before 1914. Immediately after the war, by a stroke of good luck, I made the acquaintance of Raymond Mortimer;[3] and about the same time Lytton Strachey, lecturing at Oxford, met Ralph Partridge. I do not know who discovered Stephen Tomlin: but I remember well how Keynes brought Sebastian Sprott and F.L. Lucas from Cambridge to stay at a house in Sussex shared by him with my wife, myself and Duncan Grant. I think it may have been through Francis Birrell that we came to know a brilliant girl from Newnham, Frances Marshall (later Mrs Ralph Partridge).

Now whether all or most of the people I have named are the people publicists have in mind when they speak of 'Bloomsbury' is not clear. In fact that is one of the questions I am asking. But from words let fall in broadcasts and articles I infer a tendency to lump together the two generations and call the lump 'Bloomsbury'. We can be sure of nothing till the journalists and broadcasters and the high authorities too have favoured us with their lists. I have given mine; and so doing have given what help I can and set a good example. I have named the friends who were intimate before 1914 and have added the names of those, or at any rate most of those, who became friends of *all* these friends later. Naturally, with time and space at their familiar task, the bonds of sympathy loosened – though I think they seldom snapped – and so the friends of 'the twenties' were even less like a group than the friends of the pre-war period. That, as I have said, has not prevented some critics lumping them all together, and calling the combination or compound, which it seems exhaled a mephitic influence over the twenties, 'Bloomsbury'. It is impossible, I repeat, to know whom, precisely, they have in mind; but, assuming their list to be something like mine, again I put the question: What had these friends in common that was peculiar to these friends?

Not much, I believe you will agree, if you will be so kind as to read my chapter to the end. For beyond mutual liking they had precious little in common, and in mutual liking there is nothing peculiar. Yes, they did like each other; also they shared a taste for dis-

3 Raymond Mortimer reminds me that, after the first war, he was brought to 46 Gordon Square by Aldous Huxley. That was our first meeting.

cussion in pursuit of truth and a contempt for conventional ways
of thinking and feeling – contempt for conventional morals if you
will. Does it not strike you that as much could be said of many collections of young or youngish people in many ages and many lands?
For my part, I find nothing distinctive here. Ah, say the pundits,
but there was G.E. Moore the Cambridge philosopher; Moore was
the all-pervading, the binding influence; 'Moorism' is the peculiarity
the Bloomsberries have in common. I should think there was G.E.
Moore; also the influence of his *Principia Ethica* on some of us was
immense – on some but not on all, nor perhaps on most. Four of
us certainly were freed by Moore from the spell of an ugly doctrine
in which we had been reared: he delivered us from Utilitarianism.
What is more, you can discover easily enough traces of Moorist ethics
in the writings of Strachey and Keynes and, I suppose, in mine. But
not all these friends were Moorists. Roger Fry, for instance, whose
authority was quite as great as that of Lytton Strachey was definitely
anti-Moorist. So, in a later generation, was Frances Marshall who,
beside being a beauty and an accomplished ballroom dancer, was
a philosopher. Assuredly Raymond Mortimer, Ralph Partridge and
Stephen Tomlin – all three Oxford men – were not devout believers
in *Principia Ethica*; while F.L. Lucas, who in those 'twenties' may
well have heard himself called 'Bloomsbury', at that time called himself a Hedonist. I doubt whether either of the Miss Stephens gave
much thought to the all important distinction between 'Good on
the whole' and 'Good as a whole'. Also it must be remembered that
Bertrand Russell, though no one has ever call him 'Bloomsbury', appeared to be a friend and was certainly an influence.

Lytton Strachey, I have agreed, was a Moorist. Of him I have written
at some length elsewhere and have said that, being a great character,
amongst very young men he was inevitably a power. But at Cambridge, and later among his cronies in London, his influence was
literary for the most part. He inclined our undergraduate taste away
from contemporary realism towards the Elizabethans and the eighteenth century. But when, about 1910, Roger Fry and I became fascinated by what was being written in France he did not share our
enthusiasm. Quite the contrary: and as for contemporary painting,
Lytton, who had a liking, a literary liking, for the visual arts, thought
that we were downright silly about Matisse and Picasso, and on occasions said so.[4] It begins to look – does it not? – as though this

4 Well do I remember Lytton drawing me aside and saying: 'Cannot you or Vanessa
  persuade Duncan to make beautiful pictures instead of these coagulations of dis-

thing called 'Bloomsbury' was not precisely homogeneous. Maynard
Keynes, whose effect on economic theory was, I understand, immense,
bore no sway whatever amongst his friends in the West Central district. They liked him for his cleverness, his wit, the extraordinary
ingenuity with which he defended what they often considered absurd
opinions, and his affectionate nature. They disliked other things. He
had very little natural feeling for the arts; though he learnt to write
admirably lucid prose, and, under the spell of Duncan Grant, cultivated a taste for pictures and made an interesting collection. Said
Lytton once: 'What's wrong with Pozzo' – a pet name for Maynard
which Maynard particularly disliked – 'is that he has no aesthetic
sense'. Perhaps Lytton was unjust; but with perfect justice he might
have said the same of Norton. On the other hand, Pozzo and Norton
might have said of some of their dearest friends that what was wrong
with them was that they were incapable of wrestling with abstractions.
You see we were not so much alike after all.

I have done my best to name those people who certainly were friends
and of whom some at any rate have often been called 'Bloomsbury'.
I have suggested that the people in my list held few, if any, opinions
and preferences in common which were not held by hundreds of their
intelligent contemporaries: I emphasize the words 'in common'.
Wherefore, if my list be correct, it would seem to follow that there
can be no such thing as 'the Bloomsbury doctrine' or 'the Bloomsbury point of view'. But is my list correct? It should be. And yet
I cannot help wondering sometimes whether the journalists and
broadcasters who write and talk about Bloomsbury have not in mind
some totally different set of people. There are critics and expositors,
for instance that leader-writer in *The Times Literary Supplement*,
who describe Bloomsbury as a little gang or clique which despises
all that is old and venerable and extols to the skies, without discrimination, the latest thing whatever that thing may be – the latest in
art or letters or politics or morals. Also, according to this school
of critics, the writers of Bloomsbury delight in a private and cryptic
language, unintelligible to the common reader, while mocking at
whatever is clear and comprehensible. Now who are these crabbed
and wilfully obscure writers who despise all that is old? Surely not
those reputed pillars of Bloomsbury, Lytton Strachey, Roger Fry,

tressing oddments?' Duncan Grant at that time was much under the influence of the
Post-Impressionists and had been touched by Cubism even.

Maynard Keynes, David Garnett? I beseech the *Supplement* to give us the names.[5]

There are other critics, of whom I know as little as they appear to know of the reputed pillars of Bloomsbury, who hold a clean contrary opinion. I write from hearsay; but I am told there are brisk young fellows, authorities on the 'twenties', whose distressing accents are sometimes heard on the wireless by those who can stand that sort of thing, who explain that in 'the twenties' there still existed in England a gang or group which for years had devoted itself to stifling, or trying to stifle, at birth every vital movement that came to life. Oddly enough this gang, too, goes by the name of Bloomsbury. Now who can these baby-killers have been? Obviously not Roger Fry who introduced the modern movement in French painting to the British public, nor Maynard Keynes, who, I understand, revolutionized economics. Nor does it seem likely that the critics are thinking of Lytton Strachey who, far from being reactionary, went out of his way to help the cause of Women's Suffrage when that cause was reckoned a dangerous fad, or of Leonard Woolf who was a Fabian long before British socialism had become what the Americans call a racket. Whom can these castigators of 'Bloomsbury' have in mind? Clearly not Virginia Woolf who invented what amounts almost to a new prose form; nor, I hope, certain critics who, long before 1920, had appreciated and defended the then disconcerting works of Picasso and T.S. Eliot.

Once more I cry aloud: Who were the members of Bloomsbury? For what did they stand? In the interests of history, if common decency means nothing to them, I beseech the Bloomsbury-baiters to answer my questions; for unless they speak out and speak quickly social historians will have to make what they can of wildly conflicting fancies and statements which contradict known fact. Thus, disheartened by the impossibility of discovering opinions and tastes common and peculiar to those people who by one authority or another have been described as 'Bloomsbury', the more acute may well be led to surmise that Bloomsbury was neither a chapel nor a clique but merely a collection of individuals each with his or her own views and likings. When to this perplexity is added the discovery that no two witnesses

---

5 A week or so after this leading article appeared Mr Oliver Strachey made the same request, and received from the *Supplement* (31st July 1948) what I can only consider a disingenuous reply.

agree on a definition of the 'Bloomsbury doctrine', historians are
bound to wonder whether there ever was such a thing. At last they
may come to doubt whether 'Bloomsbury' ever existed. And did it?

Leonard Woolf: Cambridge Friends and Influences

*The five volumes of Leonard Woolf's autobiography, all published
in the 1960s, contain the fullest and most riable account of Bloomsbury's origins and development. In the excerpts collected here from*
Sowing, *the first volume, Woolf sets forth the Cambridge backgrounds
of Bloomsbury. Three of Woolf's Trinity/Bloomsbury friends, Saxon
Sydney-Turner, Thoby Stephen, and Clive Bell, are characterized; the
fourth, Lytton Strachey, has been omitted because of an earlier account
of him given by Woolf in the next section of this collection. After
the description of his friends comes Woolf's eloquent exposition of
G.E. Moore's deep influence on them (and on Desmond MacCarthy,
an older friend also described by Woolf in the next section). For Leonard Woolf, G.E. Moore was 'the only great man whom I have ever
met or known in the world of ordinary, real life' (Sowing, 131). And
in explaining Moore's importance Woolf takes issue with Keynes's account in 'My Early Beliefs.'*

. . . I must return to Cambridge in the autumn and winter of 1899.
I felt terribly lonely in my first few days at Trinity. . . . But suddenly
everything changed and almost for the first time one felt that to be
young was very heaven. The reason was simple. Suddenly I found
to my astonishment that there were a number of people near and
about me with whom I could enjoy the exciting and at the same
time profound happiness of friendship. It began casually in what
was called the screens, the passage through the Hall from Trinity
Great Court to Neville's Court. I was looking at the notices on the
board after dining in Hall and said something to a man standing
next to me. We walked away together and he came back to my rooms.
He was a scholar from Westminster, Saxon Sydney-Turner. Saxon
was a very strange character with one of the strangest minds I have
met with. He was immensely intelligent and subtle, but had little
creativeness. In one of the university scholarship examinations they
set us for Greek translation a piece from a rather obscure writer which
had a riddle in it. Saxon won one of the scholarships and it was
said that he was the only person to get the riddle bit right. It was
characteristic of him. When, years later, crossword puzzles were invented and became the rage, he was a champion solver. And it was

characteristic of him that he was a champion solver, never an inventor, of crossword puzzles and other mental gymnastics, including the art of writing. He had an immense knowledge of literature, but he read books rather in the spirit in which a man collects stamps. He would tell you casually that last night he had read for the second time in three weeks Meister Eckhart's *Buch der gottlicher Tröstung und von den edlen Menschen* much in the tone of voice in which a great stamp collector might casually remark – to *épater* his fellow collectors – that yesterday afternoon he had bought for 2s. 6d in a shop in a back street of Soho two perfect specimens of a very rare 1d Cape of Good Hope stamp. Later in life, when he was in the Treasury and lived in Great Ormond Street, he was an inveterate concert and opera goer in London and Bayreuth. He kept a record, both on paper and in his head, of all the operas he had ever been to. Normally with other people he was reserved, spoke little, and fell into long and unobtrusive silences. But sometimes he would begin to talk almost volubly about opera. He would tell you that last night he had been at Covent Garden and heard *Siegfried* for the thirty-fifth time. X had sung Brünnhilde; the great duet in the last act was quite good. X sang well and reminded him of Y whom he had heard sing the same part at Bayreuth, in 1908, Z being Siegfried, when he had been to *Siegfried* for the seventh time. The best performance he had ever heard of the opera was his twelfth, also at Bayreuth; Y was again Brünnhilde and there was the greatest of all Siegfrieds, W. The fourteenth time he saw the opera was . . . and so on.

The rooms which Saxon lived in for many years in Great Ormond Street consisted of one big sitting-room and a small bedroom. On each side of the sitting-room fireplace on the wall was an immense picture of a farmyard scene. It was the same picture on each side and for over thirty years Saxon lived with them ever before his eyes, while in his bedroom there were some very good pictures by Duncan Grant and other artists, but you could not possibly see them because there was no light and no space to hang them on the walls. As time went on, Saxon acquired more and more books and, since he suffered from a variety of ailments, more and more medicine bottles. His bookcases filled up and soon a second and third row, one behind the other, became necessary, and then piles and piles of books covered the floor. There were books upon the tables and chairs, and everywhere there were empty medicine bottles on the books, and the same two pigs, the same two sheep, and the same two dogs looked down upon, one presumes, the unseeing Saxon from the same two pictures on either side of the mantelpiece.

I was up at Trinity for five years. The first two years I had rooms in New Court; in the last three years Saxon and I had a double set of rooms in Great Court. It had one very large room on the first floor and two small bedrooms on the second. Saxon was a short, thin man with a very pale face and straw-coloured hair. He seemed to glide, rather than walk, and noiselessly, so that one moment you were alone in a room and next moment you found him sitting in a chair near you though you had not heard the door open or him come in. We saw very little of each other except in the evenings for he used to get up very late as a rule whereas I was up at eight. We hardly ever had a meal together for he ate very little and at the most erratic hours.

Both physically and mentally Saxon was ghost-like, shadowy. He rarely committed himself to any positive opinion or even statement. His conversation - if it could rightly be called conversation - was extremely spasmodic, elusive, and allusive. You might be sitting reading a book and suddenly find him standing in front of you on one leg in front of the fire knocking out his pipe into the fireplace and he would say without looking up: 'Her name was Emily'; or perhaps: 'He was right.' After a considerable amount of cross-examination, you would find that the first remark applied to a conversation weeks ago in which he had tried unsuccessfully to remember the christian name of Miss Girouette in *Nightmare Abbey*, and the second remark applied to a dispute between Thoby Stephen and myself which I had completely forgotten because it had taken place in the previous term.

During the years we were at Trinity, Henry James was at the height of his powers, writing those strange, involved, elusive novels of his last period. We read *The Sacred Fount, The Wings of the Dove*, and *The Golden Bowl* as they came out. Lytton Strachey, Saxon and I were fascinated by them - entranced and almost hypnotized. I don't know whether we thought that they were really great masterpieces. My enjoyment and admiration of them have always been and still are great, but always with a reservation. There is an element of ridiculousness, even of 'phoneyness' in them which makes it impossible to rank them with the greatest or even the great novels. But the strange, Jamesian, convoluted beauty and subtlety of them act upon those who yield to them like drink or drugs; for a time we became addicts, habitual drunkards - never, perhaps, quite serious, but play-

ing at seeing the world of Trinity and Cambridge as a Jamesian phantasmagoria, writing and talking as if we had just walked out of *The
Sacred Fount* into Trinity Great Court. The curious thing was that,
whereas Lytton and I were always consciously playing a game in
talking or writing like Mrs Brissenden and Mrs Server, Saxon quite
naturally talked, looked, acted, *was* a character in an unwritten novel
by Henry James. . . .

Lytton Strachey, Thoby Stephen, and Clive Bell all came up to Trinity
in the same year as Saxon and I did and we soon got to know them
well. We were intimate friends – particularly Lytton, Saxon, and myself – but intimacy in 1900 among middle-class males was different
from what it became in generations later than ours. Some of us were
called by nicknames; for instance we always called Thoby Stephen
'The Goth', but we never used christian names. Lytton always called
me Woolf and I always called him Strachey until I returned from
Ceylon in 1911 and found that the wholesale revolution in society
and manner which had taken place in the preceding seven years involved the use of christian names in place of surnames. The difference
was – and is – not entirely unimportant. The shade of relationship
between Woolf and Strachey is not exactly the same as that between
Leonard and Lytton. The surname relationship was determined by
and retained that curious formality and reticence which the
nineteenth-century public school system insisted upon in certain matters. Now, of course, the use of christian names and their diminutives
has become so universal that it may soon perhaps become necessary
to indicate intimacy by using surnames. . . .

The characters in *The Waves* are not drawn from life, but there is
something of Lytton in Neville. There is no doubt that Percival in
that book contains something of Thoby Stephen, Virginia's brother,
who died of typhoid aged twenty-six in 1906. Thoby came up to Trinity from Clifton with an exhibition in the same year as Lytton, Saxon,
and I. He gave one an impression of physical magnificence. He was
six foot two, broad-shouldered and somewhat heavily made, with a
small head set elegantly upon the broad shoulders so that it reminded
one of the way in which the small head is set upon the neck of a
well-bred Arab horse. His face was extraordinarily beautiful and his
character was as beautiful as his face. In his monolithic character,
his monolithic common-sense, his monumental judgments he continually reminded one of Dr Johnson, but a Samuel Johnson who

had shed his neuroticism, his irritability, his fears. He had a perfect
'natural' style of writing, flexible, lucid, but rather formal, old-
fashioned, almost Johnsonian or at any rate eighteenth century. And
there was a streak of the same natural style in his talk. Any wild
statement, speculative judgment, or Strachean exaggeration would
be met with a 'Nonsense, my good fellow', from Thoby, and then
a sentence of profound, but humorous, common-sense, and a delighted chuckle. Thoby had a good sense of humour, a fine, sound, but
not brilliant mind. He had many of the characteristic qualities of
the males of his family, of his father Leslie Stephen, his uncle James
Fitzjames Stephen and his cousin J.K. Stephen. But what everyone
who knew him remembers most vividly in him was his extraordinary
charm. He had greater personal charm than anyone I have ever
known, and, unlike all other great 'charmers', he seemed, and I believe
was, entirely unconscious of it. It was, no doubt, partly physical,
partly due to the unusual combination of sweetness of nature and
affection with rugged intelligence and a complete lack of sentimentality, and partly to those personal flavours of the soul which are
as unanalyzable and indescribable as the scents of flowers or the overtones in a line of great poetry.

Thoby was an intellectual; he liked an argument and had a great,
though conservative and classical, appreciation and love of literature.
But he also, though rather scornful of games and athletics, loved the
open air – watching birds, walking, following the beagles. In these
occupations, particularly in walking, I often joined him. Walking
with him was by no means a tame business, for it was almost a Stephen
principle in walking to avoid all roads and ignore the rights of property owners and the law of trespass. Owing to these principles we
did not endear ourselves to the gamekeepers round Cambridge.
Though fundamentally respectable, conservative, and a moralist, he
was always ready in the country to leave the beaten track in more
senses than one. . . .

Clive Bell came up to Trinity the same year as we did, 1899, and
when we first got to know him he was different in many ways from
us and even from the Clive Bell whom I found married to Vanessa
Stephen and living in Gordon Square when I returned from Ceylon
in 1911. He came into our lives because he got to know Saxon, having
rooms on the same staircase in New Court. Lytton, Saxon, Thoby,
and I belonged, unconcealably and unashamedly, to that class of
human beings which is regarded with deep suspicion in Britain, and

particularly in public schools and universities, the intellectual. Clive, when he came up to Trinity from Marlborough, was not yet an intellectual. He was superficially a 'blood'. The first time I ever saw him he was walking through Great Court in full hunting rigout, including – unless this is wishful imagination – a hunting horn and the whip carried by the whipper-in. He was a great horseman and a first-rate shot, very well-off, and to be seen in the company of 'bloods', not the rowing, cricket, and rugger blues, but the rich young men who shot, and hunted, and rode in the point-to-point races. He had a very attractive face, particularly to women, boyish, goodhumoured, hair red and curly, and what in the eighteenth century was called, I think, a sanguine complexion.

Clive became great friends with Thoby, for they both were fond of riding and hunting. In those early days, and indeed for many years afterwards, intellectually Clive sat at the feet of Lytton and Thoby. He was one of those strange Englishmen who break away from their environment and become devoted to art and letters. His family of wealthy philistines, whose money came from coal, lived in a large house in Wiltshire. Somehow or other, Mr and Mrs Bell produced Clive's mind which was a contradiction in terms of theirs.[1] For his mind was eager, lively, intensely curious, and he quickly developed a passion for literature[2] and argument. We had started some reading societies for reading aloud plays, one of which met at midnight, and Clive became a member of them. In this way we came to see a good deal of him and his admiration for Lytton and Thoby began to flourish.

It is necessary here to say something about the Society – The Apostles – because of the immense importance it had for us, its influence upon our minds, our friendships, our lives. The Society was and still is 'secret', but, as it has existed for 130 years or more, in autobiographies and biographies of members its nature, influence, and membership have naturally from time to time been described. There

---

1 I do not think that I ever met either of Clive's parents, but I have heard so much about them from him and from others that I have no doubt about the truth of what I say here.

2 It is worth noting that in those days we set little or no store by pictures and painting. I never heard Clive talk about pictures at Cambridge, and it was only after he came down and lived for a time in Paris and got to know Roger Fry that his interest in art developed. Music already meant a good deal to Lytton, Saxon, and me and we went to chamber music concerts in Cambridge and orchestral concerts in London, but I do not think that it has ever meant much to Clive.

is a good deal about it in the autobiography of Dean Merivale, who was elected in 1830, and in the memoir of Henry Sidgwick, who was elected in 1856, and information about its condition in the early years of the present century can be found in *The Life of John Maynard Keynes* by R.F. Harrod, who was not himself an Apostle. . . .

When Lytton, Saxon, and I were elected, the other active undergraduate members were A.R. Ainsworth, Ralph Hawtrey, and J.T. Sheppard.[3] When Maynard Keynes came up, we elected him in 1903. Sidgwick says that the Society absorbed and dominated him, but that is not quite the end of the story. Throughout its history, every now and again an Apostle has dominated and left his impression, within its spirit and tradition, upon the Society. Sidgwick himself was one of these, and a century ago he dominated the Society, refertilizing and revivifying its spirit and tradition. And what Sidgwick did in the fifties of last century, G.E. Moore was doing when I was elected. . . .

It was, I suppose, in 1902 that I got to know Moore well. He was seven years my senior and already a Fellow of Trinity. His mind was an extraordinarily powerful instrument; it was Socratic, analytic. But unlike so many analytic philosophers, he never analyzed just for the pleasure or sake of analysis. He never indulged in logic-chopping or truth-chopping. He had a passion for truth, but not for all or any truth, only for important truths. He had no use for truths which Browning called 'dead from the waist down'. Towards the end of the nineteenth century there was an extraordinary outburst of philosophical brilliance in Cambridge. In 1902, among the Fellows of Trinity were four philosophers, all of whom were Apostles: J.E. McTaggart, A.N. Whitehead, Bertrand Russell, and G.E. Moore. McTaggart was one of the strangest of men, an eccentric with a powerful mind which, when I knew him, seemed to have entirely left the earth for the inextricably complicated cobwebs and *O altitudos* of Hegelianism. He had the most astonishing capacity for profound silence that I have ever known. He lived out of college, but he had an 'evening' once a week on Thursdays when, if invited or taken by an invitee, you could go and see him in his rooms in Great Court.

3 Ainsworth became a civil servant in the Education Office; Hawtrey, now Sir Ralph Hawtrey, a civil servant in the Treasury; Sheppard, now Sir J.T. Sheppard, Provost of King's College, Cambridge.

The chosen were very few, and Lytton, Saxon, and I, who were among them, every now and again nerved ourselves to the ordeal. McTaggart always seemed glad to see us, but, having said good evening, he lay back on the sofa, his eyes fixed on the ceiling, in profound silence. Every five minutes he would roll his head from side to side, stare with his rather protuberant, rolling eyes round the circle of visitors, and then relapse into immobility. One of us would occasionally manage to think of something banal and halting to say, but I doubt whether I ever heard McTaggart initiate a conversation, and when he did say something it was usually calculated to bring to a sudden end any conversation initiated by one of us. Yet he did not seem to wish us not to be there; indeed, he appeared to be quite content that we should come and see him and sit for an hour in silence.

In the early 1890s McTaggart's influence was great. He was six years older than Russell and seven years older than Moore, and these two in their early days at Trinity were first converted to Hegelianism by McTaggart. But Moore could never tolerate anything but truth, common-sense, and reality, and he very soon revolted against Hegel: Bertrand Russell describes the revolt in the following words:

> Moore, first, and I closely following him, climbed out of this mental prison and found ourselves again at liberty to breathe the free air of a universe restored to reality.

When I came up to Trinity, McTaggart, though regarded with respect and amused affection as an eccentric, had completely lost his intellectual and philosophical influence. The three other philosophers' reputation was great and growing, and they dominated the younger generation. In 1902 Whitehead was forty-one years old, Russell thirty, and Moore twenty-nine. It is a remarkable fact – a fine example of our inflexible irrationality and inveterate inconsistency – that, although no people has ever despised, distrusted and rejected the intellect and intellectuals more than the British, these three philosophers were each awarded the highest and rarest of official honours, the Order of Merit. 1903 was an *annus mirabilis* for Cambridge philosophy, for in that year were published Russell's *Principles of Mathematics* and Moore's *Principia Ethica*. Russell used to come to Moore's rooms sometimes in order to discuss some difficult problem that was holding him up. The contrast between the two men and the two minds was astonishing and fascinating. Russell has the quickest mind of anyone I have ever known; like the greatest of chess players he sees in a flash six moves ahead of the ordinary player and one move ahead of all the other Grand Masters. However serious he may be, his conversation scintillates with wit and a kind of puckish humour flickers through his thought. Like most people who possess this kind of mental brilliance, in an argument a slower and duller opponent may ruefully find that Russell is not always entirely scrupulous in taking advantage of his superior skill in the use of weapons. Moore was the exact opposite, and to listen to an argument between the two was like watching a race between the hare and the tortoise. Quite often the tortoise won – and that, of course, was why Russell's thought had been so deeply influenced by Moore and why he still came to Moore's rooms to discuss difficult problems.

Moore was not witty; I do not think that I ever heard him say a witty thing; there was no scintillation in his conversation or in his thought. But he had an extraordinary profundity and clarity of thought, and he pursued truth with the tenacity of a bulldog and the integrity of a saint. And he had two other very rare characteristics. He had a genius for seeing what was important and what was unimportant and irrelevant, in thought and in life and in persons, and in the most complicated argument or situation he pursued the relevant and ignored the irrelevant with amazing tenacity. He was able to do so because of the second characteristic, the passion for truth (and, as I shall show, for other things) which burned in him. The tortoise so often won the race because of this combination of clarity, integrity, tenacity, and passion.

The intensity of Moore's passion for truth was an integral part of his greatness, and purity of passion was an integral part of his whole character. On the surface and until you got to know him intimately he appeared to be a very shy, reserved man, and on all occasions and in any company he might fall into profound and protracted silence. When I first got to know him, the immensely high standards of thought and conduct which he seemed silently to demand of an intimate, the feeling that one should not say anything unless the thing was both true and worth saying, the silences which would certainly envelope him and you, tinged one's wish to see him with some anxiety, and I know that standing at the door of his room, before knocking and going in, I often took a deep breath just as one does on a cool day before one dives into the cold green sea. For a young man it was a formidable, an alarming experience, but, like the plunge into the cold sea, once one had nerved oneself to take it, extraordinarily exhilarating. This kind of tension relaxed under the influence of time, intimacy, and affection, but I do not think that it ever entirely disappeared – a proof, perhaps, of the quality of greatness which distinguished Moore from other people.

His reserve and silences covered deep feeling. When Moore said: 'I *simply* don't understand *what* he means,' the emphasis on the 'simply' and the 'what' and the shake of his head over each word gave one a glimpse of the passionate distress which muddled thinking aroused in him. We used to watch with amusement and admiration the signs of the same thing when he sat reading a book, pencil in hand, and continually scoring the poor wretch of a writer's muddled sentences with passionate underlinings and exclamation marks. I used to play fives with him at Cambridge, and he played the game with the same passion as that with which he pursued truth; after a few minutes in the court the sweat poured down his face in streams and soaked his clothes – it was excitement as well as exercise. It was the same with music. He played the piano and sang, often to Lytton Strachey and me in his rooms and on reading parties in Cornwall. He was not a highly skilful pianist or singer, but I have never been given greater pleasure from playing or singing. This was due partly to the quality of his voice, but principally to the intelligence of his understanding and to the subtlety and intensity of his feeling. He played the Waldstein sonata or sang 'Ich grolle nicht' with the same passion with which he pursued truth; when the last note died away, he would sit absolutely still, his hands resting on the keys, and the sweat streaming down his face.

Moore's mind was, as I said, Socratic. His character, too, and his influence upon us as young men at Cambridge were Socratic. It is clear from Plato and Xenophon that Socrates's strange simplicity and integrity were enormously attractive to the young Athenians who became his disciples, and he inspired great affection as well as admiration. So did Moore. Plato in the *Symposium* shows us a kind of cosmic absurdity in the monumental simplicity of Socrates; and such different people as Alcibiades, Aristophanes, and Agathon 'rag' him about it and laugh at him gently and affectionately. There was the same kind of divine absurdity in Moore. Socrates had the great advantage of combining a very beautiful soul with a very ugly face, and the Athenians of the fifth century B.C. were just the people to appreciate the joke of that. Moore had not that advantage. When I first knew him, his face was amazingly beautiful, almost ethereal, and, as Bertrand Russell has said, 'he had, what he retained throughout his life, an extraordinarily lovable smile'. But he resembled So-

crates in possessing a profound simplicity, a simplicity which Tolstoy
and some other Russian writers consider to produce the finest human
beings. These human beings are 'simples' or even 'sillies'; they are
absurd in ordinary life and by the standards of sensible and practical
men. There is a superb description of a 'silly' in Tolstoy's autobiography and, of course, in Dostoevsky's *The Idiot*. In many ways
Moore was one of these divine 'sillies'. It showed itself perhaps in
such simple, unrestrained, passionate gestures as when, if told something particularly astonishing or confronted by some absurd statement at the crisis of an argument, his eyes would open wide, his
eyebrows shoot up, and his tongue shoot out of his mouth. And Bertrand Russell has described the pleasure with which one used to watch
Moore trying unsuccessfully to light his pipe when he was arguing
an important point. He would light a match, hold it over the bowl
of his pipe until it burnt his fingers and he had to throw it away,
and go on doing this – talking the whole time or listening intently
to the other man's argument – until the whole box of matches was
exhausted. . . .

I feel that I must now face the difficult task of saying something
about Moore's influence upon my generation. There is no doubt that
it was immense. Maynard Keynes in his *Two Memoirs* wrote a fascinating, an extremely amusing account or analysis of this influence
of Moore upon us as young men. Much of what he says is, of course,
true and biographically or autobiograhically important. Maynard's
mind was incredibly quick and supple, imaginative and restless; he
was always thinking new and original thoughts, particularly in the
field of events and human behaviour and in the reaction between
events and men's actions. He had the very rare gift of being as brilliant
and effective in practice as he was in theory, so that he could outwit
a banker, business man, or Prime Minister as quickly and gracefully
as he could demolish a philosopher or crush an economist. It was
these gifts which enabled him to revolutionize economic theory and
national economic and financial policy and practice, and to make
a considerable fortune by speculation and a considerable figure in
the City and in the world which is concerned with the patronage
or production of the arts, and particularly the theatre and ballet.
But most people who knew him intimately and his mind in shirts-
leeves rather than public uniform would agree that there were in him
some streaks of intellectual wilfullness and arrogance which often
led him into surprisingly wrong and perverse judgments. To his

friends he was a lovable character and these faults or idiosyncracies were observed and discounted with affectionate amusement.

It is always dangerous to speak the truth about one's most intimate friends, because the truth and motives for telling it are almost invariably misunderstood. In all the years that I knew Maynard and in all the many relations, of intimacy and business which I had with him, I never had even the ghost of a quarrel or the shadow of unpleasantness, though we often disagreed about things, persons, or policies. He was essentially a lovable person. But to people who were not his friends, to subordinates and to fools in their infinite variety whom one has to deal with in business or just daily life, he could be anything but lovable; he might, at any moment and sometimes quite unjustifiably, annihilate some unfortunate with ruthless rudeness. I once heard him snap out to an auditor who was trying to explain to the Board of Directors of a company some item in the audited accounts: 'We all know, Mr X, that auditors consider that the object of accounts is to conceal the truth, but surely not even you can believe that their object is to conceal the truth from the Directors.'

It was this streak of impatience and wilfulness combined with a restless and almost fantastic imagination, which often induced Maynard to make absurdly wrong judgments. But once having committed himself to one of his opinions or judgments, theories or fantasies, he would without compunction use all the powers and brilliance of his mind, his devastating wit and quickness, to defend it, and in the end would often succeed in convincing not only his opponent, but himself. In several points [in 'My Early Beliefs'] in *Two Memoirs* his recollection and interpretation are quite wrong about Moore's influence, I think. His main point in the memoir is that Moore in *Principia Ethica* propounded both a religion and a system of morals and that we as young men accepted the religion, but discarded the morals. He defines 'religion' to mean one's attitude towards oneself and the ultimate, and 'morals' to mean one's attitude towards the outside world and the intermediate. Moore's religion which we accepted, according to Maynard, maintained that

> nothing mattered except states of mind, our own and other people's of
> course, but chiefly our own. These states of mind were not associated with
> action or achievement or with consequences. They consisted in timeless,
> passionate states of contemplation and communion, largely unattached
> to 'before' and 'after' . . . The appropriate objects of passionate contem-

plation and communion were a beloved person, beauty and truth, and
one's prime objects in life were love, the creation and enjoyment of aesthetic
experience and the pursuit of knowledge. Of these love came a long way
first.

Although Maynard calls this doctrine which we accepted a 'faith'
and a 'religion', he says that Moore's disciples and indeed Moore himself regarded it as entirely rational and scientific, and applied an extravagantly rationalistic, scholastic method of ascertaining what states
of affairs were or were not good. The resulting beliefs were fantastically idealistic and remote from reality and 'real' life. The effect
of this curious amalgam of extreme rationalism, unworldliness, and
dogmatic belief was intensified by our complete neglect of Moore's
'morals'. We paid no attention at all to his doctrine of the importance
of rightness and wrongness as an attribute of actions or to the whole
question of the justification of general rules of conduct. The result
was that we assumed that human beings were all rational, but we
were complete 'immoralists', recognizing 'no moral obligation on us,
no inner sanction, to conform or obey'.

In my recollection this is a distorted picture of Moore's beliefs and
doctrine at the time of the publication of his *Principia Ethica* and
of the influence of his philosophy and character upon us when we
were young men up at Cambridge in the years 1901 to 1904. The
tremendous influence of Moore and his book upon us came from
the fact that they suddenly removed from our eyes an obscuring ac-
cumulation of scales, cobwebs, and curtains, revealing for the first
time to us, so it seemed, the nature of truth and reality, of good
and evil and character and conduct, substituting for the religious and
philosophical nightmares, delusions, hallucinations, in which Jehovah, Christ, and St Paul, Plato, Kant, and Hegel had entangled
us, the fresh air and pure light of plain common-sense.

It was this clarity, freshness, and common-sense which primarily
appealed to us. Here was a profound philosopher who did not require
us to accept any 'religious' faith or intricate, if not unintelligible,
intellectual gymnastics of a Platonic, Aristotelian, Kantian, or Hege-
lian nature; all he asked us to do was to make quite certain that
we knew what we meant when we made a statement and to analyze
and examine our beliefs in the light of common-sense. Philosoph-
ically what, as intelligent young men, we wanted to know was the
basis, if any, for our or any scale of values and rules of conduct,
what justification there was for our belief that friendship or works

of art for instance were good or for the belief that one ought to do some things and not do others. Moore's distinction between things good in themselves or as ends and things good merely as means, his passionate search for truth in his attempt in *Principia Ethica* to determine what things are good in themselves, answered our questions, not with the religious voice of Jehovah from Mount Sinai or Jesus with his sermon from the Mount, but with the more divine voice of plain common-sense.

On one side of us, we were in 1901 very serious young men. We were sceptics in search of truth and ethical truth. Moore, so we thought, gave us a scientific basis for believing that some things were good in themselves. But we were not 'immoralists'; it is not true that we recognized 'no moral obligation on us, no inner sanction, to conform or obey' or that we neglected all that Moore said about 'morals' and rules of conduct. It is true that younger generations, like their elders, were much less politically and socially conscious in the years before the 1914 War than they have been ever since. Bitter experience has taught the world, including the young, the importance of codes of conduct and morals and 'practical politics'. But Moore himself was continually exercised by the problems of goods and bads as means of morality and rules of conduct and therefore of the life of action as opposed to the life of contemplation. He and we were fascinated by questions of what was right and wrong, what one *ought* to do. We followed him closely in this as in other parts of his doctrine and argued interminably about the consequences of one's actions, both in actual and imaginary situations. Indeed one of the problems which worried us was what part Moore (and we, his disciples) *ought* to play in ordinary life, what, for instance, our attitude *ought* to be towards practical politics. I still possess a paper which I wrote for discussion in 1903 and which is explicitly concerned with these problems. It asks the question whether we ought to follow the example of George Trevelyan,[4] and take part in practical politics, going down into the gloomy Platonic cave, where 'men sit bound prisoners guessing at the shadows of reality and boasting that they have found truth', or whether we should imitate George Moore, who though 'he has no small knowledge of the cave dwellers, leaves alone their struggles

4 George Macaulay Trevelyan, OM, the historian and for many years Master of Trinity College. He was four years my senior at Trinity and, when I first knew him, had just become a Fellow of the college. He was a rather fiercely political young man.

and competitions'. I said that the main question I wanted to ask was: 'Can we and ought we to combine the two Georges in our own lives?' And was it rational that George Moore, the philosopher, should take no part in practical politics, or 'right that we should as we do so absolutely ignore their questions?' My answer in 1903 was perfectly definite that we *ought* to take part in practical politics and the last words of my paper are: 'While philosophers sit outside the cave, their philosophy will never reach politicians or people, so that after all, to put it plainly, I *do* want Moore to draft an Education Bill.'

I have said that we were very serious young men. We were, indeed, but superficially we often appeared to be the exact opposite and so enraged or even horrified a good many people. After all we were young once – we were young in 1903; and we were not nearly as serious and solemn as we appeared to some people. We were serious about what we considered to be serious in the universe or in man and his life, but we had a sense of humour and we felt that it was not necessary to be solemn, because one was serious, and that there are practically no questions or situations in which intelligent laughter may not be healthily catalytic. Henry Sidgwick, in his *Memoir*, looking back in old age to the year 1856 when he was elected an Apostle wrote:

> No consistency was demanded with opinions previously held – truth as we saw it then and there was what we had to embrace and maintain, and there were no propositions so well established than an Apostle had not the right to deny or question, if he did so sincerely and not from mere love of paradox. The gravest subjects were continually debated, but gravity of treatment, as I have said, was not imposed, though sincerity was. In fact it was rather a point of the apostolic mind to understand how much suggestion and instruction may be derived from what is in form a jest – even in dealing with the gravest matters.

I am writing today just over a century after the year in which Sidgwick was elected an Apostle, and looking back to the year 1903 I can say that our beliefs, our discussions, our intellectual behaviour in 1903 were in every conceivable way exactly the same as those described by Sidgwick. The beliefs 'fantastically idealistic and remote from reality and real life', the absurd arguments, 'the extravagantly scholastic' method were not as simple or silly as they seemed. Lytton Strachey's mind was fundamentally and habitually ribald and he had developed a protective intellectual façade in which a highly personal and cynical

wit and humour played an important part. It was very rarely safe
to accept the face value of what he said; within he was intensely
serious about what he thought important, but on the surface his
method was to rely on 'suggestion and instruction derived from what
is in form a jest – even in dealing with the gravest matters'. I think
that in my case, too, there was a natural tendency to express myself
ironically – and precisely in matters or over questions about which
one felt deeply as being of great importance – for irony and the jest
are used, particularly when one is young, as antidotes to pomposity.
Of course we were young once; we were young in 1903, and we had
the arrogance and the extravagance natural to the young.

The intellectual, when young, has always been in all ages enthusiastic and passionate and therefore he has tended to be intellectually
arrogant and ruthless. Our youth, the years of my generation at Cambridge, coincided with the end and the beginning of a century which
was also the end of one era and the beginning of another. When
in the grim, grey, rainy January days of 1901 Queen Victoria lay
dying, we already felt that we were living in an era of incipient revolt
and that we ourselves were mortally involved in this revolt against
a social system and code of conduct and morality which, for convenience sake, may be referred to as bourgeois Victorianism. We did
not initiate this revolt. When we went up to Cambridge, its protag-
onists were Swinburne, Bernard Shaw, Samuel Butler in *The Way
of All Flesh*, and to some extent Hardy and Wells. We were passionately on the side of these champions of freedom of speech and freedom
of thought, of common-sense and reason. We felt that, with them
as our leaders, we were struggling against a religious and moral code
of cant and hypocrisy which produced and condoned such social
crimes and judicial murders as the condemnation of Dreyfus. People
of a younger generation who from birth have enjoyed the results of
this struggle for social and intellectual emancipation cannot realize
the stuffy intellectual and moral suffocation which a young man felt
weighing down upon him in Church and State, in the 'rules and
conventions' of the last days of Victorian civilization. Nor can those
who have been born into the world of great wars, of communism
and national socialism and fascism, of Hitler and Mussolini and Stalin, of the wholesale judicial murders of their own fellow-countrymen
or massacres of peasants by Russian communists, and the slaughter
of millions of Jews in gas-chambers by German nazis, these younger
generations can have no notion of what the long-drawn out tragedy
of the Dreyfus case meant to us. Over the body and fate of one obscure,

Jewish captain in the French army a kind of cosmic conflict went
on year after year between the establishment of Church, Army, and
State on the one side and the small band of intellectuals who fought
for truth, reason, and justice, on the other. Eventually the whole of
Europe, almost the whole world, seemed to be watching breathlessly,
ranged upon one side or other in the conflict. And no one who was
not one of the watchers can understand the extraordinary sense of
relief and release when at last the innocence of Dreyfus was vindicated
and justice was done. I still think that we were right and that the
Dreyfus case might, with a slight shift in the current of events, have
been a turning point in European history and civilization. All that
can really be said against us was that our hopes were disappointed.

It is true that in a sense 'we had no respect for traditional wisdom'
and that, as Ludwig Wittgenstein complained, 'we lacked reverence
for everything and everyone'. If 'to revere' means, as the dictionary
says, 'to regard as sacred or exalted, to hold in religious respect',
then we did not revere, we had no reverence for anything or anyone,
and, so far as I am concerned, I think we were completely right; I
remain of the same opinion still – I think it to be, not merely my
right, but my duty to question the truth of everything and the authority of everyone, to regard nothing as sacred and to hold nothing
in religious respect. That attitude was encouraged by the climate of
scepticism and revolt into which we were born and by Moore's ingenuous passion for truth. The dictionary, however, gives an alternative meaning for the word 'revere'; it may mean 'to regard with
deep respect and warm approbation'. It is not true that we lacked
reverence for everything and everyone in that sense of the word. After
questioning the truth and utility of everything and after refusing to
accept or swallow anything or anyone on the mere 'authority' of anyone, in fact after exercising our own judgment, there were many
things and persons regarded by us with 'deep respect and warm approbation': truth, beauty, works of art, some customs, friendship, love,
many living men and women and many of the dead.

The young are not only ruthless; they are often perfectionist; if
they are intelligent, they are inclined to react against the beliefs, which
have hardened into the fossilized dogmas of the previous generation.
To the middle-aged, who have forgotten their youth, the young naturally seem to be not only wrong, but wrong-headed (and indeed
they naturally often are); to the middle-aged and the old, if they are
also respectable, the young seem to be, not only wrong, but intel-

lectually ill-mannered (and indeed they often are). In 1903 we were often absurd, wrong, wrong-headed, ill-mannered; but in 1903 we were right in refusing to regard as sacred and exalted, to hold in religious respect, the extraordinary accomplishment of our predecessors in the ordering of life or the elaborate framework which they had devised to protect this order. We were right to question the truth and authority of all this, of respectability and the establishment, and to give our deep respect and warm approbation only to what in the establishment (and outside it) stood the test and ordeal of such questioning.

It will be remembered that Maynard's *Memoir*, in which he analyses the state of our minds (and Moore's) when we were undergraduates, starts with an account of a breakfast party in Bertrand Russell's rooms in Cambridge, at which only Russell, Maynard, and D.H. Lawrence were present. . . .

In this, and indeed in the whole of the *Memoir*, Maynard confuses, I think, two periods of his and of our lives. When our Cambridge days were over, there grew up in London during the years 1907 to 1914 a society or group of people which became publicly known as Bloomsbury. Later in my autobiography I shall have to say a good deal about Bloomsbury, the private nature and the public picture. Here all I need say is that Bloomsbury grew directly out of Cambridge; it consisted of a number of intimate friends who had been at Trinity and King's and were now working in London, most of them living in Bloomsbury.

Lawrence's breakfast party took place in 1914 or 1915. The people to whom he refers are not the undergraduates of 1903, but Bloomsbury, and a great deal of what Maynard wrote in his *Memoir* is true of Bloomsbury in 1914, but not true of the undergraduates of 1903. In 1903 we had all the inexperience, virginity, seriousness, intellectual puritanism of youth. In 1914 we had all, in various ways or places, been knocking about the world for ten or eleven years. A good deal of the bloom of ignorance and other things had been brushed off us. *Principia Ethica* had passed into our unconscious and was now merely a part of our super-ego; we no longer argued about it as a guide to practical life. Some of us were 'men of the world' or even Don Juans, and all round us there was taking place the revolt (which we ourselves in our small way helped to start) against the Victorian morality and code of conduct. In 1914 little or no attention was paid to Moore's fifth chapter on 'Ethics in Relation to Conduct', and pleasure, once rejected by us theoretically, had come to be accepted as a very considerable good in itself. But this was not the case in 1903.

Leonard Woolf: Old Bloomsbury

Towards the end of his discussion of Cambridge in Sowing, *Leonard Woolf wrote 'by the time I left Cambridge I had become very intimate with Thoby Stephen and Lytton Strachey and knew their families, and so the foundations of what become known as Bloomsbury were laid' (180). But during the early formation of the Group Woolf was absent. For six and a half years he was an imperial civil servant in Ceylon. He returned in 1911 and was welcomed into Bloomsbury by his old college friends. He describes what he found Old Bloomsbury to be like in* Beginning Again. *In his later discussion of the Memoir Club, however (see pp. 153-4), he decided he was actually describing a kind of 'ur-Bloomsbury'.*

Yet Beginning Again *was not the first time Leonard Woolf had described Bloomsbury, old or ur. After writing a novel about Ceylon, he published in 1914 a second novel on Bloomsbury. Entitled* The Wise Virgins: A Story of Words, Opinions, and a Few Emotions, *the novel is, I think, the first published criticism of Bloomsbury. Appropriately, this criticism comes from within the Group. An idea of the criticism Woolf directs against some of the members (but not all, for the novel is dedicated to Desmond MacCarthy) can be seen in the following description of epicurean characters who rather closely resemble Clive and Vanessa Bell, Lytton Strachey, and Virginia Woolf:*

> *These epicures in the art of emotions and the emotions of art had emancipated themselves from the convention that there are some things that men and women cannot talk about, and they had done this so successfully that a stranger might at first have been led to conclude from their practice that those are the only things that men and women of intelligence can talk about. Such a conclusion would have been hasty. It was perhaps their weakness, at any rate intellectually, that they never did those things – but then they never did anything. (80)*

This attack is qualified in the novel as being from the point of view of a young suburban Jewish outsider who is the central character of The Wise Virgins. *Yet it has some similarities to Keynes's critique*

*of Old Bloomsbury. At the very least, the passage suggests that the
Group was never a mutual admiration society.*

The excerpts from Beginning Again *in which Woolf returns to
Moore's influence on himself and his friends contain perhaps the clear-
est statement of any piece in this collection of what the nature of
the Bloomsbury Group was, though the denial of 'a communal connection' between their works is overstated.*

On Monday, July 3rd, [1911] only three weeks after I had arrived
in England, I went and dined with Vanessa and Clive Bell in Gordon
Square. I was alone with them at dinner, but afterwards Virginia,
Duncan Grant, and Walter Lamb came in. This was, I suppose, so
far as I was concerned, the beginning of what came to be called
Bloomsbury.

'What came to be called Bloomsbury' by the outside world never
existed in the form given to it by the outside world. For 'Bloomsbury' was and is currently used as a term – usually of abuse – applied
to a largely imaginary group of persons with largely imaginary objects and characteristics. I was a member of this group and I was
also one of a small number of persons who did in fact eventually
form a kind of group of friends living in or around that district of
London legitimately called Bloomsbury. The term Bloomsbury can
legitimately be applied to this group and will be so applied in these
pages. Bloomsbury, in this sense, did not exist in 1911 when I returned
from Ceylon; it came into existence in the three years 1912 to 1914.
We did ourselves use the terms of ourselves before it was used by
the outside world, for in the 1920s and 1930s, when our own younger
generation were growing up and marrying and some of our generation were already dying, we used to talk of 'Old Bloomsbury', meaning the original members of our group of friends who between 1911
and 1914 came to live in or around Bloomsbury.

Old Bloomsbury consisted of the following people: the three Stephens: Vanessa, married to Clive Bell, Virginia, who married Leonard
Woolf, and Adrian, who married Karin Costello; Lytton Strachey;
Clive Bell; Leonard Woolf; Maynard Keynes; Duncan Grant; E.M.
Forster (who will be referred to in this book as Morgan Forster or
Morgan); Saxon Sydney-Turner; Roger Fry. Desmond MacCarthy and
his wife Molly, though they actually lived in Chelsea, were always
regarded by us as members of Old Bloomsbury. In the 1920s and
1930s, when Old Bloomsbury narrowed and widened into a newer
Bloomsbury, it lost through death Lytton and Roger and added to

its numbers Julian, Quentin, and Angelica Bell, and David (Bunny) Garnett, who married Angelica.[1]

That Monday night of July 3, 1911, when I dined with Vanessa and Clive in Gordon Square, as I said, Bloomsbury had not yet actually come into existence. The reasons were geographical. At that moment only Vanessa and Clive and Saxon lived in Bloomsbury. Virginia and Adrian lived in Fitzroy Square and Duncan in rooms nearby. Roger lived in a house outside Guildford; Lytton in Cambridge and Hampstead; Morgan Forster in Weybridge; Maynard Keynes, as a Fellow of King's College, in Cambridge. I was a visitor from Ceylon. Ten years later, when Old Bloomsbury had come into existence, Vanessa, Clive, Duncan, Maynard, Adrian, and Lytton all lived in Gordon Square; Virginia and I were in Tavistock Square, Morgan in Brunswick Square; Saxon in Great Ormond Street; Roger in Bernard Street. Thus we all lived geographically in Bloomsbury within a few minutes walk of one another.

I am not, in this book, writing a history of Bloomsbury in any of its forms or manifestations, real or imaginary, and I shall have, after these first pages, very little to say about it. I am trying to write my autobiography, a true account of my life in relation to the times and the society in which I have lived, to the work I have done, and to people, whether intimates, acquaintances, or public persons. The twelve included by me in the previous paragraphs as members of Old Bloomsbury had a great influence upon my life. The account of what happened to me during the ten or twelve years after my return from Ceylon will necessarily show how we came to congregate in those nostalgic London squares and the real nature of our congregation. Here there are one or two facts about us which I want to insist upon before going on with my narrative. We were and always remained primarily and fundamentally a group of friends. Our roots and the roots of our friendship were in the University of Cambridge. Of the thirteen persons mentioned above three are women and ten men; of the ten men nine had been at Cambridge, and all of us, except Roger, had been more or less contemporaries at Trinity and King's and were intimate friends before I went to Ceylon.

---

1 There is proof of this chronological classification. We had what we called a Memoir Club, *i.e.* we met from time to time and we each in turn read a chapter, as it were, of autobiography. The original thirteen members of the Memoir Club were the thirteen members of Old Bloomsbury given above. Twenty years later the four younger persons were members.

There is another point. In the first volume of my autobiography, in dealing with my years at Cambridge, I said that it was 'necessary here to say something about the Society – The Apostles – because of the immense importance it had for us, its influence upon our minds, our friendships, our lives'. Of the ten men of Old Bloomsbury only Clive, Adrian and Duncan were not Apostles. Of the other seven of us, Desmond, Morgan, Lytton, Saxon, Maynard, and I, all overlapped more or less at Cambridge and had already grown into a peculiar intimacy there as active members of the Society. I tried in *Sowing* to give some idea of the character of G.E. Moore and of his tremendous intellectual (and also emotional) influence upon us and upon the Society of those days. The main things which Moore instilled deep into our minds and characters were his peculiar passion for truth, for clarity and common sense, and a passionate belief in certain values. I have said that Moore's influence upon us was lifelong. How profound it was is shown by what Maynard Keynes wrote in his book *Two Memoirs*. What Moore and his *Principia Ethica* gave to us as young men and what we sixty years ago embraced with the violence and optimism of youth Maynard calls a religion and he is affectionately critical of its and our adolescent one-sidedness and absurdities. But as a final summing up he writes:

It seems to me looking back that this religion of ours was a very good one to grow up under. It remains nearer the truth than any other that I know, with less irrelevant extraneous matter and nothing to be ashamed of; though it is a comfort today to be able to discard with a good conscience the calculus and the mensuration and the duty to know *exactly* what one means and feels. It was a purer, sweeter air by far than Freud cum Marx. It is still my religion under the surface.

That is the point: under the surface all six of us, Desmond, Lytton, Saxon, Morgan, Maynard, and I, had been permanently inoculated with Moore and Moorism; and even Roger, who was seven years older than Moore and highly critical of his philosophy, continually proved by his criticism of Moorism that he was 'under the surface' a Moorist. Through us and through *Principia Ethica* and four others, Vanessa and Virginia, Clive and Duncan, were deeply affected by the astringent influence of Moore and the purification of that divinely cathartic question which echoed through the Cambridge Courts of my youth as it had 2,300 years before echoed through the streets of Socratic Athens: 'What do you mean by that?' Artistically the purification can, I think, be traced in the clarity, light, absence of humbug in Virginia's literary style and perhaps in Vanessa's painting. They have the quality noted by Maynard in Moorism, the getting rid of 'irrelevant extraneous matter'.

There have often been groups of people, writers and artists, who were not only friends, but were consciously united by a common doctrine and object, or purpose artistic or social. The utilitarians, the Lake poets, the French impressionists, the English Pre-Raphaelites were groups of this kind. Our groups was quite different. Its basis was friendship, which in some cases developed into love and marriage. The colour of our minds and thought had been given to us by the climate of Cambridge and Moore's philosophy, much as the climate of England gives one colour to the face of an Englishman while the climate of India gives a quite different colour to the face of a Tamil. But we had no common theory, system, or principles which we wanted to convert the world to; we were not proselytizers, missionaries, crusaders, or even propagandists. It is true that Maynard produced the system or theory of Keynesian economics which has had a great effect upon the theory and practice of economics, finance, and politics; that Roger, Vanessa, Duncan, and Clive played important parts, as painters or critics, in what came to be known as the Post-Impressionist Movement. But Maynard's crusade for Keynesian economics against the orthodoxy of the Banks and academic economists, and Roger's crusade for Post-Impressionism and 'significant form' against the orthodoxy of academic 'representational' painters and aestheticians were just as purely individual as Virginia's writing of *The Waves* – they had nothing to do with any group. For there was no more a communal connection between Roger's 'Critical and Speculative Essays on Art', Maynard's *The General Theory of Employment, Interest and Money*, and Virginia's *Orlando* than there was between Bentham's *Theory of Legislation*, Hazlitt's *Principal Picture Galleries in England*, and Byron's *Don Juan*.

I can now return to Monday night, July 3, 1911. In Cambridge during my week-end there, as I have said, I had had the reassuring pleasure of finding men and things, truths and values, to whom or to which I had given the love or loyalty of youth, unchanged and unchanging. In Gordon Square I re-entered a society which had completely changed since I left it seven years before, but in which I found myself immediately and completely at home. Nothing is more silly than the principle, which too often fatally influences practice, that you ought to be consistent in your feelings and your likes and dislikes. Where taste is concerned there is no law of contradiction. It is absurd

to think, as many people do, that the love of cats or claret is a reason
or excuse for not loving dogs or burgundy. So I get as much pleasure
from the comfort of finding that nothing has changed as from the
excitement of finding that everything is new.

There had certainly been a profound revolution in Gordon Square.
I had dined in 46 Gordon Square with Thoby and his two sisters,
the Misses Stephen, in 1904 only a few days before I left England
for Ceylon. Now seven years later in the same rooms meeting again
for the first time Vanessa, Virginia, Clive, Duncan, and Walter Lamb
I found that almost the only things which had not changed were
the furniture and the extraordinary beauty of the two Miss
Stephens. . . .

Leonard Woolf: The Second Post-Impressionist Exhibition

*Leonard Woolf was in Ceylon during the first post-impressionist ex-
hibition. His experiences as secretary for the second complement Desmond MacCarthy's account of the first (see pp. 74–8).*

The first job which I took was a curious one. The second Post-
Impressionist Exhibition, organized by Roger Fry, opened in the
Grafton Galleries in the autumn of 1912. In Spain on our honeymoon
I got an urgent message from Roger asking me whether I would act
as secretary of the show on our return. I agreed to do so until, I
think, the end of the year. It was a strange and for me new experience.
The first room was filled with Cézanne water-colours. The highlights
in the second room were two enormous pictures of more than life-
size figures by Matisse and three or four Picassos. There was also
a Bonnard and a good picture by Marchand. Large numbers of people
came to the exhibition, and nine out of ten of them either roared
with laughter at the pictures or were enraged by them. The British
middle class – and, as far as that goes, the aristocracy and working
class – are incorrigibly philistine, and their taste is impeccably bad.
Anything new in the arts, particularly if it is good, infuriates them
and they condemn it as either immoral or ridiculous or both. As secretary I sat at my table in the large second room of the galleries
prepared to deal with enquiries from possible purchasers or answer
any questions about the pictures. I was kept busy all the time. The
whole business gave me a lamentable view of human nature, its rank

stupidity and uncharitableness. I used to think, as I sat there, how much nicer were the Tamil or Sinhalese villagers who crowded into the veranda of my Ceylon kachcheri than these smug, well dressed, ill-mannered, well-to-do Londoners. Hardly any of them made the slightest attempt to look at, let alone understand, the pictures, and the same inane questions or remarks were repeated to me all day long. And every now and then some well groomed, red faced gentleman, oozing the undercut of the best beef and the most succulent of chops, carrying his top hat and grey suede gloves, would come up to my table and abuse the pictures and me with the greatest rudeness.

There were, of course, consolations. Dealing with possible purchasers was always amusing and sometimes exciting. Occasionally one had an interesting conversation with a stranger. Sometimes it was amusing to go round the rooms with Roger and a distinguished visitor. . . . Roger came to the gallery every day and spent quite a lot of time there. We used to go down into the bowels of the earth about 4 o'clock and have tea with Miss Wotherston, the secretary, who inhabited the vast basement, and we were often joined by Herbert Cook who owned Doughty House, Richmond, and a superb collection of pictures. I saw so much of Roger that at the end of my time at the Grafton Galleries I knew him much better than when I first went there. His character was more full of contradictions even than that of most human beings. He was one of the most charming and gentle of men; born a double dyed Quaker, he had in many respects revolted against the beliefs and morals of The Friends, and yet deep down in his mind and character he remained profoundly, and I think unconsciously, influenced by them. Like his six remarkable sisters, he had a Quaker's uncompromising sense of public duty and responsibility and, though he would have indignantly repudiated this, ultimately the Quaker's ethical austerity. And yet there were elements in his psychology which contradicted all these characteristics. I was more than once surprised by his ruthlessness and what to me seemed to be almost unscrupulousness in business. For instance, we discovered, shortly after I took on the secretaryship, that when Roger had been preparing the exhibition and asking people to exhibit, owing to a mistake of his, they had been offered much too favourable terms – the figure for the Exhibition's commission on sales was much too low. When the time came to pay artists their share of the purchase amounts of pictures sold, Roger insisted upon deducting a higher commission without any explanation or apology to the painters. Most of them meekly accepted what they were given, but Wyndham Lewis, at best of times a bilious and cantankerous man, protested violently. Roger was adamant in ignoring him and his demands; Lewis never forgave Roger, and, as I was a kind of buffer between them, he also never forgave me.

Leonard Woolf: The Beginnings of the Hogarth Press

In 1915 Virginia and Leonard Woolf moved into an eighteenth-century house in the Richmond district of London. The Hogarth Press, which they started there in 1917, took its name from the house. All of Virginia's books, except her first two novels, and most of Leonard's were published by the Hogarth Press. The Press published other works of Bloomsbury, including shorter writings by Forster, Fry, and Clive Bell as well as woodcuts by Vanessa Bell, Fry, Grant, and Carrington. Vanessa also designed the dustjackets of Virginia's novels.

Leonard Woolf's story of the founding of the Hogarth Press (it was started as a manual occupation to take Virginia's mind off her writing) is an important part of the history of the Bloomsbury Group. The taste of the Press was to a large extent the taste of Bloomsbury, and the works it published reflect the wide spectrum of Bloomsbury's current interest and ideas. But the significance of the Press extends considerably beyond Bloomsbury; among its publications are some of the most influential works of twentieth-century English literature. It is worth pointing out for those who think Bloomsbury was out of sympathy with the major writers of their time that the Press published T.S. Eliot's The Waste Land *in 1923 and might have published James Joyce's* Ulysses *but were advised that no respectable English printer would print the book for them. The Hogarth Press also published translations of Rilke, the first book in English on Proust (by Clive Bell), and the standard English edition of Freud's works that Lytton's brother James translated. In later volumes of his autobiography Leonard Woolf tells the story of the various series of books the Press started, including Freud's, and also gives an account of, in his words, the 'succession of brilliant and not quite so brilliant young men' who came to the Press as assistants and managers. (For a view of Bloomsbury from the basement of the Hogarth Press, see the account by John Lehmann, pp. 386-7.)*

On March 23, 1917, we were walking one afternoon up Farringdon Street from Fleet Street to Holborn Viaduct when we passed the Excelsior Printing Supply Co. It was not a very large firm, but it sold every kind of printing machine and material, from a handpress and type to a composing stick. Nearly all the implements of printing are materially attractive and we stared through the window at them rather like two hungry children gazing at buns and cakes in a baker shop window. I do not know which of us first suggested that we should go inside and see whether we could buy a machine and type and teach ourselves. We went in and explained our desire and dilemma to a very sympathetic man in a brown overall. He was extremely encouraging. He could not only sell us a printing machine, type, chases, cases, and all the necessary implements, but also a sixteen-page pamphlet which would infallibly teach us how to print. There was no need to go to a school of printing or to become an apprentice; if we read his pamphlet and followed the instructions, we should soon find that we were competent printers. Before we left the shop we had bought a small hand-press, some Old Face type, and all the necessary implements and materials for a sum of £19.5s. 5d. The machine was small enough to stand on a kitchen table; it was an ordinary platen design; you worked it by pulling down the handle which brought the platen and paper up against the type in its chase. You could print one demy octavo page on it, and, I think, you could just squeeze in two crown octavo pages.

When the stuff was delivered to us in Richmond, we set it all up in the dining-room and started to teach ourselves to print. The Excelsior man proved to be right; by following the directions in the pamphlet we found that we could pretty soon set the type, lock it up in the chase, ink the rollers, and machine a fairly legible printed page. After a month we thought we had become sufficiently proficient to print a page of a book or pamphlet. We decided to print a paper-covered pamphlet containing a story by each of us and to try to sell it by subscription to a limited number of people whom we would circularize. Our idea was that, if this succeeded, we might go on to print and publish in the same way poems or other short works which the commercial publisher would not look at.

We set to work and printed a thirty-two page pamphlet, demy octavo, with the following title page:

Publication No. 1.

TWO STORIES

WRITTEN AND PRINTED

BY

VIRGINIA WOOLF

AND

L.S. WOOLF

HOGARTH PRESS

RICHMOND

1917

Virginia's story was *The Mark on the Wall* and mine was *Three Jews*. We even had the temerity to print four woodcuts by Carrington. I must say, looking at a copy of this curious publication today, that the printing is rather creditable for two persons who had taught themselves for a month in a dining-room. The setting, inking, impression are really not bad. What is quite wrong is the backing, for I had not yet realized that a page on one side of the sheet must be printed so that it falls exactly on the back of the page on the other side of the sheet.

We began to print *Two Stories* on May 3 in an edition of about 150 copies. We bound it ourselves by stitching it into paper covers. We took a good deal of trouble to find some rather unusual, gay Japanese paper for the covers. For many years we gave much time and care to finding beautiful, uncommon, and sometimes cheerful paper for binding our books, and, as the first publishers to do this, I think we started a fashion which many of the regular, old established publishers followed. We got papers from all over the place, including some brilliantly patterned from Czechoslovakia, and we also had some marbled covers made for us by Roger Fry's daughter in Paris. I bought a small quantity of Caslon Old Face Titling type and used it for printing the covers.

We printed a circular offering Publication No 1 for 1s 6d net and explaining that we in The Hogarth Press proposed to print and publish in the same way from time to time paper-covered pamphlets or small books, printed entirely by our two selves, which would have little or no chance of being published by ordinary publishers. We invited people to become subscribers to the publications of The Hogarth Press, either A subscribers to whom all publications would automatically be sent, or B subscribers who would be notified of each publication as it appeared. We sent this notice to people whom we knew or who, we thought, might be interested in our publications. I do not know how many people we circularized, but we published in July and by the end of the month we had practically sold out the edition for we had sold 124 copies. (The total number finally sold was 134.) I still have a list of the 87 people who bought the 134 copies and all but five or six of them were friends or acquaintances. There are some rather unexpected names among them, *e.g.* Charles Trevelyan, MP, Arthur Ponsonby, MP, Mrs Sidney Webb, and Mrs Bernard Shaw. The total cost of production was £3. 7s. od., which included the noble sum of 15s. to Carrington for the woodcuts, 12s. 6d. for paper, and 10s. for the cover paper. The two authors were not paid any royalty. The total receipts were £10. 8s. od., so that the net profit was £7. 1s. od. Eventually forty-five people became A subscribers and forty-three B subscribers. Among the A subscribers was one bookseller, James Bain of what was then King William Street, Strand, and except for him every copy of our first publication was sold to private persons at the full published price. By 1923 the Press had developed to such an extent that we had become more or less ordinary publishers, selling our books mainly to booksellers at the usual discount, and we therefore gave up the subscriber system altogether.

We so much enjoyed producing *Two Stories* and its sale had been so successful (134 copies!) that we were induced to go on to something more ambitious. Katherine Mansfield and Murry were extremely interested in what we were doing, and Katherine offered us for Publication No 2 a long short story which she had written, *Prelude*. When I look at my copy of *Prelude* today, I am astonished at our courage and energy in attempting it and producing it only a year after we had started to teach ourselves to print. For we printed only in the afternoon and even so not every afternoon; it is a sixty-eight-page book and we printed and bound it entirely with our own hands. The edition must have consisted of nearly 300 copies for, when it went out of print, we had sold 257 copies. Virginia did most of the setting and I did all the machining, though I did set when there was nothing to machine.

I did not machine *Prelude* on our small handpress; in fact, it would have taken much too long to do it page by page. I machined it on a large platen machine which printed four crown octavo pages at a time and which belonged to a jobbing printer called McDermott. . . .

By having [Virginia Woolf's short stories] *Monday or Tuesday* printed
for us [in 1921] by a commercial printer, we were, of course, aban-
doning the original idea of the Press, which was to print small books
ourselves. In fact we had been already in 1919 forced fortuitously
to take a similar step, the first step on the path which was to end
in our becoming regular and professional publishers. In 1918 we
printed two small books: *Poems* by T.S. Eliot and *Kew Gardens* by
Virginia. Of Tom's *Poems* we printed rather fewer than 250 copies.
We published it in May 1919 price 2s. 6d. and it went out of print
in the middle of 1920. Of *Kew Gardens* we printed about 170 copies
(the total sold of the first edition was 148). We published it on May
12, 1919, at 2s. When we started printing and publishing with our
Publication No 1, we did not send out any review copies, but in the
case of *Prelude*, Tom's *Poems*, and *Kew Gardens* we sent review copies
to *The Times Literary Supplement*. By May 31 we had sold 49 copies
of *Kew Gardens*. On Tuesday, May 27, we went to Asham and stayed
there for a week, returning to Richmond on June 3rd. In the previous
week a review of *Kew Gardens* had appeared in the *Literary Supplement* giving it tremendous praise. When we opened the front door
of Hogarth House, we found the hall covered with envelopes and
postcards containing orders from booksellers all over the country.
It was impossible for us to start printing enough copies to meet these
orders, so we went to a printer, Richard Madley, and got him to
print a second edition of 500 copies, which cost us £8. 9s. 6d. It was
sold out by the end of 1920 and we did not reprint.

The expansion of the Press into something which we had never
intended or originally envisaged can be seen in the following list
of books published by us in the first four years of its existence:

1917   L. and V. Woolf. *Two Stories*. Printed and bound by
         us.
1918   K. Mansfield. *Prelude*. Printed and bound by us.
1919   V. Woolf. *Kew Gardens*. 1st ed. printed and bound by us.
         T.S. Eliot. *Poems*. Printed and bound by us.
         J. Middleton Murry. *Critic in Judgment*. Printed for us.
1920   E.M. Forster. *Story of the Siren*. Printed and bound by
         us.
         Hope Mirrlees. *Paris*. Printed and bound by us.
         L. Pearsall Smith. *Stories from the Old Testament*. Printed for
         us.
         Gorky. *Reminiscences of Tolstoi*. Printed for us.

Leonard Woolf: The Memoir Club

*Although Leonard Woolf's recollection of the Memoir Club is not
quite correct in stating that its members were all the original ones
of Bloomsbury, his account of the Club valuably emphasizes the continuity of Bloomsbury.*

*In an undated one-page fragment of a paper written for the Memoir
Club, Woolf expressed himself a little more directly about the Club.
After admitting that he had experienced considerable difficulty in writ-
ing for it, he went on to explain why.*

> *The downfall – I use the word in the sense given to it by the servant class
> – of Bloomsbury was its intolerance of every one and every thing which
> was not all the time amusing. Perhaps that is an exaggeration, but it is
> true that, just as one hesitated in Moore's rooms at Cambridge to say any-
> thing amusing which was not also profound and true, so in Bloomsbury
> one hesitated to say anything true or profound unless it was also amusing.
> In my experience what is amusing is very rarely true or profound, and
> what is true or profound is hardly ever amusing.*

*Despite his caveats, or perhaps because of them, Leonard Woolf be-
came Bloomsbury's chief memoirist.*

I find some difficulty in determining exactly when what is called
Bloomsbury came into existence. In *Beginning Again* [see pp.
141-2] I treated it as having come into existence in the three years
1912 to 1914. I should now prefer to say that in those three years
a kind of ur-Bloomsbury came into existence. Of the thirteen members
of Old Bloomsbury, as we came to call it, only eight at that time
actually lived in Bloomsbury: Clive and Vanessa in Gordon Square
and Virginia, Adrian, Duncan Grant, Maynard Keynes, and myself
in Brunswick Square, with Saxon Sydney-Turner in Great Ormond
Street. It was not until Lytton Strachey, Roger Fry, and Morgan Forster came into the locality, so that we were all continually meeting
one another, that our society became complete, and that did not
happen until some years after the war. First the war scattered us completely and then Virginia's illness, by banishing us to the outer suburb
of Richmond, made any return to our day-to-day intimacy impossible.
But as Virginia's health improved and it became possible for us to
go up to London more often to parties and other meetings, what
archaeologists might call a second period of ur-Bloomsbury began.

For instance, in March 1920 we started the Memoir Club and on March 6 we met in Gordon Square, dined together, and listed to or read our memoirs.

The original thirteen members of the Memoir Club, identical with the original thirteen members of old Bloomsbury, were all intimate friends, and it was agreed that we should be absolutely frank in what we wrote and read. Absolute frankness, even among the most intimate, tends to be relative frankness; I think that in our reminiscences what we said was absolutely true, but absolute truth was sometimes filtered through some discretion and reticence. At first the memoirs were fairly short; at the first meeting seven people read. But as time went on, what people read become longer and, in a sense, more serious, so that after a few years normally only two memoirs were read in an evening. They were usually very amusing, but they were sometimes something more. Two by Maynard were as brilliant and highly polished as anything he wrote – one describing his negotiations with the German delegates and, in particular, Dr Melchior, in the railway carriages at Trèves after the 1914 War, and the other about Moore's influence upon us and our early beliefs at Cambridge – and these were after his death published, exactly as they were originally read to us, under the title *Two Memoirs*. Some of Virginia's were also brilliant, and Vanessa developed a remarkable talent in a fantastic narrative of a labyrinthine domestic crisis. The years went by and the Club changed as the old inhabitants died and the younger generation were elected. The last meeting took place, I think, in 1956, thirty-six years after the first meeting. Only four of the original thirteen members were left, though in all ten members came to the meeting.

PART TWO

Bloomsberries

Introduction

The memoirs of the previous section reveal how the individual members experienced and regarded the Bloomsbury Group. In this section various members of the Group (or in several instances their children) examine directly and obliquely the relations of the individual members to Bloomsbury. The differing nature of these connections can be illuminated by one of the central principles of G.E. Moore's *Principia Ethica*. Moore argued that the worth of what he termed an organic whole 'bears no regular proportion to the sum of the values of its parts' (79). (Moore illustrates his conception of an organic whole by explaining how the value of a whole made up of a state of consciousness of a beautiful object is not simply the sum of the value of consciousness and the object, neither of which has much value in itself.) Moore's idea is useful in assessing not only the value of Bloomsbury's individuals for the Group but also the effect that Bloomsbury had on them. The importance of these individuals and their work outside the Group bore no regular proportion to their importance within the organic whole that was Bloomsbury. Thus an examination of Bloomsbury has to include a consideration of the relations of the members to the Group and the Group to its members.

According to Clive Bell it was Molly MacCarthy who coined the word 'Bloomsberries' around 1910 or 1911 when arranging her friends topographically (see p. 117). The term remains useful to distinguish the parts of Bloomsbury from the whole. The Bloomsberries discussed in this section have been arranged by age – nearly twenty years separate the eldest from the youngest – but couples have also been placed together. The first section includes practically all the available memoirs on Bloomsbury by its members, but here, for some of the Bloomsberries, there is a considerable amount of writing from which to choose. In making selections I have tried to choose pieces that reflect the interrelations of the individuals and the Group.

Roger Fry by Virginia Woolf

After Roger Fry's death in 1934 his sister Margery asked Virginia Woolf to take up Fry's suggestion that she should 'put into practice your theories of the biographer's craft in a portrait of himself.' When a previous suggestion for a full-length Bloomsbury biography had arisen in Bloomsbury after Lytton Strachey's death, it was quickly realized that a true biography of him could never be a reticent one; yet at the time no other kind was possible. Reticence remained one of the difficulties for Virginia Woolf's life of Fry, who had a number of affairs after his wife became insane. There were pressures from Fry's sisters, and the biographer herself may have been reluctant to write of Fry's love for her own sister.

The extracts selected have mainly to do with Fry's significance as an art critic and as a friend. Both aspects show his importance for Bloomsbury. Aside from remarks about mutual admiration societies ('a mutual admiration society, if such things exist – and according to some observers they do – would have expelled Roger Fry at the first meeting' – see p. 169), Woolf does not treat Fry's relation to Bloomsbury directly, though it is implicit in almost everything that is said here.

But if Oxford rejected him [for the Slade Professorship in 1927], London accepted him. He found in these years to his amazement that he could fill the Queen's Hall when he lectured upon art. The winter exhibitions at Burlington House gave him the opportunity. He lectured on Flemish art, on French, on Italian art; and the hall was filled. The audience, as one of them records, 'was enthusiastic and rapt'. It was an astonishing feat. There was the Queen's Hall, full those winter evenings of greenish mist, echoing with the sneezings and coughings of the afflicted flock. And to entertain them there was nothing but a gentleman in evening dress with a long stick in his hand in front of a cadaverous sheet. How could contact be established? How could the world of spiritual reality emerge in those uncongenial surroundings? At first by 'personality' – the attraction, as Mr Hannay says, 'of the whole man'. 'He had only to point to a passage in a picture . . . and to murmur the word "plasticity" and a magical atmosphere was created.' The voice in which he murmured was conciliatory, urbane, humorous. It conveyed what was not so perceptible in his writing – the tolerance, the wide experience, that lay behind the hob-goblin mask of the man who had the reputation of being either a crack-brained theorist or the irresponsible champion of impossible beliefs. But as he went on it was clear that the beliefs were still there. Many listeners might have inferred that the lecturer, who looked like a 'fasting friar with a rope round his waist' in spite of his evening dress, was inviting them to the practice of a new kind of religion. He was praising a new kind of saint – the artist who leads his laborious life 'indifferent to the world's praise or blame'; who must be poor in spirit, humble, and doggedly true to his own convictions. And the penalty for back-sliding was pronounced – if he lies 'he is cut off from the chief source of his inspiration'. No Fry among all the generations of Frys could have spoken with greater fervour of the claims of the spirit, or invoked doom with more severity. But then, 'Slide, please', he said. And there was the picture – Rembrandt, Chardin, Poussin, Cézanne – in black and white upon the screen. And the lecturer pointed. His long wand, trembling like the antenna of some miraculously sensitive insect, settled upon some 'rhythmical phrase', some sequence; some diagonal. And then he went on to make the audience see – 'the gem-like notes; the aquamarines; and topazes that lie in the hollow of his satin gowns; bleaching the lights to evanescent pallors'. Somehow the black-and-white slide on the screen became radiant through the mist, and took on the grain and texture of the actual canvas.

All that he had done again and again in his books. But here there was a difference. As the next slide slid over the sheet there was a pause. He gazed afresh at the picture. And then in a flash he found the word he wanted; he added on the spur of the moment what he had just seen as if for the first time. That, perhaps, was the secret of his hold over his audience. They could see the sensation strike and form; he could lay bare the very moment of perception. So with pauses and spurts the world of spiritual reality emerged in slide after slide – in Poussin, in Chardin, in Rembrandt, in Cézanne – in its uplands and its lowlands, all connected, all somehow made whole and entire, upon the great screen in the Queen's Hall. And finally the lecturer, after looking long through his spectacles, came to a pause. He was pointing to a late work by Cézanne, and he was baffled. He shook his head; his stick rested on the floor. It went, he said, far beyond any analysis of which he was capable. And so instead of saying, 'Next slide', he bowed, and the audience emptied itself into Langham Place.

For two hours they had been looking at pictures. But they had seen one of which the lecturer himself was unconscious – the outline of the man against the screen, an ascetic figure in evening dress who paused and pondered, and then raised his stick and pointed. That was a picture that would remain in memory together with the rest, a rough sketch that would serve many of the audience in years to come as the portrait of a great critic, a man of profound sensibility but of exacting honesty, who, when reason could penetrate no further, broke off; but was convinced, and convinced others, that what he saw was there.

The success of the lectures surprised him. Perhaps he had misjudged the British public. Perhaps in its queer way the public had more feeling for art than he allowed. At any rate there was the fact –

> under certain conditions the English public becomes interested in 'high-brow' stuff. . . . Roger Fry had the power of making other people feel the importance of art . . . In spite of a complete absence of purple passages or playing to the gallery he was able to keep his audience at a high pitch of interest and curiosity.

People, drawn from all classes and callings, would fill the Queen's Hall when he lectured. And not only would they fill the Queen's Hall – they threatened to fill Bernard Street into the bargain. 'I am as usual', he wrote after one of these lectures, 'swamped by telephone calls and people at me all the time. Miss —— wishes to know if she may come and look at my Matisse. Mr —— wants advice on a lot of old masters . . . A. wants to borrow my Vlaminck. B. came to consult me about his son's education as an art student.' And there were the letters – the innumerable letters. One from a schoolgirl ran:

> Dear Mr Fry . . . Our art mistress from school took a party to the Persian art Exhibition and we were attracted in many pictures, to people with their first fingers held to their lips. Also in some designs animals are seen biting each other. If these mean anything, or are symbolical in any way, I should be very grateful if you could tell me. Another thing is, does our common cat originate from Persia?

He was delighted to answer schoolgirls' questions. He was delighted to give advice. He would show 'hordes of school marms from the USA armed with note-books seeking information', round his rooms; and then 'a very intelligent young man from Manchester' who was interested in Chinese pottery; and then go on to a committee meeting

at Burlington House to arrange the Italian Exhibition; and from that
to a committee meeting of the *Burlington Magazine*; and when he
got home in the evening, there was somebody waiting to 'ask my
advice about getting up a show of Russian ikons'. That was an ordinary day's work; and it was no wonder that at the end of a season
of such days he would exclaim 'London's impossible!'

It was an exclamation that burst forth irrepressibly every year about
February or March. It was necessary to escape from London and its
attractions and distractions if he was to have any peace at all. And
it was equally necessary if he was to continue lecturing. He must
fill his cistern from the main source; he must see pictures again. And
so he was off – to Berlin, to Tunis, to Sicily, to Rome, to Holland,
to Spain and again and again to France. The old pictures must be
seen once more; they must be seen afresh. 'I spent the afternoon in
the Louvre. I tried to forget all my ideas and theories and to look
at everything as though I'd never seen it before . . . It's only so that
one can make discoveries . . . Each work must be a new and a nameless
experience.'

His method was the same in his sixties as it had been in his thirties.
He went to the gallery as soon as it was opened; for six hours he
worked steadily round, looking at each picture in turn, and making
rough notes in pencil. When lunch-time came he was always taken
by surprise; and always, as in the old days, he compared his impressions with his companion's, and scribbled his theories down in letters
to friends at home. I'm getting my aesthetic feeling absolutely exhausted with the amount I've looked at. I doubt if I've ever had such
hard work in my life – one's absolutely driven to it by the wealth
of these museums', he wrote to Vanessa Bell from Berlin in 1928.
A long list of pictures seen and noted follows. There was a Menzel;
there was Liebermann; there was Trübner. There were 'magnificent
Cézannes'; there were Manets. There was Egyptian art; there was the
art of Central Asia. Berlin had ten galleries filled with paintings and
sculptures and miniatures, whereas the British Museum had only a
few cases. Stimulated by all these sights, theories began to form themselves; perhaps too rapidly – perhaps they might have to be scrapped.
'In fact I don't know what I'm getting at at all. All sorts of vague
hints at new aesthetics seem to be simmering in my brain . . .'

It was thus, in front of the pictures themselves, that the material
for the lectures was collected. It was from these new and nameless
experiences that vague hints at new aesthetics came into being. Then
the vagueness had to be expelled; the simmer had to be spun into

a tough thread of argument that held the whole together. And after the lecture had been given the drudgery of re-writing the spoken word would begin. The obstinate, the elusive, word had to be found, had to be coined, had to be 'curled round' the sensation. And so at last the books came out one after another – the books on French art, and Flemish art and British art; the books on separate painters; the books on whole periods of art; the essays upon Persian art and Chinese art and Russian art; the pamphlets upon Architecture; upon Art and Psychology – all those books and essays and articles upon which his claim to be called the greatest critic of his time depends.

But if, in order to write and lecture, it was necessary to see pictures 'as if for the first time', it was almost equally necessary to see friends. Ideas must be sketched on other people's minds. Theories must be discussed, preferably with someone, like Charles Mauron, who could demolish them. But even if the friend was incapable of demolishing them, they must be shared. 'He was so sociable that he could never enjoy anything without at once feeling the need to share it with those around him', as M. Mauron says. It was the desire to share, to have two pairs of eyes to see with, and somebody at hand, or at least within reach of the pen, to argue with that made him scribble those letters which it is impossible to quote in full, for they have neither beginning, middle nor end, and are often illustrated with a sketch of a landscape, or with the profile of a sausage-maker's wife at Royat, or with a few notes to indicate what he was 'getting at' in his own picture. But if the letters cannot be quoted in full, here is a complete post-card:

> In the train going to Edinburgh. I wonder whether you could send me to Edinburgh 1. my béret which is very nice for travelling. 2. Slides of Picasso's sculptures, those queer birds. They're in the Vitality series upstairs I think and still all together and on the bureau. 3. A negro head [sketch] the very blank one with no features. It's in the negro lecture which I left on the old French chest of drawers in my sitting-room. The carriage is scarcely warmed. Damn the English.

'Damn the English' – the words ceased to apply to the English – was not England the only country where free speech was allowed? But they may serve as a hint that he was not one of those characters who have, as we are told by their biographers, an instinctive love of their kind. His kind often amazed him and shocked him. His eyes, shining beneath the bushy black eyebrows, would fix themselves suddenly, and, looking as formidable as his father the Judge, he would pronounce judgment. 'You are bolstering people up in their natural beastliness', his words to Sir Charles Holmes who had given him, innocently, a book on fishing recall some awkward moments in his company. But if not gregarious he was sociable – 'incurably sociable' he called himself. His friends meant so much to him that he would give up the delights of wandering from village to village, from gallery to gallery, in order to be with them. Spring after spring he would exclaim, 'I feel very much inclined never to come back to England, just to wander on into Spain and Morocco . . .', but the sentence would end, 'if you wretches will live in London, then to London I must be dragged back'.

A list of those friends would be a long one. It would include many famous names – the names of painters, writers, men of science, art experts, politicians. But it would include many names that are quite unknown – people met in trains, people met in inns, mad poets and melancholy undergraduates. Often he had forgotten their names; names mattered less and less to him. He went out into society sometimes, but he came back disillusioned. 'Your old friend', he wrote (to Virginia Woolf), 'went to that charming Princess . . . and came back with another illusion gone – he now knows that *all* aristocrats are virtuous but incredibly boring and refuses to suffer them any more . . . the said Princess having been his last desperate throw of the net on that barren shore.' After the war his old dream of a society in which people of all kinds met together in congenial surroundings, and talked about everything under the sun, had to be given up. People were too poor, their time was too occupied, and the English moreover had little gift for discussing general ideas in public. . . .

But in London he was less ambitious. The attraction of London to him was that it was easy to get together little parties where old friends met new ones even if their names had slipped his memory. For if names mattered less and less, people mattered more and more. How much they mattered, how from one end of his life to the other he lived in his friendships, how in letter after letter he broke into praise of his friends – all that is not to be conveyed by lists of names. If certain friends – Lowes Dickinson, Desmond MacCarthy, Vanessa Bell, Philippa Strachey, the Maurons, his sister Margery – stand out, they are surrounded by so many others from so many different worlds, talking so many different languages, that to choose from among them or to say what it was that he got from each of them is impossible.

But to be with them was one of his chief pleasures. 'Do you realise what delightful little parties we shall be able to have?' he wrote when he moved to Bernard Street; and one of those little parties may stand as the type of many.

His guests found him writing. He had forgotten the time; he was trying to finish a lecture. But he was delighted to stop writing and to begin to talk. The room was as untidy as ever. Ink-bottles and coffee-cups, proof sheets and paint-brushes were piled on the tables and strewn on the floor. And there were the pictures – some framed, others stood against the wall. There was the Derain picture of a spectral dog in the snow; the blue Matisse picture of ships in the harbour. And there were the negro masks and the Chinese statues, and all the plates – the rare Persian china and the cheap peasant pottery that he had picked up for a farthing at a fair. Always there was something new to look at – a new picture, or a little panel of wood perhaps with a dim face upon it – very possibly it was the portrait of Dante, painted by Giotto and carried in Dante's funeral procession. The room was crowded, and for all Roger Fry's acute sensibility, he was curiously indifferent to physical comfort. The chairs had passed their prime; the lifts in the tube station opposite clanged incessantly; a flare of light came in from the arc-lamp in the street outside; and what he called 'the hymnology of Bernard Street' brayed from a loudspeaker next door. But it did not matter. 'The dinner', he wrote of one of those little parties, 'was a great success. The wild ducks were a trifle tough, but our friends are not really critical. And after dinner', the letter goes on,

we settled in to a good old Cambridge Apostolic discussion about existence, whether good was absolute or not. Charles [Mauron] and I representing modern science managed to make it clear that Oliver [Strachey] and Leonard [Woolf] were mystics. They could not accept the complete relativity of everything to human nature and the impossibility of talking at all about things in themselves. It's curious how difficult it is to root out that mediaeval habit of thinking of 'substances' of things existing apart from all relations, and yet really they have no possible meanings . . . Poor Oliver was horribly shocked to think he was in that *galère*. . . . It was a delightful talk. Philosophy was varied by some free criticisms of —— to begin with. He was left a good deal damaged, but with some sympathy for him as a character – when Oliver said, 'But the really wicked man is —— ' And then the hunt was up and a fine run across country. . . .

Fortunately the younger generation, his own children and the children of his friends, was growing up and proved of great help in carrying on the business of living. 'They are entirely lacking in reverence,' he noted. They had greatly improved upon his own generation. When they were small he would teach them the rudiments of chemistry, making a beautiful blue-green solution of copper sulphate, or brewing coal gas in a clay pipe plugged with plasticine on the drawing-room file. He would appear at a children's party glittering in chains and frying-pans bought at Woolworth's, a fancy dress which brought out, as fancy dress so often does, a spiritual likeness, in his case indisputably, to Don Quixote. Later he would arrive at their rooms in Cambridge and, remembering his own attitude to his elders, exclaim in delight, 'They talk about their own interest and their pleasure in life without troubling to recognize our presence'. But there he was wrong. They were well aware of his presence – of his humours, of his eccentricities; of his 'immense seriousness', and of his equally immense powers of enjoyment. He would plunge at once into his own interest and his own problems. He would make them help to translate Mallarmé, he would argue for hours on end with 'terrific Quaker scrupulosity and intellectual honesty'; and he would play chess, and through playing chess bring them to understand his views on aesthetics. 'He was extraordinarily good at gaining one's confidence,' one of those undergraduates, Julian Bell, wrote,

> principally because he always took one's ideas seriously enough to discuss them, and contradicted them if he disagreed. . . . He made one share his pleasure in thinking. . . . He had a power of analyzing poetry, of showing what was happening, that was extraordinarily useful. . . . I've never known anyone so good at making one share his enjoyments. . . . He always seemed ready to enjoy whatever was going on, food, drink, people, love affairs. I was never once bored in his company. He never grew old and cursed.

And Roger Fry returned the compliment. For Julian Bell himself he had a deep affection – 'the most magnificent human being I have known since Jem Stephen', he called him. Fresh from talk with him and his friends, he went on to reflect how much more at his ease he felt with the young than with his own generation. They made him realize 'how curiously far I have travelled from the standpoint of my own generation . . . Not that I didn't enjoy seeing [an old friend] very much, but it just showed me how much I'd joined the younger generation.

. . . If in his company, as Sir Kenneth Clark has said, 'one felt some-times that the proper answer to Tolstoy's "What is art?" was the counterquestion "What isn't?"' so in his company the proper answer to the question 'What is life?' seemed to be 'What isn't?' Everything was drawn in, assimilated, investigated. The body might creak, but the mind seemed to work with more sweep, with less friction than ever. It reached out and laid hold of every trifle – a new stitch, a zip-fastener, a shadow on the ceiling. Each must be investigated, each must be examined, as if by rescuing such trifles from mystery he could grasp life tighter and make it yield one more drop of rational and civilised enjoyment. And here fittingly, since he was no lover of vague statements, may follow his own definition 'of what I mean by life. . . . I mean the general and instinctive reaction to their surroundings of those men of any period whose lives rise to complete self-consciousness, their view of the universe as a whole and their con-ception of their relation to their kind'. Could he but live five years longer, he wrote in 1933, 'life will have done all for me that I can expect'.

Only one subject seemed to escape his insatiable curiosity; and that was himself. Analysis seemed to stop short there. Perhaps human na-ture, until we have more knowledge of psychology, is inexplicable; we are only beginning, he would insist, to know anything about this very queer animal man. He was delighted, of course, to hazard the-ories – about the effect of a puritan upbringing, about the origin of the inferiority complex which he observed cropping up in him from time to time. And if pressed, though very little interested in the past compared with the present, he would try to set down what he could remember. 'The first thing', one such fragment of autobi-ography begins, 'is the play of light on the leaves of the elm trees outside the nursery window at Highgate. . . .' He could remember many sights, and here and there an amusing incident or character – his father skating, for example, or Pierpont Morgan, with his straw-berry nose and his little red eyes, buying pictures in Italy. But the central figure remained vague. '. . . I don't pretend to know much on the subject. It so rarely interests me', he wrote when asked to explain himself. 'You say I'm wild and want to know if I'm impulsive', he went on (to Helen Anrep).

Why I should have thought, but of course I don't know, that I was impulsive (which I don't like and suspect you don't) but not wild. No, surely
not wild – infinitely sane, cautious, reasonable – what makes me look
wild is that I don't happen to accept any of the world's *idées reçues* and
values but have my own and stick to them. . . . But I should have said
impulsive, *i.e.* moved rather jerkily and suddenly by what appeals to me,
and I think it implies something wasteful and incoherent in me which
I also lament and would like you to forgive – oh, and cure, perhaps.

This lack of interest in the central figure – that central figure which
was so increasingly interested in everything outside itself – had its
charm. It made him unconscious, a perfect butt for the irreverent
laughter, in which he delighted, of the young; unaware too of the
astonishment that his appearance, clasping *le diable* in his arms, created among the respectable residents in middle-class hotels. But it
had its drawbacks, for if he ignored himself, he sometimes ignored
other people also. Thus it would be quite possible to collect from
different sources a number of unflattering portraits of Roger Fry.
They would be contradictory, of course. To some people he seemed
insincere – he changed his opinions so quickly. His enthusiasm made
the first sight so exciting; then his critical sense came into play and
made the second sight so disappointing. The swan of yesterday would
become the goose of to-day – a transformation naturally, and often
volubly, resented by the bird itself. To others he seemed on the contrary only too ruthless, too dictatorial – a Hitler, a Mussolini, a Stalin.
Absorbed in some idea, set upon some cause, he ignored feelings,
he overrode objections. Everybody he assumed must share his views
and have the same ardour in carrying them out. Fickle and impulsive,
obstinate and overbearing – the unflattering portraits would be drawn
on those lines.

And he was the first to realize that there was some truth in them.
He was impulsive, he knew; he was obstinate; he was, he feared, egotistical. 'I suddenly see,' he wrote, 'the curious twisted egotism that
there is somewhere in me that used to come out when I was little
in my indignation against "the twinges", as I used to call Isabel and
Agnes, for wanting to play with my things.' Also he was 'cross, fussy,
stingy, pernickety and other things'. Perhaps psycho-analysis might
help; or perhaps human nature in general and his own in particular
was too irrational, too instinctive, either to be analyzed or to be cured.
And he would go on to deplore the natural imperviousness of the
human mind to reason; to gird at the extraordinary morality with

which human beings torture themselves, and to speculate whether
in time to come they may not accept the simple gospel 'that all decency and good come from peoples gradually determining to enjoy
themselves a little, especially to enjoy their intellectual curiosity and
their love of art'. In such speculations about the race in general, Roger
Fry lost sight of himself in particular. Certainly he would have refused
to sit for the portrait of a finished, complete or in any way perfect
human being. He detested fixed attitudes; he suspected poses; he was
quick to point out the fatal effect of reverence. And yet whether he
liked it or not he would have had to sit for the portrait of a man
who was greatly loved by his friends. Truth seems to compel the admission that he created the warmest feeling of affection and admiration in the minds of those who knew him. It was Roger Fry, to
sum up many phrases from many letters, who set me on my feet again,
and gave me a fresh start in life. It was he who was the most actively,
the most imaginatively helpful of all my friends. And they go on
to speak of his considerateness, of his humanity, and of his profound
humility. So though he made some enemies and shed some acquaintances, he bound his friends to him all the more for the queer strains
of impulsiveness and ruthlessness that lay on the surface of that very
deep understanding.

But there was the other life – the artist's. He felt no need to apologize
for his conduct there. A work of art was a work of art, and nothing
else: personal considerations counted for nothing there. He was a
difficult man, it is easy to believe, on committees. He gave his opinion
uncompromisingly; he gave it wittily and pungently, or sometimes
he gave it sufficiently with one deep groan. He had no respect for
authority. 'If you said to him, "This must be right, all the experts
say so, Hitler says so, Marx says so, Christ says so, *The Times* says
so", he would reply in effect, "Well, I wonder. Let's see" . . . You
would come away realizing that an opinion may be influentially
backed and yet be tripe.' Naturally, artists and art critics being what
they are, he was bitterly attacked. He was accused of caring only
for the Old Masters or only for the latest fashions. He was always
changing his mind and he was obstinately prejudiced in favour of
his friends' work. In spite of failings that should have made his opinion worthless, it had weight – for some reason or other Roger Fry
had influence, more influence, it was agreed, than any critic since
Ruskin at the height of his fame.

How, without any post to back it he came to have such influence,
is a question for the painters themselves to decide. The effect of it

is shown in their works, and whether it is good or bad, no one, it is safe to say, will hold that it was negligible. To the outsider at any rate, the secret of his influence seemed based, in one word, upon his disinterestedness. He was among the priests, to use his own definition, not among the prophets, or the purveyors. By ignoring personalities and politics, success and failure, he seemed to penetrate beyond any other critic into the picture itself. To this the outsider could also add from direct observation another characteristic – he did not indulge in flattery. Friends he had – he cannot be acquitted of liking some people better than others. But a mutual admiration society, if such things exist – and according to some observers they do – would have expelled Roger Fry at the first meeting. He was as honest with his friends' work as with his enemies'. He would look long and searchingly, and if he liked what he saw, he would praise generously, dispassionately. But if he did not like what he saw, he was silent; or his one word of condemnation was enough. But his detachment, his disinterestedness was shown most impressively by his own attitude to his own work. His painting was beyond comparison more important to him than his criticism. He never lost hope that he had 'a little sensation', as he called it, or that he had at last been able to express it. He would set his own canvas on the easel and await the verdict. It was often adverse; those whose praise he would have valued most highly were often unable to give it. How keenly he minded that silence is shown again and again in his letters. But it made no difference. His own picture would be set with its face to the wall, and he would turn to the work of those who had been unable to praise his own. He would consider it with perfect single-mindedness, and if he liked it, he praised it, not because it was a friend's work, but because he admired it. 'One thing I can say for myself', he wrote. 'There are no pangs of jealousy or envy when I see someone else doing good work. It gives me pure delight.' There perhaps lay the secret of his influence as a critic.

But his influence as a human being – his own words, 'We know too little of the rhythms of man's spiritual life', remind us of the perils of trying to guess the secret that lay behind that. He did not believe with all his knowledge that he could guess the secret of a work of art. And human beings are not works of art. They are not consciously creating a book that can be read, or a picture that can be hung upon the wall. The critic of Roger Fry as a man has a far harder task than any that was set him by the pictures of Cézanne. Yet his character was strongly marked; each transformation left some-

thing positive behind it. He stood for something rare in the general life
of his time – 'Roger Fry's death is a definite loss to civilization', wrote
E.M. Forster. 'There is no one now living – no one, that is to say, of
his calibre – who stands exactly where he stood.' He changed the taste
of his time by his writing, altered the current of English painting by his
championship of the Post-Impressionists, and increased immeasur-
ably the love of art by his lectures. He left too upon the minds of those
who knew him a very rich, complex and definite impression. . . .

Roger Fry by Clive Bell

*The art criticism of Roger Fry is more closely associated with that
of Clive Bell than is any other work in Bloomsbury, except maybe
the painting of Vanessa Bell and Duncan Grant. Clive Bell's tribute
to Fry, first published in 1952, allows an unusual view of a Bloomsbury relationship. There were more than enough causes for bad feeling
between Bell and Fry in personal as well as professional matters, yet
the friendship endured. Bell's estimate of Fry, though quite critical
of his creative endeavours and puritanism, is nevertheless appreciative
of Fry's sensibility and vitality. And like Virginia Woolf's biography,
Bell's recollections obliquely indicate Fry's place in Bloomsbury by
describing his qualities as a friend and a critic.*

*Bell's essay also brings out one of the most important ideas of
Bloomsbury: their formalist aesthetics. The idea appears clearly in
Bell's redefinition of his famous term 'significant form.' The closeness
of Bell and Fry, in the eyes of one observer at any rate, is represented
in the Max Beerbohm cartoon that Bell reproduced as the frontispiece
to* Old Friends. *The cartoon shows Fry and Bell talking; the dialogue,
appropriately entitled 'Significant Form', is as follows:*

> Mr Clive Bell: *I always think that when one feels one's been carrying a
> theory too far, then's the time to carry it a little farther.*
> Mr Roger Fry: *A little? Good heavens, man! Are you growing old?*

*Three passages from Bell's essay have been omitted here – a description
of being in Paris in 1904, a digression on the Courtauld Collection,
and another anecdote on Fry's gullibility.*

'You knew him well, why don't you give us your picture of him?' said
an American friend with whom I was talking about Roger Fry. Because,
said I, Virginia Woolf wrote a biography which, besides being as com-

plete an account of Fry's life as for the present it would be seemly
to publish, happens to be a masterpiece: I have no notion of entering
into competition with one of the great writers of my age. Of course
I knew well enough that what my friend had in mind was something
utterly unlike Mrs Woolf's biography; what he expected of me was
an appetising lecture, fifty-five minutes of lively gossip, a chapter
from my unpublished memoirs. But here again a lion was in the
way: for though, as a matter of fact, I did jot down soon after Fry's
death, for the amusement of my friends and his, a handful of anecdotes
intended to illustrate just one facet of his nature – the lovably absurd
– I felt that to enjoy these fantastic tales it was necessary to have
known the hero and to have known him well. Now Virginia Woolf
made us know him so well that she was able to avail herself of my
collection – which was of course at her service – dropping delicately
here an absurdity there an extravagance with telling effect: but I am
not Virginia Woolf. I cannot bring the dead to life, and so I cannot
effectively retell my own stories. All I can do is to give, or try to
give, the impression made on me by the man, the critic and the
painter, drawing more on my recollection of what he said and did
than on what he published, which is after all accessible to all and
I hope familiar to most. For his ideas I must go sometimes to his
books; but of his character and gifts I will try to give an account
based on what I remember of his sayings and doings.

'How did Roger Fry strike you?' That, I suppose, is the question.
It is not easily answered. That fine, old sport of analyzing characters
and reducing them to their component qualities or humours is out
of fashion, and was, I admit, as a method, unsubtle. Still, no one
who knew Roger is likely to quarrel with me if I say that some of
the things that come first to mind when one thinks of him are intelligence, sweetness, ardour and sensibility; nor I believe will it be
denied that one of the first things to catch the attention of anyone
who was becoming acquainted with him was likely to be his prodigious and varied knowledge. To be sure, the very first thing that
struck me was his appearance. He was tall – about six foot I dare
say; but did not look his height. Maybe he stooped a little; he was
well made, by no means lanky, anyhow he certainly did not give
the impression of a very tall man. What one noticed were his eyes
which were both round and penetrating – an uncommon combination
– and were made to appear rounder by large circular goggles. One
noticed his hair too – once black, I believe, but greyish when I met
him – which, long, rebellious and silky, somehow accentuated his
features which, in profile at all events, were very sharply defined.

He was clean shaven. There was something the air of a judge about him, but still more the air of one who is perpetually surprised by life - as indeed he was. At moments he reminded me of a highly sagacious rocking-horse. He wore good clothes badly. Obviously they had been made by the right tailor, but there was always something wrong with them. It might be a too decorative tie fashioned out of some unlikely material, or a pair of yellow brown sandals worn when black shoes would have been more appropriate. His hats were peculiar; broad-brimmed, round, Quakerish and becoming. Only in full evening dress - white tie, white waistcoat, boiled shirt and collar - did he appear smart. Then, with his silvery hair carefully brushed, he looked infinitely distinguished.

So much for the impression made at first meeting. Acquaintance ripening to friendship, you would probably note a restless activity of mind and body. Ardent he was, as I have said, intelligent, sensitive, sweet, cultivated and erudite: these qualities and attainments revealed themselves sooner or later, and soon rather than late, to everyone who came to know him, and of them I must speak first. But what charmed his intimate friends almost as much as his rare qualities was his boundless gullibility: of that I shall speak later.

I have said that his knowledge was what might well have struck you in the beginning. One was surprised by the amount he knew before one realized that it was a mere means to something far more precious - to culture in the best sense of the word. Roger Fry was what Bacon calls 'a full man'; but his various erudition was only a means to thought and feeling and the enrichment of life. Knowledge he knew added immensely to the fun of the fair, enabling one to make the most of any odd fact that comes one's way by seeing it in relation to other facts and to theories and so fitting it into the great jig-saw puzzle. But he never cared much to be given a result unless he could learn how that result had been obtained; and therein you will recognize one of the essential qualifications of a scholarly critic. At Cambridge his studies had been scientific: that is something to have in mind for it helps to an understanding of the man, his merits and some of his defects. He took a first in the Natural Science tripos. To do that, I am assured, requires more than smattering a little Botany and cutting up a few frogs: to have done it is, I suspect, to have given the mind a bent which the most varied and thrilling experiences of later life will hardly rectify.

I shall ask you to bear in mind, then, that Roger Fry was a man of science by training and to some extent by temper. I shall not ask you to bear in mind that he was intelligent and lovable, because intelligence and charm are the very oil and pigment in which the picture of his life is to be painted. These qualities, I hope, will make themselves felt without demonstration as my tale proceeds. His old friends will not be surprised if I do not insist on them; what may surprise some is that I did not put first among his qualities, Sensibility. That Fry had acquired exquisite sensibility was clear to all who knew him or read his writings or listened to his lectures, and clearer still to those who worked with him. To watch, or rather catch, him – for in such matters his methods were summary – disposing of a foolish attribution, was to realize just how convincing a decision based on trained sensibility and knowledge can be. I have seen a little dealer, with all due ceremony, reverence and precaution, produce from a triply locked safe what purported to be a Raphael Madonna; I have seen Fry give it one glance or two and heard him say sweetly but firmly 'an eighteenth-century copy and a bad one at that'; and I have seen the dealer, himself for the moment convinced, fling the picture back into the safe without so much as bothering to lock the door. Such was the force of Fry's sensibility – trained sensibility supported by intelligence and knowledge. His possession of that has never been called in question so far as I know. What perhaps he did not possess, in such abundance at all events, was that innate sensibility, that hankering after beauty, that liking for art which resembles a liking for alcohol, that 'gusto' as Hazlitt would have called it, which is the best gift of many second- and third-rate painters and of some critics even – Théophile Gautier for instance. . . .

His first approach to art was so hampered by family tradition, lofty and puritan, that it was I dare say inevitable that he should make some false starts and fall into some pits from which a normal, barbarous upbringing might have saved him. Also the climate of Cambridge in the 'Eighties', and even later, was not altogether favourable to growth of the aesthetic sense. Also he was reading science. All this I take into account: and all this notwithstanding I do feel, re-reading the story of his early years, that his blunders of commission and omission, his baseless enthusiasms and blind spots, were not those of a very young artist but of an intellectual at any age. Assuredly the admirations and anathemas of the very young are never to be brought up against them; but in 1892 Fry was twenty-six and, what is more, had for some time been an art-student, which makes it hard to believe that, had sensibility been innate, he could have spent months in Paris – at Jullian's too – without feeling a thrill for the

Impressionists and could have found in the Luxembourg nothing more exciting than Bastien Lepage.

I spoke of family tradition lofty and puritan: the puritan strain in Roger's character his friends might like but could not ignore. To his hours of abandon even it gave an air of revolt. His paganism was protestant – a protest against puritanism. Intellectually the freest of men, and almost indecently unprejudiced, he made one aware of a slight wrench, the ghost of a struggle, when he freed his mind to accept or condone what his forbears would have called 'vile pleasures'. It is on this streak of puritanism the devil's advocate will fasten when Roger comes up, as come up he will, for canonisation. He was open-minded, but he was not fair-minded. For though, as I have said, he was magnificently unprejudiced, he was not unprincipled; and he had a way of being sure that while all his own strong feelings were principles those of others, when they happened to cross his, were unworthy prejudices. Thanks to his puritanical upbringing he could sincerely regard his principles as in some sort the will of God. From which it followed that anyone who opposed him must have said, like Satan, 'Evil be thou my good'. People who happened not to agree with him found this annoying.

Few of us are all of a metal; most, as Dryden puts it, are 'dashed and brewed with lies'. The best founded even are flawed with some disharmony. The cup is just troubled with an 'aliquid amari', and the bitterness will now and then catch in the throat and spoil the flavour of life as it goes down. A tang of puritanism was in Roger's cup: it was barely appreciable, yet to it I believe can be traced most of his defects as man and critic. Not all: there are defects that can be traced to his scientific training and temper, but here there is gain to record as well as loss. The pure unscientific aesthete is a sensationalist. He feels first; only later, if he happens to be blest – or curst – with a restless intellect, will he condescend to reason about his feelings. It would be false and silly to suggest that Roger Fry's emotions were at the service of his theories; but he was too good a natural philosopher to enjoy seeing a theory pricked by a fact. Now the mere aesthete is for ever being bowled over by facts: the facts that upset him being as a rule works of art which according to current doctrine ought not to come off but which somehow or other do (e.g. the Houses of Parliament or the works of Kipling). The aesthete, sensationalist that he is, rather likes being knocked down by an outsider. He picks himself up and goes on his was rejoicing in an adventure. Roger Fry did not altogether like it. He entered a gallery with a generalization in his head – a generalization which, up to that moment, was, or should be, a complete explanation of art. He was not the man to deny facts, and he was much too sensitive to overlook the sort I have in mind; but I do think he was inclined to give marks to pictures which, because they were right in intention, ought to have been right in achievement, and sometimes, I think, he was rather unwilling to recognize the patent but troublesome beauty of works that seemed to be sinning against the light. Nine times out of ten this tendency towards injustice was due to a puritanical aversion from charm, and to counter it the spirit of science had made him magnificently open-minded. He was the most open-minded man I ever met: the only one indeed who tried to practise that fundamental precept of science – that nothing should be assumed to be true or false until it has been put to the test. This made him willing to hear what anyone had to say even about questions on which he was a recognized authority, even though 'anyone' might be a schoolboy or a housemaid: this also made him a champion gull – but of that later. Had he fallen in with a schoolboy – a manifestly sincere and eager schoolboy – in the Arena Chapel at Padua, and had that boy confessed that he could see no merit in the frescos, Roger would have argued the question on the spot, panel by panel: and this he would have done in no spirit of amiable complacency. Always supposing the boy to be serious and ardent, the great critic would have been attentive to the arguments and objections of the small iconoclast: convinced, I suppose, he would have modified his judgment and, if necessary, recast his aesthetic.

About that aesthetic, which gave him so much trouble, I shall soon have a word to say. But first let me given an example of open-mindedness and integrity which will, I hope, make some amends for what I have said or shall say concerning his slightly biased approach to works of art. Always he had disliked Indian art: it offended his sense of reasonableness and his taste. Late in life, having enjoyed opportunities of studying more and better examples may be, or perhaps merely having studied more happily and freely examples that were always within his reach, he changed his mind. That done, the next thing to do was to 'own up'. And 'own up' he did in a discriminating lecture. When you remember that at the time of writing this palinode Roger Fry was getting on for seventy and was the foremost critic in Europe, I think you will agree that he gave proof of considerable open-mindedness and a lesson to us all. The scientific spirit is not without its uses in the appreciation of the fine arts: neither is character.

Indeed he was open-minded; which is not to say, as jealous fools

were at one time fond of saying, that he was a weather-cock, slave
to every gust of enthusiasm. It is a memorable fact, to which Sir
Kenneth Clark sorrowfully calls attention in his preface to [Fry's]
Last Lectures, that, try as he would, Fry could never bring himself
greatly to admire Greek sculpture. He would have been glad to admire
it: for Greek civilization, for the Greek view and way of life, for Greek
prose and verse, philosophy and science, he felt what all intelligent
and well educated people must feel. He realized that Athens was man's
masterpiece. And so, towards the end of his life, he went with three
friends – one an accomplished Hellenist and all highly intelligent
– to see whether he could not prove himself wrong. The will to admire
was there: but honesty, but fidelity to his personal reaction, proved
the stronger. He found Greek sculpture, whether archaic or of what
is called 'the great age', comparatively dull. And he said so.

Roger Fry was troubled by aesthetics; anyone who cares for art
yet cannot keep his intellect quiet must be. Roger cared passionately,
and positively enjoyed analysing his emotions: also he did it better,
I think, than anyone had done it before. Having analyzed he went
on to account for his feelings, and got into that fix which everyone
gets into who makes the attempt: *experto credite*. Art is almost as
wide as life; and to invent a hypothesis which shall comprehend it
may be as difficult, just as it may appear as simple, as to explain
the universe. The place where Roger stuck is where we all stick. There
is a constant in art just as, once upon a time, there was supposed
to be a constant in life. I have a notion they called it 'C': anyhow
that was a long time ago. But I feel pretty sure that in those far
off days the difference between Organic and Inorganic was determined
by the presence or absence of a definable somewhat; and still it is
permissible to say that a work of art cannot exist unless there be
present what I used to call 'significant form', and you call by any
name you please – provided that what you mean by your name is
a combination of lines and colours, or of notes, or of words, in itself
moving, *i.e.* moving without reference to the outside world. Only,
to say that, is no more to answer the question 'What is art?' than
to chatter about what 'C' is, or ever was, or to answer the question
'What is life?' Renoir, painting pictures of girls and fruit, concentrated his attention exclusively on their forms and colours. But implicit in those forms and colours, for Renoir inseparable from them,
was appetizingness – the feeling that girls are good to kiss and peaches
to eat. Easy enough to see that when a painter sets out to make you
feel that his girls would be nice to kiss he ceases to be an artist and

becomes a pornographer or a sentimentalist. Renoir never dreams of trying to make you feel anything of that sort; he is concerned only with saying what he feels about forms and colours. Nevertheless, he does feel, consciously or subconsciously, embedded in those forms and colours, deliciousness. All that he feels he expresses. Now all that an artist expresses is part of his work of art. The problem is turning nasty, you perceive; complicate it, multiply instances and diversify them, and you will be near where Roger stuck. He never quite swallowed my impetuous doctrine – Significant Form first and last, alone and all the time; he knew too much, and saw raw morsels stuck in his scientific throat. He came near swallowing it once; but always he was trying to extend his theory to cover new difficulties – difficulties presented, not only by an acute and restless intellect, but by highly trained sensibility playing on vast experience. Need I say that his difficulties were always ahead of his explanations? In wrestling with them he raised a number of interesting questions; better still – far better – he threw a flood of brilliant light on art in general and on particular works. Read again that masterly chapter in *Transformations* called 'Some Questions in Aesthetics', a matter of fifty pages, in which he goes deeper into the subject than anyone had gone before or has gone since – I am not forgetting Max Eastman whom I greatly admire. You will find the destructive criticism entirely satisfying; you will be enlightened by the analysis of aesthetic experience; you will enjoy seeing the finest mince-meat made of Mr Richards's simple-minded psychological explanations, which boil down to the absurd conclusion that our responses to works of art are the same as our responses to life; and when it comes to justification let Fry speak for himself:

> As to the value of aesthetic emotion – it is clearly infinitely removed from those ethical values to which Tolstoy would have confined it. It seems to be as remote from actual life and its practical utilities as the most useless mathematical theorem. One can say only that those who experience it feel it to have a peculiar quality of 'reality' which makes it a matter of infinite importance in their lives. Any attempt I might make to explain this would probably land me in the depths of mysticism. On the edge of that gulf I stop. (*Vision and Design*).

Certainly his wrestlings helped to give muscle to the body of Fry's criticism; but to the building of that body went many rare aliments – trained sensibility, intellect, peculiar knowledge, wide general culture, the scientific spirit and honour. Virginia Woolf speaks of 'his power of making pictures real and art important'. Words could not give better a sense of just what it was Roger Fry did for my generation and the next. Having learnt to feel intensely the beauty and glory and wonder of a work of visual art he could, so to speak, unhook his emotion and hold it under, I will not say a microscope, but an uncommonly powerful pair of spectacles. That done, he could find, and sometimes invent, words to convey feelings and analyses of feelings into the apprehension of the reader – or listener: it was even better to be a listener than a reader. I am not thinking of those unforgettable conversations and discussion before particular works of art in churches or galleries, but of his lectures. Roger Fry's lectures were his best critical performances: he was the perfect lecturer almost. And the lecture with slides is the perfect medium for pictorial exegesis, permitting, as it does, the lecturer to bring before the eyes of his audience images of the objects about which he is speaking, thinking and feeling. To hear a lecture by Roger Fry was the next best thing to sight-seeing in his company. He stuck but loosely to his text, allowing himself to be inspired by whatever was on the screen. It was from a sensation to a word. Almost one could watch him thinking and feeling.

To say the excruciatingly difficult things Fry set himself to say he was obliged to work language pretty hard. In my opinion he worked it well. His prose was lucid and lively, and on occasions he could be delightfully witty and verbally felicitous. His biographer glances, critically but affectionately, at his habit of repeating favourite phrases. The fault is unavoidable in the prose of an art-critic since there is no vocabulary of art-criticism. If such terms as 'plastic sequence', 'plastic unity', 'inner life', 'structural planes' keep cropping up, that is because they are the only symbols available for subtle and complex things which themselves keep cropping up. It is essential to understanding that readers or listeners should know precisely what the critic is referring to; and only by repeatedly describing in the same terms the same concepts can he hope to give these terms anything like generally accepted significance. To some extent the art-critic must create his own vocabulary.

Writing, as a fine art, was Roger's foible. Of prose and verse rhythms he was indistinctly aware; but he liked spinning theories about them. Of his translations of Mallarmé the less said the better: the one significant thing about them is that he believed them to be adequate. They have made me think of Bentley editing Milton; for, after all,

Bentley was a great, a very great critic, and in some ways understood Greek poetry as it never had been understood by a modern. Having named Milton I find myself thinking of some gibberish Roger once wrote – for the benefit of intimate friends only – gibberish which did possess recognizable similarity of sound with the *Ode on the Nativity* but did not possess what he firmly believed it to possess, *i.e.* all, or almost all, the merits of the original. The gibberish was, of course, deliberate gibberish – a collection of sounds so far as possible without meaning. It was highly ingenious, and I am bound to reckon the theory behind it pretty, seeing that it was much the same as one I had myself propounded years earlier as an explanation of visual art. Only, at the time Roger's experiment was made we were deep in the Twenties and the fine frenzy of Post-Impressionism was a thing of the past. There was now no controversial axe to grind. Simply, Roger liked the theory because he felt it was one in the eye for 'magic'. It came from the heart rather than the head and he wanted to believe it. Now it was this gibberish, and his opinion of it, and the passion with which he defended his opinion, that finally opened my eyes to a truth which had, I suppose, always been plain to those who did not love him: Roger's feeling for poetry was puritanical. The charm, the romance, the imagery, the glamour, the magic offended the quaker that was in him; wherefore he was very willing to believe that all that signified could be reduced to clean, dry bones.

Having said so much about writing and lecturing, I must say something, I suppose, about painting. It is an unenviable task; for, preposterous as it must seem to those who know him only by his achievement, Roger Fry took his painting more seriously than he took his criticism. It was the most important thing in his life, or at any rate he thought it was. He said so and his friends were bound to believe him; yet some of them wondered: surely he knew that he was the best critic alive, and, at the bottom of his heart, can he have believed that he was a very good painter? He knew that those whose opinion he valued did not think so. To me it seems that his early work, especially his water-colours and paintings on silk, are his happiest productions. They are frankly eclectic; the influence of some master, of some English water-colourist as a rule, being acknowledged at every turn. But in most of these works – things done before 1910 shall we say? – there are pleasing qualities which later I seek in vain. Unashamed, in those unregenerate days, he could utilize his knowledge, and exploit his taste, the delicacy of his perceptions, his sleight of hand. All these assets contributed to a tentative style which did in

some sort express a part of his nature. The Post-Impressionist revolution which set free so many of his latent capacities overwhelmed
these modest virtues. it set free his capacity for living and enjoying,
but it did no good to his painting. On the contrary, that movement
which was to liberate the creative powers of all those young and youngish artists who possessed any powers worth liberating, that movement of which in this country he was the animator, did Fry's painting
harm, driving it into uncongenial ways. He tried to paint in a manner
which he understood admirably and explained brilliantly but could
not make his own. No longer decked in the rather antiquated finery
which had fitted his temper on one side at any rate, his painting
gift appeared naked, and we perceived to our dismay that it amounted
to next to nothing. His very energy and quickness, qualities elsewhere
profitable, here served him ill. He worked too fast. Neither had he
that ruminating enjoyment which lingers over a subject till the last
oozings of significance have been tasted, nor yet the patience which
will elaborate a design to its last possibilities. I have seen him, out
of sheer conscientiousness, or in some desperate hope of a miraculous
revelation, work on at a picture to which he knew he could add nothing, for all the world like an examination candidate who has written
all he knows and vainly strives to improve the appearance of his
paper by writing it all over again. Roger knew that he had added
nothing. Maybe he knew too much.

Roger Fry was a good, though impatient, craftsman, proper of his
hands and quick to learn a trade. His best productions in this sort
are the white pots and plates he made for the Omega; and it is to
be hoped that a few will be preserved in some public collection, for
they grow rare. But no sooner did he think it necessary to embellish
a chair or a table or a chest of drawers, to beautify a curtain, a
lamp-shade or a frock, than something went wrong. There must have
been a devil, I have sometimes fancied, a demon born of puritanism
and pampered in young 'artistic' days, which lurked in his sub-
consciousness and on favourable occasions poked up its nose. At any
rate, in all that he did for the Omega, with the exception of those
plain white pots and plates, I taste an unpleasant flavour – a flavour
redolent of 'artistry'. That was the devil's revenge; and perhaps it
was this same evil spirit that forbade Fry the paradise of creation.
From that delectable country he was excluded; he could not reach
the frontiers because where art begins some perverse sub-
consciousness or self-consciousness arrested him. What was it precisely? I hardly know. Could he have believed – no, he could not

have believed nor thought either – but could he have hoped, in some dark corner of his being inaccessible to reason, that style could be imposed? A horrid fancy: that way lie art guilds and gowns, sandals, homespun and welfare-work, and at the end yawns an old English tea-room. If Roger had finished a picture before he had begun a work of art, that may have been because he could not practise what he preached so well – that in creating all the horses must be driven abreast, that you cannot hitch on style or beauty as an ostler used to hitch on a tracer. And if I am asked why Roger Fry's painting seems dead, all I can say is what Renoir said when asked whether art comes from the head or the heart: *'des couilles'* he replied.

But if Roger Fry was not an artist, he was one of the most remarkable men of his age, besides being one of the most lovable. This his biographer has established; his other friends can but bring a few flowers to the monument and cherish the inscription. I first met him appropriately enough in the morning train from Cambridge to King's Cross. It was early in 1910, a moment at which Fry was in a sense beginning a new life. The tragedy in which the old had ended, the courage and devotion with which that tragedy had been fought and for a while warded off, Mrs Woolf has most movingly recounted. In 1910 Roger Fry was in his forty-fifth year: one life was ending and a new, and perhaps more exciting, about to begin. Indeed, it was a movement at which everyone felt excitement in the air: had not I – even I – just sat down to describe the general state of affairs in an *opus* to bear the pregnant title *The New Renaissance*, an *opus* of which the bit I did publish three years later, a book called *Art*, would have formed a mere chapter. Certainly there was a stir: in Paris and London at all events there was a sense of things coming right, though whether what we thought was coming could properly be described as a 'renaissance' now seems to me doubtful. The question is academic: as usual the statesmen came to the rescue, and Mr Asquith, Sir Edward Grey and M. Viviani declared war on Germany. But in 1910 only statesmen dreamed of war, and quite a number of wide-awake people imagined the good times were just round the corner. Miracles seemed likely enough to happen; but when Roger Fry told me that morning in the train that he proposed to show the British public the work of the newest French painters, I told him that I would be proud to help in any way I could but that his scheme was fantastic. Not that there was any question of my being of serious use – Roger never needed an *État-Major*; but as I had written in praise of Cézanne and Gauguin and other 'revolutionaries' he thought I might as well give a hand. Anyhow, I was put on a committee which did nothing, and late that summer I joined Roger and Desmond Mac-Carthy in Paris: in the autumn opened the first Post-Impressionist exhibition. . . .

One result of the first Post-Impressionist exhibition was that Roger Fry became the animator and advocate of the younger British painters; but not the master. Few young painters mistook him for a master, though to him they looked for advice and encouragement and some-times for material support. With his fine intellect, culture and per-suasive ways he became spokesman for modern art – our represent-ative in the councils of the great; for he could place his word where he would. *The Times* felt bound to print letters from him in large type on the leader page. Even fine ladies, even the Prime Ministress, had to pretend to listen. And, under the wand of the enchanter, with his looks, his voice, his infinite variety and palpable good faith, those who began to listen found themselves becoming converts. It was now, in these last years of peace, that France became for him what for the rest of his life she remained – his second country; and there he made friends, deep, affectionate and charming, who later were to do much to lighten the gloom of declining years. At home, too, between 1910 and 1914 he was making friends, some of whom were to grow into close companions and collaborators; and of these most, it is to be noted, were a generation younger than his own. They were, I think, gayer, more ribald, more unshockable, more pleasure-loving and less easily impressed by grave airs and fine sentiments than the friends – whom, by the way, he never lost nor ceased to love – with whom he had grown to middle age. It was from these younger people that he learnt to enjoy shamelessly almost – yes, almost. Their blissful adiabolism helped him to ignore the nudgings of the old puritan Nick. And this I like to count some small return for all they learnt from him. He taught them much: amongst other things, by combining with an utterly disinterested and unaffected passion for art a passion for justice and hatred of cruelty, he made them aware of the beauty of goodness. That virtue could be agreeable came as a surprise to some of us. Like all satisfactory human relationships, these new friendships were matters of give and take; and I know who gave most. Nevertheless, between the first Post-Impressionist exhibition and the First War I have a notion that Roger Fry changed more than he had changed in all the years between Cambridge and that exhibition.

I have suggested that one reason why Roger was unable to elaborate a work of art and knocked off too many works of craft was that his boundless energy induced impatience. This energy, allied with pro- digious strength of will, was terrifying; and it is not surprising that his enemies, and his friends too when they chanced to be his victims, called him ruthless and obstinate; for it is provoking to be driven straight into a field of standing corn because your driver cannot admit that his map may be out of date or that he may have misread it. Of this energy and wilfulness an extract from my unpublished notes may perhaps give some idea. So,

I recall a cold and drizzling Sunday in August: I cannot be sure of the year. Roger is staying with us at Charleston, convalescent; for, like many exceptionally robust and energetic men, Roger was a valetudinarian. I re- member hearing my wife say, probably at breakfast, that she suspected him of intending to be motored some time in the afternoon to Seaford, eight or nine miles away, where dwelt his curious old friend, Hindley Smith; but that she, the weather being vile, the road slippery, the car open and ill-humoured, had no intention of obliging him. Just before lunch Frances Marshall (Mrs Ralph Partridge) who also was staying with us, and possessed, like my wife, what most would deem a will of iron, told me she had a headache and meant, the moment lunch was over, to slip off to bed, if that could be done without causing commotion. In any case she was not going to play chess with Roger. For my part I never cared about playing chess with Roger; if, by any chance, one succeeded in some little plot for surprising his queen or rook - and setting traps is what amuses all thoroughly bad players such as I - he would dismiss the strate- gem as 'uninteresting', retract a series of moves - generally to his own advantage - and so continue till on scientific and avowable principles he had beaten one to his satisfaction. Anyhow, on this dark and dismal Sun- day, lunch finished, Roger sprang to his feet - all invalid that he was he could spring when the occasion seemed to demand action - exclaiming: 'Now Frances for a game.' And, as soon as Frances had been allowed to lose in a way of which he could approve, again he sprang: 'Now, Vanessa, we've just time to go and see Hindley Smith.' Vanessa went like a lamb.

I have spoken of Roger's open-mindedness, of his readiness to listen to anyone he thought sincere: that was fine. His aptitude for dis- covering sincerity in unlikely places was fine, too, I suppose; but sometimes it landed him in difficulties. Not to mince words, he was a champion gull: gullibility was the laughable and lovable defect of a quality. Stories illustrating this weakness abound; one or two, which, I am proud to say, are drawn from my notes, appear in Virginia Woolf's biography. . . .

Inevitably one so gullible and so often gulled grew suspicious – not of the crooks, but of old friends and well meaning acquaintances. To make matters worse, Roger had no turn for practical psychology. A poorer judge of men I have seldom met, and it goes without saying he piqued himself on penetration. He was as ready as Rousseau to believe in *conspirations holbachiques,* and was given to explaining plots which he supposed to have been woven against him, and had in truth been woven in his own imagination, by facts and motives which his friends knew to be non-existent. Does this sound sinister? It was not; for his attention could be diverted with the greatest ease from private grievances to general ideas or, better still, to particular events – in plain words to gossip. In both he delighted; also his mind was far too nimble, his capacity for enjoyment too keen, his taste too pure, his sense of fun too lively, for him to dwell long on petty troubles. He was not much like Rousseau after all. But suspicious he was, and in his fits of suspicion unjust. He could be as censorious as an ill-conditioned judge: possibly the trait was hereditary. Then it was that the puritan came out from hiding undisguised and made him believe that those who differed from him must be actuated by the foulest motives. In such moods it was that he suspected those who opposed him of having said, like Satan, 'evil be thou my good'; also, it seems to me, these moods grew more frequent with the years, bringing with them a perceptible loss of magnanimity. So it seems to me. Or was it that some of his old friends were growing touchy? That explanation is admissible too.

   In this discursive chapter I hope to have given some idea of the qualities that made Roger Fry one of the most remarkable men of his age. A combination of intellect and sensibility, extensive culture not in the arts only but in history and science as well, dexterous manipulation of a fine instrument, and an unrivalled power of getting close in words to thoughts and feelings, made him indisputably our first critic. In fact he was more than the first critic of the age; so far as I can judge from my readings in three languages he was one of the best writers on visual art that ever lived. There may be Russians or Germans who have responded more delicately and analyzed their responses more acutely, who have contrived to come nearer the heart of the matter; if so, I shall be glad to study their works as soon as they have been translated. Add to these gifts, which were as one may say open to the public, those with which in private he charmed his friends, a playful intellect for instance, free fancy and a sense of fun, along with taste in food and wine, and you have beside a great critic a rare companion. Men I have known who possessed tempers to me more congenial, but none better equipped to please generally. His was, on the whole, a happy disposition, and a cause of happiness in others. One permanent anxiety beset him: it was the child of his virtues. He dreaded, especially during the last years of his life, the collapse of civilization. For civilization he cared nobly; and the prevalence of its mortal enemies – fanaticism, superstition, dogmatism, unreasonableness, the cult of violence and stupidity, contempt of truth and the ways of truth – dismayed him. In naming these vices I have indicated his virtues, which were their contraries. He was a man of many virtues; what is more, in practice he contrived to make them amiable.

Desmond MacCarthy by E.M. Forster

'He had, I suspect, a good deal to do with the genial social climate of Bloomsbury, with the reconciliation of difficult and angular characters and with the general spirit of tolerance and compromise which triumphed over the disputes and acerbities which were also a part of that environment' (Woolf, 1:103). Quentin Bell's evaluation of Desmond MacCarthy's role in Bloomsbury in illustrated by E.M. Forster's tribute to his old friend, which is taken from a Memoir Cub paper that was republished with other tributes after MacCarthy's death in 1952.

I have not many recollections of the early Desmond MacCarthy, but fortunately I can clearly remember the first time we met. It was about fifty years ago, in Cambridge, and at one of those little discussion societies which are constantly being born and dying inside the framework of the university. They still continue, I am glad to say, and I know that he too would be glad.

This particular society was called the Apennines. Its invitation card displayed a range of mountains, and there was also a pun involved, upon which I will not expatiate. I had to read a paper to the Apennines, then I was pulled to pieces, and among my critics was a quiet, dark young man with a charming voice and manner, who sat rather far back in the room and who for all his gentleness knew exactly what he wanted to say, and in the end how to say it. That was my first impression of him, and I may say it is my last impression also. The young man became an old one and a famous one, but he remained charming and gentle, he always knew his own mind, and he always sat rather far back in the room. Compare him in this respect with that trenchant critic Mr So-and-So, or with that chatty columnist Sir Somebody Something, who always manage to sit well in front. I do not think it was modesty on Desmond's part that made him retiring. He just knew where he wanted to be. Some years after the Apennines, when he was doing literary journalism, he chose for a pseudonym the name 'Affable Hawk'. Nothing could have been more apt. He was affable to his fellow writers, whenever possible. But if a book was shallow or bumptious or brutal, then down pounced the hawk, and the victim's feathers flew.

He and I were always friendly and I stayed with him in Suffolk in those far-off days, and elsewhere later on, but all my vivid memories of him are in a group with other people. So let us now move from Cambridge to London. There, in the early years of this century, I remember a peculiar organization which had been formed for the purpose of making Desmond write his novel. He wanted to write his novel. He could talk his novel – character, plot, incidents, all were fascinating: I recall a green valley in Wales where a famous picture had got hidden. But he could not get his novel on to paper. So some of his friends thought that if a society was formed at which we all wrote novels and read a fresh chapter aloud at each meeting, Desmond would be reluctantly dragged down the path of creation. Needless to say, he eluded so crude a device. Other people wrote their novels – which usually began well and fell to bits in the second chapter. He – he had forgotten, he had mislaid the manuscript, he had not the time. And he did not write his novel. And after the First World War the group was reconstituted: not to write novels but to write reminiscences.

Here Desmond was supreme. 'Memory', he often said, 'is an excellent compositor'. And in the midst of a group which included Lytton Strachey, Virginia Woolf, and Maynard Keynes, he stood out in his command of the past, and in his power to rearrange it. I remember one paper of his in particular – if it can be called a paper. Perched away in a corner of Duncan Grant's studio, he had a suit-case open before him. The lid of the case, which he propped up, would be useful to rest his manuscript upon, he told us. On he read, delighting us as usual, with his brilliancy, and humanity, and wisdom, until – owing to a slight wave of his hand – the suit-case unfortunately fell over. Nothing was inside it. There was no paper. He had been improvising.

Desmond MacCarthy by Leonard and Virginia Woolf

In the first volume of his autobiography Leonard Woolf wrote of Desmond MacCarthy's great promise. Defending this judgment in his third volume, he attempted to explain the discrepancy between Mac-Carthy's brilliant potential and disappointing achievement. Included in Leonard's description is a passage from Virginia's diary of 1919, written after the publication of MacCarthy's Remnants, *that poses again the paradox of MacCarthy's career.*

. . . It is true that Desmond did look like a dishevelled bird when he was middle-aged, and he knew it himself – hence his characteristic pen name Affable Hawk. But when I first saw Desmond – he was twenty-six and just returned from a Grand Tour of Europe – there was nothing of the dishevelled fledgling fallen from the nest about him; he looked like a superb young eagle who with one sweep of his great wing could soar to any height he chose. He not only looked it; the good fairies had lavished upon him every possible gift and particularly those gifts which every would-be writer and novelist would pray for. Why did he never fulfil his promises? Why did the splendid eagle degenerate into an affable hawk, a dishevelled fledgling?
. . . The human being is psychologically so infuriatingly complex that you can never explain his thoughts, actions, or character by trotting out a single superficial cause. One of the difficulties is that in the human mind the same element is at the same time both a cause and an effect. Thus in the case of Desmond it is probably true to say that 'his special gift of conversation' was a cause of his not writing novels, but it is also true that (1) it was an *excuse* for his not writing novels, and (2) his not writing novels was a cause of his special gift for conversation. One summer Desmond came to stay for a few days with us in the country at Asham House. He was slightly depressed when he arrived and soon told us the reason. His friend A.F. Wedgwood, the novelist, had recently died leaving a posthumous novel and Desmond had promised the widow to write an introduction and memoir of the author for the book. He had continually put off doing this; the book had been printed, was ready for binding, and was com-

pletely held up for Desmond's introduction; the publisher was desperate and desperately bombarding Desmond with reply paid telegrams. Desmond had sworn that he would write the thing over the week-end and post it to the publisher on Monday morning. He asked me to promise that next morning I would lock him up in a room by himself and not let him out until he had finished the introduction. And he told me then that he really suffered from a disease: the moment he knew that he ought to do something, no matter what that something was, he felt absolutely unable to do it and would do anything else in order to prevent himself from doing it. It did not matter what 'it' might be; it might be something which he actually wanted to do, but if it was also something which he knew he *ought* to do, he would find himself doing something which he did not want to do in order to prevent himself doing something which he ought to do and wanted to do.

Here for instance was a fairly common situation in Desmond's life: he is engaged to dine at 7.30 with someone whom he likes very much in Chelsea; he looks forward to the evening; at 7 he is sitting in a room at the other end of London talking to two or three people whom he does not very much like and who are in fact boring him; at 7.5 he begins to feel that he ought to get up and leave for Chelsea; at 7.30 he is still sitting with the people whom he does not much like and is uncomfortably keeping them from their dinner; at 8 they insist that he must stay and dine with them; at 8.5 he rings up his Chelsea friends, apologizes, and says that he will be with them in 20 minutes.

I should add that that evening at Asham Desmond recovered his spirits and was in fine form. After we had gone to bed, we heard him for a short time walking up and down the corridor groaning: 'O God! God!' Next morning he was quite cheerful when I locked him in the sitting room. An hour later he thumped on the door and shouted: 'You must let me out, Leonard, you must let me out.' He had run out of cigarettes and I weakly let him out so that he could walk over to Rodmell, a mile away, and buy some at the village shop. I cannot remember whether when he left us on Monday or Tuesday morning, he had finished the introduction. I rather think he had not.

Now one of the several reasons why Desmond never fulfilled his youthful aquiline promise and never wrote that brilliant novel which in 1903 lay embryonically in his mind was that he thought that he *ought* to write a novel and that the novel *ought* to be absolutely first class. Desmond was in many ways Moore's favourite apostle and Desmond loved and followed Moore with the purity and intensity of the disciple devoted to the guru or sage. He, as an impressionable young man, like all of us in the Cambridge of those days, took *Principia Ethica* as a bible of conduct. In *Sowing*, I tried to describe and define this influence of Moore and his book upon us [see pp. 129–41]. The book told us what we *ought* to do and what we ought not to do, and, when one thought of those words, it was impossible not to see and hear Moore himself, the impassioned shake of his head on the emphasized words as he said: 'I think one *ought* to do that,' or 'I think one ought *not* to do that.' So when Desmond sat down to write, an invisible Moore, with the 'oughts' and 'ought nots', stood behind his chair. But both as a man and a writer his gifts were of a lyrical kind; they had to be given a free hand; his imagination would not work and so he could not write on a tight, intellectual rein.

The best, said the Greeks, is the enemy of the good. The vision of the best, the ghostly echoes of *Principia Ethica*, the catechism which always begins with the terrifying words: 'What exactly do you *mean* by *that?*,' inhibited Desmond. When he wrote 'seriously', he began to labour, and the more he tinkered with what he wrote the more laboured and laborious it became. This brings me back to the point from which I started, the effect of journalism upon Desmond and writers like him. Journalism provided him with the easy way out of his difficult and complicated situation as regards writing a novel. He thought that he ought to write a novel – something serious – and as the habit grew upon him of not being able to do what he thought he ought to do, the habit of always doing something else in order to avoid doing what he ought to do, writing the weekly article for the *New Statesman* or *Sunday Times* became his refuge and shelter from his duty to be a great writer. (Of course, there was the further stage that, when the moment came at which he *ought* to begin writing the article, he had to find something else to prevent his doing so, and it was only a devoted and efficient secretary who managed somehow or other to get Affable Hawk's article, usually a few minutes after the very last moment, to an infuriated printer.)

But writing an article as a refuge for Desmond against doing what he thought he ought to do, *i.e.* writing a novel, was only part of the story. In literature he had tremendously high standards, and, if he had ever been inclined to lower them, the memories of Cambridge, Moore, and *Principia Ethica* would have warned him off. To write a book, say a novel, as a serious artist, requires a good many qualities, by no means common, besides the ability to write. However sensitive you may be to praise or blame, you have to be at some point ruthless and impervious – and ruthless to yourself. The moment comes when the writer must say to himself: 'I don't care what they say about it and me; I shall publish and be damned to them.' And he has to accept responsibility, the responsibility for what he has written; he must strip himself artistically naked before the public and take the icy plunge. People like Desmond, once they begin to doubt whether what they are writing is really any good – and such doubts occasionally torture practically all good writers – cannot stay the course. They cannot force themselves through those despairing moments of grind in the long distance race before you get your second wind and they cannot face responsibility. Here again journalism is the refuge. Even *Principia Ethica* would allow one to lower one's standards in the *Sunday Times* or *New Statesman*, where one is writing not *sub specie aeternitatis*, but for a short week-end. And in any case the responsibility is not so much yours as the editor's. Journalism is the opiate of the artist; eventually it poisons his mind and his art.

Off and on over the years I saw a good deal of Desmond, walking and talking with him at all hours of day and night, watching him try to write and even occasionally working with him. I am sure that his psychology as a writer was more or less that analyzed by me in the previous paragraphs. One can only add that the charm of the dead cannot be reproduced second-hand in words. One can only record the fact that Desmond was the most charming of men, the most amusing companion, and finally had about him in friendship the honesty and faithfulness which I associate with old sheep dogs.

When I had written this, I remembered that Virginia had once in her diaries, when after being ill she was for a time only able to write her novel for an hour a day, amused herself by writing short accounts of her friends' characters. I turned up what she had written about Desmond and this is what she said in January 1919:

> How many friends have I got? There's Lytton, Desmond, Saxon: they belong to the Cambridge stage of life; very intellectual . . . I can't put them in order, for there are too many. Ka and Rupert and Duncan, for example, all come rather later. . . . Desmond has *not* rung up. That is quite a good preface to the description of his character. The difficulty which faces one in writing of Desmond is that one is almost forced to describe an Irishman. How he misses trains, seems born without a rudder to drift wherever the

current is strongest; how he keeps hoping and planning, and shuffles along, paying his way by talking so enchantingly that editors forgive and shopmen give him credit and at least one distinguished peer leaves him a thousand in his will. . . . Where was I? Desmond, and how I find him sympathetic compared with Stracheys. It is true; I'm not sure he hasn't the nicest nature of any of us – the nature one would soonest have chosen for one's own. I don't think that he possesses any faults as a friend, save that his friendship is so often sunk under a cloud of vagueness, a sort of drifting vapour composed of times and seasons separates us and effectively prevents us from meeting. Perhaps such indolence implies a slackness of fibre in his affections too – but I scarcely feel that. It arises rather from the consciousness which I find imaginative and attractive that things don't altogether *matter*. Somehow he is fundamentally sceptical. Yet which of us, after all, takes more trouble to do the sort of kindness that comes his way? Who is more tolerant, more appreciative, more understanding of human nature? It goes without saying that he is not an heroic character. He finds pleasure too pleasant, cushions too soft, dallying too seductive and then as I sometimes feel now, he has ceased to be ambitious. His 'great work' (it may be philosophy or biography now, and is certainly to be begun, after a series of long walks, this very spring) only takes shape, I believe, in that hour between tea and dinner, when so many things appear not only possible, but achieved. Comes the daylight, and Desmond is contented to begin his article; and plies his pen with a half humorous half melancholy recognition that such is his appointed life. Yet it is true, and no one can deny it, that he has the floating elements of something brilliant, beautiful – some book of stories, reflection, studies, scattered about in him, for they show themselves indisputably in his talk. I'm told he wants power; that these fragments never combine into an argument; that the disconnection of talk is kind to them; but in a book they would drift hopelessly apart. Consciousness of this, no doubt, led him in his one finished book to drudge and sweat until his fragments were clamped together in an indissoluble stodge. I can see myself, however, going through his desk one of these days, shaking out unfinished pages from between sheets of blotting paper, and deposits of old bills, and making up a short book of table talk, which shall appear as a proof to the younger generation that Desmond was the most gifted of us all. But why did he never do anything? they will ask.

. . . The last time I saw him, not long before he died, I walked away with him from the house in Gordon Square where he had had a Memoir Club meeting. It was 11 o'clock and a cold autumn night. He was suffering terribly from asthma and was racked by a sudden

fit of it as we turned out of the Square. I made him wait while I
ran off to find him a taxi. When I put him into the taxi, he looked,
not like an affable hawk or even a dishevelled fledgling, but like a
battered, shattered, dying rook. At the corner of Gordon Square I
suddenly saw him again as a young man walking with me on the
hills above Hunter's Inn in Devonshire when we were on an Easter
'reading party' with Moore and Lytton. There are few things more
terrible than such sudden visions of one's friends in youth and vigour
through the miseries of age and illness. I left Desmond sitting in
the taxi, affectionate, dejected, unheroic, because so obviously broken
and beaten by asthma and by life; but brave in not complaining and
not pretending and in still, when he could, making his joke and his
phrase . . .

Molly MacCarthy by Leonard Woolf

*Molly MacCarthy was regarded as one of the Group's best correspond-
ents. She was also the author of a memoir, a novel, and then a series
of biographical sketches; and she organized for her husband the Novel
and then the Memoir Club. Yet she remains one of the more elusive
of the Bloomsberries she so named. One reason for this was her increasing deafness, which kept her from Bloomsbury conversation. The
difficulties of living with Desmond may have been another cause,
as Leonard Woolf's brief sketch suggests.*

[Molly MacCarthy] was one of those people whose minds go blank
the moment they are faced by the slightest crisis; her vagueness and
fluttering indecision must have been perpetually nourished by a lifetime of waiting for Desmond to return to dinner to which he had
forgotten that he had invited several friends. The way that Molly's
mind refused to work is shown by the following affectionate memory
of her. One week-end she and W.B. Yeats were both staying at Garsington. On Saturday night after dinner the poet, as his way was,
got off on one of his, to me boring, disquisitions about spirits, second
sight, and mediums. He suddenly turned to Molly and said that he
was sure that she was psychic and she must let him try to get her
to 'see' things. Much against her will Molly at last gave in and said
flutteringly that she could try. There were I suppose some ten or
twelve people sitting around in the drawing-room, and poor Molly
was seated in a chair next to Yeats who performed the usual ceremony

of mumbo jumbo. There was a moment of complete silence, and then
Yeats said: 'And now what do ye see, my dear?' Molly's mind went
absolutely blank; she saw nothing and could not even think of anything which she might see. Yeats became agitated 'Come now, my
dear, come now, ye must see something.' A long paralysing silence,
and then Molly said miserably: 'Yes, I think I do see something –
a frog.' Yeats was outraged.

E.M. Forster by Virginia Woolf

*Of all Virginia Woolf's Bloomsbury friends, E.M. Forster was the clos-
est professionally. He was the one she talked with about writing, as
she said in her letters (see p. 63). Forster was an important influence
on Woolf's development as a novelist, having written all but one of
his novels before she had published her first. Despite their differing
conceptions of fiction, they wrote some of the best criticism that has
been done of each other's work. Virginia Woolf never wrote a memoir
of Forster, but a composite picture of him can be assembled from
various diary entries that complements the moving Cambridge lecture
he gave after her death (see pp. 222–36). Woolf's diary portrait of Forster shows the affection they had for each other, and also something
of the wariness. Woolf thought Forster touchy, for example, and in
his* Commonplace Book *he called her a pythoness it would not do
to rally (54). (In the entry of 9 April 1935 Virginia refers to a comic
history of Bloomsbury that she and Leonard hoped Forster would
write for the Hogarth Press.)*

Saturday 12 July 1919 I met Morgan Forster on the platform at Waterloo yesterday; a man physically resembling a blue butterfly – I
mean by that to describe his transparency & lightness. He had been
conveying the luggage of 5 Indians from Deptford to Waterloo; Indians seem to weight him down. We exchanged compliments on our
writing – I'm surprised to find him openly liking a compliment,
though its nothing strange in myself. . . . I like Forster very much,
though I find him whimsical & vagulous to an extent that frightens
me with my own clumsiness & definiteness.

Thursday 24 July 1919 Morgan . . . is an unworldly, transparent
character, whimsical & detached, caring very little I should think
what people say, & with a clear idea of what he wishes. I don't think

he wishes to shine in intellectual society; certainly not in fashionable. He is fantastic & very sensitive; an attractive character to me, though from his very qualities it takes as long to know him as it used to take to put one's gallipot over a humming bird moth. More truly, he resembles a vaguely rambling butterfly; since there is no intensity or rapidity about him. To dominate the talk would be odious to him. He subsided in a chair; or strolled about the room, turning over the pages of a book . . . He will come to Asheham if we pay his fare. He has only £26 in the bank. I like this simple way of explaining things. And he hates Stevenson; & makes up his novels as he goes along; & sees what I mean about dialogue; there's a lot to say to him, though I don't yet know how to say it. Its absurd at my age, & I feel very middle aged, to be as easily put out & flustered as I am. It takes the form of saying things rashly. 'I want to write an article upon you' I said, & that wasn't what I meant to say.

Thursday 6 November 1919   Morgan has the artists mind; he says the simple things that clever people don't say; I find him the best of critics for that reason. Suddenly out comes the obvious thing that one has overlooked. He is in trouble with a novel of his own, fingering the keys but only producing discords so far.

Saturday 24 April 1920   Morgan came for a night. Very easy going; as sensitive as a blue butterfly. So I was pleased to write in his birthday book which is one of his tests of niceness. And he's obstinate about 'niceness' - much of a puritan. Tells the truth. I wish I could write his talk down.

Tuesday 1 March 1921   Morgan goes to India, & I think for ever. He will become a mystic, sit by the roadside, & forget Europe, which I think he half despises. In thirty years time he may turn up again, give us an amused look, & return to the East, having written a little unintelligible poetry. He has no roots here. And the news made me melancholy. I like him, & like having him about. But we shan't see him again.

Thursday 15 September 1921   A letter from Morgan this morning. He seems as critical of the East as of Bloomsbury, & sits dressed in a turban watching his Prince dance, quite unimpressed. He is not impressed by Q. Vict. [Lytton Strachey's *Queen Victoria*] either. Flimsy, he says, compared with Macaulay, which was perhaps what I meant.

Sunday 12 March 1922 Then I hit Morgan on the wing. He had come to London that very day, & so came here, & was, we thought, depressed to the verge of inanition. To come back to Weybridge, to come back to an ugly house a mile from the station, and old, fussy, exacting mother, to come back having lost your Rajah, without a novel, & with no power to write one – this is dismal, I expect, at the age of 43. The middle age of b——s is not to be contemplated without horror. But he was charming, transparent; & told us as much as we could get out. A years absence fills one too full for many drops to issue upon turning the bottle upside down.

Wednesday 27 September 1922 Then we snuggled in, & Morgan became very familiar; anecdotic; simple, gossiping about friends & humming his little tunes; Tom [T.S. Eliot] asked him to contribute to the Criterion. I was impressed by his complete modesty (founded perhaps on considerable self-assurance). Compliments scarcely touch him. He is happy in his novel [*A Passage to India*], but does not want to discuss it. There is something too simple about him – for a writer perhaps, mystic, silly, but with a childs insight: oh yes, & something manly & definite too.

Tuesday 18 September 1923 We all grow old; grow stocky; lose our pliancy & impressionability. Even Morgan seems to me to be based on some hidden rock. Talking of Proust & [D.H.] Lawrence he said he'd prefer to be Lawrence; but much rather would be himself. We discussed his novels. I don't think I am a novelist, he said. Suddenly I said 'No, I don't think you are' Ah! he exclaimed, eagerly, interested, no dashed. But L. [Leonard Woolf] denied this. 'I'm not at all downcast about my literary career', he said. I think he has made up his mind that he has much to fall back on. He is aloof, serene, a snob, he says, reading masterpieces only. We had a long gossip about servants.

Thursday 22 March 1928 Morgan was here for the week end; timid, touchy, infinitely charming. One night we got drunk, & talked of sodomy, & sapphism, with emotion – so much so that next day he said he had been drunk. This was started by Radclyffe Hall & her meritorious dull book [*The Well of Loneliness*]. . . . Morgan said Dr Head can convert the sodomites. 'Would you like to be converted?' Leonard asked. 'No' said Morgan, quite definitely. He said he thought Sapphism disgusting: partly from convention, partly because he disliked that women should be independent of men.

Tuesday 9 April 1935   I met Morgan in the London Library yesterday & flew into a passion.

'Virginia, my dear' he said. I was pleased by that little affectionate familiar tag.

'Being a good boy & getting books on Bloomsbury?' I said.

'Yes . . . Virginia, you know I'm on the Co[mmi]ttee here' said Morgan. 'And we've been discussing whether to allow ladies –

It came over me that they were going to put me on: & I was then to refuse: Oh but they do – I said. There was Mrs Green . . . [*sic*]

'Yes yes – there was Mrs Green. And Sir Leslie Stephen said, never again. She was so troublesome. And I said, havent ladies improved? But they were all quite determined. No no no, ladies are quite impossible. They wouldnt hear of it.'

See how my hand trembles. I was so angry (also very tired) standing. And I saw the whole slate smeared. I thought how perhaps M. had mentioned my name, & they had said no no no: ladies are impossible. . . . God damn Morgan for thinking I'd have taken that.

Thursday 7 November 1940   Morgan asks if he may propose me for the L[ondon] L[ibrary] Committee. Rather to my pleasure I answered No. I dont want to be a sop – a face saver. This was a nice little finish to a meeting with EMF years ago in the L.L. He sniffed about women on Cttee. One of these days I'll refuse I said silently. And now I have.

E.M. Forster by David Garnett

David Garnett's essay on Forster and Bloomsbury first appeared in a collection of essays aptly entitled Aspects of E.M. Forster *that was presented on his ninetieth birthday. The Bloomsbury aspect of Forster described by Garnett shows the extent to which Forster belonged to Bloomsbury. (A passage quoting Virginia Woolf's diary on Forster has been omitted.)*

'We did not see much of Forster at that time; who was already the elusive colt of a dark horse,' Lord Keynes wrote[1] of the years about 1902 when he was forming his early beliefs, based on the philosophy of G.E. Moore and the discussions in the Society, otherwise known

---

1 *The Two Memoirs* [see p. 85].

as the Apostles. Leonard Woolf lists the active Moorists as Maynard Keynes, Lytton Strachey, Saxon Sydney-Turner, Thoby Stephen and himself, 'and at varying distances from the centre Clive Bell, J.T. Sheppard, R.G. Hawtrey and A.R. Ainsworth orbiting at some distance beyond'. 'Forster and Desmond MacCarthy,' he adds, 'moved erratically in and out of this solar system of intellectual friendship, like comets.'[2]

The explanation of Morgan Forster's making only occasional appearances was the difference in age, which is never more important than at school or the university. He was four years older than Maynard Keynes and had gone down from Cambridge in 1901, two years before the Moorist revelation was most influential. (*Principia Ethica* was not published till 1903.) Forster would revisit Cambridge for a meeting of the Society, and, more important to him, to see Goldsworthy Lowes Dickinson, and then vanish.

Forster's friendships with Nathaniel Wedd and Dickinson were far more formative than those with any of the younger men. He must have met Moore occasionally, but he only got to know him well towards the end of Moore's life; and I have been told that Ainsworth, rather than Moore, is the model for Stewart Ansell, the young philosopher in *The Longest Journey*. Wilfred Stone has said that no one ever called Forster a Moorist, though Henry James got the two men mixed up.[3] Yet the two fundamental tenets of *Principia Ethics* underlie much of Forster's writing. By these I mean that what matter are states of mind, not necessarily associated with action, and that since it is impossible to calculate the final effects of any act one must only take into account the immediate result: thus a brutal or a barbarous action can never be justified because of its possible long-term results. Forster applies this not only to such acts as the bombing of a foreign country but to every form of unkindness.

Artists, in which term I include imaginative writers, reflect a climate of opinion rather than devote themselves to ethical propaganda; and it is the climate of opinion which Forster absorbed at Cambridge from Dickinson and his friends in the Society that one finds expressed with such subtlety in the novels.

No one has questioned that the Cambridge which produced that climate of opinion existed. But when the young men from Cambridge went to London, got married, or set up house there, did they form

2 *Sowing* (Hogarth Press, London, 1960), p. 171.
3 Wilfred Stone, *The Cave and the Mountain: A Study of E.M. Forster* (1966) pp. 65–6; and E.M. Forster, 'Henry James and the Young Men', *The Listener* LXII (1959) 103.

'Bloomsbury'? Clive Bell denied that it ever existed. But whether he
was right or wrong, it has been invented, worshipped by some and
abominated by others. If there was a Bloomsbury, it certainly centered
round No 46 Gordon Square, the house in which Clive Bell and Vanessa Stephen went to live after their marriage. It is arguable that
the factor which distinguished the group in Cambridge after they
moved to London was not a matter of space and time but the presence
of two women, the daughters of Sir Leslie Stephen, Vanessa and Virginia. There is truth in Cyril Connolly's recent description of Bloomsbury as a 'milieu which is more intense, more spacious and more
loving [than our own]. Bloomsbury was such a society, matriarchal
despite the brilliance of the courtiers, and at the centre of the maze
sat the unwobbling pivot, Vanessa Bell.'[4]

Friendships formed at the university often fall apart as life brings
new experiences and interests. Work absorbs and scatters groups of
friends. This did not happen to the 'Bloomsburies', for several reasons. Most of them were heretics who did not accept conventional
standards of art, literature, morals or ethics. They were men and
women with strong intellectual interests and great originality. They
were, moreover, attached to and interested in each other. These facts
kept them together. And then Clive Bell was extremely hospitable.

Of the others, Virginia and her brother Adrian Stephen set up house
together in Brunswick Square. Maynard Keynes, Duncan Grant and
Gerald Shove took rooms in it. The whole group went to the opera,
to the ballet, they gave parties and had play-readings and played poker
far into the night. Naturally changes took place as the years went
by. Virginia married Leonard Woolf and they had various homes,
moving out to Richmond and back to Bloomsbury; Adrian Stephen
married and came to live in No 51 Gordon Square; the Strachey family
left Hampstead and took No 50 next door; James Strachey married
and took No 41 Gordon Square. Maynard Keynes married and took
over the lease of No 46. Clive took a flat at the top of Adrian's house
and Vanessa took a lease of No 37. Roger Fry went to live in Bernard
Street, and Morgan Forster had a *pied-à-terre* in my mother-in-law's
house, No 27 Brunswick Square. It was of this period that Leonard
Woolf writes: 'it was not until Lytton Strachey, Roger Fry and Morgan
Forster came into the locality, so that we were all continually meeting
one another, that our society became complete.'[5]

4 Review of *Lytton Strachey: a Critical Biography*, vol. 2, by Michael Holroyd, in
   Sunday Times Weekly Review, 25 Feb. 1968, p. 51.
5 *Downhill All the Way* [see p. 153].

Yet Morgan Forster was on the periphery rather than at the heart of this circle. I would not describe his visits as sudden and comet-like, blazing through the solar system. He seemed to turn up when something interesting was occurring; and he himself was always interesting. The elusiveness that Maynard Keynes notes is very characteristic, and was made more noticeable by the fact that for many years, just as the party was warming up, he had to catch a train back to Weybridge. He was more like the Cheshire Cat than a comet.

The friendship that originally brought him into Bloomsbury was that with Leonard Woolf. He had known Leonard before the latter went to Ceylon, and the friendship grew after his return. Forster had met Virginia before her marriage, but his friendship with her, based largely on their both being professional writers, only grew close because she and Leonard were a couple usually seen together. For Morgan Forster, Leonard Woolf was a practical man whose advice and help he was anxious to get in any difficulty.

When, at the beginning of 1921, he was invited to go out to India as temporary private secretary to the Maharajah of Dewas Senior, Forster thought that he ought to be able to ride a horse. He consulted Leonard and asked him to give him lessons. Leonard agreed and lessons took place at Richmond. Morgan shared the trust that so many people, particularly the young and the simple, and all animals feel for Leonard. But, if he sought Leonard's advice, Virginia came to respect and depend on his criticism and good opinion of her writing more than on that of Lytton Strachey or Clive Bell or Roger Fry. . . .

It was not a one-way traffic: Morgan's value to Virginia was repaid by Leonard. After his return from India, he showed Leonard the unfinished manuscript of *A Passage to India* which he had abandoned in despair. Leonard pronounced it a great work and urged him to finish it. Moreover, the consciousness of the Bloomsbury audience consisting of his friends, Virginia and Leonard, Clive, Lytton, Maynard, and Roger had, I suspect, a restraining influence on his vein of fantasy. At the time of the early novels – 1905 to 1910, when Bloomsbury was only just coming into existence – Edward Garnett had influenced him far more than the Stracheys or Stephens ever did. In these novels and in the stories Pan, satyrs and dryads sometimes make their appearance and are always present in the wings. Even in *Howards End* there are pigs' teeth in the wych-elm. Edward Garnett had told him that these sublimations or symbolisations of sex were often out of key and unconvincing, and Bloomsbury later reinforced

his judgement. Morgan Forster himself recalls that ' "The Point of
It" was ill-liked when it came out by my Bloomsbury friends. "What
is the point of it?" they queried thinly, nor did I know how to reply'
(*Collected Short Stories*, vii). It is possible that without this restraining
influence the immanent spirit in the Marabar caves might have become an overt presence, disastrous to the credibility of *A Passage to
India*.

If Morgan Forster sought the aid of Leonard as a practical man,
the situation was sometimes reversed in his relations with Lytton Strachey. In September 1915, at the end of Lytton's tenancy of Hilton
Young's cottage in Wiltshire, Morgan not only helped him to pack
up all his possessions, but undertook to see them safely delivered
to the Strachey home in Belsize Park Gardens while Lytton went
off on a round of visits. At the beginning of the friendship Morgan
and Lytton had been rather shy of one another, but understanding
and affection grew after the war and until Lytton's death. It was
founded, not on admiration of each other's work, but on shared jokes
and sympathetic appreciation of each other's attitude to life.

Another early acquaintance which grew into friendship with the
years was that with Roger Fry. Their friendship was enhanced by
their interest in Charles Mauron, the French writer on aesthetics who
later translated *A Passage to India*.

The first time that I met Forster in Bloomsbury was at a party
given by Lady Ottoline Morrell in Bedford Square. The next day,
going to Duncan Grant's studio at the top of No 22 Fitzroy Street,
I found Forster sitting there. Then the bell sounded and I ran down
and admitted D.H. Lawrence and Frieda, who had also come to look
at Duncan's pictures. Forster was, I think, interested to meet Lawrence
again, but after one or two pictures had been set up on the easel
Lawrence began a didactic harangue, and an expression of pain came
into Morgan's face. I have often noticed him wince when someone
has said something brutal or insensitive. Usually it is only for a moment as he braces himself to face the harshness of the outside world.
But as Lawrence launched himself on a denunciation of the evil that
he discovered in Duncan's paintings the look of pain was replaced
by one of pure misery, and very soon he murmured something about
a train to Weybridge and disappeared.

Though the wince of pain is one of my most vivid memories of
Morgan Forster, the delighted appreciation of a remark which had
pleased him is a more frequent memory. His broad, rather heart-
shaped face would light up, the eyes would sparkle and a sort of

suppressed sneeze which became a surreptitious laugh would reveal how greatly he had been pleased and amused. It was a pleasure that was almost anguish. I have most often witnessed this reaction at readings of the Memoir Club. Sometimes a preliminary look of pain would be followed by the little sneeze of joy when he listened to the inspired gossip which was characteristic of Bloomsbury – gossip which its chroniclers stigmatize as malicious, but which was actually the result of an almost gourmet-like love of the foibles of old and intimate friends. What would be malicious if told about a stranger or a slight acquaintance may be free of malice if told about a loved one. Such were the anecdotes at the expense of Vanessa and Duncan and Roger Fry. And rich and varied they were.

I myself saw most of Morgan Forster when I was a bookseller and he did more than anyone in Bloomsbury, or outside it, to help Francis Birrell and me make our shop pay its way.

He was not at that time the world-renowned author he has become. One of his introductions led to our supplying the state of Hyderabad with educational books, another to our equipping Palestine with terrestrial globes. A recommendation from him got me a job as a reviewer on the *Daily Herald* at a time when I was very hard up. After I became an author he recommended a book of mine to a Danish lady who translated it. For all these considerate and generous acts I have always been grateful. But the greatest gift was to feel that one was liked, and the greatest pleasure to watch his face light up with appreciation or approval of something one had said and to provoke the little sneeze of anguished, slightly surreptitious, laughter.

Laughter was omnipresent in Bloomsbury, but how different were its individual tones. Clive had a loud uncontrolled guffaw that did one's heart good, Virginia a sudden bird-like crow. Lytton's laughter took many forms to match the wide range of his feelings which it expressed. Leonard's and Vanessa's were often reluctant. But Morgan's appreciative, anguished, but always critical laughter is the most abiding memory I have of him among his friends in Bloomsbury.

Vanessa Bell by Virginia Woolf

Although she has been described as the unwobbling pivot at the centre of the Bloomsbury maze (see p. 198), Vanessa Bell remains among the more elusive of the Bloomsberries. Her son Julian described her as follows:

And one, my best, with such a calm of mind,
And, I have thought, with clear experience
Of what is felt of waste, confusion, pain,
Faced with a strong good sense, stubborn and plain;
Patient and sensitive, cynic and kind.

The sensuous mind within preoccupied
By lucid vision of form and colour and space,
The careful hand and eye, and where resides
An intellectual landscape's living face,
Oh certitude of mind and sense, and where
Native I love and feel accustomed air.   (228-9)

But Julian Bell also said the lines could be applied to Roger Fry as well as to his mother.

Virginia Woolf wrote two introductions to the catalogues of her sister's exhibition in 1930 and 1934. In the first, reprinted here, Virginia's humorous formalist and feminist appreciation of Vanessa's work is based on an awareness of both the sensibility and the solidity of her sister that were so important for Bloomsbury and herself.

That a woman should hold a show of pictures in Bond Street, I said, pausing upon the threshold of Messrs Cooling's gallery, is not usual, nor, perhaps, altogether to be commended. For it implies, I fancy, some study of the nude, and while for many ages it has been admitted that women are naked and bring nakedness to birth, it was held, until sixty years ago that for a woman to look upon nakedness with the eye of an artist, and not simply with the eye of a mother, wife or mistress was corruptive of her innocency and destructive of her domesticity. Hence the extreme activity of women in philanthropy, society, religion and all pursuits requiring clothing.

Hence again the fact that every Victorian family has in its cupboard the skeleton of an aunt who was driven to convert the native because her father would have died rather than let her look upon a naked man. And so she went to Church; and so she went to China; and so she died unwed; and so there drop out of the cupboard with her bones half a dozen flower pieces done under the shade of a white umbrella in a Surrey garden when Queen Victoria was on the throne.

These reflections are only worth recording because they indicate the vacillations and prevarications (if one is not a painter or a critic of painting) with which one catches at any straw that will put off the evil moment when one must go into the gallery and make up one's mind about pictures. Were it not that Mrs Bell has a certain reputation and is sometimes the theme of argument at dinner tables, many no doubt would stroll up Bond Street, past Messrs Cooling's, thinking about morality or politics, about grandfathers or great aunts, about anything but pictures as is the way of the English.

But Mrs Bell has a certain reputation it cannot be denied. She is a woman, it is said, yet she has looked on nakedness with a brush in her hand. She is reported (one has read it in the newspapers) to be 'the most considerable painter of her own sex now alive'. Berthe Morisot, Marie Laurencin, Vanessa Bell – such is the stereotyped phrase which comes to mind when her name is mentioned and makes one's predicament in front of her pictures all the more exacting. For whatever the phrase may mean, it must mean that her pictures stand for something, are something and will be something which we shall disregard at our peril. As soon not go to see them as shut the window when the nightingale is singing.

But once inside and surrounded by canvases, this shillyshallying on the threshold seems superfluous. What is there here to intimidate or perplex? Are we not suffused, lit up, caught in a sunny glow? Does there not radiate from the walls a serene yet temperate warmth, comfortable in the extreme after the rigours of the streets? Are we not surrounded by vineyards and olive trees, by naked girls couched on crimson cushions, by naked boys ankle deep in the pale green sea? Even the puritans of the nineteenth century might grant us a moment's respite from the February murk, a moment's liberty in this serene and ordered world. But it is not the puritans who move us on. It is Mrs Bell. It is Mrs Bell who is determined that we shall not loll about juggling with pretty words or dallying with delicious sensations. There is something uncompromising about her art. Ninety-nine painters had nature given them her susceptibility, her sense of the lustre of grass and flower, of the glow of rock and tree, would have lured us on by one refinement and felicity after another to stay and look for ever. Ninety-nine painters again had they possessed that sense of satire which seems to flash its laughter for a moment at those women in Dieppe in the eighties, would have caricatured and illustrated; would have drawn our attention to the antics of parrots, the pathos of old umbrellas, the archness of ankles, the eccentricities of noses. Something would have been done to gratify the common, innocent and indeed very valuable gift which has produced in England so rich a library of fiction. But look round the room: the approach to these pictures is not by that means. No stories are told; no insinuations are made. The hill side is bare; the group of women is silent; the little boy stands in the sea saying nothing. If portraits there are, they are pictures of flesh which happens from its texture or its modelling to be aesthetically on an equality with the China pot or the chrysanthemum.

Checked at that point in our approach (and the snub is none the less baffling for the beauty with which it is conveyed) one can perhaps draw close from another angle. Let us see if we can come at some idea of Mrs Bell herself and by thus trespassing, crack the kernel of her art. Certainly it would hardly be possible to read as many novels as there are pictures here without feeling our way psychologically over the features of the writer; and the method, if not illicit, has its value. But here, for a second time, we are rebuffed. One says, Anyhow Mrs Bell is a woman; and then half way round the room one says, But she may be a man. One says, She is interested in children; one has to add, But she is equally interested in rocks. One asks, Does she show any special knowledge of clothes? One replies, Stark nakedness seems to please her as well. Is she dainty then, or austere? Does she like riding? Is she red haired or brown eyed? Was she ever at a university? Does she prefer herrings or Brussels sprouts? Is she – for our patience is becoming exhausted – not a woman at all, but a mixture of Goddess and peasant, treading the clouds with her feet and with her hands shelling peas? Any writer so ardently questioned would have yielded something to our curiosity. One defies a novelist to keep his life through twenty-seven volumes of fiction safe from our scrutiny. But Mrs Bell says nothing. Mrs Bell is as silent as the grave. Her pictures do not betray her. Their reticence is inviolable. That is why they intrigue and draw us on; that is why, if it be true that they yield their full meaning only to those who can tunnel their way behind the canvas into masses and passages and relations and values of which we know nothing – if it be true that she is a painter's painter – still her pictures claim us and make us stop. They give us an emotion. They offer a puzzle.

And the puzzle is that while Mrs Bell's pictures are immensely expressive, their expressiveness has no truck with words. Her vision excites a strong emotion and yet when we have dramatised it or poetised it or translated it into all the blues and greens, and fines and exquisites and subtles of our vocabulary, the picture itself escapes. It goes on saying something of its own. A good example is to be found in the painting of the Foundling Hospital. Here one says, is the fine old building which has housed a million orphans; here Hogarth painted and kind hearted Thackeray shed a tear, here Dickens, who lived down the street on the left-hand side, must often have paused in his walk to watch the children at play. And it is all gone, all perished. House breakers have been at work, speculators have speculated. It is dust and ashes – but what has Mrs Bell got to say about it? Nothing. There is the picture, serene and sunny, and very still. It represents a fine eighteenth century house and an equally find London plane tree. But there are no orphans, no Thackeray, no Dickens, no housebreakers, no speculators, no tears, no sense that this sunny day is perhaps the last. Our emotion has been given the slip.

And yet somehow our emotion has been returned to us. For emotion there is. The room is charged with it. There is emotion in that white urn; in that little girl painting a picture; in the flowers and the bust; in the olive trees; in the provencal vineyard; in the English hills against the sky. Here, we cannot doubt as we look is somebody to whom the visible world has given a shock of emotion every day of the week. And she transmits it and makes us share it; but it is always by her means, in her language, with her susceptibility, and not ours. That is why she is so tantalising, so original, and so satisfying as a painter. One feels that if a canvas of hers hung on the wall it would never lose its lustre. It would never mix itself up with the loquacities and trivialities of daily life. It would go on saying something of its own imperturbably. And perhaps by degrees – who knows? – one would become an inmate of this strange painters' world, in which mortality does not enter, and psychology is held at bay, and there are no words. But is morality to be found there? That was the very question I was asking myself as I came in.

Vanessa Bell by Quentin Bell

Quentin Bell is the family biographer of Bloomsbury, as it were. His life of his aunt, the first and certainly the best written of what were to be numerous biographies of Virginia Woolf, appeared in 1972. The following description of his mother comes from an introduction to her letters and was originally entitled with the nickname of 'Ludendorff Bell' that Keynes gave her.

'Museum 5596.'
'Can I speak to Mrs Bell?'

'I am afraid Mrs Bell is out.'

'But you are Mrs Bell; I am your brother George.'

'I am afraid Mrs Bell is out.'

'But Vanessa, I know your voice; this is George Duckworth.'

'I am afraid Mrs Bell is out.'

'But, confound it, you *are* Mrs Bell.'

'I am afraid Mrs Bell is out.'

Sir George slammed down the receiver.

It was not often that Vanessa employed an imaginary parlourmaid, and there were times when she would have responded kindly enough to almost any caller; but at that moment she had no time for anyone save the agreeable young woman who reclined naked upon a sofa. Her middle years were made happy by her ability to employ a model and to preserve those sacred hours that were dedicated to work with the help of a fictitious domestic. It was the lack of any such assistance which had brought her into sad collision with Lydia Lopokova, who was soon to become Mrs Maynard Keynes. Lydia, charming, and welcome almost everywhere, started with the enormous advantage of living in the same house as Vanessa; she needed no telephone, she was universally welcome, and she wandered innocently into the studio for a chat at almost any time of day. In the end Vanessa made what she called 'a statement' – her statements sometimes sounded more like ultimatums – and her working hours were saved, but not without some protests from Mr Keynes. This incident and others earned for Vanessa the reputation of a dragon, a terrible monster who guarded the life-room with fire and flames. I doubt whether she did much to contradict the popular legend. Nevertheless, since I did for a time work beside her, I feel it is right to say that her reputation was not entirely deserved. On two occasions I saw her throw up her morning's work in order to assist a friend in trouble. On the first occasion it was in fact a woman who had fallen into debt and other difficulties and needed sympathy; on the second, it was a last-minute theatrical crisis in which the fate of a ballet embodying the work of Blake, Vaughan Williams and Gwen Raverat was in peril. That morning Vanessa and I found ourselves painting innumerable ballet dresses in order to be ready for that night's performance. It has to be remembered that here Vanessa was responding to one of the occasional emergencies of a fellow artist. Lydia Lopokova's friendly incursions resulted from a more or less constant need to communicate, to discuss, perhaps for the hundredth time, the genius of dear Maynard, the infamy of Diaghilev, of Massine, and in fact of nearly everyone connected with the ballet in London, and the undeniable differences which might be discovered between the climate of Russia and that of England, as also between their languages, their literature and their polity. A less dedicated painter than Vanessa might have discovered, as she did, that her capacity for responding to conversational openings such as these diminished rapidly.

A time came when she decided that she no longer needed a house, or rather part of a house, in Gordon Square. In the late twenties she moved into a studio at no. 8 Fitzroy Street adjacent to one Duncan Grant had taken over from Sickert at the beginning of the decade. They were huge, tall rooms looking into a back alley and communicating with the street by means of a clanking metallic passageway. Here there was ample studio space, with room enough for a sleeping and dining area, a bathroom, and a kitchen: here too one child could be accommodated at a time, and here an imaginary parlourmaid could be employed to deal with the outside world.

I think that in many ways the time that Vanessa spent at No. 8 Fitzroy Street was the happiest of her life, although her happiness ended abruptly in 1937 when Julian was killed in Spain. The earlier years of that decade were years in which Duncan's success, always as important to her as her own, was continually growing. She saw a good deal of her children in London and a great deal of them at Charleston. Although she claimed that Bloomsbury had come to an end in 1914, there was still a good deal of it that she could see either in London or in Sussex. Those of Duncan's friends who bored her could be entertained in his part of the building. It says a good deal for her character that Duncan's lovers usually ended by becoming her intimate friends.

Like her sister Virginia, Vanessa was always anxious to dispense as far as possible with servants; the very nice woman who came in to help with domestic chores was rapid and inconspicuous. Vanessa made breakfast and lunch for herself and Duncan on the studio stove, and sometimes a more substantial meal in the evenings. She worked until the light failed, when she would sometimes design decorations or write letters. After dinner she and Duncan would often go to a movie.

Today when we think of her, I suspect that we refer to Marcel Gimond's study of her head. It is a gravely beautiful, an Olympian head, but neither the sculptor's intention nor his medium allow us to suppose that it is a head that might be distorted by laughter or by distress; and yet in thinking of Vanessa I do see her thus transformed. My elder brother, speaking with unconscious prescience, likened her to Demeter, a goddess who with terrible velocity could change from summer to winter. My earliest memories are of her summer laughter, specifically of an evening seated on a bench in Gordon Square when she told us how children were made and born, an account which she made so overwhelmingly droll that I rolled helpless with mirth off the bench.

W.B. Yeats once told Vanessa that she had supernatural gifts. A stern rationalist, she rejected the idea with indignation. I think that it was more generally felt that, although far from stupid, she was not an intellectual, and this I think was true and is not incompatible with the fact that she was on affectionate terms with the owners of brilliant minds – Keynes, Strachey, Fry, and indeed her sister. But one was always being mildly surprised by her erudition. I had never suspected that she had any Latin until my brother was preparing to enter a public school and she was able to introduce him to Virgil.

But it was in the domestic and managerial line of business that she excelled. It was here that she excited the admiration of Maynard Keynes, even though he sometimes suffered as a result of her regulations. It was he who called her Ludendorff Bell, comparing her to the Prussian commander of terrifying efficiency who manipulated the armies of Germany with such verve and skill as very nearly to break the Allied lines in 1918. She was called upon to exert these talents, which were indeed diplomatic rather than military, when in 1916 she, Duncan Grant, David Garnett, servants, children and a dog arrived at Charleston Farmhouse in order to comply with and perhaps evade the conscription laws of that year. The group was soon to be enlarged by the addition of a governess, her daughter, and her lover, and by the birth of my sister Angelica. Maynard Keynes used the house as a weekend retreat, Mr and Mrs Woolf came over from Asheham, Lytton Strachey arrived and made improper suggestions to the boys on the farm. With the coming of peace, my father would often arrive, bringing with him a number of charming strangers. Duncan, who always had an unlucky talent for attracting the lunatic and criminal classes, brought one hapless young man who believed himself to be the lineal descendant of the pharaoh Tutankhamen, and another, less sympathetic, who specialized in building illicit stills. Maynard brought catamites who ranged from the absolutely charming to the perfectly appalling. Altogether we made an unstable compound which needed to be handled with intelligent dexterity.

In a house inhabited by difficult, temperamental individuals, where

machinery consisted of a hot-water system quite as difficult and
temperamental as any of the inhabitants, no motorcar, no telephone
and no serious shops within six miles, the mere mechanics of housekeeping must have been formidable: but to placate, assuage, reason
with or charm all the inhabitants and yet to go on painting their
portraits or, what might seem better, some distant landscape, was
surely a feat of considerable magnitude.

No doubt Maynard was right when he told Vanessa that she might
command armies; but of course they would have bored her to tears.
Better to command households, and this I think she must have enjoyed
as one enjoys anything that one does well; much better to stay in
the nursery. But I am sure that she was happiest away from the world,
painting in her studio.

Duncan Grant by Roger Fry

*In Roger Fry's introduction to a selection of his paintings, Duncan
Grant is related to Bloomsbury implicitly through the discussion of
'the personality of his work' - its naturalness, spontaneity, and joyful
inventiveness. Grant's indifference to current fashions in painting or
to public taste and his passion to follow where his art led him are
thoroughly consistent with Bloomsbury's convictions.*

*Fry's commentary on Grant's painting is an example of the critical
skills he brought to bear even on the work of a close friend. The
whole enterprise of the book on Grant - the introduction, the reproduced paintings, and the publication by the Hogarth Press - is
a Bloomsbury production. To the Group's critics it illustrated the
power of a mutual admiration society; to their friends it was a demonstration of the diversity of Bloomsbury's talents.*

Duncan Grant may almost be called a popular artist. He has not,
of course, a big popularity, nor is he likely ever to obtain it. But
he has, for so pure and uncompromising an artist, a suprisingly large
circle of genuine admirers. I hasten to add that he has never done
a single stroke of work with a view to ingratiate himself. He pleases,
but merely by the accident of being what he is, never because he
has sought in any way to satisfy the possible demands of the public.
He pleases because the personality his work reveals is so spontaneous,
so unconstrained, so entirely natural and unaffected. And these happy
dispositions of his nature reveal themselves in his work - in his draw-

ings by a singularly melodious and rhythmic line, in his painting
by a corresponding fluency and elegance of handling. His naturalness
gives him his singular charm of manner. But more than this, he has
a peculiar happiness of disposition. A certain lyrical joyousness of
mood predominates in his work. And this leads him to affect and
enjoy what is beautiful in nature, and to express that delight in beauty
in his work. I use the words beautiful and beauty here in the ordinary
sense. In the more strict sense of that which is aesthetically significant,
all genuine artists love beauty and create beauty. But many artists
– and among them some of the greatest – have built their aesthetically
beautiful constructions out of material that would be called ugly.
In their outlook on life they are attracted rather by what is sinister,
ugly, or exaggeratedly characteristic than by what the layman would
call beautiful. Artists in whom the dramatic sense of life is uppermost
generally avoid what is ordinarily felt to be beautiful, whilst those in
whom the lyrical sentiments are strong are likely to affect beauty in life.

Translated into more strictly aesthetic language, this amounts, I
think, to saying that artists like Duncan Grant feel most naturally
those harmonies which are easy to grasp, which are fluent, persuasive,
and can be followed without effort. This is true not only of the quality
of Duncan Grant's design, but also of his colour. In his earlier work
particularly his colour had a peculiar pellucid clearness and gaiety.
Even when he restricted himself, as he often did, to a limited palette
of ochres, greys, and dull greens, he was able to make his tones extraordinarily resonant and gay. In his later work an effort to give
more plastic density to his forms has led him to complicate his colour
schemes, with the result of a more united effect with some loss of
purity and resonance.

Although in developing his means of expression Duncan Grant
has been very much influenced by the great modern French masters,
his talent is peculiarly English. He has, what is comparatively rare
in the French school, a great deal of invention. But I do not call
him English merely because of the fact that he has invention, since
one could, after all, cite a good many inventors among the French,
but rather because of the quality of his invention – the peculiar playful, fantastic element in it, which reminds one occasionally of the
conceits of Elizabethan poetry. This shows itself particularly in such
pictures as the 'Tight-rope Walker' or the 'Woman in the Tub', with
its odd and unexpectedly happy use of the accessories of the toilet
as elements in the design.

The very idea of invention in painting implies a literary or representational element, since the painter who is entirely preoccupied
with the manner of representation will not be likely to be at the pains
to invent motives, but will accept more or less what Nature provides.
The inventor is almost necessarily concerned to some extent with
the significance of the objects his invention brings to him mind. Having once invented his theme, he may concern himself exclusively with
the manner of presenting it, but *what* he invents is likely to retain
a certain value in the total result. I have sometimes thought that
Duncan Grant has never exploited as fully as he should his particular
gift of invention.

It was perhaps inevitable that, coming at a time when the movement
of creative artists was in favour of insisting almost exclusively upon
the formal elements of design, he should have tended to suppress
his natural inclination to fantastic and poetic invention. Fortunately,
however, this has found an outlet from time to time in his decorative
work.

Gifted as he is with a peculiarly delightful rhythmic sense and an
exquisite taste in colour, he is peculiarly fitted to apply his talents
to decoration. When he was working at the Omega workshops his
fellow-artists all recognized the peculiar charm, the unexpected originality, and the rare distinction of his ideas, and I should be inclined
to say that some of the designs which he then made for carpets, for
marquetry, and for needlework represent the high-water mark of applied design in England. Later on he has occasionally decorated
rooms, working in collaboration with Vanessa Bell, and he has, I
think, always succeeded in creating a singularly delightful atmosphere in his interiors, by reason of the unexpectedness of his fancy,
the gaiety and purity of his colour – which, however, never ceases
to be essentially discreet and sober – and the perfect adaptation of
even the oddest inventions to the decorative purposes of the work
in hand.

He has occasionally designed costumes for the ballet and given
designs for scenery. These, alas, have been all too rarely executed,
thanks to the conventionalism and timidity of producers. One of these
designs, a proposed backcloth for a Venetian ballet with eighteenth-
century costume, is reproduced. It illustrates well enough Duncan
Grant's peculiar aptitude for such work. The datum being
'Eighteenth-Century Venice', he has made a composition essentially
modern in feeling, but with a witty allusion to Guardi. In all his

costumes one finds him singularly sensitive to this allusive element, which plays so large a part in the art of dress. But his wit – for such in effect such allusions undoubtedly are – is never hard or merely brilliant. It is always tempered by that lyrical and poetic quality which characterizes his work. Naturally, he keeps as far as possible from pedantic archaism, though by a subtle hint he may let those who know into the secret of how sensitive he himself is to the art of the past.

It is indeed greatly to be regretted that so rare a talent as Duncan Grant shows for all kinds of decorative design can find so little outlet in our modern life. And in Duncan Grant's case this is peculiarly regrettable, since it is difficult for him to find scope within the limits of the easel picture for his finest gifts. He is, I think, always more inspired by having a problem of adaptation and a theme for development given to him than when he is confronted with the unlimited possibilities of canvas and oils. And, indeed, the tendency of art of the last few years had been unfavourable to him. The effort to create complete and solidly realized constructions in a logically coherent space, which has succeeded of late to the more decorative conception that derived from Gaugin, has, I think, hampered rather than helped his expression. Duncan Grant co-ordinates form more fully on the flat surface than in three dimensions. He is more plastic when he suggests relief by the quality of his contour than when he tries to realize it in all its complexity, and finally the attempt to realize a completely coherent three-dimensional whole tends to inhibit invention, which can never hope to attain quite the same completeness of realization as the rendering of the thing seen.

In the slow process of the development of an artist Duncan Grant is still young. It remains to be seen whether he will get the opportunities to utilize fully his exceptional gifts as a decorative designer, or whether, failing that, he will find – a difficult, but by no means impossible task – just that pictorial formula which will give full play to all his faculties, his charming poetic invention, his infallible tact in colour oppositions, and his melodious rhythm.

Of one thing his past assures all those who know his work, and that is, that no outward circumstances could ever make him deviate a hair's-breadth from the direction which his passion for art points out.

Clive Bell by David Garnett

Looking back, Desmond MacCarthy thought Clive Bell's part in the formation of Bloomsbury was impossible to overestimate (see p. 70). And Bell's son thought he 'helped temper the austerities' of Bloomsbury:

> He was different from the others in that he was better dressed, had a good seat on a horse, and was an excellent wing shot; for while all the rest were pretty obviously intellectual, he came from a society which hunted birds, animals, and, in his case, girls. . . . At Cambridge he was, I think, underrated by his friends; they did not look in the one direction in which he was, intellectually, more alert than they. In his rooms hung a reproduction of a painting by Degas, someone of whom most of them had probably never heard, for Cambridge at the turn of the century was aesthetically blind.   (Virginia Woolf, 1:156)

David Garnett's sketch of Clive Bell illustrates the effect of his personality on Bloomsbury. Garnett begins with a party in 1915 which introduced him to Bloomsbury.

46 Gordon Square, where the Bells lived, is a large house in the middle of the East side of one of the most pleasant squares in Bloomsbury. There was already a large party when we arrived and were ushered into the dining-room on the ground floor. I immediately noticed a cubist painting by Picasso, which I had seen reproduced in Clive's book *Art*. I also noticed a Vlaminck which I liked better. The pictures gave dignity to a room which was beautiful, although already crowded with people, among whom I recognized many old friends. . . .

Soon after that party I found myself on terms of warm friendship not only with Duncan and Maynard, but with Clive and Vanessa. 46 Gordon Square became for me a house where I felt sure of being welcome and Blanche, the thin tall housemaid who opened the door, and the children, Julian and Quentin aged six and four, soon began to greet me as a friend.

I do not think such a rapid friendship would have been possible but for Clive, whose character was in many ways complementary to Vanessa's, just as that of Jack Sprat was complementary to that of his lady who could eat no lean. Clive created the atmosphere of

Number Forty-six more than Vanessa and I shall therefore attempt a superficial sketch of his character.

In one of Hans Andersen's fairy tales there is a Princess who is so sensitive that she cannot sleep if there is so much as a crumpled rose petal beneath the mattress of her bed. Clive is like the princess, he cannot be happy if he is aware of anyone feeling unhappy in the vicinity. Thus, perhaps for selfish reasons, he does everything to create happiness about him. He is an almost perfect example of James Mill's Utilitarian theory that a man cannot become rich without enriching his neighbours. If everyone were like Clive, the theory might be generally true.

At this time Clive was not in the slightest degree interested in me and would not have cared if he had never seen me again. But if I was going to haunt Gordon Square, it was essential for his comfort that I should be feeling happy when I did. He was therefore far kinder to me than an altruistic man would have been. When the door was opened, a warm stream of Clive's hospitality and love of the good things of life poured out, as ravishing as the smell of roasting coffee on a cold morning. Heaviness, dullness, coldness, the besetting sins of English people and of the English climate, were impossible in Clive's house and Clive's company. Such jolly hearty good-fellowship is traditionally associated with fox-hunters and shooting parties and it was, in fact, from that milieu that Clive inherited his temperament. His tastes had led him into the chillier world of philosophers, mathematicians, critics and artists where the spiritual virtues of the hunt breakfast were unknown. Clive therefore provided an essential element in the formation of Bloomsbury. He brought to what might otherwise have been a bleak intellectual world

> a beaker full of the warm South
> Full of the true, the blushful Hippocrene
> With beaded bubbles winking at the brim.

He saved Bloomsbury from being another Clapham Sect, devoted, in the same cold unworldly way, to aesthetics and the pursuit of abstract truth instead of to evangelical religion. This was by no means all of Clive's contribution, for though he gives the impression of an airy quick-witted talker, he has the habits of a scholar. He always spends a good many hours a day reading. Clive's wide reading, quick wit and common sense were an essential ingredient in the brilliant talk to be heard in Bloomsbury. The other most important elements in it were the talk of Lytton, Virginia, Maynard, Desmond MacCarthy and Harry Norton. Clive cannot endure illness and he is often an absentee at the sick-beds of his nearest and dearest. Yet in other ways he is not squeamish. A secret horror of 46 Gordon Square was that the basement kitchen was infested with cockroaches. When the pest became bad, Clive would put on his shooting boots and go down in the middle of the night to stamp on them. No one else in Bloomsbury (except myself) would have done that.

Clive Bell and Duncan Grant by Angelica Garnett

Angelica Garnett's is the most involved Bloomsbury family history of anyone in the Group. Daughter of Vanessa Bell and Duncan Grant, she was raised as the daughter of Vanessa and Clive Bell in order not to jeopardize the financial support of Clive's family at Seend. After Julian Bell's death in the Spanish Civil War she was informed at eighteen of her true parentage. At twenty-two she married the recently widowed David Garnett, whose close friendship with Duncan and Vanessa began before she was born.

Angelica Garnett entitled the story of her Bloomsbury childhood Deceived with Kindness. *The chapter reprinted here was originally called 'Child of Two Fathers.'*

I remember that summer as endless, hot and tiring. One day when Vanessa was better she took me into the drawing-room at Charleston and told me that Duncan Grant, not Clive, was my real father. She hugged me close and spoke about love: underneath her sweetness of manner lay an embarrassment and lack of ease of which I was acutely aware, and which washed over my head like the waves of the sea. It is hard to say what prompted her to tell me just at that moment – how much was due to a plan conceived long ago, and how much because of her actual state of emotion. It is very likely that she felt, however obscurely, that she owed this gesture to Julian's memory. Not only would the knowledge she was about to impart help me to mature, but he would approve of the honesty of her gesture. At the same time she must have felt an immense need to unburden herself of the lie we had all been living under for the last seventeen years. Anxious about how I was going to take it, she said it need change nothing, since it was the intimacy of the present, not the facts of the past, that was important: my love for Quentin, for example, need not be affected by the fact that I now knew he was my half-brother. I remember the curious little shock this assertion gave me and I recognised the fact that I did indeed love him, though never before had I thought of saying so, which may indicate what an undemonstrative family we were. Although Julian had written to her that I was even more emotional than he was himself, I was not an outgoing child. If Vanessa expected me to show surprise at her information, she must have been disappointed: I hardly batted an eyelid, though when she left me to myself I was filled with euphoria. It was a fact which I had obscurely known for a long while. Whatever explosion there may have been occurred far below the surface: at the time I simply felt that a missing piece had been slotted into place.

Still, I did not talk to Duncan: perhaps I was afraid he would deflate my exultation. I preferred to gloat alone, unable to overcome my feeling that, with such a father, I had been marked for a special destiny. I was the little girl, red rose in hand, who falls in love with the prince, the hideous and charming beast. It never occurred to me that I was fantasising a Duncan that could never be. Nor did I realise, in my desperate need of a father figure, the true nature of my sacrifice. I should have spoken to Duncan. As it was, Vanessa said no more, he said nothing, and I remained closeted in dreams.

My relation to Duncan never got beyond this: I adored him, but the will to be his daughter was all on my side, and was received with no more than a bland serenity. It was an asexual barrier of simplicity and kindness which baffled me. I could not see round it, but – I cannot now help wondering – was there anything further to see? Assuredly there was, but it was too nebulous, private and self-centred to respond to the demands of a daughter. As a result our relationship, though in many ways delightful, was a mere simulacrum. We were not like father and daughter. There were no fights or struggles, no displays of authority and no moments of increased love and affection. All was gentle, equable, and superficial – it was indeed his ability to remain uninvolved that made him such a delicious companion. My dream of the perfect father – unrealised – possessed me, and has done so for the rest of my life. My marriage was but a continuation of it, and almost engulfed me.

So absolute was my confidence in their wisdom that I never thought of blaming either Duncan or Vanessa for their silence. Even later, when my resentment fell upon Vanessa, I never could bring myself to blame Duncan. This was years afterwards, when I had begun to realise what I had missed, and how deeply the ambiguity of the situation had sunk into me.

Although Vanessa comforted herself with the pretence that I had two fathers, in reality – emotional reality, that is – I had none. It was impossible to associate Duncan with any idea of paternity – and he never tried to assume such a role. Clive acted better, but carried no conviction, for he knew the truth. How different it would have been if we had all acknowledged it. Among other things, Duncan might have been able to show what affection he had. Vanessa never reflected that perhaps he too was inhibited by her prevarication, just as she never realised that, by denying me my real father, she was treating me even before my birth as an object, and not as a human being. No wonder she always felt guilt and I resentment, even though I did not understand the true reason for it; no wonder too that she tried to make it up to me by spoiling me, and in doing so only inhibited me.

As a result I was emotionally incapacitated – though it would be a great mistake to think that, had she told me before that my father was Duncan, my life would have been easier. My difficulties might indeed have been much the same, since his character would have remained constant. It was knowing the truth, instead of being deceived by those who had not fully considered the consequences of their lie, that would have changed everything.

But curiously enough, when the moment came, being told the truth made the world seem less and not more real. No one seemed capable of talking openly and naturally on the subject: Vanessa was in a state of apprehension and exaltation, and Duncan made no effort to introduce a more frank relationship. They gave the impression of children who, having done something irresponsible, hope to escape censure by becoming invisible.

Even Clive did not profit from my recently acquired knowledge; I was told by Vanessa that he preferred to look on me as his real daughter, and that therefore I had better say nothing to him. This was a great pity since Clive's affection was based on something better than pretence, and his relief at seeing all the cards on the table would have led to an easier relationship between us. He would have understood, if he wanted to, that there was nothing to prevent him from thinking of me as a daughter, while on my side the very real affection I had for him might have been released.

Whether Clive was aware of it or not, my attitude to him was deeply affected by the ambiguity of the situation, and because I could see Vanessa's feelings for him. I did not examine these at the time but I now understand that, while outwardly composed of trust and respect for his knowledge of the world, and an affection from which all effervescence had departed, she had, in expecting him to maintain a pretence, ridden roughshod over his finer susceptibilities. Did she never consider what was to happen at the moment when I appealed to him *as* my father, when I expected from him a moral support that he knew himself to be in no position to provide? Had anyone point this out, I think Vanessa would have said that, since Clive himself knew the truth, he had only to show his affection for me – without admitting that a permanent state of prevarication exacts its own dues. She might also have said that, had I been more precocious and more sensitive, she would have told me of it earlier, thus reducing the risks of an appeal to Clive. But she appeared to ignore the fact that, apart from and beyond affection, his answer would have been deprived of authority, and that it was this that I longed for, if only in the end to reject it.

Vanessa imagined that she herself could shoulder the entire situation, but although this was meant well, it was a gesture compounded of arrogance as well as generosity, and showed blindness, if not indifference, to reality. It would be easy to say she failed to recognise the importance of the relationship between father and daughter, but I do not think this was so – she evidently hoped that the one between myself and Clive would be fruitful – but she may not have understood that a daughter longs to be possessed by her father, and this Clive was in no position to do.

He did, however, show a greater sense of responsibility towards me than Duncan – although my general insecurity prevented me responding to it wholeheartedly. I suffered from reservations which I attributed to his inherent coldness, or to certain innuendoes and implications to sexual subjects, which I found embarrassing. Within certain limits, however, we got on very well, although as I look back on our relationship I regret that, at the time, I did not do his intentions justice.

Clive had welcomed my arrival in the world with generosity, and had continued to show a warm interest in my existence, even on rare occasions taking Vanessa's place when she wanted to go away – something Duncan never did. Of course, Nellie or Louie was always there, but as a point of reference, Clive was reliable, calm and good-humoured. When, as a very small child with mumps, appositely and without tears, I said, 'Oh dear, I've fallen out of bed,' he was delighted at my natural philosophy, and repeated the story at intervals for the next twenty years – a reiteration which irritated and blinded me to the affection that lay behind it. I remember too an occasion when

I was rude to him. I was still small, but old enough to know what not to say, yet my tongue, like a lizard's, seem to act on its own, and I came out with something now lost in the limbo of the unconscious – some remark met on his side with a blank surprise, a disbelief which showed that he was wounded, although I never heard any more about it.

On another occasion, having reached the age when Seend no longer seemed the magical place it once had been, I asked Vanessa whether I need go there for Christmas. She referred me to Clive, and with some trepidation I went to see him in his study at No. 50 Gordon Square, where he sat in his cane-backed chair puffing his pipe. Although innocent of all desire to cause pain, I have little doubt that my manner was tactless: young as I was, I did not realise that he was and always would be fond of a place and people that I, with youthful inconsistency, had just rejected. Clive looked at me over his spectacles in silence, and I knew that his feelings were hurt. Diplomatically, however, he promised that, if I went to Seend this year I need not go the next. For me it was a milestone because, even if he did not realise it, it was the first time I had talked to him as an adult, capable of doing something from choice rather than because I was told to.

If Clive had ever suffered embarrassment from our fictitious relationship, he seemed determined to disregard it now that I was growing up. For him, well-off, living half his life *en garçon* in London, it was a delight to give me my first oyster or plover's egg, and introduce me to his cosmopolitan and society friends, with whom we would lunch at the oval mahogany table, sitting long into the afternoon under the influence of still champagne, the remains of purple passion fruit crushed on our plates, our words left floating in the air. Clive enjoyed showing me off. He was also, however, sensitive to my predicament, and knowing that Duncan was incapable of showing an interest in my sexual education, gave me *Daphnis and Chloe* to read – pastoral and poetic and perfectly adapted to my stage of development. As my French improved he gave me *Manon Lescaut*, followed by the rather curious choice of *Les Liaisons Dangereuses*, which, as I might have known, was a Bloomsbury favourite. It was thanks to Clive that I became an enthusiastic admirer of Mérimée, enjoying *Carmen, Colomba, La Vénus d'Ille*, and some of the *Lettres à une Inconnue*.

It was only much later that I realised Clive was an unhappy, even a pessimistic man whose gifts had never been fully realised. One has the impression that with his friends – whose standards, though high, were also limited – he had never quite passed the acid test of being 'first-rate'. Whether this was because his literary achievements were lacking in distinction or his attitude to his love affairs hysterical is hard to say, but as time went on their criticism had its effect, and with some bitterness he recognised its justice. Together with a quick intelligence, his undoubted talents were for the observation of humanity – to which he brought the gift of common sense as well as a certain cynicism – and for the armchair variety of enjoyment, to which the more chairs that could be added, the better. Although Bunny has pointed out that his generosity was founded on selfishness, yet he was a man who preferred to enjoy himself in company, who always welcomed the unexpected guest, and who gave without stint. He loved his friends to exhibit themselves, to be what he expected them to be, and although no doubt this put a burden on them, and tended to limit their intercourse, it was a disarming form of affection: in his presence they could not help responding to his benevolence.

More than any other member of Bloomsbury, Clive was socially experienced, suave and competent, partly as a result of having money, but also because of his longing to associated with those whose style of life needed money. Unlike Vanessa or Virginia, he was unafraid of the refinement and delicacy of manners natural to the rich, although he did require a certain degree of culture and beauty to go with them. Characteristic of him though this was, however, one sometimes got the impression that his own delicacy was lacking; he so longed to impress by means of elaborate witticisms, flattery and *double entendres* that he was embarrassing, and in the end his friends were charmed more by his transparent goodwill than by his eighteenth-century manners.

There were in Clive two men, and both were at least a century out of date: one was the man about town, the dilettante, and the writer; the other, the squire, the countryman, and the sportsman. In the latter role he was, I think, more genuinely at ease, since his knowledge, skill and love of country life dated from childhood. In neither character did he quite fit into the world as it was, and one of the things that one loved him for was his refusal to recognise this, his ability to transform his surroundings either into the haunt of a sybarite or into the property of a landed gentleman.

At Charleston, where he had no property, he walked about the country as though he owned it, and the shepherd, the game-keeper, the gardener and their wives were devoted to him. If this assumption irritated Vanessa, she got her own back not only by a certain coolness but also by her ability to suggest that she might, at any time, act in such a way as to leave Clive gasping, conscious of how precarious his hold on her world was. In actual fact, however, a balance was always maintained: although Clive loved to feel on the brink, Vanessa never pushed him over.

In later life, his feeling for Vanessa was principally one of admiration that she could continue her professional life, her painting, without sacrificing her personal relationships. He never tired of her beauty and he appreciated her love for her children and her gift for organisation. He loved her for a depth which, when added to her tenderness and humour (even when not addressed to himself), gave her a distinction and mystery he never found elsewhere. In her youth, the mixture of a not unbarbed gaiety, a gentle and sometimes inspired irony, had been irresistible. Clive was not only a man of the world but a little boy, and much of Vanessa's charm lay in her ability to be discreetly maternal. If on her side this sentiment evaporated rather quickly, it was partly that it was impossible to continue loving a little boy as selfish as Clive, one who had never learned self-restraint, especially in sexual matters, and therefore lacked a sense of proportion. Neither had he, in spite of his knowledge and love of painting, any understanding of what it meant to be an artist: to him it was a mystery which he both loved and feared, because in Vanessa it was indissolubly linked to her femininity, her almost goddess-like capacity – as in the *Vénus d'Ille* – to love and to crush.

It was not only that Clive admired Vanessa's instinct for going her own way, he was also too lazy, perhaps too conscious of his own shortcomings, to stop her. He preferred her to shoulder the psychological problems of family life at the price of relinquishing his authority. It was perhaps his awareness of what was essentially an emotional failure that created in him a cold centre, a sterility which, for all his sociability and outward warmth, he could not completely conceal. And yet, though Clive suffered, his bitterness was addressed only to himself, never to her. For him she remained the only woman in whose house he could live with some semblance of contentment.

Between Clive and Duncan there was not the faintest show of jealousy – indeed it seems absurd to mention such a thing – and although this was no doubt largely because Duncan was a homosexual and that there was therefore no masculine rivalry, they also had a deep affection and understanding for each other. Clive, while he teased Duncan mercilessly for giving himself the airs of a colonel or major of some long-forgotten regiment, or for his almost uncritical catholicity of taste in art, or for any of his other idiosyncrasies, never patronised him, was always generous and never inconsiderate. It would have been only too easy for him to treat Duncan as an escaped lunatic or an *enfant terrible*, but this he never did. His respect for Duncan's personality was always evident, even if never directly spoken of. On his side, Duncan understood Clive and appreciated his sophistication, his erudition and the scope of his reading, which would often form the topic of their conversation. Neither had Duncan any prejudice against Clive's upper-class friends, with whom on occasion he was delighted to mix. He knew enough about them to enjoy Clive's reports of the latest intrigues and scandals, which often arrived at Charleston by letter, part of Clive's enormous correspondence. Often, Duncan's lightness of touch, and willingness to risk an original opinion, did more to cheer Clive than anything else. If Clive was the tinder, Duncan was the match, illuminating corners that would otherwise have been forgotten.

Virginia Woolf by E.M. Forster

E.M. Forster's Rede lecture on Virginia Woolf delivered after her death at Cambridge University during the Second World War is a public estimate of her work by the Bloomsbury friend whose professional judgment she most respected. As a good friend as well as a novelist and critic, Forster is able to present a view of Woolf that reveals her toughness, evaluates her aestheticism and her fiction, and is critical of her snobbery or her feminism. Readers surprised by Forster's misjudgment (not uncommon at the time) that her feminism was out of date should note the self-awareness with which he qualifies his old man's opinion. Despite this opinion, Forster's essay may be the best brief introduction to her work that has been written.

Forster's lecture, aptly dedicated to Leonard Woolf, is in the end a celebration of the values that Forster shared with Virginia, her husband, and their friends. (Two footnotes to the lecture have been omitted here.)

When I was appointed to this lectureship the work of Virginia Woolf was much in my mind, and I asked to be allowed to speak on it. To speak on it, rather than to sum it up. There are two obstacles to a summing up. The first is the work's richness and complexity.

As soon as we dismiss the legend of the Invalid Lady of Bloomsbury, so guilelessly accepted by Arnold Bennett, we find ourselves
in a bewildering world where there are few headlines. We think of
The Waves and say 'Yes – that is Virginia Woolf: then we think of
The Common Reader, where she is different, of *A Room of One's
Own* or the preface to *Life as We Have Known It*: different again.
She is like a plant which is supposed to grow in a well-prepared
garden bed – the bed of esoteric literature – and then pushes up suckers
all over the place, through the gravel of the front drive, and even
through the flagstones of the kitchen yard. She was full of interests,
and their number increased as she grew older, she was curious about
life, and she was tough, sensitive but tough. How can her achievement
be summed up in an hour? A headline sometimes serves a lecturer
as a life-line on these occasions, and brings him safely into the haven
where he would be. Shall I find one to-day?

The second obstacle is that the present year is not a good date
on which to sum up anything. Our judgments, to put it mildly, are
not at their prime. We are all of us upon the Leaning Tower, as
she called it, even those of us who date from the nineteenth century,
when the earth was still horizontal and the buildings perpendicular.
We cannot judge the landscape properly as we look down, for everything is tilted. Isolated objects are not so puzzling; a tree, a wave,
a hat, a jewel, an old gentleman's bald head look much as they always
did. But the relation between objects – that we cannot estimate, and
that is why the verdict must be left to another generation. I have
not the least faith that anything which we now value will survive
historically (something which we should have valued may evolve, but
that is a different proposition); and maybe another generation will
dismiss Virginia Woolf as worthless and tiresome. However this is
not my opinion, nor I think yours; we still have the word, and when
you conferred the Rede Lectureship on me – the greatest honour I
have ever received – I wondered whether I could not transmit some
honour to her from the university she so admired, and from the central
building of that university. She would receive the homage a little
mockingly, for she was somewhat astringent over the academic position of women. 'What? I in the Senate House?' she might say; 'Are
you sure that is quite proper? And why, if you want to discuss my
books, need you first disguise yourselves in caps and gowns?' But
I think she would be pleased. She loved Cambridge. Indeed, I cherish
a private fancy that she once took her degree here. She, who could
disguise herself as a member of the suite of the Sultan of Zanzibar,

or black her face to go aboard a Dreadnought as an Ethiopian –
she could surely have hoaxed our innocent praelectors, and, kneeling
in this very spot, have presented to the Vice-Chancellor the exquisite
but dubious head of Orlando.

There is after all one little life-line to catch hold of: she liked
writing.

These words, which usually mean so little, must be applied to her
with all possible intensity. She liked receiving sensations – sights,
sounds, tastes – passing them through her mind, where they encountered theories and memories, and then bringing them out again,
through a pen, on to a bit of paper. Now began the higher delights
of authorship. For these pen-marks on paper were only the prelude
to writing, little more than marks on a wall. They had to be combined,
arranged, emphasised here, eliminated there, new relationships had
to be generated, new pen-marks born, until out of the interactions,
something, one thing, one, arose. This one thing, whether it was
a novel or an essay or a short story or a biography or a private paper
to be read to her friends, was, if it was successful, itself analogous
to a sensation. Although it was so complex and intellectual, although
it might be large and heavy with facts, it was akin to the very simple
things which had started it off, to the sights, sounds, tastes. It could
be best described as we describe them. For it was not about something.
It was something. This is obvious in 'aesthetic' works, like *Kew Gardens* and *Mrs Dalloway*; it is less obvious in a work of learning, like
the *Roger Fry*, yet here too the analogy holds. We know, from an
article by Mr R.C. Trevelyan, that she had, when writing it, a notion
corresponding to the notion of a musical composition. In the first
chapter she stated the themes, in the subsequent chapters she developed them separately, and she tried to bring them all in again at
the end. The biography is duly about Fry. But it is something else
too; it is one thing, one.

She liked writing with an intensity which few writers have attained,
or even desired. Most of them write with half an eye on their royalties,
half an eye on their critics, and a third half eye on improving the
world, which leaves them with only half an eye for the task on which
she concentrated her entire vision. She would not look elsewhere,
and her circumstances combined with her temperament to focus her.
Money she had not to consider, because she possessed a private income, and though financial independence is not always a safeguard
against commercialism, it was in her case. Critics she never considered
while she was writing, although she could be attentive to them and

even humble afterwards. Improving the world she would not consider, on the ground that the world is man-made, and that she, a woman, had no responsibility for the mess. This last opinion is a curious one, and I shall be returning to it; still, she held it, it completed the circle of her defences, and neither the desire for money nor the desire for reputation nor philanthropy could influence her. She had a singleness of purpose which will not recur in this country for many years, and writers who have liked writing as she liked it have not indeed been common in any age.

Now the pitfall for such an author is obvious. It is the Palace of Art, it is that bottomless chasm of dullness which pretends to be a palace, all glorious with corridors and domes, but which is really a dreadful hole into which the unwary aesthete may tumble, to be seen no more. She has all the aesthete's characteristics: selects and manipulates her impressions; is not a great creator of character; enforces patterns on her books; has no great cause at heart. So how did she avoid her appropriate pitfall and remain up in the fresh air, where we can hear the sound of the stable boy's boots, or boats bumping, or Big Ben; where we can taste really new bread, and touch real dahlias?

She had a sense of humour, no doubt, but our answer must go a little deeper than that hoary nostrum. She escaped, I think, because she liked writing for fun. Her pen amused her, and in the midst of writing seriously this other delight would spurt through. A little essay, called *On Being Ill*, exemplifies this. It starts with the thesis that illness in literature is seldom handled properly (de Quincey and Proust were exceptional), that the body is treated by novelists as if it were a sheet of glass through which the soul gazes, and that this is contrary to experience. There are possibilities in the thesis, but she soon wearies of exploring them. Off she goes amusing herself, and after half a dozen pages she is writing entirely for fun, caricaturing the type of people who visit sick-rooms, insisting that Augustus Hare's *Two Noble Lives* is the book an invalid most demands, and so on. She could describe illness if she chose – for instance, in *The Voyage Out* – but she gaily forgets it in *On Being Ill*. The essay is slight, and was not offered for public sale, still it does neatly illustrate the habit of her mind. Literature was her merry-go-round as well as her study. This makes her amusing to read, and it also saves her from the Palace of Art. For you cannot enter the Palace of Art, therein to dwell, if you are tempted from time to time to play the fool. Lord Tennyson did not consider that. His remedy, you remember, was that the Palace would be purified when it was inhabited by all mankind, all behaving seriously at once. Virginia Woolf found a simpler and a sounder solution.

No doubt there is a danger here – there is danger everywhere. She might have become a glorified *diseuse*, who frittered away her broader effects by mischievousness, and she did give that impression to some who met her in the flesh; there were moments when she could scarcely see the busts for the moustaches she pencilled on them, and when the bust was a modern one, whether of a gentleman in a top hat or a youth on a pylon, it had no chance of remaining sublime. But in her writing, even in her light writing, central control entered. She was master of her complicated equipment, and though most of us like to write sometimes seriously and sometimes in fun, few of us can so manage the two impulses that they speed each other up, as hers did.

The above remarks are more or less introductory. It seems convenient now to recall what she did write, and to say a little about her development. She began back in 1915 with *The Voyage Out* – a strange tragic inspired novel about English tourists in an impossible South American hotel; her passion for truth is here already, mainly in the form of atheism, and her passion for wisdom is here in the form of music. The book made a deep impression upon the few people who read it. Its successor, *Night and Day*, disappointed them. This is an exercise in classical realism, and contains all that has characterized English fiction, for good and evil, during the last two hundred years: faith in personal relations, recourse to humorous sideshows, geographical exactitude, insistence on petty social differences: indeed most of the devices she so gaily derides in *Mr Bennett and Mrs Brown*. The style has been normalized and dulled. But at the same time she published two short stories, *Kew Gardens*, and *The Mark on the Wall*. These are neither dull nor normal; lovely little things; her style trails after her as she walks and talks, catching up dust and grass in its folds, and instead of the precision of the earlier writing we have something more elusive than had yet been achieved in English. Lovely little things, but they seemed to lead nowhere, they were all tiny dots and coloured blobs, they were an inspired breathlessness, they were a beautiful droning or gasping which trusted to luck. They were perfect as far as they went, but that was not far, and none of us guessed that out of the pollen of those flowers would come the trees of the future. Consequently when *Jacob's Room* appeared in 1922 we were tremendously surprised. The style and sen-

sitiveness of *Kew Gardens* remained, but they were applied to human
relationships, and to the structure of society. The blobs of colour
continue to drift past, but in their midst, interrupting their course
like a closely sealed jar, stands the solid figure of a young man. The
improbable has occurred; a method essentially poetic and apparently
trifling has been applied to fiction. She was still uncertain of the
possibilities of the new technique, and *Jacob's Room* is an uneven
little book, but it represents her great departure, and her abandonment
of the false start of *Night and Day*. It leads on to her genius of its
fullness; to *Mrs Dalloway* (1925), *To the Lighthouse* (1927), and *The
Waves* (1931). These successful works are all suffused with poetry
and enclosed in it. *Mrs Dalloway* has the framework of a London
summer's day, down which go spiralling two fates: the fate of the
sensitive worldly hostess, and the fate of the sensitive obscure maniac;
though they never touch they are closely connected, and at the same
moment we lose sight of them both. It is a civilized book, and it
was written from personal experience. In her work, as in her private
problems, she was always civilized and sane on the subject of madness.
She pared the edges off this particular malady, she tied it down to
being a malady, and robbed it of the evil magic it has acquired
through timid or careless thinking; here is one of the gifts we have
to thank her for. *To the Lighthouse* is, however, a much greater
achievement, partly because the chief characters in it, Mr and Mrs
Ramsay, are so interesting. They hold us, we think of them away
from their surroundings, and yet they are in accord with those surroundings, which the poetic scheme. *To the Lighthouse* is in three
movements. It has been called a novel in sonata form, and certainly
the slow central section, conveying the passing of time, does demand
a musical analogy. We have, when reading it, the rare pleasure of
inhabiting two worlds at once, a pleasure only art can give: the world
where a little boy wants to go to a lighthouse but never manages
it until, with changed emotions, he goes there as a young man; and
the world where there is pattern, and this world is emphasized by
passing much of the observation through the mind of Lily Briscoe,
who is a painter. Then comes *The Waves*. Pattern here is supreme
– indeed it is italicized. And between the motions of the sun and
the waters, which preface each section, stretch, without interruption,
conversation, words in inverted commas. It is a strange conversation,
for the six characters, Bernard, Neville, Louis, Susan, Jinny, Rhoda,
seldom address one another, and it is even possible to regard them
(like Mrs Dalloway and Septimus) as different facets of one single

person. Yet they do not conduct internal monologues, they are in touch amongst themselves, and they all touch the character who never speaks, Percival. At the end, most perfectly balancing their scheme, Bernard, the would-be novelist, sums up, and the pattern fades out. *The Waves* is an extraordinary achievement, an immense extension of the possibilities of *Kew Gardens* and *Jacob's Room*. It is trembling on the edge. A little less – and it would lose its poetry. A little more – and it would be over into the abyss, and be dull and arty. It is her greatest book, though *To the Lighthouse* is my favourite.

It was followed by *The Years*. This is another experiment in the realistic tradition. It chronicles the fortunes of a family through a documented period. As in *Night and Day*, she deserts poetry, and again she fails. But in her posthumous novel *Between the Acts* (1941) she returns to the method she understood. Its theme is a village pageant, which presents the entire history of England, and into which, at the close, the audience is itself drawn, to continue that history; 'The curtain rose' is its concluding phrase. The conception is poetic, and the text of the pageant is mostly written in verse. She loved her country – her country that is 'the country', and emerges from the unfathomable past. She takes us back in this exquisite final tribute, and she points us on, and she shows us through her poetic vagueness something more solid than patriotic history, and something better worth dying for.

Amongst all this fiction, nourishing it and nourished by it, grow other works. Two volumes of *The Common Reader* show the breadth of her knowledge and the depth of her literary sympathy; let anyone who thinks her an exquisite recluse read what she says on Jack Mytton the foxhunter, for instance. As a critic she could enter into anything – anything lodged in the past, that is to say; with her contemporaries she sometimes had difficulties. Then there are the biographies, fanciful and actual. *Orlando* is, I need hardly say, an original book, and the first part of it is splendidly written: the description of the Great Frost is already received as a 'passage' in English literature, whatever a passage may be. After the transformation of sex things do not go so well; the authoress seems unconvinced by her own magic and somewhat fatigued by it, and the biography finishes competently rather than brilliantly; it has been a fancy on too large a scale, and we can see her getting bored. But *Flush* is a complete success, and exactly what it sets out to be; the material, the method, the length, accord perfectly, it is doggie without being silly, and it does give us, from the altitude of the carpet or the sofa-foot, a peep at high

poetic personages, and a new angle on their ways. The biography
of Roger Fry – one should not proceed direct from a spaniel to a
Slade Professor, but Fry would not have minded and spaniels mind
nothing – reveals a new aspect of her powers, the power to suppress
herself. She indulges in a pattern, but she never intrudes her personality or over-handles her English; respect for her subject dominates
her, and only occasionally – as in her description of the divinely
ordered chaos of Fry's studio with its still-life of applies and eggs
labelled 'please do not touch' – does she allow her fancy to play.
Biographies are too often described as 'labours of love', but the *Roger
Fry* really is in this class; one artist is writing with affection of another,
so that he may be remembered and may be justified.

Finally, there are the feminist books – *A Room of One's Own* and
Three Guineas – and several short essays, etc., some of them significant. It is as a novelist that she will be judged. But the rest of her
work must be remembered, partly on its merits, partly because (as
Mr William Plomer has pointed out) she is sometimes more of a
novelist in it than in her novels.

After this survey, we can state her problem. Like most novelists
worth reading, she strays from the fictional norm. She dreams, designs, jokes, invokes, observes details, but she does not tell a story
or weave a plot, and – can she create character? That is her problem's
centre. That is the point where she felt herself open to criticism –
to the criticisms, for instance, of her friend Hugh Walpole. Plot and
story could be set aside in favour of some other unity, but if one
is writing about human beings, one does want them to seem alive.
Did she get her people to live?

Now there seem to be two sorts of life in fiction, life on the page,
and life eternal. Life on the page she could give; her characters never
seem unreal, however slight or fantastic their lineaments, and they
can be trusted to behave appropriately. Life eternal she could seldom
give; she could seldom so portray a character that it was remembered
afterwards on its own account, as Emma is remembered, for instance,
or Dorothea Casaubon, or Sophia and Constance in *The Old Wives'
Tale*. What wraiths, apart from their context, are the wind-sextet from
The Waves, or Jacob away from *Jacob's Room*! They speak no more
to us or to one another as soon as the page is turned. And this is
her great difficulty. Holding on with one hand to poetry, she stretches
and stretches to grasp things which are best gained by letting go of
poetry. She would not let go, and I think she was quite

right, though critics who like a novel to be a novel will disagree.
She was quite right to cling to her specific gift, even if this entailed
sacrificing something else vital to her art. And she did not always
have to sacrifice; Mr and Mrs Ramsay do remain with the reader afterwards, and so perhaps do Rachel from *The Voyage Out*, and Clarissa Dalloway. For the rest – it is impossible to maintain that here
is an immortal portrait gallery. Socially she is limited to the upper-
middle professional classes, and she does not even employ many types.
There is the bleakly honest intellectual (St John Hirst, Charles Tansley, Louis, William Dodge), the monumental majestic hero (Jacob,
Percival), the pompous amorous pillar of society (Richard Dalloway
as he appears in *The Voyage Out*, Hugh Whitbread), the scholar who
cares only for young men (Bonamy, Neville), the pernickety independent (Mr Pepper, Mr Banks); even the Ramsays are tried out first
as the Ambroses. As soon as we understand the nature of her equipment, we shall see that as regards human beings she did as well as
she could. Belonging to the world of poetry, but fascinated by another
world, she is always stretching out from her enchanted tree and
snatching bits from the flux of daily life as they float past, and out
of these bits she builds novels. She would not plunge. And she should
not have plunged. She might have stayed folded up in her tree singing
little songs like *Blue-Green* in the *Monday or Tuesday* volume, but
fortunately for English literature she did not do this either.

So that is her problem. She is a poet, who wants to write something
as near to a novel as possible.

I must pass on to say a little – it ought to be much – about her
interests. I have emphasized her fondness for writing both seriously
and in fun, and have tried to indicate how she wrote: how she gathered
up her material and digested it without damaging its freshness, how
she rearranged it to form unities, how she was a poet who wanted
to write novels, how these novels bear upon them the marks of their
strange gestation – some might say the scars. What concerns me now
is the material itself, her interests, her opinions. And not to be too
vague, I will begin with food.

It is always helpful, when reading her, to look out for the passages
which describe eating. They are invariably good. They are a sharp
reminder that here is a woman who is alert sensuously. She had an
enlightened greediness which gentlemen themselves might envy,
which few masculine writers have expressed. There is a little too much
lamp oil in George Meredith's wine, a little too much paper crackling
on Charles Lamb's pork, and no savour whatever in any dish of Henry
James's, but when Virginia Woolf mentions nice things they get right

into our mouths, so far as the edibility of print permits. We taste their deliciousness. And when they are not nice, we taste them equally, our mouths awry now with laughter. I will not torture this great university of Oxbridge by reminding it of the exquisite lunch which she ate in a don's room here in the year 1929; such memories are now too painful. Nor will I insult the noble college of women in this same university – Fernham is its name – by reminding it of the deplorable dinner which she ate that same evening in its Hall – a dinner so lowering that she had to go to a cupboard afterward and drink something out of a bottle; such memories may still be all too true to fact. But I may without offence refer to the great dish of Boeuf en Daube which forms the centre of the dinner of union in *To the Lighthouse,* the dinner round which all that section of the book coheres, the dinner which exhales affection and poetry and loveliness, so that all the characters see the best in one another at last and for a moment, and one of them, Lily Briscoe, carries away a recollection of reality. Such a dinner cannot be built on a statement beneath a dish-cover which the novelist is too indifferent or incompetent to remove. Real food is necessary, and this, in fiction as in her home, she knew how to provide. The Boeuf en Daube, which had taken the cook three days to make and had worried Mrs Ramsay as she did her hair, stands before us 'with its confusion of savoury brown and yellow meats and its bay leaves and its wine'; we peer down the shiny walls of the great casserole and get one of the best bits, and like William Banks, generally so hard to please, we are satisfied. Food with her was not a literary device put in to make the book seem real. She put it in because she tasted it, because she saw pictures, because she smelt flowers, because she heard Bach, because her senses were both exquisite and catholic, and were always bringing her first-hand news of the outside world. Our debt to her is in part this: she reminds us of the importance of sensation in an age which practises brutality and recommends ideals. I could have illustrated sensation more reputably by quoting the charming passage about the florist's shop in *Mrs Dalloway,* or the passage where Rachel plays upon the cabin piano. Flowers and music are conventional literary adjuncts. A good feed isn't, and that is why I preferred it and chose it to represent her reactions. Let me add that she smokes, and now let the Boeuf en Daube be carried away. It will never come back in our lifetime. It is not for us. But the power to appreciate it remains, and the power to appreciate all distinction.

After the senses, the intellect. She respected knowledge, she believed

in wisdom. Though she could not be called an optimist, she had,
very profoundly, the conviction that mind is in action against matter,
and is winning new footholds in the void. That anything would be
accomplished by her or in her generation, she did not suppose, but
the noble blood from which she sprang encouraged her to hope. Mr
Ramsay, standing by the geraniums and trying to think, is not a figure
of fun. Nor is this university, despite its customs and costumes: 'So
that if at night, far out at sea over the tumbling waves, one saw a
haze on the waters, a city illuminated, a whiteness in the sky, such
as that now over the hall of Trinity where they're still dining or washing up plates: that would be the light shining there – the light of
Cambridge.'

No light shines now from Cambridge visibly, and this prompts
the comment that her books were conditioned by her period. She
could not assimilate this latest threat to our civilization. The sub-
marine perhaps. But not the flying fortress or the land mine. The
idea that all stone is like grass, and like all flesh may vanish in a
twinkling, did not enter into her consciousness, and indeed it will
be some time before it can be assimilated by literature. She belonged
to an age which distinguished sharply between the impermanency
of man and the durability of his monuments, and for whom the dome
of the British Museum Reading Room was almost eternal. Decay she
admitted: the delicate grey churches in the Strand would not stand
for ever; but she supposed, as we all did, that decay would be gradual.
The younger generation – the Auden-Isherwood generation as it is
convenient to call it – saw more clearly here than could she, and
she did not quite do justice to its vision, any more than she did justice
to its experiments in technique – she who had been in her time such
an experimenter. Still, to belong to one's period is a common failing,
and she made the most of hers. She respected and acquired knowledge,
she believed in wisdom. Intellectually, no one can do more; and since
she was a poet, not a philosopher or a historian or a prophetess,
she had not to consider whether wisdom will prevail and whether
the square upon the oblong, which Rhoda built out of the music
of Mozart, will ever stand firm upon this distracted earth. The square
upon the oblong. Order. Justice. Truth. She cared for these abstractions, and tried to express them through symbols, as an artist must,
though she realized the inadequacy of symbols.

They come with their violins, said Rhoda; they wait; count; nod; down
come their bows. And there is ripples and laughter like the dance of olive
trees . . .

'Like' and 'like' and 'like' – but what is the thing that lies beneath the semblance of the thing? Now that lightning has gashed the tree and the flowering branch has fallen . . . let me see the thing. There is a square. There is an oblong. The players take the square and place it upon the oblong. They place it very accurately; they make a perfect dwelling-place. Very little is left outside. The structure is now visible; what is inchoate is here stated; we are not so various or so mean; we have made oblongs and stood them upon squares. This is our triumph; this is our consolation.

The consolation, that is to say, of catching sight of abstractions. They have to be symbolized, and 'the square upon the oblong' is as much a symbol as the dancing olive trees, but because of its starkness it comes nearer to conveying what she seeks. Seeking it, 'we are not so various or so mean'; we have added to the human heritage and re-affirmed wisdom.

The next of her interests which has to be considered is society. She was not confined to sensations and intellectualism. She was a social creature, with an outlook both warm and shrewd. But it was a peculiar outlook, and we can best get at it by looking at a very peculiar side of her: her Feminism.

Feminism inspired one of the most brilliant of her books – the charming and persuasive *A Room of One's Own*; it contains the Ox-bridge lunch and the Fernham dinner, also the immortal encounter with the beadle when she tried to walk on the college grass, and the touching reconstruction of Shakespeare's sister – Shakespeare's equal in genius, but she perished because she had no position or money, and that has been the fate of women through the ages. But Feminism is also responsible for the worst of her books – the can-tankerous *Three Guineas* – and for the less successful streaks in *Orlando*. There are spots of it all over her work, and it was constantly in her mind. She was convinced that society is man-made, that the chief occupations of men are the shedding of blood, the making of money, the giving of orders, and the wearing of uniforms, and that none of these occupations is admirable. Women dress up for fun or prettiness, men for pomposity, and she had no mercy on the judge in his wig, the general in his bits and bobs of ribbon, the bishop in his robes, or even on the harmless don in his gown. She felt that all these mummers were putting something across over which women had never been consulted, and which she at any rate disliked. She declined to co-operate, in theory, and sometimes in fact. She refused to sit on committees or to sign appeals, on the ground that women must not condone this tragic male-made mess, or accept the crumbs of power which men throw them occasionally from their hideous feast. Like Lysistrata, she withdrew.

In my judgment there is something old-fashioned about this extreme Feminism; it dates back to her suffragette youth of the 1910s, when men kissed girls to distract them from wanting the vote, and very properly provoked her wrath. By the 1930s she had much less to complain of, and seems to keep on grumbling from habit. She complained, and rightly, that though women today have won admission into the professions and trades they usually encounter a male conspiracy when they try to get to the top. But she did not appreciate that the conspiracy is weakening yearly, and that before long women will be quite as powerful for good or evil as men. She was sensible about the past; about the present she was sometimes unreasonable. However, I speak as a man here, and as an elderly one. The best judges of her Feminism are neither elderly men nor even elderly women, but young women. If they, if the students of Fernham, think that it expresses an existent grievance, they are right.

She felt herself to be not only a woman but a lady, and this gives a further twist to her social outlook. She made no bones about it. She was a lady, by birth and upbringing, and it was no use being cowardly about it, and pretending that her mother had turned a mangle, or that Sir Leslie had been a plasterer's mate. Working-class writers often mentioned their origins, and were respected for doing so. Very well; she would mention hers. And her snobbery – for she was a snob – has more courage in it than arrogance. It is connected with her insatiable honesty, and is not, like the snobbery of Clarissa Dalloway, bland and frilled and unconsciously sinking into the best armchair. It is more like the snobbery of Kitty when she goes to tea with the Robsons; it stands up like a target for anyone to aim at who wants to. In her introduction to *Life as We Have Known It* (a collection of biographies of working-class women edited by Margaret Llewelyn Davies) she faces the fire. 'One could not be Mrs Giles of Durham, because one's body had never stood at the wash-tub; one's hands had never wrung and scrubbed and chopped up whatever the meat is that makes a miner's supper.' This is not disarming, and it is not intended to disarm. And if one said to her that she could after all find out what meat a miner does have for his supper if she took a little trouble, she would retort that this wouldn't help her to chop it up, and that it is not by knowing things but by doing things that one enters into the lives of people who do things. And she was not going to chop up meat. She would chop it badly, and waste her time. She was not going to wring and scrub when what she liked doing and could do was write. To murmurs of 'Lucky lady you!' she replied, 'I am a lady', and went on writing. 'There aren't going to be no more ladies. 'Ear that?' She heard. Without rancour or surprise or alarm, she heard, and drove her pen the faster. For if, as seems probable, these particular creatures are to be extinguished, how important that the last of them should get down her impressions of the world and unify them into a book! If she didn't, no one else would. Mrs Giles of Durham wouldn't. Mrs Giles would write differently, and might write better, but she could not produce *The Waves*, or a life of Roger Fry.

There is an admirable hardness here, so far as hardness can be admirable. There is not much sympathy, and I do not think she was sympathetic. She could be charming to individuals, working-class and otherwise, but it was her curiosity and her honesty that motivated her. And we must remember that sympathy, for her, entailed a tremendous and exhausting process, not lightly to be entered on. It was not a half-crown or a kind word or a good deed or a philanthropic sermon or a godlike gesture; it was adding the sorrows of another to one's own. Half fancifully, but wholly seriously, she writes:

> But sympathy we cannot have. Wisest Fate says no. If her children, weighted as they already are with sorrow, were to take on them that burden too, adding in imagination other pains to their own, buildings would cease to rise; roads would peter out into grassy tracks: there would be an end of music and of painting; one great sigh alone would rise to Heaven, and the only attitudes for men and women would be those of horror and despair.

Here perhaps is the reason why she cannot be warmer and more human about Mrs Giles of Durham.

This detachment from the working-classes and Labour reinforces the detachment caused by her Feminism, and her attitude to society was in consequence aloof and angular. She was fascinated, she was unafraid, but she detested mateyness, and she would make no concessions to popular journalism, and the 'let's all be friendly together' stunt. To the crowd – so far as such an entity exists – she was very jolly, but she handed out no bouquets to the middlemen who have arrogated to themselves the right of interpreting the crowd, and get paid for doing so in the daily press and on the wireless. These middlemen form after all a very small clique – larger than the Bloomsbury they so tirelessly denounce, but a mere drop in the ocean of humanity. And since it was a drop whose distinction was proportionate to its size, she saw no reason to conciliate it.

'And now to sum up', says Bernard in the last section of *The Waves*.

That I cannot do, for reasons already given; the material is so rich
and contradictory, and ours is not a good vintage year for judgments.
I have gone from point to point as best I could, from her method
of writing to her books, from her problems as a poet-novelist to her
problems as a woman and as a lady. And I have tried to speak of
her with the directness which she would wish, and which could alone
honour her. But how are all the points to be combined? What is
the pattern resultant? The best I can do is to quote Bernard again.
'The illusion is upon me', he says, 'that something adheres for a
moment, has roundness, weight, depth, is completed. This, for the
moment, seems to be her life.' Bernard puts it well. But, as Rhoda
indicated in that earlier quotation, these words are only similes, com-
parisons with physical substances, and what one wants is the thing
that lies beneath the semblance of the thing; that alone satisfies, that
alone makes the full statement.

Whatever the final pattern, I am sure it will not be a depressing
one. Like all her friends, I miss her greatly – I knew her ever since
she started writing. But this is a personal matter, and I am sure that
there is no case for lamentation here, or for the obituary note. Virginia
Woolf got through an immense amount of work, she gave acute pleasure in new ways, she pushed the light of the English language a
little further against darkness. Those are facts. The epitaph of such
an artist cannot be written by the vulgar-minded or by the lugubrious.
They will try, indeed they have already tried, but their words make
no sense. It is wiser, it is safer, to regard her career as a triumphant
one. She triumphed over what are primly called 'difficulties', and
she also triumphed in the positive sense: she brought in the spoils.
And sometimes it is as a row of little silver cups that I see her work
gleaming. 'These trophies', the inscription runs, 'were won by the
mind from matter, its enemy and its friend.'

Virginia Woolf by Leonard Woolf

*Leonard Woolf's brief portrait of his wife was done for the BBC in
1965, while he was writing his extensive autobiographies. The picture
of Virginia Woolf in them is, of course, much fuller, but in his broadcast Leonard effectively, if a little laconically, summarizes his view
of her genius. (Subsequent bibliographical research revealed that the
Church* Guardian *was the first paper Virginia Woolf began writing
for.)*

All human beings are extremely complicated. Virginia Woolf was one of the few people I have ever met who I think was a genius, and geniuses are slightly more complicated than ordinary people. I have myself met two people whom you have to call geniuses; one was G.E. Moore the philosopher, and the other was my wife. Her mind acted in a way in which ordinary people, who are not geniuses, never let their minds run. She had a perfectly ordinary way of thinking and talking and looking at things and living; but she also at moments had a sight of things which does not seem to me to be exactly the ordinary way in which ordinary people think and let their minds go. It was partly imagination, and it worked in ordinary life in exactly the same way every now and then as it worked in her books. She would be describing what she had seen in the street, for instance, or what someone had said to her, and then go on to weave a character of the person and everything connected with them, and it would be quite amusing. Then suddenly it would become something entirely different. I always called it leaving the ground. She would weave not the sort of scene or conversation which one felt was what anyone else would have seen and described, but something entirely different. It was often extraordinarily amusing, but in a very peculiar way – almost like a fantasy, and sometimes it was extremely beautiful. In her diary, when she describes how she wrote the last page of *The Waves*, she says that suddenly, as she was writing, the pen as it were took control of her and her thoughts raced ahead of herself, and she followed her own thoughts. I think that exactly describes a genius's method of composition and imagination as opposed to that of a non-genius.

She spoke somewhere about 'the voices that fly ahead', and she followed them. She had also, and this is an important thing to remember, an insane period in her life. She had three mental breakdowns. Then, when she was at her worst and her mind was completely breaking down again the voices flew ahead of her thoughts: and she actually heard voices which were not her voice; for instance, she thought she heard the sparrows outside the window talking Greek. When that happened to her, in one of her attacks, she became incoherent because what she was hearing and the thoughts flying ahead of her became completely disconnected. Of course, people have said, from the time of the Greeks, that insanity and genius are closely allied. In my wife's case, I think one could see clearly that the two things were not disconnected.

There was a side of her which was completely like ordinary people. She liked eating and talking and going for walks, and she was fond of playing bowls and listening to music. One critic has said that she was completely withdrawn from the world and had no contact with ordinary people, but that was entirely untrue; she loved society, she loved parties, she would spend hours talking to people and would have liked to go out to parties or to theatres or to concerts every day of her life. But she had to be careful not to overtire herself, and therefore it was a perpetual struggle for her to prevent herself going into society. I have never known anyone more social with every kind of person, and the less intellectual they were, the more she liked, in a way, talking to them, because she was interested in what was going on in a person's mind. She got on extremely well with children; you cannot do that if you are withdrawn or if you do not have one side of you which is an ordinary person.

She had a very regular routine: it was dominated by her writing because writing was the most important thing to her and everything had to be regularized for it. Her day began after breakfast, at about half-past nine, when she went into her work-room, which was a very peculiar room. When we lived in Tavistock Square there was an enormous room which had been a billiards room, I imagine, and there she sat in an armchair, in the most frightful disorder – almost squalor – because the Hogarth Press's publishing business which we had started used it as a storeroom for the books, and she was by no means a tidy writer, or tidy with papers. There she would write with a pen and ink on a board on her lap for the morning; if she was well, she would probably write for two or three hours, but whenever she was at all ill, she had to be very careful not to overwork and sometimes was allowed to write only for an hour a day. Then she had lunch, and then she almost always went for a walk; she was very fond of walking about the London streets and observing things, just letting the impact of what she saw come upon her. I think her writing in her books is extraordinarily visual.

She was the most conscientious writer that I have ever known. Even where the voices flew ahead of her and the pen followed her thoughts, thoughts actually controlling her, written at the most tremendous pace, that was not the final version; sometimes she would go on for five or six revisions.

She always said that she had no education at all, and was rather pleased at the thought. It was not really true; she never went to school, I think partly because she was a very delicate child, but her father, Sir Leslie Stephen, was a literary man of the first water – a Victorian of the Victorians. He was the editor of the *Dictionary of National*

Biography; he was a very good essayist; he edited one of the quarterlies. He had a very good library of all the great English writers. His daughter, Virginia, was given the run of it, at an early age, and he would discuss with her afterwards what she had read. They used to go for walks in Kensington Gardens, and he would talk about what the children were reading and the people he had known. He married as his first wife Thackeray's daughter; she died, but the other daughter, Lady Ritchie, who had married Sir Richmond Ritchie, was a writer of some genius and very fond of my wife. She had met every conceivable person, from Charlotte Brontë downwards, and had written the most fascinating descriptions of them. Therefore, in a way, my wife was born into English literature.

She must have begun to write fairly early, but I have not found anything written by her much before 1900, when she was eighteen. She began by writing diaries. Then she taught herself to write by writing, which is, I imagine, the only way in which one can. She began writing for a paper called *The Speaker*. Then *The Times Literary Supplement* was started, and Richmond, the editor, knew the Stephen family. At any rate, she became one of his most cherished reviewers. Then when she was about twenty-five, she began writing a novel, *The Voyage Out*, but she re-wrote it, I think, seven times from end to end. I don't think one could possibly know that: the book reads as if it had just been written straight out. But she found in an old cupboard once five or six complete versions of *The Voyage Out* and burnt them.

She always got into a terrible state about a book when she had finished it. In fact, it was always one of the dangerous times for her health because the strain was terrific. When she finished *The Years*, which was one of the most popular of her novels, she thought it was hopelessly bad and got into such a state about it that we decided that she would have to stop thinking about it, and we went away and she put it out of her mind. Then she came back and started on it again and she cut out an enormous chunk in the middle. That is the only time in which she ever scrapped anything entirely.

She wrote *Orlando* as a sort of joke, and therefore was not worried about it as she was so much by other novels. If you write that kind of farce, I suppose it is easier to write, but I am quite certain that she enjoyed writing her novels immensely; it was her greatest pleasure in life. But she was hopelessly sensitive about everything, particularly about writing. Any criticism or feeling that the thing was not right was almost torture. I certainly have never felt about anything in the

world anything like what she felt about the slightest thing wrong
with anything she had written. Therefore, although the actual writing
was of enormous importance to her, there was also this torture of
having to get it right in the end.

It is difficult to know whether she knew exactly what her position
was as a writer. She knew that she had reached a very high position
among contemporary writers. I don't think she really very much worried about that; but any individual criticism or any unpleasant thing
said about her as a writer, she minded very much indeed.

I think myself that *The Waves* is a great book and has all the marks
of great literature. Whether any of the others are on the same level
I rather doubt. *To the Lighthouse* is probably a great novel; I don't
think the others are on the same level. What I mean by a great novel
is that it is on the same level as, say, a book by Charlotte Brontë
or even George Eliot or even probably *Wuthering Heights*. I don't
think one should say more than that. Also, as a critic, I think she
was very good.

Leonard Woolf by Quentin Bell

*Quentin Bell's introduction to Leonard Woolf's autobiographies
brings out the intellectual honesty, rationalism, and political interests
that uncle and nephew shared, and makes it clear why Leonard Woolf
chose Quentin Bell to write Virginia's biography. Bell's description
of Leonard's personality is supplemented by Angelica Garnett's account of the Woolfs that follows.*

Leonard Woolf was an intelligent, a sensitive and very truthful man.
This is the kind of thing that I need to say in this introduction;
this, and my reasons for saying what I do. Others are as able as or
more able than I to say that this book is a thoroughly 'good read'
(as indeed it is). But I have had to use it as biographical material
and to find out whether Leonard is indeed truthful: here then I speak
with a certain authority.

But before doing so I want to try to introduce *him*. I knew him
for about half a century, but I remember him best in middle and
old age when he was a long, thin man, finely, elegantly constructed
with a sharp semitic nose, deep grey eyes and a sensitive mouth. The
lines of his face, which fell habitually into a mournful or even a
grim expression, could be very much transformed when, as often hap-

pened, he smiled. His hands, particularly when he was gardening or driving a car, had a look of muscular intelligence like the hands of a craftsman. But the first impression, and it was an enduring impression, was of someone strange from a distant land. When I was a child I was slightly amazed to find that he could speak English so well (I may have been a little confused by having been told that he came from Ceylon). But my father also felt this; Lytton Strachey described him as a camel driver, while his future wife told him that he seemed 'foreign'.

I cannot be sure about that distant land in which my infant understanding and my adult imagination placed him. Certainly it was beyond the Hellespont, somewhere in the East, and it was gorgeous but harsh; one had laboriously to extract a meagre living amidst the bitter herbs and rocky wastes of that country and the best that one could ever hope for was a crumb or two of manna blown from across the mountains by an icy wind. To pursue this fantasy a little further, it was because he or his forebears had, as I imagined, scratched a living from that inhospitable desert, that, when he could cultivate the genial humus of Sussex, he found it child's play to make the land yield milk and honey.

There was no real incongruity in the fact that, despite this exotic appearance, Leonard was at times exceedingly British and almost John Bullish in his insistence upon the particular virtues of the English. Few people – apart from some eccentric foreigners – have ever been so insistent upon the pre-eminent merits of our cooking. Also there was an intellectual boldness, an uncomfortable intransigence about him which reminded me rather of French than of English friends. There was something unyielding and a little fierce in his way of arguing, which was intimidating, and although he could feel charm in others he did not allow it to affect his judgements, nor did he have any sympathy with weakness or procrastination. I would not like to have been a minor official when Leonard was a colonial administrator, and to have found myself having to confess to some little human weakness or official equivocation.

But 'the grissily Wolf' as Dora Carrington called him 'was charming', and this she said even at a time when she had behaved rather badly, was being examined, and had every expectation of finding Leonard both foreign and ferocious. Indeed I think that one may say that, although he would stand for no nonsense, even the most seductive nonsense, and although there were those, particularly his colleagues in the Hogarth Press, who found him difficult, still, essentially he was a very kind man. There must have been many occasions when he found me almost unbearably exasperating but I do not remember him saying anything that was really malevolent or unkind. Nor, in my experience, did he ever harbour a grudge. Indeed, some of those who knew him only in his later years may think that I have said too much of the forbidding aspect of the man. But it was real enough and so was his kindness; this latter quality earned him a kind of bonus; it is pleasant when pussy purrs upon the hearthrug; but it would be more than pleasant, it would be downright reassuring, to hear a tiger purr (if tigers do purr). Leonard's benevolence was considerable but it was made more considerable still by the intimidating gravity which he sometimes displayed; it had the charm of the unexpected. Women felt this very much, for women are in some respects less immodest than men; men tend to believe, often without the faintest justification, that they are the intellectual equals of all other men; in consequence they take it for granted that they will be taken seriously. Leonard seemed to take everyone very seriously and anyone who might meet him in discussion was treated with intellectual courtesy. Women found this astonishing and flattering and it was perhaps for this reason that, in many ways, Leonard found women better to work with than men. It must also be said that although he tried to be scrupulously fair in argument and was never either evasive or dismissive, he very rarely conceded defeat and was in truth uncommonly stubborn in his opinions. I should like to think that these few sketchy and heavily corrected contours may provide the reader with a faint image of the man, although I have hardly suggested his gift for laughter and for imaginative sympathy. The essential outline which I have attempted to describe is gaunt and severe, but that image has to be qualified by the understanding that his was a very humane and a very kindly personality. He was a person who cared for other people and for animals, even for his tiresome dogs and his perfectly horrible pet monkey. But the aspect of the man which most concerns us here was his honesty, and of his passionate desire to tell the truth on any and every subject there can, to my mind, be no doubt.

These memoirs are essays in veracity; also, and this is something different, he strove to be accurate. In 1968 I gave it as my opinion that he was our most accurate writer on Bloomsbury. This, at the time, was true, and if in the Biography, the Letters and the Diaries of Virginia Woolf we have been able at some points to supplement or even to correct his information, of his desire to write the truth there is still no doubt whatsoever. His two main sources, apart from his memory, were his own diaries and those of Virginia Woolf, and when he has these to help him he practically never goes wrong; it is when there are no diaries on which to rely that he makes mistakes. One of these, oddly enough, is the date of his return from his honeymoon. In the same way, and for the same reason, he is at times misleading when he refers to events which took place in England at a time when he was in Ceylon; but as I said these are minor errors.

Leonard valued intellectual probity and this was one of his grand characteristics. It was a passion which led him to noble and disinterested actions but it could sometimes be a source of weakness in that at times it prevented him from doing things that he wanted to do. Both as a novelist and as a politician he was in a way inhibited by his own honesty.

As a writer of fiction he entered that difficult and perplexing terrain in which, although truth is respected, it is sometimes best conveyed by means of falsehood. Just as the draughtsman must, by a species of falsification and selection, achieve the seemingly impossible task of delineating solid objects upon a flat surface, so the writer of fiction may make his events more real by imposing upon them a form which does not, or need not, exist in nature. In *The Village in the Jungle* Leonard comes so close to direct reporting of that which he has seen that we are continually held, delighted and horrified by what he has to say. It need not, I feel, have been a work of fiction and would have been better if he had not imposed a fictional form upon it. As it is, the book is damaged by the necessities of a story which lacks form. Of *The Wise Virgins* I speak without assurance; to me it seems a failure (some people say that it is a masterpiece). It was written under great stress and with some anger; he describes his family, his wife's family and himself, and everyone or almost everyone is made odious, so odious that it is difficult to feel any sympathy for anyone. Again, for the purposes of his fiction his people act in an uncharacteristic way and in truth he is not at ease with the form that he has chosen. He made some other attempts at fiction but they were few and, so it seems to me, he discovered finally that it was a genre that did not suit him. It would have been difficult under any circumstances, for Virginia's husband to have written novels.

He is certainly much more at home in the world of politics and his political works are extensive. It is rash to generalise but I fancy that he is at his best in works which are in the main historical, as for instance his admirable *Empire and Commerce in Africa*. Here he tells a plain story with force, lucidity, and some humour.

He had a passionate dislike for the kind of intellectual legerdemain which makes dogma seem respectable. In *Quack, Quack!*, a book too topical to have survived, he made a statement of faith, or rather of doubt, which, for its clarity and honesty, deserves I think to be rescued from oblivion; for here, in the last section of his book, there is an attack upon certain tendencies of thought, or perhaps one should say of rhetoric, which are still with us. We still suffer from fraudulent mystics, transcendental word-mongers, and priest-craft. Indeed if a single superstition has died during the past fifty years then I think it must be that which sees the destinies of mankind prefigured at the bottom of teacups, and this, alas, not because we have become more reasonable but because tea-bags are more convenient. Thus when Leonard denounces the dangerous windbags of his time, Spengler and Count Keyserling, Radhakrishnan and Bergson, he is denouncing the kind of intellectual confusion and chicanery which still flourishes, prospers hugely, disseminates dangerous myths and needs to be attacked.

Spengler he takes as the grand example of the intellectual-political quack; impressive, at times brilliant, he is condemned for his complete lack of intellectual probity or humility – 'my work is the result of inspiration such as has not been known in the human race for thousands of hears'. Leonard finds Spengler not only pretentious and ridiculous but also dangerous. His manner of arriving at what he calls 'truth' is to search in his blood, his guts, his solar plexus, anywhere so long as it is not his head, and to assert things because in some undefinable way he 'knows' them. The process is terribly like the deep intuitive illuminations of Hitler, the message drawn from the blood and soil of Germany. The transcendent truths of the Nordic myth have exactly the same intellectual character as the splendid certainties of Spengler, and sure enough when it became politically convenient to forget certain passages in *The Decline of the West* this feat was accomplished. Herr Spengler's doctrines became, in 1933, quite indistinguishable from those of the rulers of Germany. On a rational view this adaptation would appear to be unjustifiable, but the beauty of this kind of argument is that it rises above mere reason, and this, for someone who is anxious to placate a tyrant, is certainly a great convenience.

The metaphysical quacks of whom Bergson, Radhakrishnan and Count Keyserling are taken as examples are in their argumentative methods very similar to Spengler.

By metaphysical quackery I mean the abandonment of and contempt for reason as a means of truth in non-political speculation and the substitution for it of so-called intuition, magic and mysticism. A determined and honest application of reason to the universe as we know it seems inevitably to lead to scepticism and agnosticism, to a disbelief in what appear to be absolute truths, to a conviction that the truth which seems to us most certainly true and most rigorously proved, the belief which we are totally unable not to believe, even reason itself, all these are dubious and precarious and may well be merely delusions and superstitions, the shadow dreams of shadows.

This, as Leonard himself allows, is not a comfortable position for the intellect, and, if one accepts a scepticism which extends even to the operation of reason itself, may one not forgive those who find in the promptings of faith or intuition a way past the insurmountable difficulties which confront the sceptic? In such a tempest of doubt surely the hapless swimmer may grasp at whatever spars or whatever straws seem to give him some buoyancy – always provided that the straws and spars are of a respectable kind – a wave-born cross or a floating mantra and not a Nordic myth?

But this is just what Leonard will not permit. To say that, because we cannot know, we must assert, is in his view wholly dishonest. The fact that we should very much like to be provided with unchallengeable certainties concerning the nature of the universe does not mean that they are obtainable, and the only true conclusion that we may draw from the discovery that we do not know what we would so much like to know is quite simply that indeed we do not know.

Moreover, if we do attempt to cut the Gordian knot of doubt, arguing that since reason cannot take us where we want to go there must be a mode of apprehension which transcends reason, our conclusions are invalidated by our own argument, for to argue is to reason, and yet it is the purpose of our argument precisely to dethrone reason.

As may be imagined, Leonard is not in sympathy with religion. He regards it rather as liberal-minded men regard sodomy or drug addiction. It is all right so long as you keep your vices private. Let the solitary anchorite regard his navel or count his beads; undertaken in the privacy of a hermit's cell this is a harmless occupation. But when the religious man begins to preach or to proselytise he becomes a public danger. Scepticism is the mother of toleration; religion, and in particular organised religion, breeds persecution. Nor can it very well be otherwise, for, if we abandon reason, we cannot dispute either with rationalists or with non-conformists. In default of reason we must rely upon arguments that all can understand, those of the *Index Librorum Prohibitorum* or the stake.

I have done my best to summarise Leonard's arguments, although I am well aware that I have not the equipment needed for such a task. The attempt had to be made, partly because the argument which he developed in *Quack, Quack!* was of central importance in his view of the world and partly because the book exhibits both his strength and his limitations.

Moreover I must note in passing that while rereading that book I have been struck by its strange topicality. In the very large volume of literature devoted to the study of Virginia Woolf there is a kind of lunatic fringe, and in this of late it has been possible to find authors who are ready to denounce Leonard, to find in his rationalism an unsympathetic and insensitive quality which, so the story goes, made him incapable of making his wife happy. There is a distinct air of quackery about such writers, a rejection of reason and indeed a sublime disregard of nearly all the available evidence. They too have their place in the records of intellectual dishonesty which Leonard so carefully examined.

From this it may be perceived that, in so far as I understand them, I am in sympathy with Leonard's views. At all events I find it difficult not to admire such a dedicated pursuit of so forbidding a theory and I do think that in demolishing the prophets of the higher or transcendental nonsense he was doing something well worth doing and doing it with great force.

A deep distrust of specious argument and a passionate belief in the value of intellectual integrity seem to me to be very admirable things; but they are not, it must be allowed, a part of the usual equipment of a successful politician, and Leonard was a politician. He went into the world of practical politics, not simply as a thinker but rather to go to the grass roots. And this meant, not merely that on polling day his was one of the tiny band of motor cars which sported the Labour colours in the Lewes Constituency, but also that he was personally involved in the day to day business of the Women's Cooperative Guild or the ward Labour Party. It must be allowed that in practice, as a candidate and as an expert adviser to his party, he did not achieve success as the world usually measures that commodity.

It is easy, nor is it wholly wrong, to explain his relative failure by invoking a familiar idea of the remote intellectual, that is to say the image of one who stands upon some cold eminence from which he can see very well what his fellow men ought to be doing, but where he is so much raised above the common emotions that he cannot descend to those lower altitudes where policies are converted into effective action.

The image is at once true and false. It is true enough that Leonard never thumped a tub and that, precisely because the resonance which results from that exercise is so great and gives to arguments a force which, intellectually, is not properly theirs, he would always have found the effort too distasteful to be accomplished with the enthusiasm which is its necessary ingredient. But, this being conceded, it would be wrong to think of him as one so cerebral in his approach to life as to be quite separated from his fellows by a 'superior' Cambridge arrogance.

If he ever had that quality he lost it in Ceylon. I have only to recall the many times that I myself have heard him, patiently, quietly, without the faintest air of condescension or of 'side', explaining to the Rodmell Labour Party some difficult question concerning the League Covenant or the taxation of land. He had only one aim in view, to make a difficult proposition clear; there was an honesty and a simplicity about him to which those audiences responded. His clarity gave them greater acuteness than they knew themselves to possess; his manifest sincerity was entirely lovable.

Virginia noticed the same thing in him, as also his perfect respect for those who, without being brilliant or in any striking way successful, were in the truest sense respectable.

> Leonard went off at 10 a.m. to give his second lecture at Hampstead. The first was a great success, as I knew it would be. He finds the women much more intelligent than the men; in some ways too intelligent, & apt on that account, not to see the real point. He has another to give this afternoon, so he is staying up at Hampstead, lunching with Lilian, & perhaps seeing Janet. No one except a very modest person would treat these working women, & Lilian & Janet & Margaret as he does. Clive or indeed any other clever young man, would give himself airs; and however much he admired them pretend he didn't.

The truth about Leonard, as I suppose about any human being, is too complex to be expressed in a formula. I cannot even agree with his own estimate. At the end of a lifetime of thankless work on committees he declared that it had all been time wasted.

He was wrong. He achieved more than he would admit. The work of those who, like Leonard, will commit themselves to the prosaic side of politics, giving their wisdom and experience and asking nothing in return, is of inestimable value, and certainly the country needs such men badly. I believe that Leonard was able to persuade us to do sensible things and to prevent us from committing even greater follies than those of which we have been guilty. As an old man he returned to Ceylon; it cannot often happen that when a period of imperial rule is over and a people has won its liberty a returning civil servant, and a severe one too, is kindly received. Leonard had something like a hero's welcome. The long hours in committee rooms had after all borne some fruit.

'What a life he has led', said E.M. Forster, 'and how well he has led it.'

Virginia and Leonard Woolf by Angelica Garnett

Angelica Garnett's chapter on Virginia and Leonard Woolf in her auto-biography is entitled 'The Woolves.' It presents their household from the Charleston point of view, as it were. Although Angelica's recol-lections are more critical of Bloomsbury than her brother's, there is considerable affection in them. Included in her comparison of the Woolves is a revealing description of Vanessa and Virginia.

Our intimacy with the Woolves, as we called them, was close in spite of the fact that the atmosphere we breathed was very different. We were a family, whereas they were a couple, ranging through life with single-minded commitment. To them we, the younger generation, must have seemed disorganised and undisciplined, even egotistical, battening on to Vanessa and stretching her to the utmost. At the same time Virginia loved finding herself back in a family environment, and, feeling that an afternoon at Charleston was a holiday, her main purpose was to twang the strings and make them buzz with teasing and laughter. To her this was the breath of life, and she thoroughly enjoyed it. For us it was as though a stopper had been taken out of a bottle – criticisms, questions, and jokes poured out of her: we were exposed not only to her realms of imagination but to a mind as tough and sharp as obsidian.

Neither Virginia nor Leonard pretended to be other than they were; there was no facile morality or talking down to children – on the contrary Virginia was less remote than Vanessa and insisted on a reciprocity that filled the air with tension, which if sometimes alarming, was also stimulating. She was convinced that I inhabited a world of fantasy special to myself, and she longed to enter it. In this world she was Witcherina and I, Pixerina; we flew over the elms and over the downs, our main object, as far as I remember, being to bring back fictitious information about other members of the family. As may be imagined, this suited Virginia to perfection, for she loved inventing improbable situations in which Julian, Quentin or Vanessa might find themselves, whereas I, dazzled by her virtuosity, remained wingless, fixed to the ground.

It was at teatime that I remember Virginia's arrival at Charleston, pacing through the house, followed by Leonard and Pinka, the spaniel, whose feathered pads would slap on the bare boards beside her master's more measured footfall. Virginia, seeing myself and Vanessa sitting by the fire or under the apple tree in the garden, would crouch beside us, somehow finding a small chair or low stool to sit on. Then she would demand her rights, a kiss in the nape of the neck or on the eyelid, or a whole flutter of kisses from the inner wrist to the elbow, christened the Ladies' Mile after the stretch of sand in Rotten Row, Hyde Park, where Vanessa in the past had ridden on a horse given her by George Duckworth.

Virginia's manner was ingratiating, even abject, like some small animal trying to take what it knows is forbidden. My objection to being kissed was that it tickled, but I was only there to be played off against Vanessa's mute, almost embarrassed dislike of the whole demonstration. After a long hesitation, during which she wished that some miracle would cause Virginia to desist, she gave her one kiss solely in order to buy her off. Although she felt victimised and outwitted by her sister, she won the day by her power of resistance, and an utter inability to satisfy Virginia's desires, which completely disregarded Vanessa's feelings. She suffered mainly because, much as she loved Virginia and deep though her emotions were, she became almost unbearably self-conscious when called upon to show them. Of her love for Virginia there was no question: she simply wished that it could have been taken for granted. They were both affectionate, but Virginia had the advantage of articulateness, which Vanessa may have distrusted, having suffered from it in the past: Virginia's flashes of insight into other people's motivations could be disturbing. In one word she could say too much, whereas Vanessa, priding herself on her honesty, was inclined to say too little. Neither could Vanessa compete with Virginia's brilliance and facility; made to feel emotionally inadequate, she also imagined herself lacking in intelligence. She distrusted Virginia's flattery, in which she detected an element of hypocrisy, setting her on a pedestal for false reasons, but she did not see how to retaliate without brutality, of which she was incapable. She became more and more truculent, her exasperation masked by an ironic smile with which she tried to discourage Virginia's efforts to extract a sign of love.

When the ceremony of rights was over, conversation resumed on a gossipy, joking level, flavoured by Virginia's wit and Vanessa's logic. Once Virginia had been liberated by receiving her allowance of kisses, she became detached, quizzical, gay and intimate. Vanessa, let off the hook, relaxed the knot into which she had tied herself, and although she continued to feel waves of frustration and reserve, the hedge in which she sat, and which Virginia had been trying to break down, grew less thick and impenetrable.

Leonard, like a vigilant and observant mastiff, remained unmoved by this behaviour. He was made of different material from the rest of us, something which, unlike obsidian, couldn't splinter, and inevitably suggested the rock of ages. I know from later conversations with him that he strongly disapproved of the way in which I had been brought up, and although, had I been his own daughter, he would not have used the rod, neither would he have spoiled the child. I remember two incidents which, trivial in themselves, gave me a taste of his authority – a taste which suggested a different set of values. Once, not realising the nature of my crime, I spilled some type that he had just spent hours in sorting, and I said nothing about it. A week later I was reprimanded with a controlled annoyance which seemed to imply a standard of behaviour I was seldom expected to live up to. On another occasion, having asked for a copy of *Flush* to give a friend, I was unprepared to pay for it, but Leonard made me go home and get the money. These contacts with a sterner reality impressed me – he seemed to be the father figure who was missing in my life. And yet, had Leonard been my father I would have resembled one of his dogs, never beaten but always intimidated by the force of his personality.

For my birthday one year he gave me a splendid Victorian copy of *Pilgrim's Progress*, filled with pictures of Christian marching onwards in stiffly engraved wooden drapery. For some reason this book meant a great deal to me, and my eyes met those of Leonard across the festive tea-table in a moment of intense understanding I seldom experienced. For once I felt limpid and transparent, purged by emotion of all the dross of puerile secrecy and prevarication that usually submerged me. I had unwittingly come into contact with the passion in Leonard's character, which was both convinced and inflexible, contrasting with Vanessa's tendency to compound and procrastinate in favour of those she loved, and Duncan's ability to laugh away and ignore things he didn't like. They were conscious of a moral force in Leonard which they repudiated as narrow, philistine and puritanical. Both he and Vanessa were natural judges and both were full of prejudice, but whereas she avoided morality, Leonard clung to it, always remaining something of the administrator of the Hambantota District in Ceylon. In Bloomsbury, vowed to amorality, this may have seemed a little heavy-handed and irritating, but with it went a refreshing purity which in later years I fully appreciated.

Once every fortnight in summer we would bundle into the car and, in the chalky stillness of a Sussex afternoon, drive over to Rodmell, crossing the Ouse at Southease level-crossing. Monk's House, in the heart of the village, was, very largely for this reason, as different from Charleston as possible. The house was long and narrow: the rooms opened out of each other in succession, the whole house lower than the garden outside, so that one stepped into it rather as one steps into a boat. Plants and creepers knocked at the small-paned windows as though longing to come in, invited perhaps by the green walls. Cool and peaceful, on a hot summer's day the house seemed to bubble gently, like a sun-warmed stone that has been dropped into a pool. As a little girl I had sometimes stayed at Monk's House as a guest, and once my cousin Judith and I had discovered the amusement of rolling down the steep lawn opposite the front door, only to be scolded by our nurses because we were bright green all over. Green is the colour that comes to mind when I think of the house and garden, with its curling fig trees and level expanse of lawn overlooking the water-meadows. Green was Virginia's colour; a green crystal pear stood always on the table in the sitting-room, symbol of her personality.

For tea we sat at the long table in the dining-room, the only big room there was. Virginia, sitting at one end, poured out tea, not as Vanessa did, with a careful, steady hand, but waving the teapot to and fro as she talked, to emphasise her meaning. Our cups and saucers were of delicate china, our food less solid than at Charleston – there were biscuits instead of cake, farmhouse butter procured by

Virginia herself, and penny buns. Virginia ate little, popping small
pieces of food into her mouth like a greyhound. Before tea was over
she would light a cigarette in a long holder, and as her conversation
took fire, she herself grew hazier behind the mounting puffs of smoke.
She would describe a visit from Hugh Walpole or Ethel Smyth, or
some local scandal, and, encouraged by our comments and laughter,
rise to heights of fantasy unencumbered by realism. From Julian and
Quentin in particular the laughter became ecstatic, their chairs tipped
dangerously backward, hands raised in mock dismay at Virginia's au-
dacity or slapping their thighs in capitulation. Her brilliance was
not without malice, and her eyes shone with delight at her success.
While her mind seized on the unconscious, weaker and more vul-
nerable aspects of people, noticing details of behaviour with a brilliant haphazard appropriateness that skirted the edge of the possible,
Leonard would wait, and then describe the same incident in terms
that were factual, forthright and objective. Not that Virginia was not
capable of objectivity, but she arrived at it by a different road, and
on these occasions flung it over the windmill, intent only on enjoying
herself.

When the meal was over we all trooped into the garden, invited
by Leonard to play the ritual game of bowls. If the first half of the
entertainment had been Virginia's, the second was his. He took charge
of the game, pressing everyone to play, even the least experienced,
who were given handicaps and praised if they did better than expected. Leonard paced the doubtful distances with large, thick-soled
feet placed carefully one before the other, sometimes attended by
Pinka, who adoringly sniffed each mark on the grass, only to be
gruffly told to go and lie down. Leonard's word was law, his judgment
final, and we would continue with the gentle, decorous game while
he carried on a discussion with Julian or Quentin about the habits
of animals or local politics.

Meanwhile Virginia sat in a deckchair under the elm tree, smoking,
talking to Vanessa about cousins seen again after many years, and
laughing about them in their own quiet, throwaway fashion, like
two birds on a perch. Alternatively, Virginia, unable to tolerate boredom, did her best to inspire rivalry between Charleston and Rodmell,
preferring to squabble about houses rather than remain silent. Vanessa
hated the thought of life in a village, and, albeit reluctantly, defended
the liberty and privacy of Charleston, where we were a law unto ourselves, where no Mrs Ebbs looked over the garden wall or called out
to one on one's way up the village street, and where there were no

church bells to intrude on one's Sunday afternoon. But when I went to sit beside them Virginia would insist on trying to make me say that Rodmell was the superior of the two. In the end I would become impatient and she would say, 'Oh! Pixerina, what a devil you are! But you do love me, don't you?'

'Of course I do, Witcherina, but I can't lie to you.'

As I grew older and she grew richer, Virginia made herself responsible for my dress allowance, which was £15 a quarter, quite enough for clothes and minor pleasures. Although the money was hers, Virginia had often forgotten to bring it with her and had to ask Leonard to pay me by cheque. It was a little like extracting water from a stone. Although Leonard did not protest, he went through a process of finding and putting on his spectacles, which made him look like a hanging judge, plunging his hand into some inner pocket to draw out his cheque book, then his pen, from which he unscrewed the cap with some difficulty, and finally writing out and signing the cheque with a trembling hand in complete silence – all of which seemed a test of my endurance. In the end he handed it over with a half-smile, like the flash of a needle under water.

Leonard and Virginia's relationship was above all comradely: deeply affectionate and indivisibly united, they depended on each other. They knew each other's minds and therefore took each other for granted – they accepted each other's peculiarities and shortcomings and pretended no more than they could help. They were bound together by honesty. There was little, if any, conjugal bickering. Leonard never failed in vigilance and never fussed; neither did he hide his brief anxiety that Virginia might drink a glass too much wine or commit some other mild excess; he would say quite simply, 'Virginia, that's enough,' and that was the end of it. Or, when he noticed by the hands of his enormous watch that it was 11.00 in the evening, no matter how much she was enjoying herself, he would say, 'Virginia, we must go home,' and after a few extra minutes stolen from beneath his nose, she would rise and, as though leaving a part of herself behind, follow him and Pinka to the door.

Once I remember walking behind Virginia up the garden steps, when it suddenly occurred to me to wonder whether she had ever made love with Leonard. I assumed she had, and yet it seemed impossible – I could imagine her in bed with no one, in spite of her obvious femininity – but no doubt the absence of sexual feelings was an important factor in the success of their relationship. Virginia re-

mained a virginal, bony creature, stalking her way through life, like
a giraffe. And yet, though her head was often above the clouds, her
feet were firmly enough planted on the earth. Shabby, untidy, wispy,
her fingers stained with nicotine, she cared not a straw for her appearance, but by some curious fluke remained both distinguished and
elegant.

On one occasion I went to tea at Monk's House when Virginia
was alone. Before the evening was over she complained of a headache
and I helped her to bed, finally leaving her alone to await Leonard's
arrival from London. It was the only time I ever saw her near a breakdown. I had been shielded from knowledge of these, partly because
Virginia had needed protection when she was suffering from them.
But there was also a common family habit of referring to Virginia's
'madness', which made it seem quite unreal – and, as though that
were her intention, it became something one could not contemplate.
Seeing her suddenly threatened left me with the impression of a stoic
vanquished only for the moment, as brief a moment as she could
make it. In spite of her fragility Virginia had enormous resilience:
she could never resist the call of life itself, no matter what shape
it took. She never cut herself off from people, as we did at Charleston;
even if it threatened to destroy her, human contact was indispensable.
She searched continually for satisfying relationships, finding for the
most part only volatile if stimulating contacts in a sea that threatened
to submerge her, and which, had it not been for Leonard, would
have done so.

With hindsight I can see, though she never said so, that Virginia
was disappointed in me: she wished I was more intelligent, more
disciplined, and probably agreed with Leonard about my education.
She would have liked me to have had more enterprise and independence, to have been less predictable. Longing none the less to seduce
me, she succumbed to the more conventional ploy of trying to improve my appearance, doing things which did not come naturally
to her such as taking me to my first hairdresser, giving me jewels
and feminine knick-knacks. But she also gave me her copy of Mme
du Deffand's letters, presented to her many years before by Lytton,
and encouraged me to talk to the Rodmell Women's Institute on the
theatre, helping me with my script. She tried to probe and loosen
my ideas, and, when she forgot to be brilliant and amusing, showed
a capacity for intimacy which I found illuminating. At such moments
her critical faculties and insight were used intuitively, and never made
one feel inferior. I felt too that there was in her a toughness and

courage to which she clung through thick and thin, of which one
was aware under all the jokes and laughter.

Lytton Strachey by Leonard Woolf

*The influence of Lytton Strachey on his contemporaries at Cambridge
and afterwards was considerable. After he died, Vanessa Bell wrote
to Carrington that she had loved him since Thoby's death when 'he
came and was such an inexpressible help and made one think of the
things most worth thinking of' (Selected Letters, 371). Then, according to Clive Bell, it was Strachey who made history in Bloomsbury
by writing to him on 25 November 1906 as 'Dear Clive.' 'It was the
time of my engagement to Vanessa Stephen that we took to Christian
names, and it was entirely Lytton's doing. No question here of drifting
into a habit, the proposal was made formally when he came to con-
gratulate us. The practice became general. . . . Henceforth between
friends manners were to depend on feelings rather than conventions'
(Old Friends, 31). Virginia Woolf also testified to Strachey's influence
on the Group's language in her memoir of Old Bloomsbury (see pp.
54–5).*

*After the Bells and the Woolfs established themselves in London
and Sussex, and Strachey set up his own unusual Berkshire ménage
with Carrington, there was inevitably less interaction between him
and other Bloomsberries. It might almost be said that Strachey's sway
over Bloomsbury was inversely proportional to his fame. The celebrated ironist of* Eminent Victorians *remained very much a member
of Bloomsbury but some of the Group felt he never completely fulfilled
their high expectations.*

*If Leonard Woolf, who was among Lytton Strachey's closest friends
at Cambridge and even during his Edwardian years in Ceylon, also
thought Strachey's career was disappointing, there is no indication
of it in his tribute, which was written just after Strachey's death in
1932 for the* New Statesmen and Nation. *Woolf's emphasis on Strachey's integrity is noteworthy as coming from one who himself possessed that quality to a striking degree.*

Many of those who have written about Lytton Strachey during the
last week have said that as a writer he left a mark upon his age.
No contemporary can be certain of his judgment as to the ultimate
value in literature, biography, or history of *Eminent Victorians*,

Queen Victoria, and *Elizabeth and Essex*, but the great effect and importance of these books during the last fourteen years are shown both by the admiration and the hostility which they have roused. I think that the most significant thing about Lytton Strachey both as a person and as a writer is that his writings came so directly from himself, from the very core of his character, that years before he had achieved anything or had become famous he was impinging (as he would have said himself) upon practically everyone with whom he came in contact in exactly the same way in which he impinged upon the reading public by his books. There were two reasons for this: first, the extreme individuality of his character, a character which united in a most fascinating way a whole series of pairs of contradictory qualities; secondly, an intellectual integrity which, when he was a young man, was extraordinarily violent and passionate.

When he came up to Trinity, Cambridge, in 1899, he knew and was known to none of his contemporaries. He had never been to a public school, and Walter Headlam, at King's, a fellow and much older than Strachey, must have been, I think, the only person in Cambridge who really knew anything about him. By the end of his first year he had already an intimate circle of friends and was recognized by many undergraduates and dons in Trinity and King's as a man of very remarkable character and powers. All through the time that he was in residence at Trinity his influence increased, and it is not an exaggeration to say that in the end it had become a dominating influence upon the intellectuals of his generation. And this domination did not end when technically he had 'gone down'. He still continued to spend a good deal of his time in Cambridge, and generations of undergraduates fell under his powerful spell. Its power extended even to the characteristic intonation of his voice, and when I visited Cambridge again after a long interval in 1911, it was amusing to find half the undergraduates at King's talking in what was called the Stracheyesque voice.

One reason for his immediate effect upon his generation was his astonishing maturity. When he arrived at Trinity in 1899 he already had intellectually the equipment which made it possible for him nineteen years later to write *Eminent Victorians* and combined with this intellectual maturity he had the fiery and violent intransigence of youth. With age and success he became extremely mellow and gentle; when a young man, his external demeanour was gentle and almost diffident, but was accompanied by an intellectual prickliness and ruthlessness which was extraordinarily impressive and at times devastating. The effect was increased by his peculiar method of conversation. When he was with those whom he liked, he would talk with animation, dropping every now and then into the general stream of conversation, casually and in his low staccato voice, some maliciously illuminating and extraordinarily witty phrase or comment. But in those days, though his conversation was fascinating and brilliant, it was often difficult, for he required much, including stimulus, from the person to whom he was talking. If the person or persons with whom he found himself in contact happened not to be congenial or their remarks unintelligent, the result would often be a social disaster, painful at the moment to a third party, though extremely amusing in retrospect. His legs inextricably intertwined, he would lie back in his chair, in black gloom and complete silence, and then quite suddenly drop, this time probably into the most uncomfortable moment of silence, a sardonically witty remark which stripped the last shred of self-control and intelligence from his victim.

These combinations of ruthlessness and gentleness, silence and wit, prickliness and affection only increased the charm of his personality for those whom he liked. It was this charm, when united with his extraordinary intellectual gifts, his highly individual outlook on life, and his very definite opinions, which made him the dominating influence upon three or four generations of Cambridge undergraduates. When he first came to Trinity it was clear that he would be a writer, and his contemporaries were convicted that he would be a great writer. In those days he wrote much more poetry than prose. I think that perhaps all through his life he would have preferred to achieve something in poetry or the drama than in any other sphere of literature. But he demanded of himself the same tremendous standards that he required in others, and it is significant that, though he wrote a great deal of poetry, he never published it. He became a prose writer partly because his verse never came up to the standard which he himself demanded of poetry, and partly because the immense influence which Professor G.E. Moore and *Prinicipia Ethica* exercised upon him, as upon so many of his contemporaries, turned his mind in other directions.

As a matter of fact, prose was, I am sure, the right instrument for his thoughts, given the fact that he was living not in the eighteenth, but the twentieth century. His mind was fundamentally of the order of Swift's and Voltaire's, a critical and analytical mind which delighted to express itself with natural brilliance in satire and wit. Some of the most brilliant things which he ever wrote were Voltairean squibs and essays written when an undergraduate on subjects about which he felt deeply and violently. It was these writings which showed that, as I said, at nineteen he already possessed the intellectual equipment of the author of *Eminent Victorians* and *Queen Victoria*.

His published writings are the direct product of his character, which, by its curious combination of contradictory qualities, was always producing something rich and strange. He was an iconoclast who loved traditions, so that, for instance, on a subject like the French Revolution he could feel with Burke and think with Tom Paine. He combined extreme originality, and even eccentricity, with a true love of the elaborate manners, forms, and formalities of a highly civilised and sophisticated society. He was a realist and a cynic, and yet he was a romantic who loved the pageantry of life and history. Though the standards he set for himself and demanded of others were so high and though one of the most remarkable things about him was his intellectual integrity, he would display, on occasions, an almost contemptuous, if not unscrupulous, disregard of accuracy in detail. These qualities determined his choice of subject and moulded his biographical method and literary style. They account both for the enormous effect which the iconoclasm of *Eminent Victorians* had upon a generation and for the reaction against him as a biographer and historian which has been so marked in the last few years. His romanticism and disregard of detailed accuracy are fairly open to criticism, and it is arguable that his methods, used by others without his genius and wit, have done harm to both biography and history. But many of his critics merely convict themselves of the biographical sentimentality and the historical humbug against which much of his work was rightly and triumphantly directed. And in doing so they often showed themselves to be blind to what I have called his intellectual integrity. An example which would certainly have amused Lytton Strachey himself may be quoted. In the recent controversy on the question whether General Gordon drank too much brandy and soda, one of his critics was very angry with him. He was indignant that a mere writer should suggest that a distinguished soldier who read the Bible could drink too much brandy. And in order to clinch the argument, he asked what right Lytton Strachey had to criticize General Gordon – Lytton Strachey who had never been in the East, had never been out in the sun without an umbrella, had never been far from a cup of tea or glass of lemonade. At that moment Lytton Strachey was enduring a long, painful illness with extraordinary patience and fortitude, and, though without the consolations of either a Christian or a soldier, was facing the prospect of imminent death with courage and equanimity.

Lytton Strachey by Desmond MacCarthy

Desmond MacCarthy's account comes from an essay on Lytton Stra-
chey and the art of biography that he wrote around 1934. (MacCarthy's
introduction on the development of biography has been omitted here
along with a discussion of Strachey's poetry). MacCarthy was a few
years older than Lytton Strachey and did not know him as well as
contemporaries such as Leonard Woolf. MacCarthy's description of
Cambridge and Moore's influence also predates Strachey's Cambridge
a little. (Strachey's essay on Warren Hastings that MacCarthy refers
to was an undergraduate essay, not part of his dissertation, and it
was not included in Characters and Commentaries.*)*

As practically nothing has been written about Lytton Strachey as a
man, it may not be uninteresting if I attempt to give you some idea
of him, for I knew him well.

He was born at Clapham in 1880; he was the last but two of a
long family, and a family which for several generations had been
remarkable for ability. When Francis Galton was making his re-
searches into hereditary talent he examined, together with the Dar-
wins and the Butlers, the Pollocks and other families who had distinguished themselves for several generations, the careers of the
Stracheys.

Lytton Strachey was born, then, into what we may term the intellectual aristocracy of England, and he belonged to the adminis-
trative class. His grandfather, Edward Strachey, an Anglo-Indian of
considerable importance in his day, was a friend of Carlyle. They
made an excursion to Paris together in the pre-railroad days and –
it is Carlyle who tells the story – at the end of the journey the postilion
asked for a tip. Edward Strachey curtly refused, adding 'vous avez
drivé devlish slow'.

I repeat this small anecdote for the sake of his grandson's comment
upon it, which is characteristic of Lytton Strachey's attitude towards
all forms of John Bullishness.

'The reckless insularity of this remark', he wrote, 'illustrates well
enough the extraordinary change which had come over the English
governing classes since the eighteenth century. Fifty years earlier a cultivated Englishman would have piqued himself upon answering the
postilion in the idiom and the accent of Paris. But the Napoleonic
Wars, the industrial revolution, the romantic revival, the Victorian
spirit, had brought about a relapse from the suavity of the eighteenth
century culture; the centrifugal forces always latent in English life

had triumphed, and men's minds had shot off into the grooves of eccentricity and provincialism.'

He proceeds to notice the flux and reflux of these tendencies in the history of our literature: 'the divine amenity of Chaucer followed by the no less divine idiosyncracy of the Elizabethans; the *exquisite vigour* of the eighteenth century followed by the *rampant vigour* of the nineteenth'; and (please note these words) 'today, the return once more to the Latin elements in our culture, the revulsion from the Germanic influences which obsessed our grandfathers, the preference for what is swift, what is well-arranged, and what is not too *good*'. Too edifying, Strachey means.

I ask you to note those passages for two reasons, one connected with his own work (he himself was the chief representative of that revulsion and that preference), and the other connected with himself and his influence upon his own generation. He had been a delicate child, and after one term at a private school, he had been sent to Leamington College. This choice was probably made on grounds of health. (I know nothing of Leamington College beyond the fact that it was one of the minor public schools.) But this choice was of some importance – he thereby escaped the more powerful and possibly more agreeable influence of one of the *great* public schools. Lytton Strachey's individualism would probably have survived that. But as it was, what is called 'the public school spirit', 'team-work', 'playing the game' and so forth, remained notions, not only repulsive, but to a large extent incomprehensible, to him. He not only disliked and feared the public school spirit but thought it absurd and grotesque.

You cannot imagine a youth more utterly unsatisfactory from, say, Kipling's point of view, than the long, limp, pale young man with pince-nez and a small rather dismal moustache, who came up to Trinity, Cambridge, in 1899. He had left Leamington in 1897 for Liverpool University, where he attended Walter Raleigh's lectures and had read history in a desultory fashion; it was a letter from Walter Raleigh announcing that a distinctly remarkable undergraduate was about to join us, which largely determined Lytton Strachey's circle of friends at the university.

As he kept those friends all his life; as that London set of writers and artists, known afterwards as 'Bloomsbury', in which he was the most prominent figure, was really an off-shoot or colony of Cambridge at the beginning of the century (with Leslie Stephen's two daughters, Virginia Woolf and Vanessa Bell, added), I shall try to indicate the spirit of that Cambridge generation to which I also belonged.

We were not much interested in politics. Abstract speculation was much more absorbing. Philosophy was much more interesting to us than public causes. The wave of Fabian socialism, which affected some of Lytton Strachey's younger contemporaries like Rupert Brooke, had not reached Cambridge in my time. What we chiefly discussed were those 'goods' which were ends in themselves; and these ends, for which the rest of life was only a scaffolding, could be subsumed under three heads: the search for truth, aesthetic emotions and personal relations – love and friendship.

Those who have been to a university will remember how each decade, as far as the intellectual life of the young is concerned, tends to be dominated by some unusually gifted man. The dominating influence when Lytton Strachey came up was metaphysical, embodied in G.E. Moore and Bertrand Russell who had shaken confidence in the Idealism of McTaggart. Thus Amurath to Amurath succeeds. Lytton Strachey himself was the next influence. He remained at Cambridge after he had taken his degree, a second in History, sitting for a Fellowship at Trinity till 1905 and writing a dissertation on Warren Hastings. The curious can read that essay in his posthumous volume *Characters and Commentaries*. It is an elegant and surprisingly mature piece of work. No doubt he was attracted to the subject through the connection of his family with India, but it was not a subject particularly suited to his hand, and it failed to win him a Fellowship. Meanwhile, as I said, he had become a leader among the young, not only through his culture, his wit and the discrimination of his taste, but thanks above all to the vehement and passionate nature of his judgments upon character. The drift of his influence was away from metaphysical speculation, for though he had a clear head in argument he was not particularly fitted to follow complicated trains of abstract reasoning. His days and nights were spent in reading and in long, leisurely, laughing, intimate talks. It has been said of Edward Fitzgerald that his friendships were more like loves, and that might also be said of Lytton Strachey.

His influence, especially upon his younger contemporaries, was to fix their attention on emotions and relations between human beings. He was a master of what may be called psychological gossip, the kind which treats friends as diagrams of the human species and ranges over the past and fiction as well as history, in search of whatever illustrates this or that side of human nature. He was writing a good deal of verse too, some of it of a ribald kind, the rest emotional, and marked by that intellectual elaboration we associate with the metaphysical school of poets, the seventeenth century poets, or the classic impetuosity of such verses as Pope's 'Abelard and Héloise'.

Just as his taste in prose was towards a Gallic clarity and the Latin elements in our culture, towards the amenity and composed vigour of the eighteenth century, his taste in poetry inclined him towards the Elizabethans and their immediate successors. He loved in poetry things extreme and dazzling bright, the golden moments of emotion that shoot up and spatter the skies – though he always kept his eye on the falling stick. The poetry which was wit's forge and fire-blast, meaning's press and screw, enraptured him. . . .

The duality of his temperament found a parallel in certain physical characteristics. He spoke with two voices. The one tiny as that of the gnat in *Alice in Wonderland*; the other grave and deep. The first voice added a spice to his quick interjections, puncturing pomposity or checking impertinence. I remember, soon after he had grown that long reddish beard which added so much to the dignity of his appearance, a lady asking him 'Oh, Mr Strachey, tell me, when you go to bed, do you keep that beard of yours inside or outside the blankets?' It was in the gnat-like voice that he replied 'Come and see!'

But in reading Racine or the Elizabethan dramatists (which he did admirably and with great feeling) or at moments when he expressed indignation rather than contempt, it was his sombre and majestic tones you heard. There was a similar contrast in his demeanour; an extreme passivity bordering on lassitude was apt to be broken by the most fantastic gesticulation when he repudiated some enormity or hailed an extravagance that delighted him.

How long the pauses were between his books! He was not an ambitious man – at least, not after he had proved both to himself and his friends that the gifts they had divined in him were really there. Other feelings were far stronger in him than ambition. He did not like characters in whom ambition took control of personal relations and destroyed detachment. He had a keen eye, as his studies in human nature show, for the fantastic antics and morose stupidities that ambition inspires. He did not even like, though he excused and admired (you remember his *Florence Nightingale*) the egotism of ruthless devotion which is kin to ambition. His books are surprisingly accurate, considering how attractive as 'a note' every significant, though perhaps not well authenticated, fact must have been to him. His fine sense for what is entertaining lent his work an apparent slightness that concealed the pains he had taken in writing it. This sense of what is entertaining supported his instincts as an artist, and when writing *Queen Victoria* it directed his path through the forest of facts from 1817 to 1901. He was determined that at every turn in that path something should beguile us. Without this unerring sense of what is entertaining he would never have found his way. Where, too, he showed himself a craftsman, was in conducting his narrative (and this is seen in his short biographies also) so that we do not even miss a thorough treatment of the large unaccommodating historic facts, in front of which a lesser artist in biography would have felt bound to detain us. The miracle is that though there are omissions these are not felt as gaps. What pains he must have taken to maintain that beguiling smoothness! How deftly he used the indirect method!

'The history of the Victorian Age will never be written: we know too much about it', he wrote in the Preface to *Eminent Victorians*. '. . . It is not by the direct method of a scrupulous narrative that the explorer of the past can hope to depict that singular epoch. If he is wise he will adopt a subtler strategy.'

And he added: 'It has been my purpose to illustrate rather than to explain.' Now, since history is chiefly concerned with causality (it is this preoccupation which distinguishes the historian proper), Lytton Strachey was a painter of the past and a biographer, not a historian. Note the adjective 'singular' in the phrase he applied to the Victorian Age, that 'singular epoch'. Nobody before had seen it just like that. The Victorian Age had been lashed again and again by indignant economic historians, and almost as fiercely as by its own children, Carlyle and Ruskin; but its prestige was still imposing. When Lytton Strachey looked at it with calm amazement, many twentieth century readers discovered that they too had moved, half unconsciously, so far from the standards and convictions of the Victorian Age that the word 'singular', with its ironic inflection, described what they felt about it themselves.

Now amazement, though an enjoyable condition of mind, cannot be prolonged and continue to please, and, when maintained for the sake of flattering the sense of superiority which may accompany it, it becomes both contemptible and tiresome. We are now heartily sick of the amused and surprised smiles of any scribbling whippersnapper who chooses to turn his face towards the great Victorians. But that is no blame to Lytton Strachey, nor can he be held responsible for the cheap effects of those who have imitated him without his 'subtler strategy', his careful curiosity, his perspicuous serenity and – I am coming to that – his moral passion. A writer's imitators, as Macaulay knew, are more destructive of his reputation than his sourest critics; but, however regrettable, these results are proof of originality and fascination. Lytton Strachey's importance can be measured by his having both focused and intensified our consciousness of the differences between nineteenth and twentieth century modes of thinking and feeling, and in having changed, by his dangerous example, the methods of popular biography. That influence alone would have secured him a place in the history of literature, even if his own work did not possess the finish and freshness which preserves.

Like most original and influential men, he was bold. His boldness was effortless, and because he admired and firmly believed in certain qualities in human nature and in certain attitudes of mind, he was also the natural foe of ideals and patterns of virtue which tend to brow-beat the qualities he valued and loved. The public thought he was a frivolous and detached ironist, but he was much more of a moralist. Only in writing he avoided carefully, for aesthetic reasons, the portentous frown of the earnest writer. He did not believe in the Christian religion, and he was one of the few English writers about the past – Gibbon was another – who have allowed scepticism to colour their view of believers.

Lytton Strachey was like Voltaire in three respects: he thought beliefs absurd in others which he thought absurd in himself, and he was convinced that as long as men continued to believe absurdities they would continue to commit atrocities. As a moralist he believed that *surtout point de zèle*, except against zealots, was a trustworthy guide to right living and right judgment. The public thought this was only his naughty relish for poking destructive fun – but then the public are so immoral they do not recognize a moralist unless he bears the conventional insignia about him.

There is, by the by, not nearly so much destructive irony, and a great deal more sympathy, in his work than is generally supposed. I could quote many passages of delicate sensitive sympathy with those whose outlook upon life he did not share. (Recall the pages on Newman in *Eminent Victorians* and *passim* his fairness to the far from charming but honourable figure of the Prince Consort in *Queen Victoria*.)

Seldom has a born writer, who, as the essay on 'English Letters Writers' now shows, matured so early, had so long a period of incubating: he was thirty-seven when *Eminent Victorians* appeared. This was partly due to ill-health, but perhaps even more to the warring of those two tendencies in him – the romantic and the rational. He did not know what he wanted most to do, or, rather, he was uncertain what he could do best. He would have wished, I think, to write poetic drama. His sense of form, his passionate pre-occupation with human nature, made drama extremely attractive to him. Elizabeth and Essex was a subject which had called to him in youth.

Mr Francis Birrell, in an excellent essay which he contributed to *La Revue Hebdomadaire* in July 1932, pointed out that Strachey's *Elizabeth and Essex* is almost a sketch for a play. The long meditations attributed to Elizabeth, to Essex, to Bacon, and Cecil, are monologues inspired by those of the Elizabethan drama, where the protagonist often occupies the stage alone, delivering in poetry the passions and perplexities which divide his soul. Like Antony, Essex leaves and returns to his Queen; like Antony he dies a violent death. The passage, so carefully weighed, with which the book ends, where Cecil is seen at his writing table, brooding over the future of England and the destiny of his own house, is also an invention borrowed from the Elizabethan stage. Does not *Antony and Cleopatra* close with the triumph of Octavius, *Hamlet* with the crowning of Fortinbras? It is well to keep this parallel in mind in judging the book. It disappointed some of Strachey's admirers because, like all admirers, they wanted him to repeat himself. But I believe that as time goes on *Elizabeth and Essex* will be rated much higher. It contains some of the finest and most imaginative prose he ever wrote.

'Human beings', he wrote, 'are too important to be treated as mere symptoms of the past. They have a value which is independent of any temporal processes – which is eternal, and must be felt for its own sake. The art of biography seems to have fallen on evil times in England. We have had, it is true, a few masterpieces, but we have never had, like the French, a great biographical tradition; we have had no Fontenelles and Condorcets, with their incomparable *éloges*, compressing into a few shining pages the manifold existences of men. With us, the most delicate and humane of all the branches of the art of writing has been relegated to the journeymen of letters. . . . To preserve, for instance, a becoming brevity – a brevity which excludes everything that is redundant and nothing that is significant – that, surely, is the first duty of the biographer. The second, no less surely, is to maintain his own freedom of spirit.'

It was in this, 'the most delicate and humane of all the branches of the art of writing', that he excelled, and he did so, apart from his gifts as a writer and story-teller, thanks to 'maintaining his own freedom of spirit'. There lay his originality when he began to write. It was the custom of our biographers to curb in themselves 'freedom of spirit'. They deliberately obliterated their own attitude towards life, either adopting for the time that of the man about whom they were writing a nondescript point of view supposed to be equivalent to 'impartiality'. The lives of Conservatives were written by Conservatives, of Liberals by Liberals; those of religious leaders and reformers by writers who either shared their convictions or pretended to do so. These books might have great merits, but they could not have those of a work of art. Take, for example, Morley's *Life of Gladstone*: no one would guess from that book that Lord Morley was an ardent rationalist. His rationalism must have made many of Gladstone's judgments and emotions, and much of his behaviour, appear fantastic to him: though he might not cease to admire, Morley's admiration must have been often tinged with irony or amazement. But he was on his honour 'as a biographer' to let none of this appear in his book. A work of art cannot be created under such conditions. To Lytton Strachey biography was interpretation, and therefore the record, not only of facts, but of the biographer's deepest response to them. There could be no genuine focus otherwise, no vital principle of selection. When he says 'human beings are too important to be treated as mere symptoms of the past' he gives us the clue to his own sense of proportion. His preoccupation was with human nature itself, and only incidentally with the causes of events or of changes. These he had often to deal with in order to tell the story, and admirably he did so: witness his masterly summary of the Oxford Movement, or of the causes of the tardy change in the Liberal Government towards Gordon and the Sudan. But it is upon the effect of temperament and character on events that he invariably fixes our attention, or, again, upon the effect of events upon character, as he has shown with such skill in his *Queen Victoria*. He fulfilled the task of the biographer as Johnson defined it.

Lytton Strachey was 51 when he died. Serious as the loss to Literature was admitted to be, it was greater than at once appeared. It is likely that we have been robbed of his finest book. The poet and the novelist usually repeat themselves after maturity; their work is so dependent upon inspiration, invention and emotion, things which age slowly takes away. They may keep their skill, their insight, but they see and record for us little that they have not used before. But of the man of letters it is much truer to say 'ripeness is all'. In the work of the biographer and historian knowledge and judgment are relatively much more important, and until lassitude sets in, and

with lassitude that finished garrulity and serene laxity which are its
fatal signs, years only add to his knowledge and widen his view. I
am sure, alas, that in Lytton Strachey's case the best was yet to come.
But what an artist he had already proved himself!

Carrington by David Garnett

*Dora Carrington, who insisted on being called just Carrington, is
connected to Bloomsbury primarily through her love for Lytton Strachey with whom she lived from 1917 until his death in 1932. Two
months later she committed suicide at the age of thirty-eight. In her
diary she had written an epigraph by Henry Wotton:*

> *He first deceased, she for a little tried
> To live without him, liked it not and died.*

*Carrington's reputation as a painter has developed as interest increased
in Bloomsbury's art. With the publication of her selected letters and
diaries, she has also belatedly been recognized as a writer. David Garnett's introduction to Carrington's letters and diaries appeared in 1970.*

The reader may ask: 'Who was this woman Carrington anyway?' And
when I reply that he should read this book to find out – for all her
qualities good and bad are revealed in these letters – he may be annoyed and ask: 'But to look at? Was she beautiful?'

To provoke him still further I will say that he probably wouldn't
have thought so, but that I enjoyed looking at her.

Lady Ottoline Morrell called her 'a wild moorland pony'. Quite
good. Aldous Huxley, whose characters are closely drawn from life
as far as *appearances* go, wrote of 'the serious moonlike innocence
of her childish face', and described her bobbed hair hanging 'in a
bell of elastic gold about her cheeks' and her large china-blue eyes
'with an expression of ingenuous and often puzzled earnestness'. He
remembered that she was often out of breath when she talked and
that 'her words were punctuated with little gasps'.

Later he emphasized her childish appearance in a suit of mauve
pyjamas – the pyjamas reappear in later pages and the reader will
learn that they were drawn from life. But for private reasons Huxley
made Mary Bracegirdle an exceedingly stupid girl, unable to decide
whether he or Gertler would be a more suitable lover.

The book is *Crome Yellow* (1921); the setting is Philip and Lady

Ottoline Morrell's beautiful country house Garsington Manor and they, Mark Gertler, Dorothy Brett and others are caricatured within its pages.

Carrington's 'little gasp' had already been noted by Gilbert Cannan in his novel *Mendel*, written five years earlier. It is the story of Gertler's early life and Carrington, who was a fellow-pupil of Gertler's at the Slade School of Art, is its heroine.

'Her voice rather irritated him [Gertler]. Her accent was rather mincing and precise and between her sentences she gave a little gasp which he took for an affectation.' Cannan gives no description of her appearance but refers several times to her shyness and 'very charming air of diffidence'. The reader is meant to think her very attractive and to fall under her spell, as Cannan seems to have done.

Aldous Huxley's description is too doll-like and Carrington did not have golden hair. It was the colour of weathered straw – very pale brown with a glint of gold in it. Her complexion was pink and cream, like apple blossom. She had a broken nose and the edges of her two upper front teeth were not square but obliquely pointed, worn away at the sides.

Tens of thousands of young women have china-blue eyes, talk in little gasps and have sex trouble, but one does not want to wade through their correspondence. Carrington would have always been attractive to her friends; what makes her interesting and fascinating to subsequent generations is her relationship with Lytton Strachey, the critic who sprang into fame with *Eminent Victorians* and his biography of Queen Victoria. Carrington devoted her life to Lytton, and after his death from an undiagnosed cancer of the intestine decided that it was not worth living, and shot herself.

The reader of these letters will find himself plunged into a part of the social life of England during the First World War and the 1920s, and will want a few clues to understand Carrington's place in it.

It was a world of distinguished intellectuals, writers, painters and University men who were standing out against the war, often conscientious objectors. After the war it was reinforced by younger men who had survived, or had been born too late to take part in it.

Scarcely any of them believed that war could come again in their lifetime. It was a time of elation. The old barriers and conventions would be swept away, and could be disregarded.

In *Eminent Victorians* and *Queen Victoria* Lytton Strachey had called into question the credentials of the great men of the age which had made that slaughter almost inevitable. He instantly became famous and a leader of intellectual and pacifist dissent.

One corner of this critical British world which rejected Victorian morality, art and conventional behaviour has since been called 'Bloomsbury', from the parish in central London where many of these free-thinking heretics lived. The chief figures in this group were the sisters Vanessa and Virginia Stephen, their husbands Clive Bell and Leonard Woolf, with some of the Strachey family and the Stracheys' cousin Duncan Grant. Also Roger Fry, the great art critic, and Maynard (afterwords Lord) Keynes, who revolutionized economics.

Carrington did not quite fit into this group and entered it more as an appendage of Lytton Strachey's than in her own right. And when famous hostesses such as Lady Cunard, Margot Asquith (afterwards Lady Oxford) and Lady Colefax invited the literary lion Lytton Strachey to their houses they would no more have thought of including Carrington than of asking him to bring his housekeeper or his cook.

This did not apply to Lady Ottoline Morrell, who had got to know Carrington before the girl met Lytton Strachey and through whom she made friends with Bertrand Russell, Aldous Huxley, Katherine Mansfield, Middleton Murry and many of the intellectuals, artists and Bohemians whom Lady Ottoline delighted to entertain. Carrington was more at home in the world of Augustus John, Henry Lamb and the painters trained like her at the Slade School of Art than with the Bloomsbury painters Vanessa Bell, Duncan Grant and Roger Fry, who looked across the channel and were influenced by Cézanne, Matisse and Picasso. Carrington's painting remained insular. She was far more at home in Wiltshire, where she created Lytton Strachey's beautiful house Ham Spray and helped him to entertain large numbers of guests, than she was in Bloomsbury. Her husband Ralph Partridge fell in love with Frances Marshall and they lived together during the week in Bloomsbury from 1926 until Carrington's suicide, after which they married and lived at Ham Spray. But their weekends were very often spent at Ham Spray which was always Ralph Partridge's country home.

Frances Marshall belonged far more to the Bloomsbury world than Carrington. She was very well educated, interested in abstract ideas and was more articulate and though younger more mature.

Lytton was homosexual, but he did not dislike women: quite the contrary. Some of his happiest relationships were with such women friends as Virginia Woolf, Dorelia John, Ottoline Morrell, his cousin

Mary St John Hutchinson, and his sisters Dorothy Bussy and Pippa Strachey. By far the most important was his relationship with Carrington, with whom he fell in love in the spring and summer of 1916.

They became lovers, but physical love was made difficult and became impossible. The trouble on Lytton's side was his diffidence and feeling of inadequacy, and his being perpetually attracted by young men; and on Carrington's side her intense dislike of being a woman, which gave her a feeling of inferiority so that a normal and joyful relationship was next to impossible.

Yet for many years they were happy together. Like Matthew Arnold in Max Beerbohm's caricature, Lytton Strachey was never 'wholly serious'. Everything, including his own deep feeling and beliefs, was the subject of constant jokes and gay exaggerations. To take Lytton *au pied de la lettre* is to misunderstand him entirely. His humour appealed to Carrington and hers to him – and both did much to bind them 'indisoulubly' together. When sexual love became difficult each of them tried to compensate for what the other could not give in a series of love affairs. The first of Carrington's compensatory affairs was with Ralph Partridge, who forced her to marry him. It was not a success, but the link could not be broken.

The interest of these letters is, then, partly that of following a very complex and original character in a very intimate but strange situation. But many people will, I think, feel Carrington's fascination. Her husband, Ralph Partridge, said that once you got her into your blood it was for ever. Gerald Brenan, one of her lovers, wrote in his diary: 'Compared to her, other women seem vulgar and without taste. She has on them the same effect as Dorelia [Augustus John's wife] has . . . she does not make them seem less beautiful, not less intelligent but she deprives them of that intimate connection between beauty and intelligence which is taste . . .'

I, a casual intimate, would say that she had the strength of character that one finds in a child but that a girl often loses when she becomes a woman. When she talked to me she seemed to be confiding a secret, and I was flattered. She made me feel like a child and she was a child herself.

She had indeed many of the childish, or adolescent characteristics that afflict girls at puberty. She never overcame her shame at being a woman, and her letters are full of references to menstruation. Although her sexual desire had greatly increased between her affair with Mark Gertler and that with Gerald Brenan, and although she was in love with Brenan as she had never been with Gertler, they follow a curiously similar pattern: almost the same deceptions, excuses and self-accusations are repeated in each relationship. And in each it was the hatred of being a woman which poisoned it.

Like a child, she found it hateful to choose; and after breaking off a relationship for ever she would immediately set about starting it again.

Like a child, she would tell lies which were bound to be found out and her life was complicated by continual deceptions and imbroglios.

She is an almost textbook case of the girl who can only be happy with a 'father figure'. She loved her father, hated her mother and found her only lasting happy relationship with Lytton Strachey exaggerating their age difference.

When caught out, or in an emotional crisis, she often behaved like a child, confessing her guilt, telling more lies and appealing to Lytton for help and forgiveness.

Her sexual love was unconsciously directed to her brother Teddy, killed in 1916 in the war, who played a large part in her dream life. She thought of him always as a sailor and her last love affair was with a sailor whom she identified with Teddy and who had many of his attractive qualities.

She was uneducated, but appeared much more ignorant than she was because she misplaced the letters in spelling words: thus 'minute' is always 'minuet'.

Although she had no background of general knowledge she was a remarkably well-read young woman before she ever met Lytton, and had a very decided taste of her own in literature. She had a longing to make up for her ignorance and Lytton was an ideal teacher.

She was very secretive, and it was only to Lytton, and later to Julia Strachey, that she revealed herself almost completely; though she hid from them the romanticism which she displayed in her letters to Gerald Brenan – letters signed 'Queen of Georgia'. She was very fond of secret names. With Lytton she was at first 'votre gross Bébé', then 'your niece' until she finally settled down as Mopsa. Charming variants are found in many of these letters. She hated her own name Dora and by 1915, when I first met her, had transformed it to Doric. Later she reversed this in letters to Gerald Brenan and it became Cirod. In his diaries Brenan almost always refers to her as C.R.D. The private name with which she signs a letter usually corresponds with the temper in which it was written.

There is an equal variety in the names she applied to those she loved. Among others Lytton is 'Grandpère', a 'Yahoo', 'A Toad In The Hole', 'Old Count Bumbel', her 'rat-husband' and a 'bugger-wug'.

Though her end was tragic, for she was totally committed to Lytton, I do not think of her as primarily a tragic figure. The greatest of her, or perhaps I should say of our, misfortunes was that the men she loved and lived with after her breach with Mark Gertler cared little for painting. It did not occur to Lytton Strachey, or to Ralph Partridge, that her painting should be put first. Gertler was too much of an egoist to encourage her and work with her. At the end of her life the only painters she saw much of, Augustus John and Henry Lamb, belonged to an older generation. There was nobody to work with her as Duncan Grant worked with Vanessa Bell. It is possible that if there had been such a companionship, her psychological blockage would have been overcome. But in her isolation it increased, and she became discouraged. I think that this was the greatest harm that Lytton did her, except by dying when he did.

John Maynard Keynes by Virginia Woolf

In the spring of 1934 Virginia Woolf jotted down the initials JMK at the top of a page in one of her writing notebooks. Under them she rapidly wrote a three-page biographical sketch on themes in the current life of John Maynard Keynes. The sketch connects two of the most remarkable members of Bloomsbury and also illustrates in miniature Woolf's art of biography. 'JMK' is, to use a term from her diary, a biographical fantasy (4:180).

Admiration and affection mingle with irony in Virginia Woolf's sketch. She begins with a list of topics in the life of JMK, but develops only half a dozen or so of them. From a pig and a college, the sketch modulates to Covent Garden and Downing Street, mixes finance with book-collecting, and ends with the famous man in bed inquiring after a rare pamphlet and thinking of his engagements, of Atlantis, and of the symbols that will eventually answer all problems. The transitions are rapid, sometimes abrupt or ironic, the shifting viewpoint both impersonal and internal. Scenes are vividly if elliptically sketched in a few words. The absence of explanatory information combines with some very specific facts. Humour in the narrative ranges from understatement to hyperbole, and interconnections are suggested be-

tween the pig and the sausage being eaten, the enigmatic criss-cross of the plan in the dust and the plan of the ballet as well as the frolicking x's and y's on the board. The fantasy ends with a beginning and has a completeness that indicates 'JMK' is not a fragmentary composition. All of its techniques will be familiar to readers of Woolf's Orlando *and* Flush *as well as her essays and diaries.*

The sudden dislocations of Woolf's short narrative are explained parenthetically and apologetically at the start by the 'infancy' of the biographical art itself, which cannot proceed without the 'leading strings' that the narrator fails for the most part to provide here. Yet when Woolf's biographical fantasy of Keynes is examined closely, the factual basis of much of it emerges. Keynes, for example, had become interested in pigs as Bursar at King's College and began breeding them at his country home near Charleston. A don but never a professor, he was even before his marriage an enthusiast of ballet and a financial advisor to the government. The very specific date of 15 June reflects events in Keynes's life during this month in 1933. The World Economic Conference was meeting in London that June; it included a gala performance by the Camargo Society organized by Keynes in which Lydia Lopokova danced. The Queen attended the gala – and so did Virginia Woolf. The Conference was concerned with the stabilization of currency exchanges, and Keynes was being consulted by Downing Street in the negotiations. Again in 1933, Keynes received from his brother a very rare abstract of Hume's A Treatise on Human Nature *(but the two other known copies of the pamphlet were not in California and the Kremlin). There are further references in the sketch to Keynes's collection of works by British philosophers and economists, to his habit of working in bed in the mornings, to the centenary meetings of the Royal Statistical Society also in the summer of 1933, and to the Cézanne still life of seven (not five) apples that Keynes had bought in Paris during the war and hidden in the hedge at Charleston. Atlantis, it seems, was not one of Keynes's interests, though he made a hobby of studying the currencies of ancient civilizations. Finally, the juggle of cryptic symbols that will produce the one simple, sufficient, and comprehensive word alludes fantastically to the great* General Theory of Employment, Interest and Money *that Keynes was writing in 1933 and would publish three years later.*

Virginia Woolf sometimes thought of her novels in terms of fact and vision. 'JMK' is a work of Virginia Woolf's imagination, but the life of John Maynard Keynes in 1933 shows that much of what is visionary in the sketch consists of the way the factual is treated in it. (In transcribing Woolf's sketch I have regularized the capitalization and punctuation and omitted all of her cancellations as well as a few words that she forgot to cancel. The handwriting is very difficult to decipher in places and a few readings are conjectural.)

J M K

Politics. Art. Dancing. Letters. Economics. Youth. The Future. Glands. Genealogies. Atlantis. Morality. Religion. Cambridge. Eton. The Drama. Society. Truth. Pigs. Sussex. The History of England. America. Optimism. Stammer. Old Books. Hume.

The pig was born in Berkshire, and no doubt cost its mother a pang or two as prize pigs do. But can it be proved that the prize pig was born on the hundred of the thane from whom the College in whose Chapel the organ is even now, at Evensong, pealing stole a thicket and therefore built a town six hundred years ago? (The art of biography is in its infancy. It has not yet learnt to walk without leading strings.) To cut the matter short, the prize pig was the father of a fine litter, not in Berkshire though, nor yet in the famous town where the Chapel is one of the sights of the civilised world, so that often on a fine summer evening a little knot of tourists will hang about the door asking each other who's that who's that? as the dignitaries go in and out.

Now it is a fact that Cyrus K. Pyecroft shot a little wad of chewing gum onto the turf the other evening accompanying the Professor. Famous in New York, famous on Wall Street, famous in Chicago, famous in Boston. By gum! he said.

Yes, a very famous man, he must be, who, in the summer pausing to sketch in the dry dust with the point of his shoe the plan – but the plan of what?

When he had passed on, his head thrust forward, deep in talk, the tourists tried in vain to unriddle the criss-cross in the dust. A plan of some said one thing some another. It was none of these things though.

What was it then?

On June the 15th as the summer sun sunk over London the lights went up in Covent Garden. The Queen of England threw a rose to the ballet dancers, but the gentleman in full evening dress by her side, noted on the back of his shirt cuff that she was three quarters of an inch off the square. He was demonstrating to the most venerable of all masters – the Archbishop of the old established Russian Church of Dancing – this heresy – the fraction from the plan – when sure enough, as always happened that year between one and two in the morning – Downing Street unable to sleep, crept restlessly to the telephone, despairingly raised the receiver, and from the cavernous gloom of the deserted Cabinet Room, with Pitt ironically regarding the map that seemed on the point of being for ever rolled up, summoned the only trusty Counsellor, the one man on whom the fate of the Empire . . .

The sausage was still hot between his lips. Rose leaves and the torn muslin of ballet dancer's skirts were on the ground. He made him a tent of tulle; and there couchant, dictated. All the papers had it in large letters – next morning.

'But are you positive that the Capital A on the verso of the 10th folio is upside down?' he insisted, then sank back on his pillows.

England was off the gold standard; and he had at last, after years of research, recovered the only extant copy of the excessively rare pamphlet only three of which were in existence, one in the Kremlin, one at Pasadena – and now the third – the only known copy of that very obscure pamphlet for which he had been hunting, turning catalogues, browsing in dark booksellers' shops these twenty years.

So while they were calling the terrific news down the streets he lay, gazing at the narrow space between the great volumes – Hume, Locke, Berkeley, Malthus which swelled one after another in polished, in noble array underneath five apples by Cézanne. And then – his glance shot rapidly – there was Lady —— ——'s invitation to dinner, a little further along the shelf; and the statisticians were meeting – the philosophers and the antiquaries and the genealogists, and the explorers. There was the expedition to that spot, now all running white capped waves, underneath slept the ruins of Atlantis. An old civilisation, a better civilisation? Atlantis. Had the bells there rung to higher services than those ringing now, outside? He heard them crying the news in the street. And shrugging his shoulders applied himself to the great green board on which were pinned sheets of symbols: a frolic of xs controlled by ys and embraced by more cryptic symbols still: which, if juggled together would eventually, he was sure, positive, produce the one word, the simple, the sufficient, the comprehensive word which will solve all problems forever. It was time to begin. He began.

John Maynard Keynes by Clive Bell

Clive Bell's recollections of Keynes appeared ten years after Keynes's death in 1946 and five years after the authorized biography of him by Roy Harrod. The tone of Bell's memoir shows the same mixture of affection and criticism as his memoir of Fry, confirming again that Bloomsbury was no mutual admiration society. The faintly ironical references to 'Lord Keynes' are an example. (He had become Baron Keynes of Tilton in 1942.) Bell also reveals a fusion of moral, aesthetic, political, literary, and economic ideas that were involved in the personal relations of the Group. But he is necessarily more reticent in print than other Bloomsbury memoirists who were writing only for the Memoir Club.

In a memoir called 'My Early Beliefs' Lord Keynes, describing the company he kept at Cambridge, finds a word or phrase to fit each of his friends: 'Moore himself was a puritan and a precisian,' he writes, 'Strachey (for that was his name at that time) a Voltairean, Woolf a rabbi, myself a nonconformist, Sheppard a conformist and (as it now turns out) an ecclesiastic, Clive a gay and amiable dog, Sydney-Turner a quietist, Hawtrey a dogmatist and so on.' Now Clive may have been gay and amiable and a dog, but Maynard can have known it only by hearsay; for, oddly enough, at Cambridge we never met. Or did we meet for a moment; before dinner, before a debate? I think not; though I distinctly remember Edwin Montagu telling me that he had invited a brilliant freshman, just up from Eton, who would be of great value – when we had gone down – to the Liberal Party in the Union. That was in the late autumn of 1902, and that was the first I heard of Maynard. That we did not know each other may be accounted for perhaps by the fact that I spent a good part of my last, my fourth, year (October 1902-3) in London working at the Record Office, and when I was in Cambridge lived mostly with my old friends in Trinity, not accompanying Lytton Strachey on his excursions into King's. Be that as it may, certain I am that the first time I met Maynard to talk to was in the summer of 1906, when Lytton brought him to my chambers in the Temple. He was then, I surmise, sitting for the civil service examination, and wearing, I am sure, a light green Burberry and a bowler hat.[1]

1 May I, while correcting one mistake, irrelevantly call attention to another? On page [84 of 'My Early Beliefs'] Maynard writes – 'Many years later he (D.H. Lawrence) recorded in a letter which is printed in his published correspondence, that I was the only member of Bloomsbury who had supported him by subscribing for Lady Chatterley.' This, if I am to be reckoned a member of Bloomsbury, is, like so many things that Lawrence said, untrue. My subscription copy, duly numbered 578 and signed, stands now in my book-case.

Our acquaintance must have improved steadily. In February 1908 my elder son was born; and, as in those days it was customary for a young mother to remain in bed for perhaps a month after giving birth to a child, I took to inviting some agreeable friend who after dinner would entertain the convalescent with an hour's conversation. Maynard was one of the three or four who came. Nevertheless we cannot yet have been what I should call intimate since I remember feeling, not exactly shy, but conscious of the fact that this was the first time I had dined with him en tête-à-tête. He was still a clerk in the India Office, living in one of those dreary blocks of flats near St James's Park Station; but a few months later he returned to Cambridge, and though during the next year or two I saw him much in company I rarely saw him alone. He stayed with us in the country; he was with us at Guildford in July 1911 and he it was who, having as usual secured first look at *The Times*, told us that the Lords had passed the Parliament Act: when he took Asheham for the Easter holidays my wife and I stayed with him. Evidently in August 1913 we were on easy and amiable terms for we shared a tent on a camping-party, organized by the Oliviers of course – the Brandon Camp: I recall most vividly the discomfort. Maynard minded less, he was a better camper-out than I. On the other hand he was an even worse lawn-tennis player. We played occasionally on the hilly courts of Gordon Square – he and I, Gerald Shove, Phillip Morrell and sometimes Adrian Stephen. But Maynard was so feeble that though we always gave him for partner Phillip, by far the best of the bunch, we could not make a game of it. Maynard was dropped.

This must have been just before the first war, in the summer of 1914, when Maynard was lodging in Brunswick Square. During the winter he had served on a Royal Commission on Indian currency and consequently had begun to make friends in high places. A new Maynard, who accompanied but never displaced the old, was emerging – a man of great affairs and a friend of the great. Also, I fancy, it was about this time or a little earlier that he took to speculating. According to an account he once gave me – in whimsical mood I must confess – Maynard, who at Cambridge and in early London days had barely glanced at 'Stock Exchange Dealings', grew so weary – this is what he told me – of reading the cricket-scores in *The Times* that, while drinking his morning tea, he took to studying prices instead. You may believe it or not as you choose: anyhow it was a digression from what I was saying, that already before the war Maynard had come into contact with a part of the political and high

official world. Some of us shook our heads, not over the new interests
but over the new friendships. Would they not encourage the growth
of what we were pleased to consider false values? Would he not soon
be attaching more importance to means (power, honours, conventions, money) than to ends – i.e. good states of mind (*vide Principia
Ethica passim*)? Would he not lose his sense of proportion? But when
Maynard, having invited to dinner two of his big-wigs (Austen Chamberlain and McKenna I seem to remember), discovered at the last moment that all his Champagne had been drunk by Duncan Grant and
his boon companions – Duncan's mid-day Champagne-parties in
Brunswick Square were a feature of that memorable summer – he
took it well enough. His sense of values appeared to be intact. And
I will not doubt he realized that a subsequent party to which he
and Duncan Grant invited the St John Hutchinsons – Mrs Hutchinson was Duncan's cousin – Molly MacCarthy and myself was much
greater fun.

In September 1914 Maynard was with us at Asheham; and it pleases
me to remember that the great man – and he was a great man –
who enjoyed for years an international reputation for cool and detached judgement, rebuked me sharply for refusing to believe in the
Russian-troops-in-England fairy tale and for surmising that the war
would not soon be over. The fact is, of course, that Maynard's judgement would have been as sound as his intellect was powerful had
it really been detached; but Maynard was an incorrigible optimist.
I am not likely to forget the infectious confidence with which he
asserted in 1929 that the Liberals were bound to have more than a
hundred seats in the new House of Commons and would probably
have a hundred and fifty (in fact they had 59); for he backed his
opinion by a gamble on the Stock Exchange in which he involved
some of his impecunious friends – I was not one of them. With considerateness as characteristic as his confidence, when he realized the
awkwardness of the scrape into which his optimism had led them,
he shouldered their liabilities. In 1939, towards the middle of July,
when he was about to leave for a cure at Royat, he asked me whether
I thought war would break out that autumn or whether there would
be 'another hullabaloo'. ('Hullabaloo' seems to me quite a good name
for Munich.) I said that, having committed ourselves, foolishly in
my opinion, to defend Poland, and Hitler being obviously determined
to invade Poland forthwith, I supposed war before winter was inevitable. This time Maynard did not exactly rebuke me, but he did
call me a 'pessimist'.

During the 1914–18 war I saw a good deal of him, especially during the later part, when he and I, Sheppard and Norton, shared 46 Gordon Square. It seems not generally to be known – though Mr Roy Harrod has not attempted to conceal the fact – that Lord Keynes was a conscientious objector. To be sure he was an objector of a peculiar and, as I think, most reasonable kind. He was not a pacificist; he did not object to fighting in any circumstances; he objected to being made to fight. Good liberal that he was, he objected to conscription. He would not fight because Lloyd-George, Horatio Bottomley and Lord Northcliffe told him to. He held that it was for the individual to decide whether the question at issue was worth killing and dying for; and surely he was entitled to consider himself a better judge than the newspaper-men who at that time ruled the country. He was surprised and shocked when Mr Asquith gave way to their clamour. His work at the Treasury, which by 1917 had become of vital importance, kept him in contact with the more important ministers, and he saw right through Lloyd-George. He detested his demagogy. I remember his cutting from a French paper – *Excelsior* presumably – a photograph of 'the goat' as he always called him, in full evening dress and smothered in ribbons, speaking at a banquet in Paris; and I remember his writing under it 'Lying in state'. He pinned it up in the dining-room at forty-six. Later, in the supposed interests of the Liberal Party, he collaborated with 'the goat' who had become for certain left-wing papers and politicians a sort of 'grand old man'. No good came of that. As for his conscientious objection, he was duly summoned to a tribunal and sent word that he was much too busy to attend.

There are those who maintain that Maynard's importance during the war and familiarity with the great bred that cocksureness which was his most irritating characteristic. I do not agree. The influence of the great on Maynard was slight compared with Maynard's influence on them. The cocksureness was always there; circumstances evoked and possibly stimulated it. Certainly the habit was provoking. It was also amusing. Late one night towards the end of the first war I remember his coming up to my room in Gordon Square where Norton and I were talking quietly about, as likely as not, the meaning of meaning. He was elated; he had been dining; what is more, he had been dining with cabinet ministers. The question had arisen – 'Who finally defeated Hannibal?' No one knew except Maynard and he told them it was Fabius Maximus: 'unus homo nobis cunctando restituit rem' he declaimed, and I hope he translated it for the politicians though for us he was good enough to leave it in the original. Of course it was not the cunctator but Scipio Africanus who finally defeated Hannibal at the battle of Zama, as I obligingly pointed out. Maynard disregarded my correction in a way that did perhaps ever so slightly suggest that someone who had been dining with cabinet ministers knew better, and continued to expatiate on the pleasures of the evening, his little historical triumph, the excellent cooking and above all the wine.

Maynard laid down the law on all subjects. I dare say I minded too much: many of his friends took it as a joke. But I do think it was silly of him; for by dogmatizing on subjects about which he knew nothing he sometimes made himself ridiculous to those who did not know him well and to those who did annoying. Cocksureness was his besetting sin, if sin it can be called. Gradually it became his habit to speak with authority: a bad habit which leads its addicts to assume that the rest of us are ready to assume that their knowledge must be greater than ours. Maynard knew a good deal about a great many things, and on several subjects spoke with warranted authority. Unfortunately he got into the habit of speaking with authority whether it was warranted or not. He acquired – I do not say he cultivated – a masterful manner; and when he spoke of matters about which he knew little or nothing with the confidence and disregard for other people's opinions which were perhaps excusable when he was talking about economics or probability or rare editions, instead of appealing masterly he appeared pretentious. That, too, was a pity, for he was not pretentious; he made no boast of his superior knowledge and expected no praise for it, he merely assumed it. For my part, I was exasperated most often by his laying down the law on painting and painters; but I will not draw an example of his misplaced self-confidence from his pronouncements on art, because, aesthetic judgements being always questionable, though I am sure that his were often wrong, I am far from sure that mine are always right. Instead, I will recall a conversation – or should I say an exposition? – which remains extremely clear in my memory, and provides an instance of misplaced self-confidence the misplacedness of which is not open to dispute.

He had been staying with one of his rich city-friends – for in those days (the early 'twenties') there were still rich men in England: he had been staying in Hampshire I think but I am not sure, certainly in the south, and he returned to Charleston, the house in Sussex which for a while he shared with my wife, myself and Duncan Grant, and told us all about it. It had been a shooting party; Maynard himself never handled a gun, but he told us all about it. He told us what is done and what is not done; he told us when you might shoot and when you might not shoot, he told us how to shoot and what to shoot. And as he was under the impression – all this happened long before he had a farm and a wood of his own – that his party had been shooting grouse in Hampshire or thereabouts with rifles, you can imagine the sort of nonsense he made of it. Now it so happens I was brought up in a sporting family: I have possessed a game-licence since I was sixteen and walked with the guns since I was a child; and I do believe I have killed every game-bird in the British Isles except a capercailzie and some of the rarer duck. But if you suppose that these facts would have daunted Lord Keynes, all I can say is – you have got the great economist wrong.

My insistence on Maynard's cocksureness may have given the impression that he was spoilt by success. If so, I have given a false impression. Maynard floated happily on a sea of power and glory and considerable wealth, but never went out with the tide. Two stout anchors held him fast to shore: his old friends and Cambridge. This Mr Roy Harrod has made clear in his excellent biography. Cabinet Ministers and *The Times* might praise, but if he had an uneasy suspicion that Lytton Strachey, Duncan Grant, Virginia Woolf and Vanessa Bell did not share their enthusiasm, public flattery might appear something to be ashamed of. When he came to Charleston with Lady Keynes for the first time after his peerage had been announced he was downright sheepish. 'We have come to be laughed at' he said. And what was Cambridge thinking? Maynard cared passionately for his country, but I believe he was at greater pains to improve the finances of King's than to rescue those of the British Empire. If this be a slight exaggeration, that artistic temperament, from which I should like to be supposed to suffer, must bear the blame; but that stern, unbending economist, Mr Roy Harrod, has made it clear to all who read that Keynes valued the good opinion of his old friends far above that of the majority or the great. Mr Harrod, it seems to me, gives an excellent account of his subject – I had almost said his 'hero' – which should be read for its own sake and perhaps as a corrective to mine. Nevertheless I understand the feelings of those old and intimate friends who say – 'Maynard was not really like that, he was not like that at all.' That is what old friends will always say of official biographies; and they will be right. Mrs Thrale, who knew Johnson far longer and far more intimately than Boswell knew him, doubtless said as much. And of course Mrs Thrale was right. Only she forgot that it was Boswell's business to write a biography, to depict a man in all his activities and in his relations to all sorts of people, while it was her privilege to record a personal impression.

I, too, am recording a personal impression. I am trying to remember little things that have escaped the notice of my betters. Such things are trivial by definition, and sometimes derogatory; but, though they may be beneath the dignity of history, they matter a good deal in daily life. My recollections, I foresee, run the risk of appearing spiteful. To counteract this appearance I could of course pile up well merited compliments. But of what use would it be for me to expatiate on the power of Maynard's intellect and his services to humanity when writers far better qualified have done it already and done it with authority? Nevertheless, to escape the charge of malignity, let me say here and now what maybe I shall have occasion to repeat. Maynard was the cleverest man I ever met: also his cleverness was of a kind, gay and whimsical and civilized, which made his conversation a joy to every intelligent person who knew him. In addition he had been blest with a deeply affectionate nature. I once heard him say, humorously but I believe truly, at dinner, before a meeting of the memoir club, 'If everyone at this table, except myself, were to die tonight, I do not think I should care to go on living.' He loved and he was beloved. He did not love, though he may have rather liked, me; and I did not love him. That should be borne in mind by anyone who does this sketch the honour of a reading.

In great things he was magnificently generous; generous to his country, generous to his college, generous to servants and dependents, particularly generous to his less fortunate friends (I know two charming young men who may or may not know that they were educated – and highly education – partly at his expense). In small things, however, like many who have enjoyed the advantages and disadvantages of a serious, non-conformist upbringing, he was careful. Also, financier that he was, he loved a bargain. One summer's evening in 1919 he returned to Charleston from a day in London bearing a heavy parcel which contained innumerable minute tins of potted meat. He had bought them at a sale of surplus army-stores and he had bought them at a penny a piece. The private soldiers had not liked the stuff, and therein had shown good taste. I teased Maynard by pretending that the meat had been condemned as unfit for human consumption: and indeed, the bargain-hunter himself could barely keep it down. But at a penny a tin. . . . Again, I remember being with him at Lewes

races, and asking a farmer of my acquaintance for 'a good thing'.
Maynard did not want 'a good thing'; what he wanted was the best
bet. He wanted a bargain in odds. This rather complicated notion
puzzled my friend, and we left him puzzling. For I did not attempt
to explain that what Maynard had in mind was that there might
be some horse in some race against which the odds were longer than
need be, or rather, book-makers being what they are, less short than
might have been expected. If there were a starter at a hundred to
one which might just as well have been offered at sixty-six to one,
that horse, though standing no apparent chance of winning, was the
horse for Maynard's money. What he wanted was not a winner but
a bargain.

Lytton Strachey used to say – 'Pozzo has no aesthetic sense.'[2] That
was an exaggeration perhaps. What may be said confidently is that
he had no innate feeling for the visual arts. Had he never met Duncan
Grant he would never have taken much interest in painting. He made
a valuable collection because generally he bought on good advice;
when he relied on his own judgement the result was sometimes lamentable. Lamentable it would have been had he relied on his own
judgement to the end when he wrote that piece in *The New Statesman*
about Low's drawings; for in the original version, not only had he
compared Low with Daumier, he had likened him to Daumier, had
almost equalled him with Daumier. What he insisted on retaining
is sufficiently tell-tale.

> We all know that we have amongst us today a cartoonist in the grand
> tradition. But, as the recognition, which contributions to evening papers
> receive by word of mouth round the dinner-table, cannot reach the modest
> cartoonist, one welcomes a book like this as an opportunity to tell Low
> how much we think of him and how much we love him. He has the rare
> combination of gifts which is necessary for his craft – a shrewd and pene-
> trating intelligence, wit, taste, unruffled urbanity, an indignant but open
> and understanding heart, a swift power of minute observation with an
> equally swift power of essential simplification, and, above all, a sense and

2 Mr Roy Harrod writes in a note: 'For many years in Bloomsbury Keynes was famil-
iarly known by the name of Pozzo, having been so christened by Strachey after the
Corsican diplomat, Pozzo di Borgo – not a diplomat of evil motive or base conduct,
but certainly a schemer and man of many facets.' But it was not only, nor chiefly, of
the Corsican diplomat that Lytton and those who used the nickname were thinking.
The Italian word 'pozzo' has more than one meaning, and to English ears carries
various suggestions.

talent for beauty, which extracts something delightful even out of ugliness. One may seem to be piling it on, but Low really has these things, and it is a great addition to our lives to meet the tongue and eye of a civilized man and true artist when we open the *Evening Standard*.

Last summer Low and Kingsley Martin made a trip to Bolshieland, and this agreeable book is the outcome. Low's pencil and charcoal sketches are reproduced by some process which, whatever it may be, looks like lithograph and thereby reinforces the comparison between Low and the lithographers of the old *Charivari* of Paris – Gavarni and Daumier and their colleagues. They are *illustrations* in the literal sense of the word – pictures of the inside and of the outside of things at the same time. (Review of 'Low's Russian Sketchbook' – *New Statesman and Nation*, Dec. 10, 1932)

What one tried to point out, and Maynard could not understand, was that no two artists – to be for a moment polite and dishonest – could be much more unalike than Daumier and Low. To begin with, Low is not an artist. He possesses a prodigious knack of inventing visual equivalents for political situations and ideas; and ekes out their meaning with tags which have often the neatness of epigrams. It is a remarkable gift. But those equivalents have no aesthetic value – no value in themselves. The line is as smart and insensitive as the prose of a penny-a-liner. Daumier, who was one of the great draughtsmen of the nineteenth century, lacked entirely that gift which in old days made us buy the *Evening Standard* to see what Low was up to. Having made a beautiful drawing, which might or might not suggest some crude bit of social or political criticism, Daumier as often as not, could think of no legend to put under it. The drawing, you see, was not an illustration of something else but a work of art complete in itself. So he left the business of putting in the patter to Philipon or some other clever fellow in the office. This distinction to Maynard seemed fanciful, as it must seem to anyone who has no real feeling for visual art. Even in literature his untutored judgement was not to be trusted. During the last war he returned from America with a find – a great new novel. He had discovered a modern master, and he had brought the masterpiece home with him. It was Bemelmans' *Now I Lay Me Down to Sleep*, a piece of comicality that might, or might not, while away an hour in the train.

That Maynard Keynes has benefited all the arts by the creation of the Arts Council is a title to glory and a notorious fact which proves nothing contrary to what was said in the last paragraph. It would prove, if further proof were needed, that he was one of those uncommon human beings who have devoted great powers of organization to good purposes. Maynard's gifts were always at the service of civilization, and by long and affectionate association with artists – do not forget that Lady Keynes was a brilliant ballerina and an interesting actress – he came to realize acutely that of civilization the arts are an essential ingredient. Also this achievement, the creation of the Arts Council in time of war, of a war in which he was playing an important and exhausting part, proves – but again what need of proof? – his boundless energy and versatility, as well as his capacity for making something solid and durable out of a hint. God forbid that anyone should imagine that I am suggesting that it was I who gave the hint. At that time anxious questionings as to the future of the arts in a more or less socialist state were to be heard on all sides. I drag myself into the picture only because I recall a conversation with Maynard which led to my writing, at his suggestion, an article in *The New Statesman* of which, at that time, he was part-proprietor and, unless I mistake, a director. My argument was that, much as I disliked the idea of a Ministry of Fine Arts, the creation of such a Ministry would be, when private patronage had been destroyed by economic egalitarianism, the only means of saving the arts from extinction. The argument was neither striking nor novel; what was remarkable was that Maynard, in the midst of his preoccupations, should not only have devised but realized an institution which might nourish the arts without handing them over to civil servants and politicians. So far his contrivance has worked and worked well. Whether it will continue to evade the embrace of death – of politicians I mean – remains to be seen.

Those who have said that Maynard Keynes had no aesthetic sense may seem to have forgotten his prose. He had a fine, lucid style in which he could state persuasively and wittily the interesting things he had in mind. When he attempted to express the more delicate shades of feeling or to make a picture out of observations rather than ideas, he was, in my opinion, less convincing. Those famous portraits of Clemenceau, Wilson and Lloyd-George have never seemed to me quite the masterpieces they have seemed to other, and perhaps better, judges. They are lively and telling but scarcely subtle I think. To my taste his best book is *Essays in Persuasion*, and the best portrait he ever drew that of Alfred Marshall. In that long biographical notice, reprinted in *Essays in Biography*, his knowledge and his culture, which, though limited, had been garnered and sifted by an extraor-

dinarily powerful understanding, are most skilfully employed to en-
lighten what in other hands might have appeared a dull subject. The
result, if not precisely beautiful, is more than pleasing: in the exact
sense of the word it is admirable.

I said that his culture was limited: such judgements are always
relative, and perhaps I should try to be more explicit. As has been
intimated, in the visual arts his taste was anything but sure and his
knowledge amounted to nothing. Some believed he appreciated
music, but I have never discovered the foundations of their belief.
Literature is another matter. At Eton Maynard had been reared on
the classics, and of the Greek and Latin authors remembered as much
as clever people who have enjoyed what are called the advantages
of a public school education can be expected to remember. I have
heard that he was a fair German scholar, but of that I cannot speak.
He had very little French and no Italian. Of English he had read
much, both verse and prose. He liked poetry; but he enjoyed it as
a well education man of affairs rather than as an artist or an aesthete.
One had only to hear him read aloud – and he was fond of reading
poetry aloud – to feel that the content was what he really cared for.
His commerce with the English historians would have been more
profitable if his memory had been more retentive. He had a capacity
for forgetting, and for muddling, dates and figures, that was astonishing and sometimes rather tiresome – tiresome because, with his
invincible cocksureness, he could not dream of admitting that he mistook. To the end of his life he continued to study – or perhaps, towards
the end, merely to take an interest in – mathematics and philosophy.
Presumably he understood Wittgenstein as well as anyone understood
him – except Professor Ayer. He never called himself a Logical Pos-
itivist. Of his economic theories and constructions, that is to say of
the great work of his life, I am too ignorant to speak. I should be
able to say more about his theory of Probability than that it served
him ill at Monte Carlo, since in the years before the first war I often
heard him talk about it. And after that war, when he took up the
manuscript of his old dissertation with a view to making a book,
he would – I suppose because we were living in the same house –
occasionally hand me a much corrected sheet saying – such was his
lack of memory – 'can you remember what I meant by that?' Alas,
figures and symbols had crept into the argument and my miserable
inaptitude for sums made me unhelpful. Anyhow I am not equipped
to criticize so abstruse a theory, but I understand that [Frank] Ramsey
made a rent which caused all the stitches to run.

I dare say most readers will think I have said enough to disprove my statement that Maynard's culture was limited. Maybe I used the wrong word and should have said 'provincial'. To explain what I mean by that, perhaps I may be allowed to draw on my homely but vivid memories. At Charleston it was our habit to sit after dinner in an oblate semi-circle before a curious fire-place, devised and constructed by Roger Fry to heat with logs a particularly chilly room: strange to say, it did. Each of us would be reading his or her book, and someone was sure to be reading French. Also it so happened that, just after the old war, stimulated I think by Aldous Huxley, I had become interested in the life and through the life the plays of Alfieri; wherefore, Alfieri leading on, I might be reading some early nineteenth-century Italian. Thus, towards bed-time, could spring up talk about French or Italian ways of thinking, feeling and living. In such discussions one could not but be struck by Maynard's inability to see a foreign country from inside. France, Italy, America even, he saw them all from the white cliffs of Dover, or, to be more exact, from Whitehall or King's combination room. Compared with (say) Roger Fry, who was often of the company, he seemed ludicrously provincial. And that may be what I had in mind when I called his culture limited.

In spite of all the little annoying things that have stuck in my memory, my recollection of Maynard, vivid and persistent, is that of a delightful companion. I miss him; and I understand the feelings of those who more than miss, of those for whom the wound caused by his death never quite heals and may at any moment become painful. What I miss is his conversation. It was brilliant: that is an obvious thing to say but it is the right thing. In the highest degree he possessed that ingenuity which turns commonplaces into paradoxes and paradoxes into truisms, which discovers – or invents – similarities and differences, and associates disparate ideas – that gift of amusing and surprising with which very clever people, and only very clever, can by conversation give a peculiar relish to life. He had a witty intellect and a verbal knack. In argument he was bewilderingly quick, and unconventional. His comment on any subject under discussion, even on a subject about which he knew very little, was apt to be so lively and original that one hardly stopped to enquire whether it was just. But in graver mood, if asked to explain some technical business, which to the amateur seemed incomprehensible almost, he would with good-humoured ease make the matter appear so simple that one knew not whether to be more amazed at his intelligence or one's own stupidity. In moments such as these I felt sure that Maynard was the cleverest man I had ever met; also, at such moments, I sometimes felt, unreasonably no doubt, that he was an artist.

That Maynard Keynes was a great man is generally admitted; but in private life no one could have been less 'great-manish'. He was never pompous. His greatness no doubt revealed itself most impressively in economics – the work of his life – in organization and negotiation; but of greatness in such matters I am not competent to speak. Nor yet, alas! am I entitled to speak of what to some was his most memorable quality: for me his cleverness was what counted most, but to a few privileged men and women who knew him through and through his supreme virtue was his deeply affectionate nature. He liked a great many people of all sorts and to them he gave pleasure, excitement and good counsel; but his dearest friends he loved passionately and faithfully and, odd as it may sound, with a touch of humility.

Lydia Lopokova by Quentin Bell

The introduction of Lydia Lopokova into Bloomsbury by John Maynard Keynes, who married her in 1925, caused considerable strain in the Group. As Vanessa Bell wrote to Keynes in an unpublished, undated letter,

> *. . . Clive says he thinks it impossible for anyone of us, you, he, I or Duncan, to introduce a new wife or husband into the existing circle for more than one week at a time. He himself is prepared (no wonder) to abstain from doing so and sooner than make one of such a party he would prefer to go away alone . . . Don't think however that what I say is some kind of criticism of Lydia for it isn't. We feel that no one can come into the sort of intimate society we have without altering it (she has done so perhaps less than anyone, certainly less than any other woman could have). That is inevitable, isn't it? . . .*

Bloomsbury has been thought ungenerous in its response to Lydia by various critics. (E.M. Forster appears to have been her favourite friend in Bloomsbury.) Quentin Bell explains what some of the difficulties were. His essay is in the form of a letter to Maynard Keynes's nephew Milo, who edited a collection of essays on Lydia Lopokova in 1983.

Dear Milo,

You asked me to write about Lydia and Bloomsbury. I refused and said that I would try to write you a letter, since it seemed easier. But I find the task even harder than I had expected and the result, I dare say, will hardly be worth publishing.

The fact is that I don't want to write about Lydia. She will not read this, I know, but the circumstances are such that I shall have to say some things that would have given her pain at one time; and this makes it an awkward, unwelcome, ungrateful job.

Why then do I attempt it? The answer is that I am irritated; not a very good reason but one which it is hard to resist. What irritated me was the article by Richard Buckle in the collection of essays concerning Maynard which you published a few years ago, entitled *On Loving Lydia*. Mr Buckle thought that Bloomsbury 'missed the point' of Lydia, and this indeed argues gross hebetude; but there is worse to come: their insensibility was, as he sees it, not even honest; it arose, not from a genuine though mistaken feeling, but from a craven submission to orders; 'they' complied with the dictates of an 'autocrat' who 'ruled the roost' and in some manner enforced her wishes upon the rest of the gang. And this odious tyrant was my mother, Vanessa Bell!

Yes, as I said, I am irritated, and I am afraid that my irritation may show itself in what follows. Nevertheless I will try to confine myself to a brief account of the facts as far as I know them.

I first saw Lydia in 1918, when I was eight years old; she was I think on the stage of the Coliseum and perhaps I didn't even see her there; it doesn't matter. But a few years later I began to know her, and indeed to love her. I think that it must have been before my eleventh birthday – but again I am vague – that I was allowed to join the grown-ups at lunch at 46 Gordon Square. Lydia was there; also I believe Massine and Karsavina, my father, Clive, and Maynard. At that time there was a widespread notion that in the presence of Russian dancers one talked French. At any rate, everyone on this occasion did talk French. I don't know if you remember my father; if so, you may also recollect that when there was an excuse for talking in French he took it, and sometimes indeed he took it when there was no excuse. On this occasion he had a double motive; not only did he enjoy the chance to exhibit his command of the language, he also enjoyed the opportunity to flirt with Lydia while Maynard, whose spoken French was awkward and hesitant, could hardly get a word in. I had even less French than Maynard and for me that party was an affair of incomprehensible exclamations and laughter in which it certainly appeared that Clive 'saw the point' of Lydia, and saw it with very great enthusiasm. Maynard, not unnaturally, was vexed and at the end of the meal he exclaimed to me, his fellow-sufferer: 'Why do they jabber away in French like that? I don't believe that they really understand what they are saying themselves.'

If, as I suppose, this party took place during the summer of 1921, then in the same year I was given a first chance to improve my knowledge of French when, in the autumn of that year, the family moved to the South of France. It was here, in December 1921, that my mother and Duncan Grant learnt that Lydia had learnt English, with notable results.

Maynard, in a letter to Vanessa dated 20 December that year, wrote, '. . . my other chief news is the progress of my affair with Loppy. I told you, I think, that she came to lunch here last Sunday week. Last Friday I took her to the Savoy after the ballet where we chatted until 1 a.m. and now she has asked me to tea. What is to be done about it? I am getting terrified.' On 6 January 1922 Maynard wrote to Vanessa again: '. . . I'm in great need of much good advice from you. You needn't be afraid of marriage, but the affair is very serious, and I don't in the least know what to do about it. I begin to think it's a good thing I'm going to India. However she's very adorable.' And again on 9 January: '. . . I'm in a terribly bad plight almost beyond rescue. Clive simply grins with delight at seeing me so humbled. However I long to have a good gossip with you.'

One must no doubt allow for an element in these letters of half comic exaggeration. Nevertheless it can hardly be doubted that at this time Maynard's feelings were strangely mixed. She was indeed 'very adorable'. In another letter he speaks of her 'knowing and judicious use of English words', a playful coquetry with the language which Maynard was not alone in noticing and finding extremely attractive. Her nature was both sweet and happy; she seemed to find the world a source of perpetual and delightful astonishment; herself surprised, she was herself surprising. Gifted with tender delicacy of sentiment, which led one ballet critic in an unlucky hour to call her a 'dainty rogue in porcelain', there was all the same something sensible, honest and unpretentious, earthy even, about her. You, who knew her, will not be surprised that Maynard fell in love with her, and will agree that, certainly, there was much to adore.

Why then the terror, the appeal for rescue? Why then was the idea of marriage so swiftly (if unconvincingly) dismissed?

I don't think that one needs any very profound psychology to answer such a question. Marriage is a momentous and serious business. It has its dangers, particularly when your wife is a foreigner, never mind how delightful a foreigner: some one with entirely different interests and from an entirely different background. A few months earlier Maynard's companion had been that charming and erudite person, the late Professor Sprott, at that time a very elegant and seductive youth. Vanessa sometimes referred to him as 'Maynard's wife'. Sebastian, as he was then called, was never a member of the Bloomsbury Group, but his union with Maynard never caused the slightest difficulty with Maynard's other friends: he had been at Cambridge; he was an Apostle; he could meet those friends on their own ground and be accepted by them without difficulty. More than this, he caused not the slightest disruption to the easy, agreeable bachelor existence which Maynard had built up for himself ever since, in 1912, he had become one of the communal group which settled in Brunswick Square. That existence seemed to suit Maynard and his friends perfectly; it allowed him to be entirely independent and yet to be very sociable; it enabled him to live his own very strenuous public life, and at the same time to see a great deal of and frequently to travel abroad with his friends, and in particular with Duncan Grant and Vanessa Bell. He might persuade himself at times and attempt to persuade them that this pleasant, friendly intimacy would survive his marriage to Lydia. But in fact he must have known that it would not. Marriage would inevitably change the picture; it would no doubt bring its delights but it would demand sacrifices, sacrifices that he found it hard to contemplate. That phrase in the marriage service which enjoins the couple to 'forsake all others' would, for him, have a special and poignant meaning. He longed to see his friends and to have the benefit of their 'advice', but what could they advise but that he find some way of avoiding marriage? They were as anxious as he to continue a state of affairs which had been so pleasant for so long. Where Maynard, a man very much in love, could see the matter with such desolating clarity, his friends may perhaps be forgiven for being equally clairvoyant.

Just what happened when Duncan and Vanessa returned from France I do not know. Vanessa used to say that Maynard had implored her to extricate him, and this seems to me likely enough, although how the feat was to be performed it is hard to say. I do however remember what may have been one little attempt at extrication and, since it is first-hand evidence, it seems worth offering, even though inconclusive.

The time would be 1922 or 1923, the place Vanessa's sitting room
at No 50 Gordon Square, the actors Lydia, Vanessa and myself (a
walking-on part):

> *Lydia* (suddenly and gaily): 'Maynar' says I write to Barocchi and say to
> him: does he still consider himself married to me?'
> *Vanessa* (gravely and with meaning): 'My dear Lydia, matrimony is a very
> serious business. I should be very careful about saying or doing anything.'

I was shocked. I hadn't thought of Lydia as being married, and
she had never said anything about it to me, I who saw her every
day.

At about this time, say three years before they were finally married,
Maynard was, I think, attempting a sort of compromise policy. He
was trying to educate Lydia in the kind of things that his wife would
need to know; also I think that he was trying to transplant her, as
it were, to get her to flourish in the soil of Gordon Square. In order
to put these measures into effect Lydia was installed at No. 50 Gordon
Square; down below were Adrian Stephens, up above there were the
Bells, or at least a sample of Bells. Lydia wandered upstairs and downstairs; she spent a great deal of her time in our kitchen. But at weekends Maynard would descend upon us in order to further my education. Of course, it had to be *my* education, I was the child and
indeed sufficiently in need of education; but, of course, Lydia came
with us and could hardly dodge the splendid shower of information.
Maynard was always kind to me, ever since at the age of five I threw
his straw hat into the waters of Chichester Harbour, and I have no
doubt that he took a benevolent pleasure in my obvious delight: but
if Lydia had not been there I very much doubt whether those educational excursions would ever have taken place. We drove off in
a hired Daimler (that in itself was enough to make my day), and
we visited Westminster Abbey, Hampton Court, the Tower of London,
etc., and Maynard talked brilliantly about English History, the Constitution, the Church, and heaven knows what else. It was wholly
delightful, and I'm sure I learnt a great deal and was very sorry when
I had to go to a boarding school and stop learning. How much Lydia
gained by it I do not know, but from my point of view the thing
was an enormous success.

From my point of view it might also be said that Lydia's trans-
plantation was also a success. I have said that she was much in the
kitchen, and it is there that I chiefly remember her talking incessantly
with me and with the extremely nice young woman who was later
to become the family 'treasure' – cook-housekeeper, and much more

– our dear Grace. Sometimes Grace and I would go to the Coliseum with tickets given us by Lydia to see her transformed, etherealized, almost unrecognizably lovely upon the stage. We enjoyed this tremendously, although I cannot say that we didn't enjoy George Robey and Little Titch with equal passion. And one notable evening Maynard burst into my room and hauled me off to the first night of a revue. We had a box, and Lydia came to see us there, either before or after her act. She was there when the curtain rose upon a scene set by a lake around which were posed a score of lovelies sketchily dressed as Red Indians. The girls remained still as waxworks, there was no music, no sound in all the great house save for Lydia's reverberating whisper: 'Oaah, it makes you to *vomit.*' I think that some faces must have turned to the box from whence that appalling comment had issued. The spectators would have seen Maynard, Lydia, Vanessa, Duncan and a fat, a monstrously fat, boy with red hair cut in a fringe, his bulk tightly but untidily covered by a black and white striped football jersey and – but they would hardly have been visible – badly frayed shorts and stockings that crept in wrinkles down to dirty boots. A disturbing sight, no doubt.

I digress: let me come back to the second part of Maynard's campaign, the introduction of Lydia to Bloomsbury. As I have said, Lydia made her way into the kitchen, and here she was an unqualified success. She told us about Russia, about the Nevski Prospekt and droshkis and zakuskis and wolves and samovars. It was lovely.

But when Lydia went up another flight of stairs and, with the same artless good humour, set herself to entertain Vanessa, the results were less happy.

Vanessa, as you may know, was not a very sociable person; she devoted her time mainly to her art; to this, certain hours of the day were sacred and not to be interrupted without good reason. She could also find time for her family which in this context means her children. For Duncan, Virginia and indeed Maynard, and three or four other old friends, she could just find time, usually fairly late in the day when work was done and the younger children were in bed. A casual visitor, a dropper-in, dropping in during the daylight hours was anything but welcome. It is one of the difficulties of the art of painting that it takes a very long time and can be very seriously disturbed by any intrusions.

Maynard must surely have known this, and would, one would have thought, told Lydia that she could not always be welcome. Either he neglected to do this, or he was in some way misunderstood by

Lydia. She made herself perfectly at home; she might look in at any time of the night or day, as she was separated by no door; she was always well received in the kitchen, why not also in the sitting-room or the studio? And indeed there was always a smile for Lydia, as it would have been too cruel to deny her a friendly salute. But the constant visiting, the endless chatter, the entirely innocent annexation of every spare moment, and of moments that in truth could not be spared, became for Vanessa a misery. It seemed that it was, after all, she who had married Lydia and, while Maynard enjoyed all the comforts of matrimony, she, Vanessa, was expected to accept all the tedium. In the end Vanessa took what seemed to her to the only possible step. She went to Maynard and told him that Lydia's visits must be rationed. Personally, having known what it is like to try and produce a work of art under conditions far less difficult than those which Vanessa had to endure, I do not blame her.

All the same it was very hard on Lydia. She ceased to be a constant visitor; she moved to another house in Gordon Square, so that Vanessa was protected by a front door. One must suppose that whatever it was that Maynard had said met the case and was, therefore, distressing. If Mr Buckle got the impression that Mrs Bell was a hard-hearted woman and an autocrat, perhaps that was only to be expected.

It is a tame and a boring conclusion, but in the end it does seem to me difficult to blame either party. Lydia certainly must have known that Vanessa's door had been shut in her face, and she may well have known or divined that Vanessa was active in trying to prevent her marriage. If from time to time she said, 'Oh Wanessa, you frighten me to death,' and she did say this, one can at least understand her feelings. The tragedy is that I do not think that she could possibly have understood why it was that she exasperated Vanessa.

Leonard Woolf, in his autobiography, describes how Wittgenstein, a man with a reputation for saintly behaviour and high moral sense, once turned upon Lydia with such savagery that she burst into tears. Leonard considered that there was a nasty, sadistic streak in Wittgenstein, and since I didn't know the great philosopher and wasn't there when the tears were shed, I must allow that he knew best. But it seems to me possible that Lydia had unwittingly said things which had brought Wittgenstein himself to the verge of tears. I know that she did this to me on one occasion.

It was at Charleston in the spring of 1940. Maynard and Lydia had come over after dinner, and naturally there was talk about the war. The Germans had just invaded Norway, we had won a naval action and had landed troops at Trondheim; the circumstances were sufficiently cheerful to encourage Maynard into one of his great bursts of optimism. The Germans, he declared, were about to be crushed; they would suffer a crippling defeat from which Hitler's prestige would never recover. He was done for.

Clive, who was always irritated by what he called Maynard's hubris, took the other view; he said, and truly, that it was much too early to claim a victory and that it would be very wrong to underestimate the strength of the forces that Hitler could throw into the struggle. I dare say that Clive was rather provoking in the way in which he said this, and that he didn't choose his words as carefully as he should have, but he certainly did not deserve the reply that he got, not from Maynard, but from Lydia.

'Oaah!' (but I cannot transliterate Lydia's extraordinary vowel sounds made even more extraordinary by violent emotion) 'Clive, you shall not say that you want the Germans to win. They shall not win and you MUST NOT say it.'

Clive, astonished by this outburst, objected that he had said nothing of the kind; he had merely pointed out the dangers of being too optimistic.

But he was not allowed to finish his sentence. Every time he opened his mouth he was met by a passionate denunciation, and when he did manage to say something Lydia refused to listen; and so it went on, despite some efforts to change the conversation, or to direct it upon more rational lines. As may be imagined, the evening ended badly.

To say that I was almost reduced to tears is perhaps too much, but I, like everyone else, was profoundly exasperated. Why should our conversation be reduced to this silly shouting match?

O Diamond! Diamond! thou little knowest the mischief done! Of course, one was cross with Lydia, but one did not seriously blame her. It never occurred to her that, at a moment of intense and agonizing interest in public affairs, we were being deprived of the voice of one of the people who knew most, and could talk best, and could, despite his over-optimism, tell us things that we badly wanted to know. Indeed, it was Maynard who amazed and still amazes me. He made not the slightest attempt to stop Lydia from making a fool of herself, or Clive from losing his temper. And yet with a joke, a paradox, some very slight exercise of that incredibly brilliant mind of his, he could have set everything straight. Instead of which he sat there, almost smiling, with the bland, indulgent air of a fond parent whose spoilt child is smashing someone else's tea-cups.

I suppose that this ability to withdraw from the discussion, this readiness to allow Lydia to have her way with the conversation, was an element of the art of being married to her and may be justified by the fact that it was a very happy marriage. But, speaking as an outsider, I must say that there were moments when I wished that Maynard could have paraphrased that poet, whose name I forget, but who said to his mistress 'Sois charmante et tais toi.' I must add that, when she ventured upon what were for her dangerous topics – politics, philosophy or science – Lydia could often be absurd, but I do not think that I ever saw her so violent in the expression of her absurdity.

Do you see what I am getting at? Properly to say what I am trying to say would be a considerable feat of letters. One would have some-how to convey the fact that Lydia could be a bother, an enemy to good sense and even, as on this occasion, to good humour. But at the same time one would have to make it clear – no, rather to *insist* – that she could be, not merely good fun, but really impressive, that her natural sincerity, her gaiety, her complete lack of side, could make an evening with her not merely delightful but instructive. It was when she knew more about the subject under discussion than one did oneself that she was at her best, but let me repeat that, even at her most absurd, Lydia was thoroughly sincere, and even when tilt-ing at windmills she rode uncommonly straight. Perhaps one of your contributors will reproduce Lydia in the old days with Diagh-ilev, or the still older days in St Petersburg. And perhaps someone who saw more of her in the last years of Maynard's life will be able to paint a very different picture, for by then it was not windmills that she was charging. For my part I got no more than a glimpse of that later heroism, when she was spending all her magnificent energy and vitality in caring for Maynard and keeping that trou-blesome patient in some kind of order. At that time, undoubtedly Lydia was heroic and, whatever his previous doubts may have been, Maynard may have realized that he had a wife of whom he could most justly be proud.

There were, as you will see, two different aspects of Lydia, and if one were to try to describe the relationship between her and May-nard's older friends it would be necessary to give each its proper value.

For this you need a skilful and a highly judicious author. As I said, my own chief motive for writing was irritation; it is not a qualification for the kind of contributor you need, for how am I to escape the charge of partiality? In this matter I am not a judge, but a witness, and as such I claim merely that I have tried to tell the truth; I am in fact yours most sincerely,

Quentin

David Garnett by Henrietta Garnett

David Garnett's father, Edward, was an author and literary advisor of Galsworthy, Conrad, Ford, Hudson, Lawrence, and others; his mother, Constance, was the great English translator of Russian fiction. David became a well-known novelist with the publication of Lady into Fox *in 1922. After the death of his first wife, Ray Marshall, he married Angelica Bell, and one of their four daughters – also a novelist – describes him here after he and Angelica had separated. The occasion for her memoir was the making of Garnett's 1950s novel* Aspects of Love *into a 1980s musical by Andrew Lloyd Webber.*

When my father told me that he was 100, I was quite convinced. In fact, he was 54 when I was born, the second of his four daughters by his second marriage to Angelica Bell. His hair was white; his eyes very blue; his nose rather thick and absolutely straight. Broad-shouldered and physically powerful, he was a man of passionate feelings. He took very little trouble to disguise his emotions. I don't think he wanted or felt any need to.

We never called him anything but Bunny. As a child, he had fallen in love with Caldecott's illustration of *Bye Baby Bunting*. When his father got a rabbit skin made into a hat for him, the village children immediately called him Bunny. The nickname lasted for the rest of his life.

Bunny had a romantic notion that we should grow up proud and fearless, like the Olivier girls, the neo-Pagan friends of his youth. We were encouraged to be wild and intrepid, with the result that we were constantly in hot water. Then he would fly into a rage. This could sometimes be quite terrifying. His eyes would bulge and his face would grow brick red and his jowls purple and he would roar at us like a wild beast. But he never laid a finger on us. Although

I was very alarmed by his fury, I sometimes took a wicked pleasure in invoking his wrath and then running away. It was quite good sport if one managed to run far enough.

He was inordinately proud when my younger sisters turned out to be good shots and capable fishermen. When they bought a bayonet from a junk shop and fought with the blade unsheathed, he did not take it away from them. Our yells and battle cries must have made his life intolerable. But he failed to see that if he wanted to be the father of four Amazons, it was more than likely that they would raid his kitchen garden, plunder his orchards and generally disturb his peace.

He had also misguidedly lumbered himself with a farm. He had hankered after a herd of deer. Instead, he bought Jersey cows because he fancied their dark eyes resembled those of the deer. Unfortunately, the cows needed milking.

Bearing this in mind, perhaps it is not surprising that he did not resume writing fiction until the mid-1950s when *Aspects of Love* was first published.

It would be untrue to say that Sir George Dillingham, the aristocratic old poet in *Aspects of Love* is a self-portrait of Bunny. He is not. But having invented Sir George, Bunny began to emulate him. It was a fairly convincing performance up to a point. Bunny bought a Rolls-Royce second-hand from the local doctor. He never acquired a vineyard, but he did spend more time in France. When Sir George's Italian mistress, Giulietta, makes her speech at his funeral, much of what she says reads very much like something Bunny would have liked to have had written about him in his own obituary: 'George Dillingham was unlike most of the men of today. He did not want to change human life, or human nature, or think it wise to attempt to do so. He rejoiced in the way we are made. He did not look forward to Heaven. He was happy with the earth.

'George combined the virtues of a man of antiquity with those of a man of 50 years ago. He had, like a man of the Renaissance, an insatiable appetite for life and a belief in its goodness. He loved and understood the flesh and believed that flesh and spirit are inseparable . . . He understood and loved food and wine. More than either, he understood women and many women were enriched by his love. But unlike the men of the Renaissance, he was also a creature of great delicacy of taste and feeling . . .'

But there the resemblance ends. I am glad of it. Whatever Bunny's failings, I am infinitely happier to be his daughter than to have been Sir George's.

Like most people, Bunny loved being lionised. He was also fascinated by other people's interpretations of his work. He delighted in the ballet of his first book, *Lady Into Fox*, which Andrée Howard choreographed in 1939 to music by Honegger. Sally Gilmour danced the part of Mrs Tebrick, who suddenly changes into a vixen. Howard also did the choreography for *The Sailor's Return* in which Gilmour danced again with great success, this time in the role of Tulip, the black princess from Dahomey who follows her sailor husband back to England with dire consequences for them both. He very much admired Tom Bell's performance of the sailor, Targett, in a television adaptation of the book.

Other people wanted to film *Lady Into Fox*. Bunny was disappointed when it proved to be too difficult to train a fox of suitable size to play bezique. Again, it was a disappointment when Jean Renoir's plan of turning *Aspects of Love* into a film fell through. I can therefore imagine how pleased he would have been if he could know that Andrew Lloyd Webber has succeeded in realising his ambition to turn *Aspects of Love* into a musical.

In 1924 Bunny had bought Hilton Hall, a beautiful house with a mellow ochre Queen Ann façade, a dove house at the back and lawns leading to orchards and a hayfield beyond, situated in the dull, flat lands bordering the Fens. Although romantic, Hilton was extremely uncomfortable in those days. Bunny had a Spartan streak that made him scorn anything approaching luxury.

It is true that he was relatively poor when we were children, but I still think it rather strange of him not to have bothered about our education. I don't just mean that he sent us to stiflingly inadequate schools, but that he never evinced any interest whatsoever in our lessons. I don't remember him once asking me what I had done all day long at school. But perhaps he was right. Perhaps it didn't really matter. For if we learned anything at all, it was because we had free rein to read anything we liked from his extensive library. As well as books, the house contained many fine paintings and pieces of sculpture. If one showed any literary talent, he was full of encouragement and urged one to write more. But he kept the paper in his study and only issued a single sheet at a time. I still find this odd.

I find it odd because Bunny was one of the most generous people I have ever known. He was generous with his time and his attention

and he was an excellent host. Bunny loved giving parties and it became a tradition to give them on midsummer night's eve. They were
glorious affairs. The garden was lit with Chinese lanterns. The wine
flowed. They were large parties and people drove a long way to come
to them. The next morning, the garden was filled with guests who
stayed to lunch off the remains of the previous evening's feast, to
gossip and to drink more wine and to refresh themselves with a dip
in the pool before leaving.

He always made me feel free to invite anyone I liked to Hilton.
But I remember driving down there late one night with a friend after
having spent the evening in a London night-club. When we got to
Hilton, we found the house locked. My Amazonian upbringing came
in handy. I was about to burgle the house when the door flew open.
There was Bunny in his pyjamas aiming a shotgun straight at us.
After the initial shock, we burst into uncontrollable peals of laughter.
Bunny put away the gun and went to hunt out some claret. He enjoyed
the absurdity of the situation. He liked my friend, too. We all three
sat up talking and drinking until breakfast.

In 1970, he left Hilton and leased a cottage on the estate of the
Château de Charry in the south-west of France. It was small and
very attractive. It stood on a terrace with a tree-covered cliff behind
to the north, looking across a valley and shaded by a big oak and
some elms. The turrets of the château were visible between the trees,
which lent it a romantic aspect, as though in the vicinity of Sleeping
Beauty's castle.

I grew very fond of Charry and paid him frequent visits there. Lucky
in his neighbours, he was lucky in most of his visitors. It is indicative
of his temperament that many of the younger generation knocked
on his door. He adored playing host and only occasionally complained that the social whirl prevented him from working.

Bunny was an early riser and would breakfast off coffee, bread and
honey. He had what he called 'bee mania' and had kept bees all his
life. He still had two hives at Charry when he died. He would keep
the remains of different types of honey in their pots for my visits
and we would have great honey-tastings, comparing with the same
seriousness as wine-tasters the merits of the honey he had brought
back from his travels in Spain, Tuscany and Greece as well as the
honey from his own bees. Most of the morning he would spend writing at the long, polished table in the living-room.

In good weather, we ate lunch out of doors at a rickety round
table in the shade of the oak tree. Bunny was a good cook and proud

of it. His cooking was lavish and there was always a great deal to
eat. There was a great deal to drink too. He bottled most of his wine
which he bought locally at Parnac. But although his cooking was
delicious, the small kitchen was exceedingly untidy. The mousetraps,
baited with a variety of enticing morsels, were ignored. Instead, the
little fieldmice who came in from the cold feasted on the debris that
was left lying around to accumulate until Pierette came in to clean
up the cottage twice a week. In spite of the squalor in the kitchen,
Bunny was surprisingly domesticated. He was as interested in the
dailyness of life as in his intellectual pursuits. He did his own mend-
ing and washed most of his laundry by hand. He was once furious
with me because I brought a tombola ticket in the local fête in order
to win a washing-machine. Luckily I lost.

Our conversations at meals prolonged them. We talked of everything under the sun, from books, ethics, gossip and love affairs to
science and scandal. Of course, we did not always agree. Bunny was
often dogmatic in his views. Once, he was having a conversation with
my uncle, Quentin Bell, about Jane Austen's novel *Emma*. Bunny
claimed that Mr Woodhouse was an utterly impossible, feeble character. He attacked Emma for being a snobbish girl and for being
nasty to her dad. Quentin objected and defended Emma. He pointed
out that she had, in fact, been very nice to Mr Woodhouse. For a
moment, Bunny was stumped. Then he burst out, 'But we've only
got Jane Austen's word for it!'

We were lingering over breakfast. We had, God knows why, been
talking about the Bible. I said I thought it required reading for anyone
who wanted to understand any writer from Chaucer all the way
through Eliot. Bunny growled. He blew up and stomped outside.
About an hour later, he did concede, rather grudgingly, that perhaps
I might have a point. Nevertheless, he wished that God, as a character,
had been left out of the Bible. It is true that God gets given short
shrift in *Two by Two*, a novel he wrote in which my younger sisters
are stowaways on Noah's Ark. But in spite of such occasional differences of opinion, our talk was lively, intimate and frequently punctuated by hoots of laughter.

After lunch, Bunny sometimes took a short nap outside on a
wooden *chaise longue*, or went for a walk. If he went for a walk,
he would usually come back with something to show for it. If in
season, it would be mushrooms. Bunny was a fanatic about fungi.
As a student at Imperial College of Science, he had had the luck
to come across an unknown species of mushroom. Later, this was

known as *Discinella minutissima Ramsbottom et Garnett*. Ramsbottom was a Doctor at the Natural History Museum. As its name implies, the fungus was tiny. Bunny told me that he was prouder of this discovery than of any contribution that he had made to literature. Ceps, girolles, lurid forms of boletus, grisettes and blewits were brought back with pride and cooked with care.

Not all his guests, however, were appreciative of these culinary experiments from the wild. 'Darling Henrietta, I though you'd like to know that X & Y accuse me of having tried to murder them with intent. They came, I may say, on their own invitation. And after having lavished them with my lurid boletus, they had the cheek to complain they had been horribly ill in the night. I scorn their tracts. For while they were wrestling with saucepans in the night in order to relieve themselves decently, I stole back into the kitchen to scoff up the remains of the mushroom feast. Had I been caught, I doubt if either would ever have spoken to me again. But I disguised all smirks at breakfast and pretended with some success that I was sorry for these wretches who know nothing of the country . . .' I have to admit my sympathy comes down on the side of Bunny's guests.

Very much a country man, Bunny was never without a cat. At Hilton, there had been tribes of Siamese. At Charry, Pertinax was Bunny's last cat. He was a noble beast, a distinguished tabby. On one of my visits to Charry, Bunny was at a loose end. I reminded him that when I was a child he had read me aloud the preface of his fantasy of himself and a cat that could speak. It had seized my imagination. I persuaded him to make a novel out of it. The result was *The Master Cat*. It is an odd book and rather bloodthirsty, a far cry from his original preface. Nevertheless, it got him out of that awful hole of not knowing what to do, and he dedicated it to me.

After dinner, which was much more elaborate than lunch, we would sit in the two very pretty French armchairs by the fire. I loved that room. The fireplace was large with a splendid iron fireback and with enough space for me to crouch low beside the stack of oak logs and warm myself up. He would offer marc, prune or rum. He had brought over the familiar paintings, books and crockery from Hilton. I would light a Gitane; Bunny a Voligeur (a cheap French cigar) and we would both puff smoke at the ceiling. We talked late into the night about intimate matters, or we might read aloud to each other. Generally, we read aloud from what we had written that day or from other people's poetry. Wyatt, Donne, Blake and Yeats were favourites. Sometimes, he would recite ballads such as *Waley Waley, Lord Randal*

or *The Twa Corbies* in a quavering and crooning lilt which would
go whistling up to the rafters. He was also rather a good mimic and
would take off his friends doing something ridiculous or, perhaps,
an old woman he had seen haggling over a single turnip in the market. Although his body was large and lumbering, he could suddenly
transform himself with gesture and voice into a mouse or a peevish
lady waiting for a bus in the rain.

And he loved to talk about the past. He talked of a world now
forgotten and made it come alive. He talked of his parents. He talked
of his many visits to the pre-revolutionary Russia of his youth. He
talked of his mistresses and, with deep love, of both of his marriages.
He continued to speak with the feelings of a much younger man.
This quality enabled us to share many mutual feelings. Pertinax sat
on his knees and scratched his trousers from time to time.

Bunny was a frightful driver. In *A Rabbit In the Air*, a diary he
kept while learning how to fly, he describes quite amusingly what
a hopeless pilot he had been. But he got angry at any disparaging
remarks made about his driving. 'Get out of my way!' he would roar
in English to any oncoming traffic. Quite often, especially if he was
talking about something totally beside the point, he appeared to aim
straight at some hazard – it might be a cliff or a tree stump.

Once, I opened the door and tried to jump out of the car before
what seemed to be my inevitable death. Bunny looked amazed when
I explained that he had scared me out of my wits. Then he was very
contrite and took me to a café and gave me a slug of marc. The
rest of the way home, he drove extremely slowly, terribly badly and
bang down the middle of the road.

When he grew older, Bunny realised, with the inevitable rage of
the old, that he needed a companion. He was fortunate. He found
the writer, Joan O'Donovan, who had been living in the Dordogne.
She took care of him very well. He knew it and appreciated it. With
great tact and with care she shopped, cleaned and amused him so
intelligently that he lost sight of the fact that he had grown old and
enjoyed her company instead.

The last time that I went to visit Bunny was Christmas 1980, shortly
before he died. As usual, we were together and alone. Joan had gone
to visit friends. It was stupid of me not to have taken in quite how
much older he had grown since I had last seen him, only a few months
previously. Through the threads of his now silver hair, his pink scalp
was visible. His hands shook so that he spilled the ash of his cigar
on to his clothes. There was a faraway look in his eyes. Sometimes,

he stopped in mid-speech and would hunt for the words he had been trying to say. He spoke of a plan to go fishing with his cousin, Dicky Garnett. He told me how much he loved me and of what hopes he had for my daughter. He spoke of all the people whom he loved. It was a kind of requiem and I was so dim that I did not realise it.

It was filthy weather and freezing cold. A wild storm shook the cottage. The electricity got cut off. I lit a huge fire. I lit candles. I cooked an improvised dinner over the logs. We crouched close to the flames, drank lots of the local wine and we both enlivened the gloom with jokes and conversation. We stayed up very late. Then he shook with silent giggles and scattered more ash over his trousers.

'What is it?' I said.

'It's Joan. She's gone and left a Christmas stocking for the CAT!'

It is impossible to explain those rare moments of delight when somebody else has gone and made a boob. But we could not help ourselves. We howled with laughter. I dragged out the stuffed stocking from the airing cupboard where Joan had left it. In the toe of the stocking was a beribboned tin of sardines. Pertinax had gone out for other fish to fry. We refilled our glasses.

Two months later, a few days short of his 90th birthday, Bunny died. My brothers, my sister, my daughter and her future husband spent three weeks in the tiny cottage trying to tell him how much he had been loved. It was not an easy time. By then, he could not speak. But he could listen. I spent many hours reading aloud his favourite poems to him.

PART THREE

Bloomsbury
Observed

Introduction

The attention that Bloomsbury attracted from its contemporaries is reflected in the last section of this collection. *Bloomsbury Observed* presents views of the Bloomsbury Group by individuals who, while not uncritical, were friendly to many of its members or sympathetic to the Group's achievements. A number of the observers represented here are well-known social or literary figures, and many were close to Bloomsbury. Most of them write as outsiders, however, watching and occasionally participating in some activity of the Group.

These eyewitness accounts were written from the twenties to the nineties; they range in their descriptions from Old Bloomsbury before the First World War to well after the Second. The selections are arranged for the most part either chronologically, according to the Bloomsbury times they describe, or by subject.

Town Talker: Bloomsbury in Sussex

In 1927 Vanessa Bell wrote to Roger Fry of 'an extraordinary notice in the Westminster Gazette the other day headed "Bloomsbury in Sussex,"' which was all about the Woolfs, the Keyneses, Vanessa and her children, Duncan Grant, and some of their friends. No one in Bloomsbury knew who wrote it (Letters, 323).

The piece was part of a society column called 'The Round of the Day' by the anonymous 'Town Talker.' The column's comments are fairly well informed, apart from the misspelling of the Keyneses' name, the description of the modest Cassis farmhouse as a villa, and the tendency (which continues to this day) to identify acquaintances or associates of Bloomsbury as members of the Group. Town Talker's is possibly the first published comment on the Bloomsbury Group.

The Bloomsbury of the Country Side

Sussex has become the Bloomsbury among English counties.

Leonard and Virginia Woolf are down there for their holidays, not too far away to be able to run up to town to keep an eye on the Hogarth Press. In their absence, however, the fort is being held by Angus Davidson, one of the three talented brothers who have all started life under the most excellent auspices. Douglas lives over and studies under Duncan Grant. Malcolm was a pupil of De Reszke's, and is a prominent singer and composer.

Besides the Woolfs – or Wolves, as they are more generally called, Vanessa Bell, who is Mrs Woolf's sister, and the Keynes have houses near Lewes.

The charming gardens that sometimes figure in Mrs Bell's exhibits or the London Group are her own, and so are the children who are playing in the foreground. Mrs Bell has three children, two boys and a girl, who have all the talent and good looks of the Stephen line.

Duncan Grant's House

Talking of houses, I hear that Duncan Grant is keeping on his villa at Cassis in the South of France for five years.

His Gordon-square home is, of course, unique. On entering, the first thing one sees is a Segonzac, and from that point on there is not a square inch of wall in the place without interest.

In addition to the frescoes and pictures there is every sort of other original decorative work to be seen: tiles round the chimneys, rugs designed and worked by Bloomsbury people, and statues of some of them by others of their number.

Versatile

Apart from Frank Dobson (who, by the way, is known to his friends as 'Dobby'), the sculptor of Bloomsbury is Stephen Tomlin, who lately has married Lytton Strachey's niece. He is a most interesting and picturesque young man who can write, draw, and play the piano as well as make statues.

Among his portraits is an excellent one of Arthur Waley, and one of Beatrice Howe, whose first novel is shortly to be published by Chatto and Windus.

Stephen Tomlin's father is Mr Justice Tomlin of the Chancery division.

Raymond Mortimer: London Letter

The year 1928 saw the publication not only of Virginia Woolf's
Orlando *and Lytton Strachey's* Elizabeth and Essex *but also of the
first accurate description of the Bloomsbury Group. Raymond Mortimer's 'London Letter' to the American* Dial *enumerates for the first
time some of the convictions of Bloomsbury. His brief description
is, of course, incomplete, yet it remains more reliable than many later
accounts that have been published. The Americans had to have
Bloomsbury explained to them from the beginning; it was some time
before anyone explained Bloomsbury as clearly and fairly to the
English.*

*Mortimer is frequently mentioned as one of the younger generation
of Bloomsbury that flourished in the twenties and thirties. He eventually succeeded Desmond MacCarthy first as literary editor of the*
New Statesman *and then as senior literary critic for the* Sunday Times.
*He once commented on what Bloomsbury meant to him in a review
of Carrington's letters and diaries; after mentioning how Michael Holroyd had failed to bring out the characteristic gaiety of the Group
in his biography of Strachey, Mortimer observed 'They were the best
company I ever had the luck to find' ('Friends and Relations').*

*Raymond Mortimer supplied the following note for the reprinting
of his London Letter in the first edition of* The Bloomsbury Group:
A Collection of Memoirs, Commentary, and Criticism: *'In the years
1922 to 1929 I contributed to the* Dial *a series of London Letters.
This one includes a joke that may now need explanation. I quote
from an imaginary book published thirty-two years after the date on
which I was writing.' Curiously enough, Mortimer had a later opportunity to write at least one volume in his fictional series. In 1949
Leonard Woolf wrote to him saying his American publishers wanted
a book on Bloomsbury that would clarify the artistic and intellectual
significance of Bloomsbury through a description of the Group's personalities; Woolf told them there was only one person who could do
the book, and that was Raymond Mortimer. Mortimer never wrote
the book, but the offer is an interesting indication of Woolf's conviction, despite what he sometimes says elsewhere, that Bloomsbury
did indeed exist.*

February 1928

A small group of friends who were undergraduates at Cambridge at the beginning of the century came to have an influence on their time which can still hardly be gauged. Among these were the sons of Sir Leslie Stephen, the eminent Victorian biographer and agnostic. The Misses Vanessa and Virginia Stephen, their sisters, lived in London; and their house became the nucleus of the group, when the two brothers and their friends left Cambridge.

I am quoting from the seventh volume of Sir Raymond Mortimer's trustworthy if academic *Studies in Twentieth-Century Culture* (Hogarth Press 1960).

The young ladies, who were as remarkable for their beauty as for their intellect, married two of their brothers' friends, Clive Bell and Leonard Woolf, who were to become celebrated, the one as an apostle of contemporary art, a vigorous pamphleteer, a poet, a historian of civilization, and a psychological biographer; the other as an editor, a publisher, and a politician. An important figure in this group was Edward Morgan Forster, novelist, critic, and historian. Perhaps the most influential was Giles Lytton Strachey, who later revolutionized the art of history: he is said to have shown from the first the almost fanatical intransigence in conduct and opinion which marks the leaders of important movements. But the group was always an oligarchy – fierce mutual criticism was the breath of its existence. Another dominating figure was John Maynard Keynes, the economist and politician, who by his marriage years later with Mme Lopokova, the first dancer of her day, brought leadership in yet another of the arts into this astonishing circle. Duncan Grant, though not a member of the University, was an early intimate of the group, and so was Roger Fry, though of an older generation of Cambridge men. It thus appears that from one small band of friends have come the subtlest novelists, the most famous economist, the most influential painters, the most distinguished historian, and the liveliest critics of the post-war period in England.

I have preferred to quote from the veteran critic, because my relations with the persons concerned are too close for me to be able to speak of them easily without impertinence. But the name of Bloomsbury is becoming familiar in Berlin, Paris, and, I presume, New York as well as in London, and I think the time has come when a study of the genesis of the group and the character of those who compose it should be made public. I am certainly not the person to do this; but since I am writing a letter I may perhaps take a letter-writer's privileges and put down a few casual comments on what I see around me.

It is impossible to say where Bloomsbury begins, and where it ends. Are the painters, scholars, and journalists of a younger generation to be included? Arthur Waley? Francis Birrell? George Rylands? Douglas Davidson? Are old and intimate friends who have never become entirely imbued with the Bloomsbury spirit? And in fact what exactly is this spirit? I do not dare a definition. But I would place first a belief in Reason, and a conviction that the pursuit of Truth and a contemplation of Beauty are the most important of human activities. Obviously many of Bloomsbury's fiercest enemies might subscribe to this creed. The distinction of the leaders of the group is that they have acted upon it to an extraordinary extent. No subject of conversation has been taboo, no tradition accepted without examination, and no conclusion evaded. In a hypocritical society, they have been indecent; in a conservative society, curious; in a gentlemanly society, ruthless; and in a fighting society, pacifist. They have been passionate in their devotion to what they thought good, brutal in their rejection of what they thought second rate; resolute in their refusal to compromise. 'Narrow in their tastes, loose in their view of morals, irreverent, unpatriotic, remote, and superior,' their enemies say. And, I think, truly. For will not relentless reasoning and delicate discrimination make a man all these things?

Such vivid personalities as the leaders of the group could never of course commit themselves to any corporate doctrine of taste. But they have tended to exalt the classical in all the arts: Racine, Milton, Poussin, Cézanne, Mozart, and Jane Austen have been their more cherished artists. Already the signs of a romantic revival are everywhere perceptible. The next generation is likely to react vigorously against the intellectualism of Bloomsbury. The younger French care as little for Voltaire as they do for Anatole France. Keyserling and Maurras, Chesterton and Lawrence, are united in their hatred of intellectualism. Indeed M. Julien Benda seems almost the only important figure on the Continent whose views are akin to Bloomsbury's. But here anti-intellectualism has not yet found a champion adequately armed.

Obviously there is a romantic poet in Mrs Woolf, a mystic in Mr E.M. Forster, whereas Mr Strachey, for all his appreciation of Blake and Beddoes, remains in his outlook almost a contemporary of Voltaire. But compare these three writers with any outside the group, great Edwardians like Wells and Bennett, for instance, and a certain consonance in the Bloomsbury artists becomes, I think, apparent. For one thing they remain singularly unspotted by the world; too disillusioned to expect that their scale of values can ever command general assent. (Perhaps the fact that they almost all possessed small in-

dependent incomes gave them an initial advantage over many of their
rivals.) The east wind of Cambridge philosophy braces their nerves.
Pragmatism, Bergsonism, Oxford idealism, wither beneath it. And
the historian of Bloomsbury will have to discuss the enormous influence on the group of George Moore, the author not of *The Brook
Kerith* but of *Principia Ethica*.

Why Bloomsbury? someone who does not know London may ask.
It was Mrs Desmond MacCarthy, the author of *A Nineteenth Century
Childhood* (she and her husband have almost been intimate with the
group) who, I believe, first gave it this name from the quarter of
London where most of its members lived. It is a quarter honeycombed
with spacious squares, where houses built for the gentry in the eighteenth century declined later into boarding-houses for impoverished
foreigners and students at the University of London. The houses are
for the most part still too big to be inhabited by single families, but
the quarter is replacing Chelsea as the home of painters and writers.
On summer evenings there is tennis on the lawns, and the Vicar's
daughters can be seen playing with the bigwigs, ignorant of the dangerous company they keep. Around are figures reading and talking,
and as night falls, the mourning veils in which London soot has
dressed the Georgian façades become unnoticeable, and in these gardens you may fancy yourself in the precincts of a college. The passing
of a quarter of a century is forgotten, the quick exchanges and curious
conjectures, the vehement arguments, remake the past; and the commercial traveller arriving late at St Pancras' from the north, catches
a glimpse as he passes of an unfamiliar and unhurrying London,
of

> groups under the dreaming garden-trees,
> And the full moon, and the white evening star.

Ottoline Morrell: Artists Revels

*As the most celebrated and hospitable hostess and patron of the arts
of her time, Lady Ottoline Morrell was intimately involved with at
least two members of Bloomsbury, Roger Fry and Lytton Strachey,
and generously receptive to them all, expecially during the First World
War when Garsington, her and her husband Philip Morrell's Oxfordshire manor, became a refuge for conscientious objectors who were supposed to be doing agricultural work. She was aristocratic, eccentric,*

sentimental, extravagant – a figure of fun in Bloomsbury and else-
where. Yet there was a genuine fondness and respect for her too, as
is shown in the Times *obituary of her that Virginia Woolf wrote.*

For her part, Ottoline Morrell had reservations about Bloomsbury's
behaviour and pretensions. Her observations of pre-war Bloomsbury
given here are taken from memoirs based on diaries that she kept
at the time; the memoirs were written sometime between the mid-
twenties and her death in 1938.

I was now beginning to see more of Virginia Stephen and her friends
and to go to her Thursday evenings in Fitzroy Square, where long-
legged young men would sit in long basket-chairs smoking pipes and
talking almost inaudibly in breathless voices of subjects that seemed
to me thrilling and exciting. When the pool that lay between us grew
calm and overcast, Virginia's bell-like voice would be heard, swinging,
swinging and resonant, awaking and scattering dull thought, and
giving warning that a light would be thrown into the darkness, the
rays of which would light up her own lovely face and our stagnant
prosy minds. She would lead us swiftly along into the streets or the
lives of any she may meet, and the world of poetry, showing her
light into dull corners, and making them appear full of fantasy and
beauty. This strange, lovely, furtive creature never has seemed to me
to be made of common flesh and blood. She was rather like some
Diana of the realm of the mind who, though she had forsaken forest
and the chase of deer, now treads the ways of man still carrying hidden
under her veil her crescent of light. She comes and goes, she folds
her cloak around her and vanishes, having shot into her victim's heart
a quiverful of teasing arrows.

She walks in London streets, she travels in an omnibus, and with
her penetrating light searches the hearts of those she meets. She sees
their thoughts and feels the tenderest and frailest vibrations of emotions traversing their beings. She hears the distant song of beauty
or the sigh of despair.

To this visitant from another sphere our lives appear more strange,
more vivid and fantastically exciting than they do to oneself.

As years have gone by, and her sojourning here has inured her
to our ordinary life, she seems now to sit with almost familiar ease
in my room, and I no longer feel the fear that this enchanting and
bewildering goddess will sail away before I have recovered from her
entry and before I had caught a glimpse of her crescent light. I feel
I have made her see into my heart.

Since the days of Fitzroy Square, when she led her followers on
to the *Dreadnought* dressed up as an Eastern princess, and out to
Covent Garden at dawn to buy armfuls of flowers, she has known
the love of many, she has married, she has written, and she is now
recognized and admired. But I like to remember her in the old days
with her little circle of companions: her brother Adrian, her sister
Vanessa, Vanessa's husband, Clive Bell, that happy, flattering, good-
tempered Autolycus holding out gay leaves for us to admire. Roger
Fry, who had not yet set sail on the sea of modern French art; Lytton
Strachey and Duncan Grant – what a delightful company they seemed!

Of Lytton Strachey I used to feel most shy, for he said so little
and he seemed to live far away in an atmosphere of rarefied thought.
His voice so small and faint, but with definite accentuations and
stresses of tone, giving a sense of certainty and distinction, appeared
to come from very far away, for his delicate body was raised on legs
so immensely long that they seemed endless, and his fingers equally
long, like antennae. It was not till I knew him better that I found
how agile those long legs could be, and what passion and feeling
lay in that delicate body, and how rapidly those long and beautiful
antennae could find passages in Racine or Dryden, and the strength
and vigour of his voice when he read these passages aloud to me.
But at this time he seemed so melancholy and aloof that I hardly
dared approach him, though he would come to see me now and then.
Duncan Grant, too, was shy and vague and elusive, but always
bewitching.

It was in this year that the first Russian dancers appeared in London, not the Diaghilev Ballet, which did not arrive here until a year
or so later, but some forerunners who seemed to our unspoilt sight
as winged fairies. How lovely, how gay, how enchanting they were,
as if Conder's pictures had come to life. I was so enthusiastic about
them that night after night I took friends to see them: John and Dorelia, and Desmond MacCarthy and Roger Fry, Virginia and Duncan
Grant, were all led there. How anxiously I watched their faces to
see if they were as thrilled as I was. I often lost whole precious moments of this all too short joy by scanning the faces of those I had
taken to see the effects on them. Their appreciation never really satisfied me.

Then one day the Clive Bells asked us to go with them to Artists
Revels at the Botanical Gardens. What a picture of gaiety the two
words evoked, 'Artists Revels'. Philip and I dressed up, he in his black

velvet court suit, I in a very full black taffeta dress, with black lace mantilla.

It was my first and only experience of a fancy dress ball and I visualized a Mozartian scene of lovely gaily-dressed youths and maidens flitting in and out of dark trees lit up by coloured lights – a ballet in real life. But even at the dinner in Gordon Square with the Bells a certain disillusionment began. I felt that our companions had not chosen very appropriate costumes. Vanessa's Madonna-like beauty surely could have found a happier alias than that of a Pierrot, and Virginia was hardly suited to pose as Cleopatra, whose qualities, as I had imagined them, were just those that Virginia did not possess. Adrian, her brother, too, was not very convincing as a young Cardinal, but I excused these little lapses as high-handed carelessness on the part of intellectuals.

On arriving at the Botanical Gardens, however, the scene that I had anticipated was nowhere to be found. I searched indoors and out. I recoiled from the jumble-tumble of awkward young men waving long, raw, red arms and legs, and young women equally crude and ungainly, pretentiously and unsuitably decked out in badly adjusted garments of all ages and periods. What a different scene to the one I had expected of ordered and exquisite beauty! Has the past indeed so literally vanished that no trace of its minor arts and finery remains in our instincts? Are our ancestors so completely buried under their monuments that no spark of their delicate taste and courtly grace remains in our blood? We still live in their homes and recite their poems, but to wear their clothes clearly is a vanished art. The buoyant, athletic bodies of these young people have grown sadly unsuited to the buckram of the past. Their minds have developed their bodies into a different mould.

From behind the dark trees I caught the sound of mocking laughter. Was it from these lords and ladies whose earthly garments were being so travestied by the ungainly young revellers? I seemed to hear them say, 'You think we looked like that, do you? Silly children, how blind you are not to see and understand us better than that. Go and put on your cricket flannels and tennis skirts, your football shorts and motor goggles, and play your hoydenish games which you understand. Leave ruffs and farthingales, embroidered stomachers and waistcoats, powdered wigs and minuets to us.'

I put my arm through Philip's and drew my black lace veil close round me hoping that no one would search my face that night to read the melancholy disappointment that I felt at the sight of English artists revelling!

Perhaps, after all, I belonged to the time of hoops and loops and billowing skirts – a rare survival – one of those who were laughing from behind the trees.

Quentin Bell: The Omega Workshops

Roger Fry founded the Omega Workshops in 1913 with the help of an inheritance from his chocolate-making uncle. The name was to suggest the last word in art. Following on the two post-impressionist exhibitions, the Workshop was to subsidize young artists through their work in decorative and applied arts. All work was to be anonymous, and some of the young artists, particularly Wyndham Lewis, publicly objected to what he mistook to be Fry's practices. Bloomsbury was involved in the Omega directly through Duncan Grant and Vanessa Bell, while others patronized the Workshops. The war years were hard on the Omega, however, and Fry eventually closed it in 1919.

Quentin Bell's foreword to Judith Collin's study of the Omega Work-shops sketches some of the aesthetic history and theory behind them.

I was sick in the Omega. It must have happened sometime in January 1919. A few months later the business went into voluntary liquidation. There is no reason to connect these two *contretemps* and indeed the former is of so little interest that, even if she had been aware of it, Dr Collins would hardly have mentioned the matter – and if I allude to it now it is only because it is, as far as I can tell, the only thing about the Omega that she does not know.

Until I read this book I had supposed that I knew as much as anyone of the Omega's history, and a good deal more than most; when it has been published and read by a large public, as it assuredly will be, I shall be deprived of both these distinctions. In writing a foreword, therefore, I can no longer rely upon my ability to supply information. Looking for something to say I find myself turning from the minutiae of history (and as will have been observed, I have been compelled to gather crumbs so minute as hardly to satisfy the appetite of a wren) and looking rather to those broad commonplaces of art history which are so generally known as to be taken for granted, and which have only that novelty which derives from a general dis-inclination to dwell upon the obvious.

'There are two kinds of painting,' said Duncan Grant, 'the Northern and the Southern.' I believe that he committed this rash statement
to paper, he having been asked to write a preface for someone's exhibition, and the generalisation, as he admitted with a smile, got
him into 'a great deal of trouble'. It was indeed a bold thing to say,
but there is a rough and ready truth about it and it encourages me
to go further and to say that, for Duncan and his friends, the great
events of the year 1910 and above all the revelation to the British
public of the importance of Cézanne – events which resulted, one
might almost say which culminated, in the creation of the Omega
Workshops – signalled a new interest in this country in what he would
have called 'Southern' art. That is not quite how we see it today,
but at that time and for those people – indeed for the great mass
of the British public – the Northern element in the revolutionary
movements of the new century was either unknown or felt to be merely
ancillary to the great convulsions of French Art. They knew nothing
of Teutonic expressionism and saw all innovations as coming from
Paris and relating to a tradition which went back through Cézanne
and Poussin, the High Renaissance, Piero della Francesca, Masaccio
and Giotto to the walls of Byzantium.

It is indeed the walls that should engage our attention; the mos-
aicists of Ravenna, and their Italian heirs, express themselves naturally upon walls. The character of their work is largely determined
by the needs of the church or the palace where they find employment,
and when, in later centuries, the artist yields to the demands of a
new market which in its turn requires the frame and the easel, much
of the old architectonic discipline endures. Poussin, working on quite
small pictures, still retains those qualities of monumental order
which we find in the *Stanze*; and those who have seen Cézanne air-
borne like a bewildered astronaut in the helical corridors of the Gug-
genheim Museum will realise to what extent he assumed the existence
of and still needs a cubic and rectilinear environment with vertical
walls and horizontal floors – things which, in that museum, are strikingly absent. What I call 'Southern' art is, then, closely tied to architecture, whereas 'Northern' art, which grew up amidst coloured
windows and darkened interiors, might find a congenial home within
the pages of a book – that is to say within a framework which could
easily be transported from place to place and which invited the spectator not to look around him, as he would in a painted room, but
to bury his head in it – in a volume with its own space and, it may
be, its own world. Consider for an instant two masterpieces of these

opposing genres: Leonardo's representation of the Last Supper is in effect a remodelling, a drastic alteration of the architecture of the refectory of Sta Maria delle Grazie; if it is to have its full effect upon us it must be seen *in situ*. Compare with that the strange and moving description of what is after all a fairly banal incident of Dutch life which we call the *Night Watch*. It is a scene observed from without; we are spies peering through a glass wall. It has the private quality of a great novel.

Now this private and portable device – a painter's vision of the world and/or his imagination, separated from his environment by a band of gold (the one colour that would never find its way into the picture itself) – was the chosen vehicle of the realists and the Impressionists. They were not decorators, and hardly looked beyond the picture frame. No doubt there were at that time great decorative projects, but they did not engage the attention of the kind of painters who interested the *avant garde* at the beginning of the twentieth century. But whereas the *avant garde* in Continental Europe seemed hardly aware of the applied arts, in England it was different. The first generation of Pre-Raphaelites was already interested in the idea of adventuring into the applied arts; the second generation went boldly beyond the picture frame and tried its hand at fabrics, furniture, books and stained glass. At the same time, and again largely through British initiatives, the century found a style of its own which was not historicist and which, appropriately enough, was called *art nouveau*.

Roger Fry, who didn't care for *art nouveau* or for the Pre-Raphaelites of the Brotherhood, did always have a qualified but genuine affection for the work of Burne-Jones. His sentiment might be tiresome but his sense of design was impressive and he was, in the sense used here, very much a Southern artist looking always to Italy for inspiration. In the same way Fry was never quite happy with Impressionism; as he said when he first saw Impressionist pictures: 'I don't like having facts thrown in my face.'

I once asked Gropius whether he had had Ruskin in mind when he started the Bauhaus. He replied, with positively Irish exactitude, that 'he had him very much not in mind'. I think that the relationship between Fry and the Morris workshops was rather of that kind. Morris was trying to say something important about art and everyday life. Fry's 'message', if you can call it that, was not dissimilar, but he had no use for the language which Morris had used. He found what he needed in the pictorial idiom of Cézanne and, even more, in that

of the Fauves. The use of bold and brutal colour, the acceptance
of pictorial conventions so rude and rapid that they made questions
of verisimilitude almost irrelevant, gave the decorator a vocabulary
which could be taken without adaptation from the easel picture to
furniture, pottery, textiles, lampshades and hats. The Impressionists
(to apply the words of another revolutionary) had merely 'explained
the world, the point was to change it'.

I think that I am right in finding the genesis of this remarkable
attempt to transform the man-made world by means of unrestrained
colour and bold design in what I have called Southern art. It is a
fact that Fry and his friends did at about this time go to Ravenna
and to Constantinople, and that some of them, at all events, were
deeply influenced by the mural paintings of St. Savin. But it is also
true that a very different kind of art - the art of primitive peoples
and in particular of the Africans - was at the same time discovered
and admired. And in the creation of the Omega Workshops also there
were motives of a very different kind at work. Fry wanted to establish
a place where a young artist might earn ten shillings a week, and
for this purpose the painting of chairs was more to the point than
the painting of pictures - and there may have been other forces at
work. It is an unfortunate fact, but one that has to be faced, that
artists do not always feel and behave exactly as art historians think
they should feel and behave. The appropriate and inevitable processes
of history do not always appear to them as compelling as we may
suppose. Indeed we may on occasion be moved by the most trifling
and seemingly incongruous circumstances. Perhaps - it is just possible
- some importance should be attached to the fact that, in January
1919, a child was sick in the Omega Workshops.

Arthur Waley: Translating in Bloomsbury

*In the course of explaining how he came to study Chinese, the great
oriental scholar and translator Arthur Waley described Roger Fry's
interest in having Waley's first book,* One Hundred and Seventy Chinese Poems, *printed at the Omega Workshops. (Fry's Omega printing
was an important precursor for the Woolf's Hogarth Press.) Waley
was closely associated with Bloomsbury for many years - indeed Forster included him in the Group (see p. 81). The response to his
celebrated translations was, like most things in Bloomsbury,
varied.*

I began to make rough translations of poems that I thought would go well in English, not at all with a view to publication, but because I wanted my friends to share in the pleasure that I was getting from reading Chinese poetry. Among people who were interested by these translations were Roger Fry, Lowes Dickinson and Logan Pearsall-Smith, the author of *Trivia*. Roger Fry was at that time interested in printing. He thought verse ought to be printed in lines that undulated in a way that reinforced the rhythms, and he asked if I objected to his printing some of my translations in this way, as an experiment. The idea of their being printed at all of course thrilled me, and spell-bound by Roger's enthusiasm (as everyone was) I had not the courage to say (what was in fact the case) that I could see no point at all in the 'undulations'. A meeting of the Omega workshops was called at which about a dozen people were present. Roger Fry asked each of them in turn how many copies of translations such as mine (irrespective of 'undulation') it would be possible to sell. The highest estimate was twenty. Saxon Turner, of the Treasury, answered inaudibly. He was asked to repeat what he had said and removing his pipe from his mouth, he answered with great firmness and clarity, 'None'. Roger had been collecting estimates (with or without undulation). It was clear that in order to cover costs he must sell at least two hundred copies, so as the result of the meeting he gave up the idea of printing my translations. But I, for the first time in my life, began in consequence of this meeting to have some vague idea about the cost of getting a small work printed. For a few pounds I had about forty short poems printed in a normal way by an ordinary printer, bound the sheets in some spare wall-paper and sent the resulting booklet to a number of friends, as a sort of Christmas card. It had a mixed reception. Professor Bateson, for example, wrote on a postcard: 'I am afraid I can't get much from your translations. I don't need a Chinese poet to tell me that rivers don't turn back in their courses.' He was evidently referring to the couplet:

The hundred rivers eastward travel to the ocean;
Never shall they turn back again to the West.

He was a cultivated and benevolent man and must, I think, to write such a postcard, have been very much irritated by the poems.

I had at that time a corporate admiration for the whole Strachey family, and longed for them to be interested in what I did. I was pained, then, when Lytton Strachey wrote ribald parodies of the

poems, not intended of course for my eye; but Carrington (the pain-
tress Dora Carrington who adored Lytton and looked after him for
so long) took care that I should see them. I thought them very stupid,
and Lytton fell off his pedestal. . . .

Osbert Sitwell: Armistice in Bloomsbury

*The three Sitwells are sometimes compared or even confused with
Bloomsbury. Yet it appears from their autobiographies that Osbert
and Edith looked askance at the Group, qua Group, friends though
they were with individual Bloomsberries.*

*Bloomsbury figures briefly in Osbert Sitwell's extended autobiog-
raphy. In the following excerpt, as in many accounts of Bloomsbury,
Sitwell's early recollections of the Group in 1918 are merged with
his later, rather more acidulous attitudes towards them.*

We had found a taxicab – by no means an easy feat at the end of
the 1914-18 War – but we were obliged to crawl, so thick was the
crowd, and so numerous were the revellers who clambered round,
and rode on, the roof. Eventually we reached the Adelphi. The spacious Adam room, covered with decoration as fine as a cobweb, was
hung inappropriately with a few large pictures by the Paris School
– by Matisse, for example – and by several of the Bloomsbury Group,
its satellite and English Correspondent. There were a number of
paintings, for instance, by Mark Gertler – at that moment an artist
much patronized by the *cognoscenti*. . . . Here, in these rooms, was
gathered the élite of the intellectual and artistic world, the dark flower
of Bloomsbury. And since this name has occurred twice already in
this paragraph – as it surely must if one is to attempt to describe
the achievements or environment of the early post-war generation
– a word or two is necessary to indicate what it stood for before
its so rapid decline.

The great figures were Roger Fry, Virginia Woolf, Clive Bell, Vanessa Bell, Lytton Strachey and Duncan Grant. After them followed
a sub-rout of high-mathematicians and low-psychologists, a tangle
of lesser painters and writers. The outlook, natural in the grand ex-
emplars, and acquired by their followers, was one of great tolerance:
surprise was never shown at any human idiosyncrasy, though an
amused wonder might be expressed at the ordinary activities of mankind. The chief, most usual phrases one heard were 'ex-quisitely civ-

ilized', and 'How *simply too* extraordinary!', the first applying to
some unusual human concatenation, the second to some quite common incident of burgess life, such as a man going to a railway station
to meet his wife returning after a long absence from home. But, no
less than by the sentiments themselves, the true citizens of Bloomsbury could be recognized by the voice in which they were expressed.
The tones would convey with supreme efficacy the requisite degree
of paradoxical interest, surprise, incredulity: in actual sound, analyzed, they were unemphatic, save when emphasis was not to be expected; then there would be a sudden sticky stress, high where you
would have presumed low, and the whole spoken sentence would
run, as it were, at different speeds and on different gears, and contain
a deal of expert but apparently meaningless syncopation. Many sets
of people in the past have developed their own manner of talking,
almost their own language. . . . The Bloomsbury voice, too – that
characteristic regional way of speaking, as rare and ritualistic outside
the bounds of West Central London as the state voice of the Emperor
of China beyond his pleasances and palaces – originated, I believe,
more in a family than in a flock. Experts maintain that it originated
as an apanage of the Strachey family – of Lytton Strachey, that is
to say, and of his brothers and sisters, in whom it was natural and
delightful – and that from them it spread and took captive many,
acclimatizing itself first in the *haute vie intellectuelle* of King's College, Cambridge: thence it had marched on London, prospering particularly in Gordon and Mecklenburgh Squares and in the neighbouring sooty piazzas, and possessing affiliations, too, in certain
country districts – Firle in Sussex, for example, and Garsington in
Oxfordshire. The adoption by an individual of the correct tones was
equivalent, I apprehend, to an outward sign of conversion, a public
declaration of faith, like giving the Hitler salute or wearing a green
turban. Once, indeed, I was privileged to be present when one of
the Lesser – but now Greater – Bloomsburys took the plunge. I had
known him well before he joined up, and then, gently-spoken reader,
he talked as you or I do – and so judge of my surprise when, in
the middle of a dinner-party, I heard his tongue suddenly slide off
sense, making for a few moments meaningless but emphatic sounds
that somehow resembled words, and then, as quickly, creak into the
Bloomsbury groove like a tram proudly regaining its rails! . . . I wondered what initiation rites and tribal ceremonies had taken place in
the local Berlitz school.

Tonight, at Monty Shearman's, the Bloomsbury Junta was in full session. In later years, towards the moment of its disintegration, Bloomsbury, under the genial viceroyalty of my friend Clive Bell, took a trend, hitherto unexpected, towards pleasure and fashionable life: but in these days it was still austere, with a degree of Quaker earnestness latent in it. (But then Roger Fry, its leading and most engaging aesthetic apostle, came of Quaker stock.) The women were of a type different from that to be seen elsewhere. Something of the Victorian past clung to them still, though they were so much more advanced than their sisters, both in views and intelligence. Virginia Woolf, for instance, notably beautiful with a beauty of bone and form and line that belonged to the stars rather than the sun, manifested in her appearance, in spite of the modernity that was also clearly hers, a Victorian distinction. She made little effort to bring out the quality of her looks, but she could not destroy it. It has often occurred to me, when I have seen Roman patrician busts of the fourth century, how greatly she resembled them, with her high forehead, fine, aquiline nose and deep-set, sculptural eye-sockets. Her beauty was certainly impersonal, but it was in no way cold, and her talk was full of ineffable fun and lightness of play and warmth. I have never known anyone with a more sensitive perception of the smallest shadows cast in the air round her: nor could I ever understand why people were – but certainly they *were* – frightened of her; because, though there was, and I am sure she would have admitted it, a human amount of malice in her composition (and how greatly the dull-minded would have complained if there had not been!), there was very much more, and most unusual, gentleness. To the young, to poets and painters, but not to dons, she was invariably kind; kind, moreover, to the extent that, in spite of the burden of her own work and correspondence, she would take trouble for them. She would, I am aware – for I have been present – lay traps for the boastful and the blunted, and greatly she enjoyed the snaring of them (I once had great difficulty in rescuing alive a popular American novelist, whose name was at that time written as a sky-sign round the roofs of Cambridge Circus): but for the most part they deserved their fate. She possessed, too, a beautiful, clear, gentle speaking voice. Though sometimes, when many people were present, she could be seen swaying a little, preparing herself with nervous effort to say the words, to break through the reserve that lay over her, yet I have heard her dare to make a speech. It was at a dinner for the London Group of painters about a year later than the party. Roger Fry, who was president or chairman, had asked me to be present and to speak. When I arrived, I found to my great

pleasure that I was sitting next to Virginia. But she was pitiably nervous that night because of the prospect of having to make a speech;
her distress was obvious. I felt miserable on her behalf and tried,
indeed, to comfort her: for after having just fought an election, oratory
held temporarily few terrors for me. I concluded – and it may have
been the case – that she was unused to the strain of these occasions,
and had only consented to speak because Roger was one of her oldest
friends. If so, what happened was the more astonishing. I spoke first,
and adequately, I hope, in a matter-of-fact sort of way. The audience
laughed at the jokes I made. Then I sat down, and the moment I
had dreaded for Virginia arrived. She stood up. The next quarter
of an hour was a superb display of art and, more remarkable, of
feeling, reaching heights of fantasy and beauty in the description of
the Marriage of Music to Poetry in the time of the Lutanists, and
how, in the coming age, Painting must be similarly united to the
other arts. It was a speech beautifully prepared, yet seemingly spontaneous, excellently delivered, and as natural in its flow of poetic
eloquence as is a peacock spreading its tail and drumming. Somehow
I had not foreseen this *bravura*; it was a performance that none present
will ever forget, and, as she sat down, I almost regretted the sympathy
I had wasted on her.

There were few women of a distinction equal to Virginia's in the
room tonight: but all, pretty or *fade* or plain, wore their own clothes,
either more fashionable than elsewhere, without fashion, or smacking
of Roger's Omega workshop, wholesome and home-made. Some of
the men were in uniform, but a proportion – equally courageous
in their way – had been conscientious objectors and so were able
to appear in ordinary clothes – if *ordinary* is not, perhaps, a misnomer
for so much shagginess (the suits, many of them, looked as if they
had been woven from the manes of Shetland ponies and the fringes
of Highland cattle in conjunction), and for such flaming ties as one
saw. It was a singular dispensation – though welcome to me, because
I admired their moral bravery, sympathized with the standard they
upheld with a singular toughness, and liked them personally – that
in the next few years several of the chief artistic and literary lions
of the fashionable world, itself in every country then invariably chau-
vinistic, had been conscientious objectors: but the war, thank heaven,
was over, and a moratorium on patriotism set in for about fifteen
years. Those present tonight included several, I recall, who had
worked at farming in the Arcadian colony presided over by Lady
Ottoline Morrell. At Garsington during the war some of the best

brains of the country were obliged to apply themselves to digging
and dunging, to the potato patch or the pig-sty. . . .

Some of the donnish farm-labourers . . . had gathered here tonight.
All equally, soldiers, Bloomsbury beauties, and conscientious objectors – all except Diaghilev – danced. I remember the tall, flagging
figure of my friend Lytton Strachey, with his rather narrow, angular
beard, long, inquisitive nose, and air of someone pleasantly awaking
from a trance, jigging about with an amiable debility. He was, I think,
unused to dancing. Certainly he was both one of the most typical
and one of the rarest persons in this assembly. His individual combination of kindness, selfishness, cleverness, shyness and sociability
made him peculiarly unlike anyone else. As I watched him, I remember comparing him in my mind to a benevolent but rather irritable pelican. A man now of about forty, he had achieved no renown
(though he had possessed a high reputation for wit, learning and
personality among his own friends from Cambridge), nor had sought
any until the publication of *Eminent Victorians* raised him to the
zenith of fame and popularity with a generation no longer tolerant
of either the pretensions or the achievements of the Victorian great.
Some chapters of this book I had, in the autumn of 1917, been given
the pleasure of hearing him read aloud – rather faintly, for he was
recovering from an attack of shingles, and sat in an armchair in front
of a large fire, with a Shetland shawl draped round his shoulders.
I remember that our hostess, a cousin of Lytton's, pressed her lively
young daughter of seven to allow him to see her imitation of him.
While the precocious mimic showed off, Lytton watched the child
with a look of the utmost distaste, and when asked by the mother
what he thought of the performance – one of real virtuosity – remarked in a high, clear, decisive voice, 'I expect it's amusing, but
it isn't at all *like!*' . . .

Edith Sitwell: Bloomsbury Taken Care Of

*The ambivalence of Edith Sitwell's comments on Bloomsbury is char-
acteristic of her own literary personality as well as being typical of
the observations of others who watched the growing fame of Bloomsbury as a literary and social group.*

*The excerpts here are taken from her posthumous autobiography
entitled* Taken Care Of.

Intellectual society was, at that time, divided into several camps, and
to none of these did I, by nature, belong. On the one side was the
bottle-wielding school of thought to which I could not, owing to
my sex, upbringing, tastes, and lack of muscle, belong. On another
side was the society of Bloomsbury, the home of an echoing silence.
This section of society was described to me by Gertrude Stein as 'the
Young Men's Christian Association – with Christ left out, of course'.

Some of the more silent intellectuals, crouching under the
umbrella-like deceptive weight of their foreheads, lived their toadstool
lives sheltered by these. The appearance of others aroused the conjecture that they were trying to be foetuses. But to what rebirth and
subsequent life they looked forward, I do not know. One intellectual
lighthouse, as an American admirer called him, was immensely tall,
and if he had not been so inert one would have supposed him to
have been involved in a death-struggle with a lamp-post. They seemed
to be inextricably intertwined. From the top of this edifice from time
to time a few dim sparks emerged, but they did not cast much light
on anything.

In this world of superior intellect there were several models. There
was, for instance, the amphibian model – with gaping mouth, glassy
eyes staring at nothing in particular, and with a general air of slip-
periness and, at the same time, scaliness.

There was, too, the village idiot model, drooling, and with a boastful exhibition of mental deficiency – also the deliberately awkward
and blundering good sportsman and cricketer-model.

The ladies of this world were not, to my mind, attractive. For the
most part they had faces like fawn-coloured felt hats that had been
inadvertently sat upon. They sepnt their time in chronicling the doings of the unexciting female chatterboxes of previous centuries –
passed over by history (that terrible mill in which sawdust rejoins
sawdust), and remarkable only because of their inexhaustible enthusiasm for dossing down in every ditch with every little frog disguised
as a bull. . . .

I knew the painter and distinguished art critic, Roger Fry, well, for
I sat to him for several portraits. For one of these I wore a green
evening dress, the colour of the leaves of lillies, and my appearance
in this, in the full glare of the midsummer light of midday, in Fitzroy
Square, together with the appearance of Mr Fry, his bushy, long grey
hair floating from under an enormous black sombrero, caused great

joy to the children of the district as we crossed from Mr Fry's studio to his house for luncheon.

Imagining us to be strayed revellers, they enquired at moments (perhaps not unnaturally) if our mothers knew we were out. At other moments they referred to the fifth of November, when, according to them, our appearance would have been better timed.

Mr Fry was a most delightful companion, learned and courteous: he had a great gift for attracting and retaining friendship. Warm-hearted, generous-minded and kindly, he was always espousing some lost cause, championing some unfortunate person, rushing at some windmill with a lance. In other respects he was dreamy and vague, incapable of noticing any but a spiritual discomfort. I remember an incident when I was lunching at his house after a sitting. Mr Fry's slippers could not be found anywhere, and a game of hunt-the-slipper ensued. In the midst of the fun, a loud crash was heard, and a hoarse voice said 'Coal Sir!' 'Put it, my good man,' said Mr Fry, whirling round and round like a kitten chasing its tail, losing his spectacles, and speaking in a voice weak from fatigue – 'Oh, well, put it on the bed.'

At this point I found the slippers in the milk-jug, and the fun stopped. . . .

Virginia Woolf had a moonlit transparent beauty. She was exquisitely carved, with large thoughtful eyes that held no fore-shadowing of that tragic end which was a grief to everyone who had ever known her. To be in her company was delightful. She enjoyed each butterfly aspect of the world and of the moment, and would chase the lovely creatures, but without damaging the coloured dust on their wings. Whenever anyone present said anything pregnant, she would clasp her long delicate hands together and laugh with pleasure. In her own talk she always went straight to the point. For instance, on the first occasion when I met her, at a dinner party given by Osbert and Sacheverell, she asked me 'Why do you live where you do?' 'Because I have not much money.' 'How much money a year have you?' I told her. 'Oh well, I think we can do better for you than that' she said thoughtfully.

However, nothing came of this project, and I remained in Bayswater.

That, I think, was as well. I do not think I should have 'fitted into' the closely serried company of Bloomsbury. I was not an un-

friendly young woman, but I was shy, and yet, at unexpected moments, was not silent – and silence was much prized, sometimes to
the embarrassment of persons outside the inner circle of Bloomsbury.

I suppose I was always rather odd to look at, from a conventional
point of view – (and nothing was more unconventionally conventional than the company of Bloomsbury). Looking back on myself
I can see that I had an untidy elegance like that of a tall thin bird
– and was a being who appeared to have but a few friends, a few
snowflakes, perhaps, as I have said, and a small bough of early flowering almond blossom.

The company of Bloomsbury were kind-hearted, and from time
to time I entered it on sufferance.

Lytton Strachey was a major Bloomsbury idol of this time. I knew
him but slightly, and don't like his work. Also his letters to Virginia
Woolf, now published, make me blush from head to foot, with the
exclamations of 'oh deary Mary me!' and the enumeration of Count-
esses known and dimly related to them.

Visually, he made the impression on me of having strayed from
the companionship of the kindly demons in the Russian ballet 'Children's Tales', who existed only in profile, and had long beards of gardener's bass – (actually I think he saw the beings of whom he wrote,
with the exception of Queen Victoria, in profile only, never full face).
He seemed to have been cut out of very thin cardboard. He wasted
no words in conversation. A young a robust friend of ours, Constant
Lambert, meeting him at a party, said 'You don't remember, Mr Strachey? We met four years ago.'

'Quite a nice interval, I think, don't you?' remarked Mr Strachey
pleasantly, and passed on. . . .

Vita Sackville-West and Harold Nicolson: The Vitality of Bloomsbury

*Vita Sackville-West became acquainted with Bloomsbury through her
intense friendship with Virginia Woolf – a friendship that led, among
other things, to the writing of* Orlando. *The Hogarth Press published
her successful fiction and poetry as well as a pamphlet by her husband
Harold Nicolson on biography. Yet neither Vita nor Harold was ever
part of Bloomsbury. As Harold Nicolson wrote in his diary in 1940,*

Vita says that our mistake was that we remained Edwardian for too long,

*and that if in 1916 we had got in touch with Bloomsbury, we should have
profited more than we did carrying on with . . . Edwardian relics. We are
amused to confess that we had never even heard of Bloomsbury in 1916.
But we agree that we have had the best of both the plutocratic and the
Bohemian worlds, and that we have had a lovely life. (110)*

*The following letter of Vita Sackville-West to her husband in 1938
describes her admiration for Bloomsbury together with the inevitable
qualifications. (The blanks are those of the original editor.)*

Oh my dear, what an enchanting person Virginia is! How she weaves
magic into life! Whenever I see her, she raises life to a higher level.
How cheap she makes people like —— seem! And Leonard too: with
his schoolboyish love for pets and toys (gadgets), he is irresistably
young and attractive. How wrong people are about Bloomsbury, saying that it is devitalized and devitalizing. You couldn't find two people
less devitalized or devitalizing than the Wolves - or indeed people
more vitalizing than Roger Fry, for example. I think that where
Bloomsbury has suffered is in its hangers-on like —— and equivalent
young men, and of course the drooping Lytton must have done its
cause a great deal of harm. I hated Lytton.

Nigel Nicolson: Vita and Virginia and Vanessa

*Vita Sackville-West's involvement with Virginia Woolf has had literary
consequences for both of her sons. Virginia's series of letters to Ben
Nicolson (see pp. 64-5) defined her attitude towards Bloomsbury at
the end of her life. And her letters were eventually coedited by Nigel,
Vita and Harold's second son. Nigel Nicolson has become his family's
historian. After editing his father's extensive journals, he produced
in* Portrait of a Marriage *an edition of, and commentary on, his mother's autobiography. More recently he has edited the letters of his parents. The following account of Vita's relations with the Stephen sisters,
which was originally given as a talk at Charleston, alludes to the famous garden Vita created at Sissinghurst and to Knole, the great an-
cestral home of the Sackvilles that Virginia Woolf made use of in*
Orlando.

My mother, Vita Sackville-West, had very little to do with Charleston
or its garden, and Vanessa never asked for her advice. But she did

have quite a lot to do with Monks House garden, not with great
success, because she never ceased to despair about the lack of visual
taste in either of the Woolves. She once commented that Leonard
was attempting to reproduce Versailles in a quarter acre of Sussex.

However, I really want to discuss her relationship with the two
sisters, Virginia and Vanessa. With Vanessa, of course, it was more
difficult, because Vita was extraordinarily modest about her intellectual attainments and was scared of Vanessa in a way that she wasn't
of Virginia. Vanessa had a 'marmoreal chastity', to use Virginia's
phrase, which could be very intimidating. One knew, even I as a
child, who met her very seldom, that any false step could not easily
be retrieved, as happened, for instance with John Rothenstein, who
remarked, I think on his very first visit to Charleston, that Titian
didn't know how to draw, a remark which Vanessa never forgot or
forgave. There's no doubt that her almost instant judgements and
frighteningly high standards could make people who were well disposed to her into people who quaked in her presence.

There was one occasion which has been quite frequently referred
to in the memoirs, biographies and diaries. It was in Berlin in 1929,
when both the Woolves, Duncan and Vanessa, Quentin, and my first
cousin Eddie Sackville-West and my mother and father all gathered
together in that just pre-Hitler city. We were there, my brother Ben
and I, as children. One evening we went to see a Russian film called
Sturm über Asien – Storm Over Asia – a propoganda film with certain
spicy interludes which were not thought suitable for people under
the age of twelve. The day we went to this film happened to be my
twelfth birthday, and there was a dispute at the door between my
mother and the custodian on whether I should be admitted, being
only just of age. The answer, in pre-Nazi days, remember, was No.
Now, very often, people who are recollecting an event which happened when they were, say, thirty, are not really recollecting it at
all, but recollecting what they remember of that event when they were
fifty. But on this occasion, I can assure you, although I was only
twelve, I remember it precisely. The awful night: it was raining, there
had previously been snow, slush in the gutters, it was cold, it was
dark, and everybody there had conceived for each other a certain
apprehension, even dislike. Vanessa did not approve of the Nicolsons.
She wrote an account of this awful evening to Roger Fry in which
she said, 'I see no reason at all why Virginia has introduced these
people into our society.' That was very evident. Leonard refused to
come to a party which my father, who was then Chargé d'Affaires

at the Embassy in Berlin, had arranged for him to meet leading German politicians. My mother dragged Virginia off, that very day before the film, to Sans Souci, much to the annoyance of everybody else, and we, the boys, were bored and tired. I was refused permission to enter the cinema. My mother could be very fierce about this sort of thing. We stood on the pavement arguing. Vita said, 'Well, if he can't go in, I won't go in either.' That was very like her; she always thought that she could score off people by refusing to indulge in something that somebody else was forbidden to indulge in.

It was therefore an awkward relationship between Vanessa and Vita. Vita very seldom went to Charleston; on only two occasions that I can remember. I know I never went there at all until after Duncan's death. They met again in Rome in 1935, six years after the Berlin disaster. Vanessa wrote to Boris Anrep after this Rome visit: 'Harold isn't a bad creature, but my impression is that he could be led or pushed in any direction. Vita is as masterful as Mussolini, and has him under complete control.' How wrong people can get other people! My father was not at all pliable at that time. He was at the height of his professional competence, he'd just been elected to Parliament, he was a leading opponent of the appeasement policy. He was almost formidable, not at all the wincing creature that Vanessa suggested.

As for Vita's being Mussolini, she did have a certain imperious quality, I must admit. I remember her once at Sissinghurst, at about that time, seeing the stag hounds streaming across our fields. The stag leapt into the lake pursued by the hounds, swimming, and by the huntsman, who had taken our rowing boat which was tethered to the bank, and Vita, seeing this, seized her rifle, strode down to the lake and fired not at the stag, not at the hounds, not at the huntsman, but at our own rowing boat and sank it. Then she shouldered her still smoking rifle, while my father looked on amazed.

That, if you like, was the Mussolini side of her. But there was another, very gentle, reticent side. At the end of the War, when my brother Ben and I had returned from three years abroad in the Army in Africa and Italy, we said to her, 'Let's give a party.' We'd never given a party at Sissinghurst before, and she said, 'Good heavens, why?'

'Well, we won the war and now we're back safe and sound.'

Then she said, 'What sort of a party?' 'A cocktail party.' 'But we don't know how to make cocktails.'

Ben said, 'Well, people have written whole books on the subject, and we can find out.' And then my mother said, putting every obstacle in the way of this outlandish proposal, 'But we don't know anybody to ask', which was almost true, because, although we had many London friends, we had carefully avoided getting to know any of our neighbours.

We said, 'We know three people.' We would ask them to bring their friends; so she had to agree. Everybody who was invited naturally accepted, because they wanted to see what went on in this curious place. The party took place in the Long Library. It was terrible: we couldn't introduce anybody to anybody else, because we didn't know who they were. The cocktails were undrinkable. And at the beginning of the party a lady came up to my mother and said, 'I wonder if you can tell me who that lady in blue over there is?' 'Oh, yes,' said Vita, delighted to recognize one of the three women whom she did know, 'that's Mrs Hamilton Price.' 'No,' said the lady, 'I'm Mrs Hamilton Price.' The party never really recovered from that, and in her lifetime we never held another.

But to return to her relationship with Vanessa. They came closest on two occasions. One was when Julian Bell was killed in Spain, and Vita wrote a letter of condolence to Vanessa. Vanessa replied in a much more intimate and warmer way than she'd ever used to Vita before. She said, 'These past few weeks have been really terrible, as you can imagine. But I don't think I could have survived them without Virginia's constant presence and help. But I can't tell Virginia that. Will you tell her?' What a flood of light that throws upon the relationship of the two sisters. So close were they and yet so far apart that one couldn't express to the other her profoundest feeling of gratitude. That Vanessa should choose Vita as the intermediary was very striking, because she hardly knew her. But she knew that Vita meant to Virginia probably more than any other person in her lifetime outside her own family.

The second occasion, of course, was when Virginia herself died. A correspondence, quite brief, an exchange of about three or four letters on each side, ensued after her suicide. Vanessa asked Vita to come to Charleston. I think it was only about the second time she'd ever been there. We know very little about what transpired between them on that occasion, but it was obviously for both of them a highly emotional moment in which both were as guarded as their natures dictated, but felt that they were creating between them a bond which could never be severed. Those letters have been little quoted. I wrote a short article for the *Charleston Newsletter* about them some years ago, and I think that Frances Spalding used one or two. But in their entirety that are so moving that I think that one day they ought to be published, and I offer them now to any future biographer who cares to make use of them.

That was really the end of the relationship between Vanessa and Vita. Vita's relationship with Virginia was totally different, much closer, much warmer, and they were lovers, for about three years, between 1925 and 1928. It still seems to me to be one of the strangest affairs that we know about. Virginia had always been rather frigid in her physical relationships. She had had, as far as we know, no lesbian affair with anybody before. I can't really count that with Violet Dickinson. It led to nothing so traumatic as it did with Vita. And Virginia's relationship with Ethel Smyth had nothing of that character in it. And yet she took to this three-year relationship with Vita very calmly, without any sense of shock, or certainly not of shame, and without any fear of the consequence; but Vita had that fear. She sensed very strongly that she might trigger off in Virginia some fantasy, perhaps, which would lead to a new attack of madness. It never in fact came to anything like that, but this was constantly in my mother's mind. And so they formed this relationship based, on Vita's side, on immense admiration for Virginia as a person and as a writer. She recognized her genius, of course. She had no envy for it. She was a woman without envy. And, more humanly, as she once wrote to my father about Virginia, 'She has a sweet and childlike nature from which her intellect was completely separated.' But, she went on, of course nobody would believe this except perhaps Vanessa and Leonard.

I recognize so well that childlike nature in Virginia Woolf which was manifest even to me as a child. She was wonderful with children. It was only after you were seventeen or eighteen that she could become formidable. I well recollect times when she visited us at Long Barn, our earlier house, when she could say to my mother, 'Go away, Vita, can't you see that I'm talking to Ben and Nigel?' Now what could be more flattering to children of ten, eleven, twelve years old? We recognized that she was the leading novelist of her day. The word genius was used of her in her own lifetime. That she should want to devote hours of her time to exploring the empty minds of two little boys was something that I shall never forget. It wasn't wholly altruistic. What she was gathering was copy. As she once said to me, 'What's it like to be a child?' I said to her, 'Virginia, you know what it's like, because you've been a child. But I don't know what it's like to be grown up, because I've never been grown up.' She replied that it was something that everybody had experienced but nobody could

recapture. And so she made me go through the whole of my day:
'What woke you up?', 'How did you dress?', 'Which sock did you
put on? Left or right?', 'What did you have for breakfast?' Every detail,
until I walked into the room and found her there. This was, of course,
her method not only with children but with adults too; she longed
to explore the detail and the intimacy of their lives. Once she said
to me, 'Nothing has really happened until its been described.' She
meant described in writing. She meant that one must keep a diary.
She said:

> You must write letters, to your mother and father and brother, and they
> must keep them, and you keep theirs. The whole of your life, which you
> will never be able to recover later, must be put into writing. When you
> write you must imagine yourself knocking up in the squash court by your-
> self, trying out strokes, verbal strokes, without fear that other people are
> looking on to mock you. You must write, write and write.

Not very much of Bloomsbury intruded upon our lives as children.
My mother called it Gloomsbury. She transmitted to us some of her
own fear of these clever people. It was rather scarifying. The one
person who rescued us from that was Clive Bell. I recall one occasion
at Long Barn. I must have been eight, I think, and there was a large
party and a lot of Bloomsbury people were there at luncheon, and
they made thirteen. For some reason people in those days minded
sitting down thirteen at table, and I was brought down to make the
fourteenth, beside my mother at the end of the table. Opposite to
me there was an extraordinary woman, like a parakeet, with a very
made-up face, a great beak nose and a huge hat. It was of course
Ottoline Morrell. Suddenly there was a pause in the general conversation, and into the silence I dropped the words, 'Mummy, is that
lady a witch?' Everybody heard it. Even Bloomsbury was a little taken
aback. Then Clive said from the other end of the table: 'Of course
she is, of course she is, and we've all longed to say so. And you,
Nigel, have now the truth.' That saved the situation. He was very
much like that.

But perhaps the most lasting memory I have of that group is when
Virginia was writing *Orlando*. We didn't know – naturally, in 1928
I was eleven years old – the precise relationship between Vita and
Virginia. A woman who was a friend of both of them, who should
have known much better, said to me once at that time, 'I suppose
you realize that Virginia loves your mother?' I replied, with the in-

nocence of eleven years old, 'Well, of course she does, we all do.'
That was how, slowly and gradually, the realization of their relationship dawned upon us.

Virginia took us to Knole – I have a photograph of the occasion
– and she took us through the rooms, and looked at all the portraits
on the walls and asked us who they all were, these long dead Sackvilles. Of course we didn't really know, but we and she made up
stories about them. Then we came back, and the book was published.
Even Vita had not read a single word of it or knew any more than
that she was the subject of it until she received a copy of it, and
the manuscript fully bound, on publication day. Then we read it
too. I remember that my only reaction was one of distress, because
at the very end of the book, as you may remember, Orlando has a
child, a son. And we protested: 'But, Virginia, there are two of us.
Where's the other?'

Those are a few recollections of my mother in this company to
which she didn't really belong. She was accepted as Virginia's friend.
She never became, except for the two occasions that I've mentioned,
intimate with Vanessa. She was frightened of Leonard Woolf, whom
she thought, quite wrongly, grim. But with Virginia she established
and maintained a relationship even long after their love affair had
ended which was beautiful in its simplicity and the genuine pleasure
they took in each other's company. The honesty of it – Virginia's
honesty about Vita's writing, which she could convey without offence.
And Vita's love for her which was sustained after many, many years.
When Vita had fallen in love with other people Virginia remained
the person who was central to her life, apart from my father. You
can still see her photograph upon her desk at Sissinghurst.

Beatrice Webb: J.M. Keynes, E.M. Forster, Leonard and Virginia Woolf

*There were fundamental differences between Bloomsbury's values and
those of the Fabian socialists such as Beatrice and Sidney Webb or
Bernard Shaw. Desmond MacCarthy admired Shaw's drama, for example, but complained that his transvaluation failed to distinguish
between*

> *what is good as an end and what is only good as a means to that end. . . .
> Any one who judges the values of things from the point of view of their*

results, and hardly ever asks himself whether they have any value in them-
selves, must often get his scale of values wrong. (Court Theatre, *113-14*)

MacCarthy's assessment can be illustrated with an entry of Virginia
Woolf's diary. During a walk Beatrice Webb maintained that

> marriage was necessary as a waste pipe for emotion, as security in old age
> when personal attractiveness fails, & as a help to work. We were entangled
> at the gates of the level crossing when she remarked, 'Yes, I daresay an
> old family servant would do as well.' (*1:196*)

The differences between Bloomsbury and Fabian ways of life from
Beatrice Webb's point of view can, in turn, be illustrated by her letter
to Forster after the publication of his biography Goldsworthy Lowes
Dickinson *in 1934:*

> Why don't you write another great novel (analogous to the Passage to India)
> giving the essence of the current conflict all over the world between those
> who aim at exquisite relationships within the closed circle of the 'elect'
> and those who aim at hygienic and scientific improvement of the whole
> of the race? (Forster, Dickinson, 224)

Yet the political convictions of the Fabians and at least some of
the Bloomsberries overlapped. MacCarthy, though a Liberal, was able
to be the dramatic critic then literary editor of the Fabian New Statesman, *and Leonard Woolf served for a while as the Fabian expert*
on colonial affairs, though he came to disagree with the Webbs and
Shaw over their tolerance for imperialism and their admiration for
Soviet communism. The similarities of beliefs and backgrounds be-
tween the Webbs and the Woolfs make the dissension between them
over ends and means, individualism and collectivism, all the more
interesting. Beatrice Webb's penetrating diary descriptions of J.M.
Keynes, E.M. Forster, and the Woolfs – especially Virginia – are
among the most illuminating observations of Bloomsbury by their
contemporaries.

9 *August* [1926]   There must be scarcity of politically constructive
minds if J.M. Keynes seems such a treasure! Hitherto he has not attracted me – brilliant, supercilious, and not sufficiently patient for
sociological discovery even if he had the heart for it, I should have
said. But then I had barely seen him; also I think his love marriage

with the fascinating little Russian dancer has awakened his emotional
sympathies with poverty and suffering. For when I look around I
see no other man who might discover how to control the wealth of
nations in the public interest. He is not merely brilliant in expression
and provocative in thought; he is a realist: he faces facts and he has
persistency and courage in thought and action. By taste an administrator, by talent a man of science, with a remarkable literary gift,
he has not the make-up of a political leader. Not that he lacks 'personality' – he is impressive and attractive, he could impose himself
on an audience and gather round him a group of followers and disciples; if he could tolerate a political party as God makes it, he could
lead it. But he is contemptuous of common men, especially when
gathered together in herds. He dislikes the human herd and has no
desire to enlist the herd instinct on his side. Hence his antipathy
to trade unions, to proletarian culture, to nationalism and patriotism
as distinguished from public spirit. The common interests and vulgar
prejudices of aristocracies and plutocracies are equally displeasing
to him – in fact he dislikes all the common-or-garden thoughts and
emotions that bind men together in bundles. He would make a useful
member of Cabinet, but would he ever get there? Certainly not as
a member of one of the present Front Benches. I do not know which
one – Conservative or Labour – he would despise most. As for the
rank and file! Heaven help them. What Keynes might achieve is a
big scheme of social engineering; he might even be called in to carry
it out, but as an expert and not as a representative.

As an ardent lover of the bewitching Lydia Lopokova this eminent
thinker and political pamphleteer is charming to comtemplate.

6 February [1927]   The Leonard Woolfs spent the week-end here –
we had lost sight of them and were glad to renew relations with this
exceptionally gifted pair. A dozen years ago, when we first saw them,
they were living under a cloud – she on the borderline of lunacy,
he struggling desperately to keep her out of a mental home. For some
years it seemed doubtful whether he would succeed. Now the cloud
has passed away. Her appearance has altered: instead of a beautiful
but loosely knit young woman, constantly flushing and with a queer,
uncertain, almost hysterical manner, she is, though still beautiful,
a spare, self-contained ascetic-looking creature, startlingly like her
father, Leslie Stephen; the same tall, stooping figure, exquisite profile; refined, an almost narrow and hard intellectuality of expression.
Woolf also is matured and has lost his nervous shyness. Wholly un-

conventional in their outlook on life and manners, belonging rather
to a decadent set (Clive Bell is her brother-in-law) but themselves
puritanical, they are singularly attractive to talk to. In one matter
they are not up-to-date, for they are rigid secularists, regarding the-
ology or even mysticism as *l'infâme*. Here his Jewish blood comes
in: he quite clearly is revolted by the Christian myth, the anger of
a Jew at an apostate from the Judaic faith. (Considering the persecution of the Jews right up to the nineteenth century by the Christian Church, I wonder why they are not more obsessed by hatred
of the author of Christianity.) He is an anti-imperialist fanatic but
otherwise a moderate in Labour politics – always an opponent of
'workers' control' and 'proletarianism'. She is uninterested in politics
– wholly literary – an accomplished critic of style and a clever artist
in personal psychology, disliking the 'environmental' novel of late
Victorian times, especially its latest exponent, Arnold Bennett. Like
other works of the new school of novelists, I do not find her work
interesting outside its craftsmanship, which is excellent but *précieuse*.
Her men and women do not interest me – they don't seem worth
describing in such detail; the mental climate in which they live seems
strangley lacking in light, heat, visibility and variety; it is a dank
mist of insignificant and monotonous thoughts and feelings, no pre-
dominant aims, no powerful reactions from their mental environment, a curious impression of automatic existence when one state
of mind follows another without any particular reason. To the aged
Victorian this soullessness is depressing. Doubtless our insistence on
a purpose, whether for the individual or the universe, appears to
them a delusion and a pernicious delusion.

The last hours with them were spent in a raging argument about
denominational education and the validity of religious mysticism.
They were against toleration. What was 'manifestly false' was *not*
to be *taught* at the public expense and not to be *thought* by persons
above a certain level of intelligence who claimed to be honest with
themselves and other people. I pleaded for 'the endowment of error',
and threatened them with fundamentalism, or Roman Catholicism,
if they insisted on universal and compulsory sectarianism.

28 May. 3 a.m. [1928]   *To the Lighthouse* by Virginia Woolf represents the latest fashion in the technique of novel-writing. The story,
so far as there is a story, is told by a running description of the 'stream
of consciousness' in the principal person's mind. When this person
dies, then another mind is taken as the medium; in this book both

are women. To me this method is objectionable because it assumes
that the author *can* see into and describe another's mind and record
what happens, exactly as a person's behaviour can be watched and
his words recorded, and his surroundings and what happens to him
retailed. What one suspects is that Virginia is telling you of her *own*
stream of consciousness, the only one she knows 'of her own view
and knowledge'. And that brings me to the question: could I record
my own consciousness? So often it seems too vague and diverse and
disconnected – there are currents on currents, continuously rising or
falling in relative vividness, sometimes pictorial, sometimes vocal,
sometimes aloof or detached, sometimes part of a pattern made up
of personal contacts and relative positions, sometimes intellectual,
concrete or abstract or emotional, personal or impersonal. All in all
even one's own consciousness defies description. . . .

1 April [1931]   Leonard and Virginia Woolf here for the week-end.
Leonard a distinguished Jew – a saint with very considerable intelligence; a man without vanity or guile, wholly public-spirited, lacking perhaps in humour or brilliancy but original in thought and
always interesting. She stands at the head of literary women, fastid-
iously intellectual with great literary artistry, a consummate craftsman. (She is beautiful to look at.) Coldly analytical, we felt she was
observing us with a certain hostility; she is also extremely sensitive
– apt, I think, to take offence at unintentional rudeness. . . .

11 May [1931]   . . . E.M. Forster came down to lunch and tea; a tall
big-boned man with significant and attractive features and troubled
expression, ultra-refined, exquisite hands (of which he is aware), interested in many things but uncertain as to ultimate values – aesthetic
or social reformer, which is uppermost? Ostensibly he came to enquire about Lowes Dickinson's attachment to the London School of
Economics, how and why he had occasionally lectured there almost
from its very beginning in the 90s. But we talked politics and economics – U.S.S.R., Germany, U.S.A., the state of mind of the young
men at the university (he is Fellow of King's Cambridge), a state of
mind just at present which he admits is definitely revolutionary to
the left or the right, Communist or Fascist. I urged him to go back
from the essay to the novel. *A Passage to India* was a great novel.
Why not another? The present political situation in all countries had
certain dramatic possibilities. With moderate means, independent of
authorship, he lives with an old mother near Dorking. We disputed

the relative value of tenderness and loyalty in life; he valued tenderness. I retorted that without loyalty, tenderness might easily, as with D.H. Lawrence, be transformed into conscious cruelty, and that was almost worse than mere animalism – i.e. sexual passion followed by indifference. I would rather have a relationship of *polite consideration* between individuals, and nothing more, from start to finish, than a passionate friendship ending in hatred, malice and all uncharitableness. . . .

13 August [1938] . . . Here is E.M. Forster's view of *personal relationships*, which he regards as the main ingredient of an enjoyable life:

> All history, all our experience, teaches us that no human relationship is constant, it is unstable, as the living beings who compose it, and they must balance like jugglers if it is to remain; *if it is constant it no longer is human relationship but a social habit, the emphasis in it has passed from love to marriage.* (The italics are mine.)

Clearly Sidney and I prefer a *social habit* to a *personal relationship*: a preference which has made our mutual relations perfect and enduring. In old age and infirmity we love each other more tenderly than we did in the prime of life. It is only fair to add that neither Sidney nor I, in our contacts with other people, have had those absorbing personal relationships of which Forster speaks; we are both of us impersonal, though, I think, not unkind or disloyal to fellow workers. Sidney tends to ignore personalities and I study them as specimens. Our main end and preoccupation has been to discover how to change society in order to increase the well-being, energy and dignity of the human race. Lowes Dickinson and E.M. Forster would say that this outlook on life – the perfecting of social habits – makes the Webbs' work dry dull stuff without beauty or charm. The tenderness which two aged mortals have for each other, just because they have been comrades in work and faith for near fifty years, would seem to these devotees to emotional and necessarily transient relationships simply queer, even laughable. They would say this constancy may be ethical but it is not aesthetic. It is the presence of beauty of soul and body they desire, not a comfortable code of conduct or desirable social habits. That may be so. The individual human being is very limited: one virtue or gift may exclude others. Perhaps man cannot be at once aesthetic and ethical? It is worth observing that neither Lowes Dickinson nor E.M. Forster have married and both the one and the other are believed to have been homosexuals. They are both violently anti-Christian; upholders of individual liberty, by which they always mean the absence of restraint for the elect, not the presence of opportunity for the multitude. . . .

27 October [1939] [The Woolfs] had expressed a desire to meet me again. Leonard was looking terribly ill with his trembling hands, but was as gently wise as ever. I told him how interested I had been in his last volume of *After the Deluge*. But I hoped in his next, dealing with the period 1832-92, he would bring in the *Housekeeping State* provided by the Municipal Corporation Act of 1835 – which changed local government from being manorial or chartered trade guilds with law enforced by magistrates in town and country, into *associations of consumers* with compulsory powers to regulate and to provide public services for the whole community. He demurred: the local authority of Lewes, their neighbouring town, was corrupt and incompetent. I retorted that the corruption and ill will of many municipal corporations had not prevented the upgrowth of beneficial public services, health and education, housing and lighting, drainage and water, parks and libraries, and the prevention of nuisances. These services to the community could not have been achieved by voluntary associations of consumers. In fact, it was the proved incapacity of voluntary associations of householders in cities to do the job that led them to apply for local acts giving the compulsory power of levying rates and regulating conduct. . . .

Virginia seemed troubled by an absence of any creed as to what was right and what was wrong. I asked her whether she was going to write a second volume of *Years*. I longed to hear how the family she described so vividly would respond to this new war. Would they be as unconcerned as they were during the great war of 1914-18? She gave me no answer except that she did not know her own mind about what was happening – so how could she describe the mind of others! . . . This gifted and charming lady, with her classic features, subtle observation and symphonic style, badly needs a living philosophy. Brought up in the innermost circle of the late Victorian intellectuals, in revolt against the Christian religion with its superstitions and its hypocritical conventions, they were between *laissez-faire* and *laissez-aller* in all the circumstances of life. *Absence of restraint* was to them the one and only meaning of liberty, for they personally enjoyed the presence of opportunity to lead the life they

liked, or thought they liked. Virginia Woolf realizes that this creed
has broken down; but she sees no way out . . . We all aim at max-
imizing human happiness, health, loving kindness, scientific certainty
and the spirit of adventure together with the appreciation of beauty
in sight and sound, in word and thought. Where we differ is how
to bring about this ideal here and now. . . .

7 April [1941]   In the morning news: 'Mrs Virginia Woolf, missing
from her home since Friday 28th . . . assumed drowned in the river
Ouse.' During the day and for some days afterwards, ghosts from
the past haunted me – that tall, talented woman with her classic features, her father Leslie Stephen, also tall, good-looking, highly cultured, with whom in the 80s I used to discuss English history in
the house of Alice Green in Kensington Square. An old man, seemingly kind and courteous to a young writer but pictured as a supreme
egotist towards his family by his daughter with a bitter pen in *To
the Lighthouse,* perhaps her most successful novel.

Virginia was a beautiful woman and a writer of great charm and
finesse – in her *uniqueness* the most outstanding of our women novelists. The Woolfs stayed with the Webbs, and the Webbs with the
Woolfs, and Leonard was one of Sidney's most intimate colleagues
in international propaganda during the great war; but we never became sympathetic friends. I think we liked them better than they liked
us. In a way which I never understood. I offended Virginia. I had
none of her sensitiveness, her understanding of the inner life of the
subjective man, expressed in the birth, life and death of social in-
stitutions. Also we clashed with Leonard Woolf in our conception
of what constitutes human freedom: the absence of restraint for the
intellectual or the presence of opportunity for the ordinary man –
which element was to be the foremost object of the social reformer?
In particular, he abhorred Soviet Communism. But in spite of this
mental aloofness from the Woolfs I am pained by the thought of
that beautiful and brilliant Virginia yielding to the passion for death
rather than endure the misery of continued life. Twenty years ago
her devoted husband had nursed her through a period of mental der-
angement and suicidal mania. In middle age she became a vigorous
and seemingly self-assured woman, an eminently successful author
and a devoted companion to her distinguished husband. What led
to the tragedy? And what is happening to the ultra-refined, public-
spirited and gifted Leonard Woolf? The last time I saw them both
was at a luncheon at Barbara's about eighteen months ago. Her last

words to me, as she and Leonard met, were 'I have no living philosophy' – which may probably account for her voluntary withdrawal
from life. Can man continue happy without some assured faith as
to what should be the right relation of man to man, also of man's
relation to the universe? On the first I have a clearly defined conclusion; on the other I am a religious agnostic. I do not know, I
only have an emotional feeling that there *is* a spirit of love at work
in the universe, and I pray from time to time that it may help me
to act rightly to my fellow men. But if I were not supremely fortunate
in my circumstances, would that vague and intermittent faith save
me from despair during these days of death and destruction, by day
and by night? . . .

Gerald Brenan: Bloomsbury in Spain and England

*After the First World War Gerald Brenan, an impecunious, heroic
young English officer from a well-to-do family, settled in a primitive
mountain village south of Granada called Yegen with the aim of becoming a writer. Brenan, who had gone to war rather than university,
met Ralph Partridge in the war and through him came to know various members of Bloomsbury. For a time he was intensely involved
in Lytton Strachey's ménage through his love for Carrington.*

*Brenan's writings include books on the background of the Spanish
Civil War, Spanish literature, and St John of the Cross, several novels,
poetry, and three volumes of autobiography. The first two excerpts
of his Bloomsbury recollections come from* South from Granada *and
the rest from* Personal Record: 1920–1972, *which overlaps his Spanish
memoir. Brenan sent some draft pages of* South from Granada *to Leonard Woolf, who enjoyed them but wrote to Brenan that it was untrue
Bloomsbury regarded most people as beyond the pale:*

> It is true that Lytton had a façade of arrogance and that he did more or
> less condemn large numbers of people to outer darkness. I personally over
> and over again abused him for doing so. The general statement is quite
> untrue of Virginia, Roger, Desmond, Clive, Duncan, Morgan or myself,
> who after all were all 'Bloomsbury' (Desmond and Morgan were certainly
> regarded by all of us as 'Bloomsbury' by the way). It is not true that Blooms-
> bury despised people who fought in the war. Personally I was not a C.O.
> and was twice rejected on medical grounds. (Letters, 497)

Brenan altered his book but did not include MacCarthy and Forster
in Bloomsbury. Though there are further inaccuracies in Personal
Record, *Brenan's autobiographies still offer interesting observations*
of a variety of Bloomsbury members over the years.

I cannot recollect now how I came to know Carrington, for we had
other friends in common besides Ralph, but I remember very well
going over to Tidmarsh for the first time and meeting Lytton Strachey. It was one of those heavily overcast English summer days. The
trees and the grass were steeped in a vivid green, but the purplish
clouds overhead shut out the light and made the interiors of the
houses dark and gloomy. Carrington with her restless blue eyes and
her golden-brown hair cut in a straight page-boy bob came to the
door – she suggested to me one of the lute-playing angels, the fourth
from the left, in Piero della Francesca's *Nativity* – and I was shown
into the sitting-room. At the further end of it there was an extraordinary figure reclining in a deep armchair. At the first glance, before
I had accustomed my eyes to the lack of light, I had the illusion
– or rather, I should say, the image came into my mind – of a darkly
bearded he-goat, glaring at me from the bottom of a cave. Then I
saw that it was a man and took in gradually the long, relaxed figure,
the Greco-ish face, the brown sensitive eyes hidden behind thick
glasses, the large, coarse nose and ears, the fine, thin, blue-veined
hands. Most extraordinary was the voice which was both very low
and in certain syllables very high-pitched, and which faded out at
the end of sentence, sometimes even without finishing it. I never attuned my ears to taking in everything that he said.

Tea was laid in the dining-room – farm butter, honey in the comb,
home-made cakes and jam and currant loaf, served in a pink lustre
tea-service. Carrington was a devotee of Cobbett, and her housekeeping and furnishing expressed not only the comfort but the poetry
of cottage and farmhouse life. Her very English sensibility, in love
with the country and with all country things, gave everything she
touched a special and peculiar stamp. But what struck me more
strongly about her than anything else was the attention she paid to
Lytton. Never have I seen anyone who was so waited on hand and
foot as he was by her, or whose every word and gesture was received
with such reverence. In a young woman who in all other respects
was fiercely jealous of her independence, this was extraordinary.

How is one to describe the first beginnings of a long friendship?
Later impressions fuse with earlier ones and distort them. Besides,

I have to keep within the framework of this book, which requires that I put down only what will be necessary to make Lytton Strachey's visit to my remote and primitive village come alive. Scouring my memory then, I seem to remember that as I sat at the tea-table on that dark summer's afternoon I was puzzled by the contrast presented by the three people in front of me and wondered whether their peculiar relation (adopted father and married children, as it came in time to be) could last. They were in every way so extremely different from one another: Ralph with his look of an Oxford hearty - dirty white shorts, nondescript shirt and then rather stylized way of speaking which contrasted with the Rabelaisian laugh, rolling blue eyes and baritone voice in which he sang a jazz song or a ballad: Carrington with her simple, pre-Raphaelite clothes and her coaxing voice and smile that concealed so many intense and usually conflicting feelings: Lytton, elegant in his dark suit, gravely remote and fantastic, with something of the polished and dilettante air of a sixteenth-century cardinal. It was not any similarity of temperament or upbringing that had brought these three together, and Lytton's London friends, who resented their week-ends at Tidmarsh being diluted by people whom they looked on as outsiders, could not understand it. 'Bloomsbury' was still a small, closely guarded set, united both by old friendships and by a private philosophy, and it showed a strong resistance to accepting on an intimate footing people whom it did not regard as suitable.

It was February when I learned of my friends' expected visit, and this at once produced a crisis in my arrangements. Only two rooms of my house were as yet furnished and I should need to buy more things of every sort and in particular more beds and bedding. . . .

. . . When we had exhausted the first burst of mutual communication, the problem of transporting Lytton Strachey to Yegen came up. He sat there silent and bearded, showing no signs of enthusiasm. In the end we decided to engage a carriage for the following morning to convey us as far as Orgiva and to send on two mules to meet us there and take us the rest of the journey.

We picked up the mules and then the question arose as to which route we should take. The shortest - it saved an hour - required us to ford the Rio Grande instead of crossing the bridge. According to the muleteers this was feasible, but when we reached the ford and the mules went in almost to their girths in the racing water, Lytton drew back. There was nothing to be done but to eat our lunch under

the olive trees and return to the hotel, arranging with the men to
make a fresh start on the following day.

The evening passed in general low spirits. Everyone's nerves were
on edge. Ralph and Carrington were having a lovers' quarrel and
Lytton was gloomy because, though he had been eager to see Spain,
he had been most unwilling to come on this expedition. His stomach
was delicate, Spanish food had disagreed with him, and he was not
feeling in the mood for adventures. But Ralph, who was very loyal
to his friends, was determined to visit me, and Lytton had refused
to be left behind at Granada even if Carrington, in whose capacities
he had little confidence, remained with him. This clinging to male
protection was characteristic. Under his self-possessed manner he was
a timid man who had arranged his life so that he should never be
obliged to do anything that he found difficult. Now one of the things
that he could not do was to speak to people who were outside of
his particular range of interests. Thus, though he had been toying
for some time with a Spanish grammar, nothing would have induced
him even to order a cup of coffee in that language. In France he
refused to utter a word of French although, naturally, he knew it
well and read it aloud with a fair accent. He could not even give
an order to an English servant. When, in his own house, he wanted
some tea, he told Carrington and she told the maid and, if he was
by himself, he went without. To avoid the risk of being spoken to
in trains he always, even when he was badly off, travelled first class.
Such were the rules he had drawn up for himself. From an early
age he had planned his life, his career, even his appearance, and
this plan required that he should keep strictly within that small circle
of people where he could fly under his own colours and make himself
understood without effort. No doubt the peculiarities of his voice
and intonation as well as his dislike of any sort of social pretence
made communication with the world at large difficult for him.

That evening, then, at Lanjarón, was spoiled by recriminations.
Did I really know the road? Ralph asked me. Were the muleteers
to be trsuted? Would there be beds and eatable food when we arrived?
The conveyance of the great writer to my mountain village began
to assume more and more the appearance of a difficult military operation. Carrington, caught between two fires, became clumsily ap-
peasing and only Lytton said nothing. As for myself, I never doubted
my powers to go anywhere or do anything of a physical sort that
I wished to, but under my friends' bombardment I felt my unfitness
for assuming responsibility for other people.

It was in this harassed and ruffled frame of mind that we set off once more on the following morning. For the first hour or so everything went well. As the carriage rolled along, the sun lit up the silver leaves of the olive trees and the birds rose and sank like shuttles between them and the tall bean plants below. But no sooner had we left the carriage and descended into the river valley than our difficulties began. Lytton found he could not ride on mule-back because he suffered from piles, so that every time the track crossed the river, which happened about every half a mile, he had laboriously to climb onto the animal and then dismount again. This delayed us. It was not till a little before sunset that we reached Cádiar and then he felt so exhausted that he declared that he could not go any further. We drew up at the *posada* and looked at its best bed, but one glance at it made him change his mind and decide to go on.

The day was coming to an end so rapidly that we did not dare to take the short and comparatively easy track through Yátor. There was nothing to be done but climb straight up the mountainside to hit the end of the main road some 2,500 feet above. It was a dramatic ascent by a steep path often bordered by precipices and no one could do it sitting side-saddle on a mule, as Lytton and Carrington had to, without an unpleasant feeling inside. Slowly, as we climbed, the light faded. A rosy band mounted in the sky behind us, and the chasms and pinnacles took on a shadowy depth and height. Then the stars came out just as we reached the road, and Carrington and I hurried on to give warning of our arrival and get a meal prepared. The distance was still some six miles. When at length we reached the village and stood looking down in the starlight on its flat, greyish roofs, only the tiniest occasional glow from the smallest oil lamp in the glassless foot-square of a window showed that it was still awake.

I do not remember much about the next few days. Lytton was tired and therefore not in a mood for talking much. We went for a walk up the mountain-side and Carrington took some photographs. One of them, if I remember right, showed him sitting side-saddle on a mule, bearded, spectacled, very long and thin, with his coarse red nose, holding an open sunshade above him. Even in England he was a strange figure to meet on a country ramble: here he looked exotic, aristocratic, Oriental rather than English, and above all incongruous.

On his last evening, however, cheered by the thought that his visit was drawing to an end, he relaxed and became almost lively. When he was in the mood, his conversation had great charm. The delicacy and precision of his mind came out much better than they usually

did in his books, because in these he subordinated sensitivity of language and spontaneity of phrase to a preconceived pattern. He was
not, like Virginia Woolf, a natural writer, and even in his letters his
pen never ran away with him. But in conversation he was himself.
He needed more than most people an attuned and sympathetic audience, but, given this, he became the most easy of companions, listening as much as he talked, making whimsical or penetrating comments and creating around him a feeling of naturalness and intimacy.
One remembered afterwards his doubts and hesitations, his refusals
to dogmatize, his flights of fantasy, his high, whispering voice fading
out in the middle of a sentence, and forgot the very definite and well-
ordered mind that lay underneath. But it is beyond my power to give
any real account of so complex a character who, through some thick-
ness in the needle, perhaps some deliberate plan of writing down
to his readers, records himself with too poor fidelity in his literary
works. One observed a number of discordant features – a feminine
sensibility, a delight in the absurd, a taste for exaggeration and melodrama, a very mature judgement and then some lack of human substance, some hereditary thinness in the blood that at times gave people
who met him an odd feeling in the spine. He seemed almost indecently
lacking in ordinariness.

However, what I remember best about Lytton Strachey – for though
I was never on intimate or even on easy terms with him, I had opportunities for seeing him in his own house and elsewhere over many
years – was the great gentleness of his tone and manner when he
was with people whom he liked. As a young man he had, I understand, shown a bitter and satirical vein and when, as often happened,
he was unwell, he could be peevish and irritable. But friendship drew
out his best qualities. There was a good deal in his cautiously he-
donistic attitude to life that recalled the teachings of Epicurus. His
world, like the Garden of that valetudinarian philosopher, consisted
of a small, carefully chosen set of people whose society he enjoyed.
Some of these were young men of good looks and intellectual promise
whom he drew out and encouraged, for there was something of the
teacher in him. Others were literary figures, such as Virginia Woolf,
Maynard Keynes, Desmond and Molly MacCarthy and E.M. Forster.
Outside this he would make sallies into a wider field – luncheons
with Lady Oxford or Lady Ottoline Morrell, dinner parties at Lady
Colefax's and even at ducal houses – and return home full of mis-
chievous and ironical comments. But within these limits he remained.
Although, as a Strachey, he took a certain interest in public affairs

and stood by his very moderate Liberal opinions, I got the impression that privately he thought of the world with its incomprehensible stupidity as something which it was best to keep at a distance. Unlike Voltaire, whom he admired so greatly, he regarded it as irreformable, and it was this attitude, I suspect, that angered Bertrand Russell and led him to speak harshly of him in a recent broadcast. The two men, who often met at Lady Ottoline's, were not made to like or understand one another, in spite of their sharing the same pacifist attitude to the War.

The day for my friends' departure came. A car arrived and took them to Almeria, where they caught the train for Madrid. The visit had been something of a strain for everyone. Much though I knew that I should miss Ralph and Carrington, whose presence in my house, in spite of all the difficulties, had given me the deepest pleasure, I breathed again at the thought that I should no longer be responsible for finding dishes that would suit Lytton's delicate digestion. The ruthless cuisine of Spanish villages, with its emphasis on potato omelettes, dried cod and unrefined olive oil, had made my task a difficult one. And he must have been even more relieved at making his escape. When, three years later, Leonard and Virginia Woolf were preparing to come out and stay with me, he advised them strongly against attempting it, declaring in his high-pitched voice that 'it was death'.

* * *

It was in the spring of 1923 that Leonard and Virginia Woolf came out to see me. I met them at Granada at the house of some friends of mine, the Temples, who wished to discuss the African colonies with Leonard, and after a couple of nights there we came on by bus and mule to Yegen. This time the journey went smoothly, without any of the difficulties that had marked Lytton Strachey's passage three years before, and it was evident that they enjoyed it.

The first thing that comes to mind when I think of Virginia as she was in those days, and particularly as I saw her in the quiet seclusion of my house, is her beauty. Although her face was too long for symmetry, its bones were thin and delicately made and her eyes were large, grey or greyish blue, and as clear as a hawk's. In conversation they would light up a little coldly while her mouth took an ironic and challenging fold, but in repose her expression was pensive and almost girlish. When in the evening we settled under the hooded chimney and the logs burned up and she stretched out her hands to the blaze, the whole cast of her face revealed her as a poet.

There are writers whose personality resembles their work, and there are others who, when one meets them, give no inkling of it. Virginia Woolf belonged strikingly to the first category. When one had spent half an hour in a room with her one could easily believe that it was she who, as one was told, had scribbled quickly in purple ink in the summer house at Rodmell that fresh and sparkling article that had just appeared in *The Nation,* and when one saw her in a reflective or dreamy mood one recognized only a little less slowly the authoress of *To the Lighthouse.* One reason for this was that her conversation, especially when she had been primed up a little, was like her prose. She talked as she wrote and very nearly as well, and that is why I cannot read a page of *The Common Reader* today without her voice and intonation coming back to me forcibly. No writer that I know of has put his living presence into his books to the extent that she has done.

Not, however, that what she said was ever bookish. She talked easily and naturally in a pure and idiomatic English, often, like many of her friends, in a lightly ironical tone. Irony, it will be remembered, plays a great and important part in her writings. There it is of a gay and playful kind, sometimes verging on facetiousness, but in her conversation it became personal and took on a feminine, and one might almost say flirtatious, form. Leaning sideways and a little stiffly in her chair she would address her companion in a bantering tone, and she liked to be answered in the same manner. But whatever her vein, all the resources of her mind seemed to be at her immediate disposal at every moment. One felt a glass-like clarity, but it was not the clarity of a logician, but rather that of a kaleidoscope which throws out each time from the same set of pieces a different pattern. Much later, when she was, I think, working on *The Waves,* she told me that her difficulty lay in stopping the flow of her pen. She had been reading, she said, a life of Beethoven and envied his power of drawing up into his score by constant revision and correction themes which resisted being brought to the surface. I imagine that for her correction meant simply shaking the kaleidoscope and producing a new, more appropriate passage.

Perhaps because Virginia lacked the novelist's sense for the dramatic properties of character and was more interested in the texture of people's minds, she was much given to drawing them out and documenting herself upon them. She asked me a great many questions – why I had come to live here, what I felt about this and that, and what my ideas were about writing. I was conscious that I was being studied and even quizzed a little and also that she and Leonard were trying to decide whether I showed any signs of having literary talent. If so, I must publish with them. Yet it must not for a moment be thought that she was patronizing. On the contrary her deference to the views of the callow and rather arrogant youth with whom she was staying was quite surprising. She argued with me about literature, defended Scott, Thackeray and Conrad against my attacks, disagreed with my high opinion of *Ulysses* on the grounds that great works of art ought not to be so boring, and listened humbly to my criticisms of her own novels. That was the great thing about 'Bloomsbury' – they refused to stand on the pedestal of their own age and superiority. And her visit was followed by a succession of highly characteristic letters in which she continued the theme of our dicussions.

I want to emphasize Virginia's real friendliness on this occasion and the trouble she took to advise me, because her recklessness in conversation – when she was overexcited she talked too much from the surface of her mind – made some people think that she lacked ordinary sympathies. I was young for my age, and rather earnest. The isolation in which I lived had made me self-centred, and like all people who are starved for conversation I was very talkative. She on the other hand was a writer of great distinction, approaching the height of her powers. Yet she and her husband not only concealed the impatience they must often have felt, but treated me as though I was their intellectual equal. Of course, one might say, they believed in encouraging young writers and spotting the winners among them. Virginia had a strong sense of the continuity of literary tradition and felt it a duty to hand on what she had received. She was also intensely and uneasily aware of the existence of a younger generation who would one day rise and sit in judgment on her. It may be, therefore, that she thought that my strange way of life and my passion for literature showed that I might have something to give. If so, however, both she and Leonard decided a few years later that they had been mistaken.

As I sit here, trying to collect my scattered memories of this fortnight, a few scenes come before me with vividness. I recall Virginia's face in the firelight, then the gaily bantering tone in which she spoke, and Leonard's easy, companionable one. Her manner at such times was vivaciously, though rather chillily, feminine, and her voice seemed to preen itself with self-confidence in its own powers. With a little encouragement it would throw off a cascade of words like the notes of a great pianist improvising, and without the affectation

- born of delight in verbal mastery - that sometimes crept into the style of her novels. Leonard, on the other hand, was very steady, very masculine - a pipe-smoking, tweed-dressing man who could conduct an argument to a finish without losing the thread and who had what is called at Cambridge 'a good mind'. Moreover - and this impressed me more than anything - he could read Aeschylus without a crib.

Then, scrambling on the hillside among the fig trees and the olives, I see a rather different person. An English lady, country-bred and thin, her wide-open eyes scanning distance, who has completely forgotten herself in her delight at the beauty of the landscape and at the novelty of finding herself in such a remote and Arcadian spot. She seemed, though quiet, as excited as a schoolgirl on a holiday, while her husband's serious, sardonic features had become almost boyish. On these walks they talked of themselves and of their life together with great frankness - to have no secrets from friends was another 'Bloomsbury' characteristic - and among other things I recall Virginia telling me how incomplete she felt in comparison to her sister Vanessa, who brought up a family, managed her house, and yet found plenty of time left in which to paint. Although I doubt if she ever lost this sense of her own inadequacy, of not being quite, in every sense of the word, a person of flesh and blood, she was practical and could cook and run a house better than most women, as well as lead a social life that often probably outran her strength.

It used to be said by those that were not invited to its parties that 'Bloomsbury' was a mutual admiration society who pushed one another's works. This charge, which has recently been repeated, is simply not true. Virginia Woolf greatly admired E.M. Forster's novels, which seemed to her to have the qualities of 'reality' which she perhaps felt hers lacked, and she also admired Roger Fry's writings on art as well as his marvellously eager and stimulating conversation. But she had a poor opinion of Lytton Strachey's biographies, though she was greatly attached to him personally, and praised the fineness and subtlety of his mind and his discrimination as a critic. One evening, I remember, while the Woolfs were at Yegen, the subject of his *Queen Victoria* came up. Both Leonard and Virginia pronounced decisively against it, declaring that it was unreadable. Although I did not care for its flat, spongy style, which gave me the sensation of walking on linoleum, this charge seemed to me absurd: readable was precisely what it was. Yet they maintained that they had been unable to finish it. Lytton, on the other hand, greatly admired most of Virginia's writings, but could not read Forster in spite of his strong

personal friendship for him. I remember him saying, after looking
through his little guide to Alexandria, *Pharos and Pharillon*, that
it was a pity that he had taken to novel-writing when he was so
much better at history. And he disliked both Roger Fry and his work.

Virginia had much to say of T.S. Eliot, of whom she was seeing
a good deal at this time. She praised him warmly as a man, and
spoke of his remarkable intelligence, but seemed a little half-hearted
about *The Waste Land*, which the Hogarth Press was then publishing.
Like myself, she had a poor opinion of D.H. Lawrence. The boring
prophetic mantle he wore, the streams of slovenly and sentimental
writing that poured from his pen obscured the sometimes extraordinary freshness of insight that showed itself in one or two of his
novels and short stories. Nor had his admirers helped his reputation,
for as usually happens in such cases, they had been more impressed
by his bad books – those which contained his 'message' – than by
his good ones. Yet she could change her mind, and when, some years
later, she came across *Sons and Lovers*, she wrote an article on it
which, though perhaps not very understanding, praised it highly.
Has there ever been an age, one might ask, in which writers have
admired more than one or two of their contemporaries?

To appreciate Virginia Woolf's brilliance as a talker one had to
see her in her own circle of friends. It was a regular custom for five
or six of these to meet every week after dinner either at her house
or at her sister Vanessa's, and usually one or two of the younger generation would be invited to be present. In that capacity I went several
times. The aces were Roger Fry, Duncan Grant, Vanessa Bell, Clive
Bell, Lytton Strachey, Maynard Keynes, and occasionally one or two
people such as Desmond MacCarthy and Morgan Forster who did
not, I think, regard themselves as 'belonging to Bloomsbury', though
they were accepted by the others on the same footing. The arrangements were informal, yet everyone was aware of the purpose of the
meeting, which was to make good conversation. With this idea, for
literary people at this time were very sober, no drinks except coffee
were provided.

I very soon got the impression that these conversaziones were really
of the nature of orchestral concerts. One might almost say that the
score was provided, for the same themes always came up – the difference between the younger and the older generation, the difference
between the painter and the writer, and so forth. The performers too
were thoroughly practised, for they had been meeting every week or
even more often over a space of many years to discuss the same not,

one would have thought, very inspiring subjects. Thus they had each of them learned what part he must play to conduce to the best general effect and also how to stimulate and give the cue for the others. The solo instruments, one might say (both strings), were Virginia Woolf and Duncan Grant: they could be relied on to produce at the appropriate moment some pieece of elaborate fantasy, contradicting the serious and persistent assertions of the other instruments. Roger Fry would drive forward on one of his provocative lines: Vanessa Bell, the most silent of the company, would drop one of *mots*, while Clive Bell, fulfilling the role of the bassoon, would keep up a general roar of animation. His special function in the performance was to egg on and provoke Virginia to one of her famous sallies.

What one got from these evenings was, if my youthful judgment is to be relied on, conversation of a brilliance and (in spite of the rehearsals) spontaneity which, I imagine, has rarely been heard in England before. I have known other good talkers, one of them perhaps the equal of any of these, but they have always given solo performances. What 'Bloomsbury' evenings offered was the concert in which each talked to produce himself and to draw the best out of the others. I imagine that only continual practice by people who share the same general attitude to life and who are pleased by their friends' performance as by their own can provide anything like it.

For a young writer even a slight acquaintance with such a group of people was an education, though not perhaps a stimulus. They had standards – honesty, intelligence, taste, devotion to the arts, and social sophistication. They never, in their written judgments, let their vanity or their private friendships or their political or religious prejudices run away with them, and they were none of them out to compensate for their own weaknesses and deficiencies by attacking others. Yet it must, I think, be admitted that they lived – not singly, which would not have mattered, but collectively – in an ivory tower. Maynard Keynes and Leonard Woolf had roots outside it in the world of politics, and Roger Fry was too active and public spirited a man to let himself be confined. The others, however, were prisoners of their close web of mutual friendships and of their agreeable mode of life and also of their rather narrow and (as they held it) smug Cambridge philosophy. Virginia Woolf, it is true, was always aware of the typist queueing for her lunch in the cheap tea-shop and of the shabby old lady weeping in the third-class railway carriage, yet she too was tied to her set by her birth, her social proclivities, her craving for praise and flattery, and could only throw distant and uneasy glances outside it. Her sense of the precariousness of things, which gives her work its seriousness, came from her private life – from the shock of her brother Thoby's death and from her experience of madness. But the ethos of her group and indeed her whole cultured Victorian upbringing cut her off from the hard view of human nature that the novelist needs and drove her to develop her own poetic and mystical vision of things in what I at least feel was too subjective a way. Thus when one re-reads her novels now one feels again the ease and beauty of much of the writing and gets a certain muffled, Calderon-like impression of life being no more than a dream, yet one is left dissatisfied. For if one is to be convinced that life is a dream, one must first be shown, and pretty sharply, that what is set before one is life.

Looking back today it is not, I think, difficult to see that the weakness inherent in the splendid flower of English culture thrown up by 'Bloomsbury' lay in its being so closely attached to a class and mode of life that was dying. Already by 1930 it was pot-bound. Its members were too secure, too happy, too triumphant, too certain of the superiority of their Parnassian philosophy to be able to draw fresh energies from the new and disturbing era that was coming in. They had escaped the shock of the first German War either by being unfit for military service or by joining the ranks of the pacifists, and had not taken warning from the prophets who announced that the snug rationalist world they lived in was seriously threatened. When they should, therefore, have been in their prime, they were on their way to being an anachronism, even Virginia Woolf – the most open-minded of all except Maynard Keynes – being limited by some deep-seated doubt (connected possibly with her fits of madness) about the reality of almost everything except literature. Yet, I imagine, if the cobalt bomb does not obliterate everything, future ages will feel an interest in these people because they stand for something that the world always looks on with nostalgia – an *ancien régime*. They carried the arts of civilized life and friendship to a very high point, and their work reflects this civilization. Then, surely, two of them at least, Virginia Woolf and Maynard Keynes, possessed those rare imaginative gifts that are known as genius. . . .

* * *

In June Saxon Sydney-Turner came out to visit me. He was one of the Cambridge Apostles and a member of 'Bloomsbury', and Leonard Woolf has drawn a portrait of him in the first volume of his autobiography. He was a curious, perverse creature and one of the greatest bores I have ever known. Something, evidently an attack of schizophrenia, had happened to him when he was young which had killed all that was human and vital in his mind and left only the machine. In the course of time I got to know him pretty well and came to see that he was not only aware that he was a bore but that he was proud of being one and enjoyed dealing out his death packets to other people, whose vital qualities he despised. On this visit I had looked forward to talking to him about the Greek dramatists whose works I was reading in Leconte de Lisle's translation. I knew that he was a first-rate classical scholar, but what I had not been told was that he would never discuss literature and in fact all I could get out of him was a long, dry exposition of the intricacies of the Greek accent, which naturally was of no interest at all to a person who could not read Greek. Many years later he took to going every summer to Finland, coming back each time with a collection of snapshots that showed nothing but fir trees of varying heights and small railway stations. When he arrived at Lytton's house for the weekend he would bring these photographs with him and one dreaded the moment when he would fetch them out and display them one by one, very slowly, in that muffled yet persistent voice of his, with brief comments: 'I took that one of a railway station in the tundra because when I first went to Finland it had not been built.'

Saxon throws an interesting light on the mores of Bloomsbury. In that circle, which lived and met for good conversation, to be a bore was the worst accusation that could be levelled at anyone. Yet because he had been an Apostle, loyalty required that he should be frequently asked down for weekends by both Lytton Strachey and the Woolfs. Nothing, I think, shows better how rooted they were in that little Cambridge society. For Arthur Waley, though not an Apostle, had been at Cambridge at the same time as Lytton and Leonard. He lived in Gordon Square, next door to the Stracheys and three minutes' walk from the Woolfs, and was not only one of the most intelligent of men, but a fine prose writer and the best translator of poetry England has had since the Elizabethan Age. Yet because he was a little too obsessed with Chinese things to suit many people, he was put down as a bore, and more or less excluded from their society. Why then was Saxon preferred to him? I can only conjecture that every group or society feels the need for a private bore of its own, who belongs solely to them. His death-dealing visits, the awful discomfort and agony he causes provide a subject for wonder and humorous self-commiseration. A pride is felt in him, he is regarded as a perverse family pet who must be tolerated and cherished. If that is so, no one could have been found who was more suited to the role than Saxon. . . .

The set I moved in, which centred round that small group of older people later known as the 'Bloomsbury Group', had certain things in common. They had all of them been at either Oxford or Cambridge, they were much better off than I was and they had none of them fought in the war. Some had been medically unfit, others pacifists, one had served in the Red Cross, others were too young to have been called up. For many years I met no one except Ralph who had been at the front. Not only did the war seem to have been entirely forgotten, but those who had fought in it were slightly looked down on as people who had taken part in a shabby and barbarous enterprise. I on the other hand was proud of having been through it and felt that there was something thin and unreal about those who had not done so. They had missed the great experience of the age and that, I said to myself when I was in a priggish mood, was one of the reasons for their futility. Their comfortable incomes, their cliquishness, their suspicion of new adventures in literature, their lack of any connections with the larger world made me feel that, much as I liked and admired many of them, it would not do for me as a writer to get too involved with them. I wanted to have my own life, not to move in a small literary set or to become anyone's disciple. Yet, bound to Carrington as I was, I was becoming partly absorbed by them.

The ones among them I most admired were Leonard and Virginia Woolf. I was seeing them fairly often that summer so I will quote two extracts from my letters to Carrington that relate to them. The first is dated May 6th, 1924.

I saw Virginia last night, sitting in her dressing gown and looking rather ruffled and stormtossed, like a bird that has just crossed the sea in a gale. She was very nice and asked me to come to her parties in the evenings. I said I would like to come if I need not talk. 'But really, Gerald, you know you are a perfect chatterbox.' I walked round the square with Leonard and came home and read for *Teresa*.

I have described in *South from Granada* these Bloomsbury after-dinner gatherings at the Woolfs' house, so now I will quote from my second letter, dated June 3rd.

I went to see Virginia. Mrs Joad [who acted as their secretary] was there and Adrian Stephen and George Sanger. Leonard now takes pleasure in putting me through various tests as though I were some new and quaint form of animal. When he opened the street door he quickly stepped behind it. But I saw him and asked him why he did that. 'To see what you would do,' he said. I see now that his treatment of me and possibly of all new people consists in a series of elaborately arranged tests or experiments, from each of which he draws some conclusion. No doubt he arranges them in a kind of series like those keys for discovering the names of flowers at the beginning of botany books: one is sifted from genus to sub-genus, and as each experiment is supposed to be conclusive and irrevocable, the result is at last a pure fantasy. Far from resenting this, I find it gives me pleasure. Leonard's unflattering remarks could offend nobody, and every time I see him I like him better.

When you told me that he liked cactuses, you threw a great deal of light on his character, for what interests him in men is what they share with these plants – variety, quaintness, hard-cut outlines, immobility.

Virginia was discussing her favourite subject – the difference between the younger and the older generations. 'Look at Gerald . . .', she began. 'Gerald', said Leonard, 'is completely disoriented – he lives upside down on his head.' Though I did not agree, I thought I could guess what he meant, but he went on, 'All the younger generation are like him. Marjorie (Mrs Joad) is just the same. They are all disoriented.' And then I understood nothing. For that the quality (invisible to me) which I have in common with Mrs Joad and Ralph and many others should be called 'disorientation' was quite incomprehensible.

'They are less subtle, less sensitive, but more downright and more intelligent,' went on Virginia. 'As for intelligence,' said Leonard, 'I would back myself against all of them.'

Leonard, I thought to myself, will always be, wherever he is, the most intelligent person in the room, even when Roger Fry or Bertie Russell are present. And this is because, having a head so clear that no one could have a clearer, he has energy to spare for watching and comparing the speakers and their psychological motives: that is to say, he is detached and this gives him a feeling of superiority, of being in some sense more intelligent than even people like B.R., whose mental capacity he sums up under the rather disparaging word 'brilliant'. . . .

All through that summer and autumn [of 1924] I was spending weekends at Tidmarsh and after that at Ham Spray. This meant that I was seeing a good deal of Lytton Strachey. In *South from Granada* I have described the startling and even grotesque impression he first made on me, but as I got to know him better I lost my sense of his strangeness and was rather struck by his elegance. It was an elegance of mind as well as of body, of conversation as well as of face. However I did not find him easy to talk to. He made no efforts to communicate with those who could not tune in to his wave-length. I was one of these for, though I never felt that he disliked me, he had nothing to say to me because, like many other people, I was tongue-tied in his presence. Still, I could watch him and listen to him. His conversation, with its sudden drops in the voice, its strong stress accents, its variations of tone and its unfinished sentences was unlike anyone else's. There was something theatrical about the emphasis he put on certain words and there was also something one could call feminine, yet the mind behind this curious, wavering utterance was exceptionally clear and well ordered. Only the mood was unpredictable. Lytton talked in a great variety of styles – gentle and persuasive with those he liked, calm and dispassionate when engaged in discussion, fantastic or melodramatic if in high spirits, cryptic or cynical in moments of pessimism. And he was often silent. But the overriding impression that I got from listening to him was of his maturity.

This could in part be accounted for by his delicate health, which had given him leisure for reading and reflecting, as well as by his saturation in seventeenth- and eighteenth-century French literature. From these he had acquired a good judgement, a strong vein of scepticism and a distaste for dogmatic opinions. He had no patience with those who saw the world in sharply contrasting colours. His bent was for psychological interpretations rather than for moral ones – indeed one might cite him as an illustration of what Pascal calls *esprit de finesse*. Thus there was subtlety and discrimination in his conversation, as well as sometimes a hesitation to commit himself, which I find blunted in his books, chiefly because he was not a spontaneous writer. For this reason his rather set and formal paragraphs, which were composed in his head before he began to write and never altered afterwards, fail to take on the colour of his mind. He defended his use of clichés, but too many of these give a book a mechanical air.

Yet there was, I would say, one serious limitation to Lytton's mind. He was so strongly imbued with the views of Gibbon and Voltaire that he could not come to any kind of terms with historical Christianity, but regarded it as an unpleasant and monstrous superstition and nothing else. This meant that when he read Donne or Blake he was unable to enter sympathetically into what they said or find in his own mind an equivalent for their religious feelings and idiom. Although he admired them, he could only do so by separating the content of their verse from 'the poetry'. Thus he was in the same position as those Greek philosophers who accused Homer of having taught false and evil doctrines when he had represented the Gods as having human faces and passions. Lacking, as their age did, a sense for history, these men could not see that Homer's anthropomorphism had been a victory over the faceless and terror-striking *numina* of the Mediterranean peasants and thus a powerful contribution to the rise of Greek humanism. But Lytton lived in a history-conscious age and was himself a historian. Yet he had imprisoned himself so rigidly and dogmatically in the rationalism of the eighteenth century that he was unable to make the imaginative effort necessary to take over temporarily the mode of feeling of a poet who wrote out of his religious convictions. All religion was to him pernicious nonsense so that when *The Waste Land* and *Ash-Wednesday* came out he could find nothing to admire in them.

But I can see that in my brief sketch of Lytton's character I have failed to give a picture of what he was like to meet. His charm when he felt attracted to anyone, his aloofness when he was not, his long silences, his gift for intimacy with chosen people, his love of rhetorical exaggeration and melodrama, his irritability when he was not well, his gentleness at other times, his wit which one had to listen for, his mature judgement, his knowledge of the world and of the heart – all these elude description. Enclosing those perpetually changing and varying things, his moods, there was a definite face and voice and style of speech and gesture that fix and pin down one's impressions and which nothing but an album of snapshots and a recording of his conversation can suggest. I can therefore only say that, in spite of his having a core of clear and definite beliefs and a well-ordered mind, he was, in Montaigne's phrase, a man of *diverse et ondoyant* constitution. . . .

My friends at this time were for the most part Oxford or Cambridge men and they were all of them a good deal better off financially than I was. The older generation had got what were called first-class minds, lucid, reliable and orderly, whereas I had a vague and intermittent one which only became articulate in flashes. I was never able to join in discussions on abstract or philosophic subjects although I could follow them, and generally talked my best with women, whose style of conversation on the whole I preferred. Yet I must have been able to hold my own sometimes, for I was still

seeing a certain amount of Leonard and Virginia Woolf and was getting to know Roger Fry pretty well, though this last association was
due to my close friendship with Helen Anrep, who left her husband
Boris that spring and settled down with Roger in a house in Guilford
Street.

My diary does not give much space to Bloomsbury parties or
conversaziones, but here is a brief account of one which I will quote:

Jan 28 [1926]   At 10 a small party at Angus Davidson's for conversation.
Virginia, Vanessa, Julia Strachey, Mme Raverat, Edith Sitwell and one
foreigner: the rest men, for it is not easy to put women in a room with
the Stephen sisters. Lytton and his young man Philip Ritchie, Leonard
Woolf, Duncan Grant, James and Oliver Strachey, Raymond Mortimer
and one or two others. It was amusing. Virginia leaning stiffly sideways
attacked the painters: how fantastic they were, how only the smallest details
interested them, how they argued about everything. Vanessa and Duncan
will talk for an hour on end simply on a cat. 'Only three legs!' 'Yes, and
a white spot on its tail.' 'I'm sure I don't know how it catches mice.'
'But it doesn't.' 'Oh, but I've seen it.' 'You're quite wrong about that,
Duncan!'

   Wherever Virginia goes she undoes a knot like a Lapland witch and
lets out a war: an old well-practised war, whose tactics have been polished
up by many previous encounters. If it is not the Older Generation v. the
Younger, it is Writers v. Painters or even Men v. Women. It is these well-
worn topics that produce the most brilliant and fantastic conversation that
one can hear anywhere in England.

Another member of Bloomsbury of whom I had seen a certain
amount up to now was E.M. Forster or, as his friends called him,
Morgan. He was a dry, friendly little man, rather ordinary and insignificant at first sight, with a spinsterish manner which came from
his having been brought up at Weybridge by two maiden aunts. If
it was difficult to see his distinction, that perhaps was because he
was more interested in listening to and sizing up other people than
in expressing his own views, which would only appear in some ob-
lique comment. I had read *Howards End* and had not liked it. Then
– it must have been in 1924 – he gave me a copy of *A Passage to
India* and later came round to my rooms to ask if I had liked it.
I had not and felt obliged to say so, with the consequence that I
have not seen him since. Today I have changed my mind about this
book, which seems to me a masterly production, conveying all the

ambiguities which lie in the Indian mind and their clash with English moral positivism as well as Forster's own uncertain and enigmatic views about the Universe. How I can have been so stupid not to see this at once I do not know. All I can say in my excuse is that in those days I was too much glued to the notion of concrete and vivid expression to appreciate a novel written in a quiet tone on a sociogiocal theme.

Morgan's letters, of which I received about a dozen, are characteristic. They are written in a rather mannered style with odd turns of phrase which bring out the elusive and elfish side of his nature. Like his conversation they are dry with now and then little sharp, deflating points in them. When I first knew him his approach to people was impersonal and neutral – it was said because he had not yet faced up to his homosexuality. But this was to change and, according to Lytton Strachey, the increased bite and hardness of *A Passage to India* and its lack of sentimentality are due to his having meanwhile had a love affair with an Indian.

I was always divided in my loyalty to 'Bloomsbury', considered as a group. There could be no doubt about the high level of their intelligence, while their cult of good conversation made them very stimulating people to know. But I thought that Maynard Keynes' description of them as 'water spiders swimming gracefully on the surface of the stream' contained a good deal of truth. Civilized, liberal, agnostic or atheist like their parents before them, they had always stood too far above the life of their day, had been too little exposed to its rough-and-tumble to really belong to it. Thus, though they thought of themselves as new brooms and innovators, they quickly found they were playing the part of a literary establishment. What I chiefly got from them was their respect for the truth. Yet this – they gave the word a capital letter – was defined in a narrow and exclusive way so that anyone who held views that could not be justified rationally was regarded as a wilful cultivator of illusions and therefore as a person who could not be taken seriously. Religion in particular was anathema. The subject was finished, closed, or existed merely as a personal weakness or as a hangover from early associations, like not washing or continuing to play with dolls or tin soldiers. That psychological pressures could drive people to believe things that could not be proved rationally or scientifically was something that they refused to allow. Scepticism was a moral duty. They thus found themselves out of touch both with large areas of the world they lived in and with most of the past. For if history showed, as they thought, a slow progress from superstition to enlightenment, why bother to understand the impulse that drove people to religious belief, much less to communism or Nazism? By saying 'they're so stupid', they imagined that they had disposed of them.

This attitude was illustrated for me by their opinion of Joyce's *Ulysses*. Lytton dismissed it by saying that he could not find a single intelligent sentence in it. Virginia was more hesitant, yet disliked it for being vulgar and lower class. Morgan Forster attacked it as a book that covered the universe with filth and mud. Not one of my friends, except Arthur Waley, had a good word to say for it. Yet for me Joyce was, after Proust, the greatest novelist of the century and their incapacity to see any merit in him showed how conventional their minds were. They lived by good taste and I saw with regret that I was being carried along the same road and being obliged to live by it too.

What I also found lacking in these élite circles was the range and variety of human types which a painter or writer rubs shoulders with in a Bohemian or merely more open world. They all smelt of the University. They had been brain-washed and class-conditioned there. . . .

It was about this time [1928] that I got to know Desmond MacCarthy and his wife Molly. Desmond was the editor of *Life and Letters*, the chief literary magazine of the day, and he was also one of the original members of 'Bloomsbury'. As a literary critic he was sensible without being inspiring and I never saw in him any trace of those imaginative gifts which, according to Leonard Woolf, he had possessed at Cambridge. But then Leonard has always confused the brilliance of mind that counts at universities with those exploratory faculties that nourish literary talent. In my opinion Desmond simply did not have in him the stuff of a writer.

As a talker, however, it was very different, for his conversation was the most entrancing I have ever listened to. To begin with he always had the air of being completely relaxed and at ease in company. He could talk to anyone and, what was more difficult, make them talk back. He once told me that the reason for his being invited to political luncheons was that he was the only man in England who could draw out Mrs Baldwin. However that may be, shyness and constraint vanished from the room when he opened his mouth. He had a beautiful voice and his timing was perfect. Everything he said was adjusted to the capacities and interests of his audience. One listened and was charmed, without knowing exactly why, for he was discursive rather than witty and never rose to those flights of fancy which his future secretary Cyril Connolly is apt to break into. But Desmond had another string to his bow for, with Compton Mackenzie, he was the best raconteur I have ever heard. I shall never forget his account of a conversation he had overheard at his club between Yeats and that ultra-rationalist zoologist, Ray Lankester, in which Yeats had described his encounters with fairies. I have also heard him give imitations of Henry James's conversation which told one more about that novelist's circumlocutory style of writing and thinking and his neurotic terror of committing himself to a statement of fact than several volumes of criticism could do.

There is one other thing that I should like to say about him, because it has not always been recognized. He could be direct and forthright in expressing his opinions and had little tolerance for what he regarded as nonsense and pretentiousness in contemporary writing – and this included most *avant-garde* prose and poetry – but he was never malicious. When people talk as well as he did they do not have to amuse at the expense of other people's lives and characters.

Desmond's wife Molly was as delightful to meet as he was and I came in time to know her a good deal better. She was a plump, warm-hearted, motherly woman who lived in a cloud of vagueness and indecision, out of which she would emerge in short, erratic flights of wit and fancy which ended, like a hedge sparrow's song, suddenly. Her husband, as was the custom for social entertainers in those days, would accept invitations to lunch and dinner in which she was not included, but she did not appear to feel any resentment at this, perhaps because she was so diffident of her own capacities. Then she became deaf and wore a hearing aid which she would switch off when the conversation bored her. During the 'thirties my wife and I saw a good deal of her – that is, whenever we were in England – and we both became very attached to her. She was a better writer than her husband, for all his greater range of mind, and one of her books, *A Nineteenth Century Childhood*, is a little masterpiece. . . .

I had got to know Roger [Fry] pretty well over the past eight years and had become very attached to him. He was one of the pure – a man whose whole mind and soul were given to painting and to the arts in general. His selfless devotion to them, his uncompromising honesty, together with a strain of Quakerish austerity that was only contradicted by his love of French cooking, gave him something of the character of a saint. But unlike most saints he had an unusually open mind and, since the natural failing of the open-minded is gullibility, he was continually being taken in by the most extravagant and quackish of notions, much to the delight and amusement of his friends. He would believe it did not matter what absurdity, provided that an ingenious explanation could be given for it, because out of sheer excess of scepticism he felt drawn to any idea, the more paradoxical the better, that would demolish the conventional view. For him the charm of science lay in its being a chain of revolutionary subversion and discovery which proved that nothing was what it seemed. Virginia Woolf in her biography of him has given several examples of his credulity which I will not repeat.

Roger was also a man who lacked the faculty which enables one to understand other people's characters or to see into their minds, so that he needed the assistance of a woman's intuition to explain them to him. There had been altogether three principal women in his life – his wife, who had been languishing in a mental home for some thirty years, Vanessa Bell, with whom he had fallen in love in 1912 and never ceased to regard as a kind of oracle, and Helen Anrep, whose close friendship with me was my passport to him. He found her perverse, provoking, intriguingly feminine and admired her skill in cooking and house management as well as her social gifts. He was also deeply attached to Virginia Woolf, whom he regarded as a pure genius and therefore wayward and capricious in her judgements – a being who lived in a fantasy world of her own and was incapable of real contact with other people. This was the general Bloomsbury view of her, but her *Diary* has shown that it was wrong, for under the glittering and erratic surface of her conversation she was a woman of feeling and understanding, deeply devoted to her friends in spite of the malicious remarks she sometimes made about them. Roger was also drawn to Gamel [Woolsey Brenan, Gerald's wife] for her calm beauty and receptive mind, and it was from him that she learned to appreciate painting and to visit picture galleries whenever she had the opportunity.

I have never known anyone whose conversation I enjoyed more than Roger's. He was not a brilliant talker though he possessed a great range of knowledge and information which he could draw on with lucidity and accuracy, enunciating the words in a rich, persuasive voice full of gently ironical inflections. But his special gift lay in getting people to talk better than they were normally capable of doing. Every new idea excited him and, since he treated everyone present as being as intelligent as he was himself, he would seize on some chance remark made in the course of conversation and develop it so that it appeared more interesting than it had really been. This made him, especially for the young, the most stimulating of talkers and there was no subject on which he did not have something to say.

He had taken science both at his public school and at Cambridge and this training in the scientific method gave his mind a clarity and vigour which benefitted his art criticism. Till he began to write, painting had been judged in England mainly by its literary content, but he restored the primacy of purely pictorial values, although in the course of doing so he underrated the literary ones, which had always been stressed by the painters of the past, possibly because no language for expressing pictorial values had then been evolved. Thus he opened the way to abstract painting, of which however he did not approve because he believed that it could only lead to decoration and flatness of surface. Since in his view Cézanne was the greatest of modern painters, he drew the conclusion that the supreme aim of painting must lie in the realization of the third dimension in the picture space.

Roger Fry was also a superb lecturer. During the last years of his life he could hold large audiences. If there is such a widespread interest among English people in painting today, it is chiefly because he did so much to educate public opinion in it. His honesty was only equalled by his politeness. I have listened to him addressing the directors and patrons of a municipal art gallery and making the most devastating comments upon their recent acquisitions – all in the gentlest and most persuasive tone imaginable, which of course only irritated them the more and led to his making many enemies. Yet he did not really enjoy writing or lecturing on art. He undertook it as a duty imposed on him by his high conception of public service, for he thought of himself as a painter rather than as an art critic and was only completely happy when he was at work upon a canvas. It was the great disappointment of his life that his pictures were so little admired.

He never lost his interest in science and, since he had little time for reading books upon it, he liked to have friends who would keep him up to date about its latest discoveries. For this reason one often met Gerald Heard at his house. Heard had been, I believe, a secretary to the Irish poet George Russell (A.E.) and his wide knowledge of the latest scientific developments concealed a substratum of pseudo-mystical or Vedantic notions which in Roger's presence he kept to himself. I found him a rather negative person without any of that charm of conversation for which Irishmen are famous and besides quite sexless. But Roger would not have been aware of that: he liked men less for what they were than for the ideas they expressed. Other people one met at his house were Bertrand Russell, Arthur Waley, Aldous Huxley and Kenneth Clark – all top-rank minds – as well as his old Cambridge friend Goldsworthy Lowes Dickinson, or Goldie as he was always called, whose gentle, woolly high-mindedness and frequent quotations from Goethe I found trying.

I must not end this brief sketch of Roger Fry without mentioning his deep admiration for France and for everything French. This often led him to run down things that were English. I shared this prejudice with him, though less strongly, for at this time I preferred French prose writers to English ones and my favourite poets were Racine and Baudelaire. . . .

Peter Stansky and William Abrahams: A Bloomsbury Childhood

Though not observers of Bloomsbury themselves, Peter Stansky and William Abrahams have provided a revealing view of Bloomsbury by basing their account of Julian Bell's childhood on the recorded observations and recollections of those who knew Charleston. Stansky and Abrahams's description is from their dual biography of Julian Bell and John Cornford, both young English poets killed in the Spanish Civil War. In reviewing Journey to the Frontier, *Julian's brother Quentin noted how extraordinarily well the authors had been able to catch the brief lives of Bell and Cornford; he found only one fault with their treatment of Bloomsbury: 'It is a dangerous thing, and one of the few mistakes that these authors make, to treat Bloomsbury as a homogeneous entity. Indeed Clive Bell's* Civilization *is very nearly a summary of all that Julian Bell most detested' ('Brief Lives,' 698).*

Stansky and Abrahams's introduction and discussion of Julian's schooling have been omitted here.

'I stay myself – '
These are the opening words of Julian Bell's poem, 'Autobiography', which appeared in his second and, as it proved, his final volume, *Work for the Winter* (1936). The remark is characteristic of his strong sense of individuality: 'I stay myself – ' Yet at the same time he recognizes that he is also

> . . . the product made
> By several hundred English years,
> Of harried labourers underpaid,
> Of Venns who plied the parson's trade,
> Of regicides, of Clapham sects,
> Of high Victorian intellects,
>   Leslie, FitzJames.

This, of course, is the Stephen inheritance. And it is equally characteristic of Julian that he should acknowledge it with a kind of
sweeping inclusiveness: from the missionary austerities of the Clapham Sect to the violence of the regicides. We are dealing with something very different here from 'the enlightenment of Bloomsbury'.
His mother and his aunt might accept as just the praise accorded
their father, Sir Leslie; they would be less likely to respond to praise
for their uncle, Sir James Fitzjames Stephen, who, as a conservative
Utilitarian, had a decidedly more authoritarian cast of mind. Bloomsbury, with Lytton Strachey in the forefront, had attempted to discredit
at least the immediate past, while Julian, one might almost say, revels
in it, revels in it all. 'I stay myself, the product made . . .' On the
one hand there are 'high Victorian intellects'; on the other, 'not
among such honoured, marble names'

> That cavalry ruffian, Hodson of Hodson's Horse,
> Who helped take Delhi, murdered the Moguls . . .

He was 'At least a soldiering brigand' – a category for which Julian
would always entertain a certain fondness. 'There were worse,' he
goes on to say,

> Who built a country house from iron and coal:
> Hard-bitten capitalists, if on the whole
> They kept the general average of their class.

This, of course, is the Bell inheritance, his father's side, very different from the Stephens, representing a family which had made
its money in coal, and at whose large, ugly, Victorian country house,
at Seend in Wiltshire, the Clive Bells and their children spent some
vacations and Christmases. To his parents, Clive appeared a wild
radical and a dangerous advocate of a new aestheticism: thus they
interpreted the fame he had won as the author of such books as *Art*

and *Civilization*, as an exponent of the idea of 'significant form', and as a sponsor of the notorious exhibitions of Post-Impressionist painting which introduced Cézanne, Matisse and Picasso to England in the years before the First World War. But if he seemed a black sheep to his own family, to the Stephen side he seemed almost a little too conventional – in his 'huntin, shootin, fishin' interests, some of which he conveyed to his son, and in his comparatively conservative political views. Virginia Woolf, in a memoir of Julian written for Vanessa immediately after his death, felt he owed a great deal to the Bell inheritance. This differentiated him from her beloved Thoby, whose death, thirty years earlier, had had such a profound and lasting effect upon her. 'In fact Julian was much rougher, more impulsive, more vigorous than Thoby. He had a strong element of the Bell in him. What do I mean? I think I mean that he was practical and caustic and shrewd . . . He had much higher spirits. He was much more adapted to life. He was much less regularly beautiful to look at. But then he had a warmth, an impetuosity that the Stephens don't have.

This is to give the Bell inheritance its due. But it must be said that Julian's family, in its loyalties and intimacies, almost seemed to exclude the non-Stephen part of it. Clive did not completely fit into the Stephen inheritance of 'Clapham sects/Of high Victorian intellects', nor did Leonard Woolf. Clive and Leonard were certainly original progenitors of Bloomsbury, of undoubted brilliance and importance; nevertheless one feels the slightest sense of unease in their relationships with their wives, the Stephen sisters, who were, whatever its Cambridge intellectual masculine origins, the heart of Bloomsbury. If Clive was a little too much to the right in his political thinking, perhaps Leonard went a little too far in his interests in the practice of radical socialism. And if Clive's squire background did not exactly fit with the Stephen inheritance, neither did the London professional and mercantile background of the Woolfs. In her memoir of Julian, Mrs Woolf speaks of 'L's family complex which made him eager, no, on the alert, to criticize [the Bell] children because he thought I admired them more than his family'. But it seems not to have occurred to her that this preference of hers was almost certainly the case, and, more importantly, that there was a Stephen 'family complex', of mutual affection and admiration, that must have appeared formidable (as well as enviable) to an outsider.

The most important person in Julian's life, from its very beginning to its very end, was his mother, the gifted and beautiful Vanessa Bell. Theirs was a relationship without a break and without concealment: in it the full implications of Bloomsbury candour were taken to their limits, and the connection between mother and son never weakened. It was an extraordinary rapport which one cannot but admire, and impressive testimony to Bloomsbury's belief in personal relations. Yet in some ways the relationship was so perfect that it may have truncated others, provided a standard impossible to achieve elsewhere. The possibility will have to be considered in its place, many years later, in the history of Julian's grand and casual passions; here it can be disregarded.

From the first his mother took great pains with his upbringing, intending it to be as 'natural' and undogmatic as possible: he was not to be Victorianized, a miniature grown-up, seen but not heard, in a spotless pinafore. Yet for all their intellectual adventuresomeness, the Bells were still a well-to-do upper-middle-class family in the comfortable years before the First World War. There were maids, and a series of governesses – one of whom Julian got rid of by pushing into a ditch. And whatever they might think of religion 'upstairs', Julian found it impossible to escape completely the religion of his country 'downstairs' – although it would leave no permanent mark upon him. In a fragment of autobiography written shortly before going out to Spain, he remarks: 'I remember as independent ideas – more or less – a Darwinian argument with Mabel and Flossie – our nurses – which must have been very early – pre-war Gordon Square.' In other words, this memory dates from before Julian was six. 'Though obdurate I was secretly frightened of Jehovah, and even asked to be taught prayers. (Later, learning the Lord's Prayer, I used it as a magic defence against ghosts, and still do: or as a soporific.)' But religion was hardly very significant in Julian's life. Far more important was the education he received from his mother. He writes of this same pre-war time, 'The great liberating influence was the reading aloud by Nessa of elementary children's astronomies and geologies'. And there was a similar intellectual excitement when she read aloud to him a shortened translation of the *Odyssey*. Before he was able to read himself, he made Flossie read to him a school textbook of history. History, like astronomy, was a passion. 'There was also the famous occasion when Roger [Fry] demonstrated a home chemisty box, and brewed coal gas; Mabel was sent out and brought a clay pipe from a pub; it was tamped with plasticine, and, being cooked over the fire, eventually produced a jet of flame.' In 1916, when he was eight years old, he had what he called his 'first, definite, in-dependent idea. It was a solution of the desire for immortality. I worked out a possible cycle by which a human body would return through grass and sheep, into another human body.'[1] But it would be very misleading to give a picture of a male blue-stocking pondering his science, classics and history at a tender age. Rather, it would be more accurate to see him as an extremely adventurous, reckless child bounding from activity to activity, with his parents anxious to in-troduce him, through explanations and discussion, to the Blooms-bury dictum of rationality, which held that even irrational behaviour should be understood.

David Garnett, in a memoir of Julian, describes him as

a wilful child, swift and erratic in his movements; he looked at one from large eyes and planned devilment . . . Julian was shrill, sometimes noisy, always rather catlike and quick. My first row with him was when I found him standing, unconscious of evil-doing, on some vegetable marrow plants that he had trampled to pieces . . . He had in those days often to be ex-horted to reason, often to listen to tedious explanations about the con-sequences of his violent experiments. He flung newly-hatched ducklings into the pond and after they had raced ashore flung them in again and again until one or two were drowned. He was not punished as a child, but reasoned with: one saw on his face the lovely sulky look of a half-tame creature.[2]

And Mrs Woolf had a similar memory of about the same time – or when Julian was slightly older:

We were packing up the tea things. He took a bottle of water and smashed it. He stood there in his knickerbockers with long naked legs looking de-fiant and triumphant. He smashed the bottle completely. The water or milk spread over the path . . . He stood quite still smiling. I thought, This is the victorious male; now he feels himself the conqueror. It was a determined bold gesture, as though he wanted to express his own force and smiled at the consternation of the maids.

One should not make too much either of the enthusiasm for astron-omy and history, or of the mischief and high spirits, of a little boy,

1 Julian Bell, *Essays, Poems and Letters* (London, 1938), p.10
2 *Ibid.*, p.3

although it is of some interest that Julian himself should remember
the former, and those of his parents' generation the latter. Still, it
does not seem too fanciful to read into the division the first hints
of a theme that was to figure importantly in Julian's life, and in
the lives of many of his contemporaries: how to reconcile the conflicting demands of the life of the mind and the life of action.

The Bells made their home in Bloomsbury, but they were often in
the country, and Julian, in his attachment to the land, grew up much
more a child of the country than of the city – there would always
be something equivocal about his feelings for London; certainly they
did not go very deep. Whatever the attractiveness of Bloomsbury for
the grown-ups, the children found life more exciting and memorable
in the country: at Seend, the house of their Bell grandparents, and
at a variety of rented houses – Asheham, near Lewes in Sussex, rented
by the Woolfs from 1912 to 1918; Wissett in Suffolk, rented briefly
in 1916 by Duncan Grant; and finally, Charleston, a short distance
from Asheham, which the Bells began to rent in the autumn of 1916,
and was thereafter their place in the country. For Julian, as for his
brother Quentin, two years younger than he, and his sister Angelica,
born in 1918, Charleston meant childhood.

   In his poem 'Autobiography', he recalls 'the passage of those country years'. England was at war; and his, as he acknowledged, was
'a war-time boyhood'; but apart from this reference, the details he
chose to record (in the poem) were timeless, of

   . . . orchard trees run wild,
   West wind and rain, winters of holding mud,
   Wood fires in blue-bright frost and tingling blood,
   All brought to the sharp senses of a child.

These are the simplicities of a child's (and a poet's) world. For his
parents and their friends the War brought a more complex experience:
a true crisis of conscience. On the whole, Bloomsburyans, as we have
earlier suggested, tended to live at a certain aloof distance from the
world. (This attitude is not to be mistaken for unworldliness. If they
had little desire for luxury, or even the creature comforts, they did
not scorn the world in its more amiable, civilized aspect: civilization,
as they defined it, taking in the pleasures of food and wine and conversation. And Clive Bell was a great believer in *savoir vivre* and
savoir faire, with an English Francophile's conviction that living and

doing were done better across the Channel.) Apart from Keynes and Leonard Woolf, they were indifferent to the day-to-day or even the month-to-month practice of politics: the demands of the private life left one no time for that sort of public interest; one lived *au dessus de la mêlée*. The war changed all that – at least for the duration. After 1914, an attitude of aloofness became increasingly difficult to maintain, even untenable.

Maynard Keynes, Bloomsbury's authority on the subject, predicted a short war brought to an end by economic causes. This must have been some consolation in the beginning, for Bloomsbury was opposed to war in general ('the worst of the epidemic diseases which afflict mankind and the great genetrix of many of the others')[3] and to this war in particular. But Keynes's optimism was confounded by events. The war was prolonged from one year to the next, and it required increasing tough-mindedness to withstand popular pressure to conform to the war enthusiasm. Not unexpectedly, Bloomsbury, with its belief in the importance of the private life and private convictions, proved extremely good at this. But in 1916, for the first time in British history, conscription was introduced, and thereafter the men of Bloomsbury were compelled to make public their consciences: that is, to declare themselves Conscientious Objectors to military service.

As such they came to public attention. At Trinity College, Cambridge, for example, Bertrand Russell's lectureship was not renewed, and it is hard to avoid the impression that his unpopular pacifist opinions had something to do with the College's action. Lytton Strachey, called before the Hampstead Tribunal to prove his conscientious objections, made in passing his celebrated reply to the Military Representative ('What would you do, Mr Strachey, if you saw an Uhlan attempting to rape your sister?' 'I should try to interpose my own body') and he, like various other members of Bloomsbury, was ordered to do work of National Importance. He and Russell both sought refuge at the farm attached to Garsington Manor, the home of their friends Philip and Lady Ottoline Morrell, outside Oxford. Clive Bell was at Garsington also. A pacifist, who had argued in his pamphlet *Peace at Once* (1915) that 'the war ought to be brought to an end as quickly as possible by a negotiated peace', he was working on the land, under the provisions of the Military Service Act. And Duncan Grant and David Garnett (who earlier had been with a Friends'

---

3 David Garnett, *The Flowers of the Forest* (London, 1955), p. 1

Ambulance Unit in France) rented Wissett Lodge, outside a remote little village in Suffolk, where they meant to become fruit-farmers.

That summer (1916) Vanessa, with Julian, Quentin and the maid Blanche, came down from London to Wissett to keep house for Duncan and Bunny. The Lodge was 'a little early Victorian house with numerous small, exceptionally dark, rooms',[4] shadowed by an enormous ilex, which Julian and Quentin called 'the safety tree', for there, in its branches, they were safe from the grown-ups. Life went cheerfully at Wissett. Vanessa painted; the men worked hard in the orchard, kept bees, kept fowls – a large flock of white Leghorns: there were frequent visitors: Oliver and Lytton Strachey, Saxon Sydney-Turner, Lady Ottoline Morrell. For Julian it was a memorable time: 'orchard trees run wild, West wind and rain . . .' Long afterwards, with astonishing vividness, he recalled his first evening's fishing at Wissett,

> when I must have caught a couple of dozen roach . . . Bunny was fishing also: Clive advised me. They started to bite hard in the evening: that pond had never been fished before. I think my second was a big one – perhaps an eighth of a pound; impressive enough to a child. We filled a bucket, slimy fishy smelling; there is something extraordinarily sensual and thrilling about a fish's body in one's hand: the cold, the vigour and convulsive thumping, the odd smell, the gasping open mouth you jag the hook out of.

It was at Wissett too that he read Gardiner's *History of England from Henry VIII to the Corn Laws* ('God knows how much I understood'), and it was there that he first developed 'a passion for war and war games'.[5] The irony of this, a war-minded child in a conscientiously objecting household, needn't be insisted upon: Julian himself saw it as 'a reaction'. He knew, of course, that his family and their friends were COs: it explained 'the isolation, and later, at Charleston, the expectation of hostility'. The war game, which grew increasingly complex and took a variety of forms over the years, originated with Quentin, with Julian as an enthusiastic and inventive collaborator. In one version it was played on a board, moving counters about; in another, it was played 'life-size'. Perhaps its very beginning can be traced back to an afternoon when Bunny Garnett mounted fire-

---

4 *Ibid.*, p. 112
5 Julian Bell, *Essays, Poems and Letters*, pp. 11–13

crackers on shingles and sailed them across the pond. There was the normal desire of little boys to play soldiers, to re-enact historical battles ('the Armada . . . the Roman wall with oak-apple armies'), although, out of deference to the household, contemporary history was not drawn upon: the opposing sides were never English and German. What is remarkable about the war game is that the interest in it should have continued well beyond childhood, and that war and military strategy fascinated Julian until the day of his death.

The fruit-farming at Wissett proved unsatisfactory: it had been entered upon, at Keynes's suggestion, to ensure the two men exemption from military service. But the Appeals Tribunal, to which their cases were referred, 'declared that though the Wissett Lodge holding might qualify as work of national importance, it was out of the question for us' – we are quoting from Garnett – 'to be our own employers'. The solution appeared simple enough: to continue doing work of National Importance, that is, to continue farming, but on someone else's farm. So Wissett was abandoned. It was thought 'preferable', Garnett explains, 'to go back to the neighbourhood of Asheham, where Leonard and Virginia were living, and where Vanessa had pre-war acquaintances among the Sussex farmers, rather than to seek work in Suffolk'.[6]

Thus it was that the Bells came to Charleston.

Charleston was rented by the Bells in the autumn of 1916. Until 1918 they lived there without interruption, having given up Gordon Square; thereafter they divided their time between Charleston and London, and in the later 1920s, a house in France, at Cassis on the Mediterranean. But for Julian, Charleston came to represent childhood, holidays from school as he grew older, the long summers: it was the place in which he was most happy, the most loved of his homes.

Charleston, which is owned by Lord Gage of Firle Place, is at the end of a dirt road off the main Lewes-Eastbourne road, right beneath the looming green eminence of Firle Beacon, the highest point on the Sussex downs. At the turn of the century the house had been a simple country hotel, and many of the small, low-ceilinged rooms still retain porcelain number plates on their doors. There was an orchard, a walled garden, and, across the patch of lawn from the

6 David Garnett, *Flowers of the Forest*, p. 124

front door, a small pond – large enough, however, for naval engagements. There was also, fulfilling the immediate needs of the household, a farm near by, and there the conscientious objectors loyally carried on work of National Importance until 11 o'clock on the morning of 11th November, 1918.

In the first decade of the post-war period, Charleston became the centre of what Quentin Bell calls 'Bloomsbury-by-the-Sea'. It was a triangular outpost, populated by the Charlestonians (the Bells and their frequent visitors, such as Duncan Grant and Roger Fry), the Tiltonians (Maynard and Lydia Keynes, who took up residence at Tilton on a branch of the dirt road leading to Charleston) and the Rodmellians (Leonard and Virginia Woolf, who moved from Asheham to Monk's House at Rodmell, on the other side of Lewes). The house, rambling in its construction and haphazard-seeming in its additions and out-buildings, was full of many oddly placed and sized rooms (not a disadvantage) and provided (apart from the usual bedrooms, sitting-rooms and a dining-room with an immense fireplace) a library for Clive Bell, and studios for Vanessa Bell and Duncan Grant, who, when they were not busy painting canvases, were painting walls, bedsteads, cupboards, tables, chairs, plates and almost any other flat surface they could find. The result of their industry was to give the house a colour and a magic (in its unexpectedness) that is unlike anything else: one has no sense, nor is one meant to have, of the self-conscious work of art, as in the Peacock Room of Whistler, or even, perhaps, in the rooms at Kelmscott. The children found the house, its grounds, and the surrounding countryside a perfect place for endless activity: for adventures, walks, war games, butterfly hunting, capture of animals – when older, shooting of birds – and noise: so much noise that poor Clive Bell, in desperation, built himself a little study apart from the house, in which he hoped to gain some quiet.

The children, along with the grown-ups, were at the centre of life at Charleston: that is its immediately distinguishing quality. They were not put to one side, categorized, or patronized, taken up enthusiastically and unceremoniously let down. That this did not happen is a tribute in part to their own charm, which appears to have been considerable, and even more to the character of the grown-ups, who had not only the ability to love children, but also, which is rarer, the ability to respect and to sympathize with them, to educate and to entertain them. Of all the grown-ups, it was Vanessa, naturally, who came first in their affections; and after her, Aunt Virginia. Mrs Woolf's arrivals 'were a signal for rejoicing on the part of Julian and Quentin who had secrets to share with her. Thus she was always led aside and from the corner of the walled garden where they were ensconced came her clear hoot of laughter – like the mellow hoot of an owl – and Julian's loud explosions of merriment, protests and explanations.'[7] There were relationships of rare closeness, too, with Clive, Bunny, Duncan and Roger Fry. (Indeed, all that seems to have been lacking in this childhood was the presence of other children. When the Desmond MacCarthys came to visit, they would bring their daughter Rachel; one hears also, when Julian was eleven, of the daughter of a woman who was at Charleston to help in the house: with her, the daughter, Julian fenced and wrestled. But such encounters were the exception not the rule. On the whole, the children depended on each other, and the grown-ups, for company.)

Something of the spirit of Charleston can be glimpsed in the daily newspaper that Julian, the Editor, and Quentin, the Illustrator, put out quite regularly whenever they were in residence throughout the twenties, although one feels that in its later period it was carried on with more devotion by Quentin than by his elder brother. Only one copy was printed – i.e., typewritten – and it was handed round for the enjoyment and edification of its readers, usually at the lunch table. There were weather reports, nature notes, news of arrivals and departures ('Today Mr Raymond Mortimer arrived to the great joy of the family'), accounts of Duncan's difficulties in building an ornamental pool ('Grant's Folly'), Clive's search for peace, the foibles and adventures of the servants, with particular emphasis on the attraction of Grace, the housekeeper, for most of the male population of Lewes and the surrounding countryside. Mortality was not neglected ('We regret greatly the death of Marmaduke, the perroquet, who expired suddenly through unknown causes this afternoon. We fear he will be much missed'), daily events were chronicled ('Angelica triumphed again yesterday, she succeeded without difficulty to persuade Nessa to cut her hair short. Afterwards, she danced a triumphal "black-bottom" to celebrate her victory.') and there was even an occasional advertisement:

7 *Ibid.*, p. 161

The Life and Adventures of J. Bell by

VIRGINIA WOOLF
profusely illustrated by Quentin Bell, Esq.

Some press notices.

. . . a profound and moving piece of work
. . . psychological insight.
WESTERN DAILY NEWS

. . . superb illustrations . . . unwavering truth
. . . worthy of royal academy
. . . clearly the work of a pupil of Professor Tonks
ARTIST AND CRAFTSMAN

The paper, which began as the *Charleston Bulletin*, changed its name quite early in its history to the *New Bulletin*. It did not, however, until a later issue, state its credo: '"The Bulletin" is unique among daily papers in being controlled by no millionaire or political party. It is not perhaps unique in having no principles.'

The *New Bulletin* did not confine itself to the activites of the residents of Charleston and their visitors, but spread the circulation, and coverage, of its single copy to Tilton and Rodmell:

> The local countryside is now menaced by a new peril. Following Nessa's sensational purchase of a Renault the Woolves have purchased a Singer. And the denizens of Tilton are now the proud owners of a secondhand Morris Cowley. Whatever we may think of the problem of pedestrian traffic and the missuse [*sic*] of motor-cars, we must all agree that the car will be a great asset to the house and a permanent source of instruction and amusement to the rats in the duck shed [at Charleston, which was being used as a garage].

Towards Tilton, where the style of life was somewhat grander than at Charleston and Rodmell, the young Editor and Illustrator maintained an attitude of amused tolerance: 'We learn that Mr and Mrs Keynes are putting their chauffeur in livery. We remind our more absentminded readers that the Keynes arms are as follows: Innumerable £s rampant, numberless $$$ sinister in concentric circles *or*; Field

black. Crest St George Killing the Dragon.' Julian and Quentin were
quite aware of Keynes's importance in the world: hence the references
to Economic Consequences and Conferences that are slyly introduced
into accounts not only of the 'Squire and his lady', but of the major-
domo of the household, Harland, who assumes mythological pro-
portions in the paper as a drunkard, bore and unsuccessful suitor
for the favours of the alluring Grace. In 1925, while at Charleston
for Christmas, they recorded a pheasant shoot in Tilton wood:

> We have heard from certain sources that Mr Maynard Keynes and some
> of his business friends formed the party. From the same source we learn
> that the bag consisted of: 2 pheasants, 4 rabbits, a blackbird, a cow, 7
> beaters, 19 members of the party (including leaders, onlookers, etc.) and
> 1 dog (shot by mistake for a fox).

In the next number, along with the familiar teasing, there is a clear
reflection of Keynes's bitter and justified opposition to the return of
Britain to the Gold Standard:

> We learn that the story that the Keynes are at Tilton has now been fully
> authenticated. The reason they are not flying a flag to indicate that they
> are in residence (as, we believe, they intend to in future) is that the price
> of Union Jacks has risen owing to the introduction of the Gold standard,
> and only red flags are obtainable.

Towards the Rodmellians, Leonard and Virginia Woolf, the *New
Bulletin* was more benign, although it entertained a somewhat equivocal attitude towards their dog Grizel. (Tiltonian dogs, too, were
looked at askance: 'A stray mongrel, possibly the property of the Keynes's, appeared in the orchard this evening. If seen again it is to be
shot at sight and the remains returned to its presumed owners.') Perhaps Mrs Woolf appears most memorably in these pages as: 'The
Disappearing Aunt.' On 15th August 1925, the *New Bulletin* reported

> On Sunday the Woolves paid a visit to the Squire. Virginia, unable to
> face a Tilton tea with Harland in the offing, decided to walk over to Charle-
> ston. She was seen on the road by Angelica and Louie, and her voice is
> thought to have been heard by Duncan. She failed to appear at tea, how-
> ever, and did not afterwards return to Tilton. The most widely accredited
> theory is that she had a sudden inspiration and sat down on the way to
> compose a new novel.

The next day a sequel was given:

> Nessa and the Illustrator visited the Woolves this afternoon and found
> the disappearing aunt safe and sound. It appears that for some whim she
> decided to eat her tea under a hay stack instead of in Charleston dining
> room. The difference, however, is not great, and it is even possible that
> she mistook the one for the other.

Let this stand for what, in fact, it was: the charming world of the
private joke, the private reference, the intimacy and reassurance
within a closely-knit family, the glorious private world of childhood;
and let it also stand for the *badinage*, the chaffing, yet the deep sense
of intellectual and emotional community that existed among the
Bloomsbury family and friends – and most particularly at the very
nucleus, Virginia, Vanessa and the Bell children. It was in precisely
this spirit of playfulness and affection that Mrs Woolf, in the splendidly ironic Preface to *Orlando* (1928), acknowledged, along with a
galaxy of famous names, 'the singularly penetrating, if severe, criticism of my nephew Mr Julian Bell . . . my nephew Mr Quentin Bell
(an old and valued collaborator in fiction) . . . Miss Angelica Bell,
for a service which none but she could have rendered'.

Ann Synge: Childhood on the Edge of Bloomsbury

Ann Synge was the daughter of Adrian Stephen and Karin Costelloe,
whose mother, Mary Pearsall Smith, later married Bernard Berenson,
and whose aunt was Bertrand Russell's first wife. (Karin's sister was
the feminist Ray Strachey, wife of Lytton's older brother Oliver.) Ad-
rian and Karin remained outside the inner circle of Bloomsbury, Leo-
nard Woolf later explained to Ann Synge, because 'the Bloomsbury
mandarins – Vanessa, Virginia, Lytton' – disapproved of the marriage
between the lethargic, resentful Adrian and the energetic, gregarious
*Karin (*Letters, *531).*

For one reason or another, the 'Bloomsbury Group' did not produce
many children. I suppose, though, that I was one of the few, being
the daughter of Adrian and Karin Stephen. What is more, we lived
in the heart of Bloomsbury, in No. 50 Gordon Square, with Clive
and his concubines upstairs and the formidable Lady Strachey and
several of her offspring, including Lytton, next door at No. 51. In

spite of all this, I did not feel that our family was really part of this distinguished fellowship. Indeed, it was hard to think of my family as an entity at all. Mother and father were so ill-assorted and so far away from us children that the only things we had in common were the house and the servants.

When I was about three, my sister Judith was born and my parents, who were in their thirties by then, began to study medicine with a view to becoming psychoanalysts. We children were entrusted to the care of a nurse, Daisy, the younger sister of my previous nurse and, indeed, the youngest of the seven Selwood sisters, several of whom were, at one time or another, in service with Bloomsbury families and their friends.

The study of medicine is a hard slog at the best of times, as I know from experience, but for my parents it must have been especially hard. For one thing, they did not want to be doctors, and so felt that the facts they were called upon to memorize and the inferences they were called upon to make had no relevance to their future work. For another, Ernest Jones, who was the virtual dictator of the psychoanalytical world in Britain, had accepted James and Alix Strachey for training as analysts without insisting that they take a medical qualification first. (Later, when my mother went to America, she found that being a doctor made so much difference to the way in which she was accepted that she felt the whole enterprise had been worthwhile. All the same, she never forgave Ernest Jones.) My parents' greatest handicap, however, was that mother was extremely deaf at that time and could not hear much of what was said at lectures, tutorials and ward rounds, so father had to explain it all to her afterwards. He was very patient though, and she exceptionally able, and at last they both qualified.

This very hardworking life was one of the reasons why father lost touch, to some extent, with his sisters and their husbands and friends, but, in any case, mother never really felt comfortable with them, nor they with her. Not only did they lose contact with father's former associates, but they failed to make contact with their own children. There is a lot to be said for the view, put forward by a family friend, that we were orphans from the beginning. Not altogether orphans, though, for I can remember having my hair curled in ringlets and being dressed in my best blue silk dress with the swansdown trimmings and being taken upstairs by Daisy for 'Dinner in the Diningroom' on Sundays. All the same, I do not remember this as a very joyful experience, even though it was a privilege Judith was not allowed to share because she was too little.

Until I went to boarding school at nine, Judith and I spent most of our time with the servants, listening to their gossip with Daisy's sisters and with the other servants and charwomen who worked in the neighbourhood of Gordon Square. In this way we heard a lot about our distinguished relations and neighbours, in whom the servants took a proprietary interest and pride. Even so, they were always rather nebulous and awe-inspiring characters to me, in spite of the fact that they were often to be seen walking about in the Square or sitting and talking on the benches.

From time to time, especially in the summer, we were sent away with Daisy to stay in the country, usually to Mud House, the home of our cousins Barbara and Christopher Strachey (their mother, Ray, was our mother's sister). We also went to Chilling, the summer home of Aunty Loo (Alys Russell) and Uncle Logan (Pearsall Smith), where we would be shown off to our grandmother (Mary Berenson) on her annual visit to England from Italy. Occasionally, I believe, we went to Charleston, but I have only the faintest recollection of it. I do remember, though, that I envied our cousins and the other children to whose houses we went for tea parties and the like, because their mothers took so much more notice of them than ours did, making cakes and clothes, reading stories and playing games. One didn't expect much from fathers, and I think I was rather afraid of mine. Certainly I was scared of the giants who appear in story books and my father was exceptionally tall. He was, however, prepared to play 'Be-a-wizard-be-a-lizard'. We shouted 'Be a wizard' and he stretched himself up to his full height, shrieking spells, but, when this became too terrifying, we had only to shout 'Be a lizard' and he would become a humble and pathetic reptile.

John Lehmann: Working for the Hogarth Press

The increasing success of the Hogarth Press a few years after its beginning in 1917 meant that Leonard and Virginia Woolf had to employ others to help them. (There are a number of memoirs by those who worked at the Hogarth Press in one capacity or another; the most irreverent is Richard Kennedy's illustrated account, A Boy at the Hogarth Press, *which describes the life of a gofer at the Press in 1928.) Ralph Partridge from Lytton Strachey's ménage à trois was one of the earliest assistants in 1920. He was succeeded by G.W.H.*

'Dadie' Rylands, whom Leonard Woolf described as 'by no means the least brilliant' (Downhill, 172). Next was Angus Davidson, who remained from 1924 to 1929. Finally, the most important of all, Julian Bell's Cambridge friend the poet John Lehmann joined the Press in 1931. Leonard Woolf later wrote how Lehmann 'helped us to bring into the Hogarth Press some of the best writers of his generation' (Downhill, 174). Lehmann stayed two years, then returned in 1938 as a partner, buying Virginia Woolf's share. After her death the arguments with Leonard increased; Lehmann then offered to purchase Leonard Woolf's interest in the Press, but Leonard sold out to Chatto and Windus instead.

John Lehmann has told the story of his involvement with the Press three times. The earliest accounts are in his autobiographies The Whispering Gallery *and* I Am My Brother, *from which excerpts have been reprinted here. Lehmann revised his autobiographies into one volume entitled* In My Own Time: Memoirs of a Literary Life *in 1969, and them, using additional letters from Leonard Woolf, published* Thrown to the Woolfs *in 1978. In this last version Lehmann disputes Leonard Woolf's interpretation of their disagreement in his autobiography,* The Journey Not the Arrival Matters.

Julian and I used to carry on endless discussions whenever we were together as well as by letter: walking along the Backs, in his room at King's or in mine overlooking the Great Court of Trinity. I lured him during the vacation to Fieldhead [Lehmann's home] and I visited him in return at Charleston. Life at Fieldhead in those days was not very formal, but nevertheless a sense of the formality of big country houses in Edwardian times still lingered about the softly carpeted corridors and the dining-room with its silver candlesticks on polished taables and its ring of onlooking family portraits; even though the occasions were rare when we dressed for dinner, and old James with his serio-comic grand manner and jingling keys was no longer there to carve the joint on the sideboard. The contrast of Charleston's bohemian atmosphere was an agreeable stimulus to me. I have always enjoyed being able to be the citizen of several worlds at the same time, and found a special pleasure a few years later in being accepted intimately in the working-class life of Vienna and the literary life of London. It amused me at this time to move between Charleston and Fieldhead and the even more traditional atmosphere of my sister Helen's comfortable home in Northamptonshire, from where I wrote to Julian: 'I'm here in the middle of the hunting country,' when I would sometimes find myself, inexplicably, discussing the merits of the various Hunts in the Southern Midlands with one of the grooms. There were no grooms touching their caps on the porch at Charleston, nor pink coats hanging up in the cupboards, and the discussion was about *The Nature of Beauty, Vision and Design* and *The Ego and the Id* rather than the way in which the Grafton or the Bicester was run by the latest MFH [Master of the Foxhounds] or the impact of rich American horsey enthusiasts on the ancient pattern of country life. The half-finished canvases by Duncan Grant, or Julian's mother Vanessa, or his brother Quentin piled carelessly in the studios, and the doors and fireplaces of the old farm-house transformed by decorations of fruit and flowers and opulent nudes by the same hands, the low square tables made of tiles fired in Roger Fry's Omega workshops, and the harmony created all through the house by the free, brightly coloured post-impressionist style that one encountered in everything from the huge breakfast cup one drank one's coffee from to the bedroom curtains that were drawn in the morning, not by a silent-footed valet or housemaid but by one's own hand to let in the Sussex sunshine, excited the suppressed painter that lurked in my breast. They seemed to suggest how easily life could be restored to a paradise of the senses if one simply ignored the conventions that still gripped one in the most absurd ways, clinging from a past that had been superseded in the minds of people of clear intelligence and unspoilt imagination. . . .

One morning I received a letter from Leonard, which informed me not only that he and Virginia liked my poems very much and wanted to publish them, but also that they had heard that I might be interested in working in the Hogarth Press, and would I come and discuss it with them? I wrote off triumphantly to Julian:

> I have heard from the Woolfs, and they say they will be glad to publish my poems. Bless them. I'm cheered, I don't mind saying. It won't be till the autumn – I'd rather it were the spring – but it scarcely matters, will be an admirable experience in patience for myself, and I'm grateful to have them published at all. I gather they are now being inspected by Lady G. Whether, if she disapproves of them, they'll publish them on their own, I know not. But I suppose having said they'll publish them, they will. Bear with my selfish pleasure.

'Lady G.' – Dorothy Wellesley (now the Duchess of Wellington), to whose patronage the series of Hogarth Living Poets owed its existence – announced her approval in spite of my fears. Gone at once were the rather sobering visions of a lifetime dedicated to etching and aquatint in the dusty recesses of the British Museum, banished forever the idea of following my uncles and cousins into the service of His Britannic Majesty, as I rushed off to see the Woolfs in 52 Tavistock Square at the beginning of January. Immediately I sent a report to Julian:

> I would have written to you before about your poems, if the end of last week had not been so hectic – interviews – consultations – calculations. I expect you know substantially what the offer of the Woolves was going to be: I was surprised when they made it to me – on Friday, at tea, when I met them both for the first time,and thought them most charming, Virginia very beautiful – and not a little excited. I've now decided I'm going to make every effort to accept the offer . . . I really can't imagine any work that would interest me more, and to be a partner with them, with a voice in what's to be published (and how) and what isn't – it seems an almost unbelievable stroke of luck.

The consultations and calculations continued intensively for the next few days. There were problems to be solved about raising the money, but I found my mother sympathetic in general and pleased to see me launched on something that I obviously cared about so much. Looking back on it now, it seems to me that everything was settled with astonishing speed, for only six days later I could announce to Julian:

> This week has been a fevered one – I emerge with an agreement in my pocket, by which I become Manager of the Hogarth Press in October – if not fired after eight months of apprenticeship. And I have the option of becoming a partner in a year or two. And I start in on Wednesday as ever is! Your advice was just what I wanted – very welcome. As a matter of fact Leonard had lost confidence in his first proposition even before my Trustee turned a dubious eye on it, so I think both parties feel better under the present agreement that we argued out in a series of interviews. I pray that I shall be a success: hard work, but congenial . . . and Leonard is giving me good holidays, long enough to get some writing done, I hope. But there's so much I want to say, that I can't say it all in a letter, and must wait till I see you. I was charmed by both Leonard and Virginia, and hope they liked me.

The year before, I had been staying in London with my sister Beatrix in St George's Square. Now I moved into the house in Heathcote

Street, just off the Gray's Inn Road, that was occupied by Douglas
Davidson, the painter, and his brother Angus, skilled translator from
the Italian and author of an excellent book on Edward Lear. There
the room which had previously been occupied by Dadie was made
over to me. The advantage of Heathcote Street was that it was only
a few minutes' walk from Tavistock Square. Every morning I set out
to reach the Woolfs' house at 9.15 AM., passing through a disused
graveyard filled with ancient tombstones of the seventeenth and eighteenth centuries, its half-effaced inscriptions and funeral ornaments
dappled with moss and lichen. The Burial Ground of St George-
the-Martyr had become a quiet garden, and some old people used
to sit there all day when the sun was shining: I would see the same
faces on my return after work as I had observed on my setting out.

At No 52 the Press occupied the basement, formerly the kitchen
and servants' quarters; a friendly firm of solicitors were installed on
the ground and first floors, while on the top two floors Leonard and
Virginia had their own living quarters. The basement was cold and
draughty and ramshackle. My own office, as apprentice manager, was
a small back room that had once been a pantry and cupboard room
– the cupboards were piled high with the dusty files of the activities
of the Press ever since it had started in 1917. It was badly in need
of redecorating, it had a jammed window that looked out on a narrow
outside passage and a gloomy wall, and a decrepit gas-fire in front
of which Leonard would attempt, without any striking success, to
warm his hands when he came in to see me the day's correspondence
soon after my arrival. My mother was appalled when she first visited
me there; but to me nevertheless it was sacred ground. I was at last
part of a publishing firm, and the one that seemed to me the most
glamorous of all; I was associated every day with the – to me – the
legendary Leonard and Virginia Woolf; in the former scullery up
the passage an actual printing-machine was installed, with its trays
of type beside it, and there on many an afternoon Leonard could
be found rolling off the firm's stationery, writing paper, invoices,
royalty forms and review slips; while every now and then Virginia
herself could be glimpsed setting the type for one of the small books
of poetry that the Press still produced at home – at that time it was,
I think, Vita Sackville-West's *Sissinghurst* – in spite of the fact that
it had grown into a large business dealing with many of the biggest
printers and binders. All round me, in all the rooms and down the
dark corridors, were the piled packages of finished books as delivered
from the binders. It gave me a special pleasure to explore among

them, noting on the labels the names of books that were already precious to me, such as Virginia's *Monday or Tuesday* (not many of these) and *To the Lighthouse* in their original editions, and occasionally coming across a single, opened package of some early publication that had long been famous, Ivan Bunin's *The Gentleman from San Franciso*, or E.M. Forster's *Pharos and Phaillon*, or *The Notebooks of Anton Chekhov*, though not, alas, Katherine Mansfield's *The Prelude* or T.S. Eliot's *The Waste Land*, long out of print but tantalizing advertised at the back of some of the other books. And I persuaded Leonard to allow me to make a collection of the early hand-set volumes of poetry, all different shapes and sizes in their prettily decorated paper covers, John Crowe Ransom's *Grace After Meat*, Herbert Read's *Mutations of the Phoenix*, Robert Grave's *Mockbeggar Hall*, curiosities such as Clive Bell's *Poems* and Nancy Cunard's *Parallax*, and many others, of which I can think of one instance, Fredegond Shove's *Daybreak*, unjustly forgotten today. By far the largest piles were in the studio room at the back where (as I have described elsewhere) Virginia has her work-desk; and I would slip in, with carefully controlled eagerness and as silently as possible, to hunt out some books that were suddenly needed on the packing-table in the front room, feeling that I was entering the holiest part of the house, the inmost ark of its presiding deity. I was even allowed, later, to work at the desk when they were both away.

No one could have been a kinder or more sympathetic teacher than Leonard. There was no nonsense of formal 'business relations' in the Press, and he would explain to me how to prepare estimates and contracts (on his own highly individual patterns), how to design a book-page and an advertisement and how to organize the flow of books to the shops, with steady patience and an assumption of intimate interest in everything we published. He described the authors, the printers' and paper-makers' travellers and all the other people with whom I was to have to deal, including the persistent and unsnubbable bores, at length and with characteristically caustic comment. The absurd conventions of the trade, the prejudices of certain important booksellers and reviewers, the inexplicably chancy ups and downs of success and failure in the fortunes of books, would rouse him at all times to exasperated and withering wit; and it was due to his teaching that I learnt early on to face with a certain detached philosophy the irrational behaviour that almost everyone who has to do with books is so frequently capable of. In fact I learnt the essentials of publishing in the most agreeable way possible: from a

man who had created his own business, had never allowed it to grow
so big that it fell into departments sealed off from one another, and
who saw it all as much from the point of view of an author and
amateur printer as of someone who had to make his living by it.
If Leonard had a fault, it was in allowing detail to loom too large
at times. A small item that could not be accounted for in the books,
a misunderstanding about a point of production would, without apparent reason, irritate him suddenly to the extreme, he would worry
it like a dog worrying a rat, until indeed he seemed to be the rat
and the detail the dog; and betray, I felt after one or two such experiences, the long nervous tension he had lived under in caring so
devotedly for the genius of his wife.

My relations with Virginia began with an ardent youthful hero-
worship; but gradually, as I got to know her better, this turned into
a feeling of real affection as well as respect. At first she was irradiated
in my eyes with the halo of having written *Jacob's Room*, *To the
Lighthouse* and *Mrs Dalloway*. No other books seemed to me to express with anything like the same penetration and beauty the sensibility of our age; it was not merely the conception that underlay
those works, of time and sorrow and human longing, but also the
way she expressed it, the paramount importance in her writing of
technical change and experiment; almost everything else seemed, after
I had read them, utterly wide of the target and inadequately aware
of what was needed. I was influenced, of course, as a poet, by the
skill with which she managed to transform the material of poetry
into the prose-form of the novel; but that in itself seemed to me one
of the major artistic problems of our time, arising out of the terror
and tension, the phantasmagoria of modern life. I devoured the three
novels again and again, and always with fresh delight, valuing them
far higher than *The Common Reader*, *A Room of One's Own*,
Orlando and even *Flush*, which, much as I enjoyed them and popular
as they were, seemed to me of far less significance. In those early
days I revered Virginia as the sacred centre, the most gifted and adored
(and sometimes feared) of the Bloomsbury circle. But, as time went
on, the feeling she inspired in me was more one of happy release
than of reverence. I found her the most enchanting of friends, full
of sympathy and understanding for my own personal problems and
the problems I was up against in my job, with an intense curiosity
about my own life and the lives of my friends in my generation (many
of whom were, of course, known and even related to her). She liked
to hear all about what we wanted to do in poetry, in painting, in

novel-writing. She would stimulate me to talk, she had an unique gift for encouraging one to be indiscreet, and would listen with absorption and occasionally intersperse pointed and witty comments. Some of the happiest times I can remember in those years were the luncheons and teas I would be invited up to in the Woolfs' part of the house, where the walls were painted with frescoes by Duncan Grant and Virginia's sister Vanessa Bell, discussing the plans of the Press, the books submitted to us, and all the histories and personalities involved. She was always bubbling with ideas, longing to launch new schemes and produced books that no one had thought of before, that would startle the conventional business minds of the book world. She found an all-too-ready response in me, and had sometimes quietly to be checked on the rein by Leonard.

There were days, however, when she seemed withdrawn behind a veil, and it was hard to draw out her interest in the activities of the Press or ignite the gaiety which at other times was so characteristic of her. Sometimes this veil concealed her preoccupation with the problems of whatever she was writing at the momenmt; at other times it was darker and more opaque, bringing an uneasy atmosphere of strain and misery to the house. It is not for me to explain or explore the moods of fathomless melancholy that overcame Virginia Woolf at various periods during her life, and nearly always began with a series of acute headaches; I can only record the anxiety and distress they caused me for her own sake and for Leonard, who had fought them with her for so long, and my wonder that she managed to achieve so much with that perpetual threat hanging over her, always dropping nearer when she was in the throes of her finest creative achievement.

One of the worst of these fits of melancholy attacked her in the last stages of her work on *The Waves,* and Leonard decided that she must abandon it altogether for a time. The crisis passed, and she was able to get the book, to me the most daring if not the most successful of all her experiments, ready for press in the late summer. I could hardly contain my impatience to read it; it was for me the great event of the year, even though my own first book of poems was coming out in September. At last, at the beginning of the month, the advance copies arrived, just after I had spent a week-end with her and Leonard at Rodmell, and in writing to thank her I mentioned that I was in the middle of reading it. She immediately sent me a note insisting that I should write down for her exactly what I thought about it. I was deeply stirred by the book, and wrote her a long letter in which I tried, no doubt naively, to describe the impression it had made on me. In the same letter, I suggested that it was high time for her to define her views about modern poetry, which we had discussed so often together. I received the following letter in reply, dated 17th September:

Dear John,

I'm most grateful to you for your letter. It made me happy all yesterday. I had become firmly convinced that *The Waves* was a failure, in the sense that it wouldn't convey anything to anybody. And now you've been so perceptive, and gone so much further and deeper in understanding my drift than I thought possible that I'm immensely relieved. Not that I expect many such readers. And I'm rather dismayed to hear we've printed 7,000: for I'm sure 3,000 will feed all appetites; and then the other 4 will sit round me like decaying corpses for ever in the studio (I cleared up the table – for you, not the corpses). I agree that it's very difficult – bristling with horrors, though I've never worked so hard as I did here, to smooth them out. But it was, I think, a difficult attempt – I wanted to eliminate all detail; all fact; and analysis; and myself; and yet not be frigid and rhetorical; and not monotonous (which I am) and to keep the swiftness of prose and yet strike one or two sparks, and not write poetical, but purebred prose, and keep the elements of character; and yet that there should be many characters and only one; and also an infinity, a background behind – well, I admit I was biting off too much.

But enough, as the poets say. If I live another 50 years I think I shall put this method to some use, but as in 50 years I shall be under the pond, with the goldfish swimming over me, I daresay these vast ambitions are a little foolish, and will ruin the press. That reminds me – I think your idea of a Letter most brilliant – 'To a Young Poet' – because I'm seething with immature and ill considered and wild and annoying ideas about prose and poetry. So lend me your name – (and let me sketch a character of you by way of frontispiece) – and then I'll pour forth all I can think of about you young, and we old, and novels – how damned they are – and poetry, how dead. But I must take a look into the subject, and you must reply, 'To an Old Novelist' – I must read Auden, whom I've not read, and Spender (his novel I swear I will tackle tonight). The whole subject is crying out for letters – flocks, volleys of them, from every side. Why not get Spender and Auden and Day Lewis to join? But you must go to Miss Belsher, and I must go to my luncheon.

This is only a scribble to say how grateful I am for your letter.

Yrs.
Virginia Woolf.

* * *

From time to time I went down to Rodmell, to discuss Hogarth affairs
with her and Leonard. In theory, I had bought Virginia out of the
Press, but in fact she continued to be as keenly interested in all its
activities as ever before, and every evening we would settle down in
the little sitting-room upstairs, where the shelves were filled with
books in Virginia's own binding and the tables and window-sills covered with the begonias, gloxinias and rare giant lilies that Leonard
raised in his greenhouses, and we would discuss books and authors
and the opportunities that were open to us in the new situation.
Leonard stretched out his feet towards the fire in his armchair on
one side, and puffed at his pipe; Virginia on the other lit another
home-rolled cigarette in her long holder. Occasional visitor though
I was, I had come to be very fond of Monk's House, the old village
cottage they had bought just after the First War and rebuilt to make
an ideal home for two authors to live and work in: I loved the untidy
warm, informal atmosphere of the house, with books and magazines
littered about the rooms, logs piled up by the fireplaces, painted furniture and low tables of tiles designed by the Bloomsbury artists,
and writing down in sunny, flower-filled, messy studios. A smell of
wood smoke and ripe apples lingered about it, mixed with the fainter
under-perfume of old bindings and old paper. We ate our meals always at the stove end of the long kitchen-scullery. I remember one
Autumn evening there, just after Leonard's book *Barbarians at the
Gate* had come out: I had been moved by the persuasive force of
the argument he developed, the lucidity of the style and the underlying warmth, and I told him so, and how important I felt his warning
was at a time when people were all too easily allowing themselves
to believe that any means were justified by the ends. Virginia was
splashing gravy in large dollops over my plate as I talked, and joined
in with her praise. 'You know, Leo, it's a wonderful book', while
Leonard himself sat in modest silence, with lowered eyes, like a
schoolboy praised by the headmaster at an end-of-term prize-giving.

During those months Virginia alternated between cautious confidence and weary depression about the Roger Fry biography, very
much as she always did when at work on a new book; but sometimes
the depression seemed so deep that both Leonard and I encouraged
her to leave it for a while, to put down on paper her objections
to my generation of writers, and to prepare a third *Common Reader*
collection of essays; the idea of a change nearly always lightened her
mood. When *Roger Fry* was finished, however, just before Christmas,
she was transformed: radiant and buoyant, full of teasing malice and

the keenest interest in what her friends were doing, and finding a
startling new beauty in London – the squares and side-streets in the
black-out on a clear night – a transfigured look in the faces of the
men and women she passed – the smartness of uniforms of every
sort.

Stephen Spender: Bloomsbury in the Thirties

*Stephen Spender's observations of Bloomsbury are from the point of
view of a young poet in the thirties. The Hogarth Press (Spender's
story of its being founded on sweepstake winnings is fanciful) published anthologies of poetry in the early thirties that brought to public
attention the work of Spender, W.H. Auden, C. Day Lewis, William
Plomer, John Lehmann, William Empson, and others, including Julian Bell. Several of those socially conscious poets, as Spender describes
them, were critical of the politics and snobbery of some members of
Bloomsbury, and some in Bloomsbury – especially Virginia Woolf
– were in their turn critical of the literary implications of these poets'
social consciences. There was, nevertheless, a considerable sympathy
between the older and younger generations, as is shown not just in
Spenders's recollections, but in Lehmann's and Plomer's too (see pp.
383–92 and 403–9). (There are allusions in Spender's recollections to
F.R. Leavis's periodical* Scrutiny *and Roy Campbell's satirical poem*
The Georgiad.)*

. . . In this century, generation succeeds generation with a rapidity
which parallels the development of events. The Georgian poets were
a pre-1914 generation. The War of 1914–18 produced a generation
of War Poets, many of whom were either killed by the War or unable
to develop beyond it. The 1920s were a generation to themselves. We
were the 1930s.

Rather apart from both the 1920s and the 1930s, was the group
of writers and artists labelled 'Bloomsbury'. Bloomsbury has been
derided by some people and has attracted the snobbish admiration
of others: but I think it was the most constructive and creative influence on English taste between the two Wars.

The label 'Bloomsbury' was applied to people more by others than
by themselves. Nevertheless if one examines the reasons for regarding
Bloomsbury as a serious tendency, if not as a self-conscious movement,
the label is meaningful.

The names most usually associated with Bloomsbury are Virginia Woolf, Roger Fry, Lytton Strachey, Clive Bell, Vanessa Bell, Duncan Grant, Raymond Mortimer, and perhaps David Garnett. E.M. Forster and T.S. Eliot are associated with it rather than 'belonging' to it, if 'belonging' may be said of a free association of people with similar tastes and talents.

Bloomsbury represented a meeting of certain influences and an adoption of certain attitudes which became almost a cult.

Not to regard the French impressionist and post-impressionist painters as sacrosanct, not to be an agnostic and in politics a Liberal with Socialist leanings, was to put oneself outside Bloomsbury. For this reason Eliot was too dogmatic in religion and too Conservative in politics to fit in. It is more difficult to say why Forster does not quite fit. He was perhaps too impish, too mystical, too moralizing.

But the positive qualities of Bloomsbury were shared not only by Forster and Eliot, but by nearly all the best talent of this period. Roger Fry, Lytton Strachey and T.S. Eliot, in their different ways, introduced the influences of French impressionism, French prose, and in poetry the French symbolists. All these writers were pre-occupied with re-examining and restating the principles and aims of art and criticism. They were interested in experiment, and were amongst the first to discuss and defend James Joyce and Proust. Their attitude towards an easy-going conventionality masquerading as traditionalism was critical: at the same time, they were deeply concerned with traditional values which they studied and restated with a vigour which made the old often have the force of the revolutionary. They insisted on the necessity of expressing past values in the imagery and idiom of today.

Most of these writers had begun writing before 1914, though they did not become widely known until after the War. They had sympathized with pacifism. Leonard Woolf, an intellectual Socialist who was at heart a Liberal, Maynard Keynes, the economist who denounced the Treaty of Versailles, Bertrand Russell and Harold Nicolson, were amongst their friends and colleagues who discussed politics, economics, philosophy, history and literature with them. In this way Bloomsbury was like the last kick of an enlightened aristocratic tradition. Its purism was founded on a wide interest in ideas and knowledge of affairs. Reading the essays of Lytton Strachey, Virginia Woolf, Clive Bell, Raymond Mortimer, and even Forster, one sees how inevitably they interested themselves in the eighteenth-century French salons and the English Whig aristocrats.

Like a watered-down aristocracy they made moderate but distinct claims on society. They were individualists who asked for themselves (and usually by their own efforts, from themselves) the independence in which to do their best work, leisure for reading, and pleasure. In order to produce a few works which seem likely to live, and a great many witty, intelligent and graceful conversation pieces, they needed to nourish themselves on a diet of the arts, learning, amusement, travel, and good living. They certainly were not malicious exploiters of their fellow men, and they expected less reward than the bureaucratically favoured Soviet writer receives today. At the same time, their standard of 'five hundred pounds a year and a room of one's own' (Virginia Woolf's formula in a well-known essay) made them decidedly unwilling to sacrifice their independence to the cause of the working-class struggle. They were class-conscious, conscious even of a social gulf which divided them from one of their most talented contemporaries – D.H. Lawrence, the miner's son. Despite their Leftist sympathies the atmosphere of Bloomsbury was nevertheless snobbish. They were tolerant in their attitude towards sexual morals, scrupulous in their personal relationships with each other.

To them there was something barbarous about our generation. It seemed that with us the thin wall which surrounded their little situation of independence and which enabled them to retain their air of being the last of the Romans had broken down. A new generation had arisen which proclaimed that bourgeois civilization was at an end, and which assumed the certainty of revolution, which took sides and which was exposed even within its art to the flooding-in of outside public events, which cared but little for style and knew nothing of Paris. . . .

Strachey, with his long russet-brown beard and his high, squeaky voice, was certainly the most astonishing of the Bloomsbury group. He combined strikingly their gaiety with their intermittent chilliness. Sometimes he would play childish games such as 'Up Jenkins', which we played one Christmas. Often he would gossip brilliantly and maliciously. At times there was something insidious about his giggling manner; at times he would sit in his chair without saying a word. He was delicate and hypochondriacal. Wogan Philipps, who was given to Celtic exaggeration, told me once that Strachey had an arrangement by which the wires of his bed under the mattress were electrically heated: so that lying in bed he was agreeably grilled all night long.

Thus I began to enter into this civilized world of people who lived in country houses, pleasantly modernized, with walls covered with areas of pale green, egg-shell blue, or pale pink distempering, upon which were hung their paintings and drawings of the modern French school, and a Roger Fry, Vanessa Bell, or Duncan Grant. They had libraries and good food and wine. They discussed few topics outside literature, and they gossiped endlessly and entertainingly about their friends. In my mind these houses in the south and south-west of England, belonging to people who knew one another and who maintained approximately the same standards of living well, talking well, and believing passionately in their own kind of individualism, were connected by drives along roads which often went between hedges. At night the head-lamps would project a hundred yards in front of us an image of what looked like a luminous grotto made of crystal leaves, coloured agate or jade. This moved always in front of us on the leaves and branches. Delight in a vision familiar yet mysterious of this kind was the object of much of their painting, writing and conversation so that when we drove in the country at night, and I watched that moving brilliant core of light, I felt often that I was looking into the eyes of their sensibility. . . .

Sometimes I dined with Leonard and Virginia Woolf at their house in Tavistock Square. They lived in the upper half of this, the lower half being occupied by the offices of their publishing firm, the Hogarth Press. Their drawing-room was large, tall, pleasant, square-shaped, with rather large and simple furniture, giving, as I recollect it now, an impression of greys and greens. Painted panels by Duncan Grant and Vanessa Bell represented mandolins, fruit, and perhaps a view of the Mediterranean through an open window or a curtain drawn aside. These were painted thickly and opaquely in browns and terracottas, reds and pale blue, with a hatch work effect in the foreground with shadows of the folds of a curtain. These decorations were almost a hall-mark of Bloomsbury. Similar ones were to be found in the house of Lytton Strachey. They represented a fusion of Mediterranean release with a certain restraint and austerity. Looking at them, one recollected that Roger Fry was of a family of Quakers, and that Virginia Woolf was the daughter of Leslie Stephen.

When her guests arrived, Virginia Woolf would be perhaps nervous, preoccupied with serving out the drink. Her handshake and her smile of welcome would be a little distraught. Now when I recall her face it seems to me that there was something about the tension of the muscles over the fine bones of the skin which was like an instrument tautly strung. The greyish eyes had a sometimes limpid, sometimes

wandering, sometimes laughing, concentration or distracted-
ness.

When we had gone upstairs and had sat down to dinner, she would
say to William Plomer (we were often invited together): 'If you and
Stephen insist on talking about Bloomsbury, I shall label you "the
Maida Vale group".' 'Really,' Plomer said, raising his eyebrows and
laughing. 'I am not aware of having talked of Bloomsbury, but you
know how much one has to write these days . . .' Well then, if it's
not you, it's Stephen!' 'Oh, Stephen. How like him! But still, please
don't include him with me; I can assure you we are very different
kettles of fish! Still, I can imagine nothing more charming than an
essay by you, Virginia, on the Maida Vale group.' Then the conversation wandered a little. Perhaps the name of a critic who ran a small
literary magazine in which he had made a scurrilous attack on her
would be mentioned, and she would say aciduously: 'Why do you
mention that name? Surely we have more interesting things to discuss.' The uncomfortable moment passed and she answered, with a
warmer interest, someone's question whether adverse criticism annoyed her: 'Of course it annoys me for the moment. It is as though
someone broke a china vase I was fond of. But I forget about it afterwards.' Then another name was dropped into the conversation,
that of a poet, later to become a supporter of General Franco, who
had written a satire directed at two friends whose crime was that they
had lent him for an indefinite period of small house in their garden
where he might work. 'What ungrateful people writers are!' she said.
'They always bite the hand that feeds them'. She looked pensive. As
I write this it suddenly occurs to me, by the kind of intuition which
remembering things across a gulf of years brings in the very act of
writing, what she may have been thinking at that moment. For the
people who had been ungratefully attacked were the Nicolsons: and
her novel *Orlando* is a fantastic meditation on a portrait of Vita
Sackville-West; and in this novel there is an account of a poet who
comes to stay with Orlando, accepting his/her hospitality and then
writing a cruel satire on the visit.

Did she say that when she wrote *Orlando* she began writing the
first sentences without knowing how she would continue? Or am I
thinking of something else? How Julian Green told me that he wrote
his novels without in the least knowing how the story would develop?
Or how Vita Sackville-West, who owned the manuscript of *Orlando*,
showed me, written across the first page, a brief note explaining the
idea for a novel, whose hero-heroine should live for three hundred
years of English history, experiencing half-way through this life a

change of sex, from hero to heroine. The excitement with which she embarked straight from this note on to her voyage of three centuries of English history, is shown by the letter which she wrote to Vita Sackville-West the same day: 'I dipped my pen in the ink, and wrote these words, as if automatically, on a clean sheet: *Orlando: A Biography*. No sooner had I done this than my body was filled with rapture and my brain with ideas. I wrote rapidly till 12.'

In recalling Virginia Woolf there is something which causes my memory to become even more a kind of reverie than most of what I write here. It is necessary to remind myself that often she served the meal herself efficiently, and that she cooked it well. The dining-room was a lighter, perhaps more successful, room than the drawing-room. There was a pleasant table of painted wood, the work of her sister, Vanessa Bell, who also had designed the dishes. The pink blodges, small black dots, lines like brackets, characteristic of this style of decoration, were extremely successful on the creamy white surface of the china. Then Virginia described the beginning of the Hogarth Press, and at the age I then was, I listened like a child entranced. Her husband, Leonard Woolf, had won a prize in the Calcutta Sweepstake. With this they bought a printing press and some type, and in the house where they then lived at Richmond they had printed stories by Virginia herself and by Leonard Woolf, T.S. Eliot's *The Waste Land*, and several other small volumes. She described how they had done this with little thought except to please themselves, and then one book (I think it was her own *Kew Gardens*) had been well reviewed in the *Times Literary Supplement*. She described running downstairs and seeing the door-mat deep in letters bringing orders for more copies. They then had to farm out the printing of a second edition with a local printer: and hence they found that they had become, not amateur printers who sold their own work privately, but The Hogarth Press, a small but flourishing firm which even produced a few best-sellers.

From publishing the conversation turned to writing. She asked: 'How do you write, William?' 'How do I write?' 'Yes, what do you do when you write? Do you look out of the window? Do you write while you are walking in the street? Do you cross out a lot? Do you smoke when you are writing? Do you start by thinking of one phrase?'

When William and I had both been examined, we would ask her how she wrote. She came out with something like this:

I don't think there's any form in which the novel has to be written. My idea is to make use of every form and bring it within a unity which is that particular novel. There's no reason why a novel shouldn't be written partly in verse, partly in prose, and with scenes in it like those in a play. I would like to write a novel which is a fusion of poetry and dialogue as in a play. I would like to experiment with every form and bring it within the scope of the novel.

She said that no one should publish before he or she is thirty. 'Write till then, but scrap it or put it aside.' She herself had covered reams of paper with what she called 'just writing for the sake of writing', and she had scrapped it all. She said she believed that prose was more difficult to write than poetry.

Then after dinner we would go down to the drawing-room again, and Virginia would smoke a cheroot. There would be talk perhaps of politics, that is to say, of war. For Leonard and Virginia were among the very few people in England who had a profound understanding of the state of the world in the 1930s; Leonard, because he was a political thinker and historian with an almost fatalistic understanding of the consequences of actions. So that when, in 1934, I asked him whether he thought there would be a war he replied: 'Yes, of course. Because when the nations enter into an armaments race, as they are doing at present, no other end is possible. The arms have to be used before they become completely out of date.' Virginia had also a profound political insight, because the imaginative power which she shows in her novels, although it is concentrated often on small things – the light on the branches of the tree, a mark upon a whitewashed wall – nevertheless held at bay vast waters, madness, wars, destructive forces.

While Leonard was talking about war, labour, League of Nations, Virginia would fall silent. There was often after dinner this kind of political intermezzo. She had a little the air of letting the men talk: still more that of listening to Leonard.

The conversation passed from politics to gossip about personalities, quite possibly to Hugh Walpole. Now some stories seem so familiar to me that they have become inseparable from this life of literary London, as though it were woven out of them. For example, the story of how Hugh Walpole sat up all of one night reading an advance copy of Somerset Maugham's *Cakes and Ale,* to recognize himself in the cruel analysis of the career of the best-selling novelist.

Virginia had a passionate social curiosity, about the 'upper', the 'middle', and the 'lower' (I think these distinctions of class were sharply present in her mind). The Royal Family was a topic of intense interest to her. This preoccupation could be embarrassing – if one

is embarrassed by snobbishness. Yet her interest in royalty was largely
due to the fact that royalty, surrounded by an atmosphere of radiant
adoration as though bathed in a tank of lambent water, were peculiar
and exotic in precisely the way in which people are strange and luminous in her writing. The little episode in *Mrs Dalloway* where
a chauffeur extends a small disc to a policeman, and the car shoots
on ahead of the stopped traffic, exactly expresses like a minute phrase
in a descriptive symphony what fascinated her – the privileged special
life sealed off in the limousine whose driver had a pass. Indeed, her
Mrs Dalloways and Mrs Ramsays are by nature queens shut off from
other people who gaze at them with wonder, as through a window.
The wonder of life is a wonder of royal self-realization, which has
something akin to a gaping crowd staring at a lady dressed in ermine.
When she writes – in her essay in *The Common Reader* – of Dr Johnson, and Fanny Burney, and the Elizabethans – one is staring at exotic
fish swimming in their tank.

'Why are we so interested in them – they aren't so different from
us?' she would exclaim after the talk on the Royal Family had bordered almost on tedium. The answer was 'because they are held up
to our gaze', or 'because they are like a living museum of flesh and
blood dressed in the clothes of past history', or 'because after all,
their heredity does make them extraordinary'.

There was a division between her and other people which she attempted – not quite satisfactorily perhaps – to bridge by questions.
She enquired of everyone endlessly about his or her life: of writers
how and why they wrote, of a newly married young woman how
it felt to be a bride, of a bus conductor where he lived and when
he went home, of a charwoman how it felt to scrub floors. Her
strength and her limitations were that she didn't really know how
it felt to be someone else. What she did know was how it felt to
be alone, unique, isolated, and since to some extent this is part of
universal experience, to express this was to express what many feel.
But she was lacking in the sense of a solid communal life, divided
arbitrarily into separate bodies, which all nevertheless share. What
bound people together escaped her. What separated them was an object of wonder, delight and despair.

She seemed as detached from herself as from everyone else. Thus
she would talk about herself with an objectivity which was unambiguous in her but which in others would have seemed uneasy. She
was simply interested in the point she was making or the story she
was telling, and the fact that she herself might be deeply involved
in it seemed irrelevant. Once the conversation having turned to Ru-

pert Brooke, she said: 'He was very keen on living "the free life".
One day he said, "Let's go swimming, quite naked".' 'And did you,
Virginia?' William asked. 'Of course,' she answered, and then she
added: 'Lytton always said that Rupert had bandy legs. But I don't
think that was so.' She said that Rupert Brooke was writing at this
time his poem which begins 'These have I loved', in which he lists
a catalogue of sensations which had given him pleasure. She said
that he was quite external in his way of making this list and that
he surprised her by asking what was the brightest thing in nature,
as he needed a dazzling image for his poem. She looked up at the
sky and saw a poplar tree with white underleaves rotating to shimmer
against the light. She said: 'Bright leaves against the sky.'

She seemed to hate her dinner parties to come to an end. Sometimes
they would go on until two AM. She gave her guests an impression
of gaiety which could plunge at any moment into the deepest seriousness. She would tell stories of things which amused her until
the tears ran down her cheeks. Usually these stories concerned one
or two people who played a kind of jester's role in her life. There
was a trace of cruelty in her feeling towards them. One of these was
Hugh Walpole, concerning whom I have quoted one of her stories,
and another, Dame Ethel Smyth. There was always some new item
about Dame Ethel. Once, when Dame Ethel was already eighty-four,
Virginia had just received a letter from her, announcing that she had
become attached to a lady aged eighty who lived next door. 'And
to think that we have been close neighbours for five years,' Dame
Ethel's letter complained, 'and that we might have met when she was
seventy-five and I only seventy-nine.' Dame Ethel was a highly eccentric character. On one occasion the Woolfs invited her to dine
at their house at Rodmell near Lewes, Sussex. Dame Ethel bicycled
the twenty miles from the village where she lived to Rodmell, dressed
in rough tweeds. About two miles from her destination she decided
that perhaps she was not suitably dressed for a dinner party. She
thought that possibly corsets were required to smarten up her figure.
Accordingly, she went into a village shop and asked for some corsets.
There were none. Distressed, she looked round the shop and her eye
lighted on a bird cage, which she purchased. About twenty minutes
later, Virginia went into her garden to discover Dame Ethel in a state
of undress in the shubbery struggling with the bird cage, which she
was wrenching into the shape of corsets and forcing under her tweeds.

Virginia Woolf was a most scrupulous artist who demanded high
standards of artistic integrity from others. Once I submitted to The
Hogarth Press a novel which was rejected. It interested her and she
spent some part of an afternoon discussing it with me. As she made

several favourable comments, I asked how I could re-write it. 'Scrap it!' she exclaimed with force. 'Scrap it, and write something completely different.' When she said 'Scrap it!' I had a glimpse of the years during which she had destroyed her own failures.

She composed, I imagine, like a poet. That is to say, her writing proceeds from the organic development of images growing out of her subject matter. These become symbols in a discussion which often takes her beyond the subject itself. I have in front of me an essay called *The Leaning Tower*, which is the written version of a lecture given in 1939. The essay develops from the apparently simple image of a writer sitting in a chair at his desk. This image proliferates into further ones of the pen, the paper, and the writer's chair even: and these all become symbols of the writer's high calling, expressed in terms of the simple machinery of his trade, scarcely altering through the ages, and joining him to past writers. Within this symbolism there is a further symbol of the hand holding a pen: and through the veins of the hand there flows the blood which is the whole life of the literary tradition joining the writer, sitting at his desk, with Shakespeare. Such writing, dependent for its truth on the inter-relation of ideas in the structure of thought, developed parallel with the inter-relation of the images: the chair, the desk, the pen, etc., can only 'grow' like a poem. And I have heard that there were as many drafts of some of Virginia Woolf's essays as most poets make of a poem.

But just as my lack of belief in Original Sin divided me from the views of Eliot, so my attitude to politics divided me from Virginia Woolf. Not that we disagreed about the political issues themselves: for she hated Fascism, sympathized with the the Spanish Republicans, and held much the same political views as we did. But she objected to the way in which our writing was put to the service of our views, and she discerned that my generation were 'sold' to a public sometimes more on account of their views than for the merit of their writing. Indeed all of us irritated her in this respect, and she sometimes showed her irritation. It occurs first in the *Letter to a Young Poet*, where she quotes Auden, Day Lewis, John Lehmann and myself in order to criticize us for our impatience, our preoccupation with external social factors, and with our desire to set the world right. She returns to the assault, less directly, in *A Room of One's Own*, where she discerns in George Eliot and Charlotte Brontë a desire to preach (though she excuses this as being the result of the position of women in their time). At the beginning of the war, in the essay I have mentioned, *The Leaning Tower*, she returns to the attack more directly. She felt that though we were aware of the calamitous condition of the world, we reacted to it with our intellects and wills, before we had experienced it fully through our sensibilities. 'You have to be beaten and broken by things before you can write about them,' she once said to me. To hold strong views and feel deeply about what, however significant and important, was outside the range of one's experience, was not enough. I might have replied – though I did not – that, often passing Edith Cavell's monument near Charing Cross, with its inscription of *Patriotism is not enough,* I reflected that I would like to have *Sensibility is not enough* engraved on my tombstone.

She and her circle formed a group of friends who shared the same ideas and who, within a common appreciation of high values, had a deep loyalty for one another. Living in their small country houses, their London flats, full of taste, meeting at week-ends and at small parties, discussing history, painting, literature, gossiping greatly, and producing a few very good stories, they resembled those friends who at a time of the Plague in Florence withdrew into the countryside and told the stories of Boccaccio. Our generation, unable to withdraw into exquisite tale-telling and beautiful scenery, resembled rather the *Sturm und Drang* generation of Goethe's contemporaries, terribly in-volved in events and oppressed by them, reacting to them at first enthusiastically and violently, later with difficulty and disgust . . .

William Plomer: Evenings in Tavistock Square

The novelist, poet, critic, and editor William Plomer came to England from South Africa. He shared none of his countryman Roy Campbell's animus towards Bloomsbury, however (see pp. 67 and 396). The Ho-garth Press had accepted Plomer's first novel while he was still in South Africa. In his memoir At Home *Plomer provides amusing glimpses of Bloomsbury, its inhabitants and its neighbours. The de-scription of E.M. Forster, for example, is well known: 'incurious fellow passengers in a train, seeing him in a cheap cloth cap and a scruffy waterproof, and carrying the sort of little bag that might have been carried in 1890 by the man who came to wind the clocks, might have thought him a dim provincial of settled habits and taken no more notice of him.' When Forster showed this description to his mother, she remarked, 'There! You see what Mr Plomer says. How often have I told you, Morgan dear, that you really ought to brush your coat?' (303). Plomer's description of Virginia Woolf in Tavistock Square is from a chapter in which he compares her home with Lady Ottoline Morrell's literary salon in Gower Street.*

At Home *was later revised and combined with an earlier memoir,* Double Lives, *into one volume entitled* The Autobiography of William Plomer. *The excerpts printed here are taken from their first appearance in* At Home.

. . . I was now just twenty-six, and several years had passed since the publication in London of my first novel, the manuscript of which had travelled some six thousand miles to the Hogarth Press. I had also published two books of short stories. Like the novel they had been well received – at least in some quarters and I had therefore in some respects more self-confidence than I should have had if I had not yet published anything. To have known from the first that Leonard and Virginia Woolf believed in me as a writer had been much; to have been published by them was more still. The welcome they gave me when I returned to England, and their subsequent friendship, I value as much as anything in my life. Leonard Woolf used to send me books for review in the *Nation*, of which he was then literary editor, and soon after my return they had been good enough to invite me to the first of a long series of evenings in Tavistock Square. Besides enjoying their beautiful manners, incomparable conversation, and delicious food and wine, I was enabled to meet there for the first time many persons of literary distinction or unusual character. For a young writer, obscure, socially and by experience and temperament rather isolated, poor, curious, and both leisurely and energetic, these evenings were of such benefit and pleasure, such an education in themselves, that I strongly hope there are young writers today who find themselves half as delightfully and fruitfully entertained.

In the upper room to which withdrawal was made after dinner the lighting was fairly subdued, otherwise attention might have been unduly distracted by the mural decorations from the hand of Virginia Woolf's sister, Mrs Bell. In fact these rough trellises and wavy lines, two-handled vases, guitars, fans, and sketchy floral motifs, made their contribution to the unsolemn atmosphere of a room not quite like any other. Virginia Woolf, equally adept at entertaining and being entertained, unobstrusively kept those present as active, or attentive, as an orchestra, and unless some visitor was awkward, shy, or moody, the tempo was lively and the tone gay.

A card would have reached me, and her handwriting, sharp, delicate, and rhythmical as her prose, was pleasing in itself – the more so because it had formed an invitation; and there was often added, as if by way of an afterthought, 'X is coming.' X was almost always somebody eminent in the sphere of writing. . . . A card of invitation reached me. 'Lytton Strachey is coming,' it said.

Strachey was then still in his forties, but his beard and spectacles made him look older. Although he was lanky and Edward Lear was rotund, I imagine that Lear's beard and spectacles may also have seemed to create a certain distance between himself and others. About Strachey's eyelids, as he looked out through the windows of his spectacles over the quickset hedge of his beard, there was a suggestion of world-weariness: he had in fact just two more years to live. To me he did not seem like a man in early middle age, and although his beard made him look older than he was, I did not think of him in terms of a sum of years but as an intelligence alert and busy behind the appendage of hair and the glass outworks. A glint came into his eyes, the brain was on the move as swiftly as a bat, with something of the radar-like sensitivity of bat, and when he spoke it was sometimes in the voice of a bat.

There was a story that in the First World War he had been summoned before some military tribunal, and had appeared before it tall, sad, spectacled, bearded, and carrying a tartan travelling rug and an air cushion. Applying the air cushion to the aperture of his beard he had slowly and gravely inflated it, had then put it on the seat, subsided gently upon it, and carefully, and deliberately arranged the rug over his knees. A brisk military voice had then fired at him from the bench:

'We understand, Mr Strachey, that you are against *all* wars?'

'No,' came the piercing little voice of the pipistrel from the thicket. 'Only this one.'

I am glad to have set eyes upon this wit and revolutionary biographer, a master of English prose, so entertaining and such an influence. It happened that much later in my own life I was to have a particular reason for pondering over the working of Strachey's mind in regard to certain historical characters. Benjamin Britten's opera *Gloriana*, which was produced at the time of Queen Elizabeth II's coronation, and for which I wrote the libretto, owed much to Strachey's *Elizabeth and Essex*.

Quite a different voice from Strachey's came crackling, dry and vibrant and precise, out of the intellectual head of Roger Fry, whose spectacles seemed to magnify both ways. To look him in the eyes was to look through twin lenses of two keen and magnified visual organs and simultaneously to be conscious of exposure to expert scrutiny. If one had been anywhere overpainted, or badly varnished, or if one had been wearing the exasperating label of a false attribution, one could hardly have gone on looking him in the face. His devotion to 'significant form' is pleasantly illustrated by the story that he was seen in the National Gallery lecturing about the composition of a large religious masterpiece to a docile squad of gaping self-improvers. Indicating with his long wood pointer the presiding figure of God the Father, he was heard to say, 'Now, this important mass . . .'

Fry's own pictures have generally seemed to me saddish confections, like those of an amateur cook with sound training and well tried recipes but without the least spark of inspiration. He had been engaged by the Hogarth Press to design the dust jacket for my book of short stories on Japanese themes, *Paper Houses*. Though not at all Japanese in feeling, it was a pleasing design in blue and white, and aroused regret that dust jackets are such perishable things. . . .

Once when Virginia Woolf was sitting beside Lady Ottoline on a sofa their two profiles were suddenly to be seen, one in relief against the other, like two profiles on some Renaissance medal – two strange, queenly figures evolved in the leisured and ceremonious days of the nineteenth century. Each, by being herself, won an allegiance to herself in the twentieth. Both faces were aristocratic, but in that chance propinquity Virginia Woolf's appeared much the more fine and delicate. The two women admired one another, with reservations on one side at least; and they were affectionate in manner when together, though one appeared more affectionate than the other. They had a good deal in common. Both had what old-fashioned people used to call *presence* – a kind of stateliness, a kind of simple, unfussy dignity. Lady Ottoline Morrell, not always discriminating about people, recognized the uniqueness of Virginia Woolf. Virginia Woolf spoke admiringly of the independence and force of character which had enabled Lady Ottoline to emerge from the grand but narrow world into which she had been born (and of which she retained the panache) into a more varied world in which ideas and talent counted more than property or background.

Both had an insatiable curiosity about their fellow creatures, and both a love of gossip and the capacity to be amused or astonished which goes with that virtue. In the exercise of this curiosity the difference of approach was as striking as the difference in their profiles. Lady Ottoline would ask the most personal, direct questions, not in a hectoring way, but without the slightest compunction, and with the manner of a feudal grandee who had a right to be told what she wanted to know. Because most people like talking about themselves to a sympathetic listener she often got what she wanted, but not, as I have indicated, from me. Virginia Woolf's approach was less blunt and more ingenious. With a delicious and playful inventiveness she would often improvise an ironical fantasy about the life and habits of the person to whom she was talking, and this was likely to call forth protests, denials, and explanations which helped to make up something like a confession. Lady Ottoline, less tense and less discerning, was an easier mixer: Virginia Woolf sometimes frightened people by aloofness or asperity, for which they had sometimes their own clumsiness to blame. Yet she could show the most graceful restraint. In the course of several hours of the company of an individual who, she afterwards told me, caused her alternating emotions of anger, laughter, and utter boredom, she showed no sign of the first two and only a faint trace of the last – which is the most difficult of the three to hide.

The fact that Virginia Woolf did not make, either in social life or in her books, any concession to vulgarians, or offer any foothold to a banal understanding, or bait any traps for popularity, probably helped to create a legend about herself among the uninformed, the envious, and the ignorant, that she was some sort of precious and fragile being, ineffably superior and aloof, and quite out of touch with 'ordinary' life – whatever that may be. This legend has been completely dispersed. It is now understood that her life was rich in experience of people and places, and that her disposition, as is sometimes the case with those who are highly strung and have an inclination to melancholy, was genial. Her biographers, so far from having to chronicle the life of an etiolated recluse, may be embarrassed by the quantity and variety of their material. Clearly no adequate biography will be possible until her immense diary has been published in full. From her conversation I recall many interesting glimpses and facets of her earlier life – how, as a young girl, in an agony of shyness, she drove alone at night in a cab with straw on the floor to a ball at one of the great London houses, wearing no jewellery except a modest string of pearls ('but they were *real* pearls'); how she had Greek lessons with Clara, the sister of Walter Pater, in Canning Place, in a setting of blue china, Persian cats, and Morris wallpapers; how she took part in the *Dreadnought* hoax, one of the world's great practical jokes and a superb piece of acting, a demonstration that high-ranking hearts of oak at Portsmouth were accompanied by heads of the same material, since they were unable

to see through a bogus Negus of Abyssinia and his preposterous
'suite'; how she went bathing with Rupert Brooke, whose profile was
not quite lived up to by his legs, those being perceptibly bowed; how
she sat up all night in a Balkan hotel reading the *Christian Science
Monitor* to cheat the bugs; and how there was a murder under her
window in Euboea.

Speaking of writing as a profession, she once remarked to me that
one is bound to upset oneself physically if one works for more than
two hours a day. She put so much of herself into her work that it
must have taken much out of her, and was in fact a prodigiously
hard worker. The volume of her published and unpublished writings,
including her letters and diary, is as impressive as the sustained high
level of all that has so far been printed. She was as energetic as her
father, to whom mountains were no obstacles, nor mountains of facts
either. To be so active, one's nature must be integrated. In each of
us there are two beings, one solitary and one social. There are persons
who cannot bear to be with others, and turn into hermits or something
worse; most cannot bear to be alone, and become common or shallow,
or both. In Virginia Woolf the two beings seemed to have an equal
life and so to make her into a complete person. She could be detached
and see things in perspective; and she could enter into things, into
other people's lives, until she became part of them. The two beings
can be perceived in her writings, sometimes distinct, sometimes
merged. The special genius of her rare and solitary spirit reached
its purest expression in *The Waves*, an exquisite, subjective book
nearer to poetry and music than to to what is generally meant by
'the novel'. The social being in Virginia Woolf, and (in my opinion)
the novelist, can be seen most clearly not in her fiction but in *The
Common Reader*. Those essays are full of shrewdness and knowledge
of the world and of human nature, qualities which, though discern-
ible in her novels, are less important to them than her own sensitivity,
as an instrument to the vibrations of the external world.

The old masters of fiction – Shakespeare, Balzac, Tolstoy – are
such because, besides all the other gifts, they are imaginative men
of the world with an exceptional robustness and gusto. They have
also an extreme preoccupation with sociology. This, when it goes
more with finesse than with animal spirits, produces novelists like
Jane Austen, Flaubert, or Proust, and it was to such writers that Virginia Woolf was in some ways akin. It may be argued that her myth-
making faculty was chiefly applied to sensations rather than to characters, and that her passion for sociology was in a sense scientific.

Although she enjoyed embroidering facts about people, sometimes in a poetic or a fantastic or a censorious or an ironical way, she was really devoted to the facts themselves. The solitary being was a poet, the social being was a sort of scientist: the former discovered poetic truth, the latter anthropological truth.

During the last ten years of her life Virginia Woolf often told me how much more she enjoyed reading autobiographies than novels. She once said that she thought almost any autobiography more satisfying than a novel. When autobiographical memoirs were written by people she knew and found congenial – Lady Oxford, for instance (and what a sharp profile there!) or the bluff and breezy Dame Ethel Smyth – she not only had the pleasure of getting to know them better, but her appetite for social knowledge and reminiscence was much gratified. A passionate precision in collecting data about society (very strong in Flaubert and Proust) made her delight in anything that helped it.

At those evenings in Tavistock Square she was at her best with persons who, like herself, were not merely articulate but articulate in a new way. She had a gift for making the young and obscure feel that they were of value too. She admired physical as well as intellectual beauty. She could charm away diffidence, and, since she was something of a feminist, could be notably sympathetic with young women, in particular young women from Cambridge. A strong sense of the proper functions of literature and a highly and constantly cultivated taste gave her a proper pride (derived in part no doubt from her literary father and background) in her own gifts, but she was without arrogance, and wore her rare beauty without ostentation.

It is not enough to say that she was a hard-working writer, and that she always read a great deal. She also worked as a publisher, and even at times as a printer, with her husband. She examined a great number of typescripts and even of manuscripts for the Hogarth Press, books from which rightly bore the imprint of 'Leonard and Virginia Woolf'. No writer, known or unknown, could have wished for a more encouraging publisher's reader, or one with more openness to new ideas. She seemed unimpeded by prejudice and guided always by the knowledge that the true writer is a precision instrument with something unfamiliar to record. As early as 1930 she and her husband expressed some annoyance at the way the Hogarth Press was developing. They even seemed rather annoyed by the increasingly profitable sales of Hogarth Press books, and were seriously considering reducing the press to its original and remarkable dimensions – a hand press in a basement at Richmond, worked by themselves as amateurs. This was before John Lehmann was inducted into the business and began his long and conspicuous career as a publisher and editor. From the time I first saw him he showed an interest in my writings which has continued to this day, and I am only one of innumerable writers whom he has helped.

The nervous vitality of Virginia Woolf was greater than her physical strength. If it had not been so, she would not have gone on evoking such a response from the responsive in so many parts of the world. To write about her briefly is to be inadequate. She was complex. She looked for truth. She loved London and the country, her relations and friends; she loved her domestic surroundings; she loved the written word. She liked good talk, good food, and good coffee. I see her in a shady hat and summer sleeves, moving between the fig tree and the zinnias at Rodmell; I see her sitting over a fire and smoking one of her favourite cheroots; I see the nervous shoulders, the thin, creative wrists, the unprecedented sculpture of the temples and eye sockets. I see her grave and introspective, or in such a paroxysm of laughter that the tears came into her eyes. But her eyes are shut, and I shall never see her again.

Christopher Isherwood: E.M. Forster and Virginia Woolf

Christopher Isherwood's distinctive third-person fictive autobiographical technique is employed in his memories of E.M. Forster to explain Forster's influence on himself and on the writer closely associated with Isherwood, Wystan Hugh Auden. While Isherwood and Auden were in China in 1938, Auden dedicated a sonnet to Forster that described how 'still you speak to us, / Insisting that the inner life can pay, . . .' and 'when we are closeted with madness, / You interrupt us like the telephone' (157).

Isherwood's second novel, The Memorial, *which Forster had liked, was published by the Hogarth Press, which went on to publish four more of his books, including Isherwood's famous Berlin stories. When Virginia Woolf died, Isherwood was asked to write about her for a magazine. He did but was later tempted to alter his article because, as he explained in an introduction,*

> an attempt to speak simultaneously as the public eulogist and the private mourner is almost foredoomed to falseness; all the more so when you feel

*you are addressing strangers who could never really understand or care.
One sentence in particular nauseates me as much as anything I have ever
written: 'she was, as the Spanish say, "very rare" . . .' This bit of jargon
was undoubtedly inspired by Hemingway's* For Whom the Bell Tolls. . . .
To ape the affectations of great writers is never excusable. (124)

*Isherwood also explains that Jeremy in his article was a pseudonym
for the novelist Hugh Walpole, whom Virginia Woolf fondly teased
and who was an early influence on Isherwood himself.*

On September 14 [1932], Christopher wrote a postcard to Stephen
[Spender] – who must have been out of town for a day or two:

> Yesterday evening, Plomer and I visited an opium-den. Today he is taking
> me to see E.M. Forster. I shall spend the entire moring making-up.

I have only the dimmest memory of the alleged opium den. I think
it was a pub somewhere in the dockland area, frequented by local
Chinese and visiting Asian seamen. Plomer liked to keep the outskirts
of his life hidden in an intriguing fog of mystery; now and then
he would guide you through the fog to one of his haunts, with the
casualness of a habitué. No doubt, opium was obtainable there, but
I am sure that he and Christopher didn't smoke any . . . By 'making-
up' I suppose Christopher merely meant that he would try in every
way to look and be at his best for this tremendous encounter.

It *was* tremendous for Christopher. Forster was the only living
writer whom he would have described as his master. In other people's
books he found examples of style which he wanted to imitate and
learn from. In Forster he found a key to the whole art of writing.
The Zen masters of archery – of whom, in those days, Christopher
had never heard – start by teaching you the mental attitude with
which you must pick up the bow. A Forster novel taught Christopher
the mental attitude with which he must pick up the pen.

Plomer had been able to arrange this meeting because Forster had
read *The Memorial* – at his suggestion, probably – and had liked
it, at least well enough to be curious about its author. (Thencefor-
ward, Christopher was fond of saying, 'My literary career is over –
I don't give a damn for the Nobel Prize or the Order of Merit –
I've been praised by Forster!' Nevertheless, Christopher's confidence
in his own talent easily survived the several later occasions when
Forster definitely didn't like one of his other books or when he praised
books by writers whom Christopher found worthless.)

Forster must have been favourably impressed by Christopher; otherwise, he wouldn't have gone on seeing him. And Christopher made
a good disciple; like most arrogant people, he loved to bow down
unconditionally from time to time. No doubt he gazed at Forster with
devoted eyes and set himself to entertain him with tales of Berlin
and the boy world, judiciously spiced with expressions of social concern – for he must have been aware from the start that he had to
deal with a moralist.

Forster never changed much in appearance until he became stooped
and feeble in his late eighties. He was then fifty-three but he always
looked younger than his age. And he never ceased to be babylike.
His light blue eyes behind his spectacles were like those of a baby
who remembers his previous incarnation and is more amused than
dismayed to find himself reborn in new surroundings. He had a baby's
vulnerability, which is also the invulnerability of a creature whom
one dare not harm. He seemed to be swaddled, babylike, in his ill-
fitting suit rather than wearing it. A baby with a mustache? Well,
if a baby *could* have a mustache, it would surely be like his was,
wispy and soft . . . Nevertheless, behind that charming, unalarming
exterior, was the moralist; and those baby eyes looked very deep into
you. When they disapproved, they could be stern. They made Christopher feel false and tricky and embarrassed. He reacted to his embarrassment by trying to keep Forster amused. Thirty-eight years later,
a friend who was present at the last meeting between them made
the comment: 'Mr. Forster laughs at you as if you were the village
idiot.'

I suppose that this first meeting took place in Forster's flat, and
that, on the wall of its living room, there hung Eric Kennington's
pastel portrait of T.E. Lawrence's bodyguard, quarrelsome little Mah-
mas, with his fierce eyes and naked dagger. This was the original
of one of the illustrations to the privately printed edition of *Seven
Pillars of Wisdom*. Lawrence had given copies of the book away to
his friends, including Forster. Christopher left the flat clasping this
magic volume, which Forster had lent him. . . .

During their [Isherwood's and Auden's] arguments, Christopher
sometimes invoked the example of Forster: Morgan, he said, was incapable of having any truck with 'such Fascist filth.' I wonder, now,
if Wystan then believed what he stated in a letter to Christopher many
years later, in explanation of Forster's declared agnosticism: 'As I
see him, Morgan is a person who is so accustomed to the Presence
of God that he is unaware of it; he has never known what it feels

like when that Presence is withdrawn.' If Wystan did already believe this in 1938, he wisely kept his mouth shut. I can imagine the yell of protest Christopher would have uttered, on hearing such an outrageous accusation against his Master.

* * *

Virginia Woolf is dead – and thousands of people, far outside the immediate circle of her friends and colleages, will be sorry, will feel the loss of a great and original talent to our literature. For she was famous, surprisingly famous when one considers that she was what is called 'a writer's writer'. Her genius was intensely feminine and personal – private, almost. To read one of her books was (if you liked it) to receive a letter from her, addressed specially to you. But this, perhaps, was just the secret of her appeal.

As everybody knows, Mrs Woolf was a prominent member of what journalists used to call 'The Bloomsbury Group' – which included Lytton Strachey, Vanessa Bell, Duncan Grant, E.M. Forster, Arthur Waley, Desmond MacCarthy and Maynard Keynes. Actually, the 'Group' was not a group at all, in the self-conscious sense, but a kind of clan; one of those 'natural' families which form themselves without the assistance of parents, uncles and aunts, simply because of few sensitive and imaginative people become aware of belonging to each other, and wish to be frequently in each other's company. It follows, of course, that these brothers and sisters under the skin find it convenient to settle in the same neighbourhood – Bloomsbury, in this case. It is a district just behind and beyond the British Museum. Its three large squares, Gordon, Bedford and Tavistock, have something of the dignity and atmosphere of Cambridge college courts.

Open *To the Lighthouse*, *The Common Reader*, or *The Waves*, read a couple of pages with appreciation, and you have become already a distant relative of the Bloomsbury Family. You can enter the inner sanctum, the Woolf drawing-room, and nobody will rise to greet you – for you are one of the party. 'Oh, come in,' says Virginia, with that gracious informality which is so inimitably aristocratic, 'you know everybody, don't you? We were just talking about Charles Tansley . . . poor Charles – such a prig . . . Imagine what he said the other day . . .' And so, scarcely aware, we float into our story.

The Bloomsbury Family held together by consanguinity of talent. That you could express yourself artistically, through the medium of writing, or painting, or music, was taken for granted. This was the real business of life: it would have been indecent, almost, to refer to it. Artistic integrity was the family religion; and in its best days

it could proudly boast that it did not harbour a single prostitute,
pot-boiler or hack. Nevertheless one must live. Some of the brothers
and sisters had very odd hobbies. Keynes, for example, whose brilliant
descriptive pen could touch in an unforgettable and merciless portrait
of Clemenceau on the margin, as it were, of an economic report to
the Versailles treaty-makers – Keynes actually descended into that sor-
did jungle, the City, and emerged a wealthy man! And Virginia –
the exquisite, cloistered Virginia – became a publisher. True, the thing
happened by gradual stages. It began as a sort of William Morris
handicraft – with Leonard and Virginia working their own press,
and Virginia's delicate fingers, one supposes, getting black with printer's ink. But all this was ancient history, and the hand-press was
stowed away in the cellar under dust-sheets before the day in the
early 'thirties when I first walked timidly up the steps of the house
in Tavistock Square.

It is usually easy to describe strangers. Yet, although I didn't meet
Virginia more than half-a-dozen times, I find it nearly impossible
to write anything about her which will carry the breath of life. Which
century did she belong to? Which generation? You could not tell:
she simply defied analysis. At the time of our first meeting, she was,
I now realize, an elderly lady, yet she seemed, in some mysterious
way, to be very much older and very much younger than her age.
I could never decide whether she reminded me of my grandmother
as a young Victorian girl, or my great-grandmother – if she had taken
some rejuvenating drug and lived a hundred and twenty years, to
become the brilliant leader of an intensely modern Georgian *salon*.

One remembers, first of all, those wonderful, forlorn eyes; the slim,
erect, high-shouldered figure, strangely tense, as if always on the alert
for some distant sound; the hair folded back from the eggshell fragility
of the temples; the small, beautifully-cut face, like a Tennysonian
cameo – Mariana, or The Lady of Shalott. Yes, that is the impression
one would like to convey – an unhappy, high-born lady in a ballad,
a fairy-story princess under a spell, slightly remote from the rest of
us, a profile seen against the dying light, hands dropped helplessly
in the lap, a shocking, momentary glimpse of intense grief.

What rubbish! We are at the tea table. Virginia is sparkling with
gaiety, delicate malice and gossip – the gossip which is the style of
her books and which made her the best hostess in London; listening
to her, we missed appointments, forgot love affairs, stayed on and
on into the small hours, when we had to be hinted, gently, but firmly,
out of the house. This time, the guest of honour is a famous novelist,

whose substantial income proves that Art, after all, can really pay. He is modest enough – but Virginia, with sadistic curiosity, which is like the teasing of an elder sister, drags it all out of him: how much time New York publishers gave, how much the movie people, and what the King said, and the Crown Prince of Sweden – she has no mercy. And then, when it is all over, 'You know, Jeremy,' she tells him, smiling almost tenderly, 'you remind me of a very beautiful prize-winning cow. . . .' 'A cow, Virginia . . . ?' The novelist gulps but grins bravely at me; determined to show he can take it. 'Yes . . . a very, very fine cow. You go out into the world, and win all sorts of prizes, but gradually you coat gets covered with burrs, and so you have to come back again into your field. And in the middle of the field is a rough old stone post, and you rub yourself against it to get the burrs off. Don't you think, Leonard . . .' she looks across at her husband, 'that that's our real mission in life? We're Jeremy's old stone scratching-post.'

What else is there to say about her? Critics will place her among the four greatest English women writers. Friends will remember her beauty, her uniqueness, her charm. I am very proud to have known her. Was she the bewitched princess, or the wicked little girl at the tea party – or both, or neither? I can't tell. In any case she was, as the Spaniards say, 'very rare', and this world was no place for her. I am happy to think that she is free of it, before everything she loved has been quite smashed. If I wanted an epitaph for her, taken from her own writings, I should choose this:

'It was done; it was finished. Yes, she thought, laying down her brush in extreme fatigue, I have had my vision.'

T.S. Eliot: Virginia Woolf and Bloomsbury

T.S. Eliot's observations on Virginia Woolf and Bloomsbury come from a note he wrote for Cyril Connolly's Horizon *magazine shortly after her death. Though Eliot was never really a member of the Group, the Hogarth Press published his early poetry, including* The Waste Land, *as well as some of his criticism. He was also welcomed and respected by the Woolfs, Clive Bell, Lytton Strachey, Maynard Keynes, and others in Bloomsbury. Eliot's description of the nature and significance of the Group is among the most important statements by a contemporary on Bloomsbury.*

. . . The future will arrive at a permanent estimate of the place of Virginia Woolf's novels in the history of English literature, and it will also be furnished with enough documents to understand what her work meant to her contemporaries. It will also, through letters and memoirs, have more than fugitive glimpses of her personality. Certainly, without her eminence as a writer, and her eminence as the particular kind of writer she was, she would not have occupied the personal position she held among contemporaries; but she would not have held it by being a writer alone – in the latter case it would only be the cessation of work which would here give cause for lament. By attempting to enumerate the qualities and conditions which contributed, one may give at first a false impression of 'accidental advantages' concurring to reinforce the imaginative genius and the sense of style which cannot be contested, to turn her into the symbol, almost myth, which she became for those who did not know her, and the social centre which she was for those who did. Some of these advantages may have helped to smooth the path to fame – though when a literary reputation is once established, people quickly forgot how long it was in growing – but that fame itself is solidly enough built upon the writings. And these qualities of personal charm and distinction, of kindness and wit, of curiosity about human beings, and the particular advantage of a kind of hereditary position in English letters (with the incidental benefits which that position bestowed) do not, when enumerated, tell the whole story: they combined to form a whole which is more than the sum of the parts.

I am well aware that the literary-social importance which Virginia Woolf enjoyed, had its nucleus in a society which those people whose ideas about it were vague – vague even in connection with the topography of London – were wont, not always disinterestedly perhaps, to deride. The sufficient answer *ad hoc* – though not the final answer – would probably be that it was the only one there was: and as I believe that without Virginia Woolf at the centre of it, it would have remained formless or marginal, to call attention to its interest to the sociologist is not irrelevant to my subject. Any group will appear more uniform, and probably more intolerant and exclusive from the outside than it really is; and here, certainly, no subscription of orthodoxy was imposed. Had it, indeed, been a matter of limited membership and exclusive doctrine, it would not have attracted the exasperated attention of those who objected to it on these supposed grounds. It is no part of my purpose here either to defend, criticize

or appraise *élites*; I only mention the matter in order to make the
point that Virginia Woolf was the centre, not merely of an esoteric
group, but of the literary life of London. Her position was due to
a concurrence of qualities and circumstances which never happened
before, and which I do not think will ever happen again. It maintained the dignified and admirable tradition of Victorian upper
middle-class culture – a situation in which the artist was neither the
servant of the exalted patron, the parasite of the plutocrat, nor the
entertainer of the mob – a situation in which the producer and the
consumer of art were on an equal footing, and that neither the highest
nor the lowest. With the death of Virginia Woolf, a whole pattern
of culture is broken: she may be, from one point of view, only the
symbol of it; but she would not be the symbol if she had not been,
more than anyone in her time, the maintainer of it. Her work will
remain; something of her personality will be recorded, but how can
her position in the life of her own time be understood by those to
whom her time will be so remote that they will not even know how
far they fail to understand it? As for us – *l'on sait ce que l'on perd.
On ne sait jamais ce que l'on rattrapera.*

Frances Partridge: Bloomsbury and Their Houses

*Frances Marshall Partridge has become Bloomsbury's latter-day au-
tobiographer. In a series of memoirs and diaries beginning in 1978
and continuing into her and the century's nineties, she has presented
her view of Bloomsbury. Born in Bloomsbury, Frances Partridge encountered members of the Group in the 1920s originally through her
sister Ray, who married David Garnett. After studying philosophy
at Cambridge, she went to work at the book shop of Francis Birrell
and Garnett, where she met Ralph Partridge while he was working
for the Hogarth Press. It was at this time that E.M. Forster described
her as 'a Bloomsbury hanger on' (see p. 80). She became involved
in Lytton Strachey's* ménage *through Partridge and married him after
the deaths of Lytton and Carrington. Eventually she became a younger
member of the Memoir Club.*

*Two separate extracts from Frances Partridge's recollections are in-
cluded here: first, her introduction to Bloomsbury from* Memories *and
then an essay on Bloomsbury houses written later for the* Charleston
Newsletter.

. . . Our clientèle [at Birrell and Garnett's bookshop] was therefore limited almost entirely to friends, and friends of friends, and were for the most part denizens of Bloomsbury, both physically and spiritually.

Thus it was that I first got to know these remarkable people – for such I'm convinced they were, however much attitudes to them may change. They all bought their books from us – the 'Woolves', the Bells, Duncan Grant, Maynard Keynes, the Desmond MacCarthys, the Adrian Stephens, the Stracheys, Anreps and Saxon Sydney-Turner. These, I reflected, were the sort of people I would like to know and have friends among, more than any others I had yet come across. I was instantly captivated and thrilled by them. It was as if a lot of doors had suddenly opened out of a stuffy room which I had been sitting in far too long.

The bookshop was a centre for friendliness and conversation, and I soon began to be invited to dine with Clive Bell or Leonard and Virginia Woolf, and to spend weekends at Charleston or Lytton Strachey's house at Tidmarsh, to both of which I went in some trepidation. I asked Bunny for advice.

'You'll find they all spend a lot of time – anyway the mornings – shut away in their studios or libraries, engaged on their own activities,' he said. 'So take something of your own to do – something to write, one of your patchwork quilts, perhaps. They'll go for walks and talk, but they won't "entertain" you otherwise.' It was good advice.

So much has been written about Bloomsbury – far too much, say some – that I propose only to select from the *personal* impressions I received at the time, to which I have added some later comments and analytical notes aimed at giving an idea how *Then* appears to me *Now*.

To begin with, they were not a group, but a number of very different individuals, who shared certain attitudes to life, and happened to be friends or lovers. To say they were 'unconventional' suggests deliberate flouting of rules; it was rather that they were quite uninterested in conventions, but passionately in ideas. Generally speaking they were left-wing, atheists, pacificists in the First War (but few of them also in the Second), lovers of the arts and travel, avid readers, Francophiles. Apart from the various occupations such as writing, painting, economics, which they pursued with dedication, what they enjoyed most was talk – talk of every description, from the most abstract to the most hilariously ribald and profane. I had never, even at Cambridge, come across people who set such a high value on rationalism (a word that now raises many eyebrows), integrity and originality. Their standards were as high as their spirits. In my home circle even the more civilised had shied away from words like 'good' and 'beautiful' and would veil their appreciation of works of art in phrases such as 'That's rather a jolly bit,' or 'Isn't this amusing?' But the Bloomsburies called spades spades and said what they thought; they didn't keep afloat in a social atmosphere by the wing-flapping of small talk – if they were bored by the conversation they showed it. This disconcerted the unconfident and gave them a justified reputation for rudeness, nor do I think it any more admirable now than I found it then; but they could nearly all of them be extraordinarily kind at times, if they liked you – even the alarming Virginia, who was full of curiosity about other people's lives and liked to question 'the young', partly perhaps motivated by an unconscious desire to make fools of them.

Comfort didn't rank high in Bloomsbury houses (though beauty did), but there would be good French cooking, and wine at most meals (often imported in the cask and bottled at home), homemade bread and jams (Virginia was good at making both). In winter you might suffer seriously from the cold, and the bathroom pipes might be clad in old newspapers, but you would find a superb library, as good talk as I've heard anywhere, and a great deal of laughter. They valued friendship extremely highly, but saw no reason why it should annihilate their critical faculties. Very far from it. So they laughed at one another often, but on the whole affectionately, and told stories about their friends that may seem (and sometimes certainly were) malicious. And since they believed marriage to be a convention and convenience and never celebrated it in church, love, whether heterosexual or homosexual, took precedence over it and its percepts. They were serious but never solemn, and nothing was sacrosanct or immune from mockery and fun, certainly not themselves. Nor were they 'indoor' people, as has sometimes been supposed. Clive Bell was a good rider and shot, Arthur Waley an expert skier, and Ralph Partridge was chosen to row for Oxford. Even Lytton Strachey played badminton in a style all his own on the Ham Spray lawn, where Lydia Lopokova distinguished herself by never getting the shuttlecock over the net once. Lawn bowls was popular both at Rodmell and Ham Spray.

What then were these 'individuals' like? Lytton Strachey was by no means ugly, as some have implied. Tall, willowy, and with very long and beautiful hands, he displayed a peculiar elegance in the way he used to walk, or rather stalk, across the lawn under a white sunshade lined with green, and fold his long legs away into a deck chair. His velvety brown eyes were full of expression. He spent most of his mornings reading or writing in his library, which was lined with a fine collection of French and English books.

'How many of them have you read?' I once boldly asked him. 'All,' was his reply. He told Ralph Partridge that when writing a book he would pace up and down the room thinking out a whole paragraph in his head, and not put pen to paper until it was complete. This, he felt, was conducive to the *enchaînement* as he always called it – to him a vital ingredient in good writing. In the afternoons he usually went for a walk with his devoted companion Carrington; more reading or writing followed tea, and in the evening – when poker or piquet were not being played – he sometimes read aloud in a surprisingly deep and emotional voice, emphasising the crucial phrases with movements of his long hands. Shakespeare, Donne, Sterne, Racine – the range was wide. Lytton was alarming to be with because he was shy as well as somewhat arrogant, but if asked for guidance in reading no-one could be more helpful, and he had a brand of comedy all his own, expressed by fantastic gestures, a few arpeggios sketched on the dinner-table before leaving it, and a characteristic vocabulary, including such words as 'macabre', 'funeste' and 'abject'. Children in general were given the dismissive title of 'petit peuple'. His literary references could be surprising. Once when Carrington offered me a choice of puddings I said they both looked delicious and it was 'all one to me'. Lytton laughed and said, 'I see you're like Hippocleides – at his betrothal feast he stood on his head and waved his legs in the air, and when told this had lost him his wife he said, "It's all one to Hippocleides!"' Perhaps this character from Herodotus was a special favourite in Bloomsbury, for I later heard Leonard Woolf declare, 'I'm like Hippocleides, who stood on his head and said, "Hippocleides doesn't care!"' I preferred Lytton's translation and said so, but Leonard was obstinate. 'You see, I had a Classical education,' he told me. . . .

I do not feel I can add anything to all that has been written about the Woolves. Brilliant as she was, I found Virginia less lovable than her sister Vanessa, whose passion for colour she emulated in words. I think perhaps she was really a little jealous of Vanessa for actually having the power to squeeze her colours from a tube on to the canvas. Both the sisters were apparently unself-conscious about their remarkable beauty, but their two faces reflected an essential difference of character. Virginia's bore the stigmata that are to be seen in many who have been gravely mad – a subtly agonised tautness, something twisted; the way she held herself, turned her head or smoked a cigarette struck one as awkward even while it charmed and interested one. As Julia Strachey said of her, she 'was not at home in her body'. The lines of Vanessa's beautiful face had been graven by human emotions, and responses to other people, with the traces also of her expected bursts of hilarity and recklessness. She was famous for her mixed metaphors (like 'the longest worm has its turning' and 'in that house one meets a dark horse in every cupboard') and she could be delightfully witty too. As she got old and moved more slowly, it was as if one of the statues from the Acropolis had stepped down from her pedestal and was taking a stately walk.

In Virginia'a house there was always electricity in the air, and though enthralled by the display of lightning, few people were entirely at their ease there, or could fail to wonder where the next flash would strike. She seemed at her best with Clive Bell, of whom she was genuinely fond, and who would act as midwife to her verbal fantasies with a gentle 'Ye-e-e-es, Virginia?' But then Clive was a born host, with the rare gift of wanting his guests to shine rather than trying to do so himself. He was in some ways an eighteenth-century character, part country squire and part man of unusually wide reading, particularly in French history and memoirs. I always envied him his amazing memory for what he read, and until the day of his death (when I visited him in hospital) his mind remained perfectly clear and he never lost his consideration for others. He was a staunch friend, and above a great *enjoyer*, whose enjoyment was as infectious as his laughter. Even his more comic habits were endearing, though we might laugh at them – the French phrases that larded his conversation ('entre la poire et le café' was a favourite, which sometimes emerged as 'entre le café et la poire') or his gestures to emphasise a point, such as a hand sweeping towards far horizons, the compulsive pulling-up of his sock-suspenders as if his life depended on them, and anxious rearrangement of the thick carroty hair that grew on only part of his cranium, and had a way of getting out of place, much to his agitation.

Since Leonard Woolf outlived many of his friends, his fine Rabbinical appearance in old age, with his bright eyes, melodious but slightly tremulous voice and even more tremulous hands, became familiar to many. He had roots in both animal and vegetable worlds, as he showed by his pleasure in his splendid flower-garden and in the smelly old dogs which he treated to occasional kindly kicks.

Anyone who heard Roger Fry lecture on art must owe him an immense debt of pure pleasure, for he had the rare gift of conveying his own love for paintings, even when their attractions were not obvious, even when the slides were put in upside down. But his admiration had limits. When I went to India a few years ago I saw exactly what he meant by 'the nerveless and unctuous sinuosity of the rhythms' of Indian sculpture. I don't think he was ever reconciled to it. Yet his mind was much more 'open' than most, and among his wilder beliefs were that Shakespeare's Sonnets were just as good in French as in English, and that if a doctor was going to do something particularly unpleasant to him a brick under the bed would absorb the pain. He was a keen chess-player, and sometimes got me to play with him. He liked to win, and generally did, but if the issue was in doubt he would say, 'Oh, I don't think it was wise to move your *bishop*. Better go there with your knight', and that would do the trick. He was charming to children, enjoying talking to them and always taking their remarks seriously and laughing at their jokes. For instance he was much amused by a record owned by the Anrep children* called *The Song of the Prune*, especially by the lines 'We have wrinkles on our face. Prunes have them every place.'

There was something avian about both Desmond and Molly MacCarthy: they reminded me of a pair of china birds on the chimney-piece, partly because they were more complementary than alike, and both sharply observant as all birds are. Molly's varnish of conformity concealed an original and unexpected response that was close to genius. Desmond's feathers were often somewhat ruffled, though he spent much more time than any other Bloomsbury in the houses of the rich and great. He was a first-rate conversationalist, who used his voice like a musician, with rubato, pause and diminuendo as an essential part of his talk. No wonder that the typist, hidden in a corner on a famous occasion to record his words, failed to convey their quality. He also had an exceptional gift for sympathetic understanding – something which is often attributed to women, though its most sensitive exponents may be men. Molly's deafness interfered greatly with her happiness and sometimes with other people's. At one time she had a deaf-aid in the form of a small box, which she would push eagerly towards her neighbour at the dinner-table. Then, after listening for a few moments, she would sigh deeply and switch off.

* Baba and Igor, children of Boris and Helen.

The effect was both amusing and crushing, but she had a brilliant
talent for extracting the humour from people and situations, which
would turn her face scarlet, with tears running down her cheeks.
She was the creator of the term 'Bloomsberries', and also the Memoir
Club, where a few of us met and read papers supposed to reveal
the whole truth about some part of our lives.

Duncan Grant's charm was legendary. He never stopped painting,
even during those years when his work was out of favour and his
name unknown to the young; nor did it seem to affect him when
fame returned to him. And he loved music. When he was well over
eighty I invited him to the opera. Undeterred by having spent five
mortal hours that day carefully studying an exhibition at the Tate,
he arrived by Underground and on foot (not dreaming of taking a
taxi), looking as usual remarkably like a tramp, with hair that seemed
never to have known a brush, sat through the opera with unfaltering
attention, and came back to supper afterwards with two much
younger guests whom he easily outdid in animation.

E.M. Forster appeared to dress himself carefully to look like 'the
man in the street', in impossiblly dull grey suits, a woolly waistcoat
perhaps and a cloth cap, yet there was no mistaking him for one
of his similarly-attired fellows. Was it the curious shape of his head
– large at the top and tapering to neck and chin – or the disconcerting
gaze of his light blue eyes? I have run into him in unexpected places,
like the quay at Dover or emerging from the caves at Lascaux, and
recognised him instantly from afar. The sentimentality which is sometimes distressing in his books never appeared in his conversation or
his letters – even the wording of a postcard announcing the time
of his train had originality, as did his handwriting. He accompanied
his most amusing remarks with a look of anguish and a high explosion something like a sneeze, which seemed to express amusement
and self-depreciation at one at the same time. He was more musical
than most Bloomsburies, with the possible exception of Saxon
Sydney-Turner, a ghostly figure who hardly ever spoke (though he
often nodded emphatically), but if he did could tell you at the drop
of a hat who sang Brünnhilde or Don Giovanni in any year or opera
house during the past century.

All these people bought their books from Birrell and Garnett . . .

*   *   *

An empty house is in one sense merely a shell – but, shells have
their own beauty, and also, speaking pesonally, I am more than glad

that Haworth Parsonage, Rydal Mount and Yasnaya Polyana (to take three at random) have been preserved to give us their richly stimulating impression of the lives of the Brontës, Wordsworth and the Tolstoys respectively – for I find they linger in my mind like a picture or a cinema film perhaps, and have a certain quality of indelibility possessed by few biographies. The fact is that the connection between a house and the individuals it has fostered is a unique and potent one.

So naturally students of Bloomsbury want to come to Charleston. But all Bloomsbury didn't live at Charleston; nor did the Bells and Duncan Grant live here *all* the time. What of the other houses that sheltered their friends, and were in different ways connected with it? And what, above all, of that eponymous district of London where they so often forgathered? I shall try to give some sort of answer to these questions, and say a little about Charleston's relations – those other houses (and their life-styles) linked to it not so much by geography as by friendship and common interests and values. Those I have in mind are Tidmarsh Mill House, Monks House, Ham Spray and most of the north-east side of Gordon Square. I shall begin with the last, for it was chronologically the first, and since the ground is well-trodden I will confine myself to my own recollections.

When Vanessa bought 46 Gordon Square in 1904, she set going a process of gradual but thriving colonization, which I myself only came in contact with a good deal later, in 1921. This was the year when I came down from Cambridge, and took a job as accountant, delivery girl and dogsbody in Francis Birrell's and David Garnett's bookshop, situated just off Gordon Square, and built to a more or less matching architectural pattern. By this time several houses in the square were in occupation by those who soon became the chief – I might almost say the *only* – customers of our shop, which somehow failed to look enough like Bumpus or Hatchards to invite the casual passer-by. But such visitors as we had were extremely interesting and lively, and the talk they obviously so enjoyed was brilliant and amusing; so that if I happened to be sitting at my desk in the corner struggling to make the accounts meet, even when Frankie or Bunny had failed to enter items on the till, I forgot all about double entry and listened enthralled. At this time I was only what botanists call a 'casual' in Gordon Square. I didn't pull up my roots from my mother's house in nearby Brunswick Square and qualify as a 'denizen' until Ralph Partridge and I finally threw in our lot together and rented the first floor of No. 41 from James and Alix Strachey

some four years later. I could never imagine why they let us have
the splendid rooms on the first floor, since (both being psychoanalysts) they needed the second floor for their consulting-rooms, and
had to make do with the Yonghy Bonghy Bo simplicity of those above
to live and sleep in themselves. I really concluded they must *like*
discomfort.

On a first meeting Alix and James might strike one as aloof, but
this impression resolved itself into a combination of detachment, respect for the views of others and extremely good manners. Alix loved
argument, however, and used to support the most improbable propositions on pedestals of the purist logic, untouched by knowledge
of the world. James was much more emotional; he felt deeply about
causes and heroes (like Freud, Mozart or Lytton) and disagreement
merely turned his small round face pink beneath his silky white hair.
I think with deep affection of them both, gratitude for the help they
quietly gave Ralph and me in welding our lives together, and delight
at the memory of their flashes of eccentricity and hilarity. Their pa-
tients were something of a worry, though. One might come home
to find a desperate-looking, white-faced individual leaning against
the Square railings, trying in vain to summon up courage to ring
the door-bell. And another of them, described by James as 'refractory'
and 'threatening', caused him to take Ralph aside and beg him to
be ready to dash upstairs to his rescue at the sound of a thump of
the floor above us with the walking-stick he kept beside him for the
purpose.

James had also undertaken, and was carrying on upstairs, the stu-
pendous task of translating the *Complete Works* of Freud into English. No wonder that he became practically blind in one eye. I vol-
unteered to take the index off his hands, for I was eager to help;
but if you want to go raving mad I recommend indexing twenty-
two volumes full of abstract words like 'unconscious' and 'repression'.

Next door for a while lived Oliver Strachey and my great friend
his daughter, Julia. Their alliance was the product of *force majeure*
and not made to last; but while it did they got considerable amusement
from each other's character and behaviour – and probably exasperation as well. During some of the evenings we spent together we
would be treated to an unscripted knockabout turn, reminiscent of
the dialogue between two comedians at the Palladium; others passed
in quiet relaxation, playing word or acting games perhaps, with
Angus Davidson, one of the Cambridge boys from No. 37, or chatting
while Angus did his *petit point*.

No. 50 had a shifting population, among them Adrian and Karin Stephen, Arthur Waley and his consort, jet-black-haired Beryl de Zoete, of whom it was whispered that she 'came down from Oxford before the Boer War'. (I leave you to work *that* out.) Here too Clive Bell had his comfortable bachelor flat surrounded by his fine library, French pictures and decorations by Duncan Grant. At Charleston he habitually wore old clothes and spent his time reading, writing, walking, and perhaps shooting something 'for the pot', as he called it; but in Gordon Square he satisfied his strong social and amorous leanings and considerable skill as a host, the secret of which was that he liked his guests to shine, and that food, wine and conversation were all equally good. I doubt if he was a feminist, but I took it kindly that he always offered me a cigar after dinner. It was usually accepted.

There were parties, too, at No. 46, the Keyneses' house. These often included an elaborate entertainment: for instance a revue based on a topical *cause célèbre* but thinly disguising a satire on Bloomsbury, the hero and heroine, so far as I remember, being called Scrodger Pry and Clarissa Dell. I took part in this production, along with Barbara Bagenal and Bea Howe, in a diminutive male chorus dressed in white ties and tails, while our three strapping 'female' companions were Dadie Rylands and the Davidson brothers, in evening dress and chokers of giant pearls. Maynard and Lydia closed the proceedings with their famous performance of the Keynes-Keynes.

A very different world has hidden behind the front door of No. 51, where Lady Strachey lived with a changing selection of her children, including Lytton at times. The matriarch was monumental in more ways than one, as solid and rugged as a Rodin sculpture. A board in the hall told one who was IN and who OUT, and the maid wore a white cap and apron. It was recognized that none of the family could do a thing for themselves, so on servant's day off some member of the younger generation – probably Janie Bussy or Julia Strachey – had to come to their aid (if necessary by train) and switch on the gas stove in which the evening meal had been left ready – a feat no amount of higher education had fitted Pippa, Marjorie or Pernel (Principal of Newnham) to perform.

The ambience of Gordon Square, as Lytton noted in a letter to Virginia, was very like that of a Cambridge college, and this made it exceptionally pleasant to live in, with seclusion when wanted and congenial company at other times; with strollers or even picnickers in the Square gardens, which took the place of Quad, and where one might watch or take part in a game of tennis, fortified by the addition of Raymond Mortimer from Gordon Place, say, or Frankie Birrell from the bookshop. The latter was a better player than might have been expected from his sometimes scruffy appearance. He had learned to hit a ball at Eton, but was inclined to burst into giggles every time Arthur Waley greeted a shot that was palpably 'In' with a quick, flat 'Out'. Arthur's special technique for dealing with embarrassing facts also appeared on London's ice rinks where he and I sometimes went together. I remember an occasion when the band struck up a waltz: he seized me round the waist, but as we neither of us had the faintest idea how to dance on ice we crashed instantly to the ground in an ignominious tangle; yet Arthur remained impassive while I was helpless with laughter.

So obviously desirable a way of life did Gordon Square provide that it seems strange that its pattern should not have been copied elsewhere. Perhaps it has. As time went on the population was increased by the arrival of the Woolves at Tavistock Square just round the corner, in 1924, while in 1925 Morgan Forster became my mother's lodger in Brunswick Square.

I sometimes think of the houses of geographical Bloomsbury as if they formed a key-ring from which hung a number of keys to other establishments. The first key to slip off his ring into my hands opened the door to Tidmarsh Mill in 1924. This was the attractive old Thames valley house found by Carrington in 1917 for herself and Lytton, with the backing and occasional presence of Maynard Keynes and others, but now occupied by Lytton, Carrington and Ralph Partridge alone. It exactly resembled Carrington's well-known picture of it (reproduced on the jacket of her published letters) except that the swans floating on the mill-stream were white, instead of the exotic black creatures she converted them into. I only visited it a couple of times, not enough to get over my first shyness. I found Lytton alarming, partly because he was shy himself, and clearly just as much afraid of being left alone with me as I was with him; and though I was flattered by Ralph's attentions they were quite unlike those of any previous admirers and left me rather bewildered. Then no one had told me that every Strachey absolutely insisted on eating rice pudding at least once a day, so that the meals struck me as having a curiously nursery flavour. The conversation on the other hand was highly sophisticated, combining erudition with obscenity, the latter inclined to develop when paper games were played after dinner. Alternative evening entertainments were readings aloud from Pope or Shakespeare by Lytton (very moving and delightful) or poker played for low stakes. Lytton was kind-hearted and couldn't refrain from reimbursing any needy looking young visitors who lost. But the paper games filled me with alarm, and I remember one in particular, instigated by a young French doctor who was staying there: it was a form of the Truth game (with the answers to be written on paper), and a typical question was under what circumstances, and when, had we all lost our virginities. Being as yet unqualified to reply I was glad to be let off this one. In fact, of the company at the first weekend I found Raymond Mortimer the easiest to get along with, and the walk we took along the towpath together founded a close friendship which lasted until his death.

I shan't describe the next house I went to, which was Charleston. I can only try to evoke the impression I got on first entering the hall as a visitor - the strong feeling of life being intensely and purposefully lived, of animated talk, laughter, brilliant colour everywhere, youth. I don't think I ever felt shy there - there was so much going on, and I soon began to discover what fun it all was. There might have been a play being performed by Angelica and some school friends wearing dresses designed and made by Duncan and Vanessa. Or I sometimes rattled off with Julian and Quentin in a ramshackle little car known as 'the Pet' to swim in the nearest secluded bay; and everyone in the house seemed to enjoy that strangely unpopular but delightful sport - *arguing*. Little Angelica was musical, and I occasionally accompanied her when she sang or played her violin. She was also enchanting, and I was immensely flattered when she referred to me in a poem in the house magazine:

And then there's Miss Marshall
To whom we are partial.

Not that I was ever so addressed of course: Clive soon christened me Fanny to distinguish me from Francis Birrell, a great friend of the house. Excellent meals appeared on the large round painted dining-room table. There was always wine for dinner and the breakfast coffe warming on the hob was hot and strong. The family and their friends came down at all hours, somewhat tousled and preoccupied (Duncan's black hair without a touch of grey was a good advertisment for lack of brushing), usually hurried off afterwards to carry out their various projects, which were to occupy them most of the morning. Clive carried off *The Times* to his library, and the

painters went out into the garden – a rampant jungle of tall flowers
buzzing with bees and fruit trees bowed down with ripening apples
and pears – to collect subjects for a still life.

Only a few miles away, and in frequent touch, were the Woolves
at Monks House, which was on the same wavelength but played a
subtly different tune. There was electricity in the air, engendered by
Virginia's tense and erratic genius, and though the display of lightning was dazzling some visitors felt ill at ease, wondering where the
next flash would strike. But Leonard was a powerful influence of
calm and order, with his slow deep voice, steady gaze and trembling
hands. The lawn was always beautifully mown, his roses and dahlias
grew to supernatural size, and his doting dogs obeyed his grumbled
commands and affectionate kicks. I remember no animals at Charleston, but at Monks House they were an important element. Birds,
too, were part of the Woolves' life. On one visit I remember that
the hall door could not be shut for fear of disturbing a nesting
swallow.

And what can I say about Ham Spray – my own much loved home
for nearly thirty years? When Lytton and Ralph bought the house
jointly in 1924 I was still working at Birrell and Garnett's bookshop,
but I used to go down to Wiltshire at weekends and help paint the
inside of the house, while Carrington covered doors, furniture and
tiles with her delicate decorations, very different in style from the
bolder ones at Charleston. Meanwhile Lytton would be lovingly arranging his books in the library shelves made by the village carpenter,
over which, for purposes of reference, Carrington had mysteriously
but characteristically painted the letters of the alphabet from Z to
A. Ralph would be at work clearing away the 'vulgar' round flo-
werbeds and the superfluous trees from the lawn – they were mostly
conifers, abhorred by Lytton – so that a perfectly clear view could
be got from the pink Jane Austen front of the house and its verandah
to the Downs half a mile away, leaving nothing between that wasn't
green – the lawn, the fields and the ilex drooping gracefully over
the ha-ha. Everywhere inside the house were piles of catalogues –
Lytton's from antiquarian booksellers and Carrington's from seeds-
men. There was always at least one cat in residence.

Alas, Lytton and Carrington had a bare seven years in which to
enjoy their country peace before tragedy struck, with Lytton's fatal
illness and Carrington's suicide. The house seemed so forlorn that
it was hard to believe it would recover and even preside over a happy
life again. But the thought of deserting it was unbearable to both

Ralph and me. We left London and came to live entirely at Ham Spray. The miracle was somehow accomplished and we developed a way of life that was not so much *di*vergent as *e*mergent from the past. We brought up our son there, and our family happiness was greatly sustained by visits from friends, many of whom came from Charleston. Clive was one of our most faithful visitors, often bringing us a brace of pheasants. Julian and Quentin came too, as well as Angelica and Bunny and their four little girls, one of whom was to become my own daughter-in-law. As in Sussex we walked on the Downs, played garden bowls and not too solemn badminton at which Lytton had once displayed an unforgettable style all his own, rather as if swatting mosquitoes, and Lydia Keynes had distinguished herself by not hitting the shuttlecock once. We enjoyed the hot days in a small swimming pool with a disproportionately high diving-board. The mere hint that a local landowner had closed a right of way along the top of the Downs fired Julian's revolutionary zeal to dash off with wire-cutters and destroy it. It was hard to decoy Duncan and Vanessa away from their studios, except to go abroad, but they were specially honoured guests when they came. We owed their last visit, one icy winter weekend, to a fortunate freeze-up which made Charleston uninhabitable. I remember that we were anxious whether we should be able to keep them warm and happy, but I noted in my diary afterwards that they were the 'nicest visitors and the best company we had had for ages'.

After all there were no great differences between days spent at Charleston and at Ham Spray, but, it any existed, it lay in the way we began the mornings. At Charleston, as I have implied, they started – as they went on – creatively. Ralph and I were perhaps unusual in finding getting up and dressing the best time for conversation. It was certainly now that Ralph spouted ideas like Roman candles, it was the time when we both loved propounding theories, analysing characters, discussing books and political issues, cracking jokes. Some visitors even complained of the noise we made talking all the way down the creaking corridor that passed the spare rooms and led to the bathroom.

But, looking back, I believe there were many more similarities than differences. For after all the keys to the two houses had once dangled from the same ring – Gordon Square; and it was there, too, that Ralph's and my married life had begun, as I very often remember.

Those tall Georgian windows still stare into the Square garden between the dappled trunks and dangling bobbles of the plane trees;

but I believe the rooms are all offices or departments of the University now, and the tap of typewriters has replaced the chatter and laughter of those *very* far off days.

Richard Morphet: The Significance of Charleston

In 1936 Quentin Bell wrote a skit for Charleston entitled 'Charleston Revisited.' In it a group of tourists from the future are imagined touring the house with a guide who

> talked about the furniture, and the furniture was the audience. Maynard Keynes was, of course, a safe, Leonard and Virginia were twin bookcases labelled Fact and Fiction, my father was an 18th century escritoire, and so on. ('Charleston Revisited,' 8).

Bell recalls showing the sketch to a friend who observed it was based on an absurdity, namely that anyone would want to preserve Charleston. It was a bad play, its author admits, but at least it showed him to be a prophet.

The importance of Charleston in the history of the Bloomsbury Group has emerged clearly with the extraordinary restoration of the farmhouse and the establishment of the Charleston Trust in 1980. Thousands are now guided through Charleston every year. Richard Morphet, Keeper of the Modern Collection at the Tate Gallery, wrote of his response to Charleston in 1967, while Duncan Grant was still living there, and his article is an illuminating description and analysis of pre-restoration Charleston. The article was accompanied with photographs of the Charleston dining and garden rooms, Grant's studio, a painting of the interior of the house done by him in 1916, and examples of the Charleston decor referred to in the text.

The reawakening of interest in the achievements and life of the Bloomsbury Group involves frequent reference to Charleston, the country home near Lewes of Duncan Grant, who is now in his eighty-third year. In an exceptional degree this house, curious and individual in its decoration and mood, expresses both a pattern of life and a visual style; it makes especially evident, in a way that a museum or book cannot, the fusion of these two characteristics into a single sensibility.

Originally a farm-house, then a guest-house early in this century,

Charleston lies just beneath the South Downs on Lord Gage's estate, in an area of Sussex that has been called Bloomsbury by the sea from the proximity of a number of familiar houses – Leonard and Virginia Woolf's Monk's House at Rodmell, Maynard and Lydia Keynes's Tilton (separated from Charleston by two fields), Asheham House, taken by Virginia Woolf from 1912 to 1919, and the villa at Firle which she leased earlier still. Charleston, however, has the distinction of having entered its second half-century of continuous Bloomsbury occupation. Fifty years' activity has produced there a combination of the informal and the ingenious and of accepted simplicity and spontaneous fantasy which gives it a position fascinating in the record of English taste and invaluable in Bloomsbury studies of any kind.

In the autumn of 1916 Vanessa Bell took a lease of Charleston from Lord Gage to enable Duncan Grant and David Garnett to do work of national importance from there under war-time regulations by working as farm-labourers. The lease was continued after the war and Charleston became the settled country-home of Duncan Grant and of Clive and Vanessa Bell and their children. It was in this house of painters that Maynard Keynes wrote *The Economic Consequences of the Peace* (1919) and Lytton Strachey read aloud *Eminent Victorians* prior to publication in 1918. Perhaps especially reflective of Charleston's character is Clive Bell's *Civilization*, written largely in the early years at Charleston and published in 1928. The range of interest which these works represent and their common quality (that of Bloomsbury as a whole) of seeking to establish truth and vividness of experience, regardless of prevailing tastes and taboos, have an accurate parallel in Charleston's appearance, for the designs and the techniques employed admit of no restriction of method or source, while their directness and vigour contrast refreshingly with the mediocrity of much other English decorative work of the period.

The move to Charleston occurred only six years after the first Post-Impressionist exhibition at the Grafton Galleries and in the middle of the seven years' activity of the Omega Workshops, which were run by Roger Fry. The decorations were begun almost at once by Vanessa Bell and Duncan Grant at a time when they were bringing to English painting a much enhanced boldness and freedom of colour. At the Omega, as Professor Pevsner has shown,[1] they were creating a decorative style that foreshadowed an international one of the next decade. Nevertheless, for all their close links with these achievements

1 'Omega', *The Architectural Review*, August 1941, 90, pp. 45–48.

and with the many commissioned schemes executed by Vanessa Bell
and Duncan Grant in the inter-war period, it is a peculiar attraction
of the Charleston decorations that they have an air at once obsessive
and haphazard, of having spread informally as inspiration dictated.
Thus Charleston's overwhelming decorative unity depends not on re-
current *motifs* or related colour-schemes (each room being unexpected) but on a joyful use of colour, a visual curiosity willing to
press anything from goldfish to trumpets into decorative service and
an infinite inventiveness of concept and resourcefulness of method.
For all the odd contrasts Charleston presents, these qualities con-
stitute a highly individual style; thus decorative work by Quentin
and Angelica Bell is intermixed with that of Vanessa Bell and Duncan
Grant with complete congruity. Equally there is no obtrusive break
between adjacent items of widely differing dates.

  All the rooms at the Charleston open off passageways which retain
the simple whitewashed appearance of a farm-house. Many of the
doors bear numbers recalling the days when the house took paying
guests. The decorative condition in 1916 was uniformly simple
throughout. The extent of the change effected by Vanessa Bell and
Duncan Grant appears vividly in the contrast between a passage and
one of the earliest rooms to be decorated (1916 or 17), the library
on the first floor. Sometime earlier Vanessa Bell had been impressed
in the house or studio of either G.F. Watts or C.W. Furse by the
method, relatively unusual for the nineteenth century, of painting
the walls of a room in different plain bold colours.[2] Here the idea
is employed (the walls are grey, yellow and black), but with additional
features of some originality. Each corner contains a wide vertical band
of red; the rectangularity of the room is thus disturbed, each colour
area tending to appear independent of the wall it is on. Above and
below the principal window improbably appear an exotic bird and
a huge dog painted with unexpected spontaneity of touch. In the
upper panels of the door long painted figures bear baskets on their
heads. The baskets reappear in the panels below, three times larger
and laden with fruit. Each figure and basket stands in brilliant colours
against a black ground, and the door, made distinct by the sweep
of coloured wall, is strongly emphasized as an object. At a later date
bookcases were introduced, painted with half-discs and musicians and
filled with books bound in rich tones, and giving to a room with
so splendid a country view much of the feeling of urban Bloomsbury.

2 Information from Mr. Duncan Grant and Mr. Quentin Bell.

Some of the contrasting textiles of the rooms were designed by Vanessa Bell and Duncan Grant and were produced commercially or individually. Their designs appear on curtains, cushions, carpets, screens and even mirror-frames; and there are fabrics from Africa and the Middle East. The urge to juxtapose patterns was inseparable from an instinctive sense of order. So abrupt are the changes of scale, texture and medium that their effectiveness is indeed surprising. Yet the result, the opposite of confusion, is consistently one of heightened formal and tactile sensitivity.

The range of materials employed testifies to an exuberant sense of the possibilities inherent in hitherto unconsidered methods which inspired Vanessa Bell and Duncan Grant in about 1912; through the decades of decoration at Charleston this attitude has remained essential. In an early example, a bed-head design of Morpheus created by Duncan Grant around 1916, with its glowing wing *motif* from a distant culture, two pieces of wood are screwed on to form the god's nose and brow. At about this time Duncan Grant incorporated into a portrait of Lady Ottoline Morrell a string of pearls and a piece of wood carved in an attempt to convey the full forcefulness of the sitter's chin. Any means, he observed, was acceptable that could embody the maximum sense of reality – a principle inherent in the austerer world of Cubist collage and constructions. Painted decoration was applied not only to doors, shutters, tables, chairs, cupboards and beds, but also to screens, boxes, chests, cups, plates and tiles. Repeating patterns applied with stencils and covering the walls give certain rooms an unexpected appearance. In the garden-room, soft grey paisley shapes, set against a lighter grey and scattered with small white flowers, float to and fro with infinite gentleness. In contrast the atmosphere in the dining-room is staccato, its effect vigorous and emphatic; between grey lozenges, angular flashes of yellow jerk and jump in alternate directions against dense black. That so much activity should provide a perfect setting for paintings of more than ordinary interest appears almost miraculous. Yet a part of the rooms' effect comes from the variety and richness of the paintings and drawings they contain – by Matisse, Marchand, Matthew Smith, Maillol, Coldstream, Ingres, and including till recently Picasso's *Jugs and Lemon*, 1907, the curious petal shape of which recurs repeatedly. The cups and plates, produced by Quentin Bell, have the definite shape, thick heavy substance and sensitive textures in the ceramic tradition of Roger Fry, and the same techniques are employed even in the dining-room lampshade peppered with holes, and suspended by strings of beads over a much-painted circular table of exceptional size in proportion to that of the room. Mosaic work, stained glass and brick sculpture (also all by Quentin Bell) appear outside the house. The theories of Roger Fry of course underlie much of this remarkable variety. To counter the dreary lack of vitality of form or material of many manufactured objects in ordinary use, he passionately urged the practising artist's enjoyment in producing objects which would directly reflect individual feeling. The protruding altar-like fireplace in the garden-room and a graceful niche in the dining-room chimney-breast are Fry's own work; both are characteristically simple and direct.

Intrinsic in the imaginative character of Charleston is the impossibility of appreciating its formal innovations without encountering an abundance of artistic suggestion – or, conversely, of relishing the remarkable character of its visual conceits without one's sensitivity to form being aroused. The decorations are as it were distilled between painting and life, with an impassioned involvment in both which decorative art as a genre often seems to lack. Particularly apparent, in figures which sit, crouch, tumble or play instruments on log-box, door or overmantel, is a gift for devising postures at once fantastic, graceful and exactly apt for its enclosing space. The artist's early vivid experiences of the Russian ballet with its revelation of colour and movement, are reflected in such decorations. This exotic trend cannot be disentangled from influences in painting and architecture – a sense of the hieratic derived perhaps from Piero della Francesca, of formal and environmental harmony from the Italian Renaissance interior and of simplified form and intensified colour from Post-Impressionist painting. On one chest, painted by Duncan Grant around 1916, a swimmer, the figure a patchwork of purple, pink and green, the contours of which undulate in the surrounding water, shows a feeling for harmony between man and Nature and an originality of rhythm and colour that oddly link it with the paintings of Franz Marc. Each component decoration represents, sometimes with the directness of an individual scene, but always in the patent enthusiasm with which materials have been handled, the familiar intense pleasures of life. Raymond Mortimer might have had Charleston in mind when he wrote of Vanessa Bell and Duncan Grant in 1929, 'it is a strength of the English decorators that they reflect the varied riches of a cultured intelligence'.[3]

3 *The New Interior Decoration*, p. 29.

A further essential of Charleston's magic lies in its strangely beautiful setting. The Downs, rising behind barns on one side, the pond on another and the large walled garden on a third, provide a sequence of contrasts that parallels those indoors. There is a sense of continuity between interior and garden in the frequent representations in paintings and decorations of outdoor scenes – a door panel can appear almost as a window with a view – and in the impact of the unexpected common to both. Casts of heads which Duncan Grant found discarded (many at Lewes School of Art) stand at intervals along a wall; near by a hydrangea sprouts from inside a seemingly related torso. In an overgrown orchard lurks an extraordinary object known locally as 'the Charleston Spink', a huge upright sphinx so carved in brick (by Quentin Bell, *c.* 1929) that it merges with its pedestal as if growing from it. The round pond, well known in many paintings, is now thickly overgrown with bulrushes. It seems entirely fitting that Duncan Grant, who painted for a period from a gazebo erected for the purpose in mid-pond, should once have investigated the possibility of keeping a flock of flamingoes here. Were they now to emerge, bright and elegant from among the tall stalks, they could find no setting more congruous than this house and garden.

If Charleston gave evidence only of the combination of fantasy and formal inventiveness, which it especially does in the work of Vanessa Bell and Duncan Grant, it would have an important place in the history of art and interior design in Britain in the first half of this century. It illuminates, however, a still wider range of creative achievement – literary, philosophical, critical – among a group of friends, the significance of whose work, as it becomes the subject of widespread inquiry, is now generally acknowledged. The many decorations make apparent the inter-relation of these different concerns. But it is the unity of Charleston – of the decorations with one another and with the setting in which they were evolved – that enables the complex context from which each detail sprang to be most clearly appreciated.

Julian Bell: Monk's House and the Woolfs

Julian Bell's description of Monk's House carries Bloomsbury recollections into the third generation. Son of Anne Olivier and Quentin Bell, namesake of his uncle, Julian Bell is a painter and critic who used to live in Rodmell. His account of visiting Monk's House can be compared with that of his aunt Angelica many years before (see pp. 251–3). Julian Bell's essay, written for a Rodmell village guide, was originally illustrated with drawings and photographs of Leonard Woolf, Monk's House, and Rodmell.

A house where a writer once lived is like an abandoned pithead. Here they descended each day, to work away at the shafts of their imagination and memory: you stand at the entrance of their descent, but what really went on within, the reason and heart of their life here, is not clear to see. You can only stare into the hole they left and attempt a corresponding effort of the imagination.

Monk's House is essentially a plain piece of rural architecture: its weatherboards and steep slate roof don't set out to impose anything on the visitor beyond a spruce, upright practicality. The interiors have been arranged with faithful care, but they don't speak for themselves as do, for instance, the painters' surfaces of Charleston. How can one get at the sense of the Woolfs' life here?

My own memory tunnels back only as far as the fifties. Every August we would visit Leonard, the widower of my great-aunt. His dogs would leap up on you as you opened the gate of what seemed, more then than now, the last house in the village. I looked forward to seeing Leonard. He gave me ten-shilling notes. Handsomely too, knowing what children expected, he would present them as soon as we came inside the scented, heady jungle of the conservatory. I would clutch the crisp brown paper – real money! – and mumble thanks at his shoes. In truth his face alarmed me. It was good, but terribly strong. Lean, sallow, with a resilient shock of white hair, deep-set grey eyes, deep-etched creases to his cheeks: the whole structure of his head was chiselled, long and spare, jutting forward like some archaic weapon. And when he poured tea, there was this wild shake to his hand that you felt he was forcing the whole of his formidable will to subdue; the tea-stream juddering here and there but always just within the cup. He and my father would start talking politics, and I would go to sail boats on the pond.

Leonard believed in politics; politics and civilization. Or perhaps it was rather a business of upholding them without hope. He was stoical. I remember looking at his diaries once, and finding on every page, five days a week, fifty-two weeks a year, the tremulous black scrawl, 'Worked', 'Worked', 'Worked', just that, mostly, virtue's spare reward to itself. When my eyes got nearer to a level with his, I would stay to listen to the wise old man. Playing rather at being that very thing, he would look back over a lifetime spent advancing the cause of democratic socialism and calculate that it had been 200,000 hours of perfectly useless work. Friends and comforters would rush to demur, with stuff about the incalculable benefits somehow conferred by the mere existence of intelligensia such as himself, but I don't think such reassurances could satisfy a consistently political man. Anyhow he relished his pessimism, looking for the storm-cloud to every silver lining in a way that nevertheless managed to be personally equable and good-humoured. I remember him in 1968 or so – ahead of his time as usual – rubbing his hands gleefully at the prospect of ecological apocalypse awaiting the succeeding generation. As to civilization, he believed women were more in possession of it than men. I at the age of fifteen being a bit of a male chauvinist piglet told the venerable old gent I couldn't see why. 'In that case', he said to my trepidation, 'we must have an argument about it some day.' But that was about the last time I saw him.

I suppose his life, his most useful work, had been based on that principle. Virginia was in possession of something really precious. In tending her he was its guardian. And a vital part of the regimen he imposed on her to maintain her health was the country retreat of Monk's House, a weekend alternative to the febrile social whirl of London. Shuttled between the stimulation of the city and the tranquility of the country, she for her part duly produced. The plain shell of the house they had acquired in 1919 was gradually expanded and transformed by the profits on her novels. *Mrs Dalloway* put paid to the traditional rural sanitation of the earth closet in 1925, and at the same time afforded them the 'perfect triumph of our large combined drawing eating room, with its five windows, its beam down the middle, and flowers and leaves nodding in all around us', as her diary notes. Three years later *Orlando* became the square, rather ungainly north-east extension, with Virginia's bedroom, 'a lovely wonderful room, just what I've always hoped for'. In 1931 fame brought electricity.

> Yesterday men were in the house boring holes for electric fires. What more comfort can we acquire? And though the moralists say, when one has a thing one at once finds it hollow, I don't at all agree. I enjoy my luxuries at every turn, and think them wholly good for what I am pleased to call my soul.

One might however annotate that luxuries are nothing if not relative. When Saul Bellow came over to rent the place in the late seventies, hoping for some kind of sympathetic inspiration in its shades, he was so appalled at the palaeolithically primitive amenities and temperature that he took almost the first flight back to Chicago.

But luxury was never really part of the Woolfs' style; nor was style itself really. The visual manner of their improvements does not translate back into the literary manner that made them possible. Possessions came to them awkwardly, haphazardly, from the naive portraits that were sold with the house to the modernisitic armchair that was the laughing stock of arty friends. When in doubt in such matters Virginia turned to Vanessa, ceding much to her sister's unflappable assurance in her visual sensibilities but reserving her own unaccountable predilection for green paint. The resulting tug of influences can be seen – necessarily rationlised – in the tour of the house. What the painstaking reconstruction can't display is the muddle that was the most salient feature of the interior as I knew it in the sixties and I expect had probably not been cleared since the thirties. Great piles of books everywhere, a maze of waist-high piles to be negotiated every time you crossed the room – books interspersed with manuscripts, magazines, ashtrays, sometimes pets – an assortment apparently judged by the Woolfs' friends to be mangy and ill-favoured in the extreme, ranging from mongrels to marmosets.

But if one is trying to make sense of the place, the interior is in a way beside the point. One has to go back to June 1919, to come at the property as Virginia first inspected it. Her diary then records all kinds of hesitancies about the building, 'long and low', with 'little ceremony or precision', notes that the rooms are small, the kitchen 'distinctly bad', there is no hot water – but continues 'these prudent observations were forced to yield to a profound pleasure at the size and shape and fertility and wildness of the garden'. In other words, the primary thing about the house was not so much the being inside it as the looking from out of it. Here again, however, the mind's eye is called for. The garden suffered a period of sad neglect after Leonard's death in 1969, and the rich fruitfulness and exotic hybrids tended by Percy Bartholomew, the Woolfs' gardener, are no quick labour to restore. Leonard's sensuality was expressed in plants: the conservatory – a forties extension – was in his day a miraculous immersion into the tropics, one might imagine a recreation of the Ceylonese atmospheres of his Colonial Service. This quality is no longer there. Nor are the chief verticals of the scene, the great silly elms, brought down by gales and beetles. They ringed the churchyard and the large lawn of which Leonard used to engage all-comers in games of bowls, keeping a tally in a book of the amount of times he had defeated his wife. But beyond them, crucially, visible from Virginia's writing hut, lay the great openness of the Ouse Valley. Perhaps it's idle to speculate too closely on the relationship between someone's work and the space in which they perform it, but one can't discount the presence of this bigness before the writing desk which saw her most ambitious achievements. The Woolfs' previous dwelling in Sussex had been Asham House, three miles across the valley: a secluded place among beechwoods at the bottom of a coomb, wistful and dank. Here you reach the main lawn, and the river valley – the reclaimed marshlands between Rodmell, Lewes and Mount Caburn's round commanding hump – opens out before you, vastly.

To thus emphasize the Woolfs' private sense of space is rather to ignore the fact that Monk's House is one of the chief houses within the village; and I think that's what they themselves tended to do, at least in their earlier years at Monk's House. For much of the time their main relations with the inhabitants of Rodmell were through Percy Bartholomew and Louie Mayer, their servant. However the thirties saw Leonard and Virginia increasingly in Rodmell; he involved with it on a basis of principle, as a member of the local Labour Party; she co-opted by the ladies of the parish into the Women's Institute and the like. She became increasingly fascinated in the relaying of village gossip, even while trying to maintain a mental armslength from it. – This mental armslength extends into her work as a writer. I once illustrated a text of hers set in Rodmell – a children's story called *The Widow and the Parrot* – and found that while it seemed to mention ascertainable features of the landscape, the literal-minded illustrator would be flummoxed at every turn by the studied vagueness, cavalier inaccuracy and indeed wanton introduction of impossibilities with which she treated facts of local geography that must have been daily visible to her. How on earth could her heroine have to cross the River Ouse to walk from Lewes to Rodmell? However one can infer a teasing affection for the village. The one time the Woolfs seriously thought of moving, it was not on account of Rodmell as they found it, but rather the prospect, too awful to comtemplate, of a rival literary clique from London moving down to occupy weekend cottages of their own.

The War and the Battle of Britain brought Cockney refugees, concrete pillboxes and aerial dogfights to shatter the serenity of the Ouse Valley. With his phlegmatic precision, Leonard calculated how they would both lock themselves in the garage and gas themselves the moment they heard of a German landing. But such of course was not to be their fate. Visitors to Rodmell are forever traipsing the path to the river, impelled by some attempt to have a glimpse, if not into the depths of her imagination, at least into those of her death. Do they get closer to her, following her last steps? Can the effort ever satisfy? My friend the writer Malcolm Addison came across a macabre footnote, bringing something closer, though not Virginia. He persuaded a woman he met to write her account of a picnic party in the spring of 1941. She had been a teenager, cycling out from Lewes to Seaford with a girlfriend and three boys, along the near-deserted roads of the earlier part of the war. By Asham they 'decided to stop and have our lunch in the field near the cement works and the river. A few sandwiches and a bottle of pop later, Seaford was forgotten and we turned our energies to diverting a log from its journey along the tide.' They threw stones, 'it had become something of a challenge to get the log ashore . . . Then we realised it was not a log.' One of the boys waded out and overturned it with a stick.

'"It's a woman – a woman in a fur coat!"' The girls thought it was merely an attempt to scare them, they didn't believe it; but the boys sent them home. They called the police. 'Next day we discovered it was the body of a local authoress . . .'

You could call her that.

Charles Mauron: Remarks on Bloomsbury

The distinguished French psychological critic Charles Mauron was a close friend of both E.M. Forster and Roger Fry. Two of his works on aesthetics were published by the Hogarth Press. Mauron translated the novels of E.M. Forster as well as Virginia Woolf's Orlando *and* Flush; *he also assisted Fry in his translations of Mallarmé. The following is an unpublished excerpt from some remarks on Bloomsbury that Mauron wrote in 1965, the year before his death. Quentin Bell paid tribute to Charles Mauron's friendship for and understanding of Bloomsbury by dedicating his* Bloomsbury *to him in 1968.*

. . . The coherence of living beings – and Bloomsbury is nothing if not alive – owes but little to logical similarities; this is not the coherence of discourse. I will be criticised because we are talking about a group and not an organism. But in fact I believe that we distinguish two sorts of groups, those based, in effect, on some kind of shared thinking or interest, while the others owe their cohesiveness to the exultant pleasure of living and creating together. The human couple belongs to the second type: shared thinking and interests play an important role but are secondary compared to their love and their child. Among a group of artists like Bloomsbury, friendship replaces (at least partially) love, and aesthetic creation the child; the principle of its cohesion no less remains complementarity and creativity rather than similarity. The members of such groups cannot be added up; they are not looking for power; they do not preach a faith; their union is not their strength, it is their happiness; and that is why, moreover, they form centres of civilisation in a world where the quantitative and force triumph. . . .

Quentin Bell: The Character of Bloomsbury

'A filial tribute is, of all literary forms, the most difficult and the most perilous – censure is out of place and praise is discounted; impersonality is absurd and intimacy is embarrassing' ('Bloomsbury and the Arts,' 18). These words by Quentin Bell describe the perils he has well avoided in his invaluable writings on Bloomsbury. His familial tributes in this Bloomsbury collection and elsewhere illustrate the achievements as artist, art historian, biographer, and memoirist that have made him Bloomsbury's best living authority.

Bell's short book on Bloomsbury, the last chapter of which – minus the illustrations – is reprinted here, still provides, more than a quarter of a century after it was written, an illuminating introduction in words and pictures to what Bloomsbury was. But it is an introduction with something of a thesis; for Quentin Bell the character of Bloomsbury is to be found most clearly in those rational and pacific ideals that its members sought to maintain in a world that was becoming increasingly irrational and violent.

I imagine that I have said enough to give the reader a fair idea of what I believe to be Bloomsbury's main characteristics. Before attempting to tie my arguments together in what I hope may be a reasonably tidy knot I would like once more to emphasize the fact that I am writing about something almost impalpable, almost indefinable.

Imagine a great highway up which walks a heterogeneous crowd – the British Intellectuals. There is in that great concourse a little group of people who talk eagerly together, it is but one of many similar groups and sometimes groups seem to merge. Figures move in towards the centre and move away again to walk elsewhere; some are silent, some are loquacious. When the great ambling procession begins to march in time to a military band, the part to which we devote our attention falls out of step; this makes it, for a time, conspicuous, and yet even so it is not preferably definable. There are other groups which also become noticeably civilian; moreover, martial music is an infectious thing, and it is hard to say who is and who is not walking to its rhythms. Then, at a later stage, the group suddenly becomes enlarged. Everyone seems to be joining it, so that it is no longer a group, it has become a crowd. It dissolves, the original members disappear, and it is gone.

The image is sufficiently banal but I can find none better to convey the amorphous character of my subject.

What then had this group in common apart from the fact that it was talking? Perhaps this in itself may be a distinction, for there are groups that do not talk, they shout and yell and come to blows. Bloomsbury did none of these things. Despite tremendous differences of opinion, it talked. Indeed it did more, it talked on the whole reasonably, it talked as friends may talk together, with all the licence and all the affection of friendship. It believed, in fact, in pacific and rational discussion.

Now there is nothing remarkable about this; most of us behave quietly and carry on rational conversations. But we also do other things: we create works of art and perform acts of worship, we make love and we make war, we yell and we come to blows.

Bloomsbury sometimes did these things, too, and in fact we all live our lives upon two contradictory principles, that of reason and that of unreason. We come, as best we may, to a synthesis of opposites; the peculiar thing about Bloomsbury was the nature of its dialectic.

A creative artist in modern society can hardly be unaware of the charms of unreason. He is, by the nature of his employment, so very much more dependent upon intuition than upon ratiocination. Art in our time - I am thinking of the visual arts in particular - has broken free from any pretense of utility. The artist is bound by no rational programme, no reasonable dependence upon mimesis; his images are made in accordance with unbiddable inner necessities, they are such stuff as dreams are made on and are judged in accordance with an aesthetic which is of its nature dogmatic and impervious to reason. While this is obviously true of the musical and visual arts, in literature, where a certain tincture of thought may be apprehended, the sway of the unreasoning emotions, the 'thinking in the blood' that makes for heroism, passion, chastity, and nearly all the strong emotions that are the very stuff of tragedy, can be overwhelmingly powerful.

The irrational has an even stronger pull, in that it is so often a communal phenomenon. He who thinks much is perforce a lonely man, whereas the great unreasoning emotions of mankind bring us into a glorious brotherhood with our kind. We feel (I quote from Wyndham Lewis) 'the love and understanding of blood brothers, of one culture, children of the same traditions, whose deepest social interests, when all is said and done, are one: that is the only sane and realistic journey in the midst of a disintegrating world. That, as I interpret it, is the national socialist doctrine of *Blutsgefühl*.'[1]

These words were written at a time when it was still possible for a partial observer to ignore the uglier side of National Socialism. They may serve to remind us that the Janus-face of Social Love is Social Hatred; it is hard to create a God without creating a Devil.

In the year 1900 the world had not seen what a modern nation could do when it puts its trust in *Blutsgefühl*, but it was obvious enough that if men were to surrender to the voice of authority, to yield to the strong irrational demands of religion, or nationalism, or sexual superstition, hatred no less than love would be the result. The hatred of Christian for Christian, of nation for nation, the blind unreasoning hatred that had hounded Oscar Wilde or killed Socrates, these were all communal emotions that resulted from irrationality. The sleep of reason engenders monsters, the monsters of violence. It was therefore absolutely necessary, if charity were to survive in the world, that reason should be continually awake.

This I think was the assumption that determined Bloomsbury's attitude and gave a distinctive tone to its art and to its conversation.

No one today could for one moment suppose that the irrational forces in life, the love of death and of violence, were not present in the world, or that they do not lie somewhere within each of us, but whereas to some of us they are not merely immanent but something to be embraced and accepted with joy, connected as they are with so many great spiritual experiences, for Bloomsbury they were something to be chained, muzzled and as far as possible suppressed. The great interest of Bloombury lies in the consistency, the thor-

1 Wyndham Lewis, *Hitler* (1931), p. 109.

oughness and, despite almost impossible difficulties, the success with which this was done.

The first great step was to transfer nineteenth-century scepticism from the cosmic to the personal field. The rejection of dogmatic morality meant that the traditional sanctions of social hatred were removed. G.E. Moore's limpid intellectual honesty remained and with it a morality which excluded, or very nearly excluded, aggressive violence. As Maynard Keynes says:

> The New Testament is a handbook for politicians compared with the unworldiness of Moore's chapter on the 'Ideal'. Indeed there is, in *Principia Ethica*, a certain remoteness from the hurly-burly of everyday life, which, I suspect, results from the extraordinarily sheltered and optimistic society that was to be found in Cambridge at the beginning of the century, and this mild emotional climate was, I apprehend, an indispensable prerequisite for a society which attempted to lead a completely non-aggressive existence.

'We repudiated' – I am again quoting from Maynard Keynes – 'all versions of the doctrine of original sin, of there being insane and irrational springs of wickedness in most men.' Now this may be true, but if it is true it is surprising. It may be true, because the human mind is capable of such extraordinary feats of inconsistency, but if one considers the novels of E.M. Forster, which are deeply involved in this very question, I find it hard to believe that his contemporaries completely ignored the menace of the irrational.

Death and violence walk hand in hand through these novels; the goblins walk over the universe and although they are driven away, we know that they are still there; children are killed, young men are struck down with swords, blind hatred and blind prejudice are never far away. Where Forster differs from his friends and is not, to my mind, altogether Bloomsbury, is in his essentially reverent and optimistic attitude. His reverence is, to be sure, evasive and half veiled. But it is there all right, in the woods of Hertfordshire or the caves of Marabar; there is something that escapes his reasoning and I can just imagine him buying a rather small dim candle to burn before the alter of some rather unpopular saint – something that Lytton Strachey, for instance, could never have done.

Ethically however he seems to me altogether on the same side as Bloomsbury: conscious, deeply conscious of the dark irrational side of life but absolutely convinced of the necessity of holding fast to reason, charity and good sense.

Bloomsbury may or may not have appreciated the role of 'the insane and irrational springs of wickedness' that seem so close to the surface of life in *Howards End,* but must it not have seen them gushing forth in cascades of derisive laughter or in torrents of abuse in the Grafton Gallery Exhibition?

The public reaction to Gauguin, Cézanne and van Gogh was not founded upon any process of reasoning. The public laughed or was angry because it did not understand, and also, I think, because it *did* understand. People could hardly have been so angry, would hardly have reiterated, again and again, the charge of indecency (this hardly seems credible when we think of Cézanne's still lives) or of anarchism, unless they had become aware of some profoundly disturbing, some quite positive emotion in that which they so much hated and were later, with equal unreason, so greatly to love.

Now at first sight it would appear that when faced by such obstinate and furious aesthetic convictions reason would be powerless, and indeed speechless. Speechless she was not. Both Clive Bell and Roger Fry had plenty to say about art between 1910 and 1914. They would most willingly argue with anyone who would listen to them, and while Clive Bell elaborated his theory of significant form, Roger Fry was explaining, persuading, reasoning in talk and conversation, and in letters to the press. Here, Fry seems to be arguing a purely intellectual case. His method is to find common ground and then proceed by a process of enquiry: We both agree in liking A but you do not like B. What then is the difference between A and B? It turns out of course to be something very insubstantial and the opponent is in a perfectly nice and entirely rational way flattered. Such is the method of his argument: he refuses to be dogmatic and he refuses to be angry. He appeals continually to reason.

There was a certain element of deception here, not, I think, of conscious deception. Up to a point Roger Fry's arguments were fair enough, but at a certain point a mixture of charm and what, for lack of a better word I would call 'overwhelmingness' would clinch the victory. His friends knew this to their cost, for when Roger started some really March hare, some business of black boxes, dark stars, thaumaturgic parascientific nonsense for which he had a strong though inconsistent affection, his force of character, his air of sweet reasonableness and scientific integrity, was such that he could convince himself and his friends of the truth of whatever chimerical bee might for the moment have flown into his bonnet.

The excellence of Seurat, Cézanne and Poussin were not, in my opinion at all events, chimerical nonsense, but Fry made his hearers believe in those excellencies, made them feel them by means of a method of argument which had the purest air of scientific objectivity, in a field which, ultimately, science has no authority. Roger Fry is concerned not only to present a 'fair argument' but to argue about fair things. By this I mean that he does not readily allude to the esoteric or mysterious side of art but talks rather about sensual and easily demonstrable characteristics. His attitude to primitive art is revealing: confronted by Negro sculpture he is amazed by its plastic freedom, its 'three-dimensionalness', the intelligence with which the negro translates the forms of nature, his exquisite taste in the handling of material. Only in one brief allusive phrase does he touch on the magical purposes of these articles. Compare this with the attitude of Emil Nolde, as reported by his latest biographer:

> He saw in this art, with its abstract and rhythmic sense of ornament and color and its mystic power, an affirmation of his own anti-classical art. He was one of the first artists to protest against the relegation of primitive art objects to anthropological museums, where they were still exhibited as scientific specimens. His own 'blood and soil' mystique made him an early proponent of the indigenous art of all peoples.[2]

In fact, of course, the tendency of the Bloomsbury art critics was to look away from content altogether. It is a tendency better exemplified by Clive Bell than by Roger Fry; neither of them in fact held it with complete consistency. But undoubtedly the main tendency of their writings between, say, 1910 and 1925 is in the direction of a purely formalist attitude. The aesthetic emotion is, or at least can be and probably should be, something of almost virgin purity, a matter of harmonious relationships, of calculated patterning, entirely removed from the emotive feelings; and these, when they do occur in works of art, are not only irrelevant and 'literary' but productive of that vulgarity, sentimentality and rhetoric which is the besetting sin of nineteenth-century art. Indeed it is the existence of that kind of 'Salon Art' which, I fancy, prompted these rather hazardous generalizations. The sentimentality of Raphael and Correggio, the violence of Goya and Breughel, are not reproved but dismissed as irrelevant, or at least inessential.

2 Roger Fry, *Negro Sculpture* (1920); repr. in *Vision and Design* (1920); and Peter Selz, *Emil Nolde* (1963), p. 33.

Something of the same attitude may, I think, be traced in the actual paintings of the group. Bloomsbury finds its masters amongst the Apollonian rather than the Dionysiac painters, turning to Piero della Francesca rather than Michelangelo, Poussin rather than Bernini, Constable rather than Turner. Amongst the Post-Impressionists it looks to van Gogh and to Gauguin but above all to Cézanne.

Cézanne, whose genius is large enough to be interpreted in many ways, is used as a guide to architectonic solidity, to the careful ordering and redisposition of nature. He is not used as the Vorticists and the Germans use him, as a provider of anguished angularities, violent, emphatic, exclamatory drawing and dynamic chaos.

The insistence that art be removed from life, that painting should aspire to the condition of music, which may certainly be deduced from the writings of Clive Bell and Roger Fry, would, one might have thought, have been translated in practice into pure abstraction, but apart from a few brief essays made before 1914 Bloomsbury painting remains anchored to the visible world. For this there was an important psychological reason: the Bloomsbury painters were, I think, intensely interested in content.

Vanessa Bell continued to the last to paint landscapes and still lives, girls, children and flowers, which to me at all events seem to be replete with psychological interest, while at the same time firmly denying that the story of a picture had any importance whatsoever. Duncan Grant has always been rather less positive in his statements; his lyrical inventions are equally if not more suggestive of a highly literary mood. And the mood, which may also be observed in the work of Roger Fry, is again one of passion firmly controlled by reason, sensual enjoyment regulated by the needs of serenity.

Looking at Duncan Grant's *Lemon Gatherers* in the Tate and considering its quietly lyrical quality, the calm precision of its design, its tacit sensuality, who could doubt that in 1914 he would be a conscientious objector? The answer of course is that anyone could doubt it and that paintings do not have such clear diagnostic value as that, but I let the sentence stand because, overstatement though it is, it conveys a certain measure of truth. Bloomsbury painting, like Bloomsbury writing and Bloomsbury politics, is pacific even when it is not pacifist. It is by no means unconscious of violence, but it reacts against it either by deliberately avoiding it, or by criticism and mockery, or by trying to find a formula to contain it.

On the whole the painters shrink from violence. Roger Fry attempts to explain art in other terms; for him violence was something stupid and irrational, a means to pain when clearly pleasure is the end of life. Lytton Strachey and Maynard Keynes both fight it with ridicule, Clive Bell veers between ridicule and evasion, Virginia Woolf finds its origin in the relationship of the sexes and seeks its cure in their fusion. All turn to reason as the one possible guide in human affairs precisely because the forces of violence lie within even the best-intentioned men. As Clive Bell wrote, 'those were not naturally cruel men who burnt heretics for not agreeing with them, and witches for being vaguely disquieting, they were simply men who refused to submit prejudice to reason.'[3]

Even those who would declare that faith is in some sort a higher thing than reason would, probably, agree that there is a good deal to be said for this view – in theory. The difficulty, as anyone who surveys the world from Birmingham, Alabama to Salisbury, Rhodesia, and back again by way of Saigon, will know is that when it comes to a struggle between reason and violence reason nearly always takes a beating.

And yet this is not the whole picture. Reason does win victories and Bloomsbury has helped to win them. This paradoxically is one of the things that makes us undervalue its achievements. It would be quite easy to compile an anthology of Bloomsbury's pronouncements on prudery, sexual persecution and censorship, which would command the assent of nearly all literate people at the present day and would, for that reason, be rather dull; the audacities of one age become the platitudes of the next.

But in its larger effort, the effort to live a life of rational and pacific freedom, to sacrifice the heroic virtues in order to avoid the heroic vices, Bloomsbury was attempting something which, to the next generation, seemed unthinkable. It could only have been thought of by people in a favoured social position at a particularly favourable moment in the history of England. It could be maintained, but only just maintained, between the years 1914 and 1918 because in that war it was still possible for an intelligent man or woman to be neutral. The advocates of reason, tolerance and scepticism frequently found themselves confronted by individuals who were partly or wholly on the other side. I have mentioned Fitzjames Stephen and his generation, D.H. Lawrence, Wyndham Lewis and Rupert Brooke – a very heterogeneous collection of talents, but all united in their belief that at a certain point emotion, not reason, must be our guide, and that

3 Clive Bell, *On British Freedom* (1923), p. 47.

heroic violence is more desirable than unheroic calm. But with all of these, as also with a belligerent England, some kind of parley, some kind of communication was possible; between them and Bloomsbury there was not a complete polarity of views. With the advent of Fascism, Bloomsbury was confronted by a quarrel in which, believing what they believed, neutrality was impossible. The old pacifism had become irrelevant and the group as a group ceased to exist.

Identifications

The following are brief descriptions of the contributors to this collection and of the more significant people, places, and groups referred to in the selections.

Affable Hawk: *see* MacCarthy, Desmond.

Ainsworth, A.R., 1879-1959: Apostle, friend of G.E. Moore, educator.

Anny, Aunt: *see* Ritchie, Anny Thackeray.

Anrep, Helen, 1885-1965: companion of Roger Fry, married to the mosaicist Boris Anrep.

Apostles, The, known as The Cambridge Conversazione Society or simply as The Society: a secret Cambridge undergraduate discussion club founded in the early nineteenth century.

Asham (or Asheham) House: Woolfs' country home near Lewes, Sussex, 1912-19; demolished 1994.

Auden, W(ystan) H(ugh), 1907-73: poet, man of letters.

Bagenal, Barbara Hiles, 1891-1984: artist, friend of Saxon Sydney-Turner, married Nicolas Bagenal, later companion of Clive Bell.

Barbara: *see* Bagenal, Barbara.

Baring, Maurice, 1874-1945: poet, man of letters.

Barocchi, Randolfo: manager of Diaghilev's ballet, first husband of Lydia Lopokova.

Bedford Square: Bloomsbury square in which Ottoline Morrell's house was located, 1906-15.

Bell, Angelica: *see* Garnett, Angelica.

Bell, Clive, 1881-1964: art and literary critic, husband of Vanessa Bell, father of Julian and Quentin Bell.

Bell, Julian, (1) 1908-37: poet, son of Vanessa and Clive Bell; (2) 1953- : painter, critic, son of Quentin and Olivier Bell.

Bell, Quentin, 1910- : artist, art historian, biographer, memoirist, son of Vanessa and Clive Bell.

Bell, Vanessa, known as Nessa, 1879-1961: painter, daughter of Leslie and Julia Stephen, sister of Thoby Stephen, Virginia Woolf, and Adrian Stephen, wife of Clive Bell, companion of Duncan Grant, mother of Julian, Quentin, and Angelica Bell.

Belsize Park Gardens: Hampstead home of the Strachey family, 1907–20.

Bentinck, Lord Henry, 1863–1931: brother of Ottoline Morrell.

Bernard Street: Bloomsbury location of Roger Fry's later London home.

Bertie: *see* Russell, Bertrand.

Birrell, Francis, known as Frankie, 1889–1935: critic, co-owner of Birrell and Garnett bookshop, son of Augustine Birrell.

Bob Trevy: *see* Trevelyan, R.C.

Brenan, Gamel Elizabeth Woolsey, 1895–1968: writer, wife of Gerald Brenan.

Brenan, Gerald, 1894–1987; writer, authority on Spain, friend of Carrington and Ralph Partridge.

Brooke, Rupert, 1887–1915: Apostle, poet.

Brunswick Square: Bloomsbury square, location of the London homes at one time or another of Virginia and Adrian Stephen, Leonard Woolf, J.M. Keynes, Duncan Grant, E.M. Forster, and others.

Bunny: *see* Garnett, David.

Bussy, Dorothy Strachey, 1866–1960: writer and translator, married to Simon Bussy, sister of Lytton Strachey.

Bussy, Jane-Simone, 1906–60: painter, daughter of Dorothy and Simon Bussy.

Bussy, Simon-Albert, 1870–1945: painter, husband of Dorothy Bussy, father of Jane-Simone Bussy.

Cambridge Conversazione Society, The: *see* Apostles.

Campbell, Roy, 1901–57: poet, satirist, translator.

Carrington, Dora, known as Carrington, 1893–1932: artist, companion of Lytton Strachey, married to Ralph Partridge.

Case, Janet, 1862–1937: teacher, friend of Virginia Woolf.

Cassis-sur-mer: village near Marseille, location of La Bergère, where Vanessa Bell, Duncan Grant, and others stayed from 1927 onwards.

Cecil, David, 1902–86: critic, biographer, English professor, married to Rachel MacCarthy.

Charleston: country home near Lewes, Sussex, of Vanessa Bell, Duncan Grant, their children, and others in Bloomsbury from 1916; decorated by Vanessa, Duncan, Quentin, and Angelica, it was restored and established as the Charleston Trust in 1980.

Churchill, Winston, 1874–1965: statesman, war leader, first lord of the Admiralty 1911–15.

Clapham Sect: group of early nineteenth-century reforming Anglican evangelicals that included the great-grandfathers of E.M. Forster and the Stephen sisters.

Clive: *see* Bell, Clive.

Cole, Horace de Vere, 1881–1936: hoaxer, friend of Adrian Stephen.

Costelloe, Karin: *see* Stephen, Karin.

Costelloe, Ray: *see* Strachey, Ray.

Courtauld, Samuel, 1876–1947: industrialist, art collector, friend of Roger Fry and the Keyneses.

Cox, Katherine, known as Ka, 1887–1938: member of the Neo-Pagans, friend of Rupert Brooke, married to William Arnold Foster.

Dadie: *see* Rylands, George.

Davidson, Angus, 1898–1980: translator, art critic, writer, assistant at the Hogarth Press in the 1920s, brother of painter Douglas Davidson.

Desmond: *see* MacCarthy, Desmond.

Day Lewis, Cecil, 1904–72: poet, detective-story writer.

Dickinson, Goldsworthy Lowes, 1862–1932: Cambridge don, Apostle, writer, friend of Roger Fry, E.M. Forster, J.M. Keynes, and the Woolfs.

Dickinson, Violet: 1865–1948, early friend of Virginia Woolf, sister of Oswald Dickinson.

Dobson, Frank: 1886–1963, sculptor.

Duckworth, George, 1868–1934: son of Julia and Herbert Duckworth, brother of Gerald and Stella Duckworth, half-brother of Vanessa Bell, Virginia Woolf, and Adrian Stephen; public servant.

Duckworth, Gerald, 1870–1937: son of Julia and Herbert Duckworth, brother of George and Stella Duckworth, half-brother of Vanessa Bell, Thoby Stephen, Virginia Woolf, and Adrian Stephen; publisher.

Duckworth, Stella, 1869–1897: daughter of Julia and Herbert Duckworth, sister of George and Gerald Duckworth, half-sister of Vanessa Bell, Thoby Stephen, Virginia Woolf, and Adrian Stephen.

Duncan: *see* Grant, Duncan.

Dunnett, Nellie: nurse of Angelica Bell.

Eastman, Max, 1883–1969: American critic.

Eliot, T(homas) S(tearns), 1888–1965: poet, critic, editor, publisher.

Everest, Louie: *see* Mayer, Louie.

Firle: Sussex village near Charleston.

Fitzroy Square: Bloomsbury square where Virginia and Adrian Stephen lived, 1907–11, and where the Omega Workshops were established 1913–19.

Fitzroy Street: Bloomsbury street where Duncan Grant and Vanessa Bell had a studio 1929–40.

Forster, E(dward) M(organ), known as Morgan, 1879–1970: novelist, essayist, critic, and biographer.

Frankie: *see* Birrell, Francis.

Friday Club: established by Vanessa Bell in 1905 for the discussion of art, literature, and ideas; it held exhibitions and lasted until 1914.

Fry, Margery, 1872-1957: teacher, reformer, sister of Roger Fry.

Fry, Pamela, 1902-85: daughter of Roger and Helen Fry, married to Micu Diamond.

Fry, Roger, 1866-1934: art critic, painter, son of Edward and Mariabella Fry, brother of Agnes, Isabel, and Margery Fry, father of Julian and Pamela Fry, companion of Helen Anrep.

Garnett, Angelica Bell, 1918- : artist, writer, daughter of Vanessa Bell and Duncan Grant, married to David Garnett.

Garnett, Constance, 1862-1946: translator of Russian writers, married to Edward Garnett, mother of David Garnett.

Garnett, David, known as Bunny, 1892-1981: writer, editor, son of Edward and Constance Garnett, married (1) Ray Marshall, (2) Angelica Bell.

Garnett, Edward, 1868-1936: writer, publisher's reader, married to Constance Garnett, father of David Garnett.

Garnett, Henrietta, 1945- : writer, daughter of David and Angelica Garnett.

Garnett, Rachel Marshall, known as Ray, 1891-1940: illustrator, married to David Garnett, sister of Frances Partridge.

Garsington: Oxfordshire country home of Ottoline Morrell.

George: see either Duckworth, George, or Mallory, George.

Gertler, Mark, 1891-1939: painter.

Goat: nickname for Virginia Woolf.

Gordon Square: Bloomsbury square where the Stephens, Stracheys, Bells, Woolfs, and Keyneses all lived at various times and addresses.

Goth, The: nickname for Thoby Stephen.

Grant, Duncan, 1885-1978: painter, companion of Vanessa Bell, father of Angelica Garnett.

Great Ormond Street: Bloomsbury location of Saxon Sydney-Turner's home.

Green, Alice, 1847-1929: wife of the philosopher T.H. Green.

Guildford: Surrey location of Roger Fry's house Durbins.

Gumbo: see Strachey, Marjorie.

Ham Spray House: Lytton Strachey's country home near Hungerford, Berkshire, from 1924.

Harris, Lilian, died 1950: Women's Co-operative Guild official, friend of Margaret Llewelyn Davies.

Hawtrey, Ralph, 1879-1975: Apostle, economist, Treasury official.

Head, Henry, 1861-1940: neurologist, doctor of Virginia Woolf.

Heard, Gerald, 1889-1971: writer and intellectual.

Heretics, The: Cambridge discussion society.

Higgens, Grace, 1904-83: cook and housekeeper at Charleston.

Hiles, Barbara: see Bagenal, Barbara.

Hills, John Walter, known as Jack, 1867-1938: member of Parliament, married to Stella Duckworth.

Hogarth House: Woolf's home in Richmond, Surrey, 1915-24.

Hope, Lottie: servant of the Woolfs and the Bells.

Hutchinson, Mary Barnes, 1889-1979: writer, cousin of Lytton Strachey and Duncan Grant, married to St. John Hutchinson, companion of Clive Bell.

Huxley, Aldous, 1894-1963: novelist, critic, essayist, married to Maria Nys.

Hyde Park Gate: Kensington Gardens street, location of the Stephen family home.

Isherwood, Christopher, 1904-86: novelist, autobiographer, man of letters.

James: see Strachey, James.

Julian: see Bell, Julian (1).

Ka: see Cox, Katherine.

Keynes, J(ohn) M(aynard), known as Maynard, nicknamed Pozzo, 1883-1946: economist, Cambridge don, Treasury official, married to Lydia Lopokova.

Keynes, Lydia Lopokova, 1892-1981: ballerina, married to J.M. Keynes.

Lacket, The: Lytton Strachey's cottage in Wiltshire, 1913-15.

Lamb, Henry, 1883-1960: painter, brother of Walter Lamb.

Lamb, Walter, 1882-1961: classicist, secretary of the Royal Academy, brother of Henry Lamb.

Lawrence, D.H., 1885-1930: novelist, poet, essayist, critic.

Lee, Vernon, pen-name of Violet Paget, 1856-1935: writer.

Lehmann, John, 1907-87: poet, man of letters, editor, publisher, partner in the Hogarth Press, 1938-46.

Leonard: see Woolf, Leonard.

Lilian: see Harris, Lilian.

Llewelyn Davies, Margaret, 1861-1941: feminist, Women's Co-operative Guild leader, friend of Leonard and Virginia Woolf and also Lilian Harris.

Llewelyn Davies, Theodore, 1871-1905: Apostle, brother of Margaret Llewelyn Davies.

Lopokova, Lydia: see Keynes, Lydia.

Lottie: see Hope, Lottie.

Louie: see Mayer, Louie.

Ludwig: see Wittgenstein, Ludwig.

Lydia: see Keynes, Lydia.

Lytton: see Strachey, Lytton.

MacCarthy, Desmond, pen-name Affable Hawk, 1877-1952: literary and dramatic critic, married to Molly MacCarthy.

MacCarthy, Mary Warre-Cornish, known as Molly, 1882-1953: writer, married to Desmond MacCarthy.

MacCarthy, Rachel, 1909–82: daughter of Molly and Desmond MacCarthy, married to David Cecil.

Madge: *see* Vaughan, Margaret.

Mallory, George, 1886–1924: Apostle, mountaineer.

Mansfield, Katherine Beauchamp, 1888–1923: short-story writer, married to Middleton Murry.

Marshall, Frances: *see* Partridge, Frances.

Marshall, Rachel: *see* Garnett, Rachel.

Mary: *see* Hutchinson, Mary.

Massingham, H.W., 1860–1924: editor of the *Nation*, 1907–24.

Mauron, Charles, 1899–1966: French critic, translator of E.M. Forster and Virginia Woolf, friend of Forster and Roger Fry.

Mayer, Louie Everest, 1912– : cook for the Woolfs at Monk's House.

Mayfair: fashionable West London district.

Mayor, Robin, 1869–1947: Apostle, educator.

Maynard: *see* Keynes, J.M.

Maxse, Katherine Lushington, known as Kitty, 1867–1922: friend of the Stephen family, married to Leo Maxse, editor.

Mecklenburgh Square: Bloomsbury square, home of the Woolfs, 1939–40.

McTaggart, John McTaggart Ellis, 1866–1925: Apostle, philosopher, Cambridge don.

Memoir Club: formed in 1920 by Molly MacCarthy for members of Old Bloomsbury to read one another their memoirs; last meeting in 1956.

Midnight Society: Cambridge undergraduate society reading society, meeting around 1900.

Mill House: Lytton Strachey's country home, Tidmarsh, Berkshire, 1917–24.

Molly: *see* MacCarthy, Mary.

Monk's House (or Monks House): country home in Rodmell, near Lewes, Sussex, of the Woolfs from 1919 onwards.

Moore, G.E., 1873–1958: Apostle, philosopher, Cambridge don, author of *Principia Ethica* (1903).

Morgan: *see* Forster, E.M.

Morphet, Richard, 1938– : Keeper of the Modern Collection, Tate Gallery.

Morrell, Lady Ottoline Cavendish-Bentinck, nicknamed Ott, 1873–1938: hostess, patron of the arts, married to Philip Morrell.

Morrell, Philip, 1870–1943: barrister, member of Parliament, married to Ottoline Morrell.

Mortimer, Raymond, 1895–1980: critic, literary editor of *New Statesman*, 1935–47, succeeded Desmond MacCarthy as chief *Sunday Times* critic, companion of Harold Nicolson.

Murry, John Middleton, 1889–1957: critic, married to Katherine Mansfield.

Myers, L.H., 1881–1944: novelist.

Nellie: *see* Dunnet, Nellie.

Neo-Pagans: name given by Virginia Woolf to a group of young Cambridge friends before the First World War, including the Olivier sisters, Rupert Brooke, Ka Cox, Gwen Darwin, and Jacques Raverat.

Nessa: *see* Bell, Vanessa.

Nicolson, Benedict, 1914–78: art historian, son of Vita Sackville-West and Harold Nicolson.

Nicolson, Harold, 1886–1968: writer, diplomat, member of Parliament, married to Vita Sackville-West, father of Benedict and Nigel Nicolson, companion of Raymond Mortimer.

Nicolson, Mrs Harold: *see* Sackville-West, Vita.

Nicolson, Nigel, 1917– : writer, publisher, editor, son of Vita Sackville-West and Harold Nicolson.

Norton, Harry T.J., 1886–1937: Apostle, mathematician.

Nys, Maria, 1898–1955: friend of Ottoline Morrell, married to Aldous Huxley.

Oliver: *see* Strachey, Oliver.

Olivier sisters: Brynhild, Daphne, Margery, and Noel, daughters of Sydney and Margaret Olivier.

Omega Workshops, founded by Roger Fry in 1913, closed in 1919; Duncan Grant, Vanessa Bell, and others were involved to produce anonymous interior decorations, support young artists, and popularize post-impressionism.

Partridge, Frances Marshall, 1900– : writer, translator, married to Ralph Partridge.

Partridge, Ralph, 1894–1960: friend of Lytton Strachey and Gerald Brenan, married to (1) Carrington, (2) Frances Marshall.

Pater, Clara, 1841–1910: teacher, sister of Walter Pater.

Pernel: *see* Strachey, Pernel.

Pippa: *see* Strachey, Philippa.

Plomer, William, 1903–73: novelist, poet, and critic.

Portland Place: London location of the British Broadcasting Corporation.

Pozzo: *see* Keynes, J.M.

Quentin: *see* Bell, Quentin.

Raverat, Gwen Darwin, 1885–1957: artist, writer, married to Jacques Raverat.

Richards, I.A., 1893–1979: critic and poet.

Ritchie, Anne Thackery, known as Aunt Anny, 1837–1919: writer, daughter of William Makepeace Thackeray, sister-in-law of Leslie Stephen, married to Richmond Ritchie, the uncle of Molly MacCarthy.

Robertson, A.J., 1880–1954: Midnight Society member, businessman.

Rodmell: Sussex village near Lewes, location of the Woolfs' Monk's House.

Rowse, A.L., 1903– : Oxford and Cornish historian and essayist.

Rupert: *see* Brooke, Rupert.

Russell, Bertrand, known as Bertie, 1872–1970: Apostle, philosopher, writer, and reformer.

Rylands, G.H.W., known as Dadie, 1902– : Apostle, Hogarth Press assistant, Cambridge don, director.

Sackville-West, Vita, 1892–1962: novelist, poet, married to Harold Nicolson, friend of Virginia Woolf.

Sargant-Florence, Alix: *see* Strachey, Alix.

Savage, George, 1842–1921: physician, specialist in mental diseases, friend of the Stephen family, doctor of Virginia Woolf.

Saxon: *see* Sydney-Turner, Saxon.

Seend: Wiltshire country home of Clive Bell's parents.

Shaw, George Bernard, 1856–1950: playwright, reformer, and critic.

Sheppard, John, 1881–1968: Apostle, classicist, Provost of King's College, Cambridge.

Shove, Fredegond Maitland, 1889–1949: poet, married to Gerald Shove.

Shove, Gerald, 1887–1947: Apostle, economist, and Cambridge don, married to Fredegond Maitland.

Sichel, Edith, 1862–1914: writer.

Sickert, Walter, 1960–1942: painter.

Sidgwick, Henry, 1838–1900: Apostle, philosopher, and Cambridge don.

Sitwell, Edith, 1887–1964: poet, biographer, critic, sister of Osbert and Sacheverell Sitwell.

Sitwell, Osbert, 1892–1969: poet, autobiographer, and essayist, brother of Edith and Sacheverell Sitwell.

Smith, Logan Pearsall, 1861–1946: essayist and man of letters.

Smyth, Ethel, 1858–1944: composer, writer, feminist, friend of Virginia Woolf.

Society, The: *see* Apostles.

Spender, Stephen, 1909–95: poet, critic, autobiographer, man of letters.

Sprott, W.J.H., known as Sebastian, 1897–1971: Apostle, psychologist, don, friend of E.M. Forster and J.M. Keynes.

Stephen, Adrian, 1893–1948: psychiatrist, son of Leslie Stephen, brother of Thoby Stephen, Vanessa Bell, and Virginia Woolf, married to Karin Costelloe.

Stephen, Ann: *see* Synge, Ann Stephen.

Stephen, J.K.. known as Jem, 1859–1892: Apostle, poet, cousin of Vanessa Bell, Virginia Woolf, Thoby and Adrian Stephen.

Stephen, James Fitzjames, 1829–1894: Apostle, essayist, judge, government official, brother of Leslie Stephen, father of J.K. Stephen.

Stephen, Jem: *see* Stephen, J.K.

Stephen, Julia Jackson, 1846–1895: married to (1) Herbert Duckworth, (2) Leslie Stephen, mother of George, Stella, and Gerald Duckworth, and Vanessa Bell, Thoby Stephen, Virginia Woolf, and Adrian Stephen.

Stephen, Karin Costelloe, 1889–1953: psychiatrist, married to Adrian Stephen, sister of Ray Strachey.

Stephen, Leslie, 1832–1904: biographer, critic, historian of ideas, editor, man of letters, married to (1) Minny Thackeray, (2) Julia Jackson, father of Vanessa Bell, Thoby Stephen, Virginia Woolf, and Adrian Stephen.

Stephen, (Julian) Thoby, nicknamed the Goth, 1880–1906: son of Leslie and Julian Stephen, brother of Vanessa Bell, Virginia Woolf, and Adrian Stephen.

Stephen, Vanessa: *see* Bell, Vanessa.

Stephen, Virginia: *see* Woolf, Virginia.

Strachey, Alix Sargant-Florence, 1892–1973: psychoanalyst, married to James Strachey.

Strachey, Dorothy: *see* Bussy, Dorothy Strachey.

Strachey, James, 1887–1967: psychoanalyst, translator of Freud, brother of Dorothy, Lytton, Marjorie, Oliver, Pernel, and Philippa Strachey, married to Alix Sargant-Florence.

Strachey, Jane Maria Grant, 1840–1928: mother of Dorothy, Lytton, James, Marjorie, Oliver, Pernel, and Philippa Strachey, married to Richard Strachey.

Strachey, Julia, 1901–79: writer, daughter of Oliver Strachey, friend of Frances Partridge, married to (1) Stephen Tomlin, (2) Lawrence Gowing.

Strachey, Lytton, 1880–1932: Apostle, biographer and critic, brother of Dorothy, James, Marjorie, Oliver, Pernel, and Philippa Strachey, companion of Carrington.

Strachey, Marjorie, nicknamed Gumbo, 1882–1964: writer, teacher, sister of Dorothy, James, Lytton, Oliver, Pernel, and Philippa Strachey.

Strachey, Oliver, 1874–1960: civil servant, brother of Dorothy, Lytton, James, Marjorie, Pernel, and Philippa Strachey, married to (1) Ruby Mayer, (2) Ray Costelloe, father of Julia Strachey.

Strachey, (Joan) Pernel, 1876–1951: Principal of Newnham College, Cambridge, sister of Dorothy, Lytton, James, Marjorie, Oliver, and Philippa Strachey.

Strachey, Philippa, known as Pippa, 1872–1968: feminist, sister of Dorothy, Lytton, James, Marjorie, Oliver, and Pernel Strachey.

Strachey, Ray Costelloe, 1887–1940: writer, feminist, wife of Oliver Strachey, sister of Karin Costelloe.

Strachey, Richard, 1817–1908: Indian general, geographer, government official, married to Jane Maria Grant, father of Dorothy, Lytton, James, Marjorie, Oliver, Pernel, and Philippa Strachey.

Strachey, St Loe, 1860–1927: editor and proprietor of the *Spectator*,
   1898–1925, cousin of Dorothy, Lytton, James, Marjorie, Oliver, Pernel,
   and Philippa Strachey.
Swithin: *see* Swithinbank, B.W.
Swithinbank, B.W., 1884–1958: Indian civil servant, friend of Lytton Strachey
   and J.M. Keynes.
Sydney-Turner, Saxon, 1880–1962: Apostle, Treasury official.
Synge, Ann Stephen, 1916– : physician, teacher, peace activist, daughter of
   Adrian and Karin Stephen, married to Richard Synge.
Tavistock Square: Bloomsbury square where the Woolfs lived, 1924–39.
Tennyson, Charles, 1879–1977: lawyer, government official, writer.
Thoby: *see* Stephen, Thoby.
Tidmarsh: *see* Mill House.
Tilton: Keyneses' Sussex country home near Charleston.
Tomlin, Stephen, known as Tommy, 1901–37: sculptor, married to Julia
   Strachey.
Tonks, Henry, 1862–1937: artist and art teacher.
Trevelyan, G.M., 1876–1962: Apostle, historian, Master of Trinity College.
Trevelyan, R.C., 1872–1951: Apostle, poet, brother of G.M. Trevelyan.
Turner, Saxon: *see* Sydney-Turner, Saxon.
Turner, W.J., 1889–1946: journalist and music critic.
Vanessa: *see* Bell, Vanessa.
Vaughan, Margaret Symonds, known as Madge, 1869–1925: writer, daughter
   of John Addington Symonds, friend of Virginia Woolf, married to Virgi-
   nia's cousin W.W. Vaughan.
Virginia: *see* Woolf, Virginia.
Vita: *see* Sackville-West, Vita.
Waley, Arthur, 1889–1966: orientalist, translator, poet, companion of Beryl
   de Zoete.
Walpole, Hugh, 1884–1941: novelist, man of letters.
Watts, G.F., 1817–1904: painter and sculptor.
Waterlow, Sydney, 1878–1944: diplomat.
Webb, Beatrice Potter, 1858–1943: writer, Fabian social reformer, married to
   Sidney Webb.
Webb, Sidney, 1859–1947: writer, Fabian social reformer, government offi-
   cial, married to Beatrice Webb.
West, Rebecca, pen-name of Cecily Fairfield, 1892–1983: writer, married to
   Maxwell Andrews.
Weybridge: Surrey town where E.M. Forster lived.
Whitehead, Alfred North, 1861–1947: Apostle, mathematician, philosopher,
   don, married to Evelyn Rice.
Winston: *see* Churchill, Winston.

Wissett Lodge: Suffolk farmhouse where Duncan Grant, David Garnett, and Vanessa Bell with her children lived in 1916.

Wittgenstein, Ludwig, 1889–1951: Apostle, philosopher.

Woolf, Leonard, 1880–1969: Apostle, writer, political theorist, Labour Party advisor, critic, publisher, married to Virginia Stephen.

Woolf, Virginia Stephen, nicknamed Goat, 1882–1941: novelist, essayist, critic, and feminist, daughter of Leslie and Julia Stephen, married to Leonard Woolf, sister of Vanessa Bell, Thoby Stephen, and Adrian Stephen.

X-Society: Cambridge undergraduate discussion society meeting around 1900.

Yegen: village in Southern Spain where Gerald Brenan lived.

Young, Hilton, 1879–1960: writer and politician.

Headnote References

Works cited in the introductions and headnotes are listed below. Place of publication is London unless otherwise specified.

Auden, W.H. *Collected Poems.* Ed. Edward Mendelson. New York: Random House, 1976

Bell, Clive. Letter to Molly MacCarthy, September, 1913. Charleston Papers, King's College, Cambridge

- *Old Friends: Personal Recollections.* Chatto and Windus, 1956

Bell, Julian. *Essays, Poems and Letters.* Ed. Quentin Bell. Hogarth Press, 1938

Bell, Quentin. *Bloomsbury.* Weidenfeld and Nicolson, 1968

- 'Bloomsbury and the Arts in the Early Twentieth Century.' *Leeds Art Calendar* 55 (1964) 18-28

- 'Brief Lives.' *New Statesman* 71 (13 May 1966), 698

- 'Charleston Revisited.' *Charleston Newsletter* 17 (December 1986), 7-8

- *Virginia Woolf: A Biography.* 2 vols. Hogarth Press, 1972

- 'Who's Who in Bloomsbury.' *Charleston Newsletter* 20 (December 1987), 18-21

- and Stephen Chaplin. 'The Ideal Home Rumpus.' *Apollo* 80 (October 1964), 284-91. See also *Apollo* 82 (August 1965), 130-3, and 83 (January 1966), 75 Reprinted in *The Bloomsbury Group: A Collection of Memoirs, Commentary, and Criticism,* first edition. Toronto: University of Toronto Press, 1975, 331-6

Bell, Vanessa. Letter to John Maynard Keynes, undated. Quoted in *Charleston Papers,* Sotheby sale catalogue, 21 July 1980, #207

- *Selected Letters of Vanessa Bell.* Ed. Regina Marler. Bloomsbury, 1993

Carrington, Noel. *Carrington: Paintings, Drawings, and Decorations.* Oxford: Oxford Polytechnic Press, 1978

Forster, E.M., Bloomsbury memoir (untitled). Forster Papers, King's College, Cambridge

- *Commonplace Book.* Ed. Philip Gardner. Scholar Press, 1985

- *Goldsworthy Lowes Dickinson and Related Writings.* Ed. Oliver Stallybrass. Edward Arnold, 1973

Fry, Margaret. 'Foreword.' Virginia Woolf, *Roger Fry: A Biography*. Hogarth Press, 1940, 5

Fry, Roger. *Architectural Heresies of a Painter*. Chatto and Windus, 1921

Garnett, David. *Great Friends: Portraits of Seventeen Writers*. Macmillan, 1979

Isherwood, Christopher. *Exhumations: Stories, Articles, Verses*. Simon and Shuster, 1966

Keynes, John Maynard. *The Collected Writings*. 30 vols. Ed. D.E. Moggridge et al. Macmillan, 1971–89

MacCarthy, Desmond. *The Court Theatre, 1904–1907: A Commentary and Criticism*. A.H. Bullen, 1907

– *Portraits*. Putnam, 1931

Moore, G.E. *Principia Ethica*, revised edition. Ed. Thomas Baldwin. Cambridge: Cambridge University Press, 1993

Mortimer, Raymond. Letter to Clive Bell, 29 January 1954. Charleston Papers, King's College, Cambridge

– 'Friends and Relations.' *Sunday Times* (8 November 1970) 27

Murry, J. Middleton. 'Mr Fry among the Architects.' *Nation and Athenaeum* (27 August 1921) 776

Nicolson, Harold. *Diaries and Letters*, vol. 2. Ed. Nigel Nicolson. Collins, 1967

Plomer, William. *The Autobiography of William Plomer*. Jonathan Cape, 1975

Stephen, Adrian. *The 'Dreadnought' Hoax*. Hogarth Press, 1936

Strachey, Lytton. *Lytton Strachey by Himself: A Self-Portrait*. Ed. Michael Holroyd. Heinemann, 1971

W[oolf], L[eonard]. 'Mr. Saxon Sydney-Turner.' *The Times* (13 November 1962), 14

Woolf, Leonard. *Downhill All the Way: An Autobiography of the Years 1919–1939. Hogarth Press*, 1967

– Fragment of a Memoir Club paper. Leonard Woolf Papers, University of Sussex

– *The Journey Not the Arrival Matters: An Autobiography of the Years 1939–1969*. Hogarth Press, 1969

– *Letters of Leonard Woolf*. Ed. Frederic Spotts. New York: Harcourt Brace, 1989

– *Sowing: An Autobiography of the Years 1880–1904*. Hogarth Press, 1960

– Letter to Raymond Mortimer, 10 August 1949. Princeton University Library

– *The Wise Virgins: A Story of Words, Opinions, and a Few Emotions*. Edward Arnold, 1914; reprinted, Hogarth Press, 1979

Woolf, Virginia. *The Complete Shorter Fiction*, 2nd edition. Ed. Susan Dick. Hogarth Press, 1985

- *The Essays of Virginia Woolf*, vol. 4. Ed. Andrew McNeillie. Hogarth Press, 1994
- *The Diary of Virginia Woolf*. 5 vols. Ed. Anne Olivier Bell and Andrew McNeillie. Hogarth Press, 1977–84
- *The Letters of Virginia Woolf*. 6 vols. Ed. Nigel Nicolson and Joanne Trautmann. Hogarth Press, 1975–80

Sources of the Selections

Place of publication is London unless otherwise specified. The selections are listed in the order in which they appear.

Bloomsbury on Bloomsbury

Adrian Stephen. 'A Bloomsbury Party in 1909.' Quoted in Quentin Bell, *Virginia Woolf: A Biography*. Hogarth Press, 1972, 1:146-7
- *The 'Dreadnought' Hoax*. Hogarth Press, 1936, 16-47
Lytton, Strachey. 'Monday June 26th 1916.' *Lytton Strachey by Himself: A Self-Portrait*. Ed. Michael Holroyd. Heinemann, 1971, 139-56
- Letter to Keynes. Quoted in Michael Holroyd, *Lytton Strachey: A Critical Biography*. Heinemann, 1967, 1:396
- Letter to James Strachey, 19 September 1920. Strachey Papers, British Library
Saxon Sydney-Turner. Letter to Virginia Woolf, 9 February 1919. Monk's House Papers, University of Sussex
Roger Fry. Letter to Vanessa Bell, 12 December 1917. *Letters of Roger Fry*. Ed. Denys Sutton. Chatto and Windus, 1972, 2:423
- Letter to Virginia Woolf, 4-5 September 1921. Leonard Woolf Papers, University of Sussex
David Garnett on Bloomsbury Parties. *The Familiar Faces, Being Volume Three of The Golden Echo*. Chatto and Windus, 1962, 62-5
Virginia Woolf. 'Old Bloomsbury.' *Moments of Being*, 2nd edition. Ed. Jeanne Schulkind. Hogarth Press, 1985, 181-201
- *The Diary of Virginia Woolf*. Ed. Anne Olivier Bell and Andrew McNeillie. Hogarth Press, 1977-84, 1:105-6, 206; 3:48, 316; 4:326-7; 5:82-3, 330-1
- *The Letters of Virginia Woolf*. Ed. Nigel Nicolson and Joanne Trautmann. Hogarth Press, 1975-80, 2:451; 3:181, 337, 566; 5:91
- 'Some New Woolf Letters.' Ed. Joanne Trautmann Banks. *Modern Fiction Studies* 30 (Summer, 1984), 185
- *Letters of Virginia Woolf*, 6:62-3, 419-20

Desmond MacCarthy. 'Bloomsbury, An Unfinished Memoir.' *Memories.* MacGibbon and Kee, 1953, 172-5
- unpublished typescript with holograph revisions, MacCarthy Papers, Lilly Library, Indiana University
- 'Roger Fry and the Post-Impressionist Exhibition of 1910.' *Memories.* MacGibbon and Kee, 1953, 176-83
E.M. Forster. 'Bloomsbury, An Early Note.' *Commonplace Book.* Ed. Philip Gardner. Scolar Press, 1985, 48-9
- 'Bloomsbury, An Interview.' *Forster in Egypt: A Graeco-Alexandrian Encounter.* Ed. Hilda D. Spear and Abdel Moneim Aly. Cecil Woolf, 1987, 46-7
- *Selected Letters of E.M. Forster.* Ed. Mary Lago and P.N. Furbank. Collins, 1985, 2:105, 203
John Maynard Keynes. 'My Early Beliefs.' *Two Memoirs.* Rupert Hart-Davis, 1949; reprinted in *The Collection Writings of John Maynard Keynes,* ed. D.E. Moggridge et al. MacMillan, 1972, 10:430-50
Duncan Grant. 'Virginia Woolf.' *Horizon* 3 (June 1941), 402-6
Vanessa Bell. 'Notes on Bloomsbury.' In the possession of Angelica Grant
- Letter to Molly MacCarthy. Lilly Library, Indiana University
- *Selected Letters of Vanessa Bell.* Ed. Regina Marler. Bloomsbury, 1993, 527
Clive Bell. 'Bloomsbury.' *Old Friends: Personal Recollections.* Chatto and Windus, 1956, 126-37
Leonard Woolf on Cambridge Friends and Influences. *Sowing: An Autobiography of the Years 1880-1904.* Hogarth Press, 1960, 102-7, 119-20, 123-4, 127-9, 130, 131-7, 144-54, 155-6
- on Old Bloomsbury. *Beginning Again: An Autobiography of the Years 1911-1918.* Hogarth Press, 1964, 21-6
- on the Second Post-Impressionist Exhibition. *Beginning Again: An Autobiography of the Years 1911-1918.* Hogarth Press, 1964, 93-6
- on the Beginnings of the Hogarth Press. *Beginning Again: An Autobiography of the Years 1911-1918.* Hogarth Press, 1964, 234-7
- on The Memoir Club. *Downhill All the Way: An Autobiography of the Years 1919-1939.* Hogarth Press, 1967, 114-15

Bloomsberries

Virginia Woolf. *Roger Fry: A Biography.* Hogarth Press, 1940, 261-8, 269-70, 278-9, 288-94
Clive Bell. 'Roger Fry.' *Old Friends: Personal Recollections.* Chatto and Windus, 1956, 62-91

E.M. Forster. 'Tributes to Desmond MacCarthy, II.' *Listener* (26 June 1952), 1031

Leonard (and Virginia) Woolf on Desmond MacCarthy. *Beginning Again: An Autobiography of the Years 1911-1918*. Hogarth Press, 1964, 135-41, 143

Leonard Woolf on Molly MacCarthy. *Beginning Again: An Autobiography of the Years 1911-1918*. Hogarth Press, 1964, 142-3

Virginia Woolf on E.M. Forster. *The Diaries of Virginia Woolf*. Ed. Anne Olivier Bell and Andrew McNeillie. Hogarth Press, 1977-84, 1:291, 295, 310-11; 2:33, 96, 138-9, 171, 204, 269-70; 3:178; 4:297-8; 5:337

David Garnett. 'Forster and Bloomsbury.' *Aspects of E.M. Forster*. Ed. Oliver Stallybrass, Edward Arnold, 1969, 29-35

Virginia Woolf. 'Foreword.' *Recent Paintings by Vanessa Bell*. London Artists' Association, 1930

Quentin Bell. 'Ludendorff Bell.' *Selected Letters of Vanessa Bell*. Ed. Regina Marler. Bloomsbury, 1993, ix-xii

Roger Fry. *Living Painters: Duncan Grant*. Hogarth Press, 1923, v-ix

David Garnett on Clive Bell. *The Flowers of the Forest, Being Volume Two of The Golden Echo*. Chatto and Windus, 1955, 21-4

Angelica Garnett. 'Child of Two Fathers.' *Deceived with Kindness*. Chatto and Windus, Hogarth Press, 1984, 134-42

E.M. Forster. *Virginia Woolf, The Rede Lecture*. Cambridge: Cambridge University Press, 1942; reprinted in *Two Cheers for Democracy*, ed. Oliver Stallybrass. Edward Arnold, 1951, 1972, 238-52

Leonard Woolf. 'Virginia Woolf: Writer and Personality.' *Listener* (4 March 1965), 327-8

Quentin Bell. 'Introduction.' Leonard Woolf, *An Autobiography*, 1:1880-1911. Oxford: Oxford University Press, 1980, 1:vii-xiv

Angelica Garnett. 'The Woolves.' *Deceived with Kindness*. Chatto and Windus, Hogarth Press, 1984, 106-14

Leonard Woolf. 'Lytton Strachey.' *New Statesman and Nation* (30 January 1932), 118-19

Desmond MacCarthy. 'Lytton Strachey and the Art of Biography.' *Memories*. MacGibbon and Kee, 1953, 38-41, 43-9

David Garnett. 'Preface.' *Carrington: Letters and Extracts from Her Diaries*. Ed. David Garnett. Jonathan Cape, 1970, 9-16

Virginia Woolf. '"JMK": A Biographical Fantasy.' Ed. S.P. Rosenbaum. *The Charleston Magazine* (Spring/Summer 1995), 5-8. Virginia Woolf's Manuscript Articles and Essays, Berg Collection, New York Public Library, 7: 73-7

Clive Bell. 'Maynard Keynes.' *Old Friends: Personal Recollections.* Chatto and Windus, 1956, 42–61

Quentin Bell. 'Bloomsbury and Lydia.' *Lydia Lopokova.* Ed. Milo Keynes. Weidenfeld and Nicolson, 1983, 84–92

Henrietta Garnett. 'Aspects of My Father.' *Telegraph Weekend Magazine* (8 April 1989), 23–7

Bloomsbury Observed

Town Talker. 'The Round of the Day.' *Westminster Gazette* (29 August 1927), 5

Raymond Mortimer. 'London Letter.' *Dial* 84 (February 1928), 238–40

Ottoline Morrell. 'Artists Revels.' *The Early Memoirs of Lady Ottoline Morrell.* Ed. Robert Gathorne-Hardy. Faber and Faber, 1963, 178–81

Quentin Bell. 'Foreword.' *The Omega Workshops* by Judith Collins. Secker and Warburg, 1983, vi–x

Arthur Waley. 'Introduction.' *One Hundred and Seventy Chinese Poems.* Constable, 1962, 5–6

Osbert Sitwell. *Laughter in the Next Room.* Macmillan, 1949, 16–22

Edith Sitwell. *Taken Care Of: The Autobiography of Edith Sitwell.* Hutchinson, 1965, 81–7

Vita Sackville-West from Harold Nicolson. *Diaries and Letters: 1930–1939.* Ed. Nigel Nicolson. Collins, 1966, 350–1

Nigel Nicolson. 'Vita and Virginia and Vanessa.' *A Cézanne in the Hedge and Other Memories of Charleston.* Ed. Hugh Lee. Collins and Brown, 1992, 86–92

Beatrice Webb. *The Diary of Beatrice Webb, Volume Four: 1924–1943.* Ed. Norman and Jean MacKenzie. Virago Press, 1985, 93–4, 112–3, 144, 243, 303, 418–19, 443–4, 466–7

Gerald Brenan. *South from Granada.* Hamish Hamilton, 1957, 27–37, 139–46

- *Personal Record: 1920–1972.* Jonathan Cape, 1974, 59–60, 78–9, 89–91, 155–7, 184–5, 252–4

Peter Stansky and William Abrahams. 'A Bloomsbury Childhood.' *Journey to the Frontier: Julian Bell and John Cornford: Their Lives in the 1930s.* Constable, 1966, 5–7, 14–27

Ann Synge. 'Childhood on the Edge of Bloomsbury.' *Charleston Newsletter* 10 (March 1985), 14–15

John Lehmann. *The Whispering Gallery.* Longmans, Green, 1955, 148–9, 164–7

- *I Am My Brother.* Longmans, Green, 1960, 34–5

Stephen Spender. *World within World*. Hamish Hamilton, 1951, 139-42, 143-4, 151-9

William Plomer. *At Home*. Jonathan Cape, 1958, 43-6, 50-6

Christopher Isherwood. *Christopher and His Kind: 1929-1931*. New York: Farrar, Straus, Giroux, 1976, 104-7, 306

- *Exhumations: Stories, Articles, Verses*. Simon and Shuster, 1966, 132-5

T.S. Eliot. 'Virginia Woolf.' *Horizon* 3 (May 1941), 314-16

Frances Partridge. *Memories*. Victor Gollancz, 1981, 75-83

- 'Bloomsbury Houses.' *Charleston Newsletter* 11 (June 1985), 30-7

Richard Morphet. 'The Significance of Charleston.' *Apollo* 86 (March 1967), 342-5

Julian Bell. 'Monk's House and the Woolfs.' *Virginia Woolf's Rodmell: An Illustrated Guide to a Sussex Village*. Ed. Maire McQueeney. Rodmell, East Sussex: Rodmell Village Press, 1991, 20-7

Charles Mauron. Remarks on Bloomsbury. In the possession of Alice Mauron; translated by Susanna Eve

Quentin Bell. 'The Character of Bloomsbury.' *Bloomsbury*. Weidenfeld and Nicolson, 1968, 103-18

Bibliographies

The following is a somewhat selective bibliography of books by members of the Bloomsbury Group and a highly selective bibliography of the innumerable books of biography, bibliography, criticism, and commentary that have been devoted to the Group and its works. Unless otherwise indicated, the place of first publication is London. Dates in parentheses are of first publication.

BLOOMSBURY

Anscombe, Isabelle, *Omega and After: Bloomsbury and the Decorative Arts*, 1981
Bell, Quentin, *Bloomsbury*, 1968
- *Elders and Betters*, 1995
Bell, Quentin, Angelica Garnett, Richard Shone, *Charleston Past and Present*, 1987
Bloomsbury: The Artists, Authors, and Designers by Themselves. Ed. Gillian Naylor, 1990
Bloomsbury Group Reader, A. Ed. S.P. Rosenbaum, Oxford, 1993
Coss, Melinda, *Bloomsbury Needlepoint from the Tapestries at Charleston Farmhouse*, 1992
Garnett, Angelica, *Deceived by Kindness: A Bloomsbury Childhood*, 1984
Palmer, Alan and Veronica, *Who's Who in Bloomsbury*, Brighton, 1987
Richardson, Elizabeth P., *A Bloomsbury Iconography*, Winchester, Hampshire, 1989
Rosenbaum, S.P., *Edwardian Bloomsbury: The Early Literary History of the Bloomsbury Group*, vol. 2, 1994
- *Victorian Bloomsbury: The Early Literary History of the Bloomsbury Group*, vol. 1, 1987
Shone, Richard, *Bloomsbury Portraits: Vanessa Bell, Duncan Grant, and Their Circle*, 2nd edition, 1993
Twitchell, Beverly H., *Cézanne and Formalism in Bloomsbury*, Ann Arbor, Michigan, 1987

CLIVE BELL

BOOKS BY CLIVE BELL

Criticism
Art (1914), ed. J.H. Bullen, Oxford, 1987
Pot-Boilers, 1918
Since Cézanne, 1922
Landmarks in Nineteenth-Century Painting, 1927
Proust, 1928
An Account of French Painting, 1931
Enjoying Pictures: Meditations in the National Gallery and Elsewhere, 1934

Social and Political Writings
Peace at Once, Manchester, 1915
On British Freedom, 1923
Civilization: An Essay, 1928
Warmongers, 1938

Poetry
Editor and contributor, *Euphrosyne: A Collection of Verse*, Cambridge, 1905
Ad Familiares, privately printed, 1917
Poems, Richmond, Surrey, 1921
The Legend of Monte della Sibilla or Le Paradis de la Reine Sibille, Richmond, Surrey, 1923

Autobiography
Old Friends: Personal Recollections, 1956

WORKS ON CLIVE BELL

Bywater, William G., *Clive Bell's Eye*, Detroit, 1975
Laing, Donald A., *Clive Bell: An Annotated Bibliography of the Published Writings*, New York, 1983

VANESSA BELL

Dunn, Jane, *A Very Close Conspiracy: Vanessa Bell and Virginia Woolf*, 1990
Gillespie, Diane Filby, *The Sisters' Arts: The Writing and Painting of Virginia Woolf and Vanessa Bell*, Syracuse, New York, 1988
Selected Letters of Vanessa Bell, ed. Regina Marler, 1993

Spalding, Frances, *Vanessa Bell*, 1983
Vanessa Bell's Family Album, ed. Quentin Bell and Angelica Garnett, 1981

DORA CARRINGTON

Carrington: Letters and Extracts from Her Diaries, ed. David Garnett, 1970
Carrington, Noel, *Carrington: Paintings, Drawings, and Decorations*, Oxford, 1978
Gerzina, Gretchen, *Carrington: A Life of Dora Carrington 1893–1932*, 1989
Hill, Jane, *The Art of Dora Carrington*, 1994

E.M. FORSTER

BOOKS BY FORSTER

Collected Edition
The Abinger Edition of E.M. Forster, edited by Oliver Stallybrass and Elizabeth Heine: vol. 1: *Where Angels Fear to Tread*, vol. 2: *The Longest Journey*, vol. 3: *A Room with a View*, vol. 4: *Howards End*, vol. 4a: *The Manuscripts of 'Howards End,'* vol. 6: *A Passage to India*, vol. 6a: *The Manuscripts of 'A Passage to India,'* vol. 8: *The Life to Come and Other Stories*, vol. 9: *Arctic Summer and Other Fiction*, vol. 11: *Two Cheers for Democracy*, vol. 12: *Aspects of the Novel*, vol. 13: *Goldsworthy Lowes Dickinson*, vol. 14: *The Hill of Devi and Other Indian Writings*

Fiction
Where Angels Fear to Tread, Edinburgh, 1905
The Longest Journey, Edinburgh, 1907
A Room with a View, 1908
Howards End, 1910
The Celestial Omnibus and Other Stories, 1911
The Story of the Siren, Richmond, Surrey, 1920
A Passage to India, 1924
The Eternal Moment and Other Stories, 1928
Maurice, 1971
The Life to Come and Other Stories, 1972

Essays, Criticism, etc.
Alexandria: A History and a Guide, Alexandria, 1922
Pharos and Pharillon, Richmond, Surrey, 1923
Anonymity, 1925

Letter to Madan Blanchard, 1931
Abinger Harvest, 1936
What I Believe, 1939
England's Pleasant Land: A Pageant Play, 1940
Virginia Woolf, Cambridge, 1942
Two Cheers for Democracy, 1951
Albergo Empedocle and Other Writings, ed. George H. Thomson, New York,
   1971

Biography and Autobiography
Goldsworthy Lowes Dickinson, 1934
The Hill of Devi, Being Letters from Dewas State Senior, 1953
Marianne Thornton: A Domestic Biography, 1956
Commonplace Book, ed. Philip Gardner, 1985
Selected Letters of E.M. Forster, ed. Mary Lago and P.N. Furbank, 2 vols.,
   1983-5

WORKS ON FORSTER

*Aspects of E.M. Forster: Essays and Recollections Written for His Ninetieth
   Birthday*, ed. Oliver Stallybrass, 1969
E.M. Forster: The Critical Heritage, ed Philip Gardner, 1973
Furbank, P.N., *E.M. Forster: A Life*, 2 vols., 1977-8
Kirkpatrick, B.J., *A Bibliography of E.M. Forster*, 2nd edition, Oxford, 1968
McDowell, Frederick P.W., *E.M. Forster: An Annotated Bibliography of Writ-
   ings about Him*, De Kalb, Illinois, 1976
Stape, J.H., *An E.M. Forster Chronology*, 1993
Summers, Claude J., *E.M. Forster*, New York, 1983
Summers, Claude J., *E.M. Forster: A Guide to Research*, New York, 1991
Trilling, Lionel, *E.M. Forster*, Norfolk, Connecticut, 1943

ROGER FRY

BOOKS BY FRY

Criticism
Giovanni Bellini, 1899
Sir Joshua Reynolds, *Discourses*, introduction and notes by Roger Fry, 1905
Vision and Design (1920), ed. J.H. Bullen, Oxford, 1981
The Artist and Psycho-analysis, 1924
Art and Commerce, 1926

Transformations: Critical and Speculative Essays on Art, 1926
Cézanne: A Study of His Development, 1927
Flemish Art: A Critical Survey, 1927
Henri-Matisse, Paris, 1930
Characteristics of French Art, 1932
Reflections on British Painting, 1934
Last Lectures, Cambridge, 1939

Other Works
Twelve Original Woodcuts, Richmond, Surrey, 1921
A Sampler of Castile, Richmond, Surrey, 1923
(Translator) Stephane Mallarmé, *Poems,* with commentaries by Charles Mauron, 1936
Letters of Roger Fry, ed. Denys Sutton, 2 vols., 1972

WORKS ON FRY

Collins, Judith, *The Omega Workshops,* 1983
Laing, Donald A., *An Annotated Bibliography of the Published Writings,* New York, 1979
Spalding, Frances, *Roger Fry: Art and Life,* 1980
Woolf, Virginia, *Roger Fry* (1940), ed. Diane Filby Gillespie, Oxford, 1995

DAVID GARNETT

Fiction
Lady into Fox, 1922
A Man in the Zoo, 1924
The Sailor's Return, 1925
Go She Must!, 1927
The Old Dovecote and Other Stories, 1928
No Love, 1929
The Grasshoppers Come, 1931
A Terrible Day, 1932
Beany-Eye, 1935
Aspects of Love, 1955
A Shot in the Dark, 1958
A Net for Venus, 1959
Two by Two, A Story of Survival, 1963
Ulterior Motives, 1966
A Clean Slate, 1971

The Sons of the Falcon, 1972
Purl and Plain and Other Stories, 1973
Plough Over the Bones, 1973
Up She Rises, 1977

History and Biography
Pocahontas, Or the Nonparell of Virginia, 1933
War in the Air, September 1939 to May 1941, 1941
The Campaign in Greece and Crete, 1942

Autobiography
A Rabbit in the Air. Notes from a Diary Kept While Learning to Handle an Aeroplane, 1932
The Golden Echo, 1953
The Flowers of the Forest, Being Volume Two of The Golden Echo, 1955
The Familiar Faces, Being Volume Three of The Golden Echo, 1962
Great Friends: Portraits of Seventeen Writers, 1979

DUNCAN GRANT

Living Painters: Duncan Grant, with an introduction by Roger Fry, Richmond, Surrey, 1923
Mortimer, Raymond, *Duncan Grant,* Harmondsworth, Middlesex, 1948
Watney, Simon, *The Art of Duncan Grant,* 1990

JOHN MAYNARD KEYNES

BOOKS BY KEYNES

Collected Edition
The Collected Writings of John Maynard Keynes, ed. D.E. Moggridge et al., 29 vols. 1971–89; vol. 30 Bibliography and Index, 1971–89

Economic Writings
Indian Currency and Finance, 1913
The Economic Consequences of the Peace, 1919
A Revision of the Treaty, 1922
A Tract on Monetary Reform, 1923
The Economic Consequences of Mr Churchill, 1925
A Treatise on Money, 2 vols., 1930

Essays in Persuasion, 1931
The General Theory of Employment, Interest and Money, 1936

Biography and Autobiography
Essays in Biography, 1933
Two Memoirs, 1949

Other Writings
A Treatise on Probability, 1921
A Short View of Russia, 1925
The Arts Council: Its Policy and Hopes, [1945] 1951

WORKS ON KEYNES

Essays on John Maynard Keynes, ed. Milo Keynes, Cambridge, 1975
Keynes and the Bloomsbury Group, ed. Derek Crabtree and A.P. Thirlwall,
   1980
Mini, Piero V., *Keynes, Bloomsbury and the General Theory,* 1991
Moggridge, D.E., *Maynard Keynes: An Economist's Biography,* 1992
Skidelsky, Robert, *J.M. Keynes: Hopes Betrayed, 1883–1920; The Economist
   as Saviour, 1920–37,* 3 vols., 1983–

DESMOND MACCARTHY

BOOKS BY DESMOND MACCARTHY

Criticism
The Court Theatre 1904–1907: A Commentary and Criticism (1907), ed. Stan-
   ley Weintraub, Coral Gables, Florida, 1966
Remnants, 1918
Portraits I (no further volumes issued), 1931
Criticism, 1932
Experience, 1935
Leslie Stephen, Cambridge, 1937
Drama, 1940
Shaw, 1951
Humanities, 1953
Memories, 1953
Theatre, 1954

WORKS ON DESMOND MACCARTHY

Cecil, Hugh and Mirabel, *Clever Hearts: Desmond and Molly MacCarthy, A Biography*, 1990
Desmond MacCarthy, The Man and His Writings, ed. David Cecil, 1984

MARY MACCARTHY

BOOKS BY MARY MACCARTHY

Fiction
A Pier and a Band, 1918 (reprinted 'With an Introductory Appreciation by David Garnett,' 1931)

Autobiography
A Nineteenth-Century Childhood, 1924

Essays
Fighting Fitzgerald and Other Papers, 1930
Handicaps: Six Studies, 1936
The Festival, Etc., 1937

WORKS ON MARY MACCARTHY

Cecil, Hugh and Mirabel, *Clever Hearts: Desmond and Molly MacCarthy, A Biography*, 1990

LYTTON STRACHEY

BOOKS BY STRACHEY

Collected Edition
The Collected Works of Lytton Strachey, ed. James Strachey, 6 vols., 1948

Biography and Criticism
Landmarks in French Literature, 1912
Eminent Victorians: Cardinal Manning, Florence Nightingale, Dr. Arnold, General Gordon, 1918
Queen Victoria, 1921
Books and Characters, French and English, 1922
Elizabeth and Essex: A Tragic History, 1928

Portraits in Miniature and Other Essays, 1931
Characters and Commentaries, ed. James Strachey, 1933
Spectatorial Essays, ed. James Strachey, 1964

Verse, Fiction, and Other Writings
Contributor, *Euphrosyne: A Collection of Verse*, Cambridge, 1905
Ermyntrude and Esmeralda, 1969
The Really Interesting Question and Other Papers, ed. Paul Levy, 1972

Letters and Autobiography
Virginia Woolf and Lytton Strachey: Letters, ed. Leonard Woolf and James
    Strachey, 1956
Lytton Strachey by Himself: A Self-Portrait, ed. Michael Holroyd, 1971

WORKS ON STRACHEY

Edmonds, Michael, *Lytton Strachey: A Bibliography*, New York, 1981
Holroyd, Michael, *Lytton Strachey* (2 vols., 1967), 1994
Merle, Gabriel, *Lytton Strachey (1880–1932) biographie et critique d'un cri-
    tique et biographe*, 2 vols., Paris, 1980
Spurr, Barry, *Diabolical Art: The Achievement of Lytton Strachey*, 1994

LEONARD WOOLF

BOOKS BY LEONARD WOOLF

Social, Political, Historical, and Critical Writings
International Government: Two Reports, 1916
The Future of Constantinople, 1917
Co-operation and the Future of Industry, 1918
Economic Imperialism, 1920
Empire and Commerce in Africa: A Study in Economic Imperialism, 1920
Socialism and Co-operation, 1921
Fear and Politics: A Debate at the Zoo, 1925
Essays on Literature, History, Politics, Etc., 1927
Hunting the Highbrow, 1927
Imperialism and Civilization, 1928
After the Deluge: A Study of Communal Psychology, 2 vols., 1931, 1939 (see
    also *Principia Politica*)
Quack, Quack!, 1935
Barbarians at the Gate (Barbarians Within and Without – the American title), 1939

The War for Peace, 1940
Principia Politica: A Study of Communal Psychology (vol. 3 of *After the Deluge*), 1953

Verse, Fiction, and Drama
Contributor, *Euphrosyne: A Collection of Verse*, Cambridge, 1905
The Village in the Jungle, 1913
The Wise Virgins: A Story of Words, Opinions and Few Emotions, 1914
'Three Jews,' Virginia and L.S. Woolf, *Two Stories*, Richmond, Surrey, 1917
Stories of the East, Richmond, Surrey, 1921
The Hotel, 1939

Autobiographical Writings
Sowing: An Autobiography of the Years 1880–1904, 1960
Growing: An Autobiography of the Years 1904–1911, 1961
Diaries in Ceylon, 1908–1911: Records of a Colonial Administrator, 1963
Beginning Again: An Autobiography of the Years 1911–1918, 1964
Downhill All the Way: An Autobiography of the Years 1919–1939, 1967
The Journey Not the Arrival Matters: An Autobiography of the Years 1939–1969, 1969
Letters of Leonard Woolf, ed. Frederic Spotts, New York, 1989

WORKS ON LEONARD WOOLF

Luedeking, Leila, and Michael Edmonds, *Leonard Woolf: A Bibliography*, Winchester, Hampshire, 1992
Meyerowitz, Selma S, *Leonard Woolf*, Boston, 1982
Wilson, Duncan, *Leonard Woolf: A Political Biography*, 1978

VIRGINIA WOOLF

BOOKS BY VIRGINIA WOOLF

Collected Edition
The Shakespeare Head Press Edition of Virginia Woolf: *To the Lighthouse*, ed. Susan Dick, Oxford, 1992; *The Waves*, ed. James M. Haule and Philip H. Smith, Jr, Oxford, 1993; *Night and Day*, ed. J.H. Stape, Oxford, 1994; *Roger Fry*, ed. Diane Filby Gillespie, Oxford, 1995

Fiction
The Voyage Out, 1915
'The Mark on The Wall,' Virginia and L.S. Woolf, *Two Sisters*, Richmond,
   Surrey, 1917
Night and Day, 1919
Kew Gardens, Richmond Surrey, 1921
Monday or Tuesday, Richmond, Surrey, 1921
Jacob's Room, Richmond, Surrey, 1922
Mrs Dalloway, 1925
To the Lighthouse, 1927
Orlando: A Biography, 1928
The Waves, 1931
The Years, 1937
Between the Acts, 1941
A Haunted House and Other Short Stories, 1943
The Complete Shorter Fiction, 2nd edition, ed. Susan Dick, 1985

Essays, etc.
The Common Reader, 1925
A Room of One's Own, 1929
The Common Reader: Second Series, 1932
Three Guineas, 1938
The Death of the Moth and Other Essays, ed. Leonard Woolf, 1942
The Moment and Other Essays, ed. Leonard Woolf, 1947
The Captain's Death Bed and Other Essays, ed. Leonard Woolf, 1950
Granite and Rainbow: Essays, ed. Leonard Woolf, 1958
Contemporary Writers, ed. Jean Guiguet, 1965
The London Scene: Five Essays, New York, 1975
Books and Portraits, ed. Mary Lyon, 1977
The Essays of Virginia Woolf, 6 vols., ed. Andrew McNeillie, 1986–

Biography, etc.
Flush: A Biography, 1933
Roger Fry: A Biography, 1940
Freshwater: A Comedy, ed. Lucio Ruotolo, 1976

Autobiographical Writings
A Writer's Diary: Being Extracts from the Diary of Virginia Woolf, ed. Leo-
   nard Woolf, 1953
Virginia Woolf and Lytton Strachey, *Letters*, ed. Leonard Woolf and James
   Strachey, 1956

The Letters of Virginia Woolf, ed. Nigel Nicolson and Joanne Trautmann, 6
  vols., 1975–80
The Diary of Virginia Woolf, ed. Anne Olivier Bell and Andrew McNeillie, 5
  vols., 1977–84
Moments of Being, 2nd edition, ed. Jeanne Schulkind, 1985
The Early Journals of Virginia Woolf, ed. Mitchell A. Leaska, 1990

WORKS ON VIRGINIA WOOLF

Bell, Quentin, *Virginia Woolf: A Biography*, 2 vols., 1972
Bishop, Edward, *A Virginia Woolf Chronology*, 1989
Dick, Susan, *Virginia Woolf*, 1989
Dunn, Jane, *A Very Close Conspiracy: Vanessa Bell and Virginia Woolf*, 1990
Fuderer, Laura Sue, 'Criticism of Virginia Woolf from 1972–1990: A Selected
  Checklist,' *Modern Fiction Studies* 38 (Spring 1992), 303–42
Gillespie, Diane Filby, *The Sisters' Arts: The Writing and Painting of Vir-
  ginia Woolf and Vanessa Bell*, Syracuse, New York, 1988
Gordon, Lyndall, *Virginia Woolf: A Writer's Life*, Oxford, 1984
Kirkpatrick, B.J., *A Bibliography of Virginia Woolf*, 3rd edition, Oxford,
  1980
Majumdar, Robin, *Virginia Woolf: An Annotated Bibliography of Criticism,
  1915-1974*, New York, 1976
Virginia Woolf: A Feminist Slant, ed. Jane Marcus, Lincoln, Nebraska, 1983
Virginia Woolf: The Critical Heritage, ed. Robin Majumdar and Allen
  McLaurin, 1975
Zwerdling, Alex, *Virginia Woolf and the Real World*, Berkeley, 1986

Index of Names and Works